opposing viewpoints

# SOURCES

# soviet-american debate

opposing viewpoints

# soviet-american debate

## vol. 1

**David L. Bender**, *Publisher*
**Bruno Leone**, *Executive Editor*
**M. Teresa O'Neill**, *Senior Editor*
**Claudia Bialke Debner**, *Editor*
**Bonnie Szumski**, *Editor*
**Lynn Hall**, *Assistant Editor*
**Susan Bursell**, *Assistant Editor*
**Janelle Rohr**, *Assistant Editor*

**David Owen Kieft, Ph.D.**, *Consulting Editor*
*Associate Professor of History*
*University of Minnesota, Minneapolis*

greenhaven press, inc.

577 Shoreview Park Road
St. Paul, MN 55126

ISBN 0-89908-507-5

ISSN 0883-1270

"Congress shall make no law . . . abridging the freedom of speech, or of the press."

*first amendment to the US Constitution*

# contents

# foreword

*"It is better to debate a question without settling it than to settle a question without debating it."*

Joseph Joubert (1754-1824)

The purpose of Opposing Viewpoints SOURCES is to present balanced, and often difficult to find, opposing points of view on complex and sensitive issues.

Probably the best way to become informed is to analyze the positions of those who are regarded as experts and well studied on issues. It is important to consider every variety of opinion in an attempt to determine the truth. Opinions from the mainstream of society should be examined. But also important are opinions that are considered radical, reactionary, or minority as well as those stigmatized by some other uncomplimentary label. An important lesson of history is the eventual acceptance of many unpopular and even despised opinions. The ideas of Socrates, Jesus, and Galileo are good examples of this.

Readers will approach this anthology with their own opinions on the issues debated within it. However, to have a good grasp of one's own viewpoint, it is necessary to understand the arguments of those with whom one disagrees. It can be said that those who do not completely understand their adversary's point of view do not fully understand their own.

A persuasive case for considering opposing viewpoints has been presented by John Stuart Mill in his work *On Liberty*. When examining controversial issues it may be helpful to reflect on his suggestion:

> The only way in which a human being can make some approach to knowing the whole of a subject, is by hearing what can be said about it by persons of every variety of opinion, and studying all modes in which it can be looked at by every character of mind. No wise man ever acquired his wisdom in any mode but this.

### Analyzing Sources of Information

Opposing Viewpoints SOURCES includes diverse materials taken from magazines, journals, books, and newspapers, as well as statements and position papers from a wide range of individuals, organizations and governments. This broad spectrum of sources helps to develop patterns of thinking which are open to the consideration of a variety of opinions.

### Pitfalls to Avoid

A pitfall to avoid in considering opposing points of view is that of regarding one's own opinion as being common sense and the most rational stance and the point of view of others as being only opinion and naturally wrong. It may be that another's opinion is correct and one's own is in error.

Another pitfall to avoid is that of closing one's mind to the opinions of those with whom one disagrees. The best way to approach a dialogue is to make one's primary purpose that of understanding the mind and arguments of the other person and not that of enlightening him or her with one's own solutions. More can be learned by listening than speaking.

It is my hope that after reading this anthology the reader will have a deeper understanding of the issues debated and will appreciate the complexity of even seemingly simple issues on which good and honest people disagree. This awareness is particularly important in a democratic society such as ours where people enter into public debate to determine the common good. Those with whom one disagrees should not necessarily be regarded as enemies, but perhaps simply as people who suggest different paths to a common goal.

### The Format of SOURCES

In this anthology, carefully chosen opposing viewpoints are purposely placed back to back to create a running debate; each viewpoint is preceded by a short quotation that best expresses the author's main argument. This format instantly plunges the reader into the midst of a controversial issue and greatly aids that reader in mastering the basic skill of recognizing an author's point of view. In addition, the table of contents gives a brief description of each viewpoint, allowing the reader to identify quickly the point of view for which he or she is searching.

Each section of this anthology debates an issue, and the sections build on one another so that the anthology as a whole debates a larger issue. By using this step-by-step, section-by-section approach to understanding separate facets of a topic, the reader will have a solid background upon which to base his or her opinons. Each year a supplement of twenty-five opposing viewpoints will be added to this anthology, enabling the reader to keep abreast of annual developments.

This volume of Opposing Viewpoints SOURCES does not advocate a particular point of view. Quite the contrary! The very nature of the anthology leaves it to the reader to formulate the opinions he or she finds most suitable. My purpose as publisher is to see that this is made possible by offering a wide range of viewpoints that are fairly presented.

David L. Bender
Publisher

# introduction

*"[The Cold War] is unique in history as a national preoccupation of two supreme powers and as a national distraction for the rest."*

Saul Pett

*Editor's note: The conflict between the United States and the Soviet Union has had a major impact on the world for the past forty years. For many reasons including their vast sizes, their tremendous resources, and their involvement in the affairs of other nations, the Soviet Union and the United States have become the superpowers of the world. The policies of these two nations affect the stability, the economics, and the politics of all other nations on earth.*

*Although the Soviet-American relationship has varied over the years since the USSR became a nation in 1917, it has, except for brief periods, been characterized by contention. With the advent of the atomic bomb, the conflict has become a major determinant of the world's stability and survival. Today if the two superpowers have unsolvable differences, the impact of their incredibly devastating weapons will threaten the destruction of the entire world.*

*Soviet-American relations are of vital importance to everyone. The editors of* The Soviet-American Debate: Opposing Viewpoints SOURCES *have collected key materials that chronicle and illuminate the debate. Viewpoints from leaders and representatives of both governments, from leading scholars and journalists, from citizens both private and public, have been collected and paired in debate fashion. The editors hope in this way to enable their readers to develop an understanding of the conflict from the vantage points of both nations.*

*The book has been edited with an eye to history as well as to the present. The editors have included documents representing the official attitudes of both nations. The viewpoints debate historical episodes between the two nations that had international importance and that continue to influence policy. They continue with the issues of today including consideration of what options might be available to the two nations in their dealings with each other in the future.*

*To aid the readers' understanding of the context of the Soviet-American debate, the editors include here an excellent overview of Soviet-American relations by journalist Saul Pett. Written in commemoration of the fortieth anniversary of the end of World War II, Mr. Pett's article was published in newspapers around the country. It places today's Soviet-American debate in historical and human perspective.*

They crawled toward each other slowly and carefully along the twisted girders of the blown-up bridge, one from the west, the other from the east.

Finally, they met in the middle, two young men, one from the United States, the other from the Union of Soviet Socialist Republics. They met and they shook hands and in the touch of their fingers there came the end of two long roads on which millions had died, from Normandy and from Stalingrad.

It was a moment sweet with victory then. It has been a moment bitter with irony since. In the diabolic design of history, World War II was ending and the Cold War was beginning.

But the scent of peace would not be denied on that golden day 40 years ago, April 25, 1945, when Lt. William Robertson of the 69th Division of the U.S. 1st Army crawled along that bridge over the Elbe River. Adolf Hitler's Germany was cut in two. Total surrender was imminent.

Two great armies from two profoundly different countries were racing toward each other and between them lay the enemy that had united them, the Nazi war machine that had terrorized Europe, now crushed, beaten and in groveling disarray. German soldiers, like German civilians, were fleeing west ahead of the Soviets, begging Americans to take their surrender.

Saul Pett, "Victory Opens a New Era—The Cold War," *St. Paul Pioneer Press*, May 5, 1985. Reprinted by permission of the Associated Press.

Both the American and Soviet forces knew they were about to meet, but the Soviets, who had suffered greater casualties than any nation in history, were taking no chances.

Bill Robertson, at the head of a four-man patrol, reached the Elbe in a jeep. Seeing Russians on the other side, the Americans shouted, ''Amerikanski,'' and waved a white sheet. The Soviets fired at them.

The Americans retreated, regrouped, broke into a German drug store, liberated some colored powders, mixed them with water and then waved a sheet of approximate red, white and blue. The Soviets fired again.

Robertson climbed the tower of a nearby castle, waved the ''flag,'' and his allies across the river fired again. He did this several times with the same uncomfortable result. Then he sent Pvt. Frank Huff back to a slave labor camp liberated the day before. Huff returned with a Russian, who climbed the tower and shouted something in Russian and, in the ensuing peace, Robertson crawled across the bridge to the east bank, where the Soviet soldiers were now smiling.

## Moscow-Washington!

Watching through his binoculars, Maj. Alexei Gorlinsky of the 58th Guards Infantry Division thought the two bridge crawlers looked like acrobats. He was still not convinced the men on the west bank were Americans; the colored bed sheet looked like no flag to him.

But then he heard them shout what sounded like ''Moscow-Washington! Moscow-Washington!'' And then he knew they were Americans and he ran toward the bridge.

At another point, Pvt. Alexander Vasilyevich Olshansky and his unit crossed the Elbe with orders to find out who was on the other side. They came around a turn and there were men in uniforms they hadn't seen before walking toward them. Both groups paused cautiously. Then both started to run and they met exactly midway in a collision of joy, everybody talking at once, nobody understanding anybody, nobody needing to.

Twenty miles to the south of Robertson's bridge, Lt. Albert Kotzebue, Pvt. Joseph Polowsky and 20 other GIs of the U.S. 69th Division reached the Elbe near another destroyed bridge. Soviets on the far shore waved them over and, in a sail-less sailboat found on the bank, Kotzebue, Polowsky and two others paddled across with their rifle butts.

Near the east end of the wrecked bridge, they saw the bodies of scores of German civilians, old men, women and children, cut down in the wanton flailing of a dying war. They kept paddling and reached the Soviets and the celebrations began.

The celebrations roared on into the night wherever Americans and Russians met on the Elbe. They shook hands, they hugged, they drank vodka and schnapps and other spoils of war together, they sang to accordians and baƚalaikas, they toasted each other and they toasted Franklin Roosevelt and Josef Stalin, Harry Truman and Winston Churchill, and they drank to peace in the world and to friendship between their countries.

They exchanged liberated German pistols and cigarettes and insignia and buttons pulled off their uniforms for souvenirs. They showed each other pictures of their families. And a GI would say, ''This is my wife.'' And a Russian would say, ''This was my wife. She was killed by the Germans.''

## One-World Feeling

Bill Robertson of Los Angeles felt a ''one-world feeling'' and gave his watch to a Russian who responded with a gift of his gold wedding band. Joe Polowsky of Chicago felt tears and vowed he would never forget the day. Alexei Gorlinsky of Kiev said he could not imagine anything but peace between the victors. Alexander Vasilyevich Olshansky of Voroshilovgrad in the Ukraine savored the sudden silence of the front. ''Nobody is firing from the east, nobody,'' he said after nearly four years in combat. And in full flight, one GI wrestled an attractive, uniformed Soviet woman to the floor in search of an early detente until Al Kotzebue of Pilot Hill, Calif., removed him.

Hal Boyle and Don Whitehead of the Associated Press, writing under a double byline, found the warriors of the two nations communicating without language. ''It was enough that they were allies and had whipped the enemy.'' Andy Rooney of Stars and Stripes felt that a ''great new world was opening up.''

The celebrators could not know that two days before, in the Oval Office of the White House, President Truman had sternly berated Foreign Minister Vyacheslav Molotov for Soviet violations of agreements reached at Yalta a few months before.

But the mood of the soldiers arm in arm at the Elbe was optimistic. That same day, in San Francisco, a new international organization called the United Nations met for the first time and to many it seemed the best hope of mankind.

Four months later, Lt. Albert Kotzebue was training in a new regiment for the invasion of Japan. Like his father and uncles before him, he was planning a career in the Army. And then the atomic bomb was dropped on Hiroshima and Al Kotzebue thought he'd better find another life plan.

''There goes my Army career,'' he said. ''There won't be any more wars. There isn't going to be an Army or a Navy. Nobody would dare fight again with this thing, this atomic bomb, hanging over them.''

## The Cold War

The Cold War.

For 40 years, it has commanded the fears of people everywhere and, on one occasion, may have come close to blowing up this planet.

It is unique in history as a national preoccupation of two supreme powers and as a national distraction for the rest. It has produced four decades of tension, enmity, competition, confrontation, mutual fear, mutual distrust, staggering cost. It has brought crisis or a sense of crisis to every inhabited continent.

It has shaped and misshaped the world. It has made enemies out of allies, friends out of enemies, hostages out of neutrals, opportunists out of idealists.

It has led us to the ridges of Korea, the rice paddies of Vietnam, the craters of the moon. In bloodshed, it has cost us more than 110,000 lives and the Soviet Union none, until Afghanistan. In treasure, it has cost us more than two world wars combined.

It has stretched reason and exhausted irony. It has moved nations from dependence on a balance of power to dependence on a balance of terror. The more destructive the weapon, the more likely the deterrent. Ergo, the greater the horror, the greater the hope. Worse is better.

"If anything has reduced the chance of war," said a knowing man in the U.S. Embassy in Moscow, "it is the frightening technology, not our understanding of each other. Technology has transformed the stakes more than people have changed the politics."

The Cold War introduced sharp polemics.

"They lost China," the Republicans used to say of the Democrats, ignoring the Chinese who lost China. But then the Russians lost China. We lost Cuba. They lost Egypt. We lost Iran. They lost Albania.

## Strangers and Friends

Until the Soviet Union discovered Cuba in 1959, the two countries were virtually strangers. After that they became intimate friends. Russia subsidized a quarter of the Cuban economy. In return, a grateful Cuba sent troops where Cubans never went before, to Angola and Ethiopia.

The United States—apostle of self-determination and non-intervention—supported right-wing dictatorships in Latin America and southeast Asia because they opposed communism. But the United States also wooed communist China because it had 1 million troops along the Soviet border.

Communist Russia lets contracts to capitalist groups in Western Europe for an oil pipeline across Siberia. We are furious at the capitalists. We help the military dictatorship of Pakistan with fighter planes because the Russians in neighboring Afghanistan might try to reach the oil of the Persian Gulf. India is furious.

Thus, a ripple effect of the Cold War troubles the waters between the world's two largest democracies.

Ideology bows to expediency and expediency proclaims that "the enemy of my enemy is my friend."

In the 14th year of the Cold War, President Dwight Eisenhower said the costs of the arms race were "staggering" and if it continued indefinitely, "we could reach the breaking point." Now, in the 40th year of the Cold War, the word "staggering" seems inadequate.

Since World War II, the United States has spent about $3 trillion—that's $3,000,000,000,000—for defense. Professor William Kaufman, a Pentagon consultant and Harvard lecturer on defense planning, estimates that 60 percent of that can be charged to the Cold War.

That means $1.8 trillion spent for the military. To that, add the costs of the global competition for allies and minds, such as $265 billion in foreign aid and more than $2 billion in propaganda.

## Inevitable Conflict?

How did it all start? How did we get here? Hindsight suggests it may have been inevitable.

Start with the first and, at the time, the only socialist state in the world, born in revolution in a country rendered acutely wary, even paranoidal, by centuries of invasion. Observe that it is a system Lenin said would surely clash with the surrounding world of capitalism. Add a dictatorship needing for its control a sense of menace from the outside. The outside quickly obliged.

After World War I, the United States, England and France sent troops to Russia to overthrow the Bolshevik regime. That failed, but the Russians didn't forget.

In 1933, the United States became the very last major power to recognize the Soviet Union. In the process, the Russians agreed not to propagandize the United States or interfere with its domestic politics. They kept neither promise. The United States didn't forget.

In World War II, the two powers joined arms against Hitler in an alliance of necessity, not ideology. The Russians took horrible losses. They received $11 billion in lend-lease from the United States but repeatedly suspected their Western allies of delaying a second front in the hope that Stalin and Hitler would bleed each other white.

The United States ended lend-lease abruptly three days after the war and the Soviet Union was suddenly cut off. Stalin did not permit free elections in Eastern Europe as promised, and tightened his grip there.

Western Europe, its economy shattered by war, also looked ripe for plucking by Stalin. The United States countered with the imaginative Marshall Plan to revive Western Europe and contain the Marxist tide.

Stalin pushed and the United States pushed back. In Berlin, Greece, Iran, Turkey, the Near East, the Far East, the Congo, Cuba, Korea and Vietnam, the Soviet Union said it was trying to prevent its own encirclement. The United States said it was trying to prevent communist domination of the world.

## Equal in Power, Unequal in Comfort

Point and counterpoint, lunge and parry, they came at each other from disparate corners. They are equal only in their destructive powers. They are strikingly unequal in human comfort, security and opportunity.

The lines in Soviet stores are still long; consumer goods are frequently in short supply. Buyers wait months for a usable refrigerator and years for a reliable car. Housing has improved but many families must still share a bathroom and kitchen with neighbors. Farms are mostly unmechanized.

Life is constricted, news is censored, travel is limited. Soviet science still has difficulty making the leap from theory to application; many inventions never get out of the laboratory. Culture cannot escape the heavy hand of Big Brother and many of the most creative Soviet citizens have left. Even under the czar, Leo Tolstoy wrote in Paris, not Russia.

The Russian psyche has not recovered from the fact that Napoleon once stood on the Kremlin Wall and watched Moscow burn, and Hitler came within 22 miles of the capital.

Foreigners were not to be trusted. Foreign influences were to be avoided like dangerous contagions. The threats from abroad, it was said, made a police state necessary at home.

Josef Stalin did not let liberated Soviet prisoners of war return directly home. First, they were sent to Siberian gulags to recover from their un-Russian exposure.

## Abiding Nightmare

Deep in the Russian soul is the abiding nightmare. Four million German soldiers, tanks, cannons, planes crashing in from the west on a 1,500-mile front. One million dead in Leningrad alone. Two thousand cities and towns gutted or scorched. One third of a nation laid waste. And then the epic counteroffensive all the way to the River Elbe. Total cost: 20 million Soviet dead.

Soviet citizens do not forget World War II; the government doesn't let them. School children are told of the great victory as often as they are reminded of Lenin. Television, newspapers, magazines are full of it. The war cemeteries are vast. The memorials, the towering sculptures are heroic.

The Central Museum of the Soviet Armed Forces in Moscow devotes most of two large floors to World War II. It includes one small picture of the linkup at the Elbe. There is little else to suggest that Americans

and British were involved, that there was an invasion across Europe that began in Normandy, a long air offensive from England and a steady flow of supplies from the United States.

But visitors to the museum have no problem spotting the huge floor-to-ceiling pile of twisted metal identified as the wreckage of an American U-2 spy plane shot down over the Soviet Union.

The Cold War. What has it done to them? To us?

## Tanks Instead of Refrigerators

For them, it has meant tanks instead of refrigerators, missiles instead of housing. It has stretched an economy already gasping under the weight of Karl Marx and inept bureaucracy. It has commandeered the men and the money needed to untap the undeveloped two-thirds of the country, the vast silent places beyond the Urals.

In the battle of political systems, communism is no longer the wave of the future. Doctrine does not keep Eastern Europe in the Soviet orbit; the Red Army does. And the People's Republic of China has clearly turned soft on capitalism.

And us?

The Cold War convulsed us in a passing paroxysm of fear and fingerpointing called McCarthyism. It seems to have made other things permanent.

A huge military-industrial complex about which Eisenhower warned us, in which private enterprise and public purpose blur in a sea of green. A huge intelligence operation of untold size and cost, of spies and coups and plots, a servant of foreign policy but sometimes a rogue elephant. A vast space program of incalculable limits that began as a competition with the Soviet Union because of a small round ball called Sputnik.

In uncounted ways, the Cold War drains the treasury and diverts money and attention from poverty and education at home and, in the world, from awesome problems of hunger, creeping deserts and shrinking resources.

## Habit of War

And, finally there is a state of mind, slowly formed, vaguely perceived. It deeply concerns people like George Kennan, diplomat, historian and veteran of the Cold War:

"Despite the fact that there is no political issue in the relations between the two countries which could conceivably justify a war between them, the preparations—material and psychological—for such a war have been allowed to become an ingrained, dominating habit not just for our armed services but for large parts of our civilian society as well."

Bill Robertson is now 61, a widower and father of two sons. He is a retired neurosurgeon, living in Culver City, Calif., and he is balding and a mite paunchy to be crawling across damaged bridges.

But 10 years ago—on the 30th anniversary of the linkup at the Elbe—he and his wife were warmly received in Moscow, wined, dined and treated to the Bolshoi Ballet and circus. A good time was had by all except for one small event. This was about the time the United States was pulling out of Saigon and one of Robertson's hosts thought it fitting to bring up Vietnam. Retired or not, Robertson knew a needle when he saw one.

"I said the government there had invited us in. He said it was like Hungary, Poland and Czechoslovakia.

"I said, well, not quite. He said the Russians had liberated those countries. I said that's true but they hadn't left, not really. I said we had helped liberate France but we weren't still there. Then my wife gave me the elbow."

## Mutual Distrust

In the 40 years since they hugged at the Elbe, Bill Robertson has thought often about what has happened between the former allies. He thinks some friction is inevitable between opposing ideologies but feels strongly there has to be a way to resolve differences "where common interest come together." Soviet suspiciousness puzzles him.

"Ours is a darn open society. Surely, the Russians must see that we don't intend to go to war against them. All they have to do is read our papers and see the way we talk."

About 11,000 miles from Culver City, at the other end of puzzlement, Alexei Gorlinsky lives in a small Moscow apartment with his wife, Yekaterina. He is now 70, a retired major general of artillery, a father of three and grandfather of four.

He picks his way lovingly and proudly through blurred pictures of the Americans he met at the Elbe, shaking his head, murmuring, "History, history." Like Robertson, the man he watched crawl across the bridge 40 years ago, Gorlinsky can't understand the mistrust of former allies.

"Americans," he said, "are misinformed about us. They don't realize that in the Soviet Union we all lost one or two in our families in the war with Germany. Nobody here wants war."

## Outlawing War

Alexander Vasilyevich Olshansky is still in the army, a major general who proudly lets you know that he is a professor of military engineering at the army academy in Moscow. He remains lean and fit. He and his wife, Olga, have two children and two grandchildren.

He thinks that "science has given us the opportunity to solve all human problems as long as there is no war." He points out that the Soviet Constitution outlaws "war propaganda." He says he wishes the U.S. Constitution had a similar ban.

He does not mention the sentence in his constitution which directly precedes the injunction against war propaganda. This one says that Soviet foreign policy "is aimed at . . . consolidating the positions of world socialism, supporting the struggle of people for national liberation. . . ."

Al Kotzebue, who led a four-man amphibious force across the Elbe paddling with rifle butts, is now 61, father of five and grandfather of 14. He and his wife, Goldie, live in retirement in Pilot Hill, Calif., and he is studying law.

He has not dwelled on the irony of life since the Elbe although in his case it has been singular. He once thought that the atomic bomb meant there would be no more armies, no more navies, no more wars.

But there were, oh, yes, there were, and Kotzebue served in the war in Korea and he served in the war in Vietnam and he did not think much about the fact that behind his new enemies were his old allies.

## No Illusions

After 25 years and three wars, he retired from the army as a colonel and returned to Vietnam twice as a civilian, for the United States Agency for International Development and for army intelligence.

When he thinks of the Elbe he thinks of it as a time of great excitement and camaraderie. He did not then look at the Russians as communists, but as soldiers like himself. Still, he had no illusions; he did not think that his country and theirs would long be allies. He did not like communism or trust Soviet leaders.

For his work at the Elbe, the Russians gave Kotzebue a medal, the Order of Alexander Nevsky. "They tell me," he says, "that the medal entitles me to travel free anywhere in the Soviet Union." He does not appear to be in a hurry to try.

Joe Polowsky came back to Chicago after the big war, drove a cab, raised a family and never forgot what he called "The Oath at the Elbe." The event, he said, "took possession of me the rest of my life." He worked tirelessly for peace.

Every April 25, he stood at the Michigan Avenue bridge over the Chicago River and passed out leaflets urging nuclear disarmament. He wrote letters to members of Congress and world leaders and fellow veterans. In 1955, he went to Moscow and met with Nikita Khrushchev and Soviet alumni of the Elbe.

In 1983, Polowsky died of cancer and was buried, at his request, near the muddy river where he and his buddies paddled into history. His grave is in the middle of the Torgau cemetery in East Germany surrounded by the graves of strangers. Beyond, one sees the drab, gray buildings of an old town in need of repair and Soviet army trucks rolling in and out of a large Soviet garrison.

Nearer the river, there is a large stone monument

with inscriptions commemorating the union at the Elbe. It stands in front of the old castle, from whose tower Robertson waved a sheet 40 years ago.

Gorlinsky came from Moscow for the funeral service at the monument in which he praised Polowsky, the Chicago cab driver, as "a simple man who devoted his life to the spirit of the Elbe by working for peace between our two countries."

## The First Wreath

Then, three American and three Soviet servicemen marched to the monument to lay wreaths in Polowsky's memory, a simple ceremony that had narrowly skirted an incident.

There, on their side of the Iron Curtain, the Russians seemed for a time to be insisting that they lay the first wreath. Then, a U.S. diplomat suggested that both wreaths could be laid at the same time, and this was done. A minor chill in a long, long Cold War.

Missile crisis, Berlin Wall, Korea, Vietnam, the Middle East. Do we find safety in the stars? Will they disarm? Dare we disarm? Who will survive a first strike? Who will lay the first wreath?

*Saul Pett, Associated Press, 1985.*

*"I believe that it must be the policy of the United States to support free peoples who are resisting attempted subjugation by armed minorities or by outside pressures."*

# The Truman Doctrine: Aiding Friends Against Aggressors

Harry S. Truman

The gravity of the situation which confronts the world today necessitates my appearance before a joint session of the Congress.

The foreign policy and the national security of this country are involved.

One aspect of the present situation, which I present to you at this time for your consideration and decision, concerns Greece and Turkey.

The United States has received from the Greek Government an urgent appeal for financial and economic assistance. Preliminary reports from the American Economic Mission now in Greece and reports from the American Ambassador in Greece corroborate the statement of the Greek Government that assistance is imperative if Greece is to survive as a free nation.

I do not believe that the American people and the Congress wish to turn a deaf ear to the appeal of the Greek Government.

Greece is not a rich country. Lack of sufficient natural resources has always forced the Greek people to work hard to make both ends meet. Since 1940, this industrious, peace loving country has suffered invasion, four years of cruel enemy occupation, and bitter internal strife.

When forces of liberation entered Greece they found that the retreating Germans had destroyed virtually all the railways, roads, port facilities, communications, and merchant marine. More than a thousand villages had been burned. Eight-five percent of the children were tubercular. Livestock, poultry, and draft animals had almost disappeared. Inflation had wiped out practically all savings.

## Militant Minority Threatens Chaos

As a result of these tragic conditions, a militant minority, exploiting human want and misery, was

Harry S. Truman, from a special message to the Congress on Greece and Turkey on March 12, 1947.

able to create political chaos which, until now, has made economic recovery impossible.

Greece is today without funds to finance the importation of those goods which are essential to bare subsistence. Under these circumstances the people of Greece cannot make progress in solving their problems of reconstruction. Greece is in desperate need of financial and economic assistance to enable it to resume purchases of food, clothing, fuel and seeds. These are indispensable for the subsistence of its people and are obtainable only from abroad. Greece must have help to import the goods necessary to restore internal order and security so essential for economic and political recovery.

The Greek Government has also asked for the assistance of experienced American adminstrators, economists and technicians to insure that the financial and other aid given to Greece shall be used effectively in creating a stable and self-sustaining economy and in improving its public administration.

The very existence of the Greek state is today threatened by the terrorist activities of several thousand armed men, led by Communists, who defy the government's authority at a number of points, particularly along the northern boundaries. A Commission appointed by the United Nations Security Council is at present investigating disturbed conditions in northern Greece and alleged border violations along the frontier between Greece on the one hand and Albania, Bulgaria, and Yugoslavia on the other.

## Greek Government Can't Cope

Meanwhile, the Greek Government is unable to cope with the situation. The Greek army is small and poorly equipped. It needs supplies and equipment if it is to restore authority to the government throughout Greek territory.

Greece must have assistance if it is to become a self-supporting and self-respecting democracy.

The United States must supply this assistance. We have already extended to Greece certain types of relief and economic aid but these are inadequate.

There is no other country to which democratic Greece can turn.

No other nation is willing and able to provide the necessary support for a democratic Greek government.

The British Government, which has been helping Greece, can give no further financial or economic aid after March 31. Great Britain finds itself under the necessity of reducing or liquidating its commitments in several parts of the world, including Greece.

We have considered how the United Nations might assist in this crisis. But the situation is an urgent one requiring immediate action, and the United Nations and its related organizations are not in a position to extend help of the kind that is required.

It is important to note that the Greek Government has asked for our aid in utilizing effectively the financial and other assistance we may give to Greece, and in improving its public administration. It is of the utmost importance that we supervise the use of any funds made available to Greece, in such a manner that each dollar spent will count toward making Greece self-supporting, and will help to build an economy in which a healthy democracy can flourish.

## Democracy's Defects Always Visible

No government is perfect. One of the chief virtues of a democracy, however, is that its defects are always visible and under democratic processes can be pointed out and corrected. The government of Greece is not perfect. Nevertheless it represents 85 percent of the members of the Greek Parliament who were chosen in an election last year. Foreign observers, including 692 Americans, considered this election to be a fair expression of the views of the Greek people.

The Greek Government has been operating in an atmosphere of chaos and extremism. It has made mistakes. The extension of aid by this country does not mean that the United States condones everything that the Greek Government has done or will do. We have condemned in the past, and we condemn now, extremist measures of the right or the left. We have in the past advised tolerance, and we advise tolerance now.

Greece's neighbor, Turkey, also deserves our attention.

The future of Turkey as an independent and economically sound state is clearly no less important to the freedom-loving peoples of the world than the future of Greece. The circumstances in which Turkey finds itself today are considerably different from those of Greece. Turkey has been spared the disasters that have beset Greece. And during the war, the United States and Great Britain furnished Turkey with material aid.

Nevertheless, Turkey now needs our support.

Since the war Turkey has sought additional financial assistance from Great Britain and the United States for the purpose of effecting that modernization necessary for the maintenance of its national integrity.

That integrity is essential to the preservation of order in the Middle East.

The British Government has informed us that, owing to its own difficulties, it can no longer extend financial or economic aid to Turkey.

## US Must Provide Help

As in the case of Greece, if Turkey is to have the assistance it needs, the United States must supply it. We are the only country able to provide that help.

I am fully aware of the broad implications involved if the United States extends assistance to Greece and Turkey, and I shall discuss these implications with you at this time.

One of the primary objectives of the foreign policy of the United States is the creation of conditions in which we and other nations will be able to work out a way of life free from coercion. This was a fundamental issue in the war with Germany and Japan. Our victory was won over countries which sought to impose their will, and their way of life, upon other nations.

---

*"One of the primary objectives of the foreign policy of the United States is the creation of conditions in which we and other nations will be able to work out a way of life free from coercion."*

---

To ensure the peaceful development of nations, free from coercion, the United States has taken a leading part in establishing the United Nations. The United Nations is designed to make possible lasting freedom and independence for all its members. We shall not realize our objectives, however, unless we are willing to help free peoples to maintain their free institutions and their national integrity against aggressive movements that seek to impose upon them totalitarian regimes. This is no more than a frank recognition that totalitarian regimes imposed upon free peoples, by direct or indirect aggression, undermine the foundations of international peace and hence the security of the United States.

## Will of the Majority

The peoples of a number of countries of the world have recently had totalitarian regimes forced upon them against their will. The Government of the United States has made frequent protests against coercion and intimidation, in violation of the Yalta agreement, in Poland, Rumania, and Bulgaria. I must also state that in a number of other countries there have been similar developments.

At the present moment in world history nearly every nation must choose between alternative ways of life. The choice is too often not a free one.

One way of life is based upon the will of the majority, and is distinguished by free institutions, representative government, free elections, guarantees of individual liberty, freedom of speech and religion, and freedom from political oppression.

---

*"If we falter in our leadership, we may endanger the peace of the world—and we shall surely endanger the welfare of this Nation."*

---

The second way of life is based upon the will of a minority forcibly imposed upon the majority. It relies upon terror and oppression, a controlled press and radio, fixed elections, and the suppression of personal freedoms.

## The US Must Support Freedom

I believe that it must be the policy of the United States to support free peoples who are resisting attempted subjugation by armed minorities or by outside pressures.

I believe that we must assist free peoples to work out their own destinies in their own way.

I believe that our help should be primarily through economic and financial aid which is essential to economic stability and orderly political processes.

The world is not static, and the *status quo* is not sacred. But we cannot allow changes in the *status quo* in violation of the Charter of the United Nations by such methods as coercion, or by such subterfuges as political infiltration. In helping free and independent nations to maintain their freedom, the United States will be giving effect to the principles of the Charter of the United Nations.

## Greece's Importance

It is necessary only to glance at a map to realize that the survival and integrity of the Greek nation are of grave importance in a much wider situation. If Greece should fall under the control of an armed minority, the effect upon its neighbor, Turkey, would be immediate and serious. Confusion and disorder might well spread throughout the entire Middle East.

Moreover, the disappearance of Greece as an independent state would have a profound effect upon those countries in Europe whose peoples are struggling against great difficulties to maintain their freedoms and their independence while they repair the damages of war.

It would be an unspeakable tragedy if these

countries, which have struggled so long against overwhelming odds, should lose that victory for which they sacrificed so much. Collapse of free institutions and loss of independence would be disastrous not only for them but for the world. Discouragement and possibly failure would quickly be the lot of neighboring peoples striving to maintain their freedom and independence.

## Far-Reaching Effect

Should we fail to aid Greece and Turkey in this fateful hour, the effect will be far reaching to the West as well as to the East.

We must take immediate and resolute action.

I therefore ask the Congress to provide authority for assistance to Greece and Turkey in the amount of $400,000,000 for the period ending June 30, 1948. In requesting these funds, I have taken into consideration the maximum amount of relief assistance which would be furnished to Greece out of the $350,000,000 which I recently requested that the Congress authorize for the prevention of starvation and suffering in countries devastated by the war.

In addition to funds, I ask the Congress to authorize the detail of American civilian and military personnel to Greece and Turkey, at the request of those countries, to assist in the tasks of reconstruction, and for the purpose of supervising the use of such financial and material assistance as may be furnished. I recommend that authority also be provided for the instruction and training of selected Greek and Turkish personnel.

Finally, I ask that the Congress provide authority which will permit the speediest and most effective use, in terms of needed commodities, supplies, and equipment, of such funds as may be authorized.

If further funds, or further authority, should be needed for the purposes indicated in this message, I shall not hesitate to bring the situation before the Congress. On this subject the Executive and Legislative branches of the Government must work together.

## A Serious Course

This is a serious course upon which we embark.

I would not recommend it except that the alternative is much more serious.

The United States contributed $341,000,000,000 toward winning World War II. This is an investment in world freedom and world peace.

The assistance that I am recommending for Greece and Turkey amounts to little more than 1/10 of 1 percent of this investment. It is only common sense that we should safeguard this investment and make sure that it was not in vain.

## The Nature of Totalitarian Regimes

The seeds of totalitarian regimes are nurtured by misery and want. They spread and grow in the evil

soil of poverty and strife. They reach their full
growth when the hope of a people for a better life
has died.

We must keep that hope alive.

The free peoples of the world look to us for support
in maintaining their freedoms.

If we falter in our leadership, we may endanger the
peace of the world—and we shall surely endanger the
welfare of this Nation.

Great responsibilities have been placed upon us by
the swift movement of events.

I am confident that the Congress will face these
responsibilities squarely.

*Harry S. Truman became president of the United States
after the death of Franklin Delano Roosevelt in 1945,
and remained in the presidency until 1952. President
Truman's plea for aiding the governments of Greece and
Turkey in order to stop communist expansion remains
timely and relevant today.*

*"The Greek people have deserved [and] they should be given the opportunity to decide their internal affairs and be free in settling them."*

# The Truman Doctrine Violates International Law

### Andrei Gromyko

The United States action with regard to Greece and Turkey cannot but draw the attention of the United Nations. As it follows from the statement of the United States representative, the United States Government not only explains but also tries to justify the political course which it has decided to carry out with respect to Greece and Turkey. It tries to convince us that the action of the United States contributes to the strengthening of the United Nations and corresponds to its principles and purposes.

It is impossible to agree with such an assertion. Indeed, how is it possible to agree with this assertion, as if the action of the United States concerning Greece and Turkey contributed to the strengthening of the United Nations, since the United States Government by its move has ignored the United Nations and disregarded the authority of this Organization? The Government of the United States did not approach the United Nations regarding the question of aid to Greece and Turkey, preferring to act in this case by by-passing the Organization and informing it of the measures planned only *post factum.*

## Creating Unavoidable Suspicion

Such action by the United States not only does not contribute to the strengthening of the United Nations, but on the contrary weakens this Organization and undermines its authority. Instead of strengthening international confidence, such action brings about unavoidable suspicion with respect to its actual aims, and hampers the development of friendly relations among States. First of all, just for those very reasons, it does not correspond to the principles on which the activities of our Organization are based.

Andrei Gromyko, from a statement by the Representative of the Union of Soviet Socialist Republics to the United Nations Security Council on April 7, 1947.

The purposes and principles of the United Nations require that all nations, small and large, co-operate in the solution of international problems, and particularly of those which relate to the maintenance of international peace and security. Only such co-operation by all Member States of the Organization can ensure its success and make an effective instrument in the struggle for peace and security. Only such co-operation can contribute to the strengthening of good-neighbourly relations among nations and lead to the strengthening of international confidence which is still lacking in the activities of the United Nations and in international relations.

The United States representative tried to convince us that the so-called United States aid to Greece and Turkey would contribute to the strengthening of peace and security in that area. At the same time, he pointed to the tense situation existing in Greece, particularly in its northern part, linking that situation with the alleged existing threat to Greece from outside.

It would seem only natural and fully in accordance with the spirit and letter of the Charter to appeal in such case to an appropriate organ of the United Nations to take necessary measures in order to remove such an alleged existing threat.

But in such a case, the United States Government would be obliged to prove to the appropriate organ of the United Nations—under the circumstances, to the Security Council—that the threat, to which the United States Government refers, actually exists in so far as those countries are concerned. It would be necessary to prove the existence of such a threat, in order that the Security Council might be able to take the measures provided in the Charter in the interest of the maintenance of peace.

## Unilateral Action Adopted

However, for its part, the United States Government has evidently preferred to adopt a considerably easier method of unilateral action, instead of submitting proofs to the Security Council to the effect that the threat to Greece and Turkey actually exists. Only by those facts can one explain why the United States has ignored the United Nations in this important matter without taking into account the fact that this action deals a serious blow to the Organization's authority.

Only after the United States Government had made statements on the measures undertaken by it in regard to Greece and Turkey did it, evidently, begin to realize the fact that its action was obviously in contradiction with the principles of the United Nations Charter. Only by that circumstance can one explain the attempt of the United States representative who not only informed the Security Council of the above action *post factum* but also connected the so-called aid to Greece and Turkey with the work of the Commission of the Security Council carrying out the investigation of incidents on the northern Greek frontier.

Is it not clear that the attempt of the United States representative to connect such two different matters as the work of the Commission of Investigation, on the one hand, and the United States aid to Greece and Turkey on the other, is of an artificial nature and absolutely unfounded? In reality, the very fact that the Security Council is dealing with the question concerning the incidents on the Greek border and that a special Commission appointed by the Council is investigating the situation on the spot in Greece itself would seem to require, in the first place, that the Security Council should await the completion of the work of the Commission and, secondly, that the Security Council should take necessary measures as a result of a finding based on the conclusion of the Commission.

## United States Is Violating Law

Meanwhile, the United States Government not only considered it unnecessary to await the completion of the work of the Commission appointed by the Security Council with active participation of the United States, and to await an appropriate decision of the Security Council, but has taken measures on its part which entirely ignore the work of the Commission and the conclusions at which the Commission might arrive, as well as the future decision of the Security Council itself on the question. Such actions have nothing in common with methods of international co-operation on questions of the maintenance of peace, which every Member State is obliged to follow by its very membership in the United Nations. So much the more does this relate to the countries which are the initiators of the creation of this Organization. If those countries do not render this Organization all the necessary support, a question arises: on whose support can this Organization count first of all, and on whose support

first of all should this Organization rely?

It is impossible not to point out some other important aspects of measures undertaken by the United States in regard to Greece and Turkey. The "aid" itself which the United States Government intends to render to Greece and Turkey is of such a nature that it cannot be recognized to be consistent with the purposes and principles of the United Nations. This is apparent from the mere fact that the policy stated by the United States Government, with respect to those countries, provides, as is known, not only for economic aid, but also for military and other "aid" as well. Moreover, it follows from the statements made in Congress by United States Government representatives that the major portion of the sums assigned for Greece is intended neither for the reconstruction of the economy of that country nor for rendering material aid to the population, but for military needs. This means that the rendering of the so-called "aid" cannot bring economic recovery to Greece or improvement of the living conditions of the Greek people.

As to Turkey, it follows from the statements made in Congress by the same United States Government representatives that all sums planned for that country are intended, in fact, for military purposes only.

---

*"The Greek people have deserved to be treated with greater respect than they are being treated by the United States."*

---

I should like to draw the special attention of the Security Council to one particular kind of this "aid": namely, to the sending of United States instructors, both on civil and military matters, to Greece and Turkey. No one can dispute the fact that the sending to this or that country of civil and especially military instructors, regardless of the position taken by the Government of the country to which those instructors are sent, itself constitutes an interference in the internal affairs of that country and deals a serious blow to its actual independence.

## Greece Should Decide Its Own Affairs

The Greek people have made a large enough contribution to the common struggle of the democratic countries against the German fascist aggressors. The Greek people have considerable merits which were won in the struggle against the fascist invaders who tortured the land of Greece during the several years of brutal occupation. The Greek people have deserved to be treated with greater respect than they are being treated by the United States. In any case, the Greek people have deserved that they should be given the opportunity to decide their internal affairs and be free in settling them. We should lend our ear to the voice of Greek democratic spokesmen, who protest against the continuation of foreign interference in the affairs of Greece and justly state that the continuation of this interference would lead only to the further intensification of civil war in the country, to the increasing of sufferings of the Greek people, and to the loss of independence by Greece with all the consequences following from such a situation.

*"The measures taken by the Government of the United States with respect to Greece and Turkey seriously undermine the authority of the United Nations and inevitably produce distrust."*

It was pointed out in the statement of the United States representative that Greece had greatly suffered from the enemy occupation, that its economy had been ruined, and that it had needed aid from outside in the past and continued to be in need of such aid at the present time. Such data concerning aid to Greece from UNWRA were also given in the statement, and it was emphasized that the continuation of aid to Greece was necessary in order to save the country from ruin, further degradation, and further deterioration of its economic situation. Reference to the grave economic situation in Greece corresponds to reality. Greece, undoubtedly, suffered great destruction as a result of the war and enemy occupation. Greece, therefore, as well as other Allied countries which suffered from fascist occupation, unquestionably has the right to receive aid from outside.

## Aid Should Not Influence

It goes without saying that the aid to Greece should be rendered and used in the interests of the Greek people. That aid should in no case serve as an instrument of foreign influence in Greece. Such aid, free from the tendency to use it as a means of pressure and foreign interference in the internal affairs of Greece, would be in accord with the spirit of the Charter and with the purposes of the United Nations. Such aid could be carried out with the participation of a special commission of the Security Council which would supervise the proper realization of such aid in the interests of the Greek people.

I have already pointed out that Greece, as an Allied country which seriously suffered from the war and enemy occupation, has the right to receive aid from outside. Is it possible, however, to say the same about Turkey? As far as Turkey is concerned, we cannot say this, if we deal with the matter really objectively, and if we appraise justly and impartially

the facts characterizing Turkey's position, her role in the last war, and all other data bearing on this question.

Objectivity and justice demand recognition of the fact that Turkey has no such right to receive aid from outside, since it is not a country which has suffered in the war. Its territory was not occupied. Turkey did not assist the Allies in their struggle against hitlerite Germany. Moreover, Turkey supplied hitlerite Germany with strategic raw materials which the latter needed during the war; Turkey profiteered during the war from the help to hitlerite Germany. The efforts of the Allied Powers to persuade Turkey to take part in the common struggle of the United Nations against fascist aggressors did not bring, as is well known, positive results. The formal declaration of war by Turkey on Germany, which took place only on the eve of the final defeat and complete surrender of the latter, was, in substance, a gesture, which was not and could not be of any use to the Allies or of any assistance in their efforts to win the victory over the enemy. In the struggle of the democratic countries against the strong and brutal enemy—the German fascist hordes—Turkey was not in the camp of the democratic countries. Is it possible to ignore those facts when discussing, in the Security Council, the question of the action of the United States in respect to Turkey? No, it is not possible to ignore such facts, if we wish to give a correct and objective evaluation of that action. Thus, no sufficient reasons can be found for granting aid to Turkey.

Mr. Austin spoke extensively about the Commission of the Security Council investigating incidents on the Greek frontiers. He made a proposal on the desirability of leaving the representatives of the Commission in northern Greece, until the Security Council took an appropriate decision on the report of the Commission. Since the question about that Commission is a rather narrow and separate one, I shall express my attitude regarding that proposal in a separate statement.

## Undermining United Nations Authority

All the facts which I have stated make it necessary for me to draw the following conclusions:

The measures taken by the Government of the United States with respect to Greece and Turkey seriously undermine the authority of the United Nations and inevitably produce distrust in relations among the Member States of the United Nations.

The attempt of the United States Government to connect *post factum* its action in regard to the above countries with the work of the Commission of Investigation of the Security Council in Greece is unfounded, and only emphasizes the danger to the authority of the United Nations represented by the blow which is dealt by a unilateral move of the United States Government.

The actual material aid needed by the Greek people

can and must be real aid, and must not serve as a
screen for the purposes which have nothing in
common with aid at all. Aid must be rendered
through the United Nations, in which case it will
exclude all possibilities of any foreign influence in
that country.

*In 1947 Andrei Gromyko was a representative to the
United Nations for the Union of Soviet Socialist
Republics. The Soviet Union responded negatively and
vehemently to Truman's speech.*

# The Eisenhower Doctrine: Helping Nations Which Need Our Help

Dwight D. Eisenhower

First may I express to you my deep appreciation of your courtesy in giving me, at some inconvenience to yourselves, this early opportunity of addressing you on a matter I deem to be of grave importance to our country....

Before doing so it is well to remind ourselves that our basic national objective in international affairs remains peace—a world peace based on justice. Such a peace must include all areas, all peoples of the world if it is to be enduring. There is no nation, great or small, with which we would refuse to negotiate, in mutual good faith, with patience and in the determination to secure a better understanding between us. Out of such understandings must, and eventually will, grow confidence and trust, indispensable ingredients to a program of peace and to plans for lifting from us all the burdens of expensive armaments. To promote these objectives, our government works tirelessly, day by day, month by month, year by year. But until a degree of success crowns our efforts that will assure to all nations peaceful existence, we must, in the interests of peace itself, remain vigilant, alert and strong.

The Middle East has abruptly reached a critical stage in its long and important history. In past decades many of the countries in that area were not fully self-governing. Other nations exercised considerable authority in the area and the security of the region was largely built around their power. But since the First World War there has been a steady evolution toward self-government and independence. This development the United States has welcomed and has encouraged. Our country supports without reservation the full sovereignty and independence of each and every nation of the Middle East.

The evolution to independence has in the main

been a peaceful process. But the area has been often troubled. Persistent cross-currents of distrust and fear with raids back and forth across national boundaries have brought about a high degree of instability in much of the Mid East. Just recently there have been hostilities involving Western European nations that once exercised much influence in the area. Also the relatively large attack by Israel in October has intensified the basic differences between that nation and its Arab neighbors. All this instability has been heightened and, at times, manipulated by International Communism.

## Russia's Need to Dominate

Russia's rulers have long sought to dominate the Middle East. That was true of the Czars and it is true of the Bolsheviks. The reasons are not hard to find. They do not affect Russia's security, for no one plans to use the Middle East as a base for aggression against Russia. Never for a moment has the United States entertained such a thought.

The Soviet Union has nothing whatsoever to fear from the United States in the Middle East, or anywhere else in the world, so long as its rulers do not themselves first resort to aggression.

That statement I make solemnly and emphatically.

Neither does Russia's desire to dominate the Middle East spring from its own economic interest in the area. Russia does not appreciably use or depend upon the Suez Canal. In 1955 Soviet traffic through the Canal represented only about three-fourths of 1% of the total. The Soviets have no need for, and could provide no market for, the petroleum resources which constitute the principal natural wealth of the area. Indeed, the Soviet Union is a substantial exporter of petroleum products.

The reason for Russia's interest in the Middle East is solely that of power politics. Considering her announced purpose of Communizing the world, it is easy to understand her hope of dominating the

Dwight D. Eisenhower, from a special message to the Congress on the situation in the Middle East on January 5, 1957.

Middle East.

This region has always been the crossroads of the continents of the Eastern Hemisphere. The Suez Canal enables the nations of Asia and Europe to carry on the commerce that is essential if these countries are to maintain well-rounded and prosperous economies. The Middle East provides a gateway between Eurasia and Africa.

---

*"International Communism, of course, seeks to mask its purposes of domination by expressions of good will and by superficially attractive offers of political, economic and military aid."*

---

It contains about two-thirds of the presently known oil deposits of the world and it normally supplies the petroleum needs of many nations of Europe, Asia and Africa. The nations of Europe are peculiarly dependent upon this supply, and this dependency relates to transportation as well as to production! This has been vividly demonstrated since the closing of the Suez Canal and some of the pipelines. Alternate ways of transportation and, indeed, alternate sources of power can, if necessary, be developed. But these cannot be considered as early prospects.

## Middle East Loss of Independence

These things stress the immense importance of the Middle East. If the nations of that area should lose their independence, if they were dominated by alien forces hostile to freedom, that would be both a tragedy for the area and for many other free nations whose economic life would be subject to near strangulation. Western Europe would be endangered just as though there had been no Marshall Plan, no North Atlantic Treaty Organization. The free nations of Asia and Africa, too, would be placed in serious jeopardy. And the countries of the Middle East would lose the markets upon which their economies depend. All this would have the most adverse, if not disastrous, effect upon our own nation's economic life, and political prospects.

Then there are other factors which transcend the material. The Middle East is the birthplace of three great religions—Moslem, Christian and Hebrew. Mecca and Jerusalem are more than places on the map. They symbolize religions which teach that the spirit has supremacy over matter and that the individual has a dignity and rights of which no despotic government can rightfully deprive him. It would be intolerable if the holy places of the Middle East should be subjected to a rule that glorifies atheistic materialism.

International Communism, of course, seeks to mask its purposes of domination by expressions of good will and by superficially attractive offers of political, economic and military aid. But any free nation, which is the subject of Soviet enticement, ought, in elementary wisdom, to look behind the mask.

## Remember Nations Crushed by the USSR

Remember Estonia, Latvia and Lithuania! In 1939 the Soviet Union entered into mutual assistance pacts with these then independent countries; and the Soviet Foreign Minister, addressing the Extraordinary Fifth Session of the Supreme Soviet in October 1939, solemnly and publicly declared that "we stand for the scrupulous and punctilious observance of the pacts on the basis of complete reciprocity, and we declare that all the nonsensical talk about the Sovietization of the Baltic countries is only to the interest of our common enemies and of all anti-Soviet provocateurs." Yet in *1940*, Estonia, Latvia and Lithuania were forcibly incorporated into the Soviet Union.

Soviet control of the satellite nations of Eastern Europe has been forcibly maintained in spite of solemn promises of a contrary intent, made during World War II.

Stalin's death brought hope that this pattern would change. And we read the pledge of the Warsaw Treaty of 1955 that the Soviet Union would follow in satellite countries "the principles of mutual respect for their independence and sovereignty and noninterference in domestic affairs." But we have just seen the subjugation of Hungary by naked armed force. In the aftermath of this Hungarian tragedy, world respect for and belief in Soviet promises have sunk to a new low. International Communism needs and seeks a recognizable success.

Thus, we have these simple and indisputable facts:

1. The Middle East, which has always been coveted by Russia, would today be prized more than ever by International Communism.

2. The Soviet rulers continue to show that they do not scruple to use any means to gain their ends.

3. The free nations of the Mid East need, and for the most part want, added strength to assure their continued independence....

## The Responsibility of the US

Under all the circumstances I have laid before you, a greater responsibility now devolves upon the United States. We have shown, so that none can doubt, our dedication to the principle that force shall not be used internationally for any aggressive purpose and that the integrity and independence of the nations of the Middle East should be inviolate. Seldom in history has a nation's dedication to principle been tested as severely as ours during recent weeks.

There is general recognition in the Middle East, as

elsewhere, that the United States does not seek either political or economic domination over any other people. Our desire is a world environment of freedom, not servitude. On the other hand many, if not all, of the nations of the Middle East are aware of the danger that stems from International Communism and welcome closer cooperation with the United States to realize for themselves the United Nations goals of independence, economic well-being and spiritual growth.

If the Middle East is to continue its geographic role of uniting rather than separating East and West; if its vast economic resources are to serve the well-being of the peoples there, as well as that of others; and if its cultures and religions and their shrines are to be preserved for the uplifting of the spirits of the peoples, then the United States must make more evident its willingness to support the independence of the freedom-loving nations of the area.

## Deterring Aggression

Under these circumstances I deem it necessary to seek the cooperation of the Congress. Only with that cooperation can we give the reassurance needed to deter aggression, to give courage and confidence to those who are dedicated to freedom and thus prevent a chain of events which would gravely endanger all of the free world....

Weaknesses in the present situation and the increased danger from International Communism, convince me that basic United States policy should now find expression in joint action by the Congress and the Executive. Furthermore, our joint resolve should be so couched as to make it apparent that if need be our words will be backed by action.

## US National Security and Other Nations

It is nothing new for the President and the Congress to join to recognize that the national integrity of other free nations is directly related to our own security.

We have joined to create and support the security system of the United Nations. We have reinforced the collective security system of the United Nations by a series of collective defense arrangements. Today we have security treaties with 42 other nations which recognize that our peace and security are intertwined. We have joined to take decisive action in relation to Greece and Turkey and in relation to Taiwan.

Thus, the United States through the joint action of the President and the Congress, or, in the case of treaties, the Senate, has manifested in many endangered areas its purpose to support free and independent governments—and peace—against external menace, notably the menace of International Communism. Thereby we have helped to maintain peace and security during a period of great danger. It is now essential that the United States should manifest through joint action of the President and the

Congress our determination to assist those nations of the Mid East area, which desire that assistance.

The action which I propose would have the following features.

It would, first of all, authorize the United States to cooperate with and assist any nation or group of nations in the general area of the Middle East in the development of economic strength dedicated to the maintenance of national independence.

It would, in the second place, authorize the Executive to undertake in the same region programs of military assistance and cooperation with any nation or group of nations which desires such aid.

It would, in the third place, authorize such assistance and cooperation to include the employment of the armed forces of the United States to secure and protect the territorial integrity and political independence of such nations, requesting such aid, against overt armed aggression from any nation controlled by International Communism....

This program will not solve all the problems of the Middle East. Neither does it represent the totality of our policies for the area....

---

*"Only with [the cooperation of Congress] can we give the reassurance needed to deter aggression, . . . and thus prevent a chain of events which would gravely endanger all of the free world."*

---

The proposed legislation is primarily designed to deal with the possibility of Communist aggression, direct and indirect. There is imperative need that any lack of power in the area should be made good, not by external or alien force, but by the increased vigor and security of the independent nations of the area.

## Indirect Aggression Rarely Succeeds

Experience shows that indirect aggression rarely if ever succeeds where there is reasonable security against direct aggression; where the government disposes of loyal security forces, and where economic conditions are such as not to make Communism seem an attractive alternative. The program I suggest deals with all three aspects of this matter and thus with the problem of indirect aggression.

It is my hope and belief that if our purpose be proclaimed, as proposed by the requested legislation, that very fact will serve to halt any contemplated aggression. We shall have heartened the patriots who are dedicated to the independence of their nations. They will not feel that they stand alone, under the menace of great power. And I should add that patriotism is, throughout this area, a powerful sentiment. It is true that fear sometimes perverts true patriotism into fanaticism and to the acceptance of dangerous enticements from without. But if that fear can be allayed, then the climate will be more favorable to the attainment of worthy national ambitions.

---

*"The occasion has come for us to manifest again our national unity in support of freedom and to show our deep respect for the rights and independence of every nation—however great, however small."*

---

And as I have indicated, it will also be necessary for us to contribute economically to strengthen those countries, or groups of countries, which have governments manifestly dedicated to the preservation of independence and resistance to subversion. Such measures will provide the greatest insurance against Communist inroads. Words alone are not enough.

## Need to Use Military Force

Let me refer again to the requested authority to employ the armed forces of the United States to assist to defend the territorial integrity and the political independence of any nation in the area against Communist armed aggression. Such authority would not be exercised except at the desire of the nation attacked. Beyond this it is my profound hope that this authority would never have to be exercised at all.

Nothing is more necessary to assure this than that our policy with respect to the defense of the area be promptly and clearly determined and declared. Thus the United Nations and all friendly governments, and indeed governments which are not friendly, will know where we stand.

If, contrary to my hope and expectation, a situation arose which called for the military application of the policy which I ask the Congress to join me in proclaiming, I would of course maintain hour-by-hour contact with the Congress if it were in session. And if the Congress were not in session, and if the situation had grave implications, I would, of course, at once call the Congress into special session.

In the situation now existing, the greatest risk, as is often the case, is that ambitious despots may miscalculate. If power-hungry Communists should either falsely or correctly estimate that the Middle East is inadequately defended, they might be tempted to use open measures of armed attack. If so, that would start a chain of circumstances which would almost surely involve the United States in military action. I am convinced that the best insurance against this dangerous contingency is to make clear now our readiness to cooperate fully and freely with our friends of the Middle East in ways consonant with the purposes and principles of the United Nations. I intend promptly to send a special mission to the Middle East to explain the cooperation we are prepared to give.

## Burdens and Risks

The policy which I outline involves certain burdens and indeed risks for the United States. Those who covet the area will not like what is proposed. Already, they are grossly distorting our purpose. However, before this Americans have seen our nation's vital interests and human freedom in jeopardy, and their fortitude and resolution have been equal to the crisis, regardless of hostile distortion of our words, motives and actions.

Indeed, the sacrifices of the American people in the cause of freedom have, even since the close of World War II, been measured in many billions of dollars and in thousands of precious lives of our youth. These sacrifices, by which great areas of the world have been preserved to freedom, must not be thrown away.

In those momentous periods of the past, the President and the Congress have united, without partisanship, to serve the vital interests of the United States and of the free world.

The occasion has come for us to manifest again our national unity in support of freedom and to show our deep respect for the rights and independence of every nation—however great, however small. We seek not violence, but peace. To this purpose we must now devote our energies, our determination, ourselves.

*Dwight D. Eisenhower was president of the United States from 1953 to 1961. This pivotal speech expresses when and how the US should provide military aid to other countries.*

*"The United States wants. . .to secure a
dominant position in the capitalist world
for itself, and to reduce all its partners
in the blocs to the status of obedient
executors of its will."*

viewpoint 4

# Khrushchev on the International Position of the Soviet Union

Nikita S. Khrushchev

The emergence of socialism from within the bounds of a single country and its transformation into a world system is the main feature of our era. Capitalism has proved powerless to prevent this process of world-historic significance. The simultaneous existence of two opposite world economic systems, the capitalist and the socialist, developing according to different laws and in opposite directions, has become an indisputable fact.

Socialist economy is developing toward the ever-increasing satisfaction of the material and cultural requirements of all members of society, the continuous expansion and improvement of production on the basis of higher techniques, and closer co-operation and mutual assistance between the socialist countries.

The trend of capitalist economy is that of the ever-increasing enrichment of the monopolies, the further intensification of exploitation and cuts in the living standards of millions of working people, particularly in the colonial and dependent countries, of increased militarization of the economy, the exacerbation of the competitive struggle among the capitalist countries, and the maturing of new economic crises and upheavals. . . .

Comrades, between the Nineteenth and Twentieth Congresses of the Communist Party of the Soviet Union, very important changes have taken place in international relations.

Soon after the Second World War ended, the influence of reactionary and militarist groups began to be increasingly evident in the policy of the United States of America, Britain and France. Their desire to enforce their will on other countries by economic and political pressure, threats and military provocation prevailed. This became known as the "positions of

Nikita S. Khrushchev, from the report of the Central Committee of the Communist Party of the Soviet Union to the 20th Party Congress on February 14, 1956.

strength" policy. It reflects the aspiration of the most aggressive sections of present-day imperialism to win world supremacy, to suppress the working class and the democratic and national-liberation movements; it reflects their plans for military adventures against the socialist camp.

## International Distrust

The international atmosphere was poisoned by war hysteria. The arms race began to assume more and more monstrous dimensions. Many big U.S. military bases designed for use against the U.S.S.R. and the People's Democracies were built in countries thousands of miles from the borders of the United States. "Cold war" was begun against the socialist camp. International distrust was artificially kindled, and nations set against one another. A bloody war was launched in Korea; the war in Indo-China dragged on for years.

The inspirers of the "cold war" began to establish military blocs, and many countries found themselves, against the will of their peoples, involved in restricted aggressive alignments—the North Atlantic bloc, Western European Union, SEATO (military bloc for South-East Asia) and the Baghdad pact.

The organizers of military blocs allege that they have united for defence, for protection against the "communist threat." But that is sheer hypocrisy. We know from history that when planning a redivision of the world, the imperialist powers have always lined up military blocs. Today the "anti-communism" slogan is again being used as a smokescreen to cover up the claims of one power for world domination. The new thing here is that the United States wants, by means of all kinds of blocs and pacts, to secure a dominant position in the capitalist world for itself, and to reduce all its partners in the blocs to the status of obedient executors of its will.

The inspirers of the "positions of strength" policy assert that this policy makes another war impossible, because it ensures a "balance of power" in the world arena. This view is widespread among Western statesmen and it is therefore all the more important to thoroughly expose its real meaning.

## Peace and the Arms Race

Can peace be promoted by an arms race? It would seem that it is simply absurd to pose such a question. Yet the adherents of the "positions of strength" policy offer the arms race as their main recipe for the preservation of peace! It is perfectly obvious that when nations compete to increase their military might, the danger of war becomes greater, not lesser.

The arms race, the "positions of strength" policy, the lining up of aggressive blocs and the "cold war"—all this could not but aggravate the international situation, and it did. This has been one trend of world events during the period under review.

---

*"The fanning of war hysteria is used to justify imperialist expansion, to intimidate the masses and dope their minds in order to justify the higher taxes."*

---

But other processes have also taken place in the international arena during these years, processes showing that in the world today monopolist circles are by no means controlling everything.

The steady consolidation of the forces of socialism, democracy and peace, and of the forces of the national-liberation movement is of decisive significance. The international position of the Soviet Union, the People's Republic of China, and the other socialist countries has been further strengthened during this period, and their prestige and international ties have grown immeasurably. The international camp of socialism is exerting ever-growing influence on the course of international events.

The forces of peace have been considerably augmented by the emergence in the world arena of a group of peace-loving European and Asian states which have proclaimed non-participation in blocs as a principle of their foreign policy. The leading political circles of these states rightly hold that to participate in restricted military imperialist alignments would merely increase the danger of their countries being involved in military gambles by the aggressive forces and draw them into the maelstrom of the arms drive.

As a result, a vast Zone of Peace including peace-loving states, both socialist and non-socialist, of Europe and Asia, has emerged in the world. This zone includes vast areas inhabited by nearly 1,500 million people, that is, the majority of the population of our planet. . . .

The October Socialist Revolution struck a most powerful blow at the imperialist colonial system. Under the influence of the Great October Revolution the national-liberation struggle of the colonial peoples developed with particular force, it continued throughout the subsequent years and has led to a deep-going crisis of the entire imperialist colonial system. . . .

## Nations Freed from Colonialism

India, the country with the world's second biggest population, has won political independence. Independence has been gained by Burma, Indonesia, Egypt, Syria, the Lebanon, the Sudan, and a number of other former colonial countries. More than 1,200 million people, or nearly half of the world's population, have freed themselves from colonial or semi-colonial dependence during the last ten years.

The disintegration of the imperialist colonial system now taking place is a post-war development of history-making significance. Peoples who for centuries were kept away by the colonialists from the high road of progress followed by human society are now going through a great process of regeneration. People's China and the independent Indian Republic have joined the ranks of the Great Powers. We are witnessing a political and economic upsurge of the peoples of South-East Asia and the Arab East. The awakening of the peoples of Africa has begun. The national-liberation movement has gained in strength in Brazil, Chile and other Latin-American countries. The outcome of the wars in Korea, Indo-China and Indonesia has demonstrated that the imperialists are unable, even with the help of armed intervention, to crush the peoples who are resolutely fighting for a life of freedom and independence. The complete abolition of the infamous system of colonialism has now been put on the agenda as one of the most acute and pressing problems.

The new period in world history which Lenin predicted has arrived, and the peoples of the East are playing an active part in deciding the destinies of the whole world, are becoming a new mighty factor in international relations. In contrast to the pre-war period, most Asian countries now act in the world arena as sovereign states or states which are resolutely upholding their right to an independent foreign policy. International relations have spread beyond the bounds of relations between the countries inhabited chiefly by peoples of the white race and are beginning to acquire the character of genuinely world-wide relations.

The winning of political freedom by the peoples of the former colonies and semi-colonies is the first and most important prerequisite of their full independence, that is, of the achievement of economic independence. The liberated Asian countries are pursuing a policy of building up their own industry, training their own technicians, raising the living standards of the people, and regenerating and developing their age-old national culture. History-making prospects for a better future are opening up before the countries which have embarked upon the path of independent development.

These countries, although they do not belong to the socialist world system, can draw on its achievements to build up an independent national economy and to raise the living standards of their peoples. Today they need not go begging for up-to-date equipment to their former oppressors. They can get it in the socialist countries, without assuming any political or military commitments.

## Socialist Countries Can Aid Other Nations

The very fact that the Soviet Union and the other countries of the socialist camp exist, their readiness to help the underdeveloped countries in advancing their industries on terms of equality and mutual benefit are a major stumbling-block to colonial policy. The imperialists can no longer regard the underdeveloped countries solely as potential sources for making maximum profits. They are compelled to make concessions to them.

Not all the countries, however, have thrown off the colonial yoke. A big part of the African continent, some countries of Asia, Central and South America continue to remain in colonial or semi-colonial dependence. They are still retained as agrarian raw-material appendages of the imperialist countries. The living standard of the population in the dependent countries remains exceedingly low.

The contradictions and rivalry between the colonial powers for spheres of influence, sources of raw materials, and markets are growing. The United States is out to grab the colonial possessions of the European powers. South Vietnam is passing from France to the United States. The American monopolies are waging an offensive against the French, Belgian and Portuguese possessions in Africa. Once Iran's oil riches were fully controlled by the British, but now the British have been compelled to share them with the Americans; moreover, the American monopolists are fighting to oust the British entirely. American influence in Pakistan and Iraq is increasing under the guise of "free enterprise."

## American Monopolies

The American monopolies, utilizing their dominant position in the Central and South-American countries, have moulded the economies of many of them in a distorted, one-sided way, extremely disadvantageous for the population. They are hampering their industrial development and shackling them with the heavy chains of economic dependence.

To preserve, and in some places also to re-establish their former domination, the colonial powers are resorting to the suppression of the colonial peoples by the force of arms, a method which has been condemned by history. They also have recourse to new forms of colonial enslavement under the guise of so-called "aid" to underdeveloped countries, which brings colossal profits to the colonialists. Let us take the United States as an example. The United States renders such "aid" above all in the form of deliveries of American weapons to the underdeveloped countries. This enables the American monopolies to load up their industry with arms orders. Then the products of the arms industry, worth billions of dollars and paid for through the budget by the American taxpayers, are sent to the underdeveloped countries. States receiving such "aid" in the form of weapons, inevitably fall into dependence; they increase their armies, which leads to higher taxes and a decline in living standards.

The monopolists are interested in continuing the "positions of strength" policy; the ending of the "cold war" is to their disadvantage. Why? Because the fanning of war hysteria is used to justify imperialist expansion, to intimidate the masses and dope their minds in order to justify the higher taxes which then go to pay for war orders and flow into the safes of the millionaires. Thus, the "cold war" is a means for maintaining the war industry at a high level and for extracting colossal profits.

*"Our certainty of the victory of communism is based on the fact that the socialist mode of production possesses decisive advantages over the capitalist mode of production."*

Naturally, "aid" to underdeveloped countries is granted on definite political terms, terms providing for their integration into aggressive military blocs, the conclusion of joint military pacts, and support for American foreign policy aimed at world domination, or "world leadership," as the American imperialists themselves call it. . . .

## Peaceful Co-Existence

*The peaceful co-existence of the two systems.* The Leninist principle of peaceful co-existence of states with different social systems has always been and remains the general line of our country's foreign policy.

It has been alleged that the Soviet Union advances the principle of peaceful co-existence merely out of tactical considerations, considerations of expediency. Yet it is common knowledge that we have always, from the very first years of Soviet power, stood with equal firmness for peaceful co-existence. Hence, it is not a tactical move, but a fundamental principle of Soviet foreign policy.

This means that if there is indeed a threat to the peaceful co-existence of countries with differing social and political systems, it by no means comes from the Soviet Union or the rest of the socialist camp. Is there a single reason why a socialist state should want to unleash aggressive war? Do we have classes and groups that are interested in war as a means of enrichment? We do not. We abolished them long ago. Or, perhaps, we do not have enough territory or natural wealth, perhaps we lack sources of raw materials or markets for our goods? No, we have sufficient of all those and to spare. Why then should we want war? We do not want it, as a matter of principle we renounce any policy that might lead to millions of people being plunged into war for the sake of the selfish interests of a handful of multi-millionaires. Do those who shout about the "aggressive intentions" of the U.S.S.R. know all this?

*"We have always held and continue to hold that the establishment of a new social system in one or another country is the internal affair of the peoples of the countries concerned."*

Of course they do. Why then do they keep up the old monotonous refrain about some imaginary "communist aggression"? Only to stir up mud, to conceal their plans for world domination, a "crusade" against peace, democracy, and socialism.

## Revolutions Cannot Be Exported

To this day the enemies of peace allege that the Soviet Union is out to overthrow capitalism in other countries by "exporting" revolution. It goes without saying that among us Communists there are no supporters of capitalism. But this does not mean that we have interfered or plan to interfere in the internal affairs of countries where capitalism still exists. Romain Rolland was right when he said that "freedom is not brought in from abroad in baggage trains like Bourbons." It is ridiculous to think that revolutions are made to order. We often hear representatives of bourgeois countries reasoning thus: "The Soviet leaders claim that they are for peaceful co-existence between the two systems. At the same time they declare that they are fighting for communism, and say that communism is bound to win in all countries. Now if the Soviet Union is fighting for communism, how can there be any peaceful co-existence with it?" This view is the result

of bourgeois propaganda. The ideologists of the bourgeoisie distort the facts and deliberately confuse questions of ideological struggle with questions of relations between states in order to make the Communists of the Soviet Union look like advocates of aggression.

## The USSR Will Win

When we say that the socialist system will win in the competition between the two systems—the capitalist and the socialist—this by no means signifies that its victory will be achieved through armed interference by the socialist countries in the internal affairs of the capitalist countries. Our certainty of the victory of communism is based on the fact that the socialist mode of production possesses decisive advantages over the capitalist mode of production. Precisely because of this, the ideas of Marxism-Leninism are more and more capturing the minds of the broad masses of the working people in the capitalist countries, just as they have captured the minds of millions of men and women in our country and the People's Democracies. We believe that all working men in the world, once they have become convinced of the advantages communism brings, will sooner or later take the road of struggle for the construction of socialist society. Building communism in our country, we are resolutely against war. We have always held and continue to hold that the establishment of a new social system in one or another country is the internal affair of the peoples of the countries concerned. This is our attitude, based on the great Marxist-Leninist teaching.

*Nikita S. Khrushchev led the Soviet Union as premier and first secretary-general of the Central Committee of the Communist Party of the Soviet Union from 1953 to 1964 and was chairman of the Council of Ministers from 1958 to 1964. This speech is often quoted as the definitive Soviet position toward the US.*

*"Our foreign policy. . . must reflect our ideals, and it must reflect our purposes. We can never, as Americans, acquiesce in the suppression of human liberties."*

# The Nixon Doctrine: Cooperation Through Economic Incentives

## Richard M. Nixon

*Editor's Note: The following viewpoint is a commencement address before the US Naval Academy.*

As you set out on your noble voyage as new leaders in the defense of peace, I would like to sketch for you the outline of America's strategy for peace and the important role you will now play in advancing that strategy.

Let us look back a moment to the world in which you have grown to manhood.

When the war ended in Europe and Asia in 1945, America was the only economic and military super power in the world. Most of Europe and Japan were in ruins—economically exhausted, politically demoralized. Leadership of a whole free world fell on our shoulders, whether we wanted it or not.

Hard as it was, our task at the outset was made easier by our overwhelming material strength and by a strong, unified sense of national purpose.

Around the globe, we, as Americans, committed ourselves to halting the advance of communism, to promoting economic development, and even to encouraging other countries to adopt our economic, political, and social ideas.

## A Noble and Unselfish Goal

Simplistic and occasionally misguided as this goal may have been, it was a noble and unselfish goal in its enthusiasm. And despite some mistakes, which we came to correct, we in our hearts know—and millions in Europe and Japan and in the developing world know—that America's contribution to mankind in the quarter century after the war was of historic and unprecedented dimensions. And we can be proud that America was as generous in helping our former enemies as we were in aiding our friends.

During this same period, the face of the world changed more rapidly and dramatically than ever before in the world's history. Fifty-eight newly independent nations joined the world community. The once monolithic Communist bloc was splintered. New centers of power emerged in Europe and in Asia.

American zeal and innocence were tempered during these years, also. The war in Korea, followed by the long war in Vietnam, sapped too much of our national self-confidence and sense of purpose. Our own domestic needs commanded greater attention. And by the later 1960's, our policy of trying to solve everyone's problems all over the world was no longer realistic, nor was it necessary.

America was no longer a giant towering over the rest of the world with seemingly inexhaustible resources and a nuclear monopoly.

As our overwhelming superiority in power receded, there was a growing threat that we might turn inward, that we might retreat into isolation from our world responsibilities, ignoring the fact that we were, and are still, the greatest force for peace anywhere in the world today.

This threat of a new wave of isolationism, blind to both the lessons of the past and the perils of the future, was and remains today one of the greatest potential dangers facing our country.

## America Cannot Be Isolationist

Because in our era, American isolation could easily lead to global desolation. Whether we like it or not, the alternative to detente is a runaway nuclear arms race, a return to constant confrontation, and a shattering setback to our hopes for building a new structure of peace in the world.

When we came into office in 1969, this Administration faced a more complex, a more challenging, and yet, in some ways, a more promising world situation than that which existed in the post-

Richard M. Nixon, remarks at commencement ceremonies at the United States Naval Academy, Annapolis, Maryland on June 5, 1974.

World War II era.

While we could not and will not abdicate our responsibilities as the most powerful nation in the free world, it was apparent that the time had come to reassess those responsibilities. This was the guiding purpose of the Nixon Doctrine, a doctrine which says that those we help to enjoy the benefits of freedom should bear a fair share of the burden of its defense as well.

*"We have preserved the trust of our allies around the world by demonstrating that we are a reliable partner in the defense of liberty."*

It was also clear that both pragmatism and moral force had to be the double prongs of any American foreign policy in the new era. A sense of moral purpose is part of our heritage, and it is part of the tradition of our foreign policy. Pragmatism, realism, and technical efficiency must not be the sole touchstone of our foreign policy. Such a policy would have no roots or inspiration and could not long elicit positive support from the American people and the Congress, and more important, it would not deserve the respect of the world.

We had to remember, however, that unrealistic idealism could be impractical and potentially dangerous. It could tempt us to forgo results that were good because we insisted upon results that were perfect.

## Potential Nuclear Devastation

A blend of the ideal and the pragmatic in our foreign policy has been especially critical in our approach to the Soviet Union. The differences between our two systems of life and government are sharp and fundamental. But even as we oppose totalitarianism, we must also keep sight of the hard, cold facts of life in the nuclear age. Ever since the Soviet Union achieved equality in strategic weapons systems, each confrontation has meant a brush with potential nuclear devastation to all civilized nations. Reduction of tensions, therefore, between us has become the foremost requirement of American foreign policy.

The United States will not retreat from its principles. The leaders of the Soviet Union will not sacrifice theirs. But as we have the valor to defend those principles which divide us as nations, we must have the vision to seek out those things which unite us as human beings.

Together, we share the capacity to destroy forever our common heritage of 4,000 years of civilization. Together, we are moving to insure that this will not—because it must not—happen.

Slowly and carefully over the past 5 years, we have worked with the Soviet Union to resolve concrete problems that could deteriorate into military confrontations. And upon these bridges, we are erecting a series of tangible economic and cultural exchanges that will bind us more closely together.

The American people are a great people; the Russian people are a great people. These two great people, who worked together in war, are now learning to work together in peace. Ultimately, we hope that the United States and the Soviet Union will share equally high stakes in preserving a stable international environment.

The results of this policy have been heartening. The problem of Berlin, where our nations were at sword's point for a quarter of a century, has now been resolved by negotiation. Our two countries have concluded an historic agreement to limit strategic nuclear arms.

We and our allies have engaged the Soviet Union in negotiations on major issues of European security, including a reduction of military forces in central Europe. We have substantially reduced the risk of direct U.S.-Soviet confrontation in crisis areas. We have reached a series of bilateral cooperative agreements in such areas as health, environment, space, science and technology, as well as trade.

At the Moscow summit in 1972, our Secretary of the Navy [and] the Commander in Chief of the Soviet Navy signed an agreement on the prevention of incidents on and over the high seas—a code of conduct aimed at eliminating dangerous actions of the cold war era and a code of conduct which has already proved a success.

## More Agreements With the Soviet Union

Over the past 5 years, we have reached more agreements with the Soviet Union than in the entire postwar period preceding that, and this is a record in which all Americans can take pride.

In keeping with our efforts to bring America's foreign policy into line with modern realities, we have also sought to normalize our relation with the People's Republic of China, where one-fourth of all of the people in the world live, a country with which we shared nothing but confrontation and distrust during a quarter century of cold war.

Beginning with an official dialog opened in 1971, we have negotiated constructive agreements in the areas of trade and scientific and cultural exchanges. We established liaison offices in our respective capitals last year. We expect further progress in the years ahead.

We have also succeeded, as Admiral Mack has indicated, in ending our military involvement in Vietnam in a manner which gave meaning to the heavy sacrifices we had made and which greatly enhanced the preservation of freedom and stability in Southeast Asia.

One result is that today the 20 million people of South Vietnam are free to govern themselves and they are able to defend themselves. An even more important result is that we have proved again that America's word is America's bond.

We have preserved the trust of our allies around the world by demonstrating that we are a reliable partner in the defense of liberty; we have earned the respect of our potential adversaries by demonstrating that we are a reliable partner in the search for peace.

America's unique and essential contribution to peace is nowhere better demonstrated than in the Middle East. The hate and distrust that has for so long poisoned the relationship between Arabs and Israelis has led to war four times in the last 40 years, and the toll of death and human suffering was immense, while the tension made the Middle East a world tinderbox that could easily draw the United States and the Soviet Union into military confrontation. The need for a stable solution among the regional parties as well as between the great powers was overwhelmingly urgent.

The October war of last year, while tragic, also presented a unique opportunity, because for the first time, it was clear to us and clear to the moderate leaders of the Arab world that a positive American role was indispensable to achieving a permanent settlement in the Middle East. And it was for this reason that I sent Secretary of State Kissinger to the Middle East to offer our good offices in the process of negotiation.

The results, which reflect more than anything else the vision and statesmanship of the leaders of both sides, have been encouraging. An agreement to separate military forces has been implemented on the Egyptian-Israeli front, and now a similar accord has been negotiated between Israel and Syria. For the first time in a generation, we are witnessing the beginning of a dialog between the Arab States and Israel.

## Peace in the Middle East

Now, the road to a just and lasting and permanent peace in the Mideast is still long and difficult and lies before us. But what seemd to be an insurmountable roadblock on that road has now been removed, and we are determined to stay on course until we have reached our goal of a permanent peace in that area. The role of Secretary Kissinger in this process has presented a testament to both his remarkable diplomatic capabilities and to the soundness and integrity of our belief that a lasting structure of peace can—and must—be created.

In surveying the results of our foreign policy, it is ironic to observe that its achievements now threaten to make us victims of our success. In particular, a dangerous misunderstanding has arisen as to just what detente is and what it is not.

Until very recently, the pursuit of detente was not a problem for us in America. We were so engaged in trying to shift international tides away from confrontation toward negotiation that people were generally agreed that the overriding consideration was the establishment of a pattern of peaceful international conduct. But now that so much progress has been made, some take it for granted.

Eloquent appeals are now being made for the United States, through its foreign policy, to transform the internal as well as the international behavior of other countries, and especially that of the Soviet Union. This issue sharply poses the dilemma I outlined at the outset. It affects not only our relation with the Soviet Union but also our posture toward many nations whose internal systems we totally disagree with, as they do with ours.

## Foreign Policy and American Ideals

Our foreign policy, therefore, must reflect our ideals, and it must reflect our purposes. We can never, as Americans, acquiesce in the suppression of human liberties. We must do all that we reasonably can to promote justice, and for this reason, we continue to adhere firmly to certain humane principles, not only in appropriate international forums but also in our private exchanges with other governments—where this can be effective. But we must recognize that we are more faithful to our ideals by being concerned with results, and we achieve more results through diplomatic action than through hundreds of eloquent speeches.

*"As we have the valor to defend those principles which divide us as nations, we must have the vision to seek out those things which unite us as human beings."*

But there are limits to what we can do, and we must ask ourselves some very hard questions, questions which I know members of this class have asked themselves many times. What is our capability to change the domestic structure of other nations? Would a slowdown or reversal of detente help or hurt the positive evolution of other social systems? What price—in terms of renewed conflict—are we willing to pay to bring pressure to bear for humane causes?

## Influencing International Conduct

Not by our choice, but by our capability, our primary concern in foreign policy must be to help influence the international conduct of nations in the world arena. We would not welcome the intervention of other countries in our domestic affairs, and we cannot expect them to be cooperative when we seek to intervene directly in theirs.

We cannot gear our foreign policy to

transformation of other societies. In the nuclear age, our first responsibility must be the prevention of a war that could destroy all societies.

We must never lose sight of this fundamental truth of modern, international life. Peace between nations with totally different systems is also a high moral objective.

*"Our primary concern in foreign policy must be to help influence the international conduct of nations in the world arena."*

The concepts of national security, partnership, negotiation with adversaries are the central pillars of the "structure of peace" this Administration has outlined as its objective.

## A Structure of Peace

If a structure of peace is to endure, it must reflect the contributions and reconcile the aspirations of nations. It must be cemented by the shared goal of coexistence and the shared practice of accommodation. It must liberate every nation to realize its destiny free from the threat of war, and it must promote social justice and human dignity.

The structure of peace of which I speak will make possible an era of cooperation in which all nations will apply their separate talents and resources to the solution of problems that beset all mankind—the problems of energy and famine, disease and suffering—problems as old as human history itself.

*Richard M. Nixon was president of the United States from 1969 to 1974. In 1974, he resigned from the presidency after the Watergate scandal.*

*"We have no territorial claims on anyone whatsoever, we threaten no one, and have no intention to attack anyone, we stand for the free and independent development of all nations."*

# The Brezhnev Doctrine: Maintaining Communist Influence

Leonid Brezhnev

The features of contemporary capitalism largely spring from the fact that it is trying to adapt itself to the new situation in the world. In the conditions of the confrontation with socialism, the ruling circles of the capitalist countries are afraid more than they have ever been of the class struggle developing into a massive revolutionary movement. Hence, the bourgeoisie's striving to use more camouflaged forms of exploitation and oppression of the working people, and its readiness now and again to agree to partial reforms in order to keep the masses under its ideological and political control as far as possible. The monopolies have been making extensive use of scientific and technical achievements to fortify their positions, to enhance the efficiency and accelerate the pace of production, and to intensify the exploitation and oppression of the working people.

However, adaptation to the new conditions does not mean that capitalism has been establised as a system. *The general crisis of capitalism has continued to deepen.*

Even the most developed capitalist states are not free from grave economic upheavals. The USA, for instance, has been floundering in one of its economic crises for almost two years now. The last few years have also been marked by a grave crisis in the capitalist monetary and financial system. The simultaneous growth of inflation and unemployment has become a permanent feature. There are now almost eight million unemployed in the developed capitalist countries.

The contradictions between the imperialist states have not been eliminated either by the processes of integration or the imperialists' class concern for pooling their efforts in fighting against the socialist world. By the early 1970s, the main centres of

imperialist rivalry have become clearly visible: these are the USA—Western Europe (above all, the six Common Market countries)—Japan. The economic and political competitive struggle between them has been growing ever more acute. The import bans imposed by official US agencies on an ever growing number of products from Europe and Japan, and the European countries' efforts to limit their exploitation by US capital are only some of the signs of this struggle.

## Reactionary Imperialism

In the past five-year period, imperialist foreign policy has provided fresh evidence that imperialism has not ceased to be reactionary and aggressive.

In this context, one must deal above all with US imperialism, which in the last few years has reasserted its urge to act as a kind of guarantor and protector of the international system of exploitation and oppression. It seeks to dominate everywhere, interferes in the affairs of other peoples, high-handedly tramples on their legitimate rights and sovereignty, and seeks by force, bribery and economic penetration to impose its will on states and whole areas of the world.

Needless to say, the forces of war and aggression also exist in the other imperialist countries. In West Germany, these are the revanchists, who have been increasingly ganging up with the neo-Nazis, in Britain, these are the executioners of Northern Ireland, the suppliers of arms to the South African racists, and the advocates of the aggressive US policy; in Japan, these are the militarists who, in defiance of the constitution, which prohibits war "for all time" seek once again to push the country onto the path of expansion and aggression.

Another fact, comrades, that should also be borne in mind is that since the war militarism in the capitalist world has been growing on an unprecedented scale. This tendency has been

Leonid Brezhnev, from the report of the 24th Congress of the Communist Party, 1971.

intensified in the recent period. In 1970 alone, the NATO countries invested 103 thousand million dollars in war preparations. Militarisation has acquired the most dangerous nature in the USA. In the last five years, that country has spent almost 400 thousand million dollars for military purposes.

## Systematic Plunder

The imperialists have been systematically plundering the peoples of dozens of countries in Asia, Africa, and Latin America. Every year, they funnel thousands of millions of dollars out of the Third World. Meanwhile, according to a 1970 UN report on the world food situation, 375 million people on these continents live on the brink of death from starvation.

*"No honest man, least of all a Communist, can ever reconcile his conscience with what is being done by the US interventionists and their henchmen, who claim to represent 'Western civilisation' and the so-called 'free world.'"*

The imperialists are prepared to commit any crime in their efforts to preserve or restore their domination of the peoples in their former colonies or in other countries which are escaping from the grip of capitalist exploitation. The last five-year period has provided much fresh evidence of this. The aggression against the Arab states, the colonialist attempts to invade Guinea, and the subversive activity against the progressive regimes in Latin America—all this is a constant reminder that the imperialist war against the freedom-loving peoples has not ceased.

And the continuing US aggression against the peoples of Vietnam, Cambodia and Laos is the main atrocity committed by the modern colonialists; it is the stamp of ignominy of the United States. . . .

## US Actions in Vietnam a Disgrace

It is hard to keep a calm tone when speaking about the atrocities committed by the interventionists, who are armed to the teeth. Hundreds of thousands of tons of napalm have literally scorched into wasteland whole areas of South Vietnam. Almost 1.5 million Vietnamese have been poisoned, and many have died as a result of the use of chemical weapons. No honest man, least of all a Communist, can ever reconcile his conscience with what is being done by the US interventionists and their henchmen, who claim to represent "Western civilisation" and the so-called "free world." It is a disgrace!

Comrades, we have no doubt at all that the attempts of imperialism to turn the tide of history, to make it flow in its favour, are bound to fail. However, we Communists are well aware that there is no room for passivity or self-complacency. The fighters against capitalist oppression are confronted by the last but the most powerful of the exploiting systems that have ever existed. That is why a long and hard struggle still lies ahead.

But however hard this struggle, it continues to mount and its front is being steadily widened. In the last few years, the fighters against imperialism have written new and glorious pages into the annals of the class battles.

The *international working-class movement* continues to play, as it has played in the past, the role of time-tested and militant vanguard of the revolutionary forces. The events of the past five-year period in the capitalist world have fully borne out the importance of the working class as the chief and strongest opponent of the rule of the monopolies, and as a centre rallying all the anti-monopoly forces.

## Capitalist Chaos

In countries like France and Italy, where the traditions of the class struggle are more developed, and where strong Communist Parties are active, the working people, headed by the working class, have attacked not only individual groups of capitalists, but the whole system of state-monopoly domination. In Britain, the class struggle has reached a high state of tension, and the current strikes are comparable in scale and in the numbers involved only with the general strike of 1926. In the USA, working-class action against the monopolies has assumed great scope, and the struggle of the Negro people for equality, and of youth against the war in Vietnam is spreading with unprecedented acerbity. The mass working-class movement in the FRG is gathering momentum. For the first time in many decades, large-scale class clashes have taken place in the Scandinavian countries and in Holland. The socio-political crisis in Spain continues to sharpen. In all the class battles of the recent period, the working people's trade unions, especially those brought together within the World Federation of Trade Unions, have played a considerable and increasingly important role. . . .

Imperialism is being subjected to ever greater pressure by the forces which have sprung from the national liberation struggle, above all by the young independent and anti-imperialist-minded states of Asia and Africa.

The main thing is that *the struggle for national liberation in many countries has in practical terms begun to grow into a struggle against exploitative relations, both feudal and capitalist.*

Today, there are already quite a few countries in Asia and Africa which have taken the non-capitalist way of development, that is, the path of building a socialist society in the long term. Many states have now taken this path. Deep-going social changes, which are in the interests of the masses of people, and which lead to a strengthening of national independence, are being implemented in these countries, and the number of these changes has been growing as time goes on....

## The Struggle Against Imperialism

The great Lenin's prediction that the peoples of the colonies and dependent countries, starting with a struggle for national liberation, would go on to a fight against the very foundations of the exploitative system is coming true. And this means, of course, a most heavy blow at the positions of capitalism as a whole, as a world social system.

Comrades, success in the struggle against imperialism largely depends on the cohesion of the anti-imperialist forces, above all of *the world communist movement,* their vanguard. In the last five years, our Party together with the other fraternal Parties, has done much to strengthen this cohesion and the unity of the communist ranks....

## Ideas of Communism

Comrades, to the lot of the Communists have fallen the hardest trials of any that have ever fallen to the lot of fighters for the people's cause. We remember these words of Lenin's: "Selfless devotion to the revolution and revolutionary propaganda among the people are not wasted even if long decades divide the sowing from the harvest." The ideas of the Communists have sprouted remarkable shoots in the practice of real socialism, and in the thoughts and deeds of millions upon millions of men....

The full triumph of the socialist cause all over the world is inevitable. And we shall not spare ourselves in the fight for this triumph, for the happiness of the working people.

Comrades, in the period under review the Central Committee and the Soviet Government did their utmost to ensure peaceful conditions for communist construction in the USSR, to expose and frustrate action by the aggressive imperialist forces, and to defend socialism, the freedom of peoples and peace.

Our policy has always combined firm rebuffs to aggression, and the constructive line of settling pressing international problems, and maintaining normal, and, wherever the situation allows, good, relations with states belonging to the other social system. As in the past, we have consistently stood up for the Leninist principle of peaceful coexistence of states, regardless of their social system. This principle has now become a real force of international development.

Let me deal with the most important international problems which because of their acerbity or importance for the future have required our special attention.

To start with the events in South-East Asia. The aggressive war started by US ruling circles in that part of the world has not brought the American people any victorious laurels but tens of thousands of funeral wreaths. Anyone capable of taking a realistic view of things must realise that neither direct armed intervention, nor torpedoing of negotiations, nor even the ever wider use of mercenaries will break down the Vietnamese people's determination to become master of its own country.

The so-called Vietnamisation of the war, that is, the plan to have Vietnamese kill Vietnamese in Washington's interests, and the extension of the aggression to Cambodia and Laos—none of this will get the USA out of the bog of its dirty war in Indochina or wash away the shame heaped on that country by those who started and are continuing the aggression. There is only one way of solving the Vietnamese problem. It is clearly indicated in the proposals of the DRV Government and the Provisional Revolutionary Government of the Republic of South Vietnam, proposals which we firmly back.

The Soviet Union resolutely demands an end to the imperialist aggression against the peoples of Vietnam, Cambodia and Laos. Our country has been and will be an active champion of the just cause of the heroic peoples of Indochina....

*"The ideas of Communists have sprouted remarkable shoots in the practice of real socialism, and in the thoughts and deeds of millions upon millions of men."*

Now about the Soviet Union's relations with the United States of America. An improvement of Soviet-American relations would be in the interests of the Soviet and the American peoples, the interests of stronger peace. However, we cannot pass over the US aggressive actions in various parts of the world. In the recent period, the US Administration has taken a more rigid stance on a number of international issues, including some which have a bearing on the interests of the Soviet Union. The frequent zigzags in US foreign policy, which are apparently connected with some kind of domestic political moves from short-term considerations, have also made dealings with the United States much more difficult.

## Real Negotiations May Be Possible

We proceed from the assumption that it is possible to improve relations between the USSR and the USA. Our principled line with respect to the capitalist countries, including the USA, is consistently and fully to practise the principles of peaceful coexistence, to develop mutually advantageous ties, and to co-operate, with states prepared to do so, in strengthening peace, making our relations with them as stable as possible. But we have to consider whether we are dealing with a real desire to settle outstanding issues at the negotiation table or attempts to conduct a "position of strength" policy.

*"Whenever the imperialists need to cover up their aggressive schemes, they try to revive the 'Soviet menace' myth."*

Whenever the imperialists need to cover up their aggressive schemes, they try to revive the "Soviet menace" myth. They seek to find evidence of this threat in the depths of the Indian Ocean and on the peaks of the Cordilleras. And, of course, nothing but Soviet divisions prepared for a leap against the West are to be discovered on the plains of Europe if these are viewed through NATO field-glasses.

## USSR Has No Territorial Claims

But the peoples will not be deceived by the attempts to ascribe to the Soviet Union intentions which are alien to it. We declare with a full sense of responsibility: we have no territorial claims on anyone whatsoever, we threaten no one, and have no intention to attack anyone, we stand for the free and independent development of all nations. But let no one, for his part, try to talk to us in terms of ultimatums and strength.

We have everything necessary—a genuine peace policy, military might and the unity of Soviet people—to ensure the inviolability of our borders against any encroachments, and to defend the gains of socialism. . . .

*The Soviet Union has countered the aggressive policy of imperialism with its policy of active defence of peace and strengthening of international security.* The main lines of this policy are well known. Our Party, our Soviet state, in co-operation with the fraternal socialist countries and other peace-loving states, and with the wholehearted support of many millions of people throughout the world, have now for many years been waging a struggle on these lines, taking a stand for the cause of peace and friendship among nations. . . .

## Struggling Against Imperialism

The Soviet Union is prepared to deepen relations of mutually advantageous co-operation in every sphere with states which for their part seek to do so. Our country is prepared to participate together with the other states concerned in settling problems like the conservation of the environment, development of power and other natural resources, development of transport and communications, prevention and eradication of the most dangerous and widespread diseases, and the exploration and development of outer space and the world ocean.

Such are the main features of the programme for the struggle for peace and international co-operation, for the freedom and independence of nations, which our Party has put forward.

And we declare that, while consistently pursuing its policy of peace and friendship among nations, the Soviet Union will continue to conduct a resolute struggle against imperialism, and firmly to rebuff the evil designs and subversions of aggressors. As in the past, we shall give undeviating support to the peoples' struggle for democracy, national liberation and socialism.

Comrades, it is clear from what has been said that the past five years have been a period of vigorous and intense activity by our Party and state in the sphere of international policy.

Of course, in international affairs not everything depends on us or our friends alone. We have not advanced in every sphere as fast as we should like toward the goals we set ourselves. A number of important acts have yet to be brought to completion, and their importance will become fully evident later. But the overall balance is obvious: great results have been achieved in these five years. Our country's international position has become even stronger, its prestige has been enhanced, and the Soviet people's peaceful endeavour has reliable protection.

*Leonid Brezhnev replaced Nikita Khrushchev in 1964 and continued as president of the USSR until his death in 1982. Brezhnev claimed to adhere to the basic principles of the Soviet Union's foreign policy: peace and friendship, mutually beneficial cooperation among peoples, and respect for the sovereign rights of bigger and smaller nations.*

*"Our support for human rights in other countries is in our own national interest as well as part of our national character."*

# The Carter Doctrine: Human Rights and International Relations

James E. Carter Jr.

These last few months have not been an easy time for any of us. As we meet tonight, it has never been more clear that the state of our union depends on the state of the world. And tonight, as throughout our own generation, freedom and peace in the world depend on the state of our union.

The 1980s have been born in turmoil, strife, and change. This is a time of challenge to our interests and our values, and it's a time that tests our wisdom and our skills. At this time in Iran 50 Americans are still held captive, innocent victims of terrorism and anarchy. Also at this moment, massive Soviet troops are attempting to subjugate the fiercely independent and deeply religious people of Afghanistan. These two acts—one of international terrorism and one of military aggression—present a serious challenge to the United States of America and indeed to all the nations of the world. Together, we will meet these threats to peace.

I am determined that the United States will remain the strongest of all nations, but our power will never be used to initiate a threat to the security of any nation or to the rights of any human being. We seek to be and to remain secure—a nation at peace in a stable world. But to be secure we must face the world as it is. Three basic developments have helped to shape our challenges:

The steady growth and increased projection of Soviet military power beyond its own borders;

The overwhelming dependence of the Western democracies on oil supplies from the Middle East; and

The press of social and religious and economic and political change in the many nations of the developing world—exemplified by the revolution in Iran.

Each of these factors is important in its own right. Each interacts with the others. All must be faced together—squarely and courageously.

We will face these challenges. And we will meet them with the best that is in us. And we will not fail.

## Meeting the Challenge of the USSR

Since the end of the Second World War, America has led other nations in meeting the challenge of mounting Soviet power. This has not been a simple or a static relationship. Between us there has been cooperation, there has been competition, and at times there has been confrontation.

In the 1940s, we took the lead in creating the Atlantic alliance in response to the Soviet Union's suppression and then consolidation of its East European empire and the resulting threat of the Warsaw Pact to Western Europe.

In the 1950s, we helped to contain further Soviet challenges in Korea and in the Middle East, and we re-armed, to assure the continuation of that containment.

In the 1960s, we met the Soviet challenges in Berlin and we faced the Cuban missile crisis, and we sought to engage the Soviet Union in the important task of moving beyond the cold war and away from confrontation.

And in the 1970s, three American Presidents negotiated with the Soviet leaders in attempts to halt this growth of the nuclear arms race. We sought to establish rules of behavior that would reduce the risks of conflict, and we searched for areas of cooperation that could make our relations reciprocal and productive—not only for the sake of our two nations, but for the security and peace of the entire world.

In all these actions, we have maintained two commitments: to be ready to meet any challenge by Soviet military power and to develop ways to resolve disputes and to keep the peace.

James E. Carter Jr., from the state of the union address before a joint session of Congress on January 23, 1980.

Preventing nuclear war is the foremost responsibility of the two superpowers. That is why we've negotiated the strategic arms limitation talks—treaties SALT I and SALT II. Especially now in a time of great tension, observing the mutual constraints imposed by the terms of these treaties will be in the best interest of both countries and will help to preserve world peace. I will consult very closely with the Congress on this matter as we strive to control nuclear weapons. That effort—to control nuclear weapons—will not be abandoned.

*"We superpowers will also have the responsibility to exercise restraint in the use of our great military force."*

We superpowers will also have the responsibility to exercise restraint in the use of our great military force. The integrity and the independence of weaker nations must not be threatened. They must know that in our presence they are secure. But now the Soviet Union has taken a radical and an aggressive new step. It's using its great military power against a relatively defenseless nation. The implications of the Soviet invasion of Afghanistan could pose the most serious threat to the peace since the Second World War.

The vast majority of nations on Earth have condemned this latest Soviet attempt to extend its colonial domination of others and have demanded the immediate withdrawal of Soviet troops. The Moslem world is especially and justifiably outraged by this aggression against an Islamic people. No action of a world power has ever been so quickly and so overwhelmingly condemned.

## The Soviet Union Must Pay

But verbal condemnation is not enough. The Soviet Union must pay a concrete price for their aggression. While this invasion continues, we and the other nations of the world cannot conduct business as usual with the Soviet Union.

That's why the United States has imposed stiff economic sanctions on the Soviet Union.

I will not issue any permits for Soviet ships to fish in the coastal waters of the United States.

I've cut Soviet access to high-technology equipment and to agricultural products.

I've limited other commerce with the Soviet Union, and I've asked our allies and friends to join with us in restraining their own trade with the Soviets and not to replace our own embargoed items.

And I have notified the Olympic Committee that with Soviet invading forces in Afghanistan, neither the American people nor I will support sending an Olympic team to Moscow.

The Soviet Union is going to have to answer some basic questions: Will it help promote a more stable international environment in which its own legitimate, peaceful concerns can be pursued? Or will it continue to expand its military power far beyond its genuine security needs, and use that power for colonial conquest?

## Afghanistan Invasion Costly

The Soviet Union must realize that its decision to use military force in Afghanistan will be costly to every political and economic relationship it values.

The region which is now threatened by Soviet troops in Afghanistan is of great strategic importance. It contains more than two-thirds of the world's exportable oil. The Soviet effort to dominate Afghanistan has brought Soviet military forces to within 300 miles of the Indian Ocean and close to the Straits of Hormuz—a waterway through which most of the world's oil must flow. The Soviet Union is now attempting to consolidate a strategic position, therefore, that poses a grave threat to the free movement of Middle East oil.

This situation demands careful thought, steady nerves, and resolute action, not only for this year but for many years to come. It demands collective efforts to meet this new threat to security in the Persian Gulf and in southwest Asia. It demands the participation of all those who rely on oil from the Middle East and who are concerned with global peace and stability. And it demands consultation and close cooperation with countries in the area which might be threatened.

Meeting this challenge will take national will, diplomatic and political wisdom, economic sacrifice, and, of course, military capability. We must call on the best that is in us to preserve the security of this crucial region.

Let our position be absolutely clear: An attempt by any outside force to gain control of the Persian Gulf region will be regarded as an assault on the vital interests of the United States of America, and such an assault will be repelled by any means necessary, including military force.

During the past 3 years you have joined with me to improve our own security and the prospects for peace, not only in the vital oil producing area of the Persian Gulf region but around the world.

We've increased annually our real commitment for defense, and we will sustain this increase of effort throughout the 5-year defense program. It's imperative that the Congress approve this strong defense budget for 1981 encompassing a 5% real growth in authorizations without any reduction.

## Improving Military Capabilities

We are also improving our capability to deploy U.S. military forces rapidly to distant areas.

We have helped to strengthen NATO and our other

alliances. And recently we and other NATO members have decided to develop and to deploy modernized intermediate-range nuclear forces to meet an unwarranted and increased threat from the nuclear weapons of the Soviet Union.

We are working with our allies to prevent conflict in the Middle East. The Peace Treaty between Egypt and Israel is a notable achievement which represents a strategic asset for America and which also enhances prospects for regional and world peace. We are now engaged in further negotiations to provide full autonomy for the people of the West Bank and Gaza, to resolve the Palestinian issue in all its aspects, and to preserve the peace and security of Israel. Let no one doubt our commitment to the security of Israel. In a few days we will observe an historic event when Israel makes another major withdrawal from the Sinai and when ambassadors will be exchanged between Israel and Egypt.

We've also expanded our own sphere of friendship. Our deep commitment to human rights and to meeting human needs has improved our relationship with much of the Third World. Our decision to normalize relations with the People's Republic of China will help to preserve peace and stability in Asia and in the western Pacific. . . .

## Enhancing Independence

Finally, we are prepared to work with other countries in the region to share a cooperative security framework that respects differing values and political beliefs, yet which enhances the independence, security, and prosperity of all.

All these efforts combined emphasize our dedication to defend and preserve the vital interests of the region and of the nation, which we represent, and those of our allies in Europe and the Pacific and also in the parts of the world which have such great strategic importance to us, stretching especially through the Middle East and southwest Asia. With your help, I will pursue these efforts with vigor and with determination. You and I will act as necessary to protect and to preserve our nation's security. . . .

We also need clear and quick passage of a new charter to define the legal authority and accountability of our intelligence agencies. We will guarantee that abuses do not recur, but we must tighten our controls on sensitive intelligence information. And we need to remove unwarranted restraints on America's ability to collect intelligence.

The decade ahead will be a time of rapid change, as nations everywhere seek to deal with new problems and age-old tensions. But America need have no fear—we can thrive in a world of change if we remain true to our values and actively engage in promoting world peace.

We will continue to work as we have for peace in the Middle East and southern Africa. We will continue to build our ties with developing nations, respecting and helping to strengthen their national independence, which they have struggled so hard to achieve. And we will continue to support the growth of democracy and the protection of human rights.

## Supporting Human Rights

In repressive regimes, popular frustrations often have no outlet except through violence. But when peoples and their governments can approach their problems together—through open, democratic methods—the basis for stability and peace is far more solid and far more enduring. That is why our support for human rights in other countries is in our own national interest as well as part of our own national character.

*"We will continue to support the growth of democracy and the protection of human rights."*

Peace—a peace that preserves freedom—remains America's first goal. In the coming years as a mighty nation, we will continue to pursue peace. But to be strong abroad we must be strong at home. And in order to be strong, we must continue to face up to the difficult issues that confront us as a nation today.

The crises in Iran and Afghanistan have dramatized a very important lesson: Our excessive dependence on foreign oil is a clear and present danger to our nation's security. The need has never been more urgent. At long last, we must have a clear, comprehensive energy policy for the United States.

*James E. (Jimmy) Carter Jr. was president of the United States from 1976 to 1980. Human rights were a controversial aspect of his foreign policy. He believed that America, along with other free nations, should be the guarantors of freedom. This meant withholding aid and other economic subsidies from countries which violated human rights. During his presidency, Mr. Carter imposed economic sanctions on the Soviet Union for its invasion of Afghanistan.*

*"The Soviet people, who are dedicated. . .to the communist cause, will not allow anybody to interfere in their internal affairs, to slander their achievements, to harm Soviet society."*

# Andropov on Soviet Autonomy

Yuri Andropov

Soviet democracy, the entire Soviet social and state system, take their origin from the Great October Socialist Revolution. It is for over six decades that the Soviet people led by the Party has been steadily advancing along the path opened by that revolution.

"To follow the path of the October Revolution," Leonid Brezhnev has said, "means to strengthen the economy of this country, to enhance the productivity of labour, to advance the living standards and culture of the people.

"To follow the path of the October Revolution means to develop socialist democracy, to strengthen the friendship of Soviet nations, to educate the people persistently in the spirit of the lofty principles of communism, to cherish the unity of the Party and the people as the apple of one's eye."

Discussing the burning problems of today we go back in thought to our sources and realize with crystal clarity that our achievements, all our life are a continuation of the ideas of the October Revolution, a development of the enormous revolutionary potential it called into being, which lives on in the decisions of the Party, in all our constructive activities. . . .

## Perfection of Social Democracy

Further development and perfection of socialist democracy is one of the main directions of the activities of the Party and state. This has been laid down in the resolutions of the 24th and 25th Party Congresses and is recorded in the Constitution. There has been a corresponding growth in the role and significance of the Soviets, which Lenin described as a "form of democracy which has no match in any other country." Public organizations and labour collectives are ever more actively involved in the management of all affairs of state.

Yuri Andropov, "Under the Banner of Lenin, Under Party Leadership," from a speech at a meeting with the Stupino District constituency on February 22, 1979.

The constitutional rights and freedoms of Soviet citizens have become wider and more effective. Simultaneously the guarantees of these rights and freedoms and the democratic principles of relations between the individual and the state have been reinforced.

Exercising their rights Soviet citizens perform their duties as well. The more profound the awareness of all Soviet citizens of the interrelationship between their rights and duties and the more responsible their approach to the fulfilment of their civic duties, the more meaningful and effective is socialist government of the people which was established by the October Revolution and which has absorbed the experience of mass political creativity of over sixty years.

The socialist way of life and socialist morals have taken a firm root in this country. This is not to say, however, that we have created an ideal world inhabited by ideal people. Unfortunately, we still encounter such phenomena alien to socialism as deliberate breaches of labour discipline, drunkenness, hooliganism, bribery, embezzlement of socialist property and other anti-social acts interfering with the normal life and work of Soviet citizens.

The Communist Party and the Soviet state are doing much to eradicate crime and to prevent offences against the law. The struggle against criminal offences and anti-social behaviour, however, is a task not only for government agencies but for the whole society, a civic duty of all honest Soviet citizens, all labour collectives. The more actively this duty is performed, the earlier we shall uproot this evil.

You know what area of work I have been put in charge of by the Party and the government. Allow me to say in this context a few words about the state security agencies.

The main prerequisite for a correct political line in all activities of the state security service, for success in their work, is daily guidance by the Community Party. Speaking at the 25th CPSU Congress, Leonid Brezhnev said: "The state security agencies carry on all their work, which takes place under the Party's guidance and unflagging control, in light of the interests of the people and the state, with the support of broad masses of working people, and with strict observance of constitutional rules and socialist legality. That is the main source of their strength, and the main earnest of the successful exercise of their functions."

## Neutralizing Subversive Forces

The central task of the state security service is to neutralize the subversive operations of reactionary imperialist forces against this country. Agents of Western intelligence services, emissaries of foreign anti-Soviet organizations are attempting to ferret out our secrets, take part in organizing acts of ideological subversion, seek to "brainwash" and corrupt some unstable, weak-willed individuals. Therefore, as the CPSU Central Committee indicates, constant vigilance on the part of all Soviet citizens remains an important and pressing demand of the day.

*"The Soviet people. . . have never granted and will never grant anybody a right to harm socialism."*

Inside the Soviet Union there is no social basis for anti-Soviet activity. Nevertheless it would be wrong to ignore still existing facts of criminal offences against the state, anti-Soviet acts and misdemeanours committed under the influence of hostile forces from abroad.

There are also renegades of various kinds who maliciously slander Soviet reality and sometimes directly collaborate with imperialist secret services. Some figures in the West call the activities of such renegades "defence of human rights." The Soviet people, however, have never granted and will never grant anybody a right to harm socialism, for the triumph of which they have laid down so many lives and exerted so much effort. To safeguard society against such criminal activities is both fair and democratic. This fully accords with the rights and freedoms of Soviet citizens, the interests of society and state.

Needless to say, this does not meet the interests of the enemies of socialism. One can occasionally hear in the West hypocritical lamentations over the alleged infringements of democracy in this country and cries that the KGB is making life impossible for some "human rights champions." In fact they are worried not so much by the fact that Soviet state security agencies, acting in strict compliance with Soviet laws,

stop the criminal activities of these renegades as by the latter's resolute denunciation on the part of the whole Soviet people. This is why sad voices about the hopelessness of their activities in the USSR are heard more and more often in the West.

Soviet society is monolithic and united. The Soviet people, who are dedicated to the lofty ideals of the October Revolution, to the communist cause, will not allow anybody to interfere in their internal affairs, to slander their achievements, to harm Soviet society. . . .

## Preserving Peace

The Party's foreign policy programme expresses the vital interests of the Soviet people, who know what war brings in its wake only too well and therefore are wholly dedicated to peace. The noble and humane aim of Soviet foreign policy is to preserve peace, to prevent another war from being unleashed.

We come out in defence of peace jointly with our allies, other socialist countries, all progressive forces of mankind. Our policy of peace is opposed by a policy aimed at frustrating *detente* and countering the principles of peaceful coexistence. The danger of this policy should not be underestimated.

Under present conditions we are obliged to attach high priority to consolidating the might and defence capability of the Soviet Union. As long as the forces which threaten the peaceful work of the Soviet people and our allies are actively operating, strong and dependable defence is vitally necessary. Our defence might hold in check the most aggressive reactionary circles, compels imperialism to recognize parity in the military field, and has a sobering effect on those who have not yet abandoned for good their attempts to stop the progress of socialism by force of arms.

At the same time, our Party proceeds from the premise that peace and international security cannot be strengthened by military rivalry. The arms race undermines trust between states, poisons the international atmosphere, increases the risk of crisis situations growing into military conflicts. This is why the CPSU and the Soviet state attach paramount significance to a limitation of arms, followed by their reduction, to a peaceful settlement of disputes and conflicts, to promoting *detente* to developing mutually beneficial international co-operation. We are firmly convinced that there is no sensible alternative to this policy.

The struggle for the triumph of peace policy is not a simple matter. *Detente* has quite a few enemies, who have become appreciably more active of late. Scaring the public with the imaginary "Soviet menace" they are stepping up the arms race. Interfering in the internal affairs of foreign nations, they aggravate the general international climate. They are trying to depict *detente* as a kind of an agreement on freezing and conservation of outdated social relations and topple such regimes, they raise a hue and cry about the notorious "hand of Moscow," about KGB agents who allegedly organize social upheavals all over the world.

## Deliberate Lies

We shall not search now for those who stand behind such allegations. In some cases they are deliberate lies. In others they are the result of naivety or delusions. No, it is not "the hand of Moscow" but the bony hand of hunger, not "the intrigues of communists" but privations, oppression and suffering, that compel people to take up arms, drive them into the streets, and make radical changes inevitable. This has happened in Angola, Afghanistan and Kampuchea. This is now taking place in Iran. Nothing, absolutely nothing can stop the irresistible forces of history which eventually work their way contrary to Pinochets, Pol Pots, Smiths and the like, contrary to the attempts of reactionary forces to retard social progress.

It would be extremely unreasonable and dangerous to jeopardize *detente* and the cause of peace each time internal political changes occur in some country, which are objectionable to politicians and ideologists of the West.

We are satisfied to acknowledge that the tendency toward a relaxation of tension which emerged in the seventies is coming out with increasing clarity as the main tendency in international affairs. This is evidenced, in particular, by the situation in Europe, by the strong shoots of new relations on the continent which sprang in the period of preparation and holding of the Conference on Security and Co-operation in Europe. It is indisputable that the restructuring of relations between European states could proceed more quickly, could produce a greater political and economic effect, if it were not held back by the attempts of aggressive circles in the West to bury *detente,* to whip up the arms race, to return the world to the times of the Cold War.

However, the attempts to arrest positive changes, to resume the Cold War have failed. And we hope that the spirit of realism, a sober attitude to the pressing problems of Europe will be preserved in European capitals. As far as the Soviet Union is concerned, it will struggle with even greater persistence jointly with other socialist countries for converting Europe into a continent of peace and co-operation among nations based on equality.

## US/USSR Relations Zigzag

You know that in the last few years relations between the Soviet Union and the United States have been developing very irregularly. Vacillations and zigzags in Washington's policy have more than once resulted in declines and exacerbations and interfered with progress in matters of prime significance. Since the autumn of last year certain changes for the better

seem to have appeared in this field. Progress in preparing a new agreement on the limitation of strategic offensive arms has been stepped up.

*"It would be extremely unreasonable and dangerous to jeopardize* detente*. . .each time internal political changes occur in some country, which are objectionable to politicians and ideologists in the West."*

The Soviet government attaches great significance to improving Soviet-American relations as one of the key directions of its policy aimed at preventing nuclear war and achieving a general normalization of the international situation. Therefore, we are doing whatever is possible and necessary to resolve the major issues which have a bearing on the development of relations between the USSR and the USA.

Among the factors aggravating the international situation is China's armed attack on Vietnam. Imperialist politicians hope to use China as a tool for opposition to the Soviet Union and other socialist countries. This calculation, however, may easily turn into miscalculation.

As you see, there are quite a few complicated problems and situations in the world today. However, the complexity and at times the contradictory character of events in the world arena do not change our approach to foreign policy. The Soviet people can see ever more clearly the correctness of the policy pursued by our Party, the importance of a further consistent and determined struggle for a relaxation of international tensions, for a limitation of arms, for disarmament and the development of international co-operation.

All successes and accomplishments of the Soviet people are inseparably linked with the activities of the Leninist Party. The record of experience proves conclusively that as the scope of the Soviet Union's socioeconomic and cultural development grows, as ever new tasks in communist construction are accomplished, the Communist Party—the guiding and mobilizing force of Soviet society—has a growing part to play.

## Marxist-Leninist Doctrine

In all its theoretical and practical work the Party is invariably guided by the Marxist-Leninist doctrine. Lenin's ideas are alive today, and they will live on in the centuries to come, because they authentically reflect the objective course of history, the laws of social development and the class interests of the masses. Fidelity to Leninism, the creative development of Lenin's heritage is the dependable guarantee of new majestic accomplishments, of the triumph of communism.

The quiet and businesslike political atmosphere pervaded with communist high-principledness which has formed in the Party and country is of enormous significance for the fulfilment of all our plans. This atmosphere is the result of the purposeful activities of the Central Committee, its Politbureau and the General Secretary of the CPSU Central Committee, President of the Presidium of the USSR Soviet, Leonid Brezhnev. Many good and warm words have been said about him at today's meeting. These words are an expression of the truly nationwide recognition of his wisdom as a statesman, his political foresight and his great humaneness. The communists, all working people of this country, rightly regard Leonid Brezhnev as a political leader of the Leninist stamp, who is inseparably linked with the people, who has devoted all his life to the people, and who is doing his utmost to advance the well-being of the people and to guarantee the security of our motherland.

*"The Soviet government attaches great significance to improving Soviet-American relations as one of the key directions of its policy aimed at preventing nuclear war."*

The Communist Party of the Soviet Union is contesting the elections with a comprehensive programme of economic and cultural development, of raising the living standards of the people. It is set out in the message of the Central Committee to the electorate. The aim of this programme is to make this socialist country still more beautiful and stronger, to make the life of the Soviet people still better and fuller, to make peace on earth still stronger and more dependable. The Soviet people are well aware of that. They give their unreserved support to the Party and respond to its appeals with practical deeds. This is the most dependable guarantee that all our plans will be fulfilled, that this country will score new successes in its great onward march toward communism.

I wish you a happy life and new successes in your work for the benefit of our Soviet Motherland.

*Yuri Andropov was premier of the Soviet Union from 1982 until his death in 1984.*

*"A free market capitalist society fosters freedom."*

# Capitalism Encourages Economic Freedom

Milton Friedman

It is widely believed that politics and economics are separate and largely unconnected; that individual freedom is a political problem and material welfare an economic problem; and that any kind of political arrangements can be combined with any kind of economic arrangements. The chief contemporary manifestation of this idea is the advocacy of "democratic socialism" by many who condemn out of hand the restrictions on individual freedom imposed by "totalitarian socialism" in Russia, and who are persuaded that it is possible for a country to adopt the essential features of Russian economic arrangements and yet to ensure individual freedom through political arrangements.

Such a view is a delusion, that there is an intimate connection between economics and politics, that only certain combinations of political and economic arrangements are possible, and that in particular, a society which is socialist cannot also be democratic, in the sense of guaranteeing individual freedom.

Economic arrangements play a dual role in the promotion of a free society. On the one hand, freedom in economic arrangements is itself a component of freedom broadly understood, so economic freedom is an end in itself. In the second place, economic freedom is also an indispensable means toward the achievement of political freedom.

The first of these roles of economic freedom needs special emphasis because intellectuals in particular have a strong bias against regarding this aspect of freedom as important. They tend to express contempt for what they regard as material aspects of life, and to regard their own pursuit of allegedly higher values as on a different plane of significance and as deserving of special attention. For most citizens of the country, however, if not for the intellectual, the direct importance of economic freedom is at least comparable in significance to the indirect importance of economic freedom as a means to political freedom. . . .

## Capitalism Promotes Freedom

Viewed as a means to the end of political freedom, economic arrangements are important because of their effect on the concentration or dispersion of power. The kind of economic organization that provides economic freedom directly, namely, competitive capitalism, also promotes political freedom because it separates economic power from political power and in this way enables the one to offset the other.

Historical evidence speaks with a single voice on the relation between political freedom and a free market. I know of no example in time or place of a society that has been marked by a large measure of political freedom, and that has not also used something comparable to a free market to organize the bulk of economic activity.

Because we live in a largely free society, we tend to forget how limited is the span of time and the part of the globe for which there has ever been anything like political freedom: the typical state of mankind is tyranny, servitude, and misery. The nineteenth century and the early twentieth century in the Western world stand out as striking exceptions to the general trend of historical development. Political freedom in this instance clearly came along with the free market and the development of capitalist institutions. So also did political freedom in the golden age of Greece and in the early days of the Roman era.

History suggests only that capitalism is a necessary condition for political freedom. Clearly it is not a sufficient condition. Fascist Italy and Fascist Spain, Germany at various times in the last seventy years, Japan before World Wars I and II, tzarist Russia in

Milton Friedman, *Capitalism and Freedom.* Chicago: University of Chicago Press, 1982. Reprinted by permission.

the decades before World War I—are all societies that cannot conceivably be described as politically free. Yet, in each, private enterprise was the dominant form of economic organization. It is therefore clearly possible to have economic arrangements that are fundamentally capitalist and political arrangements that are not free.

---

*"The kind of economic organization that provides economic freedom directly, namely, competitive capitalism, also promotes political freedom."*

---

Even in those societies, the citizenry had a good deal more freedom than citizens of a modern totalitarian state like Russia or Nazi Germany, in which economic totalitarianism is combined with political totalitarianism. Even in Russia under the Tzars, it was possible for some citizens, under some circumstances, to change their jobs without getting permission from political authority because capitalism and the existence of private property provided some check to the centralized power of the state....

## Freedom of Exchange

So long as effective freedom of exchange is maintained, the central feature of the market organization of economic activity is that it prevents one person from interfering with another in respect of most of his activities. The consumer is protected from coercion by the seller because of the presence of other sellers with whom he can deal. The seller is protected from coercion by the consumer because of other consumers to whom he can sell. The employee is protected from coercion by the employer because of other employers for whom he can work, and so on. And the market does this impersonally and without centralized authority.

Indeed, a major source of objection to a free economy is precisely that it does this task so well. It gives people what they want instead of what a particular group thinks they ought to want. Underlying most arguments against the free market is a lack of belief in freedom itself.

The existence of a free market does not of course eliminate the need for government. On the contrary, government is essential both as a forum for determining the "rules of the game" and as an umpire to interpret and enforce the rules decided on. What the market does is to reduce greatly the range of issues that must be decided through political means, and thereby to minimize the extent to which government need participate directly in the game. The characteristic feature of action through political channels is that it tends to require or enforce substantial conformity. The great advantage of the market, on the other hand, is that it permits wide diversity. It is, in political terms, a system of proportional representation. Each man can vote, as it were, for the color of tie he wants and get it; he does not have to see what color the majority wants and then, if he is in the minority, submit.

## Coercive Power

It is this feature of the market that we refer to when we say that the market provides economic freedom. But this characteristic also has implications that go far beyond the narrowly economic. Political freedom means the absence of coercion of a man by his fellow men. The fundamental threat to freedom is power to coerce, be it in the hands of a monarch, a dictator, an oligarchy, or a momentary majority. The preservation of freedom requires the elimination of such concentration of power to the fullest possible extent and the dispersal and distribution of whatever power cannot be eliminated—a system of checks and balances. By removing the organization of economic activity from the control of political authority, the market eliminates this source of coercive power. It enables economic strength to be a check to political power rather than a reinforcement.

Economic power can be widely dispersed. There is no law of conservation which forces the growth of new centers of economic strength to be at the expense of existing centers. Political power, on the other hand, is more difficult to decentralize. There can be numerous small independent governments. But it is far more difficult to maintain numerous equipotent small centers of political power in a single large government than it is to have numerous centers of economic strength in a single large economy. There can be many millionaires in one large economy. But can there be more than one really outstanding leader, one person on whom the energies and enthusiasms of his countrymen are centered? If the central government gains power, it is likely to be at the expense of local governments. There seems to be something like a fixed total of political power to be distributed. Consequently, if economic power is joined to political power, concentration seems almost inevitable. On the other hand, if economic power is kept in separate hands from political power, it can serve as a check and a counter to political power.

The force of this abstract argument can perhaps best be demonstrated by example. Let us consider first, a hypothetical example that may help to bring out the principles involved, and then some actual examples from recent experience that illustrate the way in which the market works to preserve political freedom.

## Individual Rights

One feature of a free society is surely the freedom of individuals to advocate and propagandize openly for a radical change in the structure of the society—so long as the advocacy is restricted to persuasion and does not include force or other forms of coercion. It is a mark of the political freedom of a capitalist society that men can openly advocate and work for socialism. Equally, political freedom in a socialist society would require that men be free to advocate the introduction of capitalism. How could the freedom to advocate capitalism be preserved and protected in a socialist society?

In order for men to advocate anything, they must in the first place be able to earn a living. This already raises a problem in a socialist society, since all jobs are under the direct control of political authorities. It would take an act of self-denial whose difficulty is underlined by experience in the United States after World War II with the problem of "security" among Federal employees, for a socialist government to permit its employees to advocate policies directly contrary to official doctrine.

But let us suppose this act of self-denial to be achieved. For advocacy of capitalism to mean anything, the proponents must be able to finance their cause—to hold public meetings, publish pamphlets, buy radio time, issue newspapers and magazines, and so on. How could they raise the funds? There might and probably would be men in the socialist society with large incomes, perhaps even large capital sums in the form of government bonds and the like, but these would of necessity be high public officials. It is possible to conceive of a minor socialist official retaining his job although openly advocating capitalism. It strains credulity to imagine the socialist top brass financing such "subversive" activities.

The only recourse for funds would be to raise small amounts from a large number of minor officials. But this is no real answer. To tap these sources, many people would already have to be persuaded, and our whole problem is how to initiate and finance a campaign to do so. Radical movements in capitalist societies have never been financed this way. They have typically been supported by a few wealthy individuals who have become persuaded—by a Frederick Vanderbilt Field, or an Anita McCormick Blaine, or a Corliss Lamont, to mention a few names recently prominent, or by a Friedrich Engels, to go farther back. This is a role of inequality of wealth in preserving political freedom that is seldom noted—the role of the patron.

## Any Idea Can Be Heard

In a capitalist society, it is only necessary to convince a few wealthy people to get funds to launch any idea, however strange, and there are many such persons, many independent foci of support. And, indeed, it is not even necessary to persuade people or financial institutions with available funds of the soundness of the ideas to be propagated. It is only

necessary to persuade them that the propagation can be financially successful; that the newspaper or magazine or book or other venture will be profitable. The competitive publisher, for example, cannot afford to publish only writing with which he personally agrees; his touchstone must be the likelihood that the market will be large enough to yield a satisfactory return on his investment.

In this way, the market breaks the vicious circle and makes it possible ultimately to finance such ventures by small amounts from many people without first persuading them. There are no such possibilities in the socialist society; there is only the all-powerful state.

Let us stretch our imagination and suppose that a socialist government is aware of this problem and is composed of people anxious to preserve freedom. Could it provide the funds? Perhaps, but it is difficult to see how. It could establish a bureau for subsidizing subversive propaganda. But how could it choose whom to support? If it gave to all who asked, it would shortly find itself out of funds, for socialism cannot repeal the elementary economic law that a sufficiently high price will call forth a large supply. Make the advocacy of radical causes sufficiently remunerative, and the supply of advocates will be unlimited.

## Freedom to Advocate Unpopular Causes

Moreover, freedom to advocate unpopular causes does not require that such advocacy be without cost. On the contrary, no society could be stable if advocacy of radical change were costless, much less subsidized. It is entirely appropriate that men make sacrifices to advocate causes in which they deeply believe. Indeed, it is important to preserve freedom only for people who are willing to practice self-denial, for otherwise freedom degenerates into license and irresponsibility. What is essential is that the cost of advocating unpopular causes be tolerable and not prohibitive.

*"The groups in our society that have the most at stake in the preservation and strengthening of competitive capitalism are those minority groups which can most easily become the object of the distrust. . .of the majority."*

But we are not yet through. In a free market society, it is enough to have the funds. The suppliers of paper are as willing to sell it to the *Daily Worker* as to the *Wall Street Journal.* In a socialist society, it would not be enough to have the funds. The hypothetical supporter of capitalism would have to persuade a government factory making paper to sell to him, the government printing press to print his pamphlets, a government post office to distribute them among the people, a government agency to rent him a hall in which to talk, and so on.

## Only Capitalism Fosters Freedom

Perhaps there is some way in which one could overcome these difficulties and preserve freedom in a socialist society. One cannot say it is utterly impossible. What is clear, however, is that there are very real difficulties in establishing institutions that will effectively preserve the possibility of dissent. So far as I know, none of the people who have been in favor of socialism and also in favor of freedom have really faced up to this issue, or made even a respectable start at developing the institutional arrangements that would permit freedom under socialism. By contrast, it is clear how a free market capitalist society fosters freedom....

*"It is a mark of the political freedom of a capitalist society that men can openly advocate and work for socialism."*

Another example of the role of the market in preserving political freedom, was revealed in our experience with McCarthyism. Entirely aside from the substantive issues involved, and the merits of the charges made, what protection did individuals, and in particular government employees, have against irresponsible accusations and probings into matters that it went against their conscience to reveal? Their appeal to the Fifth Amendment would have been a hollow mockery without an alternative to government employment.

Their fundamental protection was the existence of a private-market economy in which they could earn a living. Here again, the protection was not absolute. Many potential private employers were, rightly or wrongly, averse to hiring those pilloried. It may well be that there was far less justification for the costs imposed on many of the people involved than for the costs generally imposed on people who advocate unpopular causes. But the important point is that the costs were limited and not prohibitive, as they would have been if government employment had been the only possibility.

## Impersonal Market

It is of interest to note that a disproportionately large fraction of the people involved apparently went into the most competitive sectors of the economy—small business, trade, farming—where the market approaches most closely the ideal free market. No one who buys bread knows whether the wheat from which it is made was grown by a Communist or a Republican, by a constitutionalist or a Fascist, or, for that matter, by a Negro or a white. This illustrates how an impersonal market separates economic activities from political views and protects men from being discriminated against in their economic activities for reasons that are irrelevant to their productivity—whether these reasons are associated with their views or their color.

As this example suggests, the groups in our society that have the most at stake in the preservation and strengthening of competitive capitalism are those minority groups which can most easily become the object of the distrust and enmity of the majority—the Negroes, the Jews, the foreign-born, to mention only the most obvious. Yet, paradoxically enough, the enemies of the free market—the Socialists and Communists—have been recruited in disproportionate measure from these groups. Instead of recognizing that the existence of the market has protected them from the attitudes of their fellow countrymen, they mistakenly attribute the residual discrimination to the market.

*Milton Friedman, well-known economist, has been the recipient of the Nobel Prize in Economics.*

*"The hardships imposed on the working people of the capitalist countries by unemployment are intensified by the growing cost of living as a result of inflation."*

# Capitalism Causes Economic Oppression

Boris N. Ponomarev

One reason why Communists are persecuted in the capitalist countries is that they are acknowledged as the political force that most consistently serves the interests of the working people.

The Communists are working not only for the long-term goal of building a socialist society, they are also dedicated to the cause of satisfying the working people's present-day social and economic needs and introducing deep-going general democratic reforms for this purpose. The Communists have no sympathy with the slogan of all or nothing that is peddled by some impatient pseudorevolutionaries. They believe it is wrong to link satisfaction of the working people's immediate needs exclusively with the future victory of socialism or with the achievement of certain intermediate objectives. In the communist view, many questions that worry the working people can be solved even today, under capitalism. So the Communists wage an active struggle for the satisfaction of the everyday needs of working people in town and country and support their mass actions on these issues.

From the great variety of immediate socioeconomic demands which the Communists put forward and for which they are fighting in various countries, we will take the most general and important.

In the forefront are problems that affect the conditions of ordinary folk, such as provision of jobs, reduction of prices, wage increases, higher pensions, improvement of living conditions and lowering of rents, free access to education, and improvement of health care and medical services.

These problems stem from the very nature of the capitalist system and the intensification of its socioeconomic contradictions. Recent years have reaffirmed the trends toward more frequent and deeper recessions in capitalist production. Structural

crises—energy, financial, currency, economic, etc.— are merging with, and giving a new edge to, the already intense cyclical crises. It is now obvious to everyone that state-monopoly regulation has proved incapable of ridding capitalism of its crises.

## Workers Suffer

As always, monopoly capital seeks to solve its problems at the expense of the workers. The fruits of the scientific and technological revolution are used to intensify exploitation. Bourgeois governments more and more often take the course of raising taxes, freezing wages, and slashing expenditure on education, health, and other social needs. This has become one of the main trends in their social policy. The result is falling living standards and stagnation, and in many capitalist countries a decline in the real incomes of the working people.

Few people are unaware that unemployment has become a problem of staggering dimensions in the capitalist world today.

Unemployment is the bugbear of the working people in the capitalist countries. By the end of 1980 the number of unemployed in the developed capitalist countries had reached the unprecedented figure of twenty-three million: over eight million jobless in the United States, more than nine million in Western Europe. According to Western experts, the jobless total in 1981 in the countries of developed capitalism increased to twenty-eight million, or 7.5-8 percent of the economically active population. Even bourgeois forecasters maintain that growing unemployment has the worst effect on young people, who often find themselves not needed by society and banned from social production even though they have an education. One can easily imagine the feelings of young men and women, full of strength and energy and eager to work but unable to do so because capitalism consigns them to the role of "redundants."

Boris N. Ponomarev, *Communism in a Changing World.* New York: Sphinx Press, Inc., 1983.

In mid-1981, there were approximately 455 million unemployed in the nonsocialist part of the world. The enforced idleness of this huge potential productive force is the tragic result of the capitalist system of social relations.

## Unemployment Escalating

The hardships imposed on the working people of the capitalist countries by unemployment are intensified by the growing cost of living as a result of inflation. In 1980 alone, prices rose generally in the EEC countries by 11 percent, and in the United States by 13.3 percent. In Italy, inflation broke all records for the postwar period with 22.5 percent in 1980. Price rises have affected mainly food, fuel, electricity, rents, consumer services, the cost of medical care, and education.

All attempts by the ruling circles in the West to cope with inflation have failed. Under the pretext of fighting inflation governments step up their attacks against the working class, the standards of living of the working people, cut social spending and unemployment benefits, etc. All this goes hand in hand with huge increases in armaments contracts for the military-industrial complex and escalation of military spending.

This policy of the ruling circles results in a lowering of real wages. For example, in 1980 in the United States, Canada, and the Federal Republic of Germany the actual hourly wage of blue- and white-collar workers fell by 4.6, 1.8, and 0.3 percent, respectively. The poverty problem has assumed dangerous proportions in a number of countries. According to figures presented by the International Labor Organization (ILO), 60 million people in the countries belonging to the Organization for Economic Cooperation and Development (OECD), i.e., 12 percent of their population, are living below the poverty line.

Housing is a real tragedy for wide sections of the population. Capitalist profit-making out of one of the most essential human needs—the need for a home—has led to constant rises in rent. Year by year rents go up in Britain, where because of high rents many buildings are standing empty while hundreds of thousands of British people have to live in wretched conditions, not to mention the 50,000 who have no homes at all.

## Monopolies' Profits Grow

Though the living standards of the working people in the capitalist countries are falling, the profits of the monopolies continue to soar. *Fortune* magazine reported that 1980 had been exceptionally good for the American oil companies thanks to the lifting of controls on the prices of home-produced oil. Some 1,200 of the major American corporations grossed profits of 123 billion dollars in 1980. In Japan, the profits of 121 top companies rose by 35.1 percent.

The result is a situation in which 1 percent of Britain's population owns more than a quarter of the national wealth, and 1.7 percent of the West German population, three-quarters of all the means of production, whereas in the United States 4 percent of Americans control property worth the fantastic sum of one trillion dollars.

In short, the realities of capitalist society, the society of "equal opportunities," mean growing difficulties for the working class, on the one hand, and further enrichment for a small privileged group, on the other.

*"The realities of capitalist society, the society of 'equal opportunities' mean growing difficulties for the working class, on the one hand, and further enrichment for a small privileged group, on the other."*

The fact that the capitalist economy is in the grip of difficulties is something capitalist society's policymakers cannot help admitting. . . .

Why do economic crises flare up? Why are crises inevitable under capitalism? Why have capitalism's economic problems taken such a sharp turn for the worse today? Some economists tell them that the oil-producing countries are to blame for everything. Some economists put the blame on the working class, on "excessive demands" put forward by labor unions. Some declare that industrial civilization in general is at fault and threatens catastrophe unless a stop is put to the expansion of production. And so on and so forth.

## Communism Based on Facts

But it is only the Communists, the Communist parties, that give the people correct, science-based answers to their questions. The causes of economic crises, the Communists explain, are rooted in the capitalist system itself. Moreover, the scientific and technological revolution and the growing monopolistic concentration of production make all the contradictions of capitalist society more acute than ever before.

This analysis is based on the well-known proposition which Karl Marx and Frederick Engels first formulated in *The Communist Manifesto*. They noted that the bourgeois relations of production hold up development of the productive forces, and that when the latter "overcome their fetters they bring disorder into the whole of bourgeois society." When attempting to remedy the situation the bourgeoisie paves the way "for more extensive and more destructive crises."

Economic crises in the form of sudden declines in the volume of production used to occur before the capitalist era too, but only episodically and as a result of crop failures, internecine wars, natural calamities, and so on. Capitalism, however, gave rise to conditions that have made economic crises inevitable. They are inevitable because of capitalism's main contradiction, that between the social nature of production and the private form of appropriation. Although the working masses create all of society's material benefits, they are cheated during the distribution of these benefits, that is, they are deprived of the fruits of their labors. Capitalism subordinates production, which is social in substance, to the interests and will of private entrepreneurs whose aim is to make maximum profits. Capitalism's basic contradiction leads to inexorably recurring economic crises of overproduction.

## Monopolies and Economics

The emergence of these crises is closely intertwined with the most characteristic features of the capitalist economy. The anarchy of capitalist production holds a special place among these features. State monopoly capitalism does not do away with uncontrolled, anarchic production in bourgeois society. On the contrary, it aggravates these features to an even greater extent within the framework of the capitalist economy as a whole and triggers sharp conflicts and clashes. Capitalism cannot be an "organized" entity. The rise of monopoly associations does not mean an end to competition and scramble among the capitalists. On the contrary, monopolies and competition go hand in hand. Monopolies aggravate the clashes between groups of capitalists and deepen the contradictions of the capitalist system. Trusts, syndicates, and cartels compete fiercely for a share of the profits, for spheres of influence, and so on. The capitalist associations fight more and more intensively for markets and sources of raw materials.

*"An important factor directly connected with the outbreak of economic crises under capitalism is the discrepancy between production and consumption."*

A furious battle goes on among the monopolies in various sectors of the economy: between those in the extractive industries and those in the manufacturing industries, etc. The whole of this struggle increases the contradictions of capitalism and aggravates the anarchy of production.

An important factor directly connected with the outbreak of economic crises under capitalism is the discrepancy between production and consumption, between the big productive potential and the limited

purchasing power of the mass of the people. The relative decline in the purchasing power of the population creates a barrier on the road of capitalist production. Vast quantities of commodities that factories and corporations manufacture as they strive for maximum profits do not find buyers. An economic crisis then sets in.

The Communist parties time and again examine the crisis of capitalism and clarify their approach to this problem in the contemporary situation. For example, the 1960 Meeting of Communist and Workers' Parties noted the growing instability of the capitalist economy; while still grappling with the consequences of an economic crisis a number of capitalist countries found themselves threatened with fresh economic upheavals.

The 1969 International Meeting of Communist and Workers' Parties pointed out that the exacerbation of capitalism's old contradictions went hand in hand with the rise of new ones. Chief among the latter, the Meeting noted, is the contradiction between the exceptional possibilities the scientific and technological revolution opens up and the obstacles capitalism places in the way of utilizing them in the interests of the whole of society because it uses the bulk of the scientific discoveries and vast material resources for military purposes, thus squandering the wealth of the nations. Another contradiction is that between the social nature of modern production and its state-monopoly regulation. Further, there are growing contradictions between labor and capital, and the increasingly deep antagonism between the interests of the overwhelming majority of the nation and those of the financial oligarchy.

What is the way out? By switching over to a new social system founded on public ownership of the means of production and on government by the working people. That system, the Meeting noted, is the only one capable of assuring planned, crisis-free economic growth in the people's interests; of guaranteeing the people's social and political rights; of making genuine democracy possible, that is, real participation by the broad mass of people in running the country; of creating the conditions for all-round development of the individual, for equality of nations and friendship among nations. . . .

## Anti-Inflationary Measures

The Communist parties . . . urge the passing of anti-inflationary measures to protect and raise the working people's living standards. The struggle for higher wages has intensified, and this is regarded not only as a means of improving living conditions but also as a way of raising effective demand, expanding the market, and safeguarding jobs. For example, the Communist Party of Austria has demanded automatic adjustment of wages to fully offset losses due to rising prices and taxes. The Communists of Britain are working for the introduction of effective price controls and a fair national minimum wage.

The Communists of the Federal Republic of Germany demand strict control of prices on goods and services that feature prominently in ordinary people's budgets (foodstuffs, rents, payments for gas and electricity, fares, and postal charges).

---

*"It is clear that the Communist parties staunchly defend a whole set of demands reflecting the immediate needs of the working people."*

---

The Communists of India are fighting against price rises, unemployment, lockouts, and dismissals. They demand a minimum wage which employers must observe and a fair wage for farm workers.

From what has been said, it is clear that the Communist parties staunchly defend a whole set of demands reflecting the immediate needs of the working people. At the same time Communists realize that any gains at this level satisfy only the partial, short-term interests of the working people. These gains are not lasting, not stable in the context of the capitalist system, for such concessions are not granted willingly by the monopolies. The Communist parties, therefore, link the struggle for immediate, partial demands with a campaign for deep-going general democratic socioeconomic and political reforms designed to restrict the omnipotence of the monopolies. . . .

It is by no means a matter of indifference to the working class and the working people in general in what form the capitalists assert their role. Lenin wrote: "We do not discard bourgeois-democratic slogans, but more consistently, fully and decisively implement what is democratic in them." Communists, while defending everything positive in bourgeois democracy, want to develop its democratic principles and make it truly representative.

*Boris N. Ponomarev is a secretary of the Central Committee of the Communist Party of the Soviet Union and an alternate member of its Political Bureau, chairman of the International Affairs Committee of the Soviet Nationalities of the USSR Supreme Soviet, and a member of the Academy of Sciences of the USSR.*

*"The real socialism built in the USSR is a vivid example of a just organisation of society in the interests of the working people."*

# Communism Is Superior to Capitalism

### Yaroslav Renkas

The real socialism built in the USSR is a vivid example of a just organisation of society in the interests of the working people. The atmosphere of genuine collectivism, integrity and friendship of all the nations and small nationalities, which consolidates with every passing day, just as the inherent spiritual health of the Soviet people—such are the obvious achievements of socialism in the USSR. Common labour for the common good, common joys and common sorrows, common aims and purposes bring the Soviet people still closer together and encourage the spirit of cooperation and mutual assistance in them.

The revolutionary experience reaffirmed that collectivism embodied in the class solidarity of the working people was and remains a powerful weapon of their struggle against capitalist oppression. The bourgeoisie goes out of its way to instill individualism in the minds of the people, which separates and alienates them. The cornerstone of individualism is private property, which divides society into two antagonistic camps—the exploiters and the exploited, the rich and the poor.

Socialism does away with the very source of individualism. V.I. Lenin stressed this aspect of socialist construction: "We shall work to do away with the accursed maxim: Every man for himself and the devil take the hindmost. We shall work to inculcate in people's minds, turn into a habit, and bring into the day-by-day life of the masses, the rule: 'All for each and each for all.'"

Seizure of power by the working class and its use for the benefit of the working masses, elimination of private ownership of the means of production and establishment of public property, the gradual evolution of a communist consciousness among the popular masses—all this opened the way to free development of the socialist collectivism.

## All People Equal

In socialist society the working people look to the future with confidence, they enjoy all constitutional rights irrespective of nationality, sex or age. It is the Soviet Union that was the first in the world to establish true equality of the people, to provide for their tangible, not illusory, rights.

Democracy established in socialist society, free from the exploiting class, ensures the growing participation of the working people in running state and public affairs. All the vital political, economic and social problems are discussed and resolved with the broad and direct cooperation of workers, farmers and intellectuals.

The material effect of socialist democracy manifests itself in the activities of the Soviets of People's Deputies. The Soviets are elective representative bodies which exercise state power at all levels. Today over 50,000 Soviets with nearly 2 million people's deputies are functioning in the USSR. They are all accountable to the electorate, while the electors have the right to recall any deputy who fails to cope with his responsibilities.

The general body of the people's deputies comprises 44.3 per cent of the workers and 24.9 per cent of the farmers. More than half of the deputies are women (50.1 per cent). Youth are also represented in the Soviets, their share amounting to 34 per cent. The majority of the deputies (57.2 per cent) are not Party members. These figures amply show that the power in the USSR belongs to the entire population, a principle enshrined in the Constitution of the USSR.

## Capitalism's Unequal Conditions

The picture is quite different in the capitalist countries. There are neither workers nor ordinary

Yaroslav Renkas, "Values of Socialism," *Soviet Military Review*, No. 9, 1984.

farmers in the United States Congress. The Americans themselves call Congress "the millionaires' club." Worker representation in the West German Bundestag is marginal. The situation is the same in the other capitalist states.

The Communist Party of the Soviet Union is not at all idealistic about what has been done or is being done in the way of promoting democracy and improving the life in the USSR. There have been and probably will be difficulties of growth arising from the limited material resources, from the state of public consciousness and culture, as well as from the existing international situation which is far from particulary favourable, but rather adverse to Soviet society, which has to grow and develop in the cold winds of the imperialism's psychologic warfare.

The CPSU regards it a primary goal to bring up every Soviet citizen in the spirit of conscious discipline, to develop the organic need for selfless constructive labour for the common good. Discipline and order are the integral aspects of socialist democracy that opens up broad opportunities for everyone in governing society and the state. The comprehensive expansion of democracy is viewed in the USSR as a powerful and effective means of the communist education, of the upbringing of the new man.

## The Right to Work

An important value of socialism is the right to work. This right is not only proclaimed but it is also guaranteed in the USSR. The planned economy makes it possible to set an industrial growth rate that would provide jobs for all able-bodied citizens. The Constitution of the USSR emphasises this right by the right to choose an occupation according to one's inclinations, capabilities, education and training and, what is no less important, in keeping with the requirements of society. Half a century ago the last labour exchange was closed in the USSR, and unemployment was forever eliminated from Soviet economic and social life.

---

*"The efforts of the Communist Party have always been primarily directed to obtain a steady rise in the material and cultural standards of the Soviet people."*

---

What can capitalism produce to counter this material advantage of socialism? According to official data, there were nearly 12 million totally unemployed and 6.5 million partially unemployed workers in the USA in 1982 and in 1983.

The growing living standard of the Soviet people is another advantage of socialism. The efforts of the

Communist Party have always been primarily directed to obtain a steady rise in the material and cultural standards of the Soviet people. The real per capita income in the USSR has grown nearly 6 times since 1940 and it has doubled during the recent 15 years. While in 1965 only 4 per cent of the population had a monthly income over 100 roubles, today half of the population is at or above this level.

## People Cared for by State

From birth and throughout his lifetime every Soviet citizen is shrouded by the care of the state and society. A widespread network of nurseries and kindergartens, free education and medical care, the world's lowest rents, free libraries and clubs are not only available but seem quite natural and routine to the Soviet people.

Here are just a few figures illustrating the state of affairs of the working people in the USA: there are 80 million people which are below a sufficient level even by American assessments, while 31.5 million live below the poverty level and 12 million exist in complete misery and hunger, over 2 million are homeless, 4.5 million children are on public relief and do not have enough food. Even these facts are enough to indicate that capitalist society is plagued by incurable ills and evils.

A major gain of socialism is free education. It is a fact that 72 per cent of the population of pre-revolutionary Russia could neither read nor write. No later than in the 30s the USSR became a fully literate country. The state introduced first elementary and then intermediate education, nowadays a complete secondary education is provided for all young people in the USSR.

Incidentally, in Great Britain, France, the Federal Republic of Germany and other advanced capitalist states only 25 to 30 per cent of the young people, mainly from the bourgeois families, have the benefit of a full secondary education. It is hard to believe, but there are 23 million totally illiterate people (over the age of 16) in the United States.

The Soviet people are proud of the spiritual gains of socialism. Today 90 million people study in different schools and universities in the USSR. Most adults have either secondary or higher education. Millions are working to create spiritual values. No wonder that within a few decades the USSR traversed a road which took other countries centuries—from a primitive wooden plough to a spaceship.

## Soviet Life and Peace

One more socialist value deserves special note—the aspiration of socialist society to peace. The peaceful nature of the Soviet Union is not a transient, temporary feature. It is organic to the humanist nature of a society free from exploitation of man by man. There are no individuals or social groups in the USSR who would profit from military conflicts, arms trade or military build-up. To attain the main goal—satisfaction of the material and spiritual needs of the working people—the Communist Party and the whole socialist society must live in peace.

That is why the CPSU and the Soviet state spare no effort to reduce substantially and eliminate the danger of nuclear war, to stop the arms race, to bring down the level of military confrontation of the two social systems. The radical steps to that effect proposed by Konstantin Chernenko, General Secretary of the CPSU Central Committee, Chairman of the Presidium of the USSR Supreme Soviet, were met with understanding and approval by the world public. However there are forces in the West that are not suited by the peaceful posture of the USSR. Influential imperialist circles and their NATO militarist stooges seek to thwart the positive developments in the world. They whip up all kinds of slanderous anti-Soviet campaigns, and endlessly raise military expenditures, thus escalating the arms build-up.

In this complex situation the Communist Party of the Soviet Union, implementing the Peace Programme, has to take the necessary steps to provide for security of the USSR and the fraternal socialist states.

*Yaroslav Renkas is a Lieutenant-Colonel in the Soviet Army.*

*"Of all the many lessons that the Free World can learn from the Soviet 'experiment'. . .the most urgent is that life under a socialist command system is far from a 'workers' paradise.'"*

# Communism Is Inferior to Capitalism

Mark Hendrickson

Of all the many lessons that the Free World can learn from the Soviet "experiment" of the last sixty-four years, the most urgent is that life under a socialist command system is far from the "workers' paradise" promised by Marxian ideologues. As Alexander Solzhenitsyn and many others have so thoroughly documented, the socialist order, trumpeted as the wave of the future, is maintained only by the most brutal measures. The fact that the socialist state depends upon force for its continued existence is powerful evidence that free individuals would promptly reject such an inhumane system.

Economically, poverty has been institutionalized in the Soviet Union. Sociologically, a well-defined class structure has emerged, with special privileges accorded at the wish of the ruling elite. Politically, individual rights have been trampled upon and extinguished by ruthless despots. Spiritually and morally, the beliefs that the state is supreme and that the end justifies the means have taken human beings to the depths of depravity, as many have become willing to betray, enslave, and even torture any number of innocent victims. Is it any wonder, then, that "Whoever can 'votes with his feet,' simply fleeing from this mass violence and destruction"?

## Economic Lessons

Economic laws, like the laws of physics, are discovered, not devised by men. The Communist rulers of the Soviet Union have tried to repeal those inexorable laws, and, in spite of their repeated failures, they persist in issuing bureaucratic decrees that attempt to revise the way the world works. In their self-deluding hubris, they act as though all action will conform to socialist planning.

It is a fact of life that human beings value more highly and will husband more carefully what they

own than what they don't own. That is why the small, privately owned garden plots which have been permitted in the USSR account for 62% of the potatoes, 32% of fruits and vegetables, 47% of the eggs, and 34% of all milk and meat produced in the country, even though these private plots constitute less than one per cent of the country's agricultural land. Yet, in spite of this impressive record and the chronic problem of food shortages in their country, the Kremlin refuses to heed the sound advice of Russian exiled dissident Alexander Solzhenitsyn to "give up the forced collective farms and leave just the voluntary ones."

The productivity of industry also languishes under its socialist directors. One major reason is the lack of incentive for workers and managers when all profit goes to the state. "Technological improvements developed in costly research institutes are ignored because no one will profit directly by introducing them." Russians naturally want to profit as do all human beings. However, they don't stand much chance of profiting by honest means, so they sometimes resort to dishonest means for personal gain. Dishonesty, of course, occurs in all countries, but Yankee ingenuity would be hard put to duplicate this mind-boggling fraud reported in a recent article:

> When senior party officials dedicated a long-awaited, badly needed tractor-repair plant last year, "Pravda" (which means "Truth") extolled it as "not a factory (but) a beautiful work of art," and the responsible comrades awarded each other the usual round of medals. No such factory existed.

Soviet experience has conclusively demonstrated that socialist production is inherently inferior to capitalist production. Lack of incentive is a major reason. But even if workers were uniformly motivated around the world, the socialist countries would be poorer because economic calculation is outlawed (de facto if not de jure).

In a capitalist order, each individual demands what

Mark Hendrickson, "Teachings of Soviet Experience," *The Freeman,* April 1982.

he values most in the marketplace. He indicates approximately how much he values different products by how much he is willing to pay for them. These approximate objectifications of value—called "price"—are the signals which communicate to producers what they need to produce, and at what cost, if they are to attract customers and stay in business. As consumers' hierarchies of values change moment by moment, these changes are transmitted through the pricing network. Entrepreneurs then seek to reorganize scarce factors of production so efficiently that they can offer a good that consumers want at a price which they are willing to pay, and still end up with a profit.

*"Soviet experience has conclusively demonstrated that socialist production is inherently inferior to capitalist production."*

Because goods which are valued highly cost dearly (depending on the available supply) they tend to be conserved and used efficiently, and so greater satisfaction (greater prosperity) results than would be the case under socialism where the value-sensitive pricing mechanism has been rejected. Production under socialism is grossly uneconomical because the decrees of state officials supplant and suppress the economic values of individuals as reflected in prices freely arrived at in the market.

Socialist planning is uneconomical also because it is totally unsuited for coping with change. Whereas the prices of commodities in the United States fluctuate moment by moment on the commodity exchanges, reflecting shifts in supply and demand, and so enabling each commodity to go to where it is most valued in the economy, in the Soviet Union, commodities are allocated by state officials who are incapable of perceiving what the most urgent needs for any given good are at any given moment. Politics supersedes economics. When considerations of value are supplanted by considerations of power, chaos in production ensues. The only reason why the blind planning of the socialist commissars in the USSR has not resulted in total chaos and much more severe poverty has been that the Soviet leaders have been able to observe the allocation of resources in the non-socialized economies of the world....

## Sociological Lessons

The social structure of the Soviet Union is an egalitarian's nightmare. Far from eliminating class distinctions, the socialist system deepens and perpetuates them. Observers differ as to how many strata or "ranks" (to use a term which is apropos for the militaristically regimented social order) but they are unanimous in acknowledging a class structure that is so rigid that Russian critics refer to "caste expediency" and a "boss class." Favors are bestowed by the state; favors are taken away by the state.

Tremendous tensions must inevitably exist because of the way the social organization, the USSR's body politic, is presently constituted. The idea of class exploiting class, which is little more than a fantasy in a capitalist system where individuals are free to excel in the competition of servicing the needs of their fellows, is a cruel, ugly reality in the USSR.

The elite minority plunders the masses, and the masses know it. Certainly, some of the victims are fatalistic about their plight, but many others bitterly resent their exploitation. The present system may endure, or it may not, but one way or the other, violence remains the central characteristic of the USSR's social organization.

The use of forced labor in Soviet Russia is as characteristic of socialism as is the impossibility of calculating value. If the 40% of the Soviet population which are forced to work the collective farms as virtual serfs cannot feed the Soviet Union's population, and managers will take credit for the construction of factories which don't even exist, one can scarcely imagine how unproductive, or even counterproductive, the labor of the zeks (the prison camp inmates) is.

In *The Gulag Archipelago Two,* Solzhenitsyn included several examples of the deliberate destructiveness of zek labor, and concluded, in something of an understatement, that the Soviet state (i.e., the people) is poorer as a result of using slave labor than it otherwise would have been. He also dispels the myth of the glory and honor of working in a socialist state, asserting, "The labor of the zeks was needed for degrading and particularly heavy work, which no one, under socialism, would wish to perform.". . .

## Political Lessons

In a system of free men, any individual who excels at satisfying the needs of his fellowman is rewarded by an impersonal market for his achievements. In such a system, service to one's fellowman determines wealth and privilege. In a socialistic command system, on the other hand, the way to privilege is to help keep one's fellowman under the subjection of Caesar. Personal favor determines wealth and privilege.

"In a country where the sole employer is the State, opposition means death by slow starvation. The old principle: who does not work shall not eat, has been replaced by a new one: who does not obey shall not eat." With those grim words, Leon Trotsky described the totalitarian grip which the communist rulers of the USSR hold on the populace of their vast territory.

That is the reality of the political order in a socialist system—a system which Karl Marx viewed as progressive. As economist George Reisman has observed, ''The complete and utter powerlessness of the plain citizen under socialism can hardly be exaggerated. Under socialism, the plain citizen is no longer the customer, 'who is always right,' but the serf, who must take his rations and like it.''

In the Soviet Union, the individual citizen is virtually without rights. This has been so ever since the Communist takeover. What the state (i.e., the ruling elite) wants, it takes. Those who once resisted the expropriation of their property in Communist Russia were liquidated. Those who object too vocally today are banished to Siberia or otherwise silenced. That is the nature of politics in a socialist state.

The public ownership of the means of production includes the public ownership of labor. Solzhenitsyn writes, ''We are slaves there from birth.'' The ultimate form of slavery in the USSR is the zek, who is subjected to treatment far worse than that endured by most of the slaves throughout history. Most slaves in ancient Greece and Rome, and in pre-Civil War United States were regarded as private property. As such, their owners at least had an incentive to keep them healthy. The zek, on the other hand, belonging to the state, is in a position in which none of his supervisors finds it in his self-interest to be concerned about the zek's well-being, and so millions of zeks have found their prison term tantamount to capital punishment.

## People Are Expendable

The experience of applied socialism in the Soviet Union demonstrates that the welfare of the propertyless citizen is of little concern to the state authorities. Subjugation is all that matters to the bosses. This has always been the case. Solzhenitsyn relates that the Volga famine of 1921 illustrated ''a typical Communist technique: to struggle for power without thinking of the fact that the productivity is collapsing, that the fields are not being sown, that the factories stand idle, that the country is sinking into poverty and famine.'' In other words, the people are expendable. What had been heralded as the ''dictatorship of the proletariat'' has in reality become a dictatorship over those proletarians who manage to survive.

For decades, the official rhetoric has assured Ivan that his grandchildren would enjoy unprecedented prosperity, yet that promise is still far from fruition, and the achievement of affluence remains in the ever-receding future. The modus operandi of the political leaders of the socialist state is to plunder its subjects in the present and offer them a rosy picture of a distant future as compensation.

The despotism of the Soviet rulers is not an esoteric matter for political scientists in the West to debate as an academic issue. Rather, it is a phenomenon of tremendous import to every single Westerner, for the objective of the Soviet Union's overlords is to extend their hegemony over the entire globe. Is it logical to suppose that tyrants who have shown no compunctions about brutalizing and enslaving their compatriots would respect the life and property of peoples of foreign lands?

## Aggressive Evil of Tyranny

Solzehenitsyn has repeatedly reminded Westerners of one of history's oft-repeated, seldom-learned lessons: that the evil of tyranny grows ever more aggressive until it is bravely confronted and defeated. Those who try to appease tyranny will eventually find themselves attacked by those very tyrants, and if they are fortunate enough to be able to vanquish the aggressors, it will only be at a cost far greater than would have been necessary had an unflinching moral stand been taken against the tyranny at the outset.

Of the present incarnation of tyranny known as Communism, Solzhenitsyn writes, ''. . .a concentration of world evil is taking place, full of hatred for humanity. It is fully determined to destroy your society.'' That may sound like melodramatic hyperbole to the average American, but it corresponds completely with the stated nature and objectives of the Communist movement, and, more importantly, it corresponds to the anti-human reality of life in the USSR and other Communist-dominated lands. Any thought that this menace will go away if it is ignored is wishful and dangerous thinking. It must be confronted. . . .

How, specifically, can the West resist the advances of Communism? Certainly by military means, but more importantly, by affirming a consistent moral position—practicing and promoting freedom of individual economic activity; not assisting the Kremlin through trade and aid; not signing treaties (such as the Helsinki accords) which legitimize Soviet aggression; refusing to live at the expense of one's fellow man; rejecting the insidious teaching that morality is relative and the end justifies the means; affirming in word and deed that all individuals have certain inalienable rights; being concerned with more than mere material ease, for liberty, if not vigilantly guarded, is lost. This is the message of Alexander Solzhenitsyn. If we heed his warning and emulate his courageous stance against Communist tyranny, the West shall indeed prevail against this aggressive, worldwide attack against individual liberty.

*Mark Hendrickson recently earned a master's degree with a thesis based on the works of Solzhenitsyn. This viewpoint is condensed from a chapter of that thesis.*

*"The ultimate aim of the Soviet Union, from its inception, has been the overthrow of capitalist societies everywhere, and the creation of a communist world."*

# Communism Threatens the US

Louis J. Walinsky

Chess, according to an old Chinese saying, is "the play of the science of war." The encyclopedia tells us that "Two chess players fighting over the board may fitly be compared to two famous generals encountering each other on the battlefield, the strategy and the tactics being not dissimilar in spirit." Significantly, the Russians take chess much more seriously than we do. Since the mid-1950s, with a brief interruption only in 1972-74, the world's chess championship has been held by Russians, and chess is reported to be an important course of study in the training of their military officers. They are better chess players than we are.

At any given stage in the course of a chess match against a formidable opponent, the grand master will base his strategy on his assessment of his opponent's strategy, and on his analysis of the relative strengths and weaknesses of his opponent's and his own positions. In like manner, the formulation of a defense strategy requires a perceptive assessment of the intentions and strategy of one's adversary and a realistic analysis of his strengths and weaknesses, as well as of one's own.

What is it the Soviet's are after? How do these intentions and objectives threaten us? What strategy are they pursuing to effectuate these purposes? What are the Soviet strengths we must evade or counter? What are the Soviet weaknesses we can exploit? How can we best utilize our own strengths, and best reduce our own vulnerabilities, as we seek to ensure our own national security?

## The Soviets' Ultimate Aim

If we begin, as we should, with the *ultimate* aim of the Soviet Union, we cannot avoid restatement of the banal. The ultimate aim of the Soviet Union, from its

Louis J. Walinsky, "Coherent Defense Strategy: The Case for Economic Denial." Reprinted by permission of Foreign Affairs, Winter 1982/83. Copyright 1983 by the Council on Foreign Relations, Inc.

inception, has been the overthrow of capitalist societies everywhere, and the creation of a communist world. (In such a world, although Marxism-Leninism is silent on this score, the Soviet Union would surely expect to play a leading, central and even dominant role.) The ideology, moreover, is quite explicit in defining how this objective is to be achieved. Capitalist societies, it holds, will be overturned by revolutions from *within*, in conditions of class conflict exacerbated by imperialist rivalries and wars—*not* by conquest from without.

Thus, the Soviet Union has naturally sought to provide leadership, encouragement and all feasible assistance to "progressive elements" in capitalist and formerly colonial nations to expedite the "inevitable" victory of the "working classes." In other words, it has tried to foment, guide, assist and exploit revolutionary or potentially revolutionary movements and situations, wherever these were considered to exist. The major Soviet threat, ideologically guided, has thus been one of subversion, rather than of direct aggression. . . .

Confronted by a rapidly reviving and dramatically strengthened Western Europe, the NATO Alliance, and the obvious appeal of the democratic idea to most of the newly independent countries, and plagued increasingly by internal economic difficulties and dissent within their satellite allies, as well as at home, the Soviet leaders were compelled to accommodate their aims to the new realities. They continued to give lip service, to be sure, to the ultimate goal of a communist world which remains the official faith, whether believed in or not, and to meddle, where they could, in troubled waters. But during the 1950s and for much of the 1960s, their real aim of necessity was reduced basically to an effort *to make the world safe for communism.* This could be paraphrased as: to safeguard the continued control of the Soviet leaders over the Soviet Union and its increasingly reluctant satellite allies, together, of course, with the continuation of their own privileged status and perquisites of power.

Starting shortly after the mid-1950s, a series of major developments favorable to the Soviet Union reversed the ebb in its international fortunes and led to the evolution of new aims and a new strategy. Sputnik gave a big boost to Soviet prestige. By the end of the 1960s, the accelerated buildup of its nuclear weaponry and power, on which the Soviet Union had embarked after its humiliation in the Cuban missile crisis of 1962, had reached a stage with which the Soviets felt much more secure. At the same time, the United States had been greatly weakened by its interminable war in Vietnam. It had lost prestige, status and respect in the international community, and its self-confidence and resolution had been eroded by internal divisiveness and civil disorder. These found their own counterparts in Europe and Japan. The failure of the West to react vigorously to the wave of Palestine Liberation Organization terrorism in the late 1960s—to the repeated hijacking of passenger planes, the taking of innocent hostages, the death toll of bombing outrages and, even worse, the unchallenged granting of asylum to the terrorists by Arab countries—all these were indicative of a loss of nerve by the Western democracies. This was confirmed by, and probably helped to encourage, the imposition of the oil embargo and the outrageous economic rape by quadrupled Organization of Petroleum Exporting Countries (OPEC) oil prices in 1973—an unparalled act of aggression to which the United States and the West supinely submitted....

## A World Safe for Communism

In combination, these and companion developments far outweighed the effects of others unfavorable to the Soviet Union. Encouraged and emboldened, the Soviet leaders progressively shifted during these years, from their basically defensive posture of the 1950s and much of the 1960s, in the direction of their earlier ultimate aims. But there was a significant difference in the position at which they arrived.

For the earlier goal of a communist world, they substituted the aim of a world dominated by communism or, at the very least, a world in which the Soviet Union would be the dominant power. Their strategy for achieving this also changed, correspondingly, in a most significant way. Abandoning hope that class conflict and revolutions within capitalist societies would seize power for communism, the new strategy would rely chiefly on a combination of intimidation by the armed might of the Soviet Union *and* subversion aimed at the destruction of morale and the erosion of the will of peoples in the democratic societies to resist, opening the door to Soviet domination. This new aim and this new strategy emerge unmistakably from an

examination of Soviet strengths and weaknesses, and from a consideration of how skillfully the Soviet leaders have exploited U.S. and Western weaknesses to negate our strengths, and used Western strengths to compensate for their own glaring weaknesses.

## Four Soviet Strengths

The greatest and most obvious of the Soviet strengths vis-à-vis the United States and the West is its awesome military power both in men under arms and in weaponry. This holds for its land, sea and air forces, whether conventional or nuclear, in both offensive and defensive deployments. Not only are its armed forces highly disciplined; their pay is low, permitting the Soviet Union to spend roughly two-thirds of its military budget on weaponry, while the relatively high pay of U.S. military personnel has consumed perhaps two-thirds of our military budgets, leaving only one-third for weaponry. The Soviet leaders also have the advantage of being able to allocate to the military as large a share of their total resources as they wish, without accountability to an electorate. (The actual military burden on the Soviet gross national product is, however, not as great as is implied by U.S. estimates of their military spending, because these are estimated in terms of what such materiel and services would cost in the United States, rather than in their actual cost to the Soviets.)

---

*"A...major strength of the Soviet Union...is the mastery of its leaders of the art of manipulating social groups and forces, especially in Western democracies, toward beliefs and in directions the Soviets desire."*

---

This enormous military strength is complemented by very important strategic locational advantages. The Soviet forces enjoy proximity to the major areas of U.S. vital interest and of potential conflict. They stand at the borders of Western Europe and the Middle East, from which the United States is separated by thousands of miles, so that it would have to deploy and supply its armed forces over seas infested by Soviet submarines. Moreover, the basic locational advantages enjoyed by the Soviet Union are enhanced by the Soviet presence, whether direct or by virtue of Cuban and East German proxies, in Angola, Ethiopia, Yemen and Afghanistan. Indeed, the ability of the Soviet Union to use proxies to advance its position and power while avoiding direct confrontation with the United States must be accounted as yet another significant element in its favor.

A third major strength of the Soviet Union, the

importance of which cannot be overestimated, is the mastery of its leaders of the art of manipulating social groups and forces, especially in the Western democracies, toward beliefs and in directions the Soviets desire. Marxist analysis has provided the Soviet leaders with an incomparable tool for selecting key groups and assessing their economic interests, ideas and value systems, as well as their disaffections, rivalries, suspicions and fears. Many decades of experience in the use of agitative propaganda have enabled the Soviets to play on these with the skill of a master programmer at a computer keyboard and with almost equal control. They have used this ability to confuse, obfuscate and mislead, all in the service of their own interests.

> *"The greatest and most obvious of the Soviet strengths. . .is its awesome military power both in men under arms and weaponry."*

Thus, they have portrayed their own expansionary and aggressive actions as essentially defensive responses to capitalist-imperialist encirclement and aggression. They have encouraged poor Third World countries to believe that their poverty and backwardness was the result of capitalist-colonialist exploitation. They encouraged the outrageous oil price and embargo actions of OPEC as acts of long overdue justice, to sabotage and weaken the economies of the West and to terrorize them by the fear that the oil lifeline might be cut off. During a decade of economic slowdown in the West, they exploited the appetites of Western producers and banks for profitable exports and loans, persuading them to work for governmental policies which made it possible for the Soviet Union and its satellites to obtain goods, technology and credits they desperately needed. They used post-Vietnam War disillusionment to foster mistrust of Western governments and institutions by their own citizens.

## USSR Plays on War

Above all, the Soviet Union has played upon universal desires for peace and fears of war, especially nuclear war. Indeed, they have been able to persuade literally millions of innocent people of goodwill throughout the West that it is their own governments, rather than the Soviet Union, whose policies threaten to lead the world to a nuclear holocaust. The effect of all this has been to develop politically significant constituencies who seriously misperceive the nature of the real struggle between the totalitarian and democratic ways of life, and to undermine their support of their governments' resolve to safeguard democracy.

Finally, we must acknowledge as an important strength of the Soviet Union that, in pursuing its strategy vis-à-vis the West—on which we shall shortly elaborate—the Soviet leadership is unhampered by sentiment or scruple, is ruthlessly objective, and is infinitely patient in its cautious pursuit of its long-term objectives. This combination of persistence, determination and caution makes it a more, not less, dangerous adversary.

## Soviet Weaknesses

Our respect for these great strengths of the Soviet Union must not, however, be permitted to cloud our eyes to its equally significant weaknesses and vulnerabilities. These concentrate heavily in economic and morale factors which must be taken importantly into account in any U.S. and Western strategy of defense.

Despite its massive manpower, rich natural resources and substantial industrial development, the economic strength of the Soviet Union is gravely flawed. First, except possibly for the military sector, the economy of the Soviet Union operates at very low levels of efficiency and productivity. (So, in general, do those of its satellites.) This results chiefly from a combination of bureaucratic rigidities, the inescapable inefficiencies of a completely controlled non-market system and low worker morale. These same factors apply to Soviet agriculture, where they are further aggravated by the utilization for crops of a vast acreage subject to the vagaries of uncertain rains and weather.

In consequence, the once rapid economic growth of the Soviet Union has slowed, in recent years, to a very low rate which is not cyclical but persistent. Moreover, low population growth rates mean correspondingly slow growth in the labor force, further inhibiting future economic growth. On the resource side, the natural resources of European Russia are already fully utilized. Large additional resources, chiefly oil, gas and minerals, are available only in far-off Siberia. Due to extreme cold, the depth of the permafrost, the need to move and settle large numbers of reluctant workers to exploit these resources, and the high cost of transportation facilities and operations, huge investments far beyond the financial and technological means of the Soviet Union are required to bring these additional resources into full production and use.

## Dependence on Capital Goods

This combination of low economic efficiency and productivity, inadequate technology, and inability to self-finance essential additional development has made the Soviet Union in recent years increasingly and heavily dependent on capital goods, technology and credits from the West, while recurring major shortages in the production of food grains have required their large-scale importation, chiefly from the United States. A final element to be noted in this economic picture is the heavy drain on Soviet economic capabilities imposed by the need to subsidize client states like Cuba and Vietnam, and to provide assistance to avert economic and possibly political collapse in allied states like Poland, Hungary and Romania. . . .

Of a lesser but not negligible order of importance in assessing the weaknesses of the Soviet Union is the fact that most Third World countries have learned to see through the sophistry and shams practiced by the Soviet Union. Even though they make use of its resources and pretensions when they can and when it serves their own purposes to do so, and while they undoubtedly respect its raw power, they clearly lack friendship or affection for it, and are unlikely to display either of these should the Soviet Union ever need them.

Lastly, we may note as a final element of significant weakness that, while the Soviet leadership may no longer really believe in the Marxist-Leninist credo, they are involuntary prisoners of it. This severely limits their flexibility in policy and action and makes their future behavior, at least in its broad patterns, quite predictable. . . .

## Economic Sanctions Necessary

The single most important conclusion which emerges from this analysis is that a U.S. and Western defense strategy cannot be based on military considerations alone. These must indeed lie at the core of such a strategy; but they must be complemented and reinforced, wherever appropriate, by economic, political and social factors. Indeed, judgments concerning the strength, composition, deployment and utilization of military forces may be influenced in significant degree by these complementary aspects of an integrated, coherent strategy.

Above all, U.S. and Western defense strategy must avoid or severely limit any actions and policies which contribute significantly to the strength of the Soviet Union and its allies or help them to overcome their weaknesses. In the first instance, this means curtailing in significant degree the flow of Western high-technology industrial goods and food grains, and the credits which facilitate and increase the volume of this flow. Such curtailment should embrace not only military technology, but civilian technology which contributes significantly, albeit indirectly, to Soviet economic and military strength as well. Such limitations, and the hardships they will inevitably impose on the Soviet Union and its allies, will reduce the volume of resources the Soviets can allocate to their military machine. At the same time, they will remove the props that have helped the Soviet leaders to maintain at least a very low level of morale among their peoples, and expose them to increasingly outspoken dissent and unrest. . . .

Instead of less than persuasive claims that the Soviet Union has achieved a position of nuclear superiority, it would be more useful for our leaders now to affirm that they do not believe the Soviet Union desires or plans or would dare to risk direct military confrontation. But they should also make it very clear to all Western peace lovers that the Soviet leaders do not understand by peace what we understand the term to mean. The venerated dogma from which they cannot escape tells them that wars are caused, inevitably, by clashing capitalist-imperialist rivalries. Peace, in their lexicon, cannot therefore be achieved until such governments are overthrown. Lenin said it very succinctly. "As an ultimate objective peace simply means communist world control." This is why, when the Soviet leaders speak of the road to peace, they refer to it always as a struggle. We must understand and make plain to all what they mean by this.

## We Shall Triumph

Real peace, as we understand it, cannot be made with Soviet leaders who adhere to such beliefs. Failing fundamental political change in the Soviet Union, the war of ideologies, between democracy and totalitarianism, between freedom and enslavement, will go on. The challenge to us is to ensure that it remains a war of ideologies only. This we can do, if we pursue policies of moderation, calm and resolve, and improve our relative strength, chiefly by restoring our economy to vigorous health and growth, and by cutting back on the economic aid and comfort we have accorded to the Soviet Union and its allies.

---

*"The challenge to us is to ensure that it remains a war of ideologies only."*

---

The Soviet Union, with our assistance, could match our military buildup, whatever its size, and maintain its military power relative to ours. But it will not be able to compensate, without serious sacrifices, for progressive withdrawals of Western goods, technology and credit. In the last analysis, we shall triumph when the peoples of the Soviet Empire decide they have lived in subjection and misery long enough, and take steps to achieve the freedom to which they too aspire.

*Louis J. Walinsky has been a vice president of Robert R. Nathan Associates, Consulting Economists; chief economic adviser to the government of Burma; and consultant to the War Production Board, the World Bank, and the Organization for Economic Cooperation and Development. He is the author of* Economic Development in Burma *and* The Planning and Execution of Economic Development.

*"The Communists have more ground for fearing the United States than we have for fearing them."*

# Communism Does Not Threaten the US

Henry Steele Commager

Since the Truman Doctrine of 1947—perhaps since Hiroshima and Nagasaki—the United States has been locked into a Cold War whose temperature has fluctuated over the years, and now theatens to become incandescent....

How are we to explain our obsession with communism, our paranoid hostility to the Soviet Union, our preoccupation with the Cold War, our reliance on military rather than political or diplomatic solutions, and our new readiness to entertain as a possibility what was long regarded as unthinkable—atomic warfare?...

Some of those assumptions have long enjoyed the dignity of official endorsement; some have been eroded in principle but linger on in official ideology—and are held together by passionate emotional harmony; some are sustained by interests so deeply entrenched that they seem invulnerable to criticism. As a body, the catechism of assumptions resembles in many respects that of the Moral Majority: it is rooted in emotion rather than in reason; it is negative rather than positive in its objectives; it is inspired by fear rather than by confidence; it is inconsistent and even contradictory in logic.

## A World Divided

Consider some of those assumptions that have proved most tenacious.

First is the assumption that the world is divided between two great ideological and power groups, one dedicated to freedom, the other to slavery. History appointed the United States to represent and defend the first. The Soviet Union, whether by appointment or not is unclear, represents the second. These two worlds have been, for thirty years, locked in fateful combat.

Henry Steele Commager, "Outmoded Assumptions," *The Atlantic Monthly*, March 1982. Copyright 1982 by the Atlantic Monthly Company, Boston. Reprinted with permission.

This simplistic picture has, over the years, been badly distorted by developments that do not fit its logic: the conflict between China and Russia; our own almost nonchalant rapprochement with China; the emergence of a new power bloc in the Middle East; and the growing reluctance of many members of the "free-world" coalition to respect either the freedom or the morality to whose defense we are committed. None of these developments has as yet persuaded many Americans to modify their original conviction that communism is the inveterate enemy.

A second assumption is implicit in the first: that communism, especially the Soviet variety, is not only dedicated to the enslavement of men but is godless and deeply immoral. Therefore the Soviet Union can never be relied upon to keep its word; it is engaged in ceaseless aggrandizement; it makes a mockery of international law and human dignity, and trusts only force. From all this it follows that for us to substitute diplomatic negotiations for military power would be to fall into a trap from which we could not extricate ourselves.

This assumption, to be sure, has deep roots in our history and our psychology. Though perhaps no other nation of modern times has had such spectacular success at the diplomatic table as the United States.

## US and USSR Equally Deplorable

As for violation of international law, treaties, and agreements, and of the territorial integrity of weaker nations, the record of the Soviet Union is indeed deplorable. Whether it differs greatly from the American record depends, no doubt, upon the point of view. Little need to rehearse that record: suffice it to say that the CIA has at least tried to be as subversive as the KGB in many parts of the globe, that intervention in Cuba, the Dominican Republic, and Guatemala was no less in violation of law than the Soviet invasions of Hungary and Czechoslovakia, and that a ten-year undeclared war in Vietnam, with casualties of some two million, both military and civilian, and bombardment with three times the tonnage dropped on Germany and Japan in World War II contrasts unfavorably with the much-condemned Soviet invasion of Afghanistan.

Nothing surprising about all this except that a people brought up, for the most part, on the New Testament should so readily ignore the question raised by Matthew: "Why beholdest thou the mote that is in thy brother's eye, but considerest not the beam that is in thine own eye?"

A third assumption is rooted in the second: that the Soviet Union is the mortal enemy of the United States and that her animosity is implacable. This assumption, implicit in innumerable statements by President Reagan and Secretary of Defense Caspar Weinberger, dictates most of our current political and military programs. The term "dictates" is appropriate, for we no longer appear to be masters of our own destiny or even in control of our policies, but react with almost Pavlovian response to the real or imagined policies of the Soviet Union. Clearly, our reaction to the Polish crisis is animated more by hostility to the Soviet Union than by compassion for Poland.

In all this we rarely ask ourselves what the Soviet Union has to gain by destroying the United States. In the past neither czarist nor Communist Russia has been an "enemy" of the United States, and in the twentieth century Russia was allied with or associated with the United States in two major wars. Nor do many Americans pause to acknowledge that the Communists have more ground for fearing the United States than we have for fearing them: after all, American military forces invaded the Soviet Union at Archangel and Vladivostok to prevent the Bolshevik takeover and remained on Russian soil for well over two years: had Communist forces invaded the United States in, let us say, Alaska or Florida, we would not be quite so forgetful. . . .

## Anti-Russian Paranoia

The exacerbation of anti-Russian paranoia by this administration is not in fact in the mainstream of American experience. We have had less excuse for it than any other major nation, for since 1815 we have never been threatened by external aggression by any nation except Japan nor, except for the Civil War, by serious ideological conflicts.

Our current crisis dramatizes the wisdom of President Washington's warning, in his Farewell Address:

> . . . nothing is more essential than that permanent, inveterate antipathies against particular nations. . . be excluded; and that in place of them just and amicable feelings toward all should be cultivated. The nation which indulges towards another an habitual hatred or an habitual fondness is in some degree a slave. It is a slave to its animosity or to its affection. . . Antipathy in one nation against another disposes each more

readily to offer insult and injury . . .

It is perhaps this enslavement to our own animosity that explains a fourth major assumption—one we might call the Dr. Strangelove syndrome: that we could fight and "win" an atomic war, that the loss of 50 million to 100 million lives would be "acceptable," that the Republic could survive and flourish after such a victory. An atomic war is no longer "unthinkable"; perhaps it never was: after all, we are the only nation ever to use the atomic weapon against an enemy. Now spokesmen of both our parties have declared that in an "emergency" we would not hesitate to use it again. In all this we are reminded of the moral of slavery: when a "necessary evil" becomes necessary enough, it ceases to be an evil.

This philosophy is a product, or a by-product, of a fifth assumption: that the most effective way, and perhaps the only way, to counter the threat of communism is neither political, economic, nor moral but quite simply military, and that the mere threat of overwhelming military might will persuade all rivals to abandon the field.

This is, to be sure, a familiar maxim: it was Voltaire who observed that God is always for the big battalions. . . .

## Threat to Security

The most serious threat to national security is in the wastage of human and the exhaustion of natural resources. It is in permitting our industrial and technological enterprises, our transportation system, our financial health, to deteriorate, our cities to decay into slums, our schools to fail of their primary functions of education, our society to be ravaged by poverty, lawlessness, racial strife, class hostilities, and injustice. It is in a leadership that lacks prudence, wisdom, and vision. It is in a society whose leaders no longer invoke, and whose people no longer take seriously, those concepts of public virtue, of the pursuit of happiness, and of the fiduciary obligation to posterity that were the all-but-universal precepts of the generation that founded the Republic.

---

*"The most serious threat to national security is in the wastage of human and the exhaustion of natural resources."*

---

A sixth assumption is a by-product of the fifth: that the security of the United States is bound up with and dependent on whatever regimes throughout the globe are ostentatiously anti-Communist. Our record here is a dismal one, yet instead of repudiating that record, the present administration seems determined to outstrip it. We persist in regarding South Korea and Taiwan as not only friends but allies; we practically forced Pakistan to accept billions of dollars for arms; we have abandoned all pretense of holding aloof from the tyrannical regimes of Chile and Argentina; we even conjure up a distinction between "authoritarian" and "totalitarian" regimes, whose only real distinction is whether they are authoritarian on our side or not.  . . .

## Our New "Imperialism"

Much of our new "imperialism" is rooted in a seventh assumption: that the United States is not only a Western but an African and an Asian power.

That the United States is a world power is incontestable. Clearly, too, it is by virtue of geography an Atlantic power and a Pacific power, and it is by virtue of history something of a European power—a fact convincingly vindicated by participation in two world wars. But the United States is no more an Asian power than China or Japan is an American power. . . .

> "We even conjure up a distinction between 'authoritarian' and 'totalitarian' regimes, whose only real distinction is whether they are authoritarian on our side or not."

Another corollary of our reliance on the military for security is dramatized by an eighth assumption: that to achieve security it is proper for government to conscript science and scholarship for the purposes of war, cold or not; that, in short, the scientific, philosophical, and cultural community should be an instrument of the State for secular purposes.

This principle was not embraced by those who founded the Republic nor, for that matter, by the philosophers of the Enlightenment in the Old World. During the American Revolution, Benjamin Franklin joined with the French minister of finance, Jacques Necker, to decree immunity for Captain Cook because he was "engaged in pursuits beneficial to mankind." . . .

## Need for Cooperation

A ninth assumption, perhaps the most intractable of all, is that any of the fundamental problems that confront us—and other nations of the globe—can be resolved within the framework of the nation-state system. The inescapable fact, dramatized by the energy crisis, the population crisis, the armaments race, and so forth, is that nationalism as we have known it in the nineteeth and much of the twentieth century is as much of an anachronism today as was States Rights when Calhoun preached it and Jefferson Davis fought for it. . . .

Every major problem that confronts us is global—energy, pollution, the destruction of the oceans and the seas, the erosion of agricultural and forest lands, the control of epidemics and of plant and animal diseases, famine in large parts of Asia and Africa and a population increase that promises to aggravate famine, inflation, international terrorism, nuclear pollution, and nuclear-arms control. Not one of these can be solved within the limits of a single nation.

*Henry Steele Commager, noted historian and educator, has taught at many universities in the United States and abroad. He is now at work on a fifty-volume work,* The Rise of the American Nation.

*"Peaceful coexistence in our day....is an objective necessity following from the present world situation."*

# The USSR Wants Peaceful Coexistence

## Nikita S. Khrushchev

Comrade Deputies, the Central Committee of the Communist Party and the Council of Ministers of the USSR have instructed me to make a statement to you on questions of the international situation and the foreign policy of the Soviet Union.

The Government of the Soviet Union, guiding itself by the Leninist policy of peace, the decisions of the Twentieth and Twenty-first Party Congresses and the directives of the Supreme Soviet of the USSR, have consistently and persistently pursued a policy aimed at relaxing international tension and abolishing the cold war, a policy aimed at improving the relations between states for the consolidation of peace and the security of peoples.

We may note with a sense of satisfaction that thanks to the efforts of the Soviet Union and the other socialist countries, and all the peaceloving forces, there has lately been a noticeable improvement in the international situation. . . .

### Reasons for International Improvement

What are the new causes of the recent changes in the international atmosphere?

The main reason lies in the growing might and international influence of the Soviet Union, of all countries of the world system of socialism. Mankind is fortunate in that in our time of great scientific discoveries and technical achievements there has appeared in the world, and is rapidly developing, the socialist system, since the desire for peace is organically inherent in socialism. And the quicker the forces of the socialist countries grow, the greater the possibilities for preserving and consolidating peace.

At the same time an increasingly greater role is played on the international scene by countries which freed themselves from colonial dependence, as well

as by other countries vitally interested in maintaining peace and preventing new wars. In our time the voice of these countries situated on all continents of the globe cannot be left unheeded. Even in the capitalist countries themselves, peaceloving forces which stand for the ending of the "cold war," for peaceful international cooperation, are of late exerting an ever increasing influence.

Finally, ever wider public circles, including many statesmen of capitalist countries, are beginning to realize that in the present conditions, with the existence of nuclear and rocket weapons, war threatens an unparalleled loss of human life and destruction, particularly in those countries that would dare to touch off a new world war.

By their peaceful policy the Soviet Union and all the socialist countries have opened to mankind the road of social development without war, on the basis of peaceful cooperation.

In our time the outstanding significance of the wisdom of the great Lenin's idea of peaceful coexistence is becoming increasingly clear to the peoples of all the world.

### The Necessity for Peaceful Coexistence

With the present balance of forces on the world scene, with the level attained by military technology, no one except those who are entirely out of touch with reality can suggest any other road of development of relations between states with different social systems than the road of peaceful coexistence.

Not infrequently one hears Western leaders discoursing about whether the Soviet Union's proposals for peaceful coexistence should be "accepted" or "not accepted." In my opinion, such talk indicates failure to understand the core of the matter. The point is that peaceful coexistence in our day is a real fact and not anyone's request or wish. It is an objective necessity following from the present

Nikita S. Khrushchev, *The International Situation and Soviet Foreign Policy*, Report given at the Third Session of the USSR Supreme Soviet on October 31, 1959.

world situation, from the present phase of development of human society. Both principal social systems now existing on earth possess weapons which would cause fatal consequences if brought into action. Those who now declare their nonrecognition of peaceful coexistence and argue against it are actually advocating war.

---

*"It is impossible to impose the dominant ideology of one state on another state."*

---

Now the question is not whether there should or should not be peaceful coexistence—it exists and will exist, if we do not want the madness of a world nuclear-missile war. The point is that we must coexist on a reasonable foundation. One can hardly regard as reasonable the fact that nations are living in a condition in which although there is no war, and rockets are at all times in readiness, in which military aircraft carrying atomic and hydrogen bombs are continually plying the heavens. And it is a fact that these aircraft not only fly but sometimes crash together with their lethal cargo, as a result of various kinds of accidents. There were a few such cases in the United States. The fact alone that such cases do occur shows how dangerous it is to stockpile such weapons and to play with them.

The Soviet Government, the entire Soviet people proceed from the Leninist principle of coexistence of states with different social systems, and are doing everything in their power to ensure a lasting peace on earth. People going to bed should not think that it is their last peaceful night, that a military catastophe can break out any moment. We want peaceful coexistence on a reasonable foundation, we want state agencies and public organizations to work in that direction, to create conditions for cooperation between nations. This cooperation must be based on the principle according to which every country chooses for itself and borrows from its neighbor what it finds necessary without anything being imposed upon it. Only then will coexistence be truly peaceful and good-neighborly.

## Realistic Approach

Naturally such coexistence of states with different social systems proceeds from the assumption of mutual concessions in the interests of peace. One might say that this calls for a realistic approach, for a sober assessment of the state of affairs, for mutual understanding and taking into consideration of each other's interests. This is a principled, but at the same time a flexible, position in the struggle for the preservation of peace.

The recognition of the existence of different systems, the recognition of the right of every people to settle independently all the political and social problems of their country, respect for sovereignty and adherence to the principle of noninterference in internal affairs, settlement of all international questions by negotiation—that is what coexistence on a reasonable foundation implies.

The principles of peaceful coexistence were well formulated at the Bandung Conference and later on were also approved by the United Nations. To put it plainly, peaceful coexistence means that states must meet each other halfway in the interests of peace.

## Mutual Concessions

Peaceful coexistence of states with different social systems in itself implies elements of mutual concession, mutual consideration of interests, since otherwise normal relations between states cannot be established.

In ideological matters we have stood and shall stand adamantly on the foundation of Marxism-Leninism. Ideological questions cannot be decided by force; it is impossible to impose the dominant ideology of one state on another state. No sober-minded person ever accepted the view that ideological disputes or questions of the government system of one or another country should be settled by war.

Capitalists do not approve of the socialist social system. Our ideology, our world outlook, are alien to them. We citizens of the socialist states equally disapprove of the capitalist order and the bourgeois ideology. But we must live peacefully, resolving international problems that arise by peaceful means only. Hence the need for reciprocal concessions.

Naturally, neither side will yield on basic social questions, questions of ideology, which divide them. I mean concessions of a different kind. For instance, we receive visits from representatives of capitalist states who express their views in statements made in our country. We do not always agree with everything they say but we are tolerant of such statements. When we visit capitalist countries, we also make speeches and frankly express our views, and they too seem to be tolerant.

The principle of peaceful coexistence of states with different social systems means noninterference in each other's internal affairs, a need for reciprocal concessions and compromises, accomodation—if you like—on the part of both sides in the sphere of relations between states in solving pressing practical issues for the preservation and consolidation of peace. V.I. Lenin taught us that the working class, both before and after winning power, must be able to pursue a flexible policy, consent to compromises, to agreements, when it is required by life, by the interests of its cause.

What does this mean as applied to present-day conditions? Take the disarmament problem, for example. The Soviet Government has submitted a proposal for general and complete disarmament. We consider that its realization would ensure peace to all peoples. But we are prepared to consider other proposals as well to achieve a mutually acceptable solution of the disarmament problem. This is a concrete instance of our readiness to make concessions when there is as yet no possibility of settling the problem as a whole, that is, to do as we think best.

On the other hand, capitalist states too make certain concessions. It will be recalled, for instance, that they recognized our Soviet state and then the majority of other socialist countries, even though the ruling capitalist circles are opponents of socialism. They have diplomatic relations with socialist countries, they negotiate with them, they participate together and discuss international problems in the United Nations. These also are concessions of course—adaptation, if you like—on the part of the capitalist states which are obliged to take account of the fact that countries of the world socialist system exist and develop.

When we speak of peaceful coexistence of socialist and capitalist states, we mean that neither of them should interfere in the other's internal affairs. It is only on this reasonable foundation that peaceful coexistence is possible.

In the relations between states with different social systems not a few questions are encountered today and will be encountered in the future on which it is necessary to meet each other halfway, to press for agreement on a mutually acceptable basis in order to prevent the development of tensions, to utilize every—even the smallest—opportunity of averting a new war.

## No Concessions in Principle

But we should not confuse reciprocal concessions for the sake of peaceful coexistence with concessions in matters of principle, in what concerns the very nature of our socialist state, our ideology. In this case there can be no question of any concessions or any adaptation. Concessions on matters of principle, questions of ideology would mean backsliding to the positions of our opponents. This would mean a qualitative change in policy, a betrayal of the cause of the working class. Those taking this road will take the road of treason to the cause of socialism and, of course, must be criticized without mercy.

We are confident of the force of our truth, we carry this socialist truth, the advantages of socialism, high aloft for the whole world to see. We do not have to fear the peoples of the socialist countries will be tempted by the capitalist devil and will renounce socialism. To think otherwise is not to believe in the strength of socialism, in the strength of the working class and its creative abilities. . . .

Some bourgeois leaders, opposing peaceful coexistence, accuse the socialist countries, and primarily the Soviet Union, of being insincere in speaking of peaceful coexistence. It is said that we advance the slogan of peaceful coexistence only from temporary, tactical considerations because Marxism-Leninism allegedly proceeds from the proposition that war is necessary for the victory of socialism.

## Marxism Against Militarism

But these assertions are nothing but a distortion of the essence of Marxism-Leninism. Marxism has always waged an implacable struggle against militarism and never has regarded war between states as necessary for the victory of the working class. The most implacable and consistent struggle against predatory wars was waged by the Russian Bolsheviks led by Lenin. . . .

We Communists know that war is paid for with blood by the working class, the toiling peasantry, the whole of the working people, while capitalists wax rich on war. But at the same time the Communists said: "If the contradictions of capitalism have led to a predatory war for repartitioning the world, the working class, the people cannot remain indifferent." The First World War was an imperialist war for a repartition of the world. The working class, according to Leninism, was to utilize this war in its interests, turn the imperialist war into a civil war, seize power and create a state wherein the working class, the working people would be the master, and then halt the war and work to make predatory wars altogether impossible.

> *"We Communists know that war is paid for with blood by the working class. . .while capitalists wax rich on war."*

The brilliant example of the practical application of these Leninist propositions by the Bolshevik Party during World War I is known to all the world. No one but the Bolsheviks, immediately after the establishment of Soviet power, addressed all the belligerents with the appeal to end the war and conclude a peace treaty. World War II was also unleashed by imperialist states for the purpose of seizing foreign territories, for the purpose of recarving the world. After the defeat of Hitler Germany, fascist Italy and militaristic Japan, great changes occurred in the world. Many countries of Europe and Asia broke away from the capitalist system and established the system of people's democracy, the socialist system.

Thus history shows that wars were unleashed not by Communists but by imperialists. . . .

Comrade Deputies, the Soviet Government believes it is its duty to the people and all mankind to strengthen the achieved relaxation of tension in international relations, to steer a course leading from relaxation to the complete elimination of international tension, to turn the achieved relaxation into a lasting peace.

For these purposes it is necessary to pursue an active policy of improving international relations;

To strive, step by step, for the solution in practice of all the pressing international questions so as to give the peoples a peaceful life;

Not to relax vigilance with regard to the forces and quarters trying to turn the march of international events back to the road of cold war and the aggravation of international relations;

*"If all the forces coming out for the peaceful settlement of international relations are brought into play, . . . a bright, radiant road to peace will be opened up to mankind."*

To show the peoples constantly the insolvency, harm and fatality to mankind of this bellicose position of the militarist quarters.

If all the forces coming out for the peaceful settlement of international relations are brought into play, if the leading quarters shaping Western policy realize the impossibility of pursuing any other policy in our time than the policy of peaceful coexistence, if the peoples raise their weighty voice against war, decisive steps will be taken shortly to eliminate the military danger, and a bright, radiant road to peace will be opened up to mankind.

*Nikita S. Khruschev led the Soviet Union as premier and first secretary-general of the Central Committee of the Communist Party of the Soviet Union from 1953 to 1964. This viewpoint is excerpted from Premier Khruschev's report to the Third Session of the USSR Supreme Soviet on October 31, 1959.*

*"[Khrushchev's] peaceful coexistence policy is based on hard calculations of winning vital advantage in the struggle with the West, and not on any softening of either the heart or the ideology."*

# The USSR's Peace Rhetoric Is a Fraud

### Foreign Policy Research Institute

For the present phase of struggle between the capitalist and Communist camps, the main strategic line is based on the concept of "peaceful coexistence." Both cajolery and threat are aimed at forcing the West to accept "peaceful coexistence" as the governing concept in relations between the two competing systems. While this concept is not new in Communist doctrine, it generally has been favored for periods of relative Soviet weakness when a "breathing spell" was needed. The fact that the peaceful coexistence concept again underlies Soviet strategy in a period when, according to Khrushchev, the Communist movement is running strong and in the full tide of success, is significant. For it demonstrates that Khrushchev has assessed the period of historical transition to Communist supremacy as one of great criticality, during which the capitalist world must be deflected from effective interference with the process of transition. What peaceful coexistence means in terms of the Communist struggle for world dominance, and how it is expected to serve this ongoing struggle under Khrushchev's leadership, therefore deserves close scrutiny.

## The Meaning of Peaceful Coexistence

Khrushchev never tires of asserting that "hostile propagandists" and "cold-war mongers" in the West are guilty of distorting the concept of peaceful coexistence, of trying to picture it as "a fraud." Any suggestion that Soviet "peace policy" represents a form of maneuver in the struggle with the non-Communist world, rather than a sincere desire to live peacefully with it, also draws pained denials from Khrushchev. At the 20th Party Congress, where peaceful coexistence was one of Khrushchev's major

themes, he addressed skeptical opinion in the West in these words:

> It has been alleged that the Soviet Union advances the principle of peaceful coexistence merely out of tactical considerations, considerations of expediency. Yet it is common knowledge that we have always, from the very first years of Soviet power, stood with equal firmness for peaceful coexistence. Hence it is not a tactical move, but a fundamental principle of Soviet foreign policy.

This assertion, with its insistence that Communists have never taken an expedient view of the peaceful coexistence principle, stands in interesting comparison with other Communist statements on the subject. At the VI World Congress of the Communist International in 1928, for example, it was stated:

> This policy (the Soviet peace policy) is the Leninist policy of the proletarian dictatorship. It is merely another—and under present conditions—a more advantageous form of fighting capitalism; a form which the U.S.S.R. has employed consistently since the October revolution.

The curiously lopsided Communist view of what a peaceful policy means is to be seen in the contention that when others talk peace they are hypocrites, but that Communists are consistently for peace even when they are preparing for war or actually waging it. The "Theses of the VI World Congress" put it in these words:

> There is a glaring contradiction between the imperialists' policy of piling up armaments and their hypocritical talk about peace. There is no such contradiction, however, between the Soviet Government's preparations for defense and for revolutionary war and a consistent peace policy. Revolutionary war of the proletarian dictatorship is but a continuation of revolutionary peace policy. "by other means."

Further insight into the reasons behind traditional Soviet pursuit of a peace policy was given on the same occasion:

> The aim of this policy is to guard the international revolution and to protect the work of building up socialism—the progress of revolutionizing the world.

Foreign Policy Research Institute of the University of Pennsylvania, *Khrushchev's Strategy and Its Meaning for America.* Washington, DC: US Government Printing Office, 1960.

It strives to put off the conflict with imperialism for as long as possible.

A similar idea was expressed by Stalin at the 15th Congress of the CPSU in 1927:

> We cannot forget the saying of Lenin to the effect that a great deal in the matter of our construction depends on whether we succeed in delaying war with the capitalist countries. . . . Therefore, the maintenance of peaceful relations with capitalist countries is an obligatory task for us. The basis of our relations with capitalist countries consists in admitting the coexistence of the two opposed systems.

## Practical Reason for Peaceful Coexistence

While these statements bear out the point that the Soviets have adverted to the principle of peaceful coexistence over a long period of time, they also make it quite clear that this principle, together with Soviet "peace policy" in general, serves the purely instrumental purpose of advancing the Communist world struggle, and not that of establishing peace as the term is generally understood in the non-Communist world.

*"Communists do not expect to stand by and wait for capitalism to collapse, but rather will continue their efforts to destroy it."*

Lenin gave perhaps the classic notation on the Communist attitude toward the instrumental use of peace tactics to serve Communist ends when he analyzed the maneuvering behind the Brest-Litovsk Treaty with Germany, which took Russia out of the war in 1918.

> . . . As every sensible man will understand, by signing this treaty we do not put a stop to our workers' revolution. . . . In war never tie your hands with considerations of formality. It is ridiculous not to know the history of war, not to know that a treaty is the means of gaining strength.

Lenin's coldblooded appraisal of his Brest-Litovsk tactics is doubtless no more cynical than many a chapter in the diplomatic history of other states. It is of particular interest in the Communist context, however, because it is so frequently cited by the Soviets as the classic example of a "wise and flexible" maneuver in the interests of peace.

## No Deviation from Leninist Principles

Khrushchev himself has recently linked his pursuit of a peaceful coexistence policy explicitly with the Brest-Litovsk example in a way which indicates that current Soviet peace policy has not deviated from the principles laid down by Lenin. In an address to the Supreme Soviet on October 31, 1959, Khruschev said:

The history of the Soviet state knows not a few examples of Lenin's wise and flexible foreign policy aimed at the solution of vital problems of peace. Thus, for example, during the periods of the Brest peace Vladimir Ilyich Lenin set the task of concluding peace with Germany to insure for the young Soviet state the possibility for peaceful construction of socialism. Lenin and the party had to wage a persistent struggle then against Trotsky, who advanced his ultra leftist objections and put forward his notorious slogan of "neither peace nor war," by which he played into the hands of the German imperialists. It is known that Trotsky's adventurist policy was used by German imperialism against the Soviet country.

What Khrushchev is saying here, among other things, is that all Communists should understand that his peaceful coexistence policy is based on hard calculations of winning vital advantage in the struggle with the West, and not on any softening of either the heart or the ideology. In fact, in the same speech, Khrushchev made it a point to stress that "in questions of ideology we have firmly stood and will continue to stand like a rock on the basis of Marxism-Leninism." To Communist initiates, this amounts to saying that the game is to be played by the old rules and for the same ends that Lenin laid down. . . .

## Reaffirmation of Revolutionary Goals

Repeatedly, Khrushchev and other Soviet leaders have reaffirmed their dedication to the revolutionary goals of communism and to unremitting class struggle, which is synonymous in Communist jargon with war on the established order. In a speech in Hungary in April 1958, Khrushchev said:

> We have always declared and continue to declare that we do not want war, but we do not renounce class warfare.

A day later, he further made clear that Communists do not expect to stand by and wait for capitalism to collapse, but rather will continue their efforts to destroy it:

> Capitalism is at its ebb, heading for collapse. This does not mean that it is already lying down with its legs stretched out. Much work has yet to be done to bring it to such a state.

At the same time that Khrushchev calls for unceasing struggle to finish off the capitalist world, he also urges sanctimoniously that:

> The principle of noninterference in the affairs of other countries must be observed by all countries, not only in words, but in deeds.

This preachment, a constantly recurring theme in the propaganda of peaceful coexistence, points up the futility of expecting coexistence on Soviet terms to bring about a real settlement of the causes of international tension. What the principle of noninterference clearly means is that the West should recognize Soviet gains, and put its seal of approval on them by signing agreements and otherwise observing the spirit of peaceful coexistence. It also means that the West should accept the Communist definition of the rules and area of future contention between the two rival systems; that is, there must be no meddling with the status quo in the Communist camp or "peace zone," but the struggle for overthrow of the status quo in the rest of the world or the "war zone" is to continue unabated.

The inverted logic of this notion of noninterference is somewhat difficult for the non-Communist mind to grasp, but to the Communist "realist" it makes perfectly good sense. He simply rejects "bourgeois" ideas of morality and ethical conduct as being in any way binding on Communist behavior, and considers that his own definition of the rules of the game bears the sanction of history. At bottom, this means that agreements register the facts of power as the Communist "realist" sees them at any given time, and not as promises to live up to one's pledged word. When the facts of power change, so will the Communist attitude toward an agreement, including any which may be reached with the West under the aegis of peaceful coexistence.

## Emphasis on Peaceful Coexistence "for the Present"

It is in this spirit that Khrushchev constantly argues that "peaceful coexistence is a hard reality" which everyone should recognize. He is not saying that he has jettisoned the Communist goal of world domination because reality in the form of nuclear weapons or other facts of power has so dictated. He is simply saying that *for the present,* until Communist power can bring about a further change in the alignment of world forces, peaceful coexistence is the expedient expression of Soviet policy.

There is no need to labor the point further. Khrushchev obviously has not reacted to "nuclear age realities" by calling off the world revolution. In fact, rather than having thus bowed to the verdict of technology by seeking a genuine settlement with the West, he is doing his best to annul this verdict. This is the sense in which peaceful coexistence can be best understood. It is the key to a strategy intended to remove the roadblock which Western nuclear power has placed in the path of Communist revolution.

## The "Mellowing" Theory of Soviet Behavior

Arnold Toynbee, the British historian, recently set forth the following optimistic evaluation of Soviet behavior in the present period of "peaceful coexistence."

> The Soviet Union now manifestly possesses power that is at least equal to that of the United States, if it is not greater. This Russian triumph has been accompanied by the new mood of relative relaxation for which Mr. Khruschev stands.
>
> This is a happy consequence, but not a surprising one. If Russia does now feel that she has mastered her security problem through her extraordinary achievements in applied physics, this is good news, not only for her, but also for the rest of us, because it is likely to make her easier to get on with.

Toynbee expresses here a view that has gained rather wide circulation in the postsputnik era of Soviet technological achievement and "peaceful coexistence" overtures. Toynbee may possibly be right. Success may have mellowed the Soviet leadership and transformed an aggressive revolutionary movement into a relaxed, live-and-let-live political system.

But Toynbee and those who hopefully subscribe to the "mellowing" theory of Soviet behavior could also be wrong. Success is a formula which may only whet the Soviet appetite for more of the same. Rather than inducing good neighborliness and relaxation—both sins of "opportunism" in the Communist doctrine of relentless class struggle and irreconcilable antagonism between Communist and "bourgeois" ideologies—success could kindle new enthusiasm for a drive to overthrow the older orders of society and establish worldwide Communist hegemony.

Why the Communist leadership should feel impelled to call off the world revolution just when history, as they see it, is giving them a new and powerful boost toward their goals, is a contradiction which even so sophisticated an historian as Professor Toynbee fails to unravel. His view amounts to saying that the Soviet leadership is content to leave history hanging in midair, as it were—to allow the dialectical process to peter out inconclusively before the final Communist "synthesis" is achieved, an outcome which the Marxist mentality of the Soviet leadership elite must find it difficult indeed to entertain.

## No Relaxation of Communist Pressure

It may, of course, be argued that ideology is not a significant element of Soviet motivation, and that any revolutionary ardor to remake the world in the Communist image has—if it ever existed at all—ceased to be an operative factor in Soviet conduct. Toynbee's framing of the mellowing concept in terms of "Russia" as a national entity rather than in terms of Communist order does, in fact, suggest that he would prefer to dismiss the influence of doctrine and ideology on Soviet aims and behavior.

*"[Khrushchev] is simply saying that for the present, . . . peaceful coexistence is the expedient expression of Soviet policy."*

Even should one choose to argue the case on exclusively nondoctrinal grounds, however, it remains to be demonstrated that Soviet success and a new sense of security in the Kremlin can be regarded as "good news" for the rest of the world. Only if one subscribes to the view that Soviet motivation is to be explained wholly in terms of a "defensive reflex" against the designs of a predatory adversary does this argument make much sense. The record of the past 40 years hardly sustains such a view.

Over the course of the last four decades, the Soviet leadership has refined its techniques of rule and developed a flexible approach to international power politics, but it has not shown the slightest inclination to relax its pressure on the free world as the power of the Communist camp has grown. On the contrary, each improvement in the Soviet position has been the signal for increased pressure on the non-Communist world in one form or another.

*"Peaceful coexistence is the key to a strategy intended to remove the remaining—and still formidable— obstacles to Communist victory and security."*

It would make more sense to suppose that a Soviet leadership flushed with success and feeling an increased security against either attack or reprisal would be a more formidable and dangerous adversary to deal with than a leadership still operating under severe restraints and uncertainty about its "security problem."

Khrushchev's peaceful coexistence campaign, superficially accepted at face value, is the obvious prop for the argument that success has made the Soviets more tractable and friendly neighbors. However, there is every indication that this campaign springs mainly from the circumstance that the Soviet leadership does not yet feel that it has mastered its security problem and got the game in the bag. Seen in this light, peaceful coexistence is the key to a strategy intended to remove the remaining—and still formidable—obstacles to Communist victory and security.

*This viewpoint is excerpted from a report by the Foreign Policy Research Institute at the University of Pennsylvania. It was prepared for a subcommittee of the Senate Committee on the Judiciary.*

*"Aggressive violations of the borders of a foreign country are a poor preparation for [a cooperative summit] meeting."*

viewpoint 17

# U-2 Flights Threaten International Cooperation

## Nikita S. Khrushchev

Comrade Deputies! Upon the instructions of the Soviet Government, I must report to you on aggressive actions against the Soviet Union in the past few weeks on the part of the United States of America.

What were these aggressive actions? The United States of America has been sending aircraft that have been crossing our state frontiers and intruding into the airspace of the Soviet Union.... 

The next-to-last aggressive act was committed by the United States of America on April 9, 1960. A United States plane intruded into the airspace of our motherland from the Afghanistan side. Of course, no sane person will think or assume that this violation was committed by Afghanistan, a country on friendly terms with us. We are convinced that this plane belonged to the United States of America, and that it was probably based somewhere on the territory of Turkey, Iran or Pakistan, which are linked to the United States through the obligations of the aggressive CENTO bloc.

When this intrusion took place, some of our comrades asked whether the United States of America should not be warned. After all, such actions are not at all in harmony with the negotiations we conducted with the U.S. President and other American statesmen when we were in the United States. We reached an agreement with the U.S. President on a summit meeting, and this meeting, as the saying goes, is literally under our nose. Aggressive violations of the borders of a foreign country are a poor preparation for such a meeting.... 

We had a discussion in the government, and we decided not to take any special measures and not to write any notes or memorandums, since we knew

Nikita S. Khrushchev, from an address to the Supreme Soviet of the USSR on May 5, 1960.

from past experience that this in fact does not produce any results. The aggressive circles, thinking they are stronger, act according to the principle: the weak complain against the strong; the strong pay no attention to this and continue their brazen actions.

## American Aggression

We then gave our military men, especially those directly responsible for the state of the country's antiaircraft defense, strict warnings that they must act resolutely and not permit unpunished intrusion of foreign planes into our airspace.

The American military apparently found this impunity in the April 9 instance to their liking, and they decided to repeat the aggressive act. The day chosen for this was the most festive day for our people and for the working people of all the countries in the world—May Day, the international holiday of the fraternal solidarity of the working class.

On this day, early in the morning, at 5:36 o'clock (Moscow time), an American plane crossed our frontier and continued its flight deep into Soviet territory. The Minister of Defense immediately reported this aggressive act to the government. The government stated: the aggressor knows what he is in for when he intrudes into foreign territory. If he goes unpunished, he will undertake new provocations. Therefore we must act—shoot down the plane! This assignment was fulfilled; the plane was shot down.

The first investigation showed that this plane belongs to the United States of America, although it bore no identification marks—the marks had been obliterated.

An expert commission is now studying all the data that fell into our hands. It has been established that this plane, like the April 9 plane, had crossed the state frontier of the Soviet Union from either Turkey, Iran or Pakistan. And these are our "good neighbors."

After all the materials now in our hands have been

studied, the Soviet Government will lodge a strong protest with the United States of America and will warn it that if similar aggressive acts against our country continue, we reserve to ourselves the right to reply to them with such measures as we may find it necessary to take in order to safeguard our country's security. I think we shall also give a stern warning to those countries that make their territory available to the United States of America for aggressive actions against our country.

## Alarming Intrusion

We believe such an event as that of May 1 will attract the attention of all the countries in the world, for it is a very alarming warning signal. Imagine what would have happened if a Soviet plane had appeared over New York, Chicago or Detroit, say, and had flown over the city. How would the United States of America have reacted?

Officials in the United States of America have repeatedly stated that they have bombers on alert, bearing atom and hydrogen bombs, which will take off at the approach of foreign planes and head for the bombing target set for each of these bombers. And this would mean the beginning of a war. I would like to ask these American officials: If you intend to take such unilateral measures in case of a hypothetical aggression against your country, then why do you not think that we can reply with the same kind of measures if a foreign plane appears over our country and threatens the security of our motherland? After all, we too do not lack those rights on whose basis you want to act in such cases.

We believe no one is in any doubt that we have the means to reply. It is true that we have no bombers on alert, but we have rockets on alert that will hit the target accurately and inevitably and that are more precise and reliable than the planes on alert....

The case of the American plane that intruded into the airspace of our country is a very alarming one. Therefore we shall place this question before the Security Council [of the United Nations], with a view to putting an end to the aggressive actions of the United States of America, since such actions are pregnant with great dangers.

It is difficult to see how such actions on the part of the aggressive forces of the United States of America should be evaluated. After all, we are to meet with Eisenhower, the President of the United States of America, on May 16 at the heads-of-government conference, yet, two weeks before this date the U.S. Air Force undertook an aggressive act against the Soviet Union. What is this, a May Day greeting? Didn't those who sent the plane understand what they were doing? They probably hoped for impunity, assuming that the plane they sent on a bandit mission would return. But such actions are completely incompatible with the goals posed before the heads of government who are to meet in Paris.

The following conclusion forces itself upon one: the aggressive imperialist circles in the United States of America have been undertaking recently the most active measures to disrupt the heads-of-government conference [proposed meeting between the Great Powers' heads of state], or, at any rate, to prevent the reaching of an agreement for which the whole world is waiting.

## Whose Responsibility?

The question arises, who sent this plane that violated the borders of the Soviet Union? Was it sent with the sanction of the Commander-in-Chief of the Armed Forces of the United States of America, who, as everyone knows, is the President, or was this aggressive act committed by the Pentagon militarists without the President's knowledge? If such actions are committed by the American military at their own risk and on their own responsibility, this is a fact that must profoundly alarm the world public....

Comrade Deputies! The impression arises that the aggressive actions newly committed by the United States of America against the Soviet Union were timed for the heads-of-government conference. This has been done in order to exert pressure on us, to try to intimidate us with their presumed military superiority and thereby to weaken our resolve in the struggle for a relaxation of international tension, for the liquidation of the "cold war" and for an end to the arms race. These actions are aimed at making agreement on the questions in dispute impossible. After all, it cannot be said that this plane was a herald of peace, that it was a messenger of good will. No! It was a true bandit flight with aggressive aims.

*"It cannot be said that this plane was a herald of peace.... No! It was a true bandit flight with aggressive aims."*

We can say to the gentlemen who sent this plane that their efforts to bend our knees and our back through pressure cannot have any effect on us. The Soviet Union has the means to give a rebuff to all those who try to attain through pressure a solution advantageous to the aggressor....

Comrades! The Soviet people and our government have always shown and continue to show their love of peace and their friendly attitude toward the United States of America. But we have been paid back for this with black ingratitude. It is understandable that we are seized with a feeling of indignation at the provocational actions of the American military. But we must not be guided in our actions by this. One must be guided not by emotions but by reason.

Statesmen who are seriously interested in

preserving peace must soberly evaluate the possible consequences of such actions and think where all this may lead to....

## Preserving the Cold War

How do we evaluate the incursion of the American plane—and not the only one but one among others? What should we consider it—a precursor of war, a precursor of an attack—that is, a repetition of what Hitler did in the past?

---

*"We go to the conference in Paris with a pure heart and with good intentions."*

---

The Soviet Government thinks that, in spite of everything, there are no grounds yet for such conclusions. A different situation, a different correlation of forces, now exists in the world. Not the smallest role in international relations is played by the peoples' will for peace. This is why we do not conclude that this was a test of strength preceding a war, or a military reconnaissance for an attack. It was a military reconnaissance to play on our nerves, to throw us back on the positions of the "cold war." It was undertaken to preserve the "cold war" icicles, to freeze them, and to return once more to tension so that the imperialists might plunder their peoples by means of taxes, continue the arms race, keep their peoples in the fear of war, keep them in submission.

The Soviet Union has no aggressive designs. We want the liquidation of the "cold war"; we want disarmament, and our proposals on this question that we submitted to the United Nations remain in force today. We emphasize once more that disarmament and effective control over it are the reliable path for securing peace throughout the world. Under such conditions no country will be able to arm unilaterally for an aggressive attack against another country.

The Soviet Union appeals anew to the Government of the United States of America to end the "cold war" and to halt provocations against other countries. Relations between states must be guided by peaceful efforts so as to ensure tranquility, peace and happiness for all the people on earth.

We address ourselves to the people of the United States of America and declare that, despite the aggressive actions that have been committed against our country, we have not forgotten the friendly encounters we had in the days of our visit to America. Even now I profoundly believe that the American people, with the exception of certain imperialist and monopolistic circles, want peace and desire friendship with the Soviet Union. And we reply to the Americans in kind. But the aggressive actions I am reporting about must put the American people on guard as well....

We want peace. But to want peace does not mean to beg for peace. Peace must be won. And peace can be won in labor, by stepping up the might of our country, by creating the latest and most reliable weapons, by raising the economy, by developing technology and science, by creating more and more new machines to ease man's work, and by providing for the satisfaction of the material and spiritual requirements of the people. If the Western powers do not want to disarm, then our soldiers, our officers, our Soviet Army must have the best arms in the world, and in the quantities necessary to deal a crushing blow to the aggressors should they draw the sword against the land of the Soviets or the socialist countries....

We go to the conference in Paris with a pure heart and with good intentions, and we shall not spare our efforts to reach a mutually acceptable agreement. But we must soberly appraise the chances and recognize that there are signs presaging that these negotiations may fail to satisfy the aspirations of the peoples of the entire world, who want to live in peace.

We have exerted and we shall exert all efforts to reach a solution of urgent questions through negotiation. We would be happiest of all if the best would happen, i.e., if an agreement were to be reached between the representatives of the powers participating in the heads-of-government conference. However, it is wrong to permit oneself to be lulled; one can become a prisoner of false illusions. As the old saying goes: "Trust in God, but don't make any mistakes yourself."

*Nikita S. Khrushchev led the Soviet Union as its premier and first secretary of the Communist Party from 1953 to 1964. This viewpoint is taken from his address to the Supreme Soviet of the USSR on May 5, 1960.*

*"It is unacceptable that the Soviet political system should be given an opportunity to make secret preparations to face the free world with the choice of abject surrender or nuclear destruction."*

# U-2 Flights Maintain International Honesty

## Christian A. Herter and Dwight D. Eisenhower

*Editor's note: The following viewpoint is taken from two sources discussing the US position on the U-2 incident. Part I is from an address by Secretary of State Christian A. Herter. Part II is from a news conference with Dwight D. Eisenhower.*

### I

On May 7 the Department of State spokesman made a statement with respect to the alleged shooting down of an unarmed American civilian aircraft of the U-2 type over the Soviet Union. The following supplements and clarifies this statement as respects the position of the United States Government.

Ever since Marshal Stalin shifted the policy of the Soviet Union from wartime cooperation to postwar conflict in 1946 and particularly since the Berlin blockade, the forceful takeover of Czechoslovakia, and the Communist aggressions in Korea and Viet-Nam the world has lived in a state of apprehension with respect to Soviet intentions. The Soviet leaders have almost complete access to the open societies of the free world and supplement this with vast espionage networks. However, they keep their own society tightly closed and rigorously controlled. With the development of modern weapons carrying tremendously destructive nuclear warheads, the threat of surprise attack and aggression presents a constant danger. This menace is enhanced by the threats of mass destruction frequently voiced by the Soviet leadership.

For many years the United States in company with its allies has sought to lessen or even to eliminate this threat from the life of man so that he can go about his peaceful business without fear. Many proposals to this end have been put up to the Soviet Union. The President's open-skies proposal of 1955 [in which all

nations would be free to fly over the others for observation purposes] was followed in 1957 by the offer of an exchange of ground observers between agreed military installations in the U.S., the U.S.S.R., and other nations that might wish to participate. For several years we have been seeking the mutual abolition of the restrictions on travel imposed by the Soviet Union and those which the United States felt obliged to institute on a reciprocal basis. More recently at the Geneva disarmament conference the United States has proposed far-reaching new measures of controlled disarmament. It is possible that the Soviet leaders have a different version and that, however unjustifiedly, they fear attack from the West. But this is hard to reconcile with their continual rejection of our repeated proposals for effective measures against surprise attack and for effective inspection of disarmament measures.

### Objectionable Secret Preparations

I will say frankly that it is unacceptable that the Soviet political system should be given an opportunity to make secret preparations to face the free world with the choice of abject surrender or nuclear destruction. The Government of the United States would be derelict to its responsibility not only to the American people but to free peoples everywhere if it did not, in the absence of Soviet cooperation, take such measures as are possible unilaterally to lessen and to overcome this danger of surprise attack. In fact the United States has not and does not shirk this responsibility.

In accordance with the National Security Act of 1947, the President has put into effect since the beginning of his administration directives to gather by every possible means the information required to protect the United States and the free world against surprise attack and to enable them to make effective preparations for their defense. Under these directives programs have been developed and put into operation

Christian A. Herter, from an official statement on May 9, 1960. Dwight D. Eisenhower, from a news conference on May 11, 1960.

which have included extensive aerial surveillance by unarmed civilian aircraft, normally of a peripheral character but on occasion by penetration. Specific missions of these unarmed civilian aircraft have not been subject to Presidential authorization. The fact that such surveillance was taking place has apparently not been a secret to the Soviet leadership, and the question indeed arises as to why at this particular juncture they should seek to exploit the present incident as a propaganda battle in the cold war.

This Government had sincerely hoped and continues to hope that in the coming meeting of the Heads of Government in Paris Chairman Khrushchev would be prepared to cooperate in agreeing to effective measures which would remove this fear of sudden mass destruction from the minds of peoples everywhere. Far from being damaging to the forthcoming meeting in Paris, this incident should serve to underline the importance to the world of an earnest attempt there to achieve agreed and effective safeguards against surprise attack and aggression.

At my request and with the authority of the President, the Director of the Central Intelligence Agency, the Honorable Allen W. Dulles, is today briefing Members of the Congress fully along the foregoing lines.

## II

I have made some notes from which I want to talk to you about this U-2 incident.

A full statement about this matter has been made by the State Department, and there have been several statesmanlike remarks by leaders of both parties.

For my part, I supplement what the Secretary of State has had to say with the following four main points. After that, I shall have nothing further to say—for the simple reason I can think of nothing to add that might be useful at this time.

### Necessity of Intelligence-Gathering

First point is this: the need for intelligence-gathering activities.

No one wants another Pearl Harbor. This means that we must have knowledge of military forces and preparations around the world, especially those capable of massive surprise attack.

Secrecy in the Soviet Union makes this essential. In most of the world no large-scale attack could be prepared in secret. But in the Soviet Union there is a fetish of secrecy and concealment. This is a major cause of international tension and uneasiness today. Our deterrent must never be placed in jeopardy. The safety of the whole free world demands this.

As the Secretary of State pointed out in his recent statement, ever since the beginning of my administration I have issued directives to gather, in every feasible way, the information required to protect the United States and the free world against

surprise attack and to enable them to make effective preparations for defense.

My second point: the nature of intelligence-gathering activities.

These have a special and secret character. They are, so to speak, "below the surface" activities.

They are secret because they must circumvent measures designed by other countries to protect secrecy of military preparations.

They are divorced from the regular, visible agencies of government, which stay clear of operational involvement in specific detailed activities.

These elements operate under broad directives to seek and gather intelligence short of the use of force, with operations supervised by responsible officials within this area of secret activities.

We do not use our Army, Navy, or Air Force for this purpose, first, to avoid any possibility of the use of force in connection with these activities and, second, because our military forces, for obvious reasons, cannot be given latitude under broad directives but must be kept under strict control in every detail.

---

*"In most of the world no large-scale attack could be prepared in secret. But in the Soviet Union there is a fetish of secrecy and concealment."*

---

These activities have their own rules and methods of concealment, which seek to mislead and obscure— just as in the Soviet allegations there are many discrepancies. For example, there is some reason to believe that the plane in question was not shot down at high altitude. The normal agencies of our Government are unaware of these specific activities or of the special efforts to conceal them.

### Distasteful but Vital Activities

Third point: How should we view all of this activity?

It is a distasteful but vital necessity.

We prefer and work for a different kind of world— and a different way of obtaining the information essential to confidence and effective deterrence. Open societies, in the day of present weapons, are the only answer.

This was the reason for my open-skies proposal in 1955, which I was ready instantly to put into effect, to permit aerial observations over the United States and the Soviet Union which would assure that no surprise attack was being prepared against anyone. I shall bring up the open-skies proposal again at Paris, since it is a means of ending concealment and suspicion.

My final point is that we must be distracted from the real issues of the day by what is an incident or a symptom of the world situation today.

This incident has been given great propaganda exploitation. The emphasis given to a flight of an unarmed, nonmilitary plane can only reflect a fetish of secrecy.

The real issues are the ones we will be working on at the summit—disarmament, search for solutions affecting Germany and Berlin, and the whole range of East-West relations, including the reduction of secrecy and suspicion.

Frankly, I am hopeful that we may make progress on these great issues. This is what we mean when we speak of ''working for peace.''

And, as I remind you, I will have nothing further to say about this matter.

*Christian A. Herter served as secretary of state under President Dwight D. Eisenhower. Mr. Eisenhower was president from 1953 to 1961.*

*"If we accept the philosophy which some people in the United States want to instill in the public, it will be... not the burglar that is guilty, but the owner of the house he broke into."*

viewpoint **19**

# The US Cannot Justify Its Spying on the USSR

Nikita S. Khrushchev

**Khrushchev:** We intend to take to the [United Nations] Security Council the question of the aggressive intrusion of an American plane within the confines of our country.

If the Security Council—on which, apparently, pressure will be exerted by the United States—does not take the right decision, we shall raise the matter in the United Nations General Assembly. Such aggressive actions by the United States of America are a highly dangerous thing.

This danger is enhanced by the fact that in his statement of May 10 the United States Secretary of State Mr. Herter not only sought to justify this act of aggression, but said also that the U.S. Government intended to continue such flights. This is an open threat to peace. We will shoot down such planes, and we will strike at the bases from which these planes will be sent to our country. You understand that if such aggressive actions continue, this might lead to war.

**Question** (one of the correspondents): May I ask you a question?

**Khrushchev:** Even two if you like.

**Question:** You have probably noticed a placard among the fragments of the plane urging assistance to the pilot. What do you think its authors meant?

**Khrushchev:** We assisted the pilot when he flew into our territory and gave him due welcome. If there are other such uninvited guests, we shall receive them just as "hospitably" as this one. We shall try him, try him severly as a spy.

**Question:** How could all this affect the summit meeting?

**Khrushchev:** Let those who sent this spy plane think this question over. Though they should have thought about the consequences beforehand. After

all, an aggression has been committed against our country. And we shall continue routing all the aggressors who dare raise a hand against us. You see how accurately our rocketeers shot down the plane without setting it on fire! The pilot is alive, the instrumentation intact; in other words, the material evidence is here for everyone to see. These are very skillful actions of our rocketeers. We are very grateful to them for this. . . .

## Bandit Tactics

There was a time—I remember it from my young days—when many criminals and other suspicious elements roamed the world. These people resorted to the following track: A bandit with a small boy would hide under a bridge and wait for someone to cross it.

Then the bandit would send the boy to the passer-by and the boy would say: "Hello, mister, give me back my watch." The natural answer would be: "What's that? Now run along!" Then the boy would insist: "But look, mister, this watch is mine. Why don't you give me back my watch?" Then the armed bandit would appear, as though attracted by the noise of the argument, and tell the passer-by: "Why do you bully the boy? Give him back his watch and hand over your coat, too!"

The United States wants to live according to this law. But we are not defenseless passers-by. Our country is a strong and mighty state which can test its strength against it. If the United States has not experienced a real war on its territory, has not experienced air raids, and if it wishes to unleash a war, we shall be compelled to fire rockets which will explode on the aggressor's territory in the very first minutes of war.

I say this because I have read Herter's statement saying: "We are compelled to fly; it is the fault of the Soviet Union itself, because it does not give us access to its secrets which we simply must know. This is why, if you please, we undertake such flights. After

Nikita S. Khrushchev, from an informal news conference in Moscow on May 11, 1960.

all, the President has said that the skies should be open—this is why we fly and shall go on flying, shall go on opening the skies." How can an official representative of a state speak in this way about another nation! We do not live according to the laws of the United States. We have our own laws and this is why we shall make everyone on our territory respect these laws—and the violators will be thrashed!

I liked the article in the British newspaper *Daily Worker*, whose theme was as follows: If we accept the philosophy which some people in the United States want to instill in the public, it will be something like this—it is not the burglar that is guilty, but the owner of the house he broke into because he locked it, thereby compelling the burglar to break in.

## Philosophy of Thieves and Bandits

But this is a philosophy of thieves and bandits!

I think that if world public opinion correctly realizes all the gravity of the situation and approaches this aggressive act of the United States policy with due responsibility, if everyone unanimously condemns this act, and if the United States Government no longer uses such methods with regard to other states, this will be a good refreshing, so to say, ozonizing tendency in international relations.

Reading American press reports these days, I see that except for a few gangsters of the pen who are whitewashing this action, the absolute majority of people writing in the American press, including those who are notorious for their past lack of objectivity, are indignant about this incident, regard it as perfidy with regard to the Soviet Union.

---

*"We have the means to cool down bandits, should they wish to use their brazen methods against us."*

---

This is a good sign. If you newsmen inform the public correctly, this incident, like every other incident, will finally be "digested." After all, gentlemen, we must live in peace, and not only in peace but also in friendship.

**Question:** Can one remain optimistic about the United States policy?

**Khrushchev:** I consider myself to be an incorrigible optimist. I regard the provocative flight of the American intelligence plane over our country not as a preparation for war, but as a probing. They have now "probed" us, and we boxed the nose of the "probers."

Some United States officials are making a big noise now. Let them! The Soviet Union is not Guatemala. They cannot send troops here. We have the means to

cool down bandits, should they wish to use their brazen methods against us. If they behave in this way, they will get this calmative.

**Question:** Mr. Khrushchev, has your estimate of President Eisenhower, which you gave upon your return from the United States, changed?

## New View of the President

**Khrushchev:** Well, the statement issued by the U.S. Department of State in connection with the intelligence plane naturally alters my belief that the United States President had nothing to do with this affair. I did not know that such an intelligence plan existed in the United States and that it included a program of reconnoitering flights over the Soviet territory. It follows from the statement of the Department of State, which was approved by the President, that flights of American intelligence planes over our country are not the whim of some irresponsible officer, but realization of a plan prepared by Allen Dulles, head of the Central Intelligence Agency, a department under the jurisdiction of the United States President.

Mr. Herter admitted that the United States President had issued directives to collect various intelligence information by all possible means.

These directives served as the basis for working out and carrying through programs which included, as Herter says, extensive aerial surveillance both peripheral and by penetration. I ask you to note this—by penetration—that is, by reconnaissance, spying flights over the territory of a state with which normal relations are maintained. And this plan was approved by the President. Incredible! Should I say after this: "What nice people you are!" To do this is to have no self-respect. I would say that Mr. Herter has taken off all the evils and removed all the paint which was used to camouflage, embellish, and make-up, as it were, the policy of the United States imperialists. Now, through his statement, he has revealed the bestial, fear-inspiring face of imperialism. So what? It turns out that this face inspires fear no longer. Such actions of the United States militarists are prompted not by the heroism of their masterminds, but by cowardice. Danger comes not from one who has his nerves at his command and relies on his powers and possibilities, but from a coward who fears everything. . . .

## Capitalist Fear of Inevitable

My conviction is that all roads lead to communism. Where else can they lead to?

This is just what the American imperialists fear. That is why they get nervous and fling themselves into reckless adventures. This shows they are not sure of their own system.

The State Department of the United States says that all countries engage in spying.

But the Soviet Union never sent its planes into the

United States or any other countries for reconnaissance purposes, nor does it do so. If there have been any individual instances of our planes inadvertently violating the airspace of other countries—this has happened on our frontier with Turkey and Iran—we have apologized to those countries and punished those responsible for such violations.

## "My conviction is that all roads lead to communism."

We want to warn those who try to send their spies into this country to think carefully of the consequences....

Some diplomats take offense and say that Khrushchev is indulging in too harsh expressions. I should like to have heard their reactions had a similar aggressive invasion been committed against their country. What do you expect of me, after all, that I should take off my hat and welcome this invasion? No, we shall meet gangsters the way they deserve. And this was a gangster, bandit raid.

Have you seen here the "air sampling instruments"? How can the authors of this lie look into our eyes after it was exposed?

### Efforts for Peace

In conclusion I have this to say: We deal harshly with those who invade the borders of our homeland, who violate our sovereignty. But we want to live in peace and friendship with all nations. I hope you will understand our attitude when we angrily condemn such aggressive action. But we take a sober view of things and realize that even the sharpest polemics are better than war.

This is why we shall do everything to relieve this strain, shall do everything to normalize the international situation and restore good relations with the United States if, of course, the United States also contributes to this.

*Nikita S. Khrushchev led the Soviet Union as its premier and first secretary of the Communist Party from 1953 to 1964. This viewpoint is taken from a press conference held in Moscow on May 11, 1960. Mr. Khrushchev spoke informally with journalists following a scheduled meeting between the press and Soviet officials who were exhibiting fragments of the U-2 airplane.*

*"If the free world failed to attempt to protect itself against [the Soviet threat], it would be inviting destruction."*

viewpoint **20**

# The US Can Justify Its Spying on the USSR

Henry Cabot Lodge

The United States has not committed any aggressive acts against the Soviet Union or any other country, either through its Air Force or through any other agency of the United States Government. And in the remarks which I am about to make I will try to show why my contention is true.

Now let me take up the Soviet representative's [Andrei A. Gromyko, Soviet Minister for Foreign Affairs] main points. He asserts first that flights over the U.S.S.R. continue to be "the State policy" of the United States. This assertion is directly and, I fear, deliberately contrary to fact. Surely the Soviet representative knows this, because he was present when President Eisenhower in Paris on May 16 said:

> . . .these activities had no aggressive intent but rather were to assure the safety of the United States and the free world against surprise attack by a power which boasts of its ability to devastate the United States and other countries by missiles armed with atomic warheads. As is well known, not only the United States but most other countries are constantly the targets of elaborate and persistent espionage of the Soviet Union.

> There is in the Soviet statement an evident misapprehension on one key point. It alleges that the United States has, through official statements, threatened continued overflights. The importance of this alleged threat was emphasized and repeated by Mr. Khrushchev. The United States has made no such threat. Neither I nor my Government has intended any. The actual statements go no further than to say that the United States will not shirk its responsibility to safeguard against surprise attack.

> In point of fact, these flights were suspended after the recent incident and are not to be resumed. Accordingly this cannot be the issue.

I will read that last paragraph once again:

> In point of fact, these flights were suspended after the recent incident and are not to be resumed. Accordingly this cannot be the issue.

Now Mr. Gromyko has just claimed, as does the Soviet memorandum, that this is merely a "tactical step," a "temporary suspension" announced with "the object of deluding world opinion."

Well, you have just heard the President's words yourselves. These flights were suspended after the recent incident and are not to be resumed. And let me say for the information of this Council that this decision was made before the President's departure for Paris and cannot be characterized in the way Mr. Gromyko has tried to characterize it.

Furthermore I am authorized to say that the United States is prepared to negotiate an open-skies treaty with the Soviet Union which would have continued force and effect and which would obviate forever the necessity of such measures of self-protection.

The U.S.S.R. asserts secondly, and I quote from its memorandum, that the United States has undertaken "flights inside frontiers of the U.S.S.R. for aggressive purposes."

## Ridiculous Concept of "Aggression"

Now I realize that the term "aggression" has never been officially defined, but any common sense definition of the term shows that the presence of a light, unarmed, single-engine, nonmilitary, one-man plane is not aggression. Yet this, Mr. President and gentlemen, this is what all the trouble in Paris and here at the United Nations is said to be all about— about this one plane.

Chairman Khrushchev said both in Moscow and Paris that he has known of these flights for a long time. These flights were not considered dangerous enough to complain about last year, when Chairman Khrushchev and the President met *privately*. Therefore it is hard to understand why such flights are suddenly described as aggressive and of urgent concern when Chairman Khrushchev met President Eisenhower *publicly*, ostensibly for peaceful negotiations. We can only speculate about Soviet

Henry Cabot Lodge, from a statement to the Security Council of the United Nations on May 23, 1960.

reasons for increasing tension now by bringing this matter to the Security Council today.

## Soviet Espionage Activity

Now, Mr. President, if we were to use the same reasoning which the Soviet Union has used, we could bring up as an aggressive act the presence of the Soviet vessel which was right off the shores of Long Island, right off Montauk Point here, a few weeks ago and which was deliberately interfering with vessels of the United States Navy. We could do that, but we will not do so.

We could, under the same interpretation of aggression, bring up as an aggressive act the repeated violations of our American *ground* space and the ground space of many other countries represented here by Soviet spies. We could, for instance, enter in detail into the cases of the following illustrative list of spies, all of whom are among those unmasked in the United States in the period of time which has elapsed since the death of Marshal Stalin. I will read a few of these names:

Amosov, Igor Aleksandrovich—he is a commander
Pivnev, Leonid Yegorovich—lieutenant colonel
Bubchikov, Ivan Aleksandrovich—colonel
Krylov, Yuriy Pavlovich—major
Kurochkin, Nikolay Ivanovich
Molev, Vasiliy Mikhaylovich
Kovalev, Aleksandr Petrovich
Martynov, Maksim Grigoryevich—he is a colonel
Petrov, Viktor Ivanovich
Gladkov, Boris Fedorovich—he is a captain
Kirilyuk, Vadim A.

## Caught in the Act

Let me point out that this agent Kirilyuk was actually caught in an act of espionage seeking data on cryptographic machines during the visit of Chairman Khrushchev to the United States—as a matter of fact, at the very moment that Chairman Khrushchev was speaking from the rostrum of the General Assembly about disarmament.

We might even make something of the fact that at least one of the agents whose name I have listed was getting photographs of United States strategic places, and, may I say, these photographs were taken at heights far lower than 65,000 feet.

We understand also that at least 360 Russian espionage agents have been convicted in different countries of the free world. All of these convictions were obtained under free court systems which means that ample proof of the charges was made.

The number of these convictions represents only a minor proportion of those cases in which Soviet espionage activity has been actually involved. We remember Fuchs, Guzenko, Petrov, and Gubichev. We do not need to recall the case of Colonel Rudolph Ivanovich Abel right here in New York.

We shall not dwell on these things or all the names

of spies caught while Marshal Stalin was in power or bring any of them up, using the logic which the Soviet Union has used, as aggressive acts.

But, Mr. President, what we do strongly deplore is the refusal of the Soviet Union to accept the President's open-sky plan in 1955: its refusal to heed General Assembly resolution 914 of the 10th session calling on it to permit aerial inspection; its rejection of the Arctic aerial inspection zone in 1958, which all 10 other members of the Security Council voted for; and its refusal to consider technical measures to prevent surprise attack at the conference in the fall of 1958. Now those are the things which we do deplore.

## Soviet Use of Force and Threats of Force

Just contemplate the situation for a moment. Here is a Government, well known for its expansionist proclivities and armed to the teeth, which has repeatedly in contravention of article 2, paragraph 4, of the charter, which is the article which forbids both the use and the threat of force, and this Government has repeatedly used force and threats of force in its relations with other sovereign states. Now that is a clear charter violation.

When such a government insists on secrecy, it is in effect also insisting on preserving its ability to make a surprise attack on humanity. If the free world failed to attempt to protect itself against such a danger, it would be inviting destruction. If it should ever be accepted that the Soviet Union can maintain a double standard whereby they have thousands of spies and subversive agents everywhere while protesting one single harmless observation flight, the free world would surely be in great and peculiar danger.

---

*"We understand also that at least 360 Russian espionage agents have been convicted in different countries of the free world."*

---

This afternoon the Soviet representative has had something to say about international law. One may ask where the Soviet Union's concern for international law was when Communist armed forces invaded the Republic of Korea in 1950 or where that concern was when the Soviet Union forcibly and brutally snuffed out the independence of Hungary in 1956.

Illegal uses of force like these violating international law and the solemn treaty obligations of the United Nations Charter cannot fail to make the rest of the world apprehensive for its safety. And this was the background against which measures were taken to try to secure information in advance of possible further Communist assaults.

Mr. President and members of the Council, that is the heart of the matter, and we shall not get very far here if we dwell on the symptoms of the disease and neglect the disease itself; and the disease is the danger of wholesale sudden death by surprise attack.

At an appropriate future time the United States intends to make proposals to get at the heart of the matter, and we hope that our proposals will appear constructive and that discussion of them will tend to reduce world tension.

## Committed to Negotiations

The United States remains committed to seek a solution of international problems through negotiations rather than force. We have said, and we repeat, that we are willing to negotiate at any time and in any place and in any manner which offers hope for agreement. We shall continue to work for progress toward the goals of general and complete disarmament with effective international controls.

*"The United States remains committed to seek a solution of international problems through negotiations rather than force."*

We will continue, Mr. President, to work toward an agreement on cessation of nuclear weapons tests. We shall continue to work toward international cooperation in the peaceful uses of outer space.

These, Mr. President, are a few of the things the United States is prepared to do. We shall cooperate with other members of the Council in seeking to create a better international atmosphere in which mankind will be freed from the specter of war.

*Henry Cabot Lodge served the United States government in many capacities. At the time of this statement, he was US representative to the United Nations.*

*"The conclusion of a German treaty will be a major step towards a final postwar settlement in Europe, for which the Soviet Union has invariably striven."*

viewpoint 21

# A German Treaty Is Essential for World Peace

Nikita S. Khrushchev

1. The delay over many years in a peace settlement with Germany has been largely responsible for the dangerous developments in Europe in the postwar period. Highly important Allied decisions on the rooting out of militarism in Germany, which the governments of the United States and the U.S.S.R. at the time regarded as an earnest of enduring peace, have been implemented only in part and are now virtually ignored in the greater part of German territory. Of the governments of the two German states which took shape after the war only the government of the German Democratic Republic recognizes and adheres to these agreements. The government of the German Federal Republic openly expresses its negative attitude to them, fosters sabre-rattling militarism and demands revision of the German frontiers, revision of the results of World War II. It seeks to build up a strong military base for its aggressive plans, to create a dangerous hotbed of conflicts on German soil and to set at loggerheads the former allies of the anti-nazi coalition.

The Western Powers have allowed the German Federal Republic to start stockpiling weapons and building an army clearly exceeding defense requirements. Other new and dangerous steps by the NATO powers are their permission for the German Federal Republic to build warships of up to 6,000 tons displacement, and also to use British, French and Italian territories for setting up military bases.

## Necessity for German Peace Treaty

2. The Soviet government sincerely strives for the elimination of the causes engendering tension between the U.S.S.R. and the United States and for constructive friendly co-operation. Conclusion of a German peace treaty would bring both countries much closer to this goal. The U.S.S.R. and the United States fought shoulder to shoulder against Nazi Germany. It is their common duty to conclude a German peace treaty and thus create a reliable guarantee that forces capable of plunging the world into another, even more destructive, war will never again emerge on German soil. If the Soviet Union's desire to strengthen peace and to prevent the unleashing of another world war in Europe does not conflict with the intentions of the United States government, it will not be difficult to reach agreement.

3. Proceeding from a realistic assessment of the situation, the Soviet government favours the immediate conclusion of a peace treaty with Germany. The question of a peace treaty is a question of the national security of the U.S.S.R. and many other states. It is no longer possible to leave the situation in Germany as it is. The conditions for the conclusion of a peace treaty have long been ripe and such a treaty must be concluded. The question is by whom and how it will be concluded and whether it will involve unnecessary hitches.

4. The Soviet government has no intention of impinging [sic] the interests of the United States or other Western Powers in Europe. It does not propose any changes in Germany or in West Berlin that would benefit only one state or group of states. The U.S.S.R. deems it necessary, for the sake of consolidating peace, to formalize the situation that has taken shape in Europe after the war, legalize and consolidate the immutability of the existing German frontiers and normalize the situation in West Berlin with due consideration for the interests of all concerned.

Desiring to reach agreement on a peace treaty, the Soviet Union does not insist on the immediate withdrawal of the German Federal Republic from NATO. Both German states could for a certain period after the conclusion of a peace treaty remain

Nikita S. Khrushchev, note handed to President Kennedy on June 4, 1961.

members of the military alignments to which they now belong.

The Soviet proposal does not link the conclusion of a peace treaty with the recognition of the German Democratic Republic or the German Federal Republic by all parties to this treaty. To recognize or not to recognize one or the other state is a matter of each government.

If the United States is not prepared to sign one peace treaty with the two German states, a peace settlement could be achieved on the basis of two treaties. In that case the member states of the anti-nazi coalition would sign a peace treaty with both or one German state at their discretion. These treaties may not have identical texts, but they must contain the same provisions on major questions of a peace settlement.

## Convert Berlin to a Demilitarized Free City

5. The conclusion of a German peace treaty would also solve the problem of normalizing the situation in West Berlin. West Berlin, deprived of a firm international status, is now a place where Bonn's revenge-seeking element constantly maintain extremely grave tension and stage all kinds of provocations fraught with serious danger for peace. We must prevent developments under which the strengthening of West-German militarism might lead to irreparable consequences because of the unsettled situation in West Berlin.

At present the Soviet government sees no better solution for the problem of West Berlin than its conversion into a demilitarized free city. Realization of the proposal for a free city would normalize the situation in West Berlin with proper regard for the interests of all parties. The occupation regime preserved there has long outlived itself; it has lost all connection with the aims for which it was created, and with the Allied agreements on Germany on the basis of which it has been operating.

---

*"It is out of the question, of course, that West Berlin should continue to be used as a base for provocative hostile activity against the U.S.S.R."*

---

Occupation rights would, of course, cease to operate with the conclusion of a German peace treaty, irrespective of whether it is signed with both German states or only with the German Democratic Republic on whose territory West Berlin is located.

The Soviet government holds that the free city of West Berlin should have free intercourse with the outside world and that its internal order should be determined by the free expression of the will of its population. The United States, like all other countries, would of course have full possibility to maintain and develop its relations with the free city. In general, West Berlin, as the Soviet government sees it, must be strictly neutral. It is out of the question, of course, that West Berlin should continue to be used as a base for provocative hostile activity against the U.S.S.R., the German Democratic Republic or any other state and remain a dangerous seat of tension and international conflicts.

The U.S.S.R. proposes the establishment of the most reliable guarantees against intervention in the affairs of the free city by any state. To guarantee the free city, token forces of the United States, the United Kingdom, France and the Soviet Union could be stationed in West Berlin. Nor would the U.S.S.R. object to the stationing in West Berlin of neutral troops under United Nations aegis for the same purpose. The status of the free city could be duly registered with the United Nations and secured by the authority of this international organization. The Soviet side agrees to discuss any other measures capable of guaranteeing the freedom and independence of West Berlin as a free demilitarized city.

A West Berlin settlement must of course take into account the necessity of respecting and strictly observing the sovereign rights of the German Democratic Republic, which is known to have expressed readiness to adhere to and respect the relevant agreement.

## Interim Solution

6. The Soviet government proposes immediate agreement on the convocation of a peace conference, conclusion of a German treaty and settlement of the question of West Berlin's status as a free city on this basis. If, for one reason or another, the governments of the United States and other Western Powers are as yet not prepared to do that, an interim solution could be worked out for a definite period.

The four powers will urge the German states to agree in any way acceptable to them on questions pertaining to a peace settlement with Germany and reunification. The four powers will declare in advance that they will recognize any agreement the Germans may reach.

In the event of a positive outcome of the talks between the German Democratic Republic and the German Federal Republic, a single peace treaty would be agreed upon and signed. If the German states are not able to agree on the aforesaid questions, measures will be taken for the conclusion of a peace treaty with both German states or with one of them at the discretion of the countries concerned.

In order not to drag out a peace settlement, it is necessary to establish a deadline for the Germans to explore the possibilities of agreement on questions within their internal competence. The Soviet government holds that a period not exceeding six months is adequate for such talks. This period is quite adequate for establishing contacts between the German Federal Republic and the German Democratic Republic and for talks between them, for the sixteen years which have elapsed since the war have created the realization that the remnants of World War II in Europe must be eliminated.

*Nikita S. Khrushchev led the Soviet Union as its premier and first secretary of the Communist Party from 1953 to 1964. This viewpoint is a note he gave to President Kennedy in Vienna on June 4, 1961.*

## "The peace treaty will specifically formalize the status of West Berlin as a free city."

7. The Soviet government is prepared to examine any constructive U.S. proposals for a German peace treaty and normalization of the situation in West Berlin. The Soviet government will display maximum good will in order to solve the German peace treaty problems by mutual agreement between the U.S.S.R., the United States and the other states concerned. The signing of a German peace treaty by all parties to the anti-nazi coalition and a settlement on this basis of the question of the neutral status of West Berlin would create better conditions for the promotion of confidence between states and solution of such major international problems as disarmament, etc. If the United States does not show an understanding of the necessity of concluding a peace treaty, we shall regret this, for then we shall have to sign a peace treaty, which it would be impossible and dangerous to delay further, not with all states but with those who want to sign it.

### Step Toward European Settlement

The peace treaty will specifically formalize the status of West Berlin as a free city, and the Soviet Union, like the other parties to the treaty, will, of course, strictly observe it, and measures will also be taken to see to it that this status is respected by other countries. At the same time this will mean the abolition of the occupation regime in West Berlin with all consequences arising therefrom. Specifically, the question of using land, water and air communications across the territory of the German Democratic Republic will have to be settled solely by appropriate agreements with the German Democratic Republic. This is but natural, since control over such communications is the inalienable right of a sovereign state.

8. The conclusion of a German treaty will be a major step towards a final postwar settlement in Europe, for which the Soviet Union has invariably striven.

*"The Soviet Union has blocked all progress toward the conclusion of a just treaty."*

# The Soviet Insistence on a German Treaty Is Deceitful

John F. Kennedy

In consultation and full agreement with its British and French allies, and with the benefit of the views of the Federal Republic of Germany, and after consultation with the other member governments of the North Atlantic Treaty Organization, the United States on Monday delivered through its Embassy in Moscow its reply to the aide memoire on Germany and Berlin received from the Soviet Government on June 4. Our reply speaks for itself and advances what I believe to be an irrefutable legal, moral, and political position. In this statement I should like to convey to the American people and the people of the world the basic issues which underlie the somewhat more formal language of diplomacy.

The Soviet aide memoire is a document which speaks of peace but theatens to disturb it. It speaks of ending the abnormal situation in Germany but insists on making permanent its abnormal division. It refers to the Four Power alliance of World War II but seeks the unilateral abrogation of the rights of the other three powers. It calls for new international agreements while preparing to violate existing ones. It offers certain assurances while making it plain that its previous assurances are not to be relied upon. It professes concern for the rights of the citizens of West Berlin while seeking to expose them to the immediate or eventual domination of a regime which permits no self-determination. Three simple facts are clear:

## Today There Is Peace

1. Today there is peace in Berlin, in Germany, and in Europe. If that peace is destroyed by the unilateral actions of the Soviet Union, its leaders will bear a heavy responsibility before world opinion and history.

John F. Kennedy, from a White House press release on July 19, 1961.

2. Today the people of West Berlin are free. In that sense it is already a "free city"—free to determine its own leaders and free to enjoy the fundamental human rights reaffirmed in the United Nations Charter.

3. Today the continued presence in West Berlin of the United States, the United Kingdom, and France is by clear legal right, arising from war, acknowledged in many agreements signed by the Soviet Union, and strongly supported by the overwhelming majority of the people of that city. Their freedom is dependent upon our exercise of these rights—an exercise which is thus a political and moral obligation as well as a legal right. Inasmuch as these rights, including the right of access to Berlin, are not held from the Soviet Government, they cannot be ended by any unilateral action of the Soviet Union. They cannot be affected by a so-called "peace treaty," covering only a part of Germany, with a regime of the Soviet Union's own creation—a regime which is not freely representative of all or any part of Germany and does not enjoy the confidence of the 17 million East Germans. The steady stream of German refugees from East to West is eloquent testimony to that fact.

The United States has been prepared since the close of the war, and is prepared today, to achieve, in agreement with its World War II allies, a freely negotiated peace treaty covering all of Germany and based on the freely expressed will of all of the German people. We have never suggested that, in violation of international law and earlier Four Power agreements, we might legally negotiate a settlement with only a part of Germany, or without the participation of the other principal World War II allies. We know of no sound reason why the Soviet Government should now believe that the rights of the Western Powers, derived from Nazi Germany's surrender, could be invalidated by such an action on the part of the Soviet Union.

The United States has consistently sought the goal

of a just and comprehensive peace treaty for all of Germany since first suggesting in 1946 that a special commission be appointed for this purpose. We still recognize the desirability of change—but it should be a change in the direction of greater, not less, freedom of choice for the people of Germany and Berlin. The Western peace plan and the all-Berlin solution proposed by the Western allies at Geneva in 1959 were constructive, practical offers to obtain this kind of fair settlement in central Germany or Berlin—our objective is the perpetuation of the peace and freedom of their citizens.

But the Soviet Union has blocked all progress toward the conclusion of a just treaty based on the self-determination of the German people and has instead repeatedly heightened world tensions over this issue. The Soviet blockade of Berlin in 1948, the Soviet note of November 27th, 1958, and this most recent Soviet aide memoire of June 4, 1961, have greatly disturbed the tranquillity of this area.

---

*"A city does not become free merely by calling it a 'free city.'"*

---

The real intent of the June 4 aide memoire is that East Berlin, a part of a city under Four Power status, would be formally absorbed into the so-called "German Democratic Republic" while West Berlin, even though called a "free city," would lose the protection presently provided by the Western Powers and become subject to the will of a totalitarian regime. Its leader, Herr Ulbricht, has made clear his intention, once this so-called "peace treaty" is signed, to curb West Berlin's communications with the free world and to suffocate the freedom it now enjoys.

The area thus newly subjected to Soviet threats of heightened tension poses no danger whatsoever to the peace of the world or to the security of any nation. The world knows that there is no reason for a crisis over Berlin today and that, if one develops, it will be caused by the Soviet Government's attempt to invade the rights of others and manufacture tensions. It is, moreover, misusing the words "freedom" and "peace." For, as our reply states, "freedom" and "peace" are not merely words—nor can they be achieved by words or promises alone. They are representative of a state of affairs.

## Free Name Not Enough

A city does not become free merely by calling it a "free city." For a city or a people to be free requires that they be given the opportunity, without economic, political, or police pressure, to make their own choice and to live their own lives. The people of West Berlin today have that freedom. It is the objective of our policy that they shall continue to have it.

Peace does not come automatically from a "peace treaty." There is peace in Germany today even though the situation is "abnormal." A "peace treaty" that adversely affects the lives and rights of millions will not bring peace with it. A "peace treaty" that attempts to affect adversely the solemn commitments of three great powers will not bring peace with it. We again urge the Soviet Government to reconsider its course, to return to the path of constructive cooperation it so frequently states it desires, and to work with its World War II allies in concluding a just and enduring settlement of issues remaining from that conflict.

*John F. Kennedy was president of the United States from 1961 until his assassination in 1963.*

*"West Berlin has been transformed into a center of subversive activity, diversion, and espionage. . . .against the G.D.R., the Soviet Union, and other socialist countries."*

viewpoint 23

# The Berlin Wall Protects the Socialist People

## The Warsaw Treaty Organization and the Soviet Government

*Editor's note: The following viewpoint consists of excerpts from two statements presenting the Soviet position on Berlin. Part I is from a statement by the Warsaw Treaty Organization, and Part II is directly from the Soviet government.*

### I

The present traffic situation on the borders of West Berlin is being used by ruling quarters of the German Federal Republic [G.F.R.] and intelligence agencies of NATO countries to undermine the economy of the G.D.R. [German Democratic Republic]. The government bodies and military concerns of the German Federal Republic, through deceit, bribery, and blackmail, induce certain unstable elements in the G.D.R. to leave for West Germany. These deceived people are compelled to serve with the Bundeswehr, and recruited for the intelligence agencies of different countries to be sent back to the G.D.R. as spies and saboteurs. A special fund has even been set up for such subversive activities against the G.D.R. and other socialist countries. Recently West German Chancellor Adenauer urged the NATO governments to increase this fund.

It is highly indicative that the subversive activities directed from West Berlin have greatly increased of late, right after the Soviet Union, the G.D.R. and other socialist countries advanced proposals for an immediate, peaceful settlement with Germany. This subversive activity not only inflicted damage on the G.D.R. but also affects the interests of other countries of the socialist camp.

In the face of the aggressive aspirations of the reactionary forces of the German Federal Republic and its NATO allies, the Warsaw Pact member states cannot but take necessary measures to guarantee

their security and, primarily, the security of the G.D.R. in the interests of the German peoples themselves.

The governments of the Warsaw Pact member states address the Peoples Chamber and Government of the G.D.R., and all working people of the G.D.R. with the proposal to establish an order on the borders of West Berlin which will securely block the way to the subversive activity against the socialist camp countries, so that reliable safeguards and effective control can be established around the whole territory of West Berlin, including its border with democratic Berlin.

It goes without saying that these measures must not affect existing provisions for traffic and control on communication routes between West Berlin and West Germany.

### Inconvenient but Necessary Measures

The governments of the Warsaw Pact member states understand, of course, that protective measures along the borders of West Berlin somewhat inconvenience the population. But the entire responsibility for the present situation rests exclusively with the Western Powers and with the German Federal Republic in the first place.

If so far the borders of West Berlin have remained open, this was done in the hope that the Western Powers would not abuse the good will of the Government of the G.D.R. But they, disregarding the interests of the German people and the population of Berlin, used the order now existing on the border of West Berlin for their own perfidious, subversive aims. An end must be put to the present abnormal situation through stronger protection and control on the border with West Berlin.

At the same time the governments of the Warsaw Pact member states find it necessary to emphasize that this necessity will disappear when a peaceful settlement with Germany is achieved and the

Declaration by the Political Consultative Committee of the Warsaw Treaty Member States on August 18, 1961. Soviet note to the United States on August 18, 1961.

questions awaiting their solution are settled on this basis.

## II

The Government of the Union of Soviet Socialist Republics considers it necessary to state the following:

1. The Soviet Government fully understands and supports the actions of the Government of the German Democratic Republic [G.D.R.] which established effective control on the border with West Berlin in order to bar the way for subversive activity being carried out from West Berlin against the G.D.R. and other countries of the socialist community.

In its measures on the borders the Government of the G.D.R. merely made sure the ordinary right of any sovereign state for the protection of its interests. Any state establishes on its borders with other states such regime as it deems necessary and responsive to its legitimate interests. As is known, the regime of state borders is one of the internal questions of any state, and its decision does not require recognition or approval on the part of other governments. Attempts by the Government of the U.S.A. to interfere in the internal affairs of the G.D.R. are therefore completely unfounded and inappropriate.

### Western Subversion

2. Doubtless the reasons are well known to the Government of the U.S.A. which made necessary and even inevitable the introduction of control over movement across the border between the G.D.R. and West Berlin. It expended no little effort itself to evoke these reasons.

West Berlin has been transformed into a center of subversive activity, diversion, and espionage, into a center of political and economic provocations against the G.D.R., the Soviet Union, and other socialist countries. Former and present West Berlin municipal leaders have cynically called West Berlin an "arrow in the living body of the German Democratic Republic," a "front city," a "violator of tranquillity," the "cheapest atom bomb put in the center of a socialist state." The gates of West Berlin have been opened to international criminals and provocateurs of all kinds, if only to sharpen international tension and widen the dimensions of the provocations and subversive acts against the countries of the socialist community. . . .

6. The G.D.R. has displayed, over the course of many years, great tolerance in the face of such a completely disgraceful and impermissible situation. Implementing its consistently peace-loving and democratic policy, it has borne enormous sacrifices to facilitate the achievement of agreement between the two German states on the questions of peaceful settlement and reunification of Germany on peace-loving and democratic foundations.

Nevertheless, and particularly recently, following the introduction of proposals on the immediate conclusion of a peace treaty with Germany and on normalization on that basis of the situation in West Berlin, subversive activity from West Berlin against the G.D.R. and other socialist countries has assumed even greater proportions. At the same time, the enemies of peace and tranquillity in this area have not missed even one opportunity to interfere with the plans for socialist construction in the G.D.R., to hinder the rise of well-being of its population, and, by every means and without stopping at anything, to complicate the situation in the Republic.

It is consequently fully understandable that the Government of the G.D.R., striving to prevent complication of the present international situation and responding to the appeal of the socialist states participants in the Warsaw Treaty, has adopted appropriate measures in defense of its state interests and the interests of the security of other socialist states.

### Rebirth of Militarism

7. Concluding their historic agreements at the end of the Second World War and following the defeat of Hitlerite Germany, the U.S.S.R., the U.S.A., Britain and France outlined a joint program for the restoration of German life on democratic peace-loving principles. This program was realized on the territory of the G.D.R. Unfortunately, in West Germany, as the Government of the U.S.S.R. has repeatedly pointed out, development took the path of a rebirth of militarism; and now there again thrive there the chauvinistic and revanchist forces, dangerous for the cause of peace, which were inspirers and organizers of Hitlerite aggression.

*"The entire responsibility for the present situation rests exclusively with the Western Powers."*

The Western Powers themselves promoted this and crudely violated all phases of the postwar quadripartite agreements. In its note of August 17, the Government of the U.S.A. attempts to invoke the quadripartite agreements on Germany which it itself violated. But is it possible, having destroyed the whole, to retain for oneself that part of an agreement advantageous to oneself? And in practice were the Government of the U.S.A. and its organs in West Berlin guided by the principles of the quadripartite agreements, to which they now appeal?

Can it be that separate monetary reform, extended to West Berlin from West Germany, accorded with quadripartite principles? Or was the creation of Bizonia and a separate magistrate in West Berlin in accordance with them? Or yet, in the opinion of the Government of the U.S.A., is it possible to reconcile with these quadripartite principles a separate tripartite occupation statute for West Berlin and the Paris agreements on the rearmament of the F.R.G. and its inclusion in NATO? Or do, perhaps, the aforementioned subversive activities from West Berlin against the U.S.S.R., the G.D.R. and other countries also accord with the principles of quadripartite cooperation?

> *"Municipal leaders have called West Berlin an 'arrow in the living body of the German Democratic Republic.'"*

It is sufficient to put these questions to understand the complete groundlessness and absurdity of references of the Government of the U.S.A. to the aforementioned agreements.

### False Concern for Germans

8. References of the Western Powers to Allied agreements are also groundless because these agreements were concluded for the period of occupation of Germany and for occupation purposes. Much has changed in the past 16½ years, including the face of Germany itself. On its territory have arisen two independent states with their own capitals and borders: the [socialist], peace-loving German Democratic Republic and the capitalistic, militaristic Federal Republic of Germany [F.R.G.]. No one has the right to interfere in the affairs of these two German states, since they relate to matters of their internal competence. These real facts can be recognized or not recognized, but they do not cease to exist for that reason.

The Government of the U.S.A. attempts in its note to represent its effort to perpetuate the occupation of West Berlin (and this 16 years after the end of the war) as a concern for the Germans and almost as a concrete expression of the right to self-determination. Such attempts in the final analysis cannot be taken seriously. And if the taking of defensive measures on the G.D.R. border with West Berlin creates certain temporary inconveniences for the city's population, blame for this rests entirely with the occupation authorities and the F.R.G. Government, which have done everything to prevent improvement of the atmosphere in this area in accordance with the legitimate interests of all states. Thus, the protest made in the note of the Government of the U.S.A. is without foundation and is categorically rejected by the Soviet Government.

9. As was already stated, measures taken by the Government of the G.D.R. are temporary. The Soviet Government repeatedly has emphasized that the conclusion of a peace treaty with Germany and normalization on such a basis of the situation in West Berlin will not infringe the interests of any of the parties and will contribute to the cause of peace and security of all peoples. To this end it appeals to the Government of the U.S.A.

*The Warsaw Treaty Organization is a mutual defense organization established in 1955. Its members include the Soviet Union and several other communist states. Part I of this viewpoint is taken from a statement by this organization. Part II is from a note from the Soviet government to the United States.*

*"The measures which have just been taken are motivated by the fact that an ever increasing number of inhabitants of East Germany wish to leave this territory."*

viewpoint **24**

# The Berlin Wall Restricts Freedom

### The United States Department of State and Chester Bowles

*Editor's note: The following viewpoint consists of excerpts from two statements about the US position on Berlin. Part I is taken from a State Department note to the Soviet Union. Part II is taken from a press conference with Under Secretary of State Chester Bowles.*

## I

On August 13, East German authorities put into effect several measures regulating movement at the boundary of the western sectors and the Soviet sector of the city of Berlin. These measures have the effect of limiting, to a degree approaching complete prohibition, passage from the Soviet sector to the western sectors of the city. These measures were accompanied by the closing of the sector boundary by a sizable deployment of police forces and by military detachments brought into Berlin for this purpose.

All this is a flagrant, and particularly serious, violation of the quadripartite status of Berlin. Freedom of movement with respect to Berlin was reaffirmed by the quadripartite agreement of New York of May 4, 1949, and by the decision taken at Paris on June 20, 1949, by the Council of the Ministers of Foreign Affairs of the Four Powers. The United States Government has never accepted that limitations can be imposed on freedom of movement within Berlin. The boundary between the Soviet sector and the western sectors of Berlin is not a state frontier. The United States Government considers that the measures which the East German authorities have taken are illegal. It reiterates that is does not accept the pretension that the Soviet sector of Berlin forms a part of the so-called "German Democratic Republic" and that Berlin is situated on its territory. Such a pretension is in itself a violation of the

solemnly pledged word of the U.S.S.R. in the Agreement on the Zones of Occupation in Germany and the administration of Greater Berlin. Moreover, the United States Government cannot admit the right of the East German authorities to authorize their armed forces to enter the Soviet sector of Berlin.

## Communist Attempt to Stop Exodus

By the very admission of the East German authorities, the measures which have just been taken are motivated by the fact that an ever increasing number of inhabitants of East Germany wish to leave this territory. The reasons for this exodus are known. They are simply the internal difficulties of East Germany.

To judge by the terms of a declaration of the Warsaw Pact powers published on August 13, the measures in question are supposed to have been recommended to the East German authorities by those powers. The United States Government notes that the powers which associated themselves with the U.S.S.R. by signing the Warsaw Pact are thus intervening in a domain in which they have no competence.

It is to be noted that this declaration states that the measures taken by the East German authorities are "in the interests of the German peoples themselves." It is difficult to see any basis for this statement, or to understand why it should be for the members of the Warsaw Pact to decide what are the interests of the German people. It is evident that no Germans, particularly those whose freedom of movement is being forcibly restrained, think this is so. This would become abundantly clear if all Germans were allowed a free choice, and the principle of self-determination were also applied in the Soviet sector of Berlin and in East Germany.

The United States Government solemnly protests against the measures referred to above, for which it holds the Soviet Government responsible. The United

United States note to the USSR on August 17, 1961. Chester Bowles replies to questions asked at the National Press Club, Washington, DC, on August 15, 1961.

States Government expects the Soviet Government to put an end to these illegal measures. This unilateral infringement of the quadripartite status of Berlin can only increase existing tension and dangers.

## II

Seen from Asian and African capitals, the Berlin crisis takes on a significance that goes far beyond our position in Europe. To this point I shall return in a moment.

First let us consider the more immediate implications of Mr. Khrushchev's maneuvers.

At no time since World War II has our nation been more directly and dangerously challenged than we are today in regard to our commitments to the people of West Berlin. Here in the heart of Europe—the cockpit of two world wars in a single generation—is a direct, total confrontation between the two greatest nuclear powers.

This is a challenge to which only one response is possible: We must adhere to our treaty rights; we must honor our commitments. Our word has been pledged to the free people of West Berlin. Unless we stand by that pledge, our word will not again be trusted by threatened peoples anywhere.

In his recent speech President Kennedy defined the terms of our response: We will carry out our promise to the people of West Berlin. If necessary we will meet force with force. But we will never close the door to honorable negotiation toward peace in central Europe or anywhere else.

### What Are Soviets Seeking?

In each country we visited on my trip, the discussions returned again and again to the central question: What are the Soviets seeking? Why have they chosen to move so far along this reckless path?

For several years now Mr. Khrushchev has been proposing what he describes as "competitive coexistence" between the Communist and non-Communist nations of the world. Such competition, he has boasted, will demonstrate the ability of a Communist society to surpass a free society in economic growth and political stability, in education and in cultural development.

---

*"We will never close the door to honorable negotiation toward peace in central Europe or anywhere else."*

---

Oddly enough, what we have had for the past 15 years—right in Mr. Khrushchev's own front yard—is precisely the competition he has been seeking. Since 1945 two Germanies—the one free and democratic, the other governed by a full-fledged Communist regime—have existed side by side.

What has been the result?

Today in West Germany we have one of the great success stories of modern times—a free, prosperous, and stable society of enormous vitality and promise.

In contrast, East Germany stands as a pathetic failure, characterized by lagging industrial development, political unrest, intellectual sterility, the frustration of its people, and their outspoken contempt for the Communist system.

### Pathetic Failure of Communism

Every day, until the border was closed, many hundreds of East Germans had been leaving their homes in what, according to Mr. Khrushchev, should by now be a Communist utopia to begin their lives anew in what, according to the Communist book, should be a capitalistic cesspool in West Germany.

These rebels against the Communist system can hardly be described as bloated capitalists. On the contrary, most of them are young people in their teens and twenties and thirties—men and women who for 15 years have presumably been brainwashed in Communist schools and universities.

It is, in fact, to contain the unfortunate East Germans that Khrushchev has now ringed Berlin with Soviet troops to make sure the borders remain closed.

This migration has been far more than a daily irritant to Khrushchev and Ulbricht. It represented in the most dramatic way a daily "plebiscite" which the Communists could never hope to win.

So here in the very heart of Europe we have had the competition for which Khrushchev has been pleading, and the results are clear: Communism has failed.

It is also clear that Mr. Khrushchev is a poor loser. Indeed he is now asking us to bail him out of his failure by agreeing to abandon the free people of West Berlin to the same system which has brought such misery to the people of East Germany.

For the last 3 weeks I have drummed these facts home in press conferences, in speeches, and in private discussions in Lagos, Rangoon, New Delhi, and Nicosia.

### Defending Self-Determination

I found that when we speak of America's legal right to remain in Berlin few Asians and Africans are impressed. But when we stress our role as defenders of the right of the West Berliners to make their own decisions, then faces light up and heads nod. For Asians and Africans know that self-determination is basic to their own independence.

To those who minimized the situation on the ground that West Berlin is only part of a city and not a country, I pointed out that there are 21 members of the United Nations with populations smaller than that of West Berlin and 58 with a smaller gross national product.

Now, the very intensity of our commitment to the

freedom of the people of West Berlin poses a problem for us in Asia, Africa, and Latin America. In our proper preoccupation with the principle of self-determination in Berlin, there is the danger that we may be persuaded to lessen our support for similar principles elsewhere.

President Kennedy recognized the urgent need to resist such pressures in his recent address to the Nation. "If new threats in Berlin or elsewhere," he warned, "should cause us to weaken our program of assistance to the developing nations who are also under heavy pressure from the same source, or to halt our efforts for . . . disarmament, or to disrupt or slow down our economy, or to neglect the education of our children, then those threats will surely be the most successful and least costly maneuver in Communist history."

These are critically important words which should be read thoughtfully by every American, by every legislator, policymaker, and administrator.

The second dimension of the Berlin crisis therefore is clear: In the weeks and months ahead we must not permit the problem of Germany to divert us from the broader struggle to build a *world* in which freedom of choice is increasingly possible. . . .

## Assault on Our Commitments

We Americans will be tested in the next few months as perhaps never before in our long history. Our will, our courage, and our military capacity will be challenged by the Soviet's frontal assault on our commitments to the people of West Berlin. Our intelligence, skill and imagination will be tested elsewhere by mankind's yearning not only for a peaceful and just resolution to the current crisis in Berlin but for the courageous application of the principle of self-determination which is at stake there to all people everywhere.

Although the ultimate verdict will rest with the historians, there is a new force in the world which will provide a more immediate judgment of our efforts, a force which can only be described as a gradually emerging world conscience. This phenomenon reflects more than common concern over the possibility of nuclear war; it reflects a common yearning for some universal standards by which the actions of nations as well as men may be judged.

If we apply the teachings of our revolutionary heritage with conviction and integrity to today's revolutionary world, I believe we can face that judgment with confidence.

These are the views which our American representatives in Asia and Africa asked me to communicate to you. . . .

## Isolation of East Berlin

I do think that we made a mistake over the years to allow the Soviet Union to isolate East Berlin from the

whole of Berlin. I think we should have been talking the last 10 years about Berlin as a whole. But nevertheless, although the barbed wire has only recently been erected, the lines were established long ago. Our guarantee and our assurances are to the people of West Berlin. We certainly are disturbed, profoundly disturbed and shocked, by what is going on in East Berlin and East Germany. I think we should realize that this is an extraordinary, fantastic defeat that the Soviet Union and communism have taken in East Germany and East Berlin. As I said before, they asked for competition; they have had it, and they have lost. And this fact is not lost on the world. I found that people in Asia and Africa understood it pretty well last week. Believe me, they understand it a whole lot better now. This doesn't make the situation any less dangerous. Indeed, in some ways it makes it more dangerous. But nevertheless, it is a fact that they have lost this contest dismally in Germany, and I think the world knows it. . . .

> "Vastly more important is the right of 2½ million people who have built that great city of West Berlin to continue as free and independent people and not to be sucked into this mess of East Germany."

I would like to know why Mr. Khrushchev has embarked on this [risky course of action in Berlin]. I think it is one of the great questions of our time. I have asked various people who have some understanding of what the Soviet mind is like, particularly in Yugoslavia, how they interepreted all this. Is this an effort simply to tidy up his backyard on Mr. Khrushchev's part? Is he simply trying to get a tidier central Europe in the face of the pressures he is receiving from the East? Or is this an all-out effort to embarrass us, to humiliate us, to drive us into a corner, to break our will?

This is the fundamental question, and I don't think anybody really has the answer. I think the answer will begin to emerge in the coming months.

## No Brinkmanship

Certainly there is no brinkmanship on our part. We have some fundamental rights there that are legal and clear. But, as I said before, vastly more important is the right of 2½ million people who have built that great city of West Berlin to continue as free and independent people and not to be sucked into this mess of East Germany.

And this right we have to stand on. When you are challenged as we have been, you can't call it brinkmanship simply to resist that challenge. If you don't resist it, you won't have any world left. The problem, of course, is to resist it in ways that are not provocative, that are responsible, that avoid recklessness. This is a time when you separate the men from the boys.

*Chester Bowles was an under secretary of state in the administration of President John F. Kennedy.*

*"The U.S.A., England, and France, utilizing uncontrolled air communications, are clearly abusing their situation in West Berlin."*

# Western Use of Berlin Air Corridors Is Aggressive

## The Soviet Government

*Editor's note: The following viewpoint consists of two notes from the Soviet government to the government of the United States. Part I was written on August 23, 1961 and Part II on September 2, 1961.*

### I

The Ministry of Foreign Affairs of the Union of Soviet Socialist Republics presents its compliments to the Embassy of the United States of America and on instruction of the Soviet Government states the following:

The Soviet Government repeatedly has drawn the attention of the Government of the U.S.A. to the illegal and inadmissible interference of the Federal Republic of Germany in the affairs of West Berlin. It is generally known that West Berlin is not part of the F.R.G. and the competence of its authorities cannot be extended to it. This is also recognized by the governments of the Western Powers.

Nevertheless, the Government of the U.S.A. has not taken proper measures for the suppression of provocative activity of certain circles of the F.R.G. in West Berlin. With the connivance of occupation organs of the Three Powers in West Berlin, this activity not only has not been ended, but recently it has been sharply increased, especially in connection with the proposal for an urgent peace settlement with Germany and a decision on this basis of the question of West Berlin. It also has assumed a scale which creates a threat of disturbing the peace and tranquillity in this area.

### Western Subversion Via Air Corridors

Over a long period the Bonn Minister of so-called All-German Affairs [Ernst] Lemmer, has acted in West Berlin, has made his residence there where provocations of different kinds are prepared and from

which leadership is exercised over subversive work against the German Democratic Republic and other socialist countries. All kinds of revanchists, extremists, saboteurs, spies, and diversionists are transported from the F.R.G. to West Berlin. For their transport the Western Powers also are using the air corridors. Thus, the U.S.A., England, and France, utilizing uncontrolled air communications, are clearly abusing their situation in West Berlin. As a result, the agreement reached in 1945 has been flagrantly violated, which agreement provided, as is known, air corridors to the three Western Powers temporarily for provision of the needs of their military garrisons, but not for subversive and revanchist goals of West German militarism and not for conducting those subversive activities which demonstratively before the eyes of the whole world, including the Germans themselves, are carried out by West German figures appearing recently almost daily in West Berlin. Official representatives of the F.R.G. [Federal Republic of Germany] Government and the "Bundestag" also arrive in West Berlin by the air corridors and directly from the airport proceed on demonstrative "inspection" tours of the city, make aggressive and hostile declarations against the G.D.R. [German Democratic Republic] and the Soviet Union. Only last week the President of the F.R.G. "Bundestag," [Eugen] Gerstenmaier, the Chairman of the CDU/CSU [Christian Democratic Union/Christian Social Union] "Bundestag" Fraktion, [Heinrich] Krone, SDP [Social Democratic Party] Chairman [Erich] Ollenhauer, FDP [Free Democratic Party] Chairman [Erich] Mende, and others assembled there.

Their arrival was accompanied by the organization of mobs and demonstrations at which appeals for aggression against peaceloving neighboring states and violence against democratic forces in West Berlin were openly proclaimed.

Intensified intrigues in the leading circles of the F.R.G. in West Berlin testify to their premeditated

Soviet notes to the United States, August 23 and September 2, 1961.

efforts to sharpen the situation in that region in order to produce the complications and conflicts and attempt to bring the Western Powers into collision with the Soviet Union, to the advantage of West German militarists and revanchists. And all this is taking place before the eyes and with the favorable support of the occupation authorities of the Three Powers in West Berlin, who, it would seem, should take into account the dangerous consequences of the aforementioned provocative activity of those circles of the F.R.G. which have made the idea of revanche the basis of their policy.

## Conniving Interference

Continuing to connive at the interference of the authorities of the F.R.G. in the affairs of West Berlin and the use of the territory of the city for international provocations, the Government of the U.S.A. takes upon itself the full responsibility for possible consequences.

The government of the U.S.S.R. insists that the Government of the U.S.A., which, at present, is exercising occupation functions in West Berlin, immediately take measures to terminate the illegal and provocative actions of the F.R.G. in that city.

## II

1. In its note [of August 26] the Government of the United States of America once more puts forward as a basic problem the question of the so-called Four Power status of Berlin. In its note of August 18 the Soviet Government adduced copious material which testifies to the fact that the Western Powers, over the course of many years, by all their actions destroyed this Four Power status, turning West Berlin into a base of divisionist, espionage, speculative, and other subversive activity against the German Democratic Republic, the Soviet Union, and other socialist states. The Government of the U.S.A. makes it appear as though it has not taken note of the incontrovertible arguments and facts adduced by the Soviet Government; obviously, it has nothing to say on the score of these facts and arguments. Thereby it confirms that it is unable to deny or dispute them, and, consequently, is unable to dispute the justice and the well-grounded character of the position of the Soviet Union, which insists on the liquidation of so impermissible a situation in West Berlin and on suppression without delay of a subversive and criminal activity, dangerous for the cause of peace, of authorities of the Federal Republic of Germany on the territory of West Berlin.

2. In the note under reference the U.S.A. once more undertakes the attempt to make domestic measures of a third sovereign state, the German Democratic Republic [G.D.R.], a subject of discussion. Such actions are in gross contradiction to generally accepted norms of international law. Even if the U.S.A. does not have normal relations with the German Democratic Republic, that does not give it the right of interference of any sort in the internal affairs of the G.D.R. If one were to admit the contrary as well-founded, that would signify the supplanting of law in international life of arbitrariness, the supplanting of international rule of law by chaos in relations between states.

*"Even if the U.S.A. does not have normal relations with the German Democratic Republic, that does not give it the right of interference of any sort in the internal affairs of the G.D.R."*

Arguments in the note of the U.S.A. regarding measures of the Government of the G.D.R. on the border with West Berlin exude the musty odor of occupation, which has long since outlived its usefulness, and an unwillingness to look true reality in the face. Old Germany no longer exists: The socialist German Democratic Republic and the capitalist Federal Republic of Germany [F.R.G.] have arisen in its place. Any realistic policy of states cannot fail to take account of the existence of these two sovereign German states, which arose not yesterday nor today but 12 years ago. This fact cannot be eliminated by exorcisms of any sort, no matter how often they might be repeated in Bonn or other capitals of the Western Powers.

## Transport of Subversives

3. The Government of the U.S.A. does not deny in its note that air corridors, which cross the territory of the G.D.R., are being used for transportation from the F.R.G. to West Berlin of revanchists, militarists, spies, and diversionists, who are active against the G.D.R. and other socialist countries. At the same time, it claims that the Western Powers, in accordance with decisions of the Control Council in Germany, have "unrestricted right" of transportation by air to West Berlin—one must understand, to transport such a type of person—and that "there has never been any limitation whatsoever placed upon their (i.e. air corridors) use by aircraft of the Western Powers."

Such assertions cannot be justified either from a juridical point of view or in substance. It is clear from the documents of the Control Council that air corridors now in use between Berlin and the Western occupation zones of Germany were temporarily assigned exclusively for the satisfaction of needs of the military garrisons of the U.S.A., Britain, and France in West Berlin, for maintenance of communications and transportation of personnel and freight of those garrisons to and from headquarters of the occupation forces of the corresponding powers in Western Germany. This is stated, in particular, in the decision of the Control Council on the report of the Military Air Directorate, unanimously adopted on November 30, 1945.

The Control Council did not adopt any quadripartite decisions on uncontrolled commercial air transport along the air corridors or on transportation along them of any German personnel or persons not in the service of the occupation authorities of the Three Powers, and still less of the West German revanchists and militarists, and such decisions simply do not exist. It is known that, at the time, organs of the Control Council discussed the question of establishment on the territory of Germany of air routes which would not be directly connected with fulfillment by the Four Powers of their occupation functions. However, the Control Council recognized that it was not competent to decide such questions.

---

## "The Soviet Government has more than once declared that it does not in any degree intend to limit the international ties of West Berlin."

---

And, in general, agreements to which the Government of the U.S.A. refers were concluded before the formation of the sovereign German states, which have already received wide international recognition. Furthermore, these agreements were concluded in the period of occupation of Germany, on termination of which respective declarations were made by the occupying powers, excluding West Berlin, in which the occupation regime has for some reason been preserved by the three Western Powers until now.

### "Wide Variety of Ties"

4. In its note the Government of the U.S.A. tries to present the matter as though the present "wide variety of ties" between West Berlin and the F.R.G. "are in no way incompatible with the Four Power status of Berlin."

The Soviet Government has already had the opportunity to point out what character this "wide variety of ties" has. It is completely obvious that ties of this kind have no more in common with the quadripartite agreements to which the American note refers than the espionage diversionary tunnel in Alt-Glienech, the activity of revanchist organizations and subversive centers in West Berlin, speculation in foreign exchange, and other such crimes.

5. The Western Powers have repeatedly acknowledged and, judging by the note of the U.S.A.,

do not now deny that West Berlin is not some sort of part of the F.R.G., cannot be governed by the latter's authorities, and, consequently, also cannot serve as residence for authorities of that kind. The question arises, however, of how such official position of the U.S.A. can be reconciled with the creation and functioning in West Berlin of West German departments and institutions under the protection of the occupation authorities, with the holding there of sessions of Parliament of the F.R.G. and of its organs, with the extension to West Berlin of the validity of Bonn laws with the claims of the Government of the F.R.G. to represent West Berlin in foreign relations, and so forth. It is clear that these are incompatible things.

It is difficult to avoid the impression that, taking such a position, the three Western Powers are trying to shield their West German allies who are carrying out activities in West Berlin which are provocative and dangerous to peace and now are trying to hide behind the back of the occupation authorities of the Western Powers.

6. The Soviet Government has more than once declared that it does not in any degree intend to limit the international ties of West Berlin in general and with the F.R.G. in particular. West Berlin, as a free city, will have the right and possibility after conclusion of a peace treaty to maintain diplomatic, economic, and cultural relations with any country of any continent. However, it cannot be a subversion center against the G.D.R. on whose territory it is located. The free city of West Berlin, of course, will have the right to maintain unobstructed communication with the outside world, but this right will not be connected with occupation, and will be based on corresponding agreements with the governments of those countries through whose territory its communications pass.

7. Confirming its note of August 23, 1961, the Government of the U.S.S.R. insists that the Government of the U.S.A., which, together with Governments of Britain and France, is at present carrying out occupation functions in West Berlin, put an end to the illegal and provocative actions of the F.R.G. in that city. The Soviet Government considers it necessary to warn the Government of the U.S.A. that it will bear full responsibility for possible consequences of the continuation of such provocative activity. The Government of the U.S.A. will be displaying too lax an approach to this entire problem of use of communications with West Berlin for provocative purposes indicated in the note of the Government of the U.S.S.R. of August 23 if it continues to adhere to the point of view expressed in the American note of August 26.

*These viewpoints were notes from the Soviet government to the United States.*

*"Air access to Berlin. . .is and has been unrestricted since the end of World War II in 1945."*

viewpoint 26

# Western Use of Berlin Air Corridors Is Legitimate

The United States Government

Air access to Berlin along the three corridors from West Germany is and has been unrestricted since the end of World War II in 1945.

West Germans who make use of this means of transporation to Berlin do so in pursuit of a variety of business, cultural, political or other normal objectives, individually chosen, in a manner which is familiar and well understood in societies where free men regulate their own lives in accordance with free choice. That the U.S.S.R. should characterize such activities as criminal does not make them so. Moreover, these ties with the Federal Republic and the outside world are of vital importance to the viability and well being of West Berlin. The attitude of the U.S.S.R. and the East German authorities toward freedom of travel is plainly shown in the recent actions by which a prison wall was built across the heart of Berlin. The authorities of the East German regime have fired on, and even killed, their fellow countrymen who were seeking no more than to enter West Berlin.

## Joint Air Access Rights

Rights with respect to air access to Berlin derive from precisely the same source as do the rights of the U.S.S.R. in East Germany and East Berlin, namely, the joint military defeat of the German Reich and the joint assumption of supreme authority over Germany. These rights are confirmed by the circumstances under which the Four Powers entered Germany, by their subsequent discussions and agreements, and by open and established practice over a period of 15 years.

The Soviet note refers to the report of the Air Directorate of the Allied Control Council (which the note incorrectly designates as the Military Air Directorate) and to the decision of the Council itself regarding flight in the corridors. These documents reveal both the nature of the rights of the respective parties and arrangements as to the exercise of these rights. Paragraph 1 of the Air Directorate report states that "Because of the increasing number of flights between the Greater Berlin area and the respective occupied zones of the four Allied Powers in Germany. . .there is a real need to ensure safety of flights. . .by means of air corridors under strict rules of flight for all aircraft using the corridors." Paragraph 3 proposes six air corridors, three to points in the Western zones and three to points outside Germany, "which could be used by aircraft of the four Allied Nations with full freedom of action."

The Coordinating Committee of the Allied Control Authority on November 22, 1945, approved the following request from the Air Directorate: "To confirm the proposals for the establishment of air corridors West of Berlin as follows: BERLIN-HAMBURG, BERLIN-BUCKEBURG, BERLIN-FRANKFURT-ON-MAIN, each twenty English miles wide. Flight over these routes (corridors) will be conducted without previous notice being given, by aircraft of the nations governing Germany." Lt. General Kutsevalov represented the U.S.S.R. On November 30, 1945, the Control Council itself approved the document with Marshal Zhukov acting for the U.S.S.R. Contrary to what is alleged by the Soviet Government, which now finds this decision inconvenient, there is no reference in this decision or in the report of the Air Directorate to any limitation upon the use of the air corridors, either as regards their duration or as regards the goods or persons to be transported by aircraft of Allied nations.

## Soviet Recognition of Western Use

Thus from the earliest days the Soviet Union recognized that the air corridors were to be used "by aircraft of the four Allied Nations with full freedom

The United States government, note to the Soviet Union on September 8, 1961.

of action." This understanding is confirmed in the records of the subsequent quadripartite meetings. For example, at the meeting of the Air Directorate on April 30, 1946, the Soviet Delegate, Ltd. General Kutsevalov stated:

> The Soviet Delegation thinks that the existing system of Air Routes through the Soviet Zone of occupation in Germany is fully sufficient, not only to meet the requirements of the Allied Troops in the Sector of Greater Berlin, but also to carry out successfully all the Allied transportation needs for commercial cargoes regardless of their volume.

In February 1947, in connection with preparations for the Council of Foreign Ministers meeting, the Western Powers renewed a recommendation for establishing additional air corridors for civil flights to Berlin by aircraft of nations other than the Four Powers. The Soviet Union objected, on the ground, as stated in the U.S.S.R. report dated February 5, 1947, that the quadripartite decisions establishing the three air corridors provided adequate facilities to meet existing requirements. The Soviet Union thus recognized that the air corridors were legitimately used by the civil aircraft of the Allied Powers.

The practice of the Western Powers is equally significant to confirming the understanding as to air access. Civil aircraft of the Allied nations had been flying to and from Berlin on special charter flights from the early days of the occupation. On May 20, 1946, the American overseas airlines inaugurated regular weekly flights. In 1947 there were 52 such flights by Pan American World Airways. In 1948 there were 549 round-trip flights by all carriers; in 1949 there were 4,776; in 1950 there were 6,974. All of these flights were processed as a matter of routine through the Berlin Air Safety Center in which the Soviet Union is represented. Civil air flights to Berlin continued unrestricted throughout the Berlin blockade and thereafter.

For the rest, the Soviet note consists merely in the repetition of many charges and allegations which the United States Government cannot accept, and which it has discussed at length in its notes of July 17, 1961, and August 26, 1961, as well as in many previous communications on this subject of Germany and Berlin.

### Divisive Wall

The Soviet Government claims that the quadripartite status of Berlin was destroyed by acts of the United States Government and its Allies. But it is plain to see what divides Berlin in two. It is the wall of barbed wire and concrete built on the sector border by East German authorities in violation of solemn obligations freely and repeatedly undertaken by the U.S.S.R. This may be "the true reality" which people living in the U.S.S.R. or under the East German authorities must "look in the face." But the United States Government cannot admit that the arbitrary application of force can alter the legal or moral foundation of rights and obligations.

The Soviet Government refers to certain relations between West Berlin and West Germany. The relations referred to are in fulfillment of the obligation undertaken by the Four Powers in Paris on June 20, 1949, after the Berlin blockade to work for "Facilitation of the movement of persons and goods and the exchange of information between the Western zones and the Eastern zone and between Berlin and the zones." The policies of the U.S.S.R. have been in flagrant violation of this undertaking. Indeed the Soviet note's criticism of normal and peaceful relations between these two parts of the same country is peculiarly inappropriate in view of the fact that the East German authorities with Soviet support have for many years maintained their headquarters in East Berlin and have stationed military and paramilitary units there, thus violating the agreed status of Berlin and seeking illegally to annex East Berlin by force. The governing authorities of West Berlin are chosen by the people of West Berlin in free elections and those authorities have freely approved relations between West Berlin and West Germany. Those relations are consistent with the legal status of Berlin.

---

*"It is plain to see what divides Berlin in two."*

---

The Soviet Government again implies that its proposed "peace treaty" with the East German authorities can somehow alter the status of West Berlin. But such a "peace treaty" can at most have certain limited effects on the relationship between the Soviet Union and its zone of occupation. The Three Western Powers recognized the principle involved when in their Convention on Relations with the Federal Republic of Germany signed in Paris on October 23, 1954, they specifically retained the rights and responsibilities exercised or held by them relating to Berlin and to Germany as a whole, thus safeguarding the positions of all countries concerned, including the Soviet Union. Indeed, the Soviet Foreign Minister, commenting on this very Convention as recently as May 25, 1959, made clear the view of the Soviet Government that agreements "concluded not with all the powers who fought against Germany but only with a group of those powers, and not with the whole of Germany but only with a part" cannot seriously be regarded "as some sort of likeness to, or substitute for, a peace treaty."

### "Freedom" Through Treaty

The United States Government is forced to conclude that the sweeping claims of the Soviet Government as to the effects of a "peace treaty" between the Soviet Union and the so-called German Democratic Republic are merely an effort to provide camouflage for the exploitation of certain advantages which the Soviet Government thinks it has because of the geographic location of Berlin. The Soviet note gives a foretaste of what the "freedom" of West Berlin would be like as a consequence of a "peace treaty" with the East German regime. Although the note asserts again that the "free city of West Berlin, of course, will have the right to maintain

*This viewpoint was a note to the Soviet Union delivered via the American Embassy in Moscow. The Embassies of France and the United Kingdom delivered identical notes to the USSR.*

*"The people of the world are by now sufficiently accustomed to the upside-down use of words in the Soviet lexicon not to be deceived by the efforts to mislead them with such labels."*

unobstructed communication with the outside world," the inference is plain that the right would not be extended to anyone to whom the U.S.S.R. or the East German authorities may choose to deny it by labelling him as a revanchist, militarist, spy, diversionist, or subversive. The people of the world are by now sufficiently accustomed to the upside-down use of words in the Soviet lexicon not to be deceived by the efforts to mislead them with such labels. Thus in Soviet usage, a "revanchist" seems to be anyone who believes in self-determination for the German people; a "militarist" seems to be one who believes in defending his home against the threat created by the large forces in East Germany; a "spy" would seem to be anyone who is curious about what goes on in the world; a "diversionist" may be anyone who publicly opposes Soviet views as to correct policy; while a "subversive" appears to be anyone who favors freedom of speech, assembly and movement.

As of today there is free and peaceful movement of persons and goods by air between West Germany and West Berlin. Any change in this situation will be the result of aggressive action against established rights by the Soviet Government and the East German regime. It is the duty of all states, especially in times like these, of increasing tensions and dangers to international peace, to refrain from unilateral action to alter existing agreements and practices which cannot but further increase such tensions. The United States Government wishes to repeat in the most solemn terms the warnings already given in its note of August 26, 1961, and the White House statement of August 24, 1961, against any action to interfere with flights in the air corridors to West Berlin.

*"The United States of America [feels it] is free to take military action against Cuba."*

# The US Is Attempting to Invade Cuba

Andrei Gromyko

A circumstance bound to arouse particular concern among the members of the United Nations gathered here for the General Assembly's seventeenth session is the statement on Cuba made by Mr. Kennedy, the President of the United States of America, at a press conference held on 13 September last. The United States of America is one of the founders of the United Nations and a permanent member of the Security Council; economically and militarily it is the most powerful of all the capitalist countries. It would seem that such a country and its statesmen, if only because of the responsibility weighing upon the United States of America as a great Power, should show particular respect for the United Nations Charter and frame their policy accordingly. But this statement by President Kennedy indicates precisely the contrary.

The Soviet Government has naturally observed that the statement of the President of the United States also contained some sound appraisals, revealing a realistic understanding of certain aspects of the Cuban question and of the situation which has developed. It must be noted that the Government of the United States of America has publicly dissociated itself from the bellicose circles in its country which have been calling for immediate armed aggression against Cuba. But the tone is set, not by these sober pronouncements, but by crude threats—which in fact cancels out what was positive in the statement. It follows from the President's words that the United States of America is free to take military action against Cuba and will decide for itself the juncture at which it regards it as necessary to undertake such an invasion. The President said that the United States Government would continue as before to collaborate with the leaders of the Cuban counter-revolution, who have found refuge in the territory of the United

States. The events of recent days do not reduce, but intensify the alarm felt by States Members of the United Nations with regard to United States policy toward Cuba. . . .

## US War Hysteria

Representatives gathered here for the General Assembly have doubtless already been able to realize the extent to which war hysteria in regard to Cuba has arisen in the United States, and what a campaign of hostility against the Cuban people is rampant in American newspapers, radio and television. Things have reached such a point that a list of pretexts which could be used to justify an invasion of Cuba has been published in advance, and this list includes everything under the sun.

For example, if the United States of America considers that Cuba is in any way "hampering" the functioning of the experimental rocket-launching pads at Cape Canaveral in Florida, that would apparently suffice for the mightiest Power of the Western hemisphere to bear down upon little Cuba with all its military strength. Of course, those who contemplate aggression against Cuba will find no difficulty in leveling any charges they wish against that country, however absurd the charges may be. In the final analysis, Cuba can be blamed for any failure of rocket tests on Cape Canaveral. Apparently, Cuba is already at fault for being situated so near to Florida.

If this logic is taken as a guide, it would appear that any State, especially a powerful one, can accuse its neighbor of hampering the execution of certain measures in a given area. But since it is impossible to remove even a small State in the way that houses, for instance, are nowadays moved from one place to another, and since Cuba cannot be moved farther away from Florida or Florida from Cuba, what is the solution? Does this mean that the stronger neighbour has the right to gobble up the weaker?

Andrei Gromyko, from an address before the United Nations General Assembly on September 21, 1962.

Another of the listed pretexts for attacking Cuba is the existence of a threat to the security of the United States military base at Guantanamo, which is maintained on the territory of Cuba without the consent of its Government. But is it not clear that any incident can be invented in the United States of America and declared to be evidence of a threat to that base?

## US Is Prepared to Attack

It is also said that the United States of America will be prepared to attack Cuba if it considers that Cuba is building up its forces to such a degree that it may constitute a threat to the United States of America, a threat to United States communications with the Panama Canal, or a threat to any State of the Western hemisphere. Any clear-thinking person knows that Cuba is pursuing neither the first, nor the second nor the third of these objectives. The statesmen of the United States of America also know this full well. They are further quite aware of the fact that the assistance rendered by the United States of America to Cuba for the strengthening of its independence has none of those objectives in view, since they are foreign to our policy.

A number of other equally trumped-up charges against Cuba could be adduced, each and all amounting to one and the same thing: that the United States of America announces the circumstances in which it may commit an act of aggression against Cuba, and that the United States itself assumed the role of judge in determining whether or not such circumstances have arisen....

## US Wants Control Over the Seas

Some statesmen of the United States speak of the need to tighten control over the whole Caribbean area, as if the Caribbean Sea were some kind of internal lake within the United States of America. Let us merely ask: Who agrees to recognize United States control over the international waters of that sea? The United States might with equal success claim the Atlantic Ocean as its own, as the self-appointed heir of the god Neptune, who in ancient mythology was the lord of the seas. The less-bridled politicians in the United States, clearly losing control of their reasoning, say, if you please, that it is necessary to control the movements of Soviet ships carrying goods to Cuba and from Cuba to the Soviet Union, and of the specialists who are helping the Cubans to put their industry and agriculture on an even keel. But who is going to permit the exercise of such control? It is not clear that such demands are a call to piracy and must be decisively condemned? It would be better if those making such demands understood their reckless nature.

And what can be said about the crude pressure exerted by the United States upon a number of other States, including its own allies in NATO, with a view

to preventing them from supplying ships for the transport of goods to and from Cuba? What value attaches to the statements of United States representatives when, under the roof of the United Nations, they speak of economic co-operation and assistance to other countries while at the same time this mighty Power tries to snatch a crust of bread from the hands of a small country.

---

*"The situation is becoming all the more dangerous in that the United States is not only using with independent and peace-loving Cuba the language of menace, but it is also engaging in concrete acts of aggression against that State."*

---

Can the United Nations tolerate the fact that one of its Members loudly proclaims its right to attack another country which is also a Member of the United Nations? And that it does so because domestic institutions of that other country conflict with the way of thinking of the United States Government and are not to its taste?...

## Concrete Acts of Aggression

The situation is becoming all the more dangerous in that the United States is not only using with independent and peace-loving Cuba the language of menace, but is also engaging in concrete acts of aggression against that State.

It is a matter of common knowledge that many cut-throats driven out by the Cuban people have found shelter in the United States or live, on American money, in neighbouring countries, whence they carry out piratical raids on the Republic of Cuba. These raids are executed with the support of the United States, which provides Cuba's inveterate enemies with all the arms and equipment they need. Full responsibility for the piratical activities and banditry of the Cuban cut-throats rests, therefore, with the Government of the United States....

## A Warning to the US

Respect for the sovereign rights of every State, renunciation of all intervention in the domestic affairs of other States, recognition of the right of Governments to establish the social and political system corresponding to the interests and wishes of their people—such must be the fixed and infringible rules of contemporary international life. Without the unswerving observance of these rules there can be neither peace, nor peaceful coexistence, nor, in the final analysis, even a United Nations.

That is why the Soviet Government considers it

necessary to raise its voice in warning and draw the attention of States Members of the United Nations to the full seriousness of the implications, for peace, of the policy pursued by the United States of America in regard to the Republic of Cuba. If the States represented here wish to preserve the United Nations and to make it an effective instrument for the preservation and strengthening of peace, then such a policy and such actions must be resolutely condemned.

*"In our time. . .we cannot lose our heads or our composure and treat questions involving war and peace as lightly as some United States political leaders."*

In our time—and this applies particularly to a great Power—we cannot lose our heads or our composure and treat questions involving war and peace as lightly as some United States political leaders treat the situation in regard to Cuba. An attack on Cuba would lead to the consequences of which the Soviet Government warned the whole world.

*Andrei Gromyko was the Soviet minister of Foreign Affairs during the Cuban missile crisis.*

*"Unilateral military intervention on the part of the United States cannot currently be either required or justified."*

# The US Is Not Attempting to Invade Cuba

### John F. Kennedy

There has been a great deal of talk on the situation in Cuba in recent days both in the Communist camp and in our own, and I would like to take this opportunity to set the matter in perspective.

In the first place it is Mr. Castro and his supporters who are in trouble. In the last year his regime has been increasingly isolated from this hemisphere. His name no longer inspires the same fear or following in other Latin American countries. He has been condemned by the OAS, excluded from the Inter-American Defense Board, and kept out of the [Latin American] Free Trade Association. By his own monumental economic mismanagement, supplemented by our refusal to trade with him, his economy has crumbled and his pledges for economic progress have been discarded, along with his pledges for political freedom. His industries are stagnating, his harvests are declining, his own followers are beginning to see that their revolution has been betrayed.

So it is not surprising that in a frantic effort to bolster his regime he should try to arouse the Cuban people by charges of an imminent American invasion and commit himself still further to a Soviet take-over in the hope of preventing his own collapse.

Ever since communism moved into Cuba in 1958, Soviet technical and military personnel have moved steadily onto the island in increasing numbers at the invitation of the Cuban government. Now that movement has been increased. It is under our most careful surveillance. But I will repeat the conclusion that I reported last week, that these new shipments do not constitute a serious threat to any other part of this hemisphere.

If the United States ever should find it necessary to take military action against communism in Cuba, all

of Castro's Communist-supplied weapons and technicians would not change the result or significantly extend the time required to achieve that result.

However, unilateral military intervention on the part of the United States cannot currently be either required or justified, and it is regrettable that loose talk about such action in this country might serve to give a thin color of legitimacy to the Communist pretense that such a threat exists. But let me make this clear once again: If at any time the Communist buildup in Cuba were to endanger or interfere with our security in any way, including our base at Guantanamo, our passage to the Panama Canal, our missile and space activities at Cape Canaveral, or the lives of American citizens in this country, or if Cuba should ever attempt to export its aggressive purposes by force or the threat of force against any nation in this hemisphere, or become an offensive military base of significant capacity for the Soviet Union, then this country will do whatever must be done to protect its own security and that of its allies.

We shall be alert to, and fully capable of dealing swiftly with, any such development. As President and Commander in Chief I have full authority now to take such action, and I have asked the Congress to authorize me to call up reserve forces should this or any other crises make it necessary.

## Preventing the Threat

In the meantime we intend to do everything within our power to prevent such a threat from coming into existence. Our friends in Latin America must realize the consequences such developments hold out for their own peace and freedom, and we shall be making further proposals to them. Our friends in NATO must realize the implications of their ships' engaging in the Cuban trade.

We shall continue to work with Cuban refugee leaders who are dedicated as we are to that nation's

John F. Kennedy, from a statement read at a news conference on September 13, 1962.

future return to freedom. We shall continue to keep the American people and the Congress fully informed. We shall increase our surveillance of the whole Caribbean area. We shall neither initiate nor permit aggression in this hemisphere.

With this in mind, while I recognize that rash talk is cheap, particularly on the part of those who did not have the responsibility, I would hope that the future record will show that the only people talking about a war and invasion at this time are the Communist spokesmen in Moscow and Havana, and that the American people, defending as we do so much of the free world, will in this nuclear age, as they have in the past, keep both their nerve and their head. . . .

> *"I have indicated that if Cuba should possess a capacity to carry out offensive actions against the United States, that the United States would act."*

I think if you read last week's statement and the statement today, I made it quite clear, particularly in last week's statement, when we talked about the presence of offensive military missile capacity or development of military bases and other indications which I gave last week, all those would, of course, indicate a change in the nature of the threat.

## Cuba's Power Cannot Be Exported

I have indicated that if Cuba should possess a capacity to carry out offensive actions against the United States, that the United States would act. I've also indicated that the United States would not permit Cuba to export its power by force in the hemisphere. The United States will make appropriate military judgments after consultation with the Joint Chiefs of Staff and others, after carefully analyzing whatever new information comes in, as to whether that point has been reached where an offensive threat does exist. And at that time the country and the Congress will be so notified. . . .

## Close Proximity a Threat

I think that the concern [over Cuba] is due to the fact that Cuba is close to the United States territory and that Cuba is obviously tying itself closer to the Communist bloc. The arrival of these weapons and technicians has caused increasing alarm by not only the Members of Congress but also by the administration and by the American people. I would think that it's part of our serious problems in which we are engaged in a tense concentration in many parts of the world at a dangerous time and it's quite natural that this action would bring a good deal of concern. I would not suggest that those who are concerned about it are motivated by political

purposes or that the Soviet judgment that they are is accurate. . . .

The United States will take whatever action the situation, as I described it, would require. As far as the threat, the United States has been living with threats for a good many years and in a good many parts of the world.

*John F. Kennedy was president of the United States from 1961 until his assassination in 1963.*

*"The arms and military equipment sent to Cuba are intended solely for defensive purposes."*

# Soviet Military Equipment Is Defensive

## The Soviet Government

The government of the U.S.S.R. considers it necessary to call the attention of all countries and of world public opinion to the provocations now being undertaken by the government of the United States of America, provocations that could plunge the world into the catastrophe of a general world war with the use of thermonuclear weapons.

Bellicose-minded reactionary forces of the United States have long been conducting unbridled propaganda in the U.S. Congress and in the American press against the Cuban Republic, calling for an attack on Cuba, an attack on Soviet ships carrying necessary goods and foodstuffs to the Cuban people—calling, in short, for war.

In the Soviet Union no particular significance was attached at first to this propaganda against peace, against humanity and humaneness....Now, however, it cannot be ignored, because the President of the United States has asked Congress to permit 150,000 reservists to be called up to the U.S. armed forces. To justify his request the President said that the United States must have "the possibility of responding quickly and effectively, if necessary, to the dangers that could arise in any part of the free world," and that he was taking this step in connection with the strengthening of the armed forces of Cuba, which, if you please, increases tension and all but creates a threat to other countries.

Such a step by the U.S. government cannot be assessed as other than a screen for the aggressive plans and intentions of the United States itself and will lead inevitably to exacerbating the international atmosphere. It is claimed that this step is intended to reduce tension. But no one has ever contended that a fire can be put out with kerosene or gasoline. It is obvious to every person in his right mind that such

steps do not lead to the relaxation of tensions but, on the contrary, serve as a means of bringing it to white heat and create a situation in which some accident could spark the catastrophe of a thermonuclear world war. Consequently, this is a provocation against peace, this is done in the interests of war, in the interests of aggression....

If one is honest and proceeds from the understanding of necessity, declared by the U.S. President himself, to live in peace, i.e., to ensure peaceful coexistence of states regardless of their social-political systems, what could have alarmed the American leaders, what is the reason for this witches' sabbath raised in Congress and in the American press around Cuba?

The trouble is, they say, that armaments and even troops are being shipped from the Soviet Union to Cuba.

### Supplying Cuba with Equipment

But we by no means hide from world public opinion that we are indeed supplying Cuba with industrial equipment and goods that are helping to strengthen her economy and raise the well-being of the Cuban people.

At the request of the Cuban government we are also sending to Cuba Soviet agronomists, machine operators, tractor drivers and zoo technicians who share their experience and knowledge with Cuban friends in order to help them improve the country's economy. We are also sending ordinary state farm workers and collective farmers to Cuba and accepting thousands of Cubans in the Soviet Union to exchange experience and teach them more progressive farming methods, to help them master the Soviet farm machinery received by Cuba.

As is known, a certain amount of armament is also being sent to Cuba from the Soviet Union at the request of the Cuban government in conection with the threats by aggressive imperialist circles. The

Statement issued by the Soviet government on September 11, 1962.

Cuban statesmen have also requested the Soviet government to send Cuba Soviet military specialists, technicians to train the Cubans in mastering up-to-date weapons, because modern weapons now require high qualifications and considerable knowledge. It is natural that Cuba does not yet have such specialists. This is why we took an understanding attitude toward this request. It must be said, however, that the number of Soviet military specialists sent to Cuba can in no way be compared with the number of agricultural and industrial personnel sent there. The arms and military equipment sent to Cuba are intended solely for defensive purposes. The President of the U.S.A. and the American military, like the military of any country, know what means of defense are. How can these means menace the United States of America?

## Soviet Union Will Extend Help

The government of the Soviet Union has authorized Tass to state also that there is no need for the Soviet Union to set up in any other country—Cuba, for instance—the weapons it has for repelling aggression, for a retaliatory blow. The explosive power of our nuclear weapons is so great and the Soviet Union has such powerful missiles for delivering these nuclear warheads that there is no need to seek sites for them somewhere beyond the boundaries of the Soviet Union. We have said and we repeat that if war is unleashed, if the aggressor attacks one or another state and the state asks for help, the Soviet Union has the capacity to extend help from its own territory to any peace-loving state, and not only to Cuba....

What reason is given for preparing aggression against Cuba? That the Soviet merchant fleet is carrying cargoes to Cuba, and in the U.S.A. these are believed to be military cargoes. But this is a purely internal affair of the states sending these cargoes and those which buy and receive them.

*"We have said and we repeat that if war is unleashed...the Soviet Union has the capacity to extend help from its own territory to any peace-loving state, and not only to Cuba."*

The whole world knows that the United States of America has surrounded the Soviet Union and other socialist countries with its military bases. What have they stationed there—tractors?...No, they have brought arms there in their ships; they are, moreover, constantly building up the stockpiles of these arms; and they claim that these armaments, set out along the frontiers of the Soviet Union...are there lawfully, by right. They consider this their right! But the U.S.A. does not allow others to do this, even in the interests of defense, and when measures are nevertheless taken to strengthen the defense capacity of one country or another, an outcry is raised in the U.S.A. and the claim is made that they want to organize an attack upon the U.S.A. What conceit! The U.S.A. apparently believes that one can turn to aggression with impunity in today's conditions....

## US Preparation Is Aggressive

The Soviet government will not follow in the path of the U.S.A., which is calling up 150,000 from the reserves. If we were to repeat the actions of the U.S.A. we would be doing apparently exactly what certain American circles want—helping them to inflame the situation. But we cannot disregard the United States' preparation of an act of aggression. The Soviet government considers it its duty to display vigilence in this situation and to instruct the Minister of Defense of the Soviet Union and the Soviet Army Command to take all measures to place our armed forces at peak military preparedness.

But these are exclusively precautionary measures. We shall do everything on our part so that peace is not disturbed.

The Soviet government appeals to the government of the United States to display common sense, not to lose self-control and to assess soberly what its actions might lead to if it unleashes war.

Instead of inflaming the situation by such actions as mobilization of reservists, which is tantamount to a threat of starting war, it would be far more sensible if the U.S. government, showing wisdom, were to make the generous gesture of establishing diplomatic and commercial relations with Cuba, the desirabiilty of which was recently stated by the Cuban government. If the American government were to show this wisdom, the peoples would assess this properly as a real U.S. contribution to relaxing international tension, to strengthening world peace.

If normal and diplomatic and trade relations were established between the United States of America and Cuba, there would be no need for Cuba to strengthen her defense capacity, her armed forces. After all, nobody would then be threatening Cuba with war or other aggressive acts and the situation would become normal.

*The Soviet government issued this statement in response to United States accusations that Soviet military equipment in Cuba was being used for offensive purposes.*

*"Cuba has been opened to a flood of Soviet weapons....Cuba has...armed itself to a degree never before seen in any Latin American country."*

# Soviet Military Equipment Is Offensive

Adlai Stevenson

The Government of the United States, like the governments of the other independent American Republics, will honor its commitments to the United Nations Charter and to the inter-American system. As we have stated so often, the United States will not commit aggression against Cuba. But let it be equally clear that the United States will not tolerate aggression against any part of this hemisphere. The United States will exercise the right of individual and collective self-defense—a right expressly recognized in the charter—against aggression in this hemisphere.

The charges made by Cuba against the United States are dictated by two factors. One is that the Castro regime has associated itself with the Communist bloc in pursuit of world domination. A tactic always used in seeking this objective is to ridicule, malign, and vilify anyone with the courage to oppose them.

The second factor is Cuba's self-inflicted exclusion from the American family of nations. The Castro regime has turned its back on its history, tradition, religion, and culture. Cuba has turned away from its neighbors, and it is at the mercy of the political riptides that sweep through the Communist world with such frequence.

Thus the other nations of the Americas are understandably anxious and alert. But vigilance cannot and should not be equated with intervention, nor alarm with aggression.

The hemisphere—and the world—were prepared to accept the original promises of the Castro government that economic and social justice would be brought to the Cuban people. But its original pledges have now been discarded by the Cuban regime, and we condemn with all the force at our command the violations of civil justice, the drumhead

executions, and the suppression of political, intellectual, and religious freedom which have been inflicted on the Cuban people.

## A Flood of Soviet Weapons

But even these excesses would not constitute a direct threat to the peace and independence of other states. However, Cuba has been opened to a flood of Soviet weapons and "technicians" and to the Soviet Union's so-called "fishing fleet," which is a long way from the fishing grounds off the north shore of Cuba. The cod and the herring, gentlemen, are a long way from the new fishing fleet's headquarters. Cuba has not only armed itself to a degree never before seen in any Latin American country, but it has also welcomed penetration by the foremost exponent of a doctrine condemned in this hemisphere as "alien" and "incompatible." What we cannot accept—and will never accept—is that Cuba has become the springboard for aggressive and subversive efforts to destroy the inter-American system, to overthrow the governments of the Americas, and to obstruct the peaceful, democratic evolution of this hemisphere toward social justice and economic development.

The statements of the President of the United States on this subject and the recent joint resolution of the Congress of the United States amply attest to this concern.

Nor can these developments be ignored by the American Republics as a whole. Let there be no doubt as to the solidarity of the nations of this hemisphere on the problem of Cuba....

In the face of this threat the foreign ministers have again unanimously reaffirmed their will to strengthen the security of the hemisphere against all aggression, from inside and outside the hemisphere, and against all developments and situations capable of threatening its peace and security.

The historic support of the members of the Organization of American States for the principles of

Adlai Stevenson, from a statement read to correspondents on October 8, 1962.

self-determination and nonintervention is well known. These principles have been enshrined in acts of inter-American conferences, antedating by decades even the conception of the United Nations.

The United States has already begun to take effective measures concerning shipping and trade with Cuba and the surveillance of traffic in arms and other strategic items in accordance with the discussions of the ministers of foreign affairs, the resolutions of the Eighth Meeting of Consultation, and other inter-American instruments.

## Defending the Hemisphere

The purpose of these measures is the collective defense of the hemisphere. As I have said, these measures have no offensive purpose.

There was incessant talk this morning about economic strangulation and economic blockade. Neither of these terms has any application to this case. The current regime in Cuba has pronounced its intention to overthrow other governments in this hemisphere. Could anyone, therefore, take part in any trade, or aid trade designed to boost the Cuban economy and to arm its military services?

To say that our self-protective actions are aggressive or a warlike gesture is absurd. It is the most normal and, indeed, the least violent way in which we can express our strong disapproval of the threats and sword rattling emanating from Cuba.

No threat to peace in this hemisphere arises out of the unanimous determination of American Republics in this regard.

---

*"Cuba has become the springboard for aggressive and subversive efforts to destroy the inter-American system."*

---

The President of Cuba professes that Cuba has always been willing to hold discussions with the United States to improve relations and to reduce tensions. But what he really wishes us to do is to place the seal of approval on the existence of a Communist regime in the Western Hemisphere. The maintenance of communism in the Americas is not negotiable. Furthermore the problem of Cuba is not a simple problem of United States-Cuban relations. It is a collective problem for all the states of this hemisphere.

If the Cuban regime is sincere in its request for negotiations and wishes to lay its grievances before the appropriate forum—the Organization of American States—I would suggest the Cuban government might start by some action calculated to awaken the confidence of the inter-American system. The obvious place to begin would be the severing of its multiple ties to the Soviet bloc.

Let no one mistake the impact of this Soviet intervention in Cuba on the hope we all share for world peace. If the Soviet Union persists in the course it has chosen, if it continues to try to prevent the peaceful social revolution of the Americas, it will increasingly excite the deep indignation of the people of my country and of other American states. The result will be to make the resolution of issues far more difficult in every other part of the world. A consequence of this gratuitous Soviet initiative is to postpone even further the hope for world stabilization. I cannot state this point with sufficient gravity.

## The Tragedy of Cuba

The tragedy of Cuba is still unfolding. How short has been the time since the two continents of the Western Hemisphere acclaimed the downfall of the Batista dictatorship and hailed what promised to be a democratic and progressive revolution. How quickly that promise was replaced by a reign of terror, confiscation, and the suppression of political, intellectual, and religious freedom.

Just as fear is the first piece of oppression, it would also have been the final price, if the Cuban oppressor had not been saved from the Cuban people by the Soviet Union. How many times in history has fear of the people's wrath driven tyrants to sell their nation to more powerful tyrants?

Can the Cuban electorate send the Russian forces home? Do the Cuban leaders dare face their people without these alien protectors? A country bristling with Soviet missiles and "protectors" is your answer.

## The Grip of Soviet Domination

We will constantly work to reassure the Cuban people that they have not been forgotten or abandoned and make clear to freedom-loving Cubans, both within and without that country, that they can count on the sympathy and support of the American people in their efforts to escape the grip of Soviet domination and recapture their own revolution. We did this for those who sought the overthrow of Batista. We can do no less today....

If the Cuban regime wishes to establish normal friendly relations in this hemisphere, let it return to the concepts and obligations of the inter-American system, let it cease its subservience to the Soviet Union, let it cease to be an avenue of intervention, which threatens the fundamental principles and the peace and security of all its neighbors with an alien doctrine.

The way is clear, and the choice is Cuba's.

*Adlai Stevenson was the US representative to the United Nations during the Kennedy Administration.*

*"Unmistakable evidence has established
the fact that a series of offensive missile
sites is now in preparation."*

viewpoint **31**

# The Soviets Must Remove
# Missile Bases from Cuba

John F. Kennedy

Good evening, my fellow citizens. This Government, as promised, has maintained the closest surveillance of the Soviet military buildup on the island of Cuba. Within the past week unmistakable evidence has established the fact that a series of offensive missile sites is now in preparation on that imprisoned island. The purpose of these bases can be none other than to provide a nuclear strike capability against the Western Hemisphere.

Upon receiving the first preliminary hard information of this nature last Tuesday morning [October 16] at 9:00 a.m., I directed that our surveillance be stepped up. And having now confirmed and completed our evaluation of the evidence and our decision on a course of action, this Government feels obliged to report this new crisis to you in fullest detail.

The characteristics of these new missile sites indicate two distinct types of installations. Several of them include medium-range ballistic missiles capable of carrying a nuclear warhead for a distance of more than 1,000 nautical miles. Each of these missiles, in short, is capable of striking Washington, D.C., the Panama Canal, Cape Canaveral, Mexico City, or any other city in the southeastern part of the United States, in Central America, or in the Caribbean area.

Additional sites not yet completed appear to be designed for intermediate-range ballistic missiles capable of traveling more than twice as far—and thus capable of striking most of the major cities in the Western Hemisphere, ranging as far north as Hudson Bay, Canada, and as far south as Lima, Peru. In addition, jet bombers, capable of carrying nuclear weapons, are now being uncrated and assembled in Cuba, while the necessary air bases are being prepared.

This urgent transformation of Cuba into an important strategic base—by the presence of these large, long-range, and clearly offensive weapons of sudden mass destruction—constitutes an explicit threat to the peace and security of all the Americas, in flagrant and deliberate defiance of the Rio Pact of 1947, the traditions of this nation and hemisphere, the Joint Resolution of the 87th Congress, the Charter of the United Nations, and my own public warnings to the Soviets on September 4 and 13.

## Contradicting Repeated Assurances

This action also contradicts the repeated assurances of Soviet spokesmen, both publicly and privately delivered, that the arms buildup in Cuba would retain its original defensive character and that the Soviet Union had no need or desire to station strategic missiles on the territory of any other nation.

The size of this undertaking makes clear that it has been planned for some months. Yet only last month, after I had made clear the distinction between any introduction of ground-to-ground missiles and the existence of defensive antiaircraft missiles, the Soviet Government publicly stated on September 11 that, and I quote, "The armaments and military equipment sent to Cuba are designed exclusively for defensive purposes," and, and I quote the Soviet Government, "There is no need for the Soviet Government to shift its weapons for a retaliatory blow to any other country, for instance Cuba," and that, and I quote the Government, "The Soviet Union has so powerful rockets to carry these nuclear warheads that there is no need to search for sites for them beyond the boundaries of the Soviet Union." That statement was false.

Only last Thursday, as evidence of this rapid offensive buildup was already in my hand, Soviet Foreign Minister Gromyko told me in my office that he was instructed to make it clear once again, as he said his Government had already done, that Soviet

John F. Kennedy, from the address to the nation on October 22, 1962.

assistance to Cuba, and I quote, "pursued solely the purpose of contributing to the defense capabilities of Cuba," that, and I quote him, "training by Soviet specialists of Cuban nationals in handling defensive armaments was by no means offensive," and that "if it were otherwise," Mr. Gromyko went on, "the Soviet Government would never become involved in rendering such assistance." That statement was also false.

## Deliberate Deception

Neither the United States of America nor the world community of nations can tolerate deliberate deception and offensive threats on the part of any nation, large or small. We no longer live in a world where only the actual firing of weapons represents a sufficient challenge to a nation's security to constitute maximum peril. Nuclear weapons are so destructive and ballistic missiles are so swift that any substantially increased possibility of their use or any sudden change in their deployment may well be regarded as a definite threat to peace.

For many years both the Soviet Union and the United States, recognizing this fact, have deployed strategic nuclear weapons with great care, never upsetting the precarious *status quo* which insured that these weapons would not be used in the absence of some vital challenge. Our own strategic missiles have never been transferred to the territory of any other nation under a cloak of secrecy and deception: and our history, unlike that of the Soviets since the end of World War II, demonstrates that we have no desire to dominate or conquer any other nation or impose our system upon its people. Nevertheless, American citizens have become adjusted to living daily on the bull's eye of Soviet missiles located inside the U.S.S.R. or in submarines.

In that sense missiles in Cuba add to an already clear and present danger—although it should be noted the nations of Latin America have never previously been subjected to a potential nuclear threat.

---

*"Our own strategic missiles have never been transferred to the territory of any other nation under a cloak of secrecy and deception."*

---

But this secret, swift, and extraordinary buildup of Communist missiles—in an area well known to have a special and historical relationship to the United States and the nations of the Western Hemisphere, in violation of Soviet assurances, and in defiance of American and hemispheric policy—this sudden, clandestine decision to station strategic weapons for the first time outside of Soviet soil—is a deliberately provocative and unjustified change in the *status quo*

which cannot be accepted by this country if our courage and our commitments are ever to be trusted again by either friend or foe.

The 1930's taught us a clear lesson: Aggressive conduct, if allowed to grow unchecked and unchallenged, ultimately leads to war. This nation is opposed to war. We are also true to our word. Our unswerving objective, therefore, must be to prevent the use of these missiles against this or any other country and to secure their withdrawal or elimination from the Western Hemisphere.

## Further Action Required

Our policy has been one of patience and restraint, as befits a peaceful and powerful nation, which leads a worldwide alliance. We have been determined not to be diverted from our central concerns by mere irritants and fanatics. But now further action is required—and it is underway; and these actions may only be the beginning. We will not prematurely or unnecessarily risk the costs of worldwide nuclear war in which even the fruits of victory would be ashes in our mouth—but neither will we shrink from that risk at any time it must be faced.

Acting, therefore, in the defense of our own security and of the entire Western Hemisphere, and under the authority entrusted to me by the Constitution as endorsed by the resolution of the Congress, I have directed that the following *initial* steps be taken immediately:

*First:* To halt this offensive buildup, a strict quarantine on all offensive military equipment under shipment to Cuba is being initiated. All ships of any kind bound for Cuba from whatever nation or port will, if found to contain cargoes of offensive weapons, be turned back. This quarantine will be extended, if needed, to other types of cargo and carriers. We are not at this time, however, denying the necessities of life as the Soviets attempted to do in their Berlin blockade of 1948.

*Second:* I have directed the continued and increased close surveillance of Cuba and its military buildup. The Foreign Ministers of the OAS in their communique of October 3 rejected secrecy on such matters in this hemisphere. Should these offensive military preparations continue, thus increasing the threat to the hemisphere, further action will be justified. I have directed the Armed Forces to prepare for any eventualities; and I trust that, in the interest of both the Cuban people and the Soviet technicians at the sites, the hazards to all concerned of continuing this threat will be recognized.

*Third:* It shall be the policy of this nation to regard any nuclear missile launched from Cuba against any nation in the Western Hemisphere as an attack by the Soviet Union on the United States, requiring a full retaliatory response upon the Soviet Union.

*Fourth:* As a necessary military precaution I have reinforced our base at Guantanamo, evacuated today the dependents of our personnel there, and ordered additional military units to be on a standby alert basis.

*Fifth:* We are calling tonight for an immediate meeting of the Organ of Consultation, under the Organization of American States, to consider this threat to hemispheric security and to invoke articles 6 and 8 of the Rio Treaty in support of all necessary action. The United Nations Charter allows for regional security arrangements—and the nations of this hemisphere decided long ago against the military presence of outside powers. Our other allies around the world have also been alerted.

*Sixth:* Under the Charter of the United Nations, we are asking tonight that an emergency meeting of the Security Council be convoked without delay to take action against this latest Soviet threat to world peace. Our resolution will call for the prompt dismantling and withdrawal of all offensive weapons in Cuba, under the supervision of U.N. observers, before the quarantine can be lifted.

## A Provocative Threat to Peace

*Seventh and finally:* I call upon Chairman Khrushchev to halt and eliminate this clandestine, reckless, and provocative threat to world peace and to stable relations between our two nations. I call upon him further to abandon this course of world domination and to join in an historic effort to end the perilous arms race and transform the history of man. He has an opportunity now to move the world back from the abyss of destruction—by returning to his Government's own words that it had no need to station missiles outside its own territory, and withdrawing these weapons from Cuba—by refraining from any action which will widen or deepen the present crisis—and then by participating in a search for peaceful and permanent solutions.

This nation is prepared to present its case against the Soviet threat to peace, and our own proposals for a peaceful world, at any time and in any form—in the OAS, in the United Nations, or in any other meeting that could be useful—without limiting our freedom of action.

We have in the past made strenuous efforts to limit the spread of nuclear weapons. We have proposed the elimination of all arms and military bases in a fair and effective disarmament treaty. We are prepared to discuss new proposals for the removal of tensions on both sides—including the possibilities of a genuinely independent Cuba, free to determine its own destiny. We have no wish to war with the Soviet Union, for we are a peaceful people who desire to live in peace with all other peoples.

But it is difficult to settle or even discuss these problems in an atmosphere of intimidation. That is why this latest Soviet threat—or any other threat which is made either independently or in response to our actions this week—must and will be met with

determination. Any hostile move anywhere in the world against the safety and freedom of peoples to whom we are committed—including in particular the brave people of West Berlin—will be met by whatever action is needed....

---

*"[Khrushchev] has an opportunity now to move the world back from the abyss of destruction. . . by withdrawing these weapons from Cuba."*

---

My fellow citizens, let no one doubt that this is a difficult and dangerous effort on which we have set out. No one can foresee precisely what course it will take or what costs or casualties will be incurred. Many months of sacrifice and self-discipline lie ahead—months in which both our patience and our will will be tested, months in which many threats and denunciations will keep us aware of our dangers. But the greatest danger of all would be to do nothing.

## Full of Hazards

The path we have chosen for the present is full of hazards, as all paths are; but it is the one most consistent with our character and courage as a nation and our commitments around the world. The cost of freedom is always high—but Americans have always paid it. And one path we shall never choose, and that is the path of surrender or submission.

Our goal is not the victory of might but the vindication of right—not peace at the expense of freedom, but both peace *and* freedom, here in this hemisphere and, we hope, around the world. God willing, that goal will be achieved.

*John F. Kennedy served as US president from 1961 until his assassination in 1963. When it became known that Soviet offensive missiles were being installed in Cuba in 1962, he ordered a naval "quarantine" of the island. At the brink of nuclear war, Premier Khrushchev ordered the removal of the missiles.*

> *"We saw a possibility of protecting the freedom-loving people of Cuba by installing rockets there so that American imperialists...would realize...the dangers of thermo-nuclear war."*

viewpoint **32**

# The US Demand Endangered Peace

Nikita S. Khrushchev

Everyone still remembers the tense days of October when mankind was anxiously listening to the news coming from the Caribbean. In those days the world was on the brink of a thermo-nuclear catastrophe.

What created this crisis? How did it develop? What lessons must be learned from it? These questions call for a penetrating analysis which will help the peace forces better to understand the resulting situation and to define their tasks in the struggle for the further maintenance and consolidation of peace....

The victory of the revolution in Cuba and her success in building a new life gave rise to an outburst of malice among the imperialist circles of the United States of America.

The imperialists are frightened of Cuba because of her ideas. They do not want to reconcile themselves to the idea that little Cuba has dared to live and develop independently, as her people want to, and not in the way which would please the American monopolies. But the question of how people are to live, what road they are to take, is an internal matter for each people!

Flouting the generally accepted standards of international relations, the United States' reactionary forces have been doing everything from the first day of the victory of the Cuban revolution to overthrow Cuba's revolutionary government and to restore their domination there. They broke off diplomatic relations with Cuba, have conducted and are conducting subversive activity and established an economic blockade of Cuba.

Threatening to apply sanctions, the United States began to press its allies not only to stop trading with Cuba, but even not to make ships available to carry food to Cuba from the socialist countries which came to the assistance of their brothers. This is an anti-human policy—a desire to starve a whole nation.

Nikita S. Khrushchev, from a report to the Supreme Soviet concerning the Cuban missile crisis on December 12, 1962.

But even this seemed insufficient to them. Assuming the functions of a policeman, they decided to take the path of military suppression of the Cuban revolution. In other words, they wanted to usurp the right to export counter-revolution.

## US Policy Unbridled and Reactionary

United States policy *vis-a-vis* Cuba is the most unbridled and reactionary policy. To declare that Cuba threatens America, or any other country, and on this plea to usurp a special right to act against Cuba, is just monstrous.

Seeking to justify its aggressive actions, American reaction is repeating that the crisis in the Caribbean was created by Cuba herself, adding that blame also rests with the Soviet Union which shipped rockets and IL-28 bombers there.

Yet is this so? It is true that we carried weapons there at the request of the Cuban government. But by what motives were we guided in doing that? Exclusively, humanitarian motives—Cuba needed weapons as a means of deterring the aggressors, and not as a means of attack. For Cuba was under a real threat of invasion. Piratical attacks were repeatedly being made on her coasts; Havana was shelled, and airborne groups were dropped from planes in order to carry out sabotage.

A large-scale military invasion of Cuba by counter-revolutionary mercenaries was launched on Cuba in April of last year. This invasion was prepared and carried out with full support on the part of the United States.

Further events have shown that the failure of the invasion did not discourage the United States imperialists in their desire to strangle Cuba. They began preparing another attack. In the autumn of this year a very alarming situation was created. Everything indicated that the United States was preparing to attack the Cuban Republic, with its own armed forces.

Revolutionary Cuba was compelled to take all measures to strengthen her defence. The Soviet Union helped her to build up a strong standing guard over the achievements of the Cuban people. In view of the mounting threat from the United States, the government of Cuba, in the summer of this year, requested the Soviet government to render further assistance.

Agreement was reached on a number of new measures, including the stationing of a couple of score of Soviet IRBMs (Intermediate Range Ballistic Missiles) in Cuba. These weapons were to be in the hands of Soviet military men.

What were the aims behind this decision? Naturally neither we nor our Cuban friends had in mind that this small number of IRBMs sent to Cuba would be used for an attack on the United States or any other country.

---

## "Our aim was only to defend Cuba."

---

Our aim was only to defend Cuba. Everybody saw how the American imperialists were sharpening their knives and threatening Cuba with a massed attack. We could not remain impartial observers in face of this bandit-like policy which was contrary to all the standards governing relations between states and contrary to the United Nations Charter. We decided to extend a helping hand to Cuba. We saw a possibility of protecting the freedom-loving people of Cuba by installing rockets there so that the American imperialists, if they really decided to invade, would realize that the war which they threatened to start stood at their own borders, so that they would realize more realistically the dangers of thermo-nuclear war. . . .

### Lies About Cuba

Some people pretend that the rockets were supplied by us for an attack on the United States. This, of course, is not wise reasoning. Why should we station rockets in Cuba for this purpose, when we were and are able to strike from our own territory, possessing as we do the necessary number of intercontinental missiles of the required range and power.

We do not in general need military bases abroad. All people who have any understanding of military matters know that in the age of intercontinental and global rockets, Cuba—that small far-away island which is only fifty kilometers wide in some places—is of no strategic importance for the defence of the Soviet Union. We stationed rockets in Cuba only for the defence of the Cuban Republic, and not for an attack on the United States. Such a small country as Cuba cannot, naturally, build up forces such as could launch an offensive against so big a country as the United States.

Only people who have taken leave of their senses can claim that the Soviet Union chose Cuba as a springboard for an invasion of the American continent—of the United States or countries of Latin America. If we wanted to start a war against the United States, we would not have agreed to dismantle the rockets installed in Cuba, which were ready for launching, for battle. We would have used them. But we did not do that, because we did not pursue such aims.

Thus, all the talk about Cuba being converted into a base for an attack on the United States of America is a vicious lie. The purpose of that lie was to cover up the plans for aggression against Cuba. We are loyal to Lenin's principles of peaceful co-existence and we consider that all disputes among states should be settled by peaceful means, by means of negotiations.

Developments in the Caribbean confirmed that there was a threat of such aggression. In the last ten days of October, a large-scale build-up of US naval and air forces, paratroopers and marines began in the south of the United States, on the approaches to Cuba. The US government sent reinforcements to its naval base at Guantanamo, lying on Cuban territory. Big military manoeuvres were announced in the Caribbean. In the course of those 'manoeuvres,' a landing was to be made on the island of Vieques. On 22 October, Kennedy's administration announced a quarantine of Cuba. The word 'quarantine,' by the way, was merely a fig-leaf in this case. Actually, it was a blockade, piracy on the high seas.

Events developed rapidly. The American command alerted all its armed forces, including its troops in Europe, and also the Sixth Fleet in the Mediterranean and the Seventh Fleet based in the area of Taiwan.

Several airborne infantry and armoured divisions, numbering about 100,000 men, were set aside for an attack on Cuba alone. Moreover, 183 warships with 85,000 naval personnel were moved to the shores of Cuba. The landing on Cuba was to be covered by several thousand military planes. Close to 20 per cent of all the planes of the US strategic air command were kept in the air round the clock, carrying atom and hydrogen bombs. Reservists were called up.

The troops of the United States NATO allies in Europe were also put on the alert. A joint command was set up by the United States and Latin American countries, and some of these countries sent warships to take part in the blockade of Cuba. As a result of these aggressive steps on the part of the US government there arose a threat of thermo-nuclear war.

### Soviet Union Only Responded

In the face of these intensified military preparations, we, for our part, had to take appropriate measures. The Soviet government instructed the USSR minister of defence to alert all the armed forces of the Soviet Union, and above all the Soviet intercontinental and strategic rocket forces, the rocket anti-aircraft defences and the fighter command, the strategic air command, and the navy. Our submarine fleet, including atomic submarines, took up assigned positions. A state of increased military readiness was announced in the ground forces, and the discharge of servicemen of senior age groups from the strategic rocket forces, the anti-aircraft defence forces and the submarine fleet was halted.

The armed forces of the Warsaw Treaty countries were also fully alerted.

In these conditions, if one or the other side had not shown restraint, had not done everything necessary to avert the outbreak of war, an explosion would have followed with irreparable consequences.

Now, when the tension caused by the events in the Caribbean has been reduced, when we are in the last stage of settling the conflict, I should like to report to the Deputies of the Supreme Soviet what the Soviet government did to extinguish the approaching flames of war.

On 23 October, immediately after the United States had proclaimed the blockade of Cuba, the Soviet government, besides taking defensive measures, issued a statement resolutely warning that the United States government was assuming a grave responsibility for the fate of the peace and was recklessly playing with fire. We frankly told the United States president that we would not tolerate piratical actions by United States ships on the high seas and that we would take appropriate measures with this object in view.

At the same time the Soviet government urged all peoples to bar the road to the aggressors. Simultaneously it took certain steps in the United Nations. The peaceful initiative of the Soviet government in settling the Cuban crisis met with full support from the socialist countries and the peoples of most other United Nations member states. The United Nations secretary-general, U Thant, made great efforts to settle the conflict.

## An Attack on Cuba

However, the government of the United States of America continued to worsen the situation. Militarist forces in the United States were pushing developments towards an attack on Cuba. On the morning of 27 October, we received informations from the Cuban comrades and from other sources which bluntly said that the invasion would be carried out within the next two or three days. We assessed the messages received as a signal of the utmost alarm. And this was a well-founded alarm.

Immediate action was needed to prevent an invasion of Cuba and to preserve peace. A message proposing a mutually acceptable solution was sent to the United States president. At that moment it was not yet too late to extinguish the fuse of war which had already been set alight. In sending this message we took into consideration the fact that the messages of the president himself had expressed anxiety and a desire to find a way out of the existing situation. We declared that if the United States undertook not to invade Cuba and would also restrain other states allied with it from aggression against Cuba, the Soviet Union would be willing to remove from Cuba the weapons which the United States described as 'offensive.'

The United States president replied by declaring that if the Soviet government agreed to remove these weapons from Cuba the American government would lift the quarantine, i.e. the blockade, and would give an assurance on renunciation of the invasion of Cuba both by the United States itself and other countries of the western hemisphere. The president declared quite definitely, and this is known to the whole world, that the United States would not attack Cuba and would also restrain its allies from such actions.

## Who Won?

But we shipped our weapons to Cuba precisely for the purpose of preventing aggression against her. That was why the Soviet government reaffirmed its agreement to remove the ballistic rockets from Cuba.

*"Cuba—that small far-away island which is only fifty kilometers wide in some places—is of no strategic importance for the defence of the Soviet Union."*

Thus, briefly speaking, a mutually acceptable solution was achieved, which meant a victory for reason, a success for the cause of peace. The Cuban question entered into the stage of peaceful talks and, as regards the United States, was, so to speak, transferred from the generals to the diplomats....

Which side triumphed? Who won? In this connection it can be said that it was reason, the cause of peace and the security of peoples that won. The two sides displayed a sober approach and took into account that unless such steps were taken as could help to overcome the dangerous development of events, a Third World War might break out....

## US and USSR Like Two Goats

Now let us imagine for a minute what could have happened had we copied diehard politicians and refused to make mutual concessions. It would have been like the two goats in the folk tale who met on a footbridge over a chasm and having locked their horns refused to make way for each other.

As is well known, both crashed into the chasm. But is this a reasonable course for human beings?

Among the ruling circles of the United States there are some politicians who are rightly called 'madmen.' The 'madmen' insisted and continue to insist on starting war as soon as possible against the Soviet Union and the countries of the socialist camp. Is it not clear that if we had taken an uncompromising position, we would only have helped the camp of the 'madmen' to take advantage of the situation in order to strike a blow at Cuba and touch off a world war?

*"We shipped our weapons to Cuba precisely for the purpose of preventing aggression against her."*

In justice, it should be noted that among the leading circles of the United States, there are also some people who take a more sane view of the situation and, considering the present balance of forces in the international arena, realize that, if the United States touched off a war, it would not win it, and would fail to achieve its purpose....

## Unwise and Dangerous

Why do I recall such rather unpleasant things as intercontinental missiles and atomic submarines? Merely because we are compelled to do this by the irresponsible statements of certain leaders of the United States and their allies.

When the events around Cuba were at their height, and danger was crackling in the air, many people in the west said it was necessary to seek a reasonable solution of disputes in order to prevent war. But now, when the shock has passed, so to speak, some of them are beginning to say that disputes should be settled on the basis of concessions by one side. This is an unwise and dangerous policy.

We are not surprised that the tune in the discordant choir of advocates of a 'tough line' is called by his like....

I should like to tell Herr 'Cold War' Chancellor that there was no cause for him to rejoice at the 'toughness' of the west which allegedly forced us to withdraw rockets from Cuba. I can assure you, Herr Chancellor, that when we decided to install forty rockets in Cuba, we did not touch the 'share,' so to speak, reserved for you, should you start aggression in Europe.

## Rockets Returned from Cuba

Now, when our rockets have returned from Cuba—to your 'satisfaction'—we have added them to the defensive means protecting our western frontiers.

Why then do you rejoice, Herr Adenauer? It would appear that you have forgotten the elementary rule of arithmetic that the sum total—in this case, the power of Soviet retaliation—does not depend on the order of the items.

It should be said that now the situation has become calmer in the world, 'toughness' is advocated not only by Adenauer, but by some other leaders as well.

Thus, the British foreign minister, Lord Home, said the other day that there are some signs that following the sobering experience of Cuba the Russians might possibly reconsider their role in the international community, that is to say, might begin to yield to the NATO bloc in everything. He said this is how the Soviet Union should 'apply' the lessons of Cuba now.

The British foreign minister should know that the Soviet Union always considers the lessons of international events. Those, however, who now advocate a 'tough policy' with regard to the Soviet Union, would do well to consider that if such a crisis recurs, and if this time it proves impossible to arrest the dangerous drift of events, Britain, together with her allies, would be plunged directly into the vortex of a catastrophe, and it would then be too late to do anything.

Warlike calls for 'toughness' have again begun to be made in the United States, too. What can we say of such imprudent boasters?

It is not precluded that some madmen may start a war. But if they start it, then even a thousand wise people will be hard put to stop it. This is known from history.

*Nikita S. Khrushchev led the Soviet Union as its premier and first secretary of the Communist Party from 1953 to 1964.*

*"Hard-headed detente must be based on a strength of arms and strength of will sufficient to blunt the threat of Soviet blackmail."*

# US Policy Toward Détente

Richard M. Nixon

The door to real peace must be unlocked. Two keys are required to open it. The United States has one; the Soviet Union has the other. Unless the superpowers adopt a new live-and-let-live relationship, the world will not see real peace in this century. If we fail to work toward that end, suicidal war is inevitable. If we succeed in reaching it, not only does world war become avoidable, but world peace becomes possible. Working against each other, the superpowers will enter a spiral of escalating differences that could lead to war. Working together, they can be an irresistible force for peace not only for themselves but for others as well.

## Difficulties of Achieving Peace

Never has real peace been so necessary and yet so difficult to achieve. The stark truth is that the ideologies and the foreign policies of the superpowers are diametrically opposed. The struggle between the Soviet Union and the United States is between an avowedly and manifestly aggressive power and an avowedly and manifestly defensive one, between a totalitarian civilization and a free one, between a state that is frightened by the idea of freedom and one that is founded on it.

The United States wants peace; the Soviet Union wants the world. Our foreign policy respects the freedom of other nations; theirs tries to destroy it. We are interested in peace as an end in itself; they are interested in it only if it serves their ends. The Soviets pursue those ends unscrupulously, by means short of all-out war. They lie, cheat, subvert governments, disrupt elections, subsidize terrorists, and wage wars by proxy. For the Soviets, peace is a continuation of war by other means.

Russians and Americans can be friends. But the governments of the Soviet Union and the United

States can never be friends because their interests are irreconcilable. The peace we seek cannot be based on mutual friendship. It can only be grounded on mutual respect for each other's strength.

We will continue to have political differences that will drive us apart. We must also recognize, however, that the United States and the Soviet Union have two common interests that can draw us together. As the world's two greatest military powers, we both want to avoid a major war that neither of us would survive. As the world's two major economic powers—each can cooperate in ways that could benefit both of us immensely.

We must not delude ourselves into believing that the East-West struggle is the result of a giant misunderstanding that can be overcome if we sit down and talk it over. We can form Soviet-American friendship societies or tip vodka glasses with Kremlin leaders, but it will not lead to peace. That approach assumes the Soviets share with the West a "sincere" desire for peace. But as Ambassador Charles Bohlen told me in 1959, "Trying to determine whether the Soviet leaders are sincere about anything is a useless exercise." Pointing to a coffee table, he added, "They are pure materialists. You can no more describe them as being sincere than you could describe that table as being sincere."

If our differences are so intractable, is peace possible? Our differences make a perfect, ideal peace impossible, but our common interests make a pragmatic, real peace achievable. We are entering a new phase of the East-West struggle. In view of the verbal missiles rocketing between Washington and Moscow, we might conclude that the chances for peace are remote. But if we look beyond the rhetoric to the realities, we can be more optimistic. The table is set for a breakthrough toward real peace.

In working for peace, we must not pursue the unachievable at the expense of the attainable. Neither we nor the Soviets can compromise our basic values.

Only if we recognize that we are not going to settle our differences can we avoid going to war over them. The most we can hope to achieve is an agreement establishing peaceful rules of engagement for our continuing conflict. If we cannot walk arm-in-arm down the road toward peace, we must try at least to walk side-by-side....

## Hard-Headed Detente

To keep the peace and defend our freedom, we need to adopt a policy of hard-headed detente. "Detente" has become a notorious codeword. The debate over the word has become so charged with emotion that substance gives way to semantics. We must therefore be clear about what hard-headed detente is and what it is not.

Hard-headed detente is a combination of detente with deterrence. It is not an entente, which is an agreement between powers with common interests, nor is it a synonym for appeasement. It does not mean that the United States and the Soviet Union *agree*. Rather it means that we profoundly *disagree*. It provides a means of peacefully resolving those disagreements that can be resolved, and of living with those that cannot.

---

*"To keep the peace and defend our freedom, we need to adopt a policy of hard-headed detente."*

---

Hard-headed detente must be based on a strength of arms and strength of will sufficient to blunt the threat of Soviet blackmail. This should be combined with a mixture of prospective rewards for good behavior and penalties for bad behavior that gives the Soviet Union a positive incentive to keep the peace rather than break it. We must make it clear to the Soviets through our strength and our will that when they threaten our interests, they are risking war. If we simultaneously engage them in a process of resolving our differences where possible, we can turn their attention toward the promise of peace.

There are those who say that detente was merely an attempt to contain the Soviet Union by tying it down in "a delicate web of interdependence." Hard-headed detente as we practiced it did not rely on anything so flimsy. We were prepared to stop Soviet aggression, direct and indirect, not only with diplomatic pressures, but also military ones. We did not reassure those who were threatening our interests that we would not use force unless attacked. Instead, we told them that we would do whatever was necessary to defend our interests and those of our allies. What was even more important, they knew we had the will to back up our words. We did not wring our hands when it became necessary to use military force or the threat of force. Our record established our credibility, and the Soviets respected it.

## Detente Worked

As we practiced it from 1969 through 1974, hard-headed detente worked. During that period, we used a combination of military and diplomatic pressures to block Soviet advances. We were prepared, if necessary, to give direct or indirect military aid to any country they threatened. We also undertook negotiations with the Soviets on a broad range of issues. Some, like arms control and the settlement of World War II debts, were of mutual interest. Others, like the granting of Most Favored Nation status and the purchase of American grain, were of particular interest to the Soviets. That gave us leverage over them. When they threatened our interests, we slowed or suspended those negotiations. When they relented, we proceeded with them.

As a result, not one nation was lost to the Soviet bloc during this period....

## Soviets Undermined Detente

The Soviet Union and its apologists are quick to blame the United States for the demise of detente. There is fault on both sides, but far more on the Soviet side....

But it was the Soviets who put the nails in the coffin of detente. They destroyed detente by their support of the North Vietnamese offensive in South Vietnam that violated the Paris peace agreements and by their expansionism throughout the Third World....

## Restoring the Military Balance

A renewed policy of hard-headed detente can reduce the other dangers greatly. Today, hard-headed detente requires us to restore fully the military balance of power and at the same time to negotiate meaningful arms control agreements. It requires us to use the West's economic power, through strictly regulated East-West trade, to give the Soviets an incentive for peace. And it requires us to establish a process of negotiation and summitry that will weave these strands together into the fabric of real peace.

*Restoring the military balance.* Our first goal must be to take the profit out of war. Aggressors wage war if they think they can gain something by it. To deter war we must remain powerful enough so that potential aggressors will conclude that they stand to lose far more than they could possibly gain from war. Thus it is essential that we restore the military balance of power....

The Soviet Union is an admittedly and avowedly offensive power. Its leaders' stated goal is world domination, and they have been pursuing that end by every means at their disposal. The Soviet Union does not arm itself for defensive reasons. The leaders in the Kremlin stand behind the aggressors in virtually every one of the world's hotspots and have instigated every postwar confrontation between the superpowers....

As President Eisenhower, no dewy-eyed dove, once said, "This country could choke itself to death piling up military expenditures just as surely as it can defeat itself by not spending enough for protection."

## Arms Control

The issue of arms control cannot be separated from the question of national security. They are intimately intertwined. Realistically conducted, arms control negotiations can contribute to real peace. Naively pursued, they can increase the risk of war....

We should not pursue arms control as an end in itself. It is dangerous to assume that any arms control agreement is better than none....

## Arms Control Can Increase War Danger

While we must seek arms control agreements, we must not overestimate what they can accomplish. A bad agreement will increase the risk of war. Not even the best agreement imaginable would solve all our problems. If the United States and the Soviet Union cut their nuclear arsenals in half, a goal that is beyond the wildest dreams of even the most optimistic arms control negotiator on either side, we would still have enough weapons to destroy each other many times over. If we were to make such drastic arms reductions, a nuclear war would be just as devastating as it would be today.

---

*"Hard-headed detente gives the Kremlin leaders a choice between aggression and restraint."*

---

If we are to reduce the risk and danger of war, we must leapfrog the sterile arms control debate and go to the heart of the problem: the political differences between the United States and the Soviet Union and the policies we can initiate that will deter the Soviets from resorting to war to resolve those differences....

Our primary goal should be to build a new relationship with the Soviets in which we will be able to prevail upon them to cease their aggression. This can only happen when the bilateral relationship with us becomes more important to them than their adventurism....

## Differences Cannot Be Overcome

A major communist head of state in Eastern Europe recently remarked to me that the last 60 years have seen a curious reversal in the rhetoric of East and West. The communists used to say that capitalism was collapsing, and now the capitalists are saying that communism is collapsing. He then observed,

"Perhaps both are wrong."

He was right. We have differences with the Soviets that we will never overcome. We will never condone their conquests and will always oppose their expansionist policies. But we cannot wish them away. They are there, so we have to deal with them. How we deal with them will determine whether we achieve real peace.

We should avoid hot rhetoric, but we should not mince words. If the world is to have real peace, the Soviets must change their aggressive ways. Their persistence in expanding their influence and control by violent means will sooner or later end in war. And the chances are good that such a war will end the world.

Winston Churchill once said, "I cannot forecast to you the action of Russia. It is a riddle wrapped in a mystery inside an enigma; but perhaps there is a key. That key is Russian national interest." Hard-headed detente is not a magic wand that will with one wave instantly make over the ruthless men in the Kremlin. It is a policy that will lead them to cooperate in the search for real peace because it is in their interest to do so.

Hard-headed detente gives the Kremlin leaders a choice between aggression and restraint. If they choose the first, the danger of war will escalate and the burden of arms will become unbearable. The world will be an increasingly perilous place to live in. If they choose the second, we can reduce the risk of war and reap the fruits of real peace. We will still have our conflicts, but these will not lead to war. If we act together, the United States and the Soviet Union can contribute to peace for ourselves and for others. If we continue to act against each other, peace has no chance.

*Richard M. Nixon was president of the United States from 1969 to 1974. He resigned in 1974 because of the Watergate scandal. One of his accomplishments was the agreements he signed with the Soviets on arms control.*

*"The Soviet Union has always been and remains a consistent champion of the cause of peace, the freedom and independence of nations."*

# USSR Policy Toward Détente

Yuri Andropov

In this country the communist has been and remains invariably the leading figure in town and country. As Leonid Brezhnev has said, the communist has never had, nor has he now, any special benefits or privileges except for one privilege and one duty—to lead the way in an attack in wartime and to give more strength and energy than others for the common cause in peacetime, to struggle and work better than others for the triumph of the great ideas of Marxism–Leninism. Today, as in the past, the communists are leading the way, setting splendid examples of selfless work, intolerance of manifestations of negligence and mismanagement, breaches of labour discipline and offenders against socialist morals. It is the duty of every communist to stand up vigorously for his convictions, to encourage people, to inspire them with confidence and determination, to lead them in all situations.

The constructive efforts of Karelia's working people are guided by the Republic's Party organization, a time-tested and battle-hardened contingent of the Leninist Party. At all stages of the formation and development of Soviet Karelia its party organization stirred its people to action in peacetime and in wartime, and led them along the right path charted by the Party's Central Committee.

There is no doubt that today too the communists of Karelia will be in the vanguard of the production front of this country. Karelia's working people will indisputably achieve still better results in all areas of communist construction.

## Inflexible Faith in Communism

The Soviet people are confronted by great and inspiring tasks. They have gained a secure foothold for attaining successfully the targets set by the 25th Party Congress. The Party pursues a time-tested economic and social policy on scientific principles in keeping with the great Marxist–Leninist theory. We have inflexible faith in our righteous cause and the wise leadership of the Soviet Communist Party.

The seventies, particularly their first half, were marked by important changes in world politics, the growth of the positive processes which have come to be known as *detente.* Relations between states belonging to different social systems have been developed with growing reliance on the principles of peaceful coexistence, which have provided the basis for developing mutually beneficial political, economic, and cultural ties. The danger of nuclear missile war has been lessened. The accords and principles recorded in the Final Act of the Helsinki Conference signed at summit level three years ago are intended to promote *detente,* to safeguard the security of nations and ensure lasting peace on earth.

It would seem that the road lying ahead is clear. This is a road of patient and constructive settlement of conflicts and differences, new steps to slow down the arms race, to widen and deepen relations between countries belonging to different social systems, between all states of the world. To make detente irreversible is the task set before mankind by history. This has been clearly and consistently stated by Leonid Brezhnev, the leader of the Soviet Communist Party and a loyal Leninist. The Soviet Union and all nations of the socialist community have got down to work with great energy and determination to accomplish this task.

The advantages of detente for the peoples of all countries have been clear in the past and today. For all that, Washington's policy has of late been departing more and more appreciably from the stance of political realism, laying emphasis on the exclusive right of the United States to lecture everybody and tending towards moves unfriendly to the Soviet Union and even attempts to put pressure on it.

Yuri Andropov, from a speech at the presentation of the order of the Red Banner of Labour to the City of Petrozavodsk on August 5, 1978.

I have no comment on the extreme, to put it mildly, naivety of those who believe that a language of lecturing and threats may be used to talk to the Soviet Union. The record of international relations since the victory of the October Revolution has proved the absolute futility of attempts to this end. All the more hopeless are such attempts today when our strength has grown immeasurably, when a new life is being built along with the Soviet Union by the fraternal socialist countries, when the scope of anti-imperialist struggle is growing in Asian, African and Latin American countries, when the movement for democracy and social progress is mounting in the capitalist countries. If anybody stands to lose from the ill-conceived actions of the Washington administration, this will certainly be the American side, the American business community in particular.

But let us discuss this question on a different, broader plane. Why is the US administration inclined to retreat under pressure from the enemies of detente? Why is the wing gravitating towards the times and practices of the Cold War growing stronger within the American ruling quarters?

The point is that by all indications American imperialism has difficulties in revising its policy to adapt it to the new realities of international life. These realities are as follows.

## Relaxing International Tensions

A relaxation of international tensions is inevitably accompanied by a change in the character of the entire system of international relations. The principles of peaceful coexistence, equality and justice are beginning to play an ever greater part in these relations, which leaves less and less room for a policy of imperialist dictation, pressure and various kinds of "power play." An easing of world tensions stimulates the process of favourable social change, increases the influence of the working class and all working people on the policy of bourgeois governments. At the same time, detente has a favourable impact not only on the general atmosphere of world politics but also on the political climate within the capitalist countries.

In other words, detente on the one hand gives free scope to the operation of progressive tendencies, and on the other hand compels the ruling circles of the capitalist world to adapt to these tendencies, to introduce corresponding amendments into their foreign and home policy.

Needless to say, different sections of the *bourgeoisie* react differently to these objective dictates of the times.

Some of them, who hold realistic views, are aware of the fact that with the present alignment of forces in the world arena there is no sensible alternative to detente and therefore capitalists must adapt to the new situation, that is to recognize the need for peaceful coexistence with the socialist countries and even for co-operation with them, to revise the

character of relations with the developing countries, to display greater flexibility on the fronts of social struggle.

Others, known as "hawks," who represent the interests of the military industrial complex, are resisting detente for all they are worth. They are calling on the West to take up whatever stick is heavier and wield it until the world lapses into a dangerous East–West confrontation and returns into the trenches of the Cold War.

Finally, there is another section, whose members realize in general outline the disastrous consequences of a global thermonuclear war. They are even prepared to reach limited agreements reducing the level of international tensions. However, they are scared of the change detente brings in its wake in international and internal affairs. Hence the instability, vacillations in policy, the growing discrepancy between word and deed, the efforts to play up to the right wing and concessions to the frankly militaristic, ultra-reactionary forces.

## The Myth of "the Soviet Menace"

Of course, in our day it is not so easy to proclaim for all to hear a renunciation of the policy of detente, to call for a retreat to the positions of the Cold War. The enemies of detente have to use cunning and to dissemble, to mislead public opinion. This is precisely the reason for reviving the myth of the "Soviet menace" and other vociferous propaganda campaigns.

*"Detente... gives free scope to the operation of progressive tendencies, and ...compels the ruling circles of the capitalist world to adapt to these tendencies."*

All this has naturally adversely affected the state of Soviet–American relations and caused relapses of international tensions. This is inseparably linked with the arms race stepped up by the imperialists, with increased imperialist interference in the life of foreign nations, with persistent attempts to play the notorious "China card" against the Soviet Union.

The CPSU Central Committee and the Soviet government are closely watching the development of the situation and the manoeuvres of the enemies of detente. We take account of vacillations in Washington's policy. At the same time, our own strategic line remains unchanged. The Soviet Union, Leonid Brezhnev has said, regards as its central aim in international affairs "Prevention of mankind's slipping to war, defence and consolidation of peace, universal, just and durable peace. This is our steadfast policy. It does not depend on any current expediency. It is legislatively laid down in the Soviet Constitution. We translate this policy into reality by all means at our disposal.

*"The struggle for detente today is a struggle against the arms race, for peace, for restructuring the system of international relations on truly democratic principles."*

The struggle for detente today is a struggle against the arms race, for peace, for restructuring the system of international relations on truly democratic principles. For the Soviet Union detente is a line of principle emanating from the very socioeconomic nature of the Soviet state, a continuation of the policy of peace proclaimed by the October Revolution and bequeathed to us by Lenin.

### Maintaining Peace on Earth

The foreign policy of the Party and the Soviet state is aimed at securing the most favourable conditions for successful implementation of the breathtaking tasks in communist construction, for maintaining international security and peace on earth.

The Soviet Union invariably comes out in the international arena side by side with other countries of the socialist community. Leonid Brezhnev's recent meetings in the Crimea with leaders of the fraternal parties of the socialist countries have demonstrated again that we have common aims, a common jointly planned strategy, that we realistically appraise the world situation with all its complexities, its pluses and minuses.

The difficulties being encountered by detente are to a certain extent inevitable. The world we live in is too heterogeneous. The contradictions dividing the two world systems are too deep-seated. The inertia of the past, the momentum of the Cold War, suspicion and mistrust are too great. We are convinced, however, that the states, social forces and political movements coming out for a relaxation of international tensions will win and secure a strong and lasting peace for all nations.

This is precisely why we display a maximum of restraint and come forward with reasonable constructive initiatives. The Soviet Union is prepared to come to an agreement based on the principle of equal security at negotiations on a variety of issues, primarily on strategic arms limitation and at the Vienna talks.

We can see that the chills coming from Washington in certain cases unfortunately affect some West European capitals. We hope, however, that their

political wisdom will enable our partners to overcome their time-serving vacillations and zigzags. The Soviet Union's European policy remains unchanged. It has repeatedly stated that a normalization of the political climate in Europe is one of the most crucial peaceful achievements of the last decade, that this achievement must be constantly supported, strengthened and widened. This is particularly important now when the enemies of detente are again exacerbating the international situation. Our stand is clear. Europe must become a continent of peace and good-neighbourly co-operation. . . .

### Soviet Union and Peace

The international positions in the country are strong and stable. Aware of its material and spiritual strength, confident of its rightness, loyal to its internationalist duty, the Soviet Union has always been and remains a consistent champion of the cause of peace, the freedom and independence of nations.

*Yuri Andropov served as head of the KGB from 1967 to 1982. He became Soviet premier in 1982, after Leonid Brezhnev's death and died in 1984.*

*"We will never know what might have been possible [for detente] had America not consumed its authority in that melancholy period."*

viewpoint 35

# Domestic Upheaval Ruined Détente

### Henry Kissinger

It is...important to recall what detente was and what it was not.

Richard Nixon came into office with the well-deserved reputation of a lifetime of anti-Communism. He despised liberal intellectuals who blamed the Cold War on the United States and who seemed to believe the Soviet system might be transformed through the strenuous exercise of goodwill. Nixon profoundly distrusted Soviet motives; he was a firm believer in negotiations from positions of strength; he was, in short, the classic Cold Warrior. Yet after four tumultuous years in office, it was this man, so unlike the conventional intellectual's notion of a peacemaker, who paradoxically was negotiating with the Soviets on the broadest agenda of East-West relations in twenty-five years. And not long afterward he found himself accused of what had been a staple of his own early campaign rhetoric: of being "soft on Communism."

The paradox was more apparent than real. We did not consider a relaxation of tensions a concession to the Soviets. We had our own reasons for it. We were not abandoning the ideological struggle, but simply trying—tall order as it was—to discipline it by precepts of national interest....

## Detente Helped Defense

The evidence proves exactly the opposite of what our critics charged: Detente helped rather than hurt the American defense effort. Before the word detente was even known in America the Congress cut $40 billion from the defense budgets of Nixon's first term; even so dedicated a supporter of American strength as Senator Henry M. Jackson publicly advocated small defense cuts and a "prudent defense posture." After the signature of SALT I, our defense budget increased and the Nixon and Ford administrations put through the strategic weapons (the MX missile, B-1 bomber, cruise missiles, Trident submarines, and more advanced warheads) that even a decade later are the backbone of our defense program and that had been stymied in the Congress *prior* to the easing of our relations with Moscow.

Detente did not prevent resistance to Soviet expansion; on the contrary, it fostered the only possible psychological framework for such resistance. Nixon knew where to draw the line against Soviet adventure whether it occurred directly or through proxy, as in Cienfuegos, Jordan, along the Suez Canal, and during the India-Pakistan war. He drew it with cool fortitude, and all the more credibly because there was national understanding that we were not being truculent for its own sake. If the Vietnam war had taught us anything, it was that a military confrontation could be sustained only if the American people were convinced there was no other choice.

## Nuclear Age Compels Coexistence

Any American President soon learns that he has a narrow margin for maneuver. The United States and the Soviet Union are ideological rivals. Detente cannot change that. The nuclear age compels us to coexist. Rhetorical crusades cannot change that, either.

Our age must learn the lessons of World War II, brought about when the democracies failed to understand the designs of a totalitarian aggressor, sought foolishly to appease him, and permitted him to achieve a military superiority. This must never happen again, whatever the burdens of an adequate defense. But we must remember as well the lesson of World War I, when Europe, *despite* the existence of a military balance, drifted into a war no one wanted and a catastrophe that no one could have imagined. Military planning drove decisions; bluster and posturing drove diplomacy. Leaders committed the cardinal sin of statecraft: they lost control over events.

An American President thus has a dual responsibility: He must resist Soviet expansionism. And he must be conscious of the profound risks of global confrontation. His policy must embrace both deterrence and coexistence, both containment and an effort to relax tensions. If the desire for peace turns into an avoidance of conflict at all costs, if the just disparage power and seek refuge in their moral purity, the world's fear of war becomes a weapon of blackmail by the strong; peaceful nations, large or small, will be at the mercy of the most ruthless. yet if we pursue the ideological conflict divorced from strategy, if confrontation turns into an end in itself, we will lose the cohesion of our alliances and ultimately the confidence of our people. That was what the Nixon Administration understood by detente.

The Nixon Administration sought a foreign policy that eschewed both moralistic crusading and escapist isolationism, submerging them in a careful analysis of the national interest. America's aim was to maintain the balance of power and seek to build upon it a more constructive future. We were entering a period when America's responsibility was to provide a consistent, mature leadership in much more complex conditions than we had ever before faced and over a much longer period of time than we ever had had to calculate.....

## Avoiding Nuclear War

How to avoid nuclear war without succumbing to nuclear blackmail, how to prevent the desire for peace from turning into appeasement; how to defend liberty and maintain the peace—this is the overwhelming problem of our age. The trouble—no, the tragedy—is that the dual concept of containment and coexistence, of maintaining the balance of power while exploring a more positive future, has no automatic consensus behind it. Historically, America imagined that it did not have to concern itself with global equilibrium because geography and a surplus of power enabled it to await events in isolation. Two schools of thought developed. The liberal approach treated foreign policy as a subdivision of psychiatry; the conservative approach considered it an aspect of theology. Liberals equated relations among states with human relations. They emphasized the virtues of trust and unilateral gestures of goodwill. Conservatives saw in foreign policy a version of the eternal struggle of good with evil, a conflict that recognized no middle ground and could end only with victory. Deterrence ran up against liberal ideology and its emotional evocation of peace in the abstract; coexistence grated on the liturgical anti-Communism of the right. American idealism drove both groups to challenge us from different directions. The mainstream of liberalism found anything

connected with the balance of power repugnant: through the early part of the twentieth century the United States thought of itself as standing above considerations of national interest. We would organize mankind by a consensus of moral principles or norms of international law. Regard for the purity of our ideals inspired conservatives, contrarily, to put communism into quarantine: there could be no compromise with the devil. Liberals worried about the danger of confrontation; conservatives about funking it.

## The Meaning of Coexistence

I sought to convey a sense of the complexity of our policy toward the USSR in a speech before the *Pacem in Terris* Conference in Washington on October 8, 1973:

> This Administration has never had any illusions about the Soviet system. We have always insisted that progress in technical fields, such as trade, had to follow—and reflect—progress toward more stable international relations. We have maintained a strong military balance and a flexible defense posture as a buttress to stability. We have insisted that disarmament had to be mutual. We have judged movement in our relations with the Soviet Union, not by atmospherics, but by how well concrete problems are resolved and by whether there is responsible international conduct.
>
> Coexistence to us continues to have a very precise meaning:
>
> —We will oppose the attempt by any country to achieve a position of predominance either globally or regionally.
>
> —We will resist any attempt to exploit a policy of detente to weaken our alliances.
>
> —We will react if relaxation of tensions is used as a cover to exacerbate conflicts in international trouble spots.
>
> The Soviet Union cannot disregard these principles in any area of the world without imperiling its entire relationship with the United States.

*"How to avoid nuclear war without succumbing to nuclear blackmail. . .how to defend liberty and maintain the peace—this is the overwhelming problem of our age."*

But our effort simultaneously to resist expansionism and to keep open the option of historical evolution—in effect, to combine the analysis and strategy of the conservatives with the tactics of the liberals—proved too ambitious in a bitter period when a domestic upheaval over Vietnam was followed immediately afterward by another upheaval over Watergate. Conservatives at least remained true to their beliefs. They wanted no truck with Communism whatever the tactical motivation. they equated negotiations with Moscow with the moral disarmament of America. They rejected our argument that if we did not take account of the global yearning for peace we would isolate ourselves internationally and divide our nation again over the same issues that had polarized America over Vietnam....

## Critics of Detente

It was the liberal community that began to find ideological flaws in the detente that for so long it had passionately championed. The argument gained currency that Nixon had "oversold" detente; that he neglected human rights in his desire to get along with the Kremlin; that the Administration was insensitive to the moral problem of dealing with Communism.

---

*"Detente is dangerous if it does not include a strategy of containment."*

---

These arguments were natural from conservatives who were seriously worried lest the erosion of dividing lines sap the Western will to resist. They came with less grace from those who had systematically opposed higher defense expenditures and who had decried the resistance to Soviet expansion in distant theaters that was the essence of our commitment to containment....

To be sure, detente is dangerous if it does not include a strategy of containment. But containment is unsustainable unless coupled with a notion of peace. The remedy is not to evade the effort to define coexistence; it is to give it a content that reflects *our* principles and *our* objectives....

## Domestic Upheaval Ruined Detente

We will never know what might have been possible had America not consumed its authority in that melancholy period. Congressional assaults on a weakened President robbed him of both the means of containment and the incentives for Soviet moderation, rendering resistance impotent and at the same time driving us toward a confrontation without a strategy or the means to back it up. The domestic base for our approach to East-West relations eroded. We lost the carrot in the debate over Jewish emigration that undercut the 1972 trade agreement with the Soviet Union. And the stick became ineffective as a result of progressive restrictions on executive authority from 1973 to 1976 that doomed Indochina to destruction, hamstrung the President's powers as Commander-in-Chief, blocked military assistance to key allies, and nearly devastated our intelligence agencies. In time the Soviets could not resist the opportunity presented by a weakened President and a divided America abdicating from foreign responsibilities. By 1975 Soviet adventurism had returned, reinforced by an unprecedented panoply of modern arms.

Partly as a result of our domestic weakness and Soviet power, for many of our allies detente became what conservatives had feared: an escape from the realities of the balance of power, a substitution of atmospherics for substance. In a period of recession induced by the oil price explosion, several European countries turned to East-West trade as an economic lifeboat, not an instrument of a well-thought-out foreign policy. Their leaders played to a domestic gallery, appearing as "mediators" between the Soviet Union and the United States.

*Henry Kissinger served as secretary of state under Presidents Nixon and Ford from 1973 to 1977. In 1973, he was awarded the Nobel Peace Prize and, in 1977, the Presidential Medal of Freedom. In 1984, President Reagan appointed Mr. Kissinger to head a bi-partisan commission on Central America. He was, and continues to be, a controversial figure because of his hard-line anti-communist attitudes.*

*"Why praise a losing policy just because the ideas that inspired it were right?"*

viewpoint

# viewpoint 36

# Détente Could Not Have Worked

### Jean-Francois Revel

In his memoirs, Kissinger compares detente to a high-wire act that the United States cannot carry off unless it hangs negotiation from one end of its balancing pole and confrontation from the other. Never, in his mind or in Nixon's, was detente what it became at the end of the 1970s: a smug, simplistic belief that all differences with the Soviet Union can be settled by negotiation alone, with nothing more than concessions, goodwill and a frantic haste always to take the first step. Detente, wrote the former Secretary of State, could not succeed without both of its components: resistance to every Soviet attempt at expansion and ceaseless negotiation with Moscow.

This marriage of two conflicting diplomatic tactics was dictated by a situation new to humanity, i.e., the coexistence of two nuclear superpowers whose political antagonism is unshakable. Even before the nuclear era, the democracies had learned to their cost how much harm can be done by too accommodating a policy. During the geopolitical face-off that preceded World War II, they thought they could bribe Hitler to be moderate by granting him concessions that, in fact, gave him the time to rearm and then, suddenly, to overrun the Continent.

That's the truth. And it is also true that many characteristics of East-West detente recall that period of disastrous blindness. But, Kissinger warns, this should not make us forget the accident of the First World War, when the nations of Europe, grouped in blocs, encased in pacts, alliances, military security and vigilant resolution, ravaged each other because they had too completely rejected the idea of negotiation. Hence the notion of double-edged detente as both a permanent channel of consultation to prevent the supreme catastrophe and a system of precautions to block Soviet encroachment.

This was a subtle, ambiguous and unusual foreign policy that could have been explained to the American people and applied to East-West relations. Unfortunately, laments Kissinger, we'll never know if it could have worked. It had hardly begun to remodel the practice of international relations when it was undermined by Watergate, which struck its indispensable protagonist, the President of the United States, with political leukemia and stripped him of the authority he needed to be conciliatory or firm as circumstances required. The machine's key part was tossed on the scrap heap, and the motor of detente went haywire, to the sole benefit of the Soviets.

Even without this stroke of fate, detente was prone to untimely compromise by the politicians. In the early 1970s, Congress, backed by the media, saw Nixon as the hawk he always had been. It withheld or haggled over the appropriations needed to modernize America's defenses, which enabled the Soviet Union first to equal the United States militarily, then to surpass it. This deprived Washington of the tools for firmness and knocked one of the components of genuine detente—a detente that was not mere sham—off the balancing pole. During Nixon's first term, Congress slashed the defense budget by forty billion dollars. The dismantling of the country's intelligence and counterespionage services, for highly respectable reasons of political morality, increased America's weakness. In addition, the government's departments, agencies, bureaucrats and the separate armed services all disagreed on a proper doctrine for negotiating the first Strategic Arms Limitation Treaty (SALT), so that the United States, in the person of Secretary Kissinger, arrived at the negotiating table without a clearly defined position.

## National Mood Changed

Then, during the latter part of the decade, the national mood flip-flopped. Congress, the media,

From *How Democracies Perish*, by Jean-Francois Revel. Translated from the French by William Byron. Copyright © 1984 by Doubleday and Company, Inc. Reprinted by permission of Doubleday and Company.

soviet-american debate/133

public opinion, all the former doves accused Kissinger of letting himself be cheated, of failing to head off a one-way system of detente that benefited only the U.S.S.R.; absorbed to a point of hypnosis by the niggling over SALT, it was said, he woke up one morning to find communism spread out over the world or, at any rate, encamped in a lot of places it had not been before. The same coalition of liberal Democrats and isolationist Republicans who in 1975 had flatly vetoed any effort to reverse the Soviet sweep in Angola now criticized the Administration for its inertia, accusing the State Department of being soft on international communism. In short, during the first half of the period the people of the United States would not hear of anything but conciliation at any price, while in the second half they demanded vigorous action and the laying down of conditions without concessions. But during the first period they had permitted the deterioration of the means needed to enforce the firm policy called for later. Neither American nor world public opinion has ever seized more than one of the two counterweights of detente at a time. But these are inseparable. On several occasions after his expulsion from office, I heard Nixon explain this complex philosophy of true detente as he and Kissinger had conceived it—which, he said, had never been put into practice.

## Detente's Final Result

However we may admire the intelligence of this definition of detente as it might have been but never was, the only question that counts now is what the final result was and is. One of the barriers to ''genuine'' detente was unforeseeable: America's political agony and Nixon's fall. But the others were thrown up by the democratic system itself. That legislatures, media, voters are neither infallible nor entirely logical, nor perfectly informed, nor consistent, that they do not always act in good faith is normal in democratic life. This is why the art of governing is partly a matter of skillful persuasion.

*"However we may admire the intelligence of the definition of detente as it might have been but never was, the only question that counts now is what the final result was and is."*

Even Nixon's removal—no U.S. President had ever before been forced to resign in mid-term—was part of the workings of democracy. That a diplomatic policy designed to defend democracy was ruined by democracy itself is a natural consequence of the system's structure. If this structure cannot be revised, then democracy is lost. If it can be corrected, then

this should have been considered. There are weaknesses hidden in the Communist system too. It is up to us to exploit them....

In an address on October 8, 1973, to the *Pacem in Terris* conference in Washington, Kissinger subordinated detente to the following three American conditions:

''We will oppose the attempt by any country to achieve a position of dominance either globally or regionally;

''we will resist any attempt to exploit a policy of detente to weaken our alliances;

''we will react if relaxation of tensions is used as a cover to exacerbate conflicts in international trouble spots.''

Just rereading these three fine resolutions gives a clear picture of the extent of the debacle. For the three dangerous situations that Kissinger said were incompatible with a healthy understanding of detente have materialized.

## Soviets and Detente

Before analyzing why, we might wonder how the Soviets saw detente, what they expected of it, and what they did not under any circumstances want it to be. Totalitarians are obliging: they declare and put in writing in advance everything they plan to do. The democracies normally make the same mistake they made with Hitler in refusing to take these detailed programs seriously because they seem so horrendous. It is a foreordained paradox that they eagerly believe the Communists' pure propaganda, reserving their skepticism for the genuinely revealing doctrinal statements. These they dismiss as mere talk, as efforts at intimidation. Or, committing the constant error of ascribing to totalitarianism the obligations and customs peculiar to democracy, they shrewdly decide that such statements are ''for domestic consumption,'' aimed at ''reassuring'' one or another faction within the Communist apparatus. But the only way to escape the uncertainties of conjecture is to compare the lists of statements and actions. In the Communists' case, they agree perfectly over the long term.

From the early years of their regime, the Soviets have never ceased declaring that capitalism and communism would have to fight to the finish for possession of the world. In this fight, Moscow is the seat of the high command of an international organization of which the Communist parties in the capitalist countries are merely one element. World conquest by the Communists may be temorarily blocked; they may be forced into tactical withdrawals, as they were when they adopted the slogan ''build socialism in a single country,'' which seemed to suggest that the U.S.S.R. would stop exporting its revolution. But this was only a pause. Conquest also includes phases of accommodation with capitalism, called ''peaceful coexistence'' or "detente." It is understood that these remain subject to two conditions that they be more advantageous to communism than to capitalism and that they impose no delay on Communist expansion. . . .

## What the Soviets Wanted from Detente

If we hesitate to follow Kissinger in what detente might have been but was not, for the West, let us try to understand what it meant to Soviet leaders by putting ourselves in their place, taking the viewpoint of their interests. What did they seek from it, and what did they receive? In any negotiations, any redefinition of foreign policy, one calculates advantages and concessions. Then, after a few years, the results are weighed to see if either side got the better deal.

What advantages did the Soviets expect when they began campaigning for detente, first with the West Germans and then with the Americans? What were their "targets of detente"?

First, international recognition of Soviet territorial gains resulting from the Second World War and from the 1945-50 period in which the Sovietization of Central Europe was completed.

Second, through negotiations on arms limitation, to profit from American goodwill to increase the U.S.S.R.'s military potential.

Third, to obtain financial, industrial, and trade contributions from the capitalist countries that would relieve or at least attenuate the shortcomings of socialist economics.

What concessions or promises did the Soviets have to make to the West in exchange for these benefits?

First, they promised to allow the Americans to conduct on-site inspections to verify that their military strength did not exceed the levels set by the agreements on strategic-arms limitation.

Next, they vowed they would adopt a general policy of restraint throughout the world, or so they led the West, especially Nixon and Kissinger, to believe in 1972-73. This was the notion of "linkage" or "attachment"—the "indissoluble nature of all aspects of detente," as Sakharov put it. Washington and Moscow specifically agreed to use their influence to prevent their respective allies and the countries with which they enjoyed special relationships from undertaking offensive actions, especially military.

## Respecting Human Rights

Finally, in the most sensational part of the Helsinki agreement, the Soviet Union had to sign a guarantee that it would respect human rights and basic freedoms in the U.S.S.R. itself and throughout the Soviet sphere of influence. Concretely, the agreement was supposed to remove obstacles to the "free circulation of persons and ideas" in both directions between East and West. Including these incredible promises in a treaty that was otherwise so advantageous for the Communists could reasonably

be seen by the Soviets as a necessary concession. Their object was to reassure people who, in the West, needed a moral justification that would consecrate the philosophy of detente.

---

*"[Soviet] conquest also includes phases of accommodation with capitalism, called 'peaceful coexistence' or 'detente.'"*

---

A quick glance at these two lists shows that, for the Soviets, the credit column in this balance sheet is incomparably more substantial than the debit column. . . .

## The Soviets' Military Expansion

As regards Soviet promises concerning military preparedness, Brezhnev could rightly boast in his report to the twenty-fifth Soviet Party Congress in 1976 that his country was achieving superiority. We have already noted that detente coincided with a boost in Soviet strategic capacity. As soon as the SALT I agreement was ratified and while talks were getting under way on SALT II, the Kremlin found ways to get around the bans and ceilings agreed on. "Two weeks after the June 1973 summit," Kissinger wrote, "the Soviets conducted their first MIRV tests on their SS-17 ICBM, the new missile that was to replace the obsolescent SS11. A *strategic revolution was now only a question of time*. . . .

How did the United States get into this fix? SALT I, signed in 1972, froze the *number* of missiles authorized for both sides but did not specify their *size*. The Soviets had merely to undertake a program of giant missiles (the SS-18s) within the original framework to attain superiority in megatonnage without violating the letter of the agreement. Behind a facade of equality, the Soviets achieved strategic superiority. This is why, when negotiations were resumed in Moscow in March 1977, just after Jimmy Carter's accession to the White House, the Americans insisted that the number of SS-18s be reduced by half so as to restore genuine parity. We recall the sensational turn events then took: the Russians "lost their tempers." Khrushchev's slogan "We will bury the United States" was not realized in the economic sphere he had in mind but in armaments.

## Soviets Benefited

Westerners opposed to reinforcing our defenses maintained that the Soviets had no intention of waging a nuclear war against the United States, which would leave three-fourths of their own territory in ruins even if they won, or of invading Western Europe. Perhaps. Why indeed would the Russians go to war if they could win without it most of what a war might bring them? They translated their military superiority into political domination.

In short, they garnered the advantages of detente without having to concede anything in return. And the West quickly formed the habit of not insisting on such concessions; even hinting at doing so soon became synonymous with provocation. Trying to link continued economic collaboration with respect for human rights or the withdrawal of Soviet troops from Afghanistan or freedom in Poland was viewed as warmongering, as imperialism. How could the Kremlin help but see detente as a great victory? What was more natural than Andropov's call, as soon as he came to power, for a "return to a policy of detente"?

## US at a Disadvantage

The democracies, on the other hand, could hardly claim they had achieved their goals for detente, which were to ensure Western security in exchange for economic, technological, and financial aid to the East, to resist nuclear blackmail while avoiding nuclear war, to restrain communism's global aggressiveness and—the supreme dream—to oblige it to respect human rights. It is very difficult for a statesman to disentangle the snarl that immediately occurs in his mind between the merits of a policy as they were originally calculated when he envisioned the future success of his plan and its final results.

*"Detente coincided with a boost in Soviet strategic capacity."*

The harder you try to focus his attention on the policy's real consequences, which are all that count for his fellow countrymen, the more energetically he refers to his earlier projections, the ones on which he wishes to be judged. Like Kissinger, Nixon maintained that "the failure was not of detente, but rather of the management of detente by U.S. policymakers." He contrasted "hardheaded" detente as he would have managed it had he remained in office to "softheaded" detente as it was conducted contrary to his ideas before and after his resignation. But when has a policy been judged on what it might have achieved?

Kissinger has no more right than Nixon or any other statesman to claim that privilege. The rule in the art of governing is to accept the verdict of results. Theory exists in action only in the action itself. It never occurs to anyone to criticize a successful policy on the grounds that the ideas behind it were wrong. Then why praise a losing policy just because the ideas that inspired it were right?

*Jean-Francois Revel is the author of a widely acclaimed multivolume history of philosophy and of the bestselling and controversial* Without Marx or Jesus, The Totalitarian Temptation, *and* Culture and Cuisine. *This viewpoint is excerpted from his new work,* How Democracies Perish.

*"It was not the democracies that invaded Afghanistan or suppressed Polish Solidarity or used chemical and toxic warfare in Afghanistan and Southeast Asia."*

viewpoint 37

# Communist USSR Is Interventionist

### Ronald Reagan

We're approaching the end of a bloody century plagued by a terrible political invention— totalitarianism. Optimism comes less easily today, not because democracy is less vigorous, but because democracy's enemies have refined their instruments of repression. Yet optimism is in order, because day by day democracy is proving itself to be a not-at-all fragile flower.

From Stettin on the Baltic to Varna on the Black Sea, the regimes planted by totalitarianism have had more than 30 years to establish their legitimacy. But none—not one regime has yet been able to risk free elections. Regimes planted by bayonets do not take root.

The strength of the Solidarity movement in Poland demonstrates the truth told in an underground joke in the Soviet Union. It is that the Soviet Union would remain a one-party nation even if an opposition party were permitted—because everyone would join the opposition party.

America's time as a player on the stage of world history has been brief. I think understanding this fact has always made you patient with your younger cousins. Well, not always patient. I do recall that on one occasion, Sir Winston Churchill said in exasperation about one of our most distinguished diplomats: "He is the only case I know of a bull who carries his china shop with him."

But witty as Sir Winston was, he also had that special attribute of great statesmen—the gift of vision, the willingness to see the future based on the experience of the past. . . .

## Threats to Our Freedom

We have not inherited an easy world. If developments like the industrial revolution which began here in England and the gifts of science and technology have made life much easier for us, they have also made it more dangerous. There are threats now to our freedom, indeed to our very existence, that other generations could never even have imagined. . . .

Now I am aware that among us here and throughout Europe there is legitimate disagreement over the extent to which the public sector should play a role in a nation's economy and life. But on one point all of us are united—our abhorrence of dictatorship in all its forms, but most particularly totalitarianism and the terrible inhumanities it has caused in our time—the great purge, Auschwitz and Dachau, the Gulag, and Cambodia.

Historians looking back at our time will note the consistent restraint and peaceful intentions of the West. They will note that it was the democracies who refused to use the threat of their nuclear monopoly in the 40's and early 50's for territorial or imperial gain. Had that nuclear monopoly been in the hands of the communist world the map of Europe—indeed, the world—would look very different today. And certainly they will note it was not the democracies that invaded Afghanistan or suppressed Polish Solidarity or used chemical and toxic warfare in Afghanistan and Southeast Asia.

If history teaches anything it teaches self-delusion in the face of unpleasant facts is folly. We see around us today the marks of our terrible dilemma— predictions of doomsday, anti-nuclear demonstrations, an arms race in which the West must, for its own protection, be an unwilling participant. At the same time we see totalitarian forces in the world who seek subversion and conflict around the globe to further their barbarous assault on the human spirit.

What, then, is our course? Must civilization perish in a hail of fiery atoms? Must freedom wither in a quiet, deadening accomodation with totalitarian evil? Sir Winston Churchill refused to accept the

Ronald Reagan, from an address to members of both houses of Parliament in the Palace of Westminster on June 8, 1982.

inevitability of war or even that it was imminent. He said: "I do not believe that Soviet Russia desires war. What they desire is the fruits of war and the indefinite expansion of their power and doctrines. But what we have to consider here today while time remains, is the permanent prevention of war and the establishment of conditions of freedom and democracy as rapidly as possible in all countries.". . .

## Decaying Soviet Experiment

The decay of the Soviet experiment should come as no surprise to us. Wherever the comparisons have been made between free and closed societies—West Germany and East Germany. Austria and Czechoslovakia, Malaysia and Vietnam—it is the democratic countries that are prosperous and responsive to the needs of their people. And one of the simple but overwhelming facts of our time is this: of all the millions of refugees we have seen in the modern world, their flight is always away from, not toward the communist world. Today on the NATO line, our military forces face East to prevent a possible invasion. On the other side of the line, the Soviet forces also face East to prevent their people from leaving.

The hard evidence of totalitarian rule has caused in mankind an uprising of the intellect and will. Whether it is the growth of the new schools of economics in America or England or the appearance of the so-called "new philosophers" in France, there is one unifying thread running through the intellectual work of these groups—rejection of the arbitrary power of the state, the refusal to subordinate the rights of the individual to the superstate, the realization that collectivism stifles all the best human impulses.

Since the exodus from Egypt, historians have written of those who sacrificed and struggled for freedom—the stand at Thermopylae, the revolt of Spartacus, the storming of the Bastille, the Warsaw uprising in World War II.

---

*"The decay of the Soviet experiment should come as no surprise to us."*

---

More recently we've seen evidence of this same human impulse in one of the developing nations in Central America. For months and months the world news media covered the fighting in El Salvador. Day after day we were treated to stories and film slanted toward the brave freedom fighters battling oppressive government forces in behalf of the silent, suffering people of that tortured country.

And then one day those silent suffering people were offered a chance to vote—to choose the kind of government they wanted. Suddenly the freedom

fighters in the hills were exposed for what they really are—Cuban-backed guerillas who want power for themselves and their backers—not democracy for the people. They threatened death to any who voted and destroyed hundreds of busses and trucks to keep the people from getting to the polling places. But on election day, the people of El Salvador, an unprecedented 1.4 million of them, braved ambush and gunfire, and trudged for miles to vote for freedom. . . .

## Struggle for Freedom

But beyond the trouble spots lies a deeper, more positive pattern. Around the world today, the democratic revolution is gathering new strength. In India a critical test has been passed with the peaceful change of governing political parties. In Africa, Nigeria is moving into remarkable and unmistakable ways to build and strengthen its democratic institutions. In the Caribbean and Central America, 16 of 24 countries have freely-elected governments. And in the United Nations, 8 of the 10 developing nations which have joined that body in the past five years are democracies.

In the communist world as well, man's instinctive desire for freedom and self-determination surfaces again and again. To be sure, there are grim reminders of how brutally the police state attempts to snuff out this quest for self-rule—1953 in East Germany, 1956 in Hungary, 1968 in Czechoslovakia, 1981 in Poland.

But the struggle continues in Poland. And we know that there are even those who strive and suffer for freedom within the confines of the Soviet Union itself. How we conduct ourselves here in the Western democracies will determine whether this trend continues.

No, democracy is not a fragile flower. Still it needs cultivating. If the rest of this century is to witness the gradual growth of freedom and democratic ideals, we must take actions to assist the campaign for democracy.

Some argue that we should encourage democratic change in right-wing dictatorships, but not in communist regimes. Well, to accept this preposterous notion, as some well-meaning people have, is to invite the argument that once countries achieve a nuclear capability, they should be allowed an undisturbed reign of terror over their own citizens.

We ask only that these systems begin by living up to their own constitutions, abiding by their own laws and complying with the international obligations they have undertaken.

We ask only for a process, a direction, a basic code of decency, not for an instant transformation.

We cannot ignore the fact that even without our encouragement there has been and will continue to be repeated explosions against repression and dictatorships. The Soviet Union itself is not immune to this reality. Any system is inherently unstable that has no peaceful means to legitimize its leaders. In such cases, the very repressiveness of the state ultimately drives people to resist it, if necessary, by force.

While we must be cautious about forcing the pace of change, we must not hesitate to declare our ultimate objectives and to take concrete actions to move toward them. We must be staunch in our conviction that freedom is not the sole prerogative of a lucky few, but the inalienable and universal right of all human beings. So states the United Nations' Universal Declaration of Human Rights, which, among other things, guarantees free elections.

The objective I propose is quite simple to state, to foster the infrastructure of democracy, the system of a free press, unions, political parties, universities, which allows a people to choose their own way to develop their own culture, to reconcile their own differences through peaceful means.

## Democracy Flourishes

This is not cultural imperialism, it is providing the means for genuine self-determination and protection for diversity. Democracy already flourishes in countries with very different cultures and historical experiences. It would be cultural condescension, or worse, to say that any people prefer dictatorship to democracy. Who would voluntarily choose not to have the right to vote, decide to purchase government propaganda handouts instead of independent newspapers, prefer government to worker controlled unions, opt for land to be owned by the state instead of those who till it, want government repression of religious liberty, a single political party instead of a free choice, a rigid cultural orthodoxy instead of democratic tolerance and diversity?

Since 1917 the Soviet Union has given covert political training and assistance to Marxist-Leninists in many countries. Of course, it also has promoted the use of violence and subversion by these same forces.

Over the past several decades, West European and other Social Democrats, Christian Democrats and leaders have offered open assistance to fraternal political and social institutions to bring about peaceful and democratic progress. Appropriately, for a vigorous new democracy, the Federal Republic of Germany's political foundations have become a major force in this effort....

We invite the Soviet Union to consider with us how the competition of ideas and values—which it is committed to support, can be conducted on a peaceful and reciprocal basis....

Now, I don't wish to sound overly optimistic, yet the Soviet Union is not immune from the reality of what is going on in the world. It has happened in the past—a small ruling elite either mistakenly attempts to ease domestic unrest through greater repression and foreign adventure, or it chooses a wiser course—it begins to allow its people a voice in their own destiny.

Even if this latter process is not realized soon, I believe the renewed strength of the democratic movement, complemented by a global campaign for freedom, will strengthen the prospects for arms control and a world at peace....

---

*"Any system is inherently unstable that has no peaceful means to legitimize its leaders. . . . The very repressiveness of the state ultimately drives people to resist it."*

---

I have often wondered about the shyness of some of us in the West about standing for these ideals that have done so much to ease the plight of man and the hardships of our imperfect world. This reluctance to use those vast resources at our command reminds me of the elderly lady whose home was bombed in the blitz. As the rescuers moved about, they found a bottle of brandy she had stored behind the staircase which was all that was left standing. And since she was barely conscious, one of the workers pulled the cork to give her a taste of it. She came around immediately and said: "here now, no, no; put it back. That's for emergencies."

Well, the emergency is upon us. Let us be shy no longer. Let us go to our strength. Let us offer hope. Let us tell the world that a new age is not only possible, but probable.

*Ronald Reagan became president of the United States in 1980 and was elected to a second term in 1984. He is an outspoken critic of the USSR.*

*"The USSR has never waged aggressive wars."*

# Communist USSR Is Not Interventionist

A. Skrylnik

As a system of ideas and views reflecting the vital interests of social classes, ideology cannot be indifferent to problems of war. The degree of its influence on war has not always been the same. In the past, when the exploiting social systems were predominant, wars were unleashed and conducted under the influence of the ruling classes' essentially exploitative ideologies.

Presently, as the confrontation and struggle between the two different social systems become ever acute and extensive, the ideologies of the rivalling classes are clashing more and more in wars.

The two ideologies—the socialist and the bourgeois—opposed each other both when the Soviet people fought against the counter-revolutionaries and foreign interventionists (1918-1920) and when they repelled the nazi invasion in the Great Patriotic War (1941-1945).

The ideology of the young freedom fighting nations is counterpoised to the ideology of imperialism. In the young developing countries progressive democratic elements form the ideological basis for consolidating different social and ethnic groups and are an effective instrument of struggle against the imperialist propaganda campaigns waged under such questionable slogans as "disinterested aid to underdeveloped countries" or "the liberating mission of the civilised states," etc.

## Ideological Aspect of Modern War

In modern warfare the ideological aspect is characteristic of one definite feature: the overall superiority of the ideas of socialism and national liberation. This was the case, for instance, during the Great Patriotic War, when the superior combat strength of the nazi armed forces in the initial period

was opposed by the far greater moral superiority of the Soviet people which enabled them to reverse the tide of the war. The overlords of nazi Germany went out of their way to ideologically submit the Soviet people. A booklet "The Political Mission of a German Soldier in the All-Out War" issued for the Wehrmacht in May 1943 stressed, apart from success on the battlefield, the decisive importance for the outcome of the war of whether "the German soldier wins the hearts of the peoples who were previously under the rule of Bolshevism."

The hopes for the victory of the "German national spirit" proved to be futile. Nazi ideology, which incorporated the most reactionary tenets of bourgeois ideology and pursued the class interests of the German monopolists claiming domination throughout the world, was doomed to defeat. It could not be otherwise, as the "spiritual potential" of nazism was based on rabid anti-communism, on paranoic "Lebensraum" dreams, on wild chauvinism and racism.

Along with the fighting on the battlefields, the struggle of ideas went on day and night. The strategic objective of this struggle was the political consciousness, the sentiments and opinions of popular masses and the armies. The main issues were the goals and nature of the war, who was responsible for it, the essence of the foreign and home policies of the belligerents, their social systems and methods of warfare, etc.

## Noble Goals of Liberation Struggle

The socialist ideology gave clear and convincing answers to all these problems. The noble goals of the patriotic liberation struggle against nazism found a ready response in the hearts and souls of all the Soviet people.

The heightened ideological consciousness in the Soviet Army and the people was ensured by the extensive efforts of the Communist Party which

A. Skrylnik, "Ideology and War," *Soviet Military Review*, No. 8, 1983.

employed a wide variety of morale-building methods in the armed forces. The daily circulation of the central newspapers alone in the Soviet Union during the war exceeded 23 million. The total circulation of army papers amounted to 3.5 million. Radio broadcasts continued 18 hours a day in 70 languages of the peoples of the USSR and in 28 foreign languages. Nearly 170 million books of fiction were published during the war.

The nazi bosses were unstinting with funds to propagate their ideas. But life proved their futility. The nazis declared all-out war on the Soviet people and were totally defeated in it, both militarily and ideologically.

## Vietnam: A Mercenary War

Vietnam is another vivid example. Year after year would the greatest capitalist power, the USA, commit to battle the most up-to-date weaponry and its best divisions brainwashed to wage any mercenary war. The people of Vietnam were subjected to severe ideological pressure by the US invaders. Suffice it to say that the US army issued and dropped tens of propaganda leaflets per every Vietnamese annually. The US propaganda machine spared no effort to distort reality, to misrepresent the policy of the socialist states so as to scare the people. But it failed to shake the combat spirit of the people and the army inspired by the ideas of socialist patriotism. The inglorious defeat of the US adventure in Vietnam was at the same time a failure of imperialist ideology. It could not be otherwise.

Ideological superiority in war is primarily dependent on the class content of the ideology, on what social aims it pursues, and on how progressive it is. The inspiring and organising power of the Marxist-Leninist ideology—the working class ideology—consists in its adherence to the vital interests of the working people, and in its devotion to the cause of social reconstruction on a socialist basis. Its genuine internationalism, humanism, justice and peaceable nature and other features attract the minds of the masses and arouse them to struggle.

## Eliminating Tensions

Marxist-Leninist ideology provides a clear understanding of the central problem of today's world—the problem of war and peace. It demonstrated real possibilities of preventing wars in our historic period and indicates the forces capable of putting these possibilities into reality. The Programme of Peace adopted at the 26th Congress of the CPSU for the 80s serves precisely these objectives. Opposed to the subversions of the militarist and aggressive forces, the Programme proclaims the path of eliminating hotbeds of tensions and military conflicts.

The living and creative Communist teaching on war and peace gives a true explanation of the facts of social life and is thus winning tremendous influence on the masses of people. It debunks all kinds of bourgeois sociological fabrications designed to conceal the true causes of the existing war threat, to get people used to the acceptability and inevitability of nuclear war.

It is not modern science and technology or human psychology that they say are responsible for destructive wars, but the capitalist system, based on private property, which gives rise to the arms build-up, militarism and political adventurism and is fraught with the dangers of a new world war. It is the division of society into antagonist classes that has caused numerous big and small wars. Today, too, imperialism is hatching up the threat of war. The militarist circles in the USA and other NATO states are building up their war arsenals and whipping up hotbeds of military conflicts in different parts of the world.

## Communist Threat Myth

The entire "case" of the advocates of militarism rests upon the "communist threat" myth. The Pentagon and NATO war hawks are trying to hammer home to the public the delirious idea of the Soviet "quest" for world domination and military superiority. They have put into operation a huge propaganda machine disseminating fantastic lies about the strength of the Soviet Armed Forces, the number of tanks, aircraft, warships, etc.

The USSR has never waged aggressive wars. It spends no more funds for military purposes than is essentially needed to ensure its security from a possible aggressive attack.

*"The Pentagon and NATO war hawks are trying to hammer home to the public the delirious idea of the Soviet 'quest' for world domination and military superiority."*

In an attempt to strengthen their positions in the struggle against socialism and national liberation and to justify the military build-up, the Western ideologists have launched in recent years a vigorous propaganda campaign against the aid the Soviet Union and other socialist states render to Angola, Ethiopia and Afghanistan. No invention is too wild for bourgeois newspapers and radio broadcasts to belittle and slander the socialist community. Threadbare and modified tales of the "growing communist menace," "military superiority of the USSR," etc. are being pushed. However, the world public begins to understand the genuine worth of this ideological drivel.

The influence of ideology is also greatly dependent on the scope of the propagation of ideas among the popular masses, which is attained by the allocation of funds for the mass media. The militarist ideological concepts are a danger to the cause of peace, for the minds of ill-informed people can become fertile soil for these concepts.

## Communism Will Succeed

Imperialists resort to every base method and means of ideological subversion to fight socialism and national liberation. The most versatile and technically equipped service of psychological warfare belongs to the United States. Its operations generally involve the activities of government bodies, private centres, intelligence services and army special units. The psychological warfare service is attached special importance in time of war. The US Army Field Manual says that at the present time psychological warfare plays an important role in all kinds of war. The struggle for people's minds attaches great significance to special activities. Success in this struggle can decisively affect the attainment of national goals.

*"Imperialists resort to every base method and means of ideological subversion to fight socialism and national liberation."*

The ideological battlefield on problems of war has no armistice or respite even in peace time.

The effects of communist ideology on the minds of millions of people is growing with each passing year. The people find in the revolutionary teachings of Marx and Lenin conclusive answers to the burning problems of present-day social development, and among them—the most acute problem of war and peace.

*A. Skrylnik is a Major General in the Soviet Armed Forces. This viewpoint appeared in the Soviet Publication* Soviet Military Review.

*"Responsibility for the present aggravation of the world situation rests with the reactionary and militarist circles in the USA and its NATO allies."*

# The US Is Interventionist

N. Kotkov

The United States of America is the biggest imperialist state, the leading power of NATO and other imperialist military-political alliances.

V.I. Lenin noted that American imperialism was remarkable even at its rise for its strong ambition to enslave other countries and peoples. At the end of the 19th century the American ruling circles zealously joined the struggle, sometimes with arms in hand, for their share of the world market, for new colonies. The Spanish-American War of 1898 unleashed by the American imperialists, was, according to Lenin, the first imperialist war for recarving a world that had been already divided.

The aggressive nature of US imperialism manifested itself with special force after World War II (1939-45). The USA had become the main stronghold of international reaction and militarism, its basic objectives being to obstruct the consolidation of positions of socialism, hold down the progressive development of the world revolutionary movement, and to check the irreversible decay of capitalism. To attain these objectives Washington sponsored the formation of aggressive military blocs in different parts of the world.

Fearful of the growing might and prestige of the world socialist system, of the scope of the international working-class and national-liberation movement, US imperialism more and more resorts to armed interference in other nations' affairs and to undermining peace in the world.

## US Provoked Conflict

After 1945 the USA initiated or was directly involved in most of the international armed conflicts. According to the Brookings Institution during the 30-year period between 1949 and 1979 the USA

directly or indirectly committed its armed forces 215 times, employment of nuclear weapons was debated 19 times in the US top administrative and military quarters, including four cases of possible nuclear strikes against the USSR.

This reaffirms Lenin's predictions that the bourgeoisie "is prepared to go to any length of savagery, brutality and crime in order to uphold dying capitalist slavery."

The imperialists' attempts to reverse the course of history failed. Owing to the Soviet Union and other socialist states, positive changes were made in the international climate. The energetic efforts of the socialist countries facilitated the improvement of the world situation and broad recognition of the principles of peaceful coexistence between states with different social systems.

The changes in the world balance of forces in favour of socialism forced the US ruling circles to adapt to the new situation in the world. A turn was effected from cold war to detente.

The imperialist powers tried to use detente to their advantage. They hoped to attain through detente what they had failed to through the cold war: to slow down the development of the socialist countries, split them, check the spread and influence of the socialist ideas in the world, hold down the world working-class and national-liberation movement and to establish neo-colonialist rule and their domination across the globe.

These schemes did not work either. The easing of international tensions presented favourable conditions for the development of cooperation among all the nations and contributed to consolidating peace and to social progress of mankind.

## US Destroyed Gains

Then the US Administration took the course of destroying all the positive achievements of the 70s. The White House first unilaterally broke off and then

N. Kotkov, "US Imperialism—The World's Vilest Enemy," *Soviet Military Review*, July 1983.

blocked the Soviet-American negotiations on a number of crucial global problems including disarmament. The most striking example of this anti-detente policy is the US refusal to ratify the SALT-2, signed in Vienna in 1979. The US Administration also frustrated negotiations on a complete ban of nuclear tests and chemical weapons, on limiting the conventional arms trade, and others.

Washington's new political line is sponsored by the most reactionary imperialist circles who seek to push international relationships off the path of detente and onto the path of confrontation and brinkmanship. Whipping up tensions in the world is regarded an instrument of pressure on the Soviet Union and other socialist states.

The NATO session held in December 1982 in Brussels approved under US pressure a plan for the deployment of nearly 600 US medium-range nuclear missiles in Western Europe. This plan, like many others along that line is intended to upset the existing parity of forces in Europe and to gain military superiority for the USA. At the same time Washington hopes to tether in this way the European countries to its hegemonistic war course and force them to tow the US adventurist line.

## US Militarist Delirium

In the heat of its militarist delirium Washington took a new step to whip up the arms race by increasing the US military budget for fiscal 1983 to a record 232 billion dollars. These funds are appropriated for the Pentagon's specific programmes, while the total military spending is to reach 263 billion dollars. The five-year programme of the US military build-up is to cost the United States over one and a half trillion dollars.

The aggressive political course is justified by a propaganda myth of a "Soviet military threat." But such inventions are not new, and have been mass produced ever since the October Revolution in Russia in 1917. These lie campaigns are brought to a peak especially when a new round of military build-up is needed.

## US Curtailed Trade

Seeking to reduce the economic potential of world socialism, the imperialist circles in the USA took to curtailing economic, scientific and cultural relations with the USSR and other socialist community countries. They are making attempts to get their NATO allies and Japan involved in their economic war against the USSR and the socialist community.

To add momentum to its anti-socialist struggle Washington has launched a wide-scale ideological campaign. Hundreds of special research centers and institutes have been set up to develop various anti-communist theories. The object is to infiltrate the socialist states and affect their internal structure and development, to disrupt their cooperation in the

fields of economy, foreign policy and party relations. Great emphasis is made on blowing up nationalistic tendencies. Ideological subversions, provocations, slander, blackmail—this is the usual tool kit of the US propaganda peddlers. A vivid example to that effect is the hullabaloo raised in the Western media about alleged human rights violations in the socialist countries. Apart from arrogant interference into other countries' home affairs this campaign represents the limit of the cynicism and hypocrisy of the self-appointed champions of human rights who do not care a straw for them at home.

*"The forces of peace are stronger than the forces of war."*

Every aspect of life in the socialist countries is shamelessly misrepresented, facts distorted and opinions grossly falsified. Especially disgraceful is the racket raised by the US propaganda machine about the events in Poland. Stepping up activities to destabilize the situation in that country and to build up an anti-Soviet hysteria, the US and NATO ruling circles hope to wrestle Poland out of the socialist community and thus change the world balance of forces in their favour. Life has proved once again that all attempts by the US imperialists to bank on a collapse of the socialist system are doomed to failure.

All these facts graphically show that responsibility for the present aggravation of the world situation rests with the reactionary and militarist circles in the USA and its NATO allies. The USSR cannot but make the appropriate conclusions.

True to the noble principles of Leninist foreign policy, the USSR will continue to do everything in its power to prevent the threat of war, to further detente, to expand peaceful coexistence and cooperation between nations.

*N. Kotkov writes for the Soviet publication* Soviet Military Review.

*"The Soviet Union has established a
vast empire . . . that from the very
beginning has grown by the artful
manipulation of symbols and the
uninhibited and skillful use of violence."* viewpoint **40**

# The US Is Not Interventionist

Jeane J. Kirkpatrick

We are the heirs of the liberal, democratic tradition, whose root is freedom. Freedom and democracy are not the only political values, any more than freedom is the only personal value. We all need community, food, shelter, human solidarity, common purpose, work under decent conditions, the basics of security and understanding.

But freedom is the prerequisite and the core in the pursuit of most of these personal and social goods, and I believe that American identity lies precisely in this tradition. The United States is the bearer of that tradition. Our identity is inextricably bound to it today. . . .

Our national identity and our importance to the defense of Western civilization make clear that it is both legitimate and important for us to be concerned about events in many places, remote as well as near. They give us a special stake in the clarity and confusion that surround our greatest adversary, the Soviet Union, and the tactics by which it operates in the contemporary world. . . .

## Soviet Foreign Policy

It is as unpleasant as it is important to remember that the Soviet Union has established a vast empire—the only empire in today's world—that extends to all continents, an empire that from the very beginning has grown by the artful manipulation of symbols and the uninhibited and skillful use of violence.

That curious statement issued in October 1983 in the name of Chairman Andropov established once again that the foreign policy of the Soviet Union is today aggressive as well as expansionist—and quite self-consciously so.

The reminder was not really necessary. We had already heard Andropov's threat of reprisal when

Western Europe refused to accept as a permanent condition the vulnerabilities imposed by the Soviet decision to deploy SS-20s in the Soviet Union and in Eastern Europe. That was a unilateral Soviet decision, taken neither in consultation with the United States in sessions on arms control, nor in consultation with the countries of Western Europe that are targeted, nor, one supposes, in consultation with the countries of Eastern Europe in which missiles may be based.

We had already heard Andropov's extraordinary threats against the West German electorate. We had heard recent Soviet menaces concerning Central America. We had had the opportunity to watch the bloody coup in Surinam that, under Cuban direction, wiped out a whole political class in that small but strategically located country. More recently, we had had the opportunity to watch an equally bloody coup in Grenada, where, as in Afghanistan a few years ago, a government that shared the ideology of the Soviet Union and was linked to it by ties of loyalty proved not quite reliably slavish enough, and was wiped out.

## Growth of Soviet Power

The growth of Soviet military-political strategic power has accelerated as it has progressed, mocking the expectations of those who explain away unseemly Soviet appetites as a result of their "understandable" insecurity. The comfortable and comforting view that the Soviets' preoccupation with armaments would diminish if only they achieved military parity has been overtaken and overwhelmed by their accelerating military buildup, as surely as some earlier expectations fashionable about the Russia of the twenties, the Cuba of the sixties, the Viet Nam of the seventies, or the Nicaragua of the eighties were overtaken and overwhelmed by experience.

Those earlier expectations featured the belief that basic human freedoms of speech, press, and assembly, the rule of law, would be restored by these

Jeane J. Kirkpatrick. "Understanding Ourselves and Our Adversaries," *Ethics and Public Policy Essay #51,* December 1983. Reprinted by permission of the Ethics and Public Policy Center.

so-called revolutionists just as soon as the monopoly of power of the relevant bourgeoisie had been smashed. As the longed for restoration of freedom has failed to occur in any country that saw the ''bourgeoisie'' displaced by Leninists, it has become clear that new explanations are required....

It is not difficult to understand the Soviet advance in the world in the abstract. That advance is based on cynical manipulation of the symbols of liberation, nationalism, and socialism. But the strategy of domination that they employ derives from a very different tradition. It derives from a tradition of oriental despotism, from a czarist synthesis of economic, social, and bureaucratic state power. The symbols manipulated by the Soviet Union speak of liberation—but the foundation and the consequence is tyranny.

## Marxism Is Not Liberal

One basic fact, hardest of all to remember, is that though Marxism itself had some roots in the European liberal socialist tradition, Marxism-Leninism and Soviet state power and the political organization ruled in their name are to the liberal-democratic tradition as antithesis is to thesis. Marxism-Leninism does not incorporate either the theory or the practice of liberalism, democracy, nationalism, or socialism; indeed, it denies all the essential elements of Western liberal-democratic, democratic-socialist, tradition.

It sees classes, not individuals, as the motor and creative principle of history; it postulates, advocates, justifies the practice of violence as the method of historical change; it spawns governments based on one-party dictatorships and never on the consent of the governed; it strictly subordinates nations and nationalism to supernational imperialism; and it grows by violence, deception, and subjugation.

There is no room today for reasonable people to misunderstand the Soviet record. The political and social events that occur in every country that has the misfortune to experience a Communist government are matters of hard fact, readily visible to all. In not one country where Marxist-Leninists have come to power have citizens been permitted free elections, a free press, free trade unions, free speech, freedom to emigrate, or any other institution-building associated with the political traditions of liberalism, democracy, democratic socialism—not one.

## Challenging Our Values

If the results are clear, so are the tactics. Not only do the Soviet leaders appeal to our values and cloak their aggressions in the symbols of liberation; they also attempt to paralyze us by creating situations in which respect for one of our basic values—say, nonintervention in the internal affairs of others—seems to require that we stand by passively while another small, relatively helpless people succumbs to

Marxist-Leninist tyranny and is ruthlessly incorporated into the Soviet empire.

That empire grows as Communists bring resources and personnel drawn from all over the Soviet block to bear on these small, helpless countries, on their indigenous political rivalries—particularly those of Third World countries. Thus the Cuban role in Nicaragua's and El Salvador's wars of ''national liberation,'' Libya's role in Chad, the Syrian role in Lebanon. Since the governments of the Third World countries are often rather weak, and the resources available to them severely limited, they are exceedingly vulnerable to destabilization by the Soviet Union and its surrogates.

---

*''The Soviet advance.... is based on cynical manipulation of the symbols of liberation, nationalism, and socialism.''*

---

This pattern is now discouragingly familiar: choose a weak government, organize a national liberation front, add a terrorist campaign to disrupt order and provoke repression, weaken an already weak economy, and then intensify the violence. The brittle institutions of many—perhaps even most—Third World governments are likely to crumble under such strains....

## Guarantee of Irreversibility

That's not all. Once a transfer of power has been achieved and a dictatorship friendly to the Soviet Union has been established, the Soviets seek to guarantee its irreversibility by providing thousands of technicians, advisors, and troops to prop up and guide the new government. Hence the extraordinary array of Soviet-bloc military and civilian personnel in Nicaragua, Angola, Benin, Ghana, Congo, Mozambique, Guinea, Cuba, South Yemen, Syria, Ethiopia. In those countries one finds extraordinary international brigades accumulated from East Germany, Czechoslovakia, Bulgaria, Viet Nam, the PLO, Libya—from all parts of the worldwide Soviet empire—brought to bear on weak institutions, weak peoples who almost invariably desire, above all, to be left alone to solve their own problems, to realize and enjoy their own national heritage.

Soviet leaders do not rely on the laws of history or the appeals of Communism to bring about what they call revolution or to insure what they call its irreversibility. Their clients can count on reliable supplies of arms and men.

*Jeane J. Kirkpatrick is the former United States Permanent Representative to the United Nations.*

*"Soviet units are in the Hungarian and Rumanian republics in accord with the Warsaw Treaty and governmental agreements."*

viewpoint 41

# The USSR Is Aiding Its Allies in Hungary

The Soviet Government

A policy of peaceful coexistence, friendship and cooperation among all states has been and continues to be the firm foundation of the foreign relations of Soviet Socialist Republics.

This policy finds its deepest and most consistent expression in the mutual relations among the socialist countries. United by the common ideals of building a socialist society and by the principles of proletarian internationalism, the countries of the great commonwealth of socialist nations can build their mutual relations only on the principles of complete equality, of respect for territorial integrity, state independence and sovereignty, and of noninterference in one another's internal affairs. Not only does this not exclude close fraternal cooperation and mutual aid among the countries of the socialist commonwealth in the economic, political and cultural spheres; on the contrary, it presupposes these things.

The system of people's democracy took shape, grew strong and showed its great vital power in many countries of Europe and Asia on this foundation after the second world war and the rout of fascism.

In the process of the rise of the new system and the deep revolutionary changes in social relations, there have been many difficulties, unresolved problems and downright mistakes, including mistakes in the mutual relations among the socialist countries—violations and errors which demeaned the principle of equality in relations among the socialist states.

The 20th Congress of the Communist Party of the Soviet Union quite resolutely condemned these violations and mistakes, and set the task of consistent application by the Soviet Union of Leninist principles of equality of peoples in its relations with the other socialist countries. It proclaimed the need for taking full account of the historical past and peculiarities of each country that has taken the path of building a new life.

The Soviet government is consistently carrying out these historic decisions of the 20th Congress, which create conditions for further strengthening friendship and cooperation among the socialist countries on the firm foundation of observance of the full sovereignty of each socialist state.

## Soviet Cooperation

As recent events have demonstrated, it has become necessary to make this declaration of the Soviet Union's stand on the mutual relations of the U.S.S.R. with other socialist countries, particularly in the economic and military spheres.

The Soviet government is prepared to discuss together with the governments of other socialist states measures ensuring further development and strengthening of economic ties among the socialist countries in order to remove any possibility of violation of the principles of national sovereignty, mutual benefit and equality in economic relations.

This principle must also be extended to advisors. It is known that, in the first period of the formation of the new social system, the Soviet Union, at the request of the governments of the people's democracies, sent these countries a certain number of its specialists—engineers, agronomists, scientists, military advisors. In the recent period the Soviet government has repeatedly raised before the socialist countries the question of recalling its advisors.

In view of the fact that by this time the people's democracies have formed their own qualified national cadres in all spheres of economic and military affairs, the Soviet government considers it urgent to review, together with the other socialist states, the question of the expediency of the further presence of U.S.S.R. advisors in these countries.

In the military domain an important basis of the mutual relations between the Soviet Union and the

Declaration by the Soviet Government on the Principles of Development and Further Strengthening of Friendship and Cooperation Between the Soviet Union and Other Socialist States, Moscow, October 30, 1956.

people's democracies is the Warsaw Treaty, under which its members adopted respective political and military obligations, including the obligation to take "concerted measures necessary for strengthening their defense capacity in order to protect the peaceful labor of their peoples, to guarantee the inviolability of their borders and territory, and to ensure defense against possible aggression."

It is known that Soviet units are in the Hungarian and Rumanian republics in accord with the Warsaw Treaty and governmental agreements. Soviet units are in the Polish republic on the basis of the Potsdam four-power agreement and the Warsaw Treaty. Soviet military units are not in the other people's democracies.

*"The Soviet government has given its military command instructions to withdraw the Soviet military units from the city of Budapest as soon as this is considered necessary by the Hungarian government."*

For the purpose of assuring mutual security of the socialist countries, the Soviet government is prepared to review with the other socialist countries which are members of the Warsaw Treaty the question of Soviet troops stationed on the territory of the above-mentioned countries. In so doing the Soviet government proceeds from the general principle that stationing the troops of one or another state which is a member of the Warsaw Treaty on the territory of another state which is a member of the treaty is done by agreement among all its members and only with the consent of the state on the territory of which and at the request of which these troops are stationed or it is planned to station them.

## Events in Hungary

The Soviet government considers it necessary to make a statement in connection with the events in Hungary. The course of events has shown that the working people of Hungary, who have attained great progress on the basis of the people's democratic system, are rightfully raising the question of the need to eliminate serious defects in the sphere of economic construction, the question of further improving the living standards of the population, the question of combating bureaucratic distortions in the state machinery. However, this legitimate and progressive movement of the working people was soon joined by the forces of black reaction and counterrevolution, which are trying to take advantage of the dissatisfaction of a part of the working people in order to undermine the foundations of the people's

democratic system in Hungary and to restore the old landowner-capitalist ways in that country.

The Soviet government, like the whole Soviet people, deeply regrets that the development of events in Hungary has led to bloodshed.

At the request of the Hungarian people's government, the Soviet government has granted consent to the entry into Budapest of Soviet military units to help the Hungarian people's army and the Hungarian agencies of government to bring order to the city.

Having in mind that the further presence of Soviet military units in Hungary could serve as an excuse for further aggravation of the situation, the Soviet government has given its military command instructions to withdraw the Soviet military units from the city of Budapest as soon as this is considered necessary by the Hungarian government.

At the same time, the Soviet government is prepared to enter into the appropriate negotiations with the government of the Hungarian People's Republic and other members of the Warsaw Treaty on the question of the presence of Soviet troops on the territory of Hungary.

## Guarding Socialist Achievements

To guard the socialist achievements of people's-democratic Hungary is the chief and sacred duty of the workers, peasants, intelligentsia, of all the Hungarian working people at the present moment.

The Soviet government expresses confidence that the peoples of the socialist countries will not permit foreign and domestic reactionary forces to shake the foundations of the people's democractic system, a system established and strengthened by the self-sacrificing struggle and labor of the workers, peasants and intelligentsia of each country. They will continue all efforts to remove all obstacles in the path of further strengthening the democratic foundations, independence and sovereignty of their countries; to develop further the socialist foundations of each country, its economy and its culture, for the sake of an uninterrupted rise in the living standards and cultural level of all the working people; they will strengthen the fraternal unity and mutual aid of the socialist countries to buttress the great cause of peace and socialism.

*The Soviet government issued this statement in response to criticism about its intervention in Hungary.*

*"There is no essential difference between what is being done by the Soviet Union today and what was done by Nazi Germany in its day."*

# The USSR Must Be Condemned for Its Intervention in Hungary

Henry Cabot Lodge

All else having failed, the General Assembly now comes to a solemn climax and must face the issue of voting a condemnation of the Soviet Union for its brutality against the tragic and valorous Hungarian people.

There can be no doubt about the two sets of facts: what has happened in Hungary and what has happened in the United Nations.

## Soviets in Hungary Like Hitler in Germany

In Hungary we have seen a sequence of events which is indistinguishable in essence from the kind of thing which was done by Adolf Hitler in World War II. We have seen the suppression of a small country by a large, powerful dictatorship; we have seen the large and powerful dictatorship put its agents in control of that small country; we have seen the local puppet government make a treaty with the large external dictatorship authorizing it to tamper in every respect with the internal affairs of the small country; and finally, we have seen the people of that country left with only their own personal valor to stand between them and the large external dictatorship. This is the kind of thing that happened under Adolf Hitler to small countries, it is what happened under Josef Stalin, and it is what is happening in Hungary now under Khrushchev. There is no essential difference between what is being done by the Soviet Union today and what was done by Nazi Germany in its day.

There is equally no doubt as to what has happened here in the United Nations. We have been extraordinarily patient and persistent in exhausting every single remedy which the charter authorizes us to use.

The record of General Assembly action on the situation in Hungary begins with the resolution adopted on November 4, the very day Russian troops began to take over the country. Since then eight more resolutions have been adopted.

## UN Actions

And in order that we may have perspective, I would like to summarize our actions here.

On November 4, in A/Res/393, this Assembly called upon the Government of the Soviet Union to stop its armed attack on the people of Hungary. It called upon the Soviet Union to withdraw all of its forces without delay from Hungarian territory. It called upon the Government of the Soviet Union and Hungary to permit observers designated by the Secretary-General to enter into Hungary, to travel freely therein, and to report their findings. It called upon all members to co-operate in making available to the Hungarian people food, medicine, and other supplies. The response of the Assembly to the tragic situation in Hungary was immediate.

On November 9, in A/Res/397, this call was repeated, and on that same day, in A/Res/398, we asked for emergency assistance to the growing number of refugees from Hungary. On November 9 also, in response to the extreme suffering to which the Hungarian people were being subjected, all members of the United Nations were asked, in A/Res/399, to participate in giving immediate aid by furnishing medical supplies, foodstuffs, and clothing.

On November 10, the item concerning the situation in Hungary was transferred to the agenda of the 11th regular session (A/Res/401), and on November 16 the Secretary-General appointed a committee of three to investigate the information available regarding the situation in Hungary (A/3339).

On November 21 we again asked for the admission of observers and demanded that the Soviet Union stop its brutal program of deportations. We

Henry Cabot Lodge, from a statement before the General Assembly of the United Nations on December 10, 1956.

demanded that those who had been deported be returned promptly to their homes. Two resolutions (A/Res/407 and 408) were passed with overwhelming support in one day.

On that same day—November 21—we urged in A/Res/409, that governments and nongovernmental organizations make contributions for the care and resettlement of Hungarian refugees. Efforts made to meet the problem of Hungarian refugees were described in a report by the Secretary-General on November 30 in document A/3405.

After receiving the report of the Secretary-General of November 30 (A/3403) noting that no information was available to him concerning steps taken in order to establish compliance with decisions of the Assembly which refer to withdrawal of troops or related political matters, the Assembly met again on December 4 to consider the situation in Hungary.

On that day, in A/Res/413, the Assembly called once more for compliance with its previous resolution. The Assembly recommended that the Secretary-General arrange for immediate dispatch to Hungary and other countries as appropriate of observers named by him pursuant to the Assembly's first resolution on Hungary. A deadline of December 7 was set for a reply from the Soviet Union and Hungary to the request for admission of observers.

## Soviet Obstruction

Since then, Mr. President, we have been met with continuing and complete obstruction by the Soviet Union. At 1 minute past midnight on last Saturday morning, the deadline of December 7 set by the Assembly for a response to the request for admission of observers passed. Although the Government of Austria has communicated its willingness to receive observers, observers have not been permitted to enter Hungary. Soviet troops have not been withdrawn. The proposed date for the Secretary-General's visit to Budapest has not been granted and has been met with a wall of silence. We have no reports of any return of deportees to Hungary.

These actions show that there has been a magnificent response by the people the world over to the plight of the Hungarian people. But all of the resolutions calling for action by the Soviet Union have been ignored by them and by their Hungarian agents. We have seen an unparalleled demonstration of the flouting by a single state of the repeatedly recorded wishes of an overwhelming majority of the nations of the world.

In the words of President Eisenhower's Human Rights Day statement, which was published in the newspapers this morning, we have seen the Soviet Union impose a terror upon Hungary—a terror, Mr. President, upon Hungary—which "repudiates and negates almost every article in the Declaration of Human Rights."

As the President said of the terror imposed by the Soviet Union on Hungary:

It denies that men are born free and equal in dignity and rights and that all should act in the spirit of brotherhood.

It denies the right to life, liberty, and security of person.

It denies the principle that no one shall be subjected to cruel, inhuman, or degrading treatment.

It denies that no person shall be arbitrarily arrested, detained, or exiled.

It denies that all are equal before the law and entitled to its equal protection.

*"The repudiation of the Soviet system by the youth of Hungary is a deadly blow to Soviet prestige."*

It denies the right to fair and public hearings by an independent and impartial tribunal.

It denies the right to freedom of thought, conscience, and religion.

It denies the right to freedom of opinion and expression.

It denies the right to freedom of peaceful assembly.

It denies that the individual may not be held in slavery or servitude.

It denies that the will of the people shall be the basis of the authority of government.

That these human rights have been so flagrantly repudiated is cause for worldwide mourning.

Yes, Mr. President, at 1 minute after midnight last Saturday morning the deadline passed for a reply authorizing the entrance of observers into Hungary—and yet the tragedy goes on.

Thomas Jefferson said, and the President quoted him, too, the human spirit knows that "the God who gave us life, gave us liberty at the same time." The President added, "The courage and sacrifices of the brave Hungarian people have consecrated that spirit anew."

The truth is that this uprising in Hungary is an uprising of youth. This makes it the deadliest of condemnations, the most abject of failures, of the whole Soviet system; of its middle-aged inability to sense the modern mood; of its ritualism; of its monstrosity; and of how completely it carries within itself the seeds of its own dissolution. That system based itself on the idea that, if what they call "the dictatorship of the proletariat" would only stay in power long enough, the new generation would grow up without ever having known anything else and would therefore be solidly, dependably Communist.

## Failure of Communism

Now, we have seen the failure of that whole idea. The trouble with this idea—and with the whole

Marxist idea, for that matter—is that it ignores that which is noble and spiritual in human nature and sees the world through the prism of Karl Marx's bitter and self-pitying frustration. It totally ignores what Abraham Lincoln called "the better angels of our nature."

Mr. President, the repudiation of the Soviet system by the youth of Hungary is a deadly blow to Soviet prestige which will continue to shrink in world standing and influence as snow melts in the summer sun.

Let us vote this resolution, Mr. President, so that the world may know of our condemnation.

*Henry Cabot Lodge served the United States government in many capacities. He made this statement as the US representative to the United Nations under President Eisenhower.*

*"The communists of the fraternal countries naturally could not allow the socialist states to remain idle... while the country was endangered by anti-socialist degeneration."*

# The USSR Serves the Cause of Peace in Czechoslovakia

## Tass and S. Kovalev

*Editor's note: The following viewpoint consists of two statements about the Russian movement of troops into Czechoslovakia. Part I is an official announcement from* Tass. *Part II is excerpted from an article in* Pravda *by S. Kovalev.*

### I

Tass is authorized to state that party and government leaders of the Czechoslovak Socialist Republic have asked the Soviet Union and other allied states to render the fraternal Czechoslovak people urgent assistance, including assistance with armed forces.

This request was brought about by the threat which has arisen to the socialist system in Czechoslovakia and to the statehood established by the constitution, a threat emanating from the counter-revolutionary forces which have entered into collusion with foreign forces hostile to socialism.

### Socialist Solidarity

The events in Czechoslovakia and around her have repeatedly been the subject of exchanges of views between leaders of fraternal socialist countries, including the leaders of Czechoslovakia. These countries are unanimous that the support, consolidation and defence of the peoples' socialist gains is a common internationalist duty of all the socialist states. This common stand of theirs was solemnly proclaimed in the Bratislava statement.

The further aggravation of the situation in Czechoslovakia affects the vital interests of the Soviet Union and other socialist states and the security interests of the states of the socialist community. The threat to the socialist system in Czechoslovakia at the same time constitutes a threat to the foundations of peace in Europe.

The Soviet government and the governments of the allied countries—the People's Republic of Bulgaria, the Hungarian People's Republic, the German Democratic Republic and the Polish People's Republic—proceeding from the principles of unbreakable friendship and co-operation and in accordance with the existing contractual commitments, have decided to meet the above-mentioned request to render the necessary help to the fraternal Czechoslovak people.

This decision is fully in accord with the right of states to individual and collective self-defence envisaged in the treaties of alliance concluded between the fraternal socialist countries. This decision is also in line with the vital interests of our countries in safeguarding peace in Europe against the forces of militarism, aggression and revanche, which have more than once plunged the peoples of Europe into war.

### Aid to Brothers

Soviet armed units, together with armed units of the abovementioned allied countries, entered the territory of Czechoslovakia on 21 August. They will be immediately withdrawn from the Czechoslovak Socialist Republic as soon as the threat that exists to the gains of socialism in Czechoslovakia and the threat to the security of the socialist commonwealth countries is eliminated and the lawful authorities find that the further presence of these armed units is no longer necessary there.

The actions which are being taken are not directed against any state and in no measure infringe the state interests of anybody. They serve the purpose of peace and have been prompted by concern for its consolidation. The fraternal countries firmly and resolutely counterpose their unbreakable solidarity to any threat from outside. Nobody will ever be allowed to wrest a single link from the commonwealth of socialist states.

Tass News Service, statement on August 22, 1968. S. Kovalev, "Sovereignty and the Internationalist Obligations of Socialist Countries," *Pravda*, October 16, 1968.

## II

In connection with the events in Czechoslovakia the question of the relationship and interconnection between the socialist countries' national interests and their internationalist obligations has assumed particular urgency and sharpness. The measures taken jointly by the Soviet Union and other socialist countries to defend the socialist gains of the Czechoslovak people are of enormous significance for strengthening the socialist commonwealth, which is the main achievement of the international working class....

## Responsibility to All

There is no doubt that the peoples of the socialist countries and the communist parties have and must have freedom to determine their country's path of development. However, any decision of theirs must damage neither socialism in their own country, nor the fundamental interest of other socialist countries nor the world-wide workers' movement, which is waging a struggle for socialism. This means that every communist party is responsible not only to its own people but also to all the socialist countries and to the entire communist movement. Whoever forgets this in placing sole emphasis on the autonomy and independence of communist parties lapses into one-sidedness, shirking his internationalist obligations....

*"Any decision of [the people of any socialist country] must damage neither socialism in their own country, nor the fundamental interest of other socialist countries."*

Each communist party is free in applying the principles of Marxism-Leninism and socialism in its own country, but it cannot deviate from these principles (if, of course, it remains a communist party). In concrete terms this means primarily that every communist party cannot fail to take into account in its activities such a decisive fact of our time as the struggle between the two antithetical social systems—capitalism and socialism. This struggle is an objective fact that does not depend on the will of the people and is conditioned by the division of the world into two antithetical social systems....

It should be stressed that even if a socialist country seeks to take an 'extra-block' position, it in fact retains its national independence thanks precisely to the power of the socialist commonwealth—and primarily to its chief force, the Soviet Union—and the might of its armed forces. The weakening of any link

in the world socialist system has a direct effect on all the socialist countries, which cannot be indifferent to this. Thus, the anti-socialist forces in Czechoslovakia were in essence using talk about the right to self-determination to cover up demands for so-called neutrality and the CSR's withdrawal from the socialist commonwealth. But implementation of such 'self-determination', i.e. Czechoslovakia's separation from the socialist commonwealth, would run counter to Czechoslovakia's fundamental interests and would harm the other socialist countries. Such 'self-determination', as a result of which NATO troops might approach Soviet borders and the commonwealth of European socialist countries might be dismembered, in fact infringes on the vital interests of these countries' peoples, and fundamentally contradicts the right of these peoples to socialist self-determination. The Soviet Union and other socialist states, in fulfilling their internationalist duty to the fraternal peoples of Czechoslovakia and defending their own socialist gains, had to act and did act in resolute opposition to the anti-socialist forces in Czechoslovakia.

## Justified Assistance

Comrade W. Gomulka, first secretary of the central committee of the Polish United Workers' Party, used a metaphor to illustrate this point:

> To those friends and comrades of ours from other countries who believe they are defending the just cause of socialism and the sovereignty of peoples by denouncing and protesting the introduction of our troops in Czechoslovakia, we reply: If the enemy plants dynamite under our house, under the commonwealth of socialist states, our patriotic national and internationalist duty is to prevent this by using any means that are necessary.

People who 'disapprove' of the actions taken by the allied socialist countries ignore the decisive fact that these countries are defending the interests of world-wide socialism and the world-wide revolutionary movement. The socialist system exists in concrete form in individual countries that have their own well-defined state boundaries and develops with regard for the specific attributes of each such country. And no one interferes with concrete measures to perfect the socialist system in various socialist countries. But matters change radically when a danger to socialism itself arises in a country. World socialism and a social system is the common achievement of the working people of all countries, it is indivisible, and its defence is the common cause of all communists and all progressive people on earth, first and foremost the working people of the socialist countries....

What the right-wing, anti-socialist forces were seeking to achieve in Czechoslovakia in recent months was not a matter of developing socialism in an original way or of applying the principles of Marxism-Leninism to specific conditions in that country, but was an encroachment on the foundations of socialism and the fundamental principles of Marxism-Leninism. This is the 'nuance' that is still incomprehensible to people who trusted in the hypocritical cant of the anti-socialist and revisionist elements. Under the guise of 'democratization' these elements were shattering the socialist state step by step; they sought to demoralize the communist party and dull the minds of the masses; they were gradually preparing for a counter-revolutionary coup and at the same time were not being properly rebuffed inside the country.

The communists of the fraternal countries naturally could not allow the socialist states to remain idle in the name of abstract sovereignty while the country was endangered by anti-socialist degeneration.

## Liberating Socialism

The five allied socialist countries' actions in Czechoslovakia are consonant with the fundamental interests of the Czechoslovak people themselves. Obviously it is precisely socialism that, by liberating a nation from the fetters of an exploitative system, ensures the solution of fundamental problems of national development in any country that takes a socialist path. And by encroaching on the foundations of socialism, the counter-revolutionary elements in Czechoslovakia were thereby undermining the basis of the country's independence and sovereignty.

The formal observance of freedom of self-determination in the specific situation that had taken shape in Czechoslovakia would signify freedom of 'self-determination' not for the people's masses and the working people, but for their enemies. The anti-socialist path, the 'neutrality' to which the Czechoslovak people were being prodded, would lead the CSR straight into the jaws of the West German revanchists and would lead to the loss of its national independence. World imperialism, for its part, was trying to export counter-revolution to Czechoslovakia by supporting the anti-socialist forces there.

The assistance given to the working people of the CSR by the other socialist countries, which prevented the export of counter-revolution from the outside, is in fact a struggle for the Czechoslovak Socialist Republic's sovereignty against those who would like to deprive it of this sovereignty by delivering the country to the imperialists.

Over a long period of time and with utmost restraint and patience, the fraternal communist parties of the socialist countries took political measures to help the Czechoslovak people to halt the anti-socialist forces' offensive in Czechoslovakia. And only after exhausting all such measures did they undertake to bring in armed forces.

## No Internal Interference

The allied socialist countries' soldiers who are in Czechoslovakia are proving in deeds that they have no task other than to defend the socialist gains in that country. They are not interfering in the country's internal affairs, and they are waging in a struggle not in words but in deeds for the principles of self-determination of Czechoslovakia's peoples, for their inalienable right to decide their destiny themselves after profound and careful consideration, without intimidation by counter-revolutionaries, without revisionist and nationalist demagoguery.

*"The allied socialists countries' soldiers who are in Czechoslovakia are proving in deeds that they have no task other than to defend the socialist gains in that country."*

Those who speak of the 'illegality' of the allied socialist countries' actions in Czechoslovakia forget that in a class society there is and can be no such thing as a non-class law. Laws and norms of law are subordinated to the laws of the class struggle and the laws of social development. These laws are clearly formulated in the documents jointly adopted by the communist and workers' parties.

The class approach to the matter cannot be discarded in the name of legalistic considerations. Whoever does so and forfeits the only correct, class-oriented criterion for evaluating legal norms, begins to measure events with the yardsticks of bourgeois law. Such an approach to the question of sovereignty means, for example, that the world's progressive forces could not oppose the revival of neo-Nazism in the FRG, the butcheries of Franco and Salazar or the reactionary outrages of the 'black colonels' in Greece, since these are the 'internal affairs' of 'sovereign states.'

*Tass is the official news agency of the Soviet Union. S. Kovalov is a Soviet journalist.*

*"[The USSR has] fabricated the claim that this invasion was requested by Czechoslovakia, with the contention that what we confront is an internal matter."*

# The USSR's Intervention Violates the Cause of Peace

George W. Ball

Six governments [Canada, Denmark, France, Paraguay, U.K., and U.S.] have requested that the item, the present serious situation in Czechoslovakia, be inscribed on the agenda of the Security Council. There is not the slightest doubt that this request is proper, that it is demanded by the present crisis, and that the inscription should be promptly accepted if the Council is to live up to the responsibilities given it by the charter.

The situation the world faces tonight is an affront to all civilized sensibilities. Foreign armies have, without warning, invaded a member state of the United Nations. If the Security Council does not seize itself of this gross violation of the charter and deal with it promptly and incisively, its vitality and integrity, its very seriousness of purpose, will be subject to serious question.

## Ugly Aggression

Rarely has a situation come before the Council where the ugly facts of aggression have been written so large and in such unmistakable characters. The Soviet Union has arrogantly announced to the world that it has sent its armies into Czechoslovakia, and the evidence is beyond question that it and its client states have done so in order to impose by force a repressive political system which is plainly obnoxious to the people and leadership of Czechoslovakia.

The Soviet Union and its Eastern European accomplices have not even tried to conceal the fact of this invasion. How could they? Rather, in a feeble and futile effort at self-justification, they have fabricated the claim that this invasion was requested by Czechoslovakia, with the contention that what we confront is an internal matter which is none of the business of the Security Council.

We all know, Mr. President, that this claim is a fraud, an inept and obvious fraud. Only a few days ago the Communist parties of the Soviet Union and her Warsaw Pact allies who joined with her in last night's aggression met with the Czechoslovak party in Bratislava. The whole world took note of the astonishing fact that present at the meeting was almost the entire Soviet Politburo and that the Czechoslovak representatives included the leading members of the Politburo of that country. This was a situation, therefore, in which the Soviet leaders and the leaders of its allies were sitting down in solemn conclave with what they clearly recognized as the authoritative leaders of Czechoslovakia. And at the conclusion of the meeting they all joined in a communique affirming their "unbreakable friendship" and their "firm resolve to do everything in their power to deepen the all-round cooperation of their countries." What is most piquant about this communique is that they made this affirmation "on the basis of the principles of equality, respect for sovereignty and national independence, territorial integrity and fraternal mutual assistance and solidarity."

Tonight most, if not all, of the Czechoslovak representatives who met at Bratislva are under detention, and the Soviet Government, having shown its respect for their "sovereignty and territorial integrity" by invading their country, is claiming that they do not speak for their country; that privilege belongs to some vague and unnamed individuals.

At Bratislava there was no question in the minds of the Soviet Union as to who were the leaders of Czechoslovakia; nor could there be, for the whole world knew the facts. Yet, did those leaders request that their country be attacked and overrun by foreign troops?

Last night, when the invasion occurred, Radio Prague, the official Government station, broadcast the following statement with regard to the invasion:

George W. Ball, from a statement to the United Nations Security Council on August 21, 1968.

"This (the invasion) happened without the knowledge of the President of the Republic, the Chairman of the National Assembly, the Premier, or the First Secretary of the Czechoslovak Communist Party Central Committee."

This morning the permanent mission of the Czechoslovak Socialist Republic to the United Nations released a declaration of the Ministry of Foreign Affairs of the Czechoslovak Government. That declaration stated that the Ministry of Foreign Affairs, with the endorsement of the President of the Republic, lodged with the embassies of the Soviet Union and its puppets in Prague a "resolute protest with the requirement that the illegal occupation of Czechoslovakia be stopped without delay and all armed troops be withdrawn from Czechoslovakia."

---

*"[The Soviet intention is] to destroy dissent, to deter free debate, to prevent mankind from uttering or facing the truth."*

---

The declaration expressed the hope that the offending Governments "will understand the seriousness of the situation created by this action which cannot be explained in any way, and all the less made stand to reason, and will make it immediately possible for the Czechoslovak people and its legitimate representatives to continue their activities without delay."

### Brave Protest

The issuance of this declaration was a brave act which all free men must applaud. But where are the responsible officials of the Czechoslovak Foreign Ministry while their country is occupied? Last night as the invading forces poured into Prague, the Embassy of a respected neutral country found itself surrounded. When the Embassy officials protested by telephone to the Czechoslovak Foreign Ministry, they were told that the officials of the Foreign Ministry could do nothing to help "since they were prisoners themselves."

Just before the Council met this evening, the permanent mission of Czechoslovakia issued an additional declaration, which reads as follows:

> The deputies of the National Assembly met and unanimously accepted the following declaration at a time when the Government and other organs cannot exercise their functions.
>
> (1) We identify ourselves with the declarations of the Presidium of the Central Committee of the Communist Party of Czechoslovakia and the Presidium of the National Assembly protesting against the occupation of Czechoslovakia by armies of the five countries of the Warsaw treaty and considering it as a violation of international law, provisions of the

Warsaw treaty and the principles of equality among nations.

> (2) We request that the constitutional representatives, primarily President of the Republic Ludvik Svoboda, Prime Minister Oldrich Cernik, Chairman of the National Assembly Josef Smrkovsky, First Secretary Alexander Dubcek, Chairman of the Central Committee of the National Front Dr. Frantisek Kriegel, Chairman of the Czech National Council Cestmir Cisar and others be released from internation and thus could exercise their constitutional functions with which the sovereign people of this country entrusted them. The delegation of the National Assembly, which we sent to the Soviet Embassy this morning, has not returned so far. We protest against the fact that the National Assembly, Government, institutions of the National Front and their representatives are prevented from exercising their legitimate rights and further from freedom of movement and assembly.
>
> (3) We categorically request immediate withdrawal of the armed forces of the five states of the Warsaw treaty and full respect for the State sovereignty of the Czechoslovak Socialist Republic.
>
> (4) We appeal to Parliaments of all countries and to the world public opinion and ask them to support our legitimate requirements.
>
> (5) We entrust the delegation of the National Assembly composed of Marie Mikova, Josef Macek, Jozef Vallo, Pavol Repos, Josef Pospichal and Vaclav Kacera to contact Chairman of the National Assembly Josef Smrkovsky, President of the Republic Ludvik Svoboda and Prime Minister Cernik in order to inform them about this decision and agree with them on further proceedings. The delegation of the National Assembly will report to the Czechoslovak people on the result of the negotiations without delay.
>
> (6) We call on all people not to resort to forcible actions against occupation armies, not be be provoked by various forces, which try to get proofs justifying the intervention, and to misuse the situation to arbitrary actions.
>
> Working people, citizens! Remain on your working places and protect your enterprises! For further development of socialism in Czechoslovakia make use of all democratic means! If necessary, you will be able to defend yourself also by a general strike. We are confident that we will overcome these serious moments with pride and character.

### Clumsy Discrepancies

Conscious as they must have been of the heavy burden of guilt and responsibility they were taking on themselves, the Soviet Union and the other invading powers made foolish mistakes of a kind that are so often committed by guilty conspirators. In their efforts to create the patently false impression that the Czechoslovak Government was requesting its own destruction and that the Czechoslovak peoples were asking for the occupation of their country, they trapped themselves by clumsy discrepancies.

An official Soviet statement published in Tass asserted, for example, that the request to invade Czechoslovakia came from certain unnamed and unidentified "party and state officials" of the Czechoslovak Government. The Polish Government, getting the message only dimly, described these ghostly "officials" as "party and state activists." The East German regime, clumsily missing the whole legal point, mutated this reference into "party and state personalities in Czechoslovakia who are loyally devoted to socialism." Confounding the issue still further, the Bulgarian Government referred to "party and state leaders of the Czechoslovak Socialist Republic."

These shadow figures who allegedly requested that their country be despoiled by foreigners have not yet been given names by Moscow. The facts are clear that the duly constituted leaders of the Czechoslovak Government, the President of the Republic, the Chairman of the National Assembly, the Premier, and even the First Secretary of the Czechoslovak Communist Party Central Committee made no such request. In fact, they knew nothing of this invasion nor of the duplicitous design which brought it about. Yet these were the men whom Mr. Kosygin and Mr. Brezhnev conferred with in solemn council and with whom they declared unbreakable friendship a few days ago. And let us not forget that leaders of all the other invading nations were also at the Bratislava meeting and endorsed this touching sentiment.

The voices that the Soviet leaders heard calling on them to invade were—if they existed at all—the voices of a new breed of quislings. The "invitation" on which the Soviet case depends—if indeed there were anything that could possibly be described as an invitation—was, as is so patently clear, a document of treason invented and written by frightened men in Moscow reacting to their own dark nightmares.

## Disgust and Revulsion

There are many poignant aspects to this tragedy, Mr. President, but not the least must be the disgust and revulsion felt by the brave and honest people of Poland and Hungary, who tried themselves, a dozen years ago, to break free from the tyranny of Moscow—disgust and revulsion that their own soldiers should be associated in such a brutal and despicable enterprise.

> "In Czechoslovakia tonight the dark and ugly visage of the Soviet intention has been sharply revealed."

I trust, Mr. President—indeed, I am confident—that this Council will not take much time to dispose of this doomed and desperate effort to frustrate its procedures.

Often in discharging the responsibilities entrusted to the Council by the U.N. Charter, we face grave and difficult problems. But, Mr. President, that is not what we face this evening. The question of inscription, which the Soviet Union has challenged, is not a grave problem but a minor one, because even the Soviet Union knows that its effort to block the Council from considering this question is both futile and absurd. Nor is it a serious question, because the issue is so clear and the answer so plain.

Let us then, Mr. President, get on with our business. In Czechoslovakia tonight the dark and ugly visage of the Soviet intention has been sharply revealed. It is the intention to destroy dissent, to deter free debate, to prevent mankind from uttering or facing the truth. I know, Mr. President, that the responsible governments represented around this Council table will never be party to such a shoddy business.

There was no Western conspiracy against Communist rule in Czechoslovakia.

There was no Czechoslovakian Government request to the Soviet Union and its allies to interfere in its internal affairs.

There was no request, as Moscow would have the world believe, to install a puppet regime in the capital of Masaryk, Benes, and Dubcek.

This Council has a heavy responsibility, as do all members of the world organization, to condemn this brazen violation of the United Nations Charter and to call on the Soviet Union and its allies to withdraw its forces immediately from Czechoslovakia.

I urge immediate adoption of the agenda, Mr. President, so that the Council can get on with the important task it has before it. Time is wasting. In light of the Soviet objection, Mr. President, I request that the adoption of the agenda be put to a formal vote.

*George W. Ball was a United States Ambassador to the United Nations. He presented this speech before the Security Council.*

*"It must be the policy of the United States to support free peoples who are resisting attempted subjugation by armed minorities or outside pressures."*

# The US Is Supporting the Vietnamese People

## Lyndon Baines Johnson

Tonight in Viet-Nam more than 200,000 of your young Americans stand there fighting for your freedom. Tonight our people are determined that these men shall have whatever help they need and that their cause, which is our cause, shall be sustained.

But in these last days there have been questions about what we are doing in Viet-Nam, and these questions have been answered loudly and clearly for every citizen to see and to hear. The strength of America can never be sapped by discussion, and we have no better nor stronger tradition than open debate, free debate, in hours of danger. We believe, with Macaulay, that men are never so likely to settle a question rightly as when they discuss it freely. We are united in our commitment to free discussion. So also we are united in our determination that no foe anywhere should ever mistake our arguments for indecision, nor our debates for weakness.

So what are the questions that are still being asked?

First, some ask if this is a war for unlimited objectives. The answer is plain. The answer is "No."

### Preventing Aggression

Our purpose in Viet-Nam is to prevent the success of aggression. It is not conquest; it is not empire; it is not foreign bases; it is not domination. It is, simply put, just to prevent the forceful conquest of South Viet-Nam by North Viet-Nam.

Second, some people ask if we are caught in a blind escalation of force that is pulling us headlong toward a wider war that no one wants. The answer, again, is a simple "No."

We are using that force and only that force that is necessary to stop this aggression. Our fighting men are in Viet-Nam because tens of thousands of invaders came south before them. Our numbers have increased in Viet-Nam because the aggression of others has increased in Viet-Nam. The high hopes of the aggressor have been dimmed, and the tide of the battle has been turned, and our measured use of force will and must be continued. But this is prudent firmness under what I believe is careful control. There is not, and there will not be, a mindless escalation.

Third, others ask if our fighting men are to be denied the help they need. The answer, again, is and will be a resounding "No."

Our great Military Establishment has moved 200,000 men across 10,000 miles since last spring. These men have, and will have, all they need to fight the aggressor. They have already performed miracles in combat. The men behind them have worked miracles of supply, building new ports, transporting new equipment, opening new roads. The American forces of freedom are strong tonight in South Viet-Nam, and we plan to keep them so.

As you know, they are led there by a brilliant and a resourceful commander, General William C. Westmoreland. He knows the needs of war, and he supports the works of peace. And when he asks for more Americans to help the men that he has, his requests will be immediately studied and, as I promised the Nation last July, his needs will be immediately met.

### Mutual Commitment

Fourth, some ask if our men go alone to Viet-Nam, if we alone respect our great commitment in the Southeast Asia Treaty. Still again, the answer is a simple "No."

We have seven allies in SEATO, and we have seen five of them give us vital support, each with his own strength and in his own way, to the cause of freedom in Southeast Asia.

Fifth, some ask about the risks of a wider war,

Lyndon Baines Johnson, from an address at a Freedom House Dinner in New York on February 22, 1966.

perhaps against the vast land armies of Red China. And again the answer is "No," never by any act of ours—and not if there is any reason left behind the wild words from Peking.

We have threatened no one, and we will not. We seek the end of no regime, and we will not. Our purpose is solely to defend against aggression. To any armed attack, we will reply. We have measured the strength and the weakness of others, and we think we know our own. We observe in ourselves, and we applaud in others, a careful restraint in action. We can live with anger in word as long as it is matched by caution in deed.

## "Our purpose in Viet-Nam is to prevent the success of aggression."

Sixth, men ask if we rely on guns alone. Still again, the answer is "No."

From our Honolulu meeting, from the clear pledge which joins us with our allies, there has emerged a common dedication to the peaceful progress of the people of Viet-Nam—to schools for their children, to care for their health, to hope and bounty for their land.

The Vice President returned tonight from his constructive and very highly successful visit to Saigon and to other capitals, and he tells me that he and Ambassador [Henry Cabot] Lodge have found a new conviction and purpose in South Viet-Nam—for the battle against want and injustice as well as the battle against aggression.

### Breeding Ground of War

So the pledge of Honolulu will be kept, and the pledge of Baltimore stands open—to help the men of the North when they have the wisdom to be ready.

We Americans must understand how fundamental is the meaning of this second war—the war on want. I talked on my ranch last fall with Secretary [Orville L.] Freeman, the Secretary of Agriculture, and in my office last week with Secretary [John W.] Gardner, Secretary of Health, Education, and Welfare, making, over and over again, the same central point: The breeding ground of war is human misery. If we are not to fight forever in faraway places—in Europe, or the far Pacific, or the jungles of Africa, or the suburbs of Santo Domingo—then we must learn to get at the roots of violence. As a nation we must magnify our struggle against world hunger and illiteracy and disease. We must bring hope to men whose lives now end at two score or less. Because without that hope, without progress in this war on want, we will be called on to fight again and again, as we are fighting tonight.

Seventh, men ask who has a right to rule in South Viet-Nam. Our answer there is what it has been for 200 years. The people must have this right—the South Vietnamese people—and no one else.

Washington will not impose upon the people of South Viet-Nam a government not of their choice. Hanoi shall not impose upon the people of South Viet-Nam a government not of their choice. So we will insist for ourselves on what we require from Hanoi: respect for the principle of government by the consent of the governed. We stand for self-determination—for free elections—and we will honor their result.

Eighth, men ask if we are neglecting any hopeful chance of peace. And the answer is "No."

A great servant of peace, Secretary Dean Rusk, has sent the message of peace on every wire and by every hand to every continent. A great pleader for peace here with us tonight, Ambassador Arthur Goldberg, has worked at home and abroad in this same cause. Their undiscouraged efforts will continue.

How much wiser it would have been, how much more compassionate toward its own people, if Hanoi had only come to the bargaining table at the close of the year. Then the 7,000 Communist troops who have died in battle since January the first, and the many thousands who have been wounded in that same period, would have lived in peace with their fellow men.

Today, as then, Hanoi has the opportunity to end the increasing toll the war is taking on those under its command.

Ninth, some ask how long we must bear this burden. To that question, in all honesty, I can give you no answer tonight.

During the battle of Britain, when that nation stood alone in 1940, Winston Churchill gave no answer to that question. When the forces of freedom were driven from the Philippines, President Roosevelt could not and did not name the date that we would return.

If the aggressor persists in Viet-Nam, the struggle may well be long. Our men in battle know and they accept this hard fact. We who are at home can do as much, because there is no computer that can tell the hour and the day of peace, but we do know that it will come only to the steadfast and never to the weak in heart.

Tenth, and finally, men ask if it is worth it. I think you know that answer. It is the answer that Americans have given for a quarter of a century, wherever American strength has been pledged to prevent aggression.

### Unchanged Purpose

The contest in Viet-Nam is confused and hard, and many of its forms are new. Yet our American purpose and policy are unchanged. Our men in Viet-Nam are there. They are there, as Secretary Dillon (former Secretary of the Treasury Douglas Dillon) told you, to keep a promise that was made 12 years ago. The Southeast Asia Treaty promised, as Secretary John Foster Dulles said for the United States, that "an attack upon the treaty area would occasion a reaction so united, so strong, and so well placed that the aggressor would lose more than it could hope to gain."

But we keep more than a specific treaty promise in Viet-Nam tonight. We keep the faith for freedom.

## Presidential Promises

Four Presidents have pledged to keep that faith.

The first was Franklin D. Roosevelt, in his State of the Union message 25 years ago. He said:

> . . . we are committed to the proposition that principles of morality and considerations for our own security will never permit us to acquiesce in a peace dictated by aggressors and sponsored by appeasers. We know that enduring peace cannot be bought at the cost of other people's freedom.

The second was Harry S. Truman, in 1947, at a historic turning point in the history of guerrilla warfare—and of Greece, Turkey, and the United States. These were his words then:

> I believe that it must be the policy of the United States to support free peoples who are resisting attempted subjugation by armed minorities or by outside pressures.
>
> I believe that we must assist free peoples to work out their own destinies in their own way.

The third was Dwight D. Eisenhower, in his first inaugural address. He promised this:

> Realizing that common sense and common decency alike dictate the futility of appeasement, we shall never try to placate an aggressor by the false and wicked bargain of trading honor for security. Americans, indeed, all free men, remember that in the final choice a soldier's pack is not so heavy a burden as a prisoner's chains.

And then 5 years ago, John F. Kennedy, on the cold bright noon of his first day in office, proclaimed:

> Let the word go forth from this time and place, to friend and foe alike, that the torch has been passed to a new generation of Americans—born in this century, tempered by war, disciplined by a hard and bitter peace, proud of our ancient heritage—and unwilling to witness or permit the slow undoing of those human rights to which this Nation has always been committed, and to which we are committed today at home and around the world.
>
> Let every nation know, whether it wishes us well or ill, that we shall pay any price, bear any burden, meet any hardship, support any friend, oppose any foe to assure the survival and the success of liberty.

This is the American tradition. Built in free discussion, proven on a hundred battlefields, rewarded by a progress at home that has no match in history, it beckons us forward tonight to the work of peace in Viet-Nam. We will build freedom while we fight, and we will seek peace every day by every honorable means. But we will persevere along the high, hard road of freedom. We are too old to be foolhardy, and we are too young to be tired. We are too strong for fear and too determined for retreat.

## Hope for Peace

Each evening when I retire, I take up—from a bedside table—reports from the battlefront and reports from the capitals around the world. They tell me how our men have fared that day in the hills and the valleys of Viet-Nam. They tell me what hope there seems to be that the message of peace will be heard and that this tragic war may be ended. I have read of individual acts of heroism—of dedicated men and women whose valor matches that of any generation that has ever gone before. I read of men risking their lives to save others—of men giving their lives to save freedom. Always among these reports are a few letters from the men out there themselves. If there is any doubt among some here at home about our purposes in Viet-Nam, I never find it reflected in those letters from Viet-Nam.

Our soldiers, our marines, our airmen, and our sailors know why they are in Viet-Nam. They know, as five Presidents have known, how inseparably bound together are America's freedom and the freedom of her friends around the world.

*"We stand for self-determination—for free elections—and we will honor their result."*

So tonight let me read you from a letter that I received from an American father, a warm friend of mine of many years, about his son, a young Army captain. He said:

> I have never known a man at war who showed less bravado in his communications with home. When he was not flying missions in his helicopter or working out of the battalion headquarters he and some of his buddies on their own visited the orphanages as individuals and played with the kids. He was deeply interested in the Vietnamese people, particularly the peasants, and he told me how sorely they wanted, more than anything else, to just be left alone in some semblance of freedom to grow their rice and to raise their families. This good young American, as thousands like him, was not on the other side of the world fighting specifically for you or for me, Mr. President. He was fighting in perhaps our oldest American tradition, taking up for people who are being pushed around.

The young captain described in this letter is dead tonight, but his spirit lives in the 200,000 young Americans who stand out there on freedom's frontier in Viet-Nam. It lives in their mothers and in their fathers here in America, who have proudly watched them leave their homes for their distant struggle.

So tonight I ask each citizen to join me, to join me in the homes and the meeting places our men are fighting to keep free, in a prayer for their safety.

I ask you to join me in a pledge to the cause for which they fight—the cause of human freedom, to which this organization is dedicated. I ask you for your help, your understanding, and for your commitment so that this united people may show forth to all the world that America has not ended the only struggle that is worthy of man's unceasing sacrifice—the struggle to be free.

*Lyndon Baines Johnson served as president of the United States from 1963 to 1969.*

*"In flagrant violation of the Geneva Agreements, the USA has piratically attacked the Democratic Republic of Vietnam and is waging a barbarous war against the people of South Vietnam."*

# The US Is an Imperialist Aggressor in Vietnam

Leonid Brezhnev and *Pravda*

*Editor's note: Part I of the following viewpoint is taken from a report by Leonid Brezhnev to the Central Committee of the Communist Party. Part II is taken from an editorial in* Pravda, *a prominent Russian newspaper.*

## I

In speaking of mounting world tension and of the threat of a world war, special mention must be made of US imperialist aggression against Vietnam. In flagrant violation of the Geneva Agreements, the USA has piratically attacked the Democratic Republic of Vietnam and is waging a barbarous war against the people of South Vietnam. This imperialist power, which styles itself a champion of freedom and civilization, is using almost all the known means of destruction and annihilation against a peace-loving country situated thousands of miles away from America, a country that has never harmed US interests. More than 200,000 US troops, US aircraft carriers, huge bombers, poison gases and napalm are being used against the heroic patriots of Vietnam. Irresponsible statements threatening to escalate military operations still further are being made in Washington. Recently the US State Department officially declared that there is a 'programme' of destroying vegetation and crops in Vietnam with chemicals in order to deprive the Vietnamese of food sources. Such is the real face of US imperialism. Through its aggression in Vietnam the US has covered itself with shame which it will never live down.

But no matter what outrages the aggressors commit they can never break the will of the Vietnamese people who have risen in a sacred struggle for the freedom of their country, for their life and honour, for the right to order their own destiny. Their heroic,

just struggle will go down in history as a splendid example of unyielding courage, staunchness and determination to achieve victory.

## Moral and Political Isolation of US

A powerful movement in support of Vietnam is mounting throughout the world. Moral and political isolation of the US aggressors is being intensified. The Vietnamese people enjoy the assistance of the Soviet Union and other socialist countries and the sympathy and support of the broad masses of all countries. Indignation against the war in Vietnam is growing among the American people as well. All this is promoting the best internationalist traditions of the world working class.

The Soviet Union and the peace-loving peoples of the whole world demand that the USA stop its aggression against Vietnam and withdraw all interventionist troops from that country. Continuation of this aggression, which the American military are seeking to extend to other South-East Asian countries, is fraught with the most dangerous consequences to world peace.

We categorically declare that if the aggressors escalate the shameful war against the Vietnamese people they will have to contend with mounting support for Vietnam from the Soviet Union and other socialist friends and brothers. The Vietnamese people will be the masters of their country and nobody will ever extinguish the torch of socialism, which has been raised on high by the Democratic Republic of Vietnam.

As a consequence of US aggression in Vietnam and other aggressive acts of American imperialism our relations with the United States of America have deteriorated. The US ruling circles are to blame for this.

## II

Recently international tension has greatly increased. Under cover of nonsense about their

Leonid Brezhnev, from "Report to the 23rd Congress of the CPSU Relating to Vietnam" on March 29, 1966. *Pravda*, editorial on August 8, 1965.

"special duties" and "special responsibility" to the so-called free world, the ruling circles of the United States are stepping up the arms race and carrying out acts of aggression in various parts of the world.

Having assumed the functions of world gendarme, they are trying—by means of the "export of counter-revolution"—to stifle the liberation movements of the peoples.

As a result, peace and the vital interests of the peoples stand in grave jeopardy.

It is only natural that this policy pursued by U.S. imperialism should meet with vigorous resistance from the U.S.S.R., the other socialist countries, the young sovereign states and the working class in the capitalist countries—from, in short, all who cherish peace, freedom and happiness on earth.

The Soviet Union has always been the main obstacle in the way of the fulfilment of world imperialism's far-reaching military and political designs, and so it remains. . . .

## Revolutionary Firmness

Characteristic of the U.S.S.R.'s Leninist foreign policy is its combination of revolutionary firmness in upholding basic principles and tackling the cardinal issues of world policy, affecting the destinies of the peoples, and the necessary flexibility in tactical actions in readiness to enter into negotiations and agreements for the peace, freedom and independence of the peoples.

By all its activity in the world arena, the U.S.S.R. is contributing to the world revolutionary movement, to the struggle of the peoples against imperialism, for peace, democracy, national independence and socialism.

In drafting and carrying out the foreign policy of the U.S.S.R., the central committee of the Communist Party of the Soviet Union and the Soviet government rely on a Marxist-Leninist analysis of the international alignment of class forces and the key objective factors of world politics.

---

*"No matter what outrages the aggressors commit they can never break the will of the Vietnamese people."*

---

Lenin once declared that "every state exists in a system of states." The existence of and struggle between two different socio-economic systems has become the definitive feature of present-day international relations, while the character of the relations between the states of these two systems has developed into the sharpest problem.

An individualist, unrealistic approach to the phenomena and events of international life is deeply foreign to our party's central committee and the Soviet government. For, as Lenin taught us, such an approach may have grave consequences; it may give rise either to vainglorious boasting or for weak nerves in the face of a war threat emanating from imperialism.

The comprehensive account it takes of the fundamental changes in the balance of forces in favour of world socialism and the anti-imperialist movement, and of the tremendous economic, political and military potentialities of the U.S.S.R. and the entire socialist system is the significant feature of Soviet foreign policy.

It gives weight to such powerful revolutionary factors as the international working-class and national liberation movements.

## Doomed Forces of Imperialism

Marxists-Leninists clearly realise that capitalism is historically doomed and that imperialism will unquestionably grow weak and decrepit as a system.

At the same time, however, in their foreign policy they cannot ignore the circumstance that imperialism, whose aggressive nature never changes, still possesses adequate strength and possibilities for unleashing local and even world wars.

In their effort to check the march of history and regain lost positions, the forces of imperialism—and first of all U.S. imperialism—are resorting more and more often to intervention in the internal affairs of other countries, and are undertaking direct acts of aggression against freedom-loving countries, thus undermining the mainstays of world peace. . . .

The Soviet government and the whole Soviet people enthusiastically and unanimously support the Vietnamese people in their heroic struggle against American imperialism.

The Soviet Union fully shares the positions of the government of the Democratic Republic of Vietnam and the National Liberation Front of South Vietnam on the problem of settlement in Vietnam—the ending of the bombing of the Democratic Republic of Vietnam, strict abidance by the Geneva Agreements, the withdrawal of all the armed forces of the United States and its allies from South Vietnam, the removal of American arms from Vietnamese territory and the granting to the Vietnamese people of the possibility of shaping their own destiny.

It is precisely the 1954 Geneva Agreements that can provide the basis for a return to normal in the situation in Vietnam. The Soviet government has repeatedly pointed out that every assistance necessary for beating back the aggression is being and will continue to be given to the Democratic Republic of Vietnam. . . .

## Support for National Liberation Movements

Together with the other countries of the socialist commonwealth, the Soviet Union is giving every possible support to the national liberation movement and is developing solidarity and co-operation with the independent countries of Asia, Africa and Latin America.

As our party's Programme indicates, the Communist Party of the Soviet Union sees fraternal alliance with peoples who have thrown off the colonial or semi-colonial yoke as a cornerstone of its international policy....

The U.S.S.R. has never been indifferent—nor will it ever be indifferent—to the aggressive actions of colonialists which threaten the independence of peoples.

The Soviet state has always opposed the imperialist policy of "exporting counter-revolution." It has given and continues to give the broadest assistance to peoples fighting for their freedom and independence against colonialism and neo-colonialism.

The Soviet Union always bases itself on the right of each people to free and independent development as a sacred right; the desire to end imperialist aggression is profoundly legitimate and completely justified.

When the imperialists compel them to take action, the peoples reply with all available means of struggle, including national liberation wars, to imperialist attempts to deprive them by force of their sacred right.

The Soviet Union has supported and will continue to support the national liberation struggle in all its forms, both peaceful and nonpeaceful. Peoples defending their independence have every reason to consider the Soviet Union their reliable friend, on whom they can always rely, for the U.S.S.R., not in words but in deeds, with all the necessary means, helps them in a real way in their struggle against imperialism.

The Soviet Union is playing an enormous role in the economic development of countries fighting for their liberation from imperialism. At the beginning of 1965, the Soviet Union had agreements on economics and technical co-operation with the governments of nearly 30 Afro-Asian countries.

## USSR Support Against Imperialism

The Soviet Union's activities in support of the struggle of the peoples against imperialism is widely known: persistent actions in the United Nations for the vigorous censure and complete ending of the shameful colonial system; its role in cutting short the Anglo-Franco-Israeli aggression against Egypt and other aggressions by imperialism in the Middle East; and support given to Indonesia's just demands on the question of Western Iran.

This is also to be seen in the Soviet Union's firm stand with regard to imperialist interference in the national liberation struggle of the people of the Congo, in the Dominican Republic and in the domestic affairs of Cyprus.

The active assistance given by the socialist countries to peoples fighting for their final liberation from political and economic oppression eases the conditions of their struggle and brings closer the hour of their final victory over the imperialist forces. At the same time, the national liberation struggle of the peoples, an integral part of the world revolutionary process, facilitates the success of this process, weakens and damages the positions of imperialism, helps to strengthen all the anti-imperialist forces and helps the peoples building socialism and communism.

*"In their effort to check the march of history and regain lost positions, the forces of imperialism. . .are resorting more and more often to intervention in the internal affairs of other countries."*

It is unnatural and dangerous for the common cause to separate and counterpose the struggle of the peoples for their liberation to the building of socialism and communism in the U.S.S.R. and in the other socialist countries and their struggle against imperialism in the international arena.

It is a common cause for the whole socialist commonwealth to give effective assistance to the national liberation movement. The unity of the countries of socialism in the struggle against the imperialist policy of "exporting counter-revolution" is necessary today as never before.

The Soviet Union has never spared its strength, nor will it spare it, in helping the peoples to defend their revolutionary gains.

## Crucial Co-Existence

The Soviet Union has regarded the putting forward of the principles of the peaceful co-existence between states with different social systems and ridding peaceful co-existence between states with different social systems and ridding mankind of the threat of a world war as one of the most important functions of its foreign policy.

Peaceful co-existence is the Leninist foundation of the policy which the Soviet Union proposes and always defends in its dealings with the capitalist states. Peaceful co-existence today is the alternative to a thermonuclear war.

In the nuclear age, the historical responsibility for the fate of present and future generations is placed on all countries, no matter how big or small in area and population.

To prevent thermonuclear war is the task and the sacred duty of the peoples of all countries. But especially great here is the responsibility of the socialist states, because the peoples see them as the most effective force in the struggle against imperialism and against its preparations for a world thermonuclear catastrophe.

Attempts are still being made to represent the policy of peaceful co-existence with the capitalist countries as renunciation of the struggle against imperialism. Such attempts cannot in any way be justified.

"Peaceful co-existence," says the Programme of the Communist Party of the Soviet Union, "serves as a basis for the peaceful competition between socialism and capitalism on an international scale and is a specific form of class struggle between them."

The policy of peaceful co-existence, directed against the most reactionary and bellicose forces of imperialism, is rooted in unarguable respect for the right of every people to choose a suitable social and state system for itself. Conditions of peaceful co-existence make for success in the liberation struggle and the fulfillment of the revolutionary tasks confronting the peoples.

Peaceful co-existence between countries with different systems is a special form of class struggle in the world arena. The struggle for the establishment of the principles of peaceful co-existence is many-sided. Its basic idea is to mobilize the masses for an active fight against each and every aggressive action of imperialism.

*"The world situation today urgently puts before the peoples and all the revolutionary forces the task of preventing a world thermonuclear war."*

Peaceful co-existence between the socialist and capitalist countries and the development of normal inter-state relations with them, presupposes rather than rules out a struggle against the aggressive plans and designs of imperialism in the international arena, it presupposes the exposure of the intrigues of militarist forces and the mobilization of the masses to struggle for peace.

### Irresponsible Military Efforts

If the imperialist politicians and strategists want to remain on the firm ground of reality, they must not hope to be able to agree with the need for peaceful co-existence with the socialist countries in words, while simultaneously increasing their military efforts, engaging in the "export of counter-revolution" and "brinkmanship"—irresponsibly hopping from step to step of the ladder of intensity of conflict, as it happens to suit their imperialist goals.

Certain western circles cherish the hope that it will be possible to enter into some sort of "peaceful co-existence" with the Soviet Union while simultaneously conducting an aggressive policy towards other countries—socialist states or newly independent states of Asia and Africa. The Soviet Union will never agree to such approach....

The world situation today urgently puts before the peoples and all the revolutionary forces the task of preventing a world thermonuclear war, of stopping the local wars unleashed by imperialism and, in the first place, by the U.S. ruling circles and of giving the utmost support to the national liberation and revolutionary struggles of all peoples.

The great socialist power, the Soviet Union, will always be in the forefront of the struggle for peace and socialism.

Objectively, the goals of Soviet foreign policy coincide completely with the vital interests of the working people of the whole world, with their desire to frustrate the aggressive tendencies of imperialism, to prevent a war conflagration and to create the most favourable conditions for the further struggle against imperialism and against all kinds of social and national oppression.

That is why Soviet foreign policy always meets with sympathy and active support from wide sections of the working people and all the peace-loving forces of the world.

*Leonid Brezhnev had a major impact on Soviet policy from his 1952 appointment to the Central Committee until his death in 1982. At his death, he was Party Chairman, the most powerful position in the USSR. Pravda is one of the Soviet Union's two largest newspapers and is an official organ of the government.*

*"If the United States government was really preoccupied with protecting the lives of...Americans, there has always been a simple way out:...to bring them back home."*

# The US Is Acting Aggressively in Cambodia

### Alexei Kosygin

In connection with the serious aggravation of the situation in south-east Asia caused by the aggressive actions of the United States against Cambodia, the Soviet government has considered it necessary to make the following statement. By order of the president of the United States, Mr. Richard Nixon, American armed forces invaded the territory of neutral Cambodia on the night of 30 April–1 May. This was announced in a radio and television address by the United States president. According to news-agency reports, the United States forces, including tanks and aircraft, are moving deep into Cambodian territory, sowing death among the Cambodian population. In these aggressive operations, the United States command is also using sizeable contingents of troops of the South Vietnamese puppet regime.

A new seedbed of war has now been created in the territory of south-east Asia. Besides Vietnam and Laos, its flames have also enveloped Cambodia.

## US Aggression

Having carried the fighting over to another state of Indo-China, the United States president voiced in his statement a threat levelled against all states that might decide to come out in support of the victims of American aggression. What is more, in the last few days, the United States has been undertaking massive air raids on some areas of the Democratic Republic of Vietnam (DRV). Thereby, it has crudely violated the obligation it assumed in accordance with the understanding which formed the basis for the four-power negotiations in Paris.

The United States administration is evidently guided by an aggressive line in policy, proceeding from the assumption that a strong power cannot act in international affairs otherwise than through the use of force. It is presumptuously believed in Washington that the United States of America merely has to use force wherever it chooses for a government that does not suit it to be removed and for its *Diktat* to be established. This course, followed in the past, has led and continues to lead the United States foreign policy to failures. That is well known and one example is the war against the Vietnamese people.

Having unleashed war in Cambodia and resumed the large-scale barbarous bombing of inhabited areas of the DRV, President Nixon is in effect also tearing up the decision of his predecessor, President Johnson, to end as of November 1968, all aerial bombing and other action involving the use of force against the DRV.

In the above-mentioned statement of the United States president, an attempt is made to justify the aggression against Cambodia, and, with this in view, arguments are marshalled whose aim is to mislead public opinion in the world and in America itself.

## Strange Logic

Washington is attempting to motivate the decision on a military invasion of Cambodia by alleging that it was necessary to save the lives of United States soldiers in South Vietnam. This logic is more than strange.

The aggressor, having first invaded the territory of one country, argues that somebody is threatening the lives of his soldiers, that is foreign invaders, and this, from the aggressor's standpoint, is an adequate pretext for invading the territory of another country, neighbouring on the first one.

And so for the United States the frontiers and the sovereignty of states, and the inviolability of their territory, lose all their meaning. But such a policy constitutes the most flagrant arbitrariness in international affairs and it must be resolutely condemned.

Alexei Kosygin, from a statement on American intervention in Cambodia, published in *Pravda* on May 5, 1970.

It is clear to everyone that with the expansion of United States aggression in Indo-China, the danger for the lives of its soldiers has not diminished at all.

The deeper the United States gets bogged down in its military gambles on the soil of Vietnam, Laos, and now in Cambodia, the more of their kith and kin will American families lose. If the United States government was really preoccupied with protecting the lives of tens and hundreds of thousands of Americans, there has always been a simple way out: not to send American soldiers to Vietnam, Cambodia or Laos, but to bring them back home.

## False Allegations

Even further away from the truth are allegations that the transfer of hostilities to the territory of Cambodia would bring the end of the war in Vietnam closer. It is made to appear as if the expansion of the theatre of war in Indo-China serves almost to reduce the scale of the fighting rather than to increase it.

As is evident from the statement of the United States president, the real meaning of the statement, and indeed of the entire policy of the United States in south-east Asia, is to eliminate progressive regimes in the countries of the region, to stifle the national liberation movement, to hamper social progress of the peoples, and through colonialist methods, to subordinate the foreign and domestic policies of the states of Indo-China to its military and strategic interests and to draw them into its military bloc.

Such are the major goals of the United States in this region. They are well known to all peoples. These are imperialist, aggressive goals alien to the interests of the peoples, and therefore they are inevitably doomed to failure.

The policy of neutrality and the peace-loving line followed by Cambodia until recently do not suit those who determine United States policies. After the American invasion of Cambodia, the connection between the subversive activities of the relevant United States services and the *coup d'etat* in Phnom Penh which resulted in the removal from office of Prince Norodom Sihanouk, the legitimate chief of state, has become all the more evident.

## Sowing Enmity

These services and their agents in Cambodia are trying to sow enmity between the Khmer people and the people of Vietnam. They have staged a bloody massacre of Vietnamese living in the territory of Cambodia, and they have set up concentration camps where peaceful inhabitants of the country are being brutally murdered.

They resort to all possible methods to set the peoples of Asia against one another. Fratricidal wars are being imposed on the countries of the region. An example of this is the United States president's doctrine of the 'Vietnamization' of the war. It is clear that any government which would allow the United States to use it as an accomplice in the policy of aggression would brand itself as an enemy of the peoples.

It would be in order to ask who gave the United States the right to be the judge of what is good and what is bad for other peoples. On what grounds does the United States assume a role that cannot be qualified otherwise than that of an international policeman? No one has given it that right and it neither had nor has any grounds for it.

The American military invasion of Cambodia arouses the indignation of all peace-loving forces throughout the world. The Soviet government believes that the expansion of the United States aggression in Indo-China makes even more pressing the need for the unity and greater cohesion of all socialist, all anti-imperialist and peace-loving forces in the struggle against aggression.

In the existing situation, all states which cherish the interests of peace and freedom of the peoples are called upon to display a high sense of responsibility for the further course of events and determination to assist in rebuffing the aggressor.

The result of the invasion of Cambodia by American troops may well be the further complication of the general international situation. In this light the question arises: how should the repeated statements of the United States president in favour of passing from an era of confrontation to an era of negotiation be understood?

---

*"Any government which would allow the United States to use it as an accomplice in the policy of aggression would brand itself as an enemy of the peoples."*

---

Is it possible to speak seriously about the desire of the United States president for fruitful negotiations to solve pressing international problems while the United States is grossly flouting the Geneva agreements of 1954 and 1962, to which it is a party, and undertaking one new act after another undermining the foundations of international security?

What is the value of international agreements which the United States is or intends to be a party to if it so unceremoniously violates its obligations?

## US Actions Conflict with Peace Claims

It is impossible not to give serious thought to the fact that President Nixon's practical steps in the field of foreign policy are fundamentally at variance with those declarations and assurances that he repeatedly made both before assuming the presidency and when he was already in the White House.

He promised the American people and the world public to do his utmost to end the war in Vietnam, to bring the American soldiers back home and to save their lives. Reality has shown that all those assurances remain meaningless phrases since in actual fact the United States government is intensifying still further its bellicose aggressive line....

*"American aggression in south-east Asia will meet with an even more resolute and effective rebuff on the part of the peoples that have fallen victim to the imperialist attack."*

Whatever trumped-up pretexts are used to cover it, it is quite clear that cynical contempt for the inalienable right of the peoples of Indo-China to be the master in their own house and a crude American *Diktat* remain the basis of United States foreign policy in that region of the world, while conspiracies, military interventions and aggression remain the instruments of its realization.

There is no doubt that the expansion of American aggression in south-east Asia will meet with an even more resolute and effective rebuff on the part of the peoples that have fallen victim to the imperialist attack, and on the part of all those who cherish the interests of peace and freedom of the peoples.

Responsibility for the aggression against the people of Cambodia has now been added to the heavy responsibility which the United States bears for the war against the Vietnamese people. The Soviet government will naturally draw the proper conclusions for its policy from this course of action of the United States in south-east Asia.

*This viewpoint is taken from a statement by Soviet Premier Alexei Kosygin on American intervention in Cambodia.*

*"We will not allow American men by the thousands to be killed by an enemy from privileged sanctuaries."*

# The US Is Acting Defensively in Cambodia

### Richard M. Nixon

*Good evening, my fellow Americans.*

Ten days ago, in my report to the Nation on Vietnam, I announced a decision to withdraw an additional 150,000 Americans from Vietnam over the next year. I said then that I was making the decision despite our concern over increased enemy activity in Laos, in Cambodia, and in South Vietnam.

At that time, I warned that if I concluded that increased enemy activity in any of these areas endangered the lives of Americans remaining in Vietnam, I would not hesitate to take strong and effective measures to deal with that situation.

## Continued Aggression

Despite the warning, North Vietnam has increased its military aggression in all these areas, and particularly in Cambodia.

After full consultation with the National Security Council, Ambassador [Ellsworth] Bunker, General [Creighton W.] Abrams, and my other advisers, I have concluded that the actions of the enemy in the last 10 days clearly endanger the lives of Americans who are in Vietnam now and would constitute an unacceptable risk to those who will be there after withdrawal of another 150,000.

To protect our men who are in Vietnam and to guarantee the continued success of our withdrawal and Vietnamization programs, I have concluded that the time has come for action.

Tonight, I shall describe the actions of the enemy, the actions I have ordered to deal with that situation, and the reasons for my decision.

Cambodia, a small country of 7 million people, has been a neutral nation since the Geneva Agreement of 1954—an agreement, incidentally, which was signed by the Government of North Vietnam.

American policy since then has been to scrupulously respect the neutrality of the Cambodian people. We have maintained a skeleton diplomatic mission of fewer than 15 in Cambodia's capital, and that only since last August. For the previous 4 years, from 1965 to 1969, we did not have any diplomatic mission whatever in Cambodia. And for the past 5 years, we have provided no military assistance whatever and no economic assistance to Cambodia.

North Vietnam, however, has not respected that neutrality.

For the past 5 years—as indicated on this map that you see here—North Vietnam has occupied military sanctuaries all along the Cambodian frontier with South Vietnam. Some of these extend up to 20 miles into Cambodia. The sanctuaries are in red, and as you note, they are on both sides of the border. They are used for hit and run attacks on American and South Vietnamese forces in South Vietnam.

## Communist Violations

These Communist occupied territories contain major base camps, training sites, logistics facilities, weapons and ammunition factories, air strips, and prisoner-of-war compounds.

For 5 years, neither the United States nor South Vietnam has moved against these enemy sanctuaries because we did not wish to violate the territory of a neutral nation. Even after the Vietnamese Communists began to expand these sanctuaries 4 weeks ago, we counseled patience to our South Vietnamese allies and imposed restraints on our own commanders.

In contrast to our policy, the enemy in the past 2 weeks has stepped up his guerrilla actions and he is concentrating his main forces in these sanctuaries that you see on this map where they are building up to launch massive attacks on our forces and those of South Vietnam.

North Vietnam in the last 2 weeks has stripped

Richard M. Nixon, from a radio address to the nation on April 30, 1970.

away all pretense of respecting the sovereignty or the neutrality of Cambodia. Thousands of their soldiers are invading the country from the sanctuaries; they are encircling the capital of Phnom Penh. Coming from these sanctuaries, as you see here, they have moved into Cambodia and are encircling the capital.

Cambodia, as a result of this, has sent out a call to the United States, to a number of other nations, for assistance. Because if this enemy effort succeeds, Cambodia would become a vast enemy staging area and a springboard for attacks on South Vietnam along 600 miles of frontier—a refuge where enemy troops could return from combat without fear of retaliation.

---

*"We take this action not for the purpose of expanding the war into Cambodia but for the purpose of ending the war in Vietnam and winning the just peace we all desire."*

---

North Vietnamese men and supplies could then be poured into that country, jeopardizing not only the lives of our own men but the people of South Vietnam as well.

## Three Options

Now confronted with this situation, we have three options.

First, we can do nothing. Well, the ultimate result of that course of action is clear. Unless we indulge in wishful thinking, the lives of Americans remaining in Vietnam after our next withdrawal of 150,000 would be gravely threatened.

Let us go to the map again. Here is South Vietnam. Here is North Vietnam. North Vietnam already occupies this part of Laos. If North Vietnam also occupied this whole band in Cambodia, or the entire country, it would mean that South Vietnam was completely outflanked and the forces of Americans in this area, as well as the South Vietnamese, would be in an untenable military position.

Our second choice is to provide massive assistance to Cambodia itself. Now unfortunately, while we deeply sympathize with the plight of 7 million Cambodians whose country is being invaded, massive amounts of military assistance could not be rapidly and effectively utilized by the small Cambodian Army against the immediate threat.

With other nations, we shall do our best to provide the small arms and other equipment which the Cambodian Army of 40,000 needs and can use for its defense. But the aid we will provide will be limited to the purpose of enabling Cambodia to defend its neutrality and not for the purpose of making it an active belligerent on one side or the other.

Our third choice is to go to the heart of the trouble. That means cleaning out major North Vietnamese and Vietcong occupied territories, these sanctuaries which serve as bases for attacks on both Cambodia and American and South Vietnamese forces in South Vietnam. Some of these, incidentally, are as close to Saigon as Baltimore is to Washington.

This one, for example [*indicating*], is called the Parrot's Beak. It is only 33 miles from Saigon.

Now faced with these three options, this is the decision I have made.

In cooperation with the armed forces of South Vietnam, attacks are being launched this week to clean out major enemy sanctuaries on the Cambodian-Vietnam border.

A major responsibility for the ground operations is being assumed by South Vietnamese forces. For example, the attacks in several areas, including the Parrot's Beak that I referred to a moment ago, are exclusively South Vietnamese ground operations under South Vietnamese command with the United States providing air and logistical support.

There is one area, however, immediately above Parrot's Beak, where I have concluded that a combined American and South Vietnamese operation is necessary.

## Essential, Non-Invasive Actions

This is not an invasion of Cambodia. The areas in which these attacks will be launched are completely occupied and controlled by North Vietnamese forces. Our purpose is not to occupy the areas. Once enemy forces are driven out of these sanctuaries and once their military supplies are destroyed, we will withdraw.

These actions are in no way directed at the security interests of any nation. Any government that chooses to use these actions as a pretext for harming relations with the United States will be doing so on its own responsibility, and on its own initiative, and we will draw the appropriate conclusions.

Now let me give you the reasons for my decision.

A majority of the American people, a majority of you listening to me, are for the withdrawal of our forces from Vietnam. The action I have taken tonight is indispensable for the continuing success of that withdrawal program.

A majority of the American people want to end this war rather than to have it drag on interminably. The action I have taken tonight will serve that purpose.

A majority of the American people want to keep the casualties of our brave men in Vietnam at an absolute minimum. The action I take tonight is essential if we are to accomplish that goal.

We take this action not for the purpose of expanding the war into Cambodia but for the purpose of ending the war in Vietnam and winning the just peace we all desire. We have made and we will continue to make every possible effort to end this war through negotiation at the conference table rather than through more fighting on the battlefield.

Let us look again at the record. We have stopped the bombing of North Vietnam. We have cut air operations by over 20 percent. We have announced withdrawal of over 250,000 of our men. We have offered to withdraw all our men if they will withdraw theirs. We have offered to negotiate all issues with only one condition—and that is that the future of South Vietnam be determined not by North Vietnam, not by the United States, but by the people of South Vietnam themselves.

The answer of the enemy has been intransigence at the conference table, belligerence in Hanoi, massive military aggression in Laos and Cambodia, and stepped-up attacks in South Vietnam, designed to increase American casualties.

This attitude has become intolerable. We will not react to this threat to American lives merely by plaintive diplomatic protests. If we did, the credibility of the United States would be destroyed in every area of the world where only the power of the United States deters aggression.

## Responsibility to Defend American Lives

Tonight, I again warn the North Vietnamese that if they continue to escalate the fighting when the United States is withdrawing its forces, I shall meet my responsibility as Commander in Chief of our Armed Forces to take the action I consider necessary to defend the security of our American men.

The action that I have announced tonight puts the leaders of North Vietnam on notice that we will be patient in working for peace, we will be conciliatory at the conference table, but we will not be humiliated. We will not be defeated. We will not allow American men by the thousands to be killed by an enemy from privileged sanctuaries.

The time came long ago to end this war through peaceful negotiations. We stand ready for those negotiations. We have made major efforts, many of which must remain secret. I say tonight that all the offers and approaches made previously remain on the conference table whenever Hanoi is ready to negotiate seriously.

But if the enemy response to our most conciliatory offers for peaceful negotiation continues to be to increase its attacks and humiliate and defeat us, we shall react accordingly.

My fellow Americans, we live in an age of anarchy both abroad and at home. We see mindless attacks on all the great institutions which have been created by free civilizations in the last 500 years. Even here in the United States, great universities are being systematically destroyed. Small nations all over the world find themselves under attack from within and from without.

If, when the chips are down, the world's most powerful nation, the United States of America, acts like a pitiful, helpless giant, the forces of totalitarianism and anarchy will threaten free nations and free institutions throughout the world.

## Test of Character

It is not our power but our will and character that is being tested tonight. The question all Americans must ask and answer tonight is this: Does the richest and strongest nation in the history of the world have the character to meet a direct challenge by a group which rejects every effort to win a just peace, ignores our warning, tramples on solemn agreements, violates the neutrality of an unarmed people, and uses our prisoners as hostages?

If we fail to meet this challenge, all other nations will be on notice that despite its overwhelming power the United States, when a real crisis comes, will be found wanting.

During my campaign for the Presidency, I pledged to bring Americans home from Vietnam. They are coming home.

I promised to end this war. I shall keep that promise.

I promised to win a just peace. I shall keep that promise.

We shall avoid a wider war. But we are also determined to put an end to this war.

In this room, Woodrow Wilson made the great decisions which led to victory in World War I. Franklin D. Roosevelt made the decisions which led to our victory in World War II. Dwight D. Eisenhower made decisions which ended the war in Korea and avoided war in the Middle East. John F. Kennedy, in his finest hour, made the great decision which removed Soviet nuclear missiles from Cuba and the Western Hemisphere.

---

*"It is not our power but our will and character that is being tested tonight."*

---

I have noted that there has been a great deal of discussion with regard to this decision that I have made and I should point out that I do not contend that it is in the magnitude as these decisions that I have just mentioned. But between those decisions and this decision there is a difference that is very fundamental. In those decisions, the American people were not assailed by counsels of doubt and defeat from some of the most widely known opinion leaders of the Nation.

## Counsels of Doubt

I have noted, for example, that a Republican Senator [George D. Aiken of Vermont] has said that this action I have taken means that my party has lost all chance of winning the November elections. And others are saying today that this move against enemy sanctuaries will make me a one-term President.

No one is more aware than I am of the political consequences of the action I have taken. It is tempting to take the easy political path: to blame this war on previous administrations and to bring all of our men home immediately, regardless of the consequences, even though that would mean defeat for the United States; to desert 18 million South Vietnamese people, who have put their trust in us and to expose them to the same slaughter and savagery which the leaders of North Vietnam inflicted on hundreds of thousands of North Vietnamese who chose freedom when the Communists took over North Vietnam in 1954; to get peace at any price now, even though I know that a peace of humiliation for the United States would lead to a bigger war or surrender later.

*"I ask for your support for our brave men fighting tonight halfway around the world—not for territory—not for glory—but so that their younger brothers and their sons and your sons can have a chance to grow up in a world of peace and freedom and justice."*

I have rejected all political considerations in making this decision.

Whether my party gains in November is nothing compared to the lives of 400,000 brave Americans fighting for our country and for the cause of peace and freedom in Vietnam. Whether I may be a one-term President is insignificant compared to whether by our failure to act in this crisis the United States proves itself to be unworthy to lead the forces of freedom in this critical period in world history. I would rather be a one-term President and do what I believe is right than to be a two-term President at the cost of seeing America become a second-rate power and to see this Nation accept the first defeat in its proud 190-year history.

## Deep National Differences

I realize that in this war there are honest and deep differences in this country about whether we should have become involved, that there are differences as to how the war should have been conducted. But the decision I announce tonight transcends those differences.

For the lives of American men are involved. The opportunity for 150,000 Americans to come home in the next 12 months is involved. The future of 18 million people in South Vietnam and 7 million people in Cambodia is involved. The possibility of winning a just peace in Vietnam and in the Pacific is at stake.

It is customary to conclude a speech from the White House by asking support for the President of the United States. Tonight, I depart from that precedent. What I ask is far more important. I ask for your support for our brave men fighting tonight halfway around the world—not for territory—not for glory—but so that their younger brothers and their sons and your sons can have a chance to grow up in a world of peace and freedom and justice.

Thank you and good night.

*Richard M. Nixon was elected president of the United States in 1970. This viewpoint was a radio address he made to the nation explaining why US troops were being used in Cambodia instead of the complete withdrawal that was pledged.*

*"Afghanistan is important to us because of its proximity to Iran and the oil which goes by tanker through the adjacent Strait of Hormuz."*

# The Afghanistan Invasion Is a Serious Event

*The Saturday Evening Post*

Afghanistan is a long way from the cornfields of Iowa. It's up in the mountains like Tibet or Outer Mongolia. There's no known oil there and little else of value. The Afghans have never been very fond of Americans. Should we care enough to sacrifice for that? Why not let the Russians have the country? Incidentally, why do *they* want it?

Afghanistan is important to us because of its proximity to Iran and the oil which goes by tanker through the adjacent Strait of Hormuz. It's not just Iranian oil passing through the Strait, but also the oil from countries like Saudi Arabia, Iraq and Kuwait.

Russia has hungered for Afghanistan for over a hundred years. It was the land bridge to India of the British Empire—now Pakistan and India. For years it was the buffer between British and Russian interests. To Russia, Afghanistan is an important chess piece in the Asian struggle between the U.S.S.R. and China. Pakistan and India are now blood enemies. Russia has befriended India. Naturally, China has aligned herself with Pakistan. Russian occupation of Afghanistan puts Russian troops on the Pakistan border—embarrassment for the Chinese, punishment for her friends.

More even than for control of Afghanistan, Russia has hungered for control of Iran and the ice-free ports on the Indian Ocean. That was even before the days when Middle East oil made this area important.

## Importance of Iran

For decades, Britain and Russia fought for control of Iran. Eventually, as temporary allies, Britain and Russia divided and occupied Iran. Harry Truman managed to force the Russians back out. The Soviets never forgot. They felt Iran, or at least part of it, belonged to them, was in their sphere of influence.

Then, in the past two decades, Iran became vastly more important. The U.S. was running out of oil. Britain had withdrawn her forces from the Indian Ocean. The oil for Japan, Western Europe and much of the U.S. flowed right by Iran's doorstep through the Strait of Hormuz. The forces of the Shah stood guard in the area.

Russia had some right to interfere in Iran—at least from her point of view. In 1921, a Soviet-Iranian treaty was signed in Moscow, and the Soviets still consider it valid. It says the Soviet Union may send armed forces into Iran if any third party does. The third power doesn't have to be America. Afghan rebels or even Kurds from Iraq might do. American forces are currently weak and weakly led. Iran's military is in shambles. Perhaps the prize may be had cheaply.

The U.S.S.R. has been getting ready for some time. Past Russian aid to Afghanistan has included highways suitable for Russian tanks leading right to the Iranian border.

## Russians Want Iran

The Iranian crisis was not all brought on by Jimmy Carter and his "human rights" binge. The Russians fish in troubled waters. They're not adverse to roiling up the water themselves. The long and the short of it—the Russians are ready to move massively into Iran from Afghanistan to the east and directly from Russia to the north. From Iran and the Strait of Hormuz, Russia could control the light switches of the Western world.

Would the Soviets plunge the world into darkness? Not necessarily, if we behave as they would like. Across the Persian Gulf from Iran is Saudi Arabia— the real "biggie" of oil production. The government of that sparsely populated country is near collapse. Beyond a doubt, the mere presence of Russian forces in Iran would push it over the edge and into the hands of the radical Yemenis, who are friends of the

*Saturday Evening Post*, "Why Afghanistan Does Matter," April 1980. Reprinted with permission from The Saturday Evening Post Company © 1980.

U.S.S.R., and Palestinians, who are being armed—at least indirectly—by the Russians.

The Russians are in Afghanistan mainly to be ready to move with massive armed forces into Iran if the time is right and the price is cheap. Must we respond to the Russians? Absolutely—unless we are satisfied to give the U.S.S.R. control of the critical balance of the world's oil. Until now it has been Western resolve—first British and then American—which has kept the Russians out of Iran. It is time to show that resolve again.

The Saturday Evening Post *is a popular feature news monthly.*

*"The days when the US could profess a
vital interest in anything that happened
anywhere in the world are over."*

viewpoint 50

# The Afghanistan Invasion
# Is Not a Serious Event

Ronald Steel

Does Afghanistan matter? Obviously not. Not in terms of any vital American interest, that is. The Soviet invasion of Afghanistan is about as threatening to the United States—and as deserving of the world's condemnation—as was the American invasion of Santo Domingo 15 years ago. In both cases a superpower sent in its troops to prop up a foundering client regime which "invited" its aid in putting down an indigenous rebellion. Both nations were exerting their right to determine what was a proper form of political independence within an area they themselves defined to be—as superpowers are wont to do—within their sphere of influence. The so-called Brezhnev Doctrine, by which the Soviets in 1968 explained their invasion of Czechoslovakia as "fraternal aid" to neighbors threatened by a hostile ideology, was not much different in theory—though far more brutal in substance—than the Johnson Doctrine by which LBJ dispatched the Marines to the Caribbean three years earlier. And it was the obvious precedent for their recent action in Afghanistan.

Now this is a very nasty way to behave. The strong should have more respect for the weak. Great powers should not be so lacking in self-confidence that they feel threatened whenever one of the pygmies in their shadow thumbs its nose at them. Unfortunately the world does not operate by such rules of restraint and decency. Great powers not only insist on dominating their neighbors, but try to extend their sphere of influence into other continents and even into other hemispheres. Witness the Soviets in Cuba and the United States in Vietnam. Such ventures are always costly and sometimes disastrous. But apparently the lure is irresistible so long as great powers define their greatness by their ability to collect clients and demonstrate their military muscle.

Ronald Steel, "Afghanistan Doesn't Matter," *The New Republic*, February 16, 1980. Reprinted by permission of THE NEW REPUBLIC, © 1980, The New Republic, Inc.

No, Afghanistan does not matter so far as America's vital interests are concerned. Indeed a few months ago it would have been hard to conceive, were one playing some Pentagon parlor game, anything that mattered less. What happens there no doubt matters to the Afghans, and to a lesser degree to their neighbors, although the Indians and Iranians and Iraqis seem far less concerned than do Arizonans and Pennsylvanians. The Pakistani dictatorship has reason to welcome an event that has reopened the apparently boundless coffers of the US Treasury and led the American government to discover a vital interest in the territorial outlines of one of the world's more artificial and unstable national entities.

Once the current hysteria dies down the world will go on very much as before, except that now the Russians will have an interminable guerrilla war on their hands which will diminish their ability to deal with more serious matters, such as the pathetic state of their economy and the growing menace of a hostile China allied to the United States. Indeed from this point of view American policymakers should welcome the Soviet folly in Afghanistan (as perhaps they secretly do). Nobody, it would seem, learns from anyone else's folly. Nor even sometimes from their own.

## Election May Be Affected

Why then has an act of such marginal significance to Americans been greeted, in President Carter's hyperbolic words, as the "most serious threat to the peace since the Second World War"? The answer, in a word, is Iran. And the answer in two words is our elections. The seizure of the Tehran embassy provided the Carter administration—which had fallen to a level of disrepute even greater than that of Nixon during the depths of Watergate—with an unexpected boon. The president discovered that talking tough paid off at the public opinion polls. Then, just about the time that talking tough was beginning to have diminishing returns and the public was beginning to lose interest, Afghanistan came along.

Seizing this manna from heaven, the administration has now found an issue on which it can ride bravely into the November elections. The public has been persuaded, for the time being at least, that the consolidation of a Soviet puppet regime in Afghanistan represents—by some still unexplained logic of extension—an effort by the Russians to seize the oil resources of the Persian Gulf. And it has responded to this orchestrated fear of dark and cold nights by approving a vast new expansion of the military budget—one that will cost an *additional* $100 billion over the next four years, stimulate inflationary pressure, erode the dollar, and further weaken the competitive position of the American economy by draining off resources from productive uses. The administration will go into the election with a war-stimulated economy. The public will pay the bill later.

## Afghanistan: A Phony Crisis?

If Afghanistan is a phony crisis, why has the public been so aroused? Clearly because of Iran. The taking of the hostages in Tehran stimulated a national mood of humiliation and anger. That mood spilled over into Afghanistan, and it was orchestrated by the administration. Without Iran the United States would have responded to Afghanistan rather as it did to the Soviet invasion of Czechoslovakia a dozen years ago: with indignation, contempt, and a realization that it did not affect the balance of power in any way. The stakes were far higher in Czechoslovakia in 1968, and that nation's geographical position was far more central to American interests. Yet no serious person in the Johnson administration suggested that the Soviets were preparing to attack Western Europe, nor was their action used to stimulate a climate of national hysteria in a presidential election year.

---

*"If Afghanistan is a phony crisis, why has the public been so aroused?"*

---

What the Carter administration has done—whether from a calculated design to cash in on the public's anxieties or from a dangerous misreading of the diplomatic stakes—is to have obliterated the distinction between a minor irritant and a vital interest. The United States, as a status quo power, has an interest in confining Soviet expansion into areas of crucial importance and of indulging its own insatiable dependence on Middle Eastern oil. It does not have a vital interest in which Marxist regime rules Afghanistan.

The days when the United States could profess a vital interest in anything that happened anywhere in the world are over. Great though our power may be, it is limited, and its real base in not military hardware but the vitality of the American economy. Restoring the draft, building the MX missile, patrolling the Indian Ocean, and funneling dollars to the dictator of Pakistan will not make the United States safer, richer, or stronger. But it will satisfy a rampant jingoism, and it may get Jimmy Carter safely past the November elections.

*Ronald Steel is a senior associate at the Carnegie Endowment for International Peace. He is the author of many articles and books on international relations.*

*"The still, breathless cornfields of Iowa and the empty $375 million stadium in Moscow are quiet weapons, but in their way they are more forceful than the rumble of artillery and napalm."*

viewpoint **51**

# American Sanctions Are an Appropriate Response to Afghanistan

*America*

Over the outrage of Afghanistan and the long, icy frustration of Iran hovers the memory of Prime Minister Neville Chamberlain, who emerged from his plane in September 1938 to tell the world that by giving the Sudetenland to Hitler he had secured "peace in our time." Of course, there was no peace. Hitler grew in strength with each sign of his enemies' weakness. According to one scenario, American inaction, seen in the Chamberlain mold as appeasement, might easily encourage the Soviet Union to new political and military adventures. A move into the vacuum in Iran and the seizure of its oil fields would inevitably be a giant step toward war with the United States. At the opposite end of political speculation, a precipitous military move by the United States in Afghanistan or Iran now might be emotionally satisfying, but it would be an unconscionable threat to world peace. Military intervention in defense of national honor in Teheran or a more independent government in Kabul is just not worth the risk of nuclear devastation. The dilemma of choosing between appeasement and overreaction is painful.

A tortuous path through this political minefield lies ahead for the United States and its allies. They must be resolute without giving provocation. They must be clear and forceful without allowing their positions to become rigid, and they must define self-interest with a stated appreciation of the legitimate national interests of the Iranians and the Afghans. This path will be a long one, for it is unlikely that the Soviet invasion force will withdraw until it has securely established an acceptable puppet government.

## Embargo Will Be Successful

So far, the American initiatives seem admirably suited to this kind of protracted silent war. By an

embargo of the $2.6 billion grain sale to the Soviet Union, the United States will not starve the enemy to its knees, but it will disrupt the next five-year plan for the Soviet economy. No Russian will go hungry as a result of the embargo, but there will be a shortage of beef as another reminder of the colossal failure of the collective farms to provide consumer goods. The tactic, then, is not morally questionable, as Senator Edward M. Kennedy (D., Mass.) implied in a campaign speech when he condemned the use of food as a weapon. It is rather an economic sanction, which may in fact enable the United States to fill its commitment to a world food bank to keep impoverished nations free from the threat of famine.

What is more, such a policy, imposed as it was so close to the crucial Iowa caucuses, has demonstrated to the Soviet leadership that the American Government is not paralyzed during an election year. President Carter was willing to act even if he did lose support from the Iowa farm vote. American grain growers may lose some income as a result of the embargo, and of course they would be tempted to blame the President for imposing a disproportionate burden on them. On the other hand, they may even stand to profit because of the Government's commitment to purchase corn for the production of ethanol for fuel. Finally, the cooperation of Australia, Canada and the Common Market has given rise to the hope that a grain cartel, along the pattern of OPEC, may be in the making as a nonviolent weapon to contain Soviet aggression. Argentina, hoping to soften U.S. criticism of its human rights policies, alone among grain-exporting nations has refused to cooperate.

## Boycotting the Olympics

The Olympic games offer another opportunity for ostracizing the Soviet Union. Moving the games from Moscow, or, failing that, withdrawing teams from the United States and other nations would be a crushing

*America*, "A Silent War Against Soviet Imperialism," January 26, 1980. Reprinted with permission of America Press, Inc., 106 West 56th St., New York, NY 10019. © 1980 All rights reserved.

blow to the Soviets' frantic search for international prestige. To maintain that the Olympics should be kept out of the political arena is a specious argument. From the days of Hitler's triumph at Nuremberg in 1936 to the present, the Olympics have always had a political undercurrent. The Soviets have consistently subsidized their athletes for the glory of the state. Withdrawing the Olympic games from Moscow would not only be a blow to Soviet propaganda, it would involve a significant loss of foreign currency, especially from American television.

The silent war will be a long one, but a war that the West is well equipped to win. The still, breathless cornfields of Iowa and the empty $375 million stadium in Moscow are quiet weapons, but in their way they are more forceful than the rumble of artillery and napalm.

America *is a monthly news and opinion magazine published by the Jesuit order of the Roman Catholic Church.*

*"Sanctions do not work unless you can have some sort of market monopoly position, and we don't have that anymore—not even in grain."*

# American Sanctions Are an Inappropriate Response to Afghanistan

## Robert Gilpin and Henry Bienen

**Norman Gall:** President Carter isn't the first U.S. chief executive to try economic sanctions as a substitute for sending in the troops.

**Robert Gilpin:** The role of economic sanctions in American foreign policymaking really goes back to the 19th century. One of the first foreign policy acts of the U.S. was the effort to use economic sanctions against the British in the War of 1812.

In contrast to Europe and Japan, the U.S. has a strong proclivity to use economic measures to promote human rights or to exert influence in other countries. I think there are several reasons for it. One is the fact that throughout most of our history there was an asymmetrical relationship between ourselves and other countries. Other countries wanted our goods more than we wanted theirs. In the 19th century it was wheat, and then as we industrialized it was American technology—and we did have the better mousetrap to sell—and other countries wanted the grain and our technology. At the same time, we were self-sufficient economically.

### Dramatic Change

Now the situation has changed dramatically. We are much less self-sufficient and there are very few areas today where we have monopolistic power. Sanctions do not work unless you can have some sort of market monopoly position, and we don't have that anymore—not even in grain.

In the past we've imported goods mainly on a cost basis. Then the big change came with the end of World War II, in materials. The U.S. shifted from its role as an overall mineral surplus producer to become a net importer. Oil is the first commodity where you would really have a major change in the American economy if those foreign materials were unavailable.

**Henry Bienen:** Economic sanctions are frequently potent as symbolic political acts, because they appear to be consequential. Whether they are potent as a weapon to coerce is very doubtful. We've looked at the cases of Rhodesia, Cuba and the sanctions imposed by the League of Nations against Italy in 1935, and they all failed. I don't think anyone in the U.S. government really believes—the President stated this himself—that today sanctions would compel the Soviet Union to withdraw from Afghanistan. Nor do I think anyone really believes that this present Iranian government—whoever is making decisions in Iran on the hostages—will be very much affected by economic sanctions. But politicians see sanctions as a statement of American commitment, an attempt to appear strong, to say something to America's allies and our own domestic constituencies, rather than a means to coerce other countries.

**Gall:** The Europeans and Japanese aren't giving us much support in this symbolic act.

**Gilpin:** Our allies are much more dependent upon this trade than we are. They also believe that such symbolic acts really are not very meaningful, that the costs are greater than the advantages of using sanctions as a way of stating your protests.

They also have been the recipients of such sanctions, and thus they are very sensitive as well. The Japanese, after all, are very much aware of the fact that the prelude to World War II was economic sanctions against Japan.

**Gall:** Okay. We've talked about sanctions as a symbolic act for consumption at home and as an alarming situation for our allies. What about its effect on its supposed target country or area?

**Gilpin:** The theory of economic sanctions is that they will cause a split within the leadership of a country, or between the leadership and the masses of people. But in almost all cases, it's been the opposite. What you have is really a rallying-around-the-flag response in these countries.

Robert Gilpin and Henry Bienen, in an interview by Norman Gall, "Economic Sanctions: An Obsolete Weapon?" Reprinted by permission of FORBES Magazine, February 18, 1980. © Forbes Inc, 1980.

**Gall:** Let's talk about grain. Isn't this one area where we really can hurt the Soviet Union with an embargo?

**Bienen:** First of all, with grain there's nothing that tells you very much about point of origin. I suppose you could tell where certain strains of wheat come from, but basically you can transship grain. The real question would be whether countries are willing and able to police their own grain exports.

Even if you get Canada and Australia and Brazil and Argentina to agree not to ship directly to the Soviet Union, there's nothing that says they can't ship to Czechoslovakia or Poland who then can ship to the Soviet Union. Sanctions don't cut off the commodity to the importing state. What they do is raise the cost. The question is, how much do they raise the cost? That really depends on the supply and demand for the particular commodity.

## Using Grain As a Weapon

**Gall:** Well, as you have said elsewhere, the U.S. remains, long run, one of the world's few dependable sources of grain exports. Doesn't this translate into real power for the U.S.?

**Bienen:** It is a power, and that's why, for all the talk about the limited aspects of sanctions, this is a weapon. It will cut different ways, but I also was trying to suggest that a relatively rich and relatively powerful country like the Soviet Union is going to be able to protect itself more than most other countries. What we've seen is that even relatively vulnerable countries like Cuba or Rhodesia under the Smith government have been able to buy and import sanctioned goods—either because a country like the Soviet Union bailed out Cuba, or in the Rhodesian case, suppliers were willing to take advantage of the markets and sell at a higher price, and South Africa helped bail them out. So that you have to ask who is vulnerable and who is relatively invulnerable, and while the U.S. does have a food weapon, and while the Soviet Union will incur some additional cost, it will be able to shift around its imports. It will be able to change its own consumption patterns to some extent. The Soviets will pay, of course, but it's not the kind of cost that's going to be really tremendous for them.

**Gall:** I'm really intrigued by some of the trade patterns that are emerging with the Russians and some of the Latin Americans, and the kind of diplomacy that the Russians conduct in Latin America compared with our own. The Russians were saddled with sending all of this oil to Cuba over maybe a 10,000-to-15,000-mile tanker route. The Cubans now have been able to establish diplomatic relations with Venezuela, and now the oil is being sent from Venezuela in a triangular trade. The Russians pay for it and it goes on a very short route, and it strategically is a very convenient relationship. There are a lot of demands on Russia's domestic oil

supplies, not only internally but from the satellites as well. They also try to earn some foreign exchange by exporting oil.

My question is, how do the Russians differ from us in trade strategy, in attitude toward embargoes?

**Bienen:** Well, one thing I think is very clear is that the Russians have a lot of flexibility as you've just pointed out, because they don't have to worry about domestic constituencies' effect on their trade. They don't have to worry about human rights concerns, whether or not they're going to do business with Chile or Argentina. As a prudent country, they'll try to extend their sources of supply and their markets for exports.

## US as Trading Partner

**Gilpin:** There's a larger consideration here and that is the U.S. is increasingly perceived as an unreliable trading partner. President Carter initially said that he would seek to minimize the impact of political considerations on trade policy in order to stimulate greater exports. But the Carter Administration, of course, has not followed through on this.

**Bienen:** It seems to me that over the last years, if anything, the U.S. has extended the range of issues on which it's willing to impose trade sanctions. The Soviet invasion of Afghanistan is one thing. One can think about that as really high policy. Major geopolitical and strategic interests are at stake. One can say this is an act of naked aggression, and one shouldn't sit still for it. Something has to be done. Everyone wants to hearken back and say, well, if only someone had stood up and had acted against Germany in the late Thirties, things might have been different.

*"The U.S. has, in the last few years, imposed sanctions on a range of human rights issues. . . . On how many issues are you going to do this?"*

But aside from invasions of sovereign states, the U.S. has, in the last few years, imposed sanctions on a range of human rights issues, in a number of countries. We've imposed sanctions to combat terrorism by imposing export restrictions to Libya, for example, because Qaddafi has been supporting terrorism in different countries.

What is an appropriate response? On how many issues are you going to do this? Have you got a policy tool which is really sensitive enough to handle issues like human rights and terrorism through trade sanctions policy? I myself am very skeptical, and the problem is, also, what targets do you pick out to deal with on these issues?

On the question of human rights, a lot of the pressure has come from Congress, which imposed a rider to prohibit trade with Uganda on an agreement to replenish funds for international lending agencies. This was not something the Executive wanted—in fact, the Secretary of State argued against this, but it was a congressional decision.

*Robert Gilpin is Eisenhower Professor of International Affairs and author of* U.S. Power and the Multinational Corporation. *Henry Bienen is director of the Woodrow Wilson School's Research Program in Developmental Studies and a consultant to the State Department.*

---

*"We are the ones who are violating our own commitment to an open world economy, more than any other country in the world today."*

---

I don't mean to suggest that one should not be concerned with human rights issues, and one shouldn't try to find appropriate policy responses to violations of human rights. Those violations seem to me to be consequential matters that Americans are and should be concerned with. The question is, what are the appropriate tools?

## Defining Interests

**Gilpin:** We are using economic sanctions and using economics in foreign policy on a broad range of issues, at the same time that the U.S., in terms of its larger national interest, is simply going to have to export more. You just can't reconcile all these things that we're doing. They just don't add up.

The U.S. must define what its interests are, defend those interests and not flip-flop around, because the perception the rest of the world has right now is that we're rudderless. If nothing else, the Russians have demonstrated they know what their interests are and they're willing to act. There's nothing in international politics like success to strengthen your position and your reputation. At the end of World War II, the U.S. defined as a major objective of American policy the depoliticization of international economics. We did so for three reasons. One is we saw that before World War II political relations were increasingly having a destructive influence upon the world economy and helped cause the war. Second, we saw our interests in terms of an open world economy. Third, we saw an open world economy as a way of binding us to our European and Japanese allies.

What is going on right now? We are the ones who are violating our own commitment to an open world economy, more than any other country in the world today. We are the ones politicizing the world economy more than any others—not the Soviet Union, but the U.S. I think that in terms of our long-term objectives it is not in the interest of the U.S. to have an increasing infringement of political factors and objectives on the world economy since we must export to live and are no longer self-sufficient in oil and other strategic materials.

*"Thanks to the Soviets, nearly half the Afghanistan people are either corpses or refugees."*

# The Soviets Are Terrorizing Afghanistan

## Robert James Bidinotto

They look like toys.

They lie on the ground where they are scattered by the helicopters: colorfully painted pens, birds, butterflies, wagons. And when the children touch the toys, they explode.

The explosions are not powerful enough to kill in most cases—just powerful enough to maim. To blow off hands and feet. That is what the "toys" are meant to do. A corpse, after all, is quickly disposed of. But living casualties tie up other people, who must care for the injured; and this diverts them from active roles in the military resistance. Besides, the sight of a maimed child traumatizes, demoralizes, terrorizes. And that is the reason for these "toys"—these gifts from the Soviet military to the children of Afghanistan.

Though history holds many sordid stories of military operations against civilian populations, there is scant precedent for military actions directed specifically against little children. But then, the Soviet mind is simply bubbling over with innovations.

### Corpses and Refugees

Since December 1979, when Soviet forces invaded Afghanistan, over 50,000 Afghan resistance fighters and 800,000 civilians (mainly women and children) have been killed in the fighting. Of a population once numbering 15 million, nearly a million have died, 3.5 million others are refugees in Pakistan and 2 million more have fled to Iran. At least another 1.5 million have become "internal exiles," forced into the cities by massive Soviet bombing of the nation's 14,000 villages. Thus, thanks to the Soviets, nearly half the Afghanistan people are either corpses or refugees.

At first glance, it is difficult to imagine what

Robert James Bidinotto, "Afghanistan and the Soviet Mind," December 10, 1984. Reprinted from ON PRINCIPLE, a pro-capitalist newsletter published bi-weekly by Amwell Publishing, Inc., Princeton Professional Park, 601 Ewing Street, Suite B-7, Princeton, NJ 08542. Subscriptions are $45.

anyone would want with a Texas-sized chunk of mountainous and barren real estate. But the landlocked country shares borders with the Soviet Union, Pakistan and Iran; and a narrow neck, the Wakhan Corridor, touches China. This strategic location makes Afghanistan a stepping-stone in Russia's path to a warm-water port in the Indian Ocean. The Soviets will need to import oil by the turn of the century, and Afghanistan now provides them with air bases from which their planes can reach the Persian Gulf shipping lanes without refueling. The next stepping stone will be the Baluchistan region south of Afghanistan, between Iran and Pakistan, where the Soviets have been recruiting students and operatives for years.

Another reason is that the Soviet Union's southern border region is a predominantly Moslem area, culturally merging with the militant Islamic hot spots of Iran and Afghanistan. The Kremlin, facing dissident rumblings throughout Eastern Europe, is alarmed at the prospect of an Islamic rebellion in its own central Asian republics; and the possibility of such an insurrection spilling over from Moslem nations along the USSR's border is an added worry.

### 1978: The Beginning

The USSR first moved into Afghanistan by proxy in 1978. Two antagonistic communist parties—the Khalq, led by Nur Mohammad Taraki, and the Parcham, headed by Babrak Karmal—had been forced by the Soviets into a shotgun wedding the year before. But in April 1978, a Parchami leader was murdered, touching off demonstrations. Taraki's right-hand man, Hafizullah Amin, with the backing of Soviet-trained air force officers, led a coup and seized power, murdering President Daoud and his family. Taraki was installed as the new president, and the Khalq faction began to jail its Parcham competitors. Babrak Karmal was put into de facto exile as ambassador to Czechoslovakia.

The government tried to paint an Islamic face on its revolution, but immediately began to arrest Muslim clerics and officers, as well as other intellectuals, and to introduce antireligious curricula in the schools. Protestors were dragged off and murdered. Even the flag was altered to eliminate Islamic symbols, which outraged the Moslem populace. The Taraki regime faced rebellions by summer, and the rural administration fell quickly into a shambles. By March of 1979, Moslem resistance forces controlled the upper Kunar Valley and Soviet tanks rushed across the border to put down an uprising in Herat. Armed rebellion spread throughout the nation, and the six major Moslem resistance groups began to form. On August 4, the military high command in Kabul tried to end the growing reign of terror and religious persecution by attempting a coup against Taraki; this was ruthlessly suppressed by Soviet aircraft. By now the entire administration was in chaos, and half the army had deserted.

---

*"That the Soviet military campaign is primarily directed against civilians is now generally acknowledged."*

---

Amin, who had been educated in American universities, was a cold-blooded thug placed in charge of putting down the resistance. On August 15, 300 members of the Hazara sect were trucked to a field near Kabul; half were doused with gasoline and set afire, the other half were buried alive by a bulldozer. The same had occurred a few days earlier at the little Village of Qal'aye Najil in the east, when 650 villagers were buried alive in sixteen big ditches. The Russians gave the orders, while Afghan soldiers did the dirty work. At the infamous Pol-e Charkhi prison, thousands were tortured and died similar deaths under the watchful eyes of Russian "advisers."

## Takeover

Taraki travelled to Cuba, then to Moscow. Brezhnev advised him to get rid of Amin, whose terrorism was stiffening the resistance. When Taraki returned in mid-September, he confronted Amin. Amin, never indecisive, shot his boss and assumed the presidency.

Trying to rationalize his takeover, Amin published a list of 15,000 prisoners at Pol-e Charkhi executed under Taraki. But the Soviets viewed Amin as a loose cannon on the deck. On November 3, they sent in troops, allegedly to help Amin put down the rebellions. In early December, more Russians entered the country. On Christmas Day, 5,000 Red Army forces invaded the country, occupying the capital and killing Amin in his palace, proclaiming him a "CIA agent." Eighty-five thousand more Soviet troops were

dispatched, and Karmal was brought back from Europe and installed as the new President. On January 5, 1980, Karmal freed his Parcham cronies from jail, accusing his predecessor of murdering a million people—and issued a new list of 17,000 *more* executed prisoners at Pol-e Charkhi.

The Soviets rationalized their invasion as a request for help from a never-before-heard-of "revolutionary council" to depose Amin and end the "CIA plot." In truth, they had simply taken over and established a reliable puppet government under Karmal. The campaign to wipe out the resistance began in earnest.

## Civilian Massacre

That the Soviet military campaign is *primarily* directed against civilians is now generally acknowledged.

For example, in a three-day period in early 1980, the civilian population of the Kunar Valley was bombed and napalmed, brutally machine-gunned by the helicopters, subjected to tear- and laughing-gas attacks, and overrun by tanks and a division of Soviet troops. Similarly, in the spring of 1983, Soviet fighter-bombers and helicopters bombed civilian settlements all over the country. Herat, the nation's third-largest city, was subjected to intensive and prolonged "carpet bombing"; at least 3,000 civilians were killed or wounded.

In October 1983, Soviet soldiers fighting in Istalef, a village north of the capital of Kabul, deliberately put to the bayonet any children found in the homes of suspected resistance fighters. Likewise, there was the highly publicized atrocity at the village of Padkhwab-e-Shana on September 13, 1982, which was confirmed by an investigation team from Europe. One hundred and five village men and boys, attempting to escape impressment into military service, hid in an underground irrigation ditch. Clapping and cheering Soviet troops covered all the exits and poured flammable liquids and powders down on the trapped villagers—then set off an underground inferno with incendiary bullets. The 105 were deliberately, methodically incinerated.

Besides the more spectacular horrors, there are the horrifying routines. Writing in the *New Republic,* Afghan authorities Roger Fenton and Maggie Gallagher report "it has become quite common for shopkeepers, farmers, and tradesmen who are too poor to satisfy Russian soldiers demanding goods without payment to be summarily shot."

Most of the civilian bloodshed has been caused by the dreaded Soviet MI-24 Hind helicopter gunship, which roams with relative immunity over the forbidding Afghan landscape. It sports 128 rockets, a rapid-fire, laser-sighted cannon and four bombs (often napalm). It can blast a village, burn its crops and mow down its people in minutes. It protects Soviet convoys, operates search-and-destroy missions and covers the countryside with camouflaged antipersonnel "butterfly" mines, aimed at both people and their flocks of farm animals. Demonstrating its marvelous versatility, the MI-24 also destroyed 6 clearly-marked French hospitals during 1980 and 1981, in an effort to suppress eyewitness accounts of the atrocities being publicized by French doctors. Those accounts include photos of the bloated, blackened bodies of poison gas victims.

## Strategy of Terror

The war on civilians is part of a *deliberate strategy of terror,* designed to isolate the Afghan resistance fighters, known as the *mujaheddin* (or "holy warriors"). This strategy is borrowed from Mao Tse Tung's writings on guerilla warfare.

Guerilla fighters pose a unique problem in modern warfare. They arise from the civilian population to launch their attacks, then melt invisibly back into that society to hide from counter-attack. Moreover, they are sustained and supplied by their civilian support system. As we discovered in Vietnam, classic counter-insurgency strategy does not work very well.

The communists, however, have found a simple solution to the problem of native resistance. Mao wrote that the guerilla in his native society was like a "fish taking to water." Thus, to follow the metaphor, if you deprive the fish of his water, he can neither hide nor long survive. "In other words," writes Dr. Claude Malhuret, a French doctor who runs a medical relief program in Afghanistan, "an effective counter-strategy in the face of guerilla action involves massive reprisals against the population, sometimes including the extermination of a large part of that population." Malhuret cites the systematic levelling of villages by the communist regime of Ethiopia, and the deliberate campaign of mass starvation by the Vietnamese in Cambodia, as examples of this strategy in action.

By emptying the Afghanistan countryside of its crops, herds and people, the Soviets intend to deprive the mujaheddin of their support system, and to break the back of the resistance. Princeton University's Louis Dupree, perhaps the foremost authority on Afghanistan, has referred to this shoot-them-or-starve-them strategy as "migratory genocide." Indeed, escaped prisoners report being told by their communist captors that if the population of Afghanistan were reduced to only 1 million, that would be sufficient to rebuild the society.

## Split Resistance

The major resistance is split between three fundamentalist Islamic groups, and three others which, while devoutly Moslem, are quite nationalistic. Most friction seems to be caused by the fanatic Gulbiddin Hekmaktyar and his Hezb-e Islami faction, which often fights other resistance groups and blocks their passage through territory under Hezb-e control. There is well-grounded suspicion that

Gulbiddin, who is heavily financed by Libya, may be a secret Soviet ally awaiting a post in the Karmal government under any negotiated settlement.

And this is relevant to a final critical question: Why hasn't the West given more aid to the dedicated, but desperately undersupplied mujaheddin? The fact is that the various resistance groups maintain headquarters in Peshawar, Pakistan; and substantial covert aid from the CIA, as well as Saudi Arabia and other nations, is channeled to a "coalition" group in Peshawar via the Pakistan government. But the government skims off most of the money and supplies first. The motives include simple greed, as well as a fear of offending the Soviets by letting too much equipment get into Afghanistan. And whatever finally reaches the coalition comes under the control of Gulbiddin, via a crony in its leadership. After more skimming, virtually nothing remains for the resistance in Afghanistan.

## Can the Mujaheddin Win?

Despite around 200,000 men, plus sophisticated weaponry, the Soviets have been fought to a virtual standstill by 90,000 underfed, undertrained, undersupplied Moslems. The biggest problem faced by the mujaheddin remains the MI-24 helicopter gunship, a threat that could be neutralized if the United States were to supply "Redeyes"—hand-launched ground-to-air missiles which could totally change the balance of power in the war. These could be shipped in surreptitiously, by air, avoiding Pakistani entanglements. But proving that Pakistan holds no monopoly in cowardice, the United States has thus far avoided sending in any Redeyes or heavier equipment— *for fear of offending Pakistan!*

The mujaheddin have survived thus far on sheer will and fanatical faith in their holy war against the Soviet "infidel." It remains to be seen if, in his second term, Mr. Reagan can muster enough resolve to help them in a decisive way.

But the Soviet genocide in Afghanistan, in exposing the ultimate corruption of the Soviet mind, inters any conceivable rationale for dealing with the USSR in any way. It obliterates any excuse for summit conferences, nuclear freezes or treaties. No nation which—as a matter of calculated policy—devises weapons specifically to cripple children, is fit for diplomatic recognition, for trade, for negotiations, for relations of any sort. The Soviet Union is indeed the focus of evil in today's world. And the sooner this sinks in, the safer the world will be.

*Robert James Bidinotto is a contributing editor to* On Principle, *a conservative monthly newsletter that deals with the merits of individual rights and capitalism.*

*"The Soviet Union came to [Afghanistan's] aid in its hour of need, in full conformity with every rule of international law."*

# The Soviets Are Deterring Aggression in Afghanistan

Boris Petkov

On April 27, 1978 and in the following days the mass media put out diverse and sometimes conflicting reports in assessing developments in Afghanistan. On one point, however, most commentators were unanimous: something important had occurred in Afghanistan's political life.

When the Chairman of the Revolutionary Council, Prime Minister Nur Mohammad Taraki, in his speech on May 9, 1978, defined the main revolutionary goals of the Democratic Republic of Afghanistan, it became clear that what had occurred in Afghanistan was not a military coup but an anti-feudal, anti-imperialist revolution.

The decrees issued soon after by the revolutionary authorities showed that the new Afghan leaders were determined to lead the people along the path of building a modern society based on principles of social justice, to uproot feudalism and abolish the exploitation of man by man.

In the first place, the revolution stretched forth a helping hand to the peasants who make up the bulk of the country's population. Under Decree No. 6 of the Revolutionary Council about eleven million peasants and members of their families, or 80-90 per cent of the rural population, had their debts to landowners and usurers cancelled.

Decree No. 8 of the Revolutionary Council marked the beginning of a fundamental reorganisation in the peasants' life. Under the decree, no one was allowed to own more than 30 dzheribs (6 hectares) of land. Excess land was confiscated and handed over free to landless and land-poor peasants.

For the urban population also much was done in the months immediately following the revolution. Control was established over the price of certain foodstuffs, and the distribution of foodstuffs at reduced prices was introduced for workers employed in the public sector.

The emancipation of women went faster. The law on marriage and the family granted women equal rights with men.

Special attention was given to solving the problem of nationalities, Afghanistan being populated by over 20 different peoples. In schools, teaching in the languages of national minorities was introduced, and newspapers and radio programmes were launched in these languages. . . .

## US Opposed Afghan Revolution

Everyone who has had the opportunity of following the developments in Afghanistan while at the same time paying attention to the reaction on the part of the Western press and news agencies, must have seen with what cynical bluntness the West changed its attitude to Afghanistan as the social reforms on behalf of the people went ahead. As soon as the first decrees had been published, Afghanistan became an object of direct and gross interference by the Western powers and China. A blatant propaganda war was unleashed against the Afghan revolution. Simultaneously, Washington and Peking began supplying the counter-revolutionaries with weapons and funds, training them and smuggling them across the border into Afghanistan. . . .

Ever since hostile acts against the Afghan republic began, Western information agencies have tried to suggest that subversive activities against the new authorities were arranged by Afghan feudal lords. In fact, the local feudal lords have at all times been incapable of concerted action, being disorganised and insulated from one another. From the outset subversive activities against Afghanistan were well organised, centralised and excellently supplied, in a way quite uncommon to the local feudal class. Whatever "standard bearers" were advanced here from among the scions of eminent Afghan families, it

Boris Petkov, *Afghanistan Today: Impressions of a Journalist.* New Delhi: Sterling Publishers Private Limited, 1983.

was immediately evident that they were mere tools or "servants" of an obviously foreign master.

## US Planned Invasion

Today we know, of course, much more than we knew in the early months following the revolution. The *Afrique-Asie* magazine, published in Paris, wrote recently that the President of Pakistan had been preparing "with the aid of the United States, the Emirates and China, an invasion of Afghanistan since May 1978."...

---

*"Facts prove...that the undeclared war by the United States against the Afghan people had started at least a year and a half before the Soviet contingent entered Afghan territory."*

---

My Afghan colleagues told me that at that time American and Chinese weapons were supplied daily to the mercenary camps through the ports of Karachi and Gwadar in Pakistan, along the Karakorum highway and by air. Some consignments of weapons, when urgently required, were delivered straight from US warships in the Indian Ocean by American helicopters and transport planes to the Pakistani military base at Manipur, from where they were shipped to the camps. Intervention in Afghanistan grew, extending to a number of provinces and threatening the revolution's very existence.

Thus, the action taken by Washington and Peking against Afghanistan as early as the summer of 1978 can be placed with good reason under the category of aggression, as defined by the UN statutes.

It is well known that the UN's definition of aggression does not only include open invasion, such as in Vietnam by the United States and subsequently by China, but such subversive actions as the "sending by or on behalf of a State of armed bands, groups, irregulars or mercenaries, which carry out acts of armed force against another State..."

## US Sponsored Aggression

Aggression by the United States in mid-1978 utterly disproves present-day US propaganda assertions to the effect that the acts against revolutionary Afghanistan, carried out jointly by the United States with Pakistan and with China, and speeded up shipments of American weapons to Pakistan were dictated by sending a limited Soviet military contingent to Afghanistan at the request of the lawful Afghan government. Facts prove beyond a shadow of a doubt that the undeclared war by the United States against the Afghan people had started at least a year and a half before the Soviet contingent entered Afghan territory, i.e., soon after the April revolution.

Afghanistan's enemies found it easier to act owing to Amin's bloody purges, which had weakened the party and the state apparatus of the republic.

Seizing power, Hafizullah Amin established dictatorial rule in the autumn of 1979, killing everyone who disagreed with him. He replaced the carrying out of reforms in late 1979 by revolutionary phrases. Even the campaign for stamping out illteracy was stopped. Manipulating socialist slogans, Amin discredited progressive ideas in the eyes of the masses, making the interventionists' offensive easier.

In December 1979, after the removal of the Amin clique, the revolution in Afghanistan entered its second stage and in January the following year aggression against the Afghan revolution on the part of the United States and China acquired fresh and dangerous forms.

How do the Afghan people repel these renewed imperialist attacks on their freedom and their achievements? How is the second stage of revolutionary change in the country developing?...

## USSR Aids Afghanistan

In December 1979—January 1980 one could witness a great fury caused in the West by the removal of Amin and by the fact that true revolutionaries appealed to all friends of Afghanistan to help curb foreign intervention against the Afghan people. We will remember the hysteria raised by the enemies of Afghanistan because the Soviet Union came to its aid in its hour of need, in full conformity with every rule of international law. Unleashing a spate of noisy propaganda, Washington and its allies wanted to convince the world that behind the aid were plans for a Soviet breakthrough to the "warm seas," to Middle Eastern oil and the Persian Gulf area. US secret service agencies fed the Western press daily with malicious inventions about the Soviet Union's "perfidious intentions."

While harping on the "Soviet threat," the United States crammed those very seas with destroyers, cruisers and aircraft carriers bearing hundreds of planes on board, established military bases there, and sped the formation of the repressive "rapid deployment force."

A few days later in Kabul, an Afghan journalist described this fuss about Afghanistan as follows.

"The imperialist circles see intervention in national liberation movements as a legitimate business, while they consider impermissible the international solidarity of the forces of progress and socialism. This strange attitude becomes understandable if you consider the West's blind hatred of the Afghan revolution. The source of this hatred is always the same, the wish to stop history, to halt the changes that have come to a head in this area. The imperialists want to stifle revolutionary Afghanistan as they wanted to stifle the revolution in Nicaragua."

Seizing upon Afghanistan as a pretext, Washington, as is known, unleashed an all-out propaganda war against Afghanistan and the Soviet Union. Even the United Nations was dragged into this war by the United States and arbitrarily made to discuss the so-called "Afghan question," contrary to the will of the lawful government of Afghanistan....

## UN Not Supportive

Nothing came of the attempts by Washington, its allies and Peking to turn the UN General Assembly into a forum for slanderous attacks on the Democratic Republic of Afghanistan. These attempts came up against the determined opposition from the socialist and many of the non-aligned countries. Vainly did Washington attempt to rally the Moslem states members of the Organisation of the Islamic Conference and sent them against Afghanistan. Instead, most of the Organisation members expressed their concern over American military power being concentrated in the Indian Ocean and about the US activities against Iran.

All large mercenary formations that had penetrated into Afghanistan were routed.

American pressure on Iran, disguised as a "concentration of power in view of the events in Afghanistan," also ended in failure.

Despite all this, the Carter Administration continued its feverish efforts to build up American military presence in the western part of the Indian Ocean, including the Persian Gulf. The Pentagon declared that the use of atomic weapons in that area was not ruled out.

The Carter Administration never ceased trying to relate all these actions to the events in Afghanistan, which, just like the mythical "Soviet threat," continued to be an object of a vociferous campaign of lies and provocation. General Secretary of the CC CPSU, Chairman of the Presidium of the Supreme Soviet of the USSR, Leonid Brezhnev, justly remarked that "had there been no Afghanistan, certain circles in the United States, in NATO would have surely found pretext to aggravate the situation in the world."

The United States and China zealously continued the undeclared war against the Afghan people, sending more and more mercenary bands, trained and armed to the teeth, across the border. Five months of the new stage of the revolution enabled me to draw definite conclusions about what had actually been accomplished by the country's new leaders. What were the results of their efforts to curb foreign intervention and rally the people to tackle the crucial problems? What was the situation in Afghanistan really like?

I got my first impressions on the flight. Far below us we could see the mountains, the bare, stark Central Asian mountains, their contours outlined distinctly, like on a map. The airhostess announced that we were flying across the Soviet-Afghan border.

"Do you know what we call this border?" my neighbour, a gray-haired, dapper Afghan said to me. "We call it pacific. As far back as I can remember, things from time to time keep happening on our other borders. Five, ten years ago, it was tension here, skirmishes there, a group of people crossing the border with ill intentions—you know how it is. But this border with the Russians was always quiet. It has never caused us Afghans any concern. When they sign a treaty, they stick to it. It has always been so. Or, rather, it has been so throughout the sixty years after their revolution."

Indeed, with the emergence of the Soviet Union the 2,000-kilometre-long border between Afghanistan and Soviet Russia became a border of stability and peace with a friend, who invariably supported the Afghans' efforts for greater independence....

In 1921 a Soviet-Afghan treaty was signed to become the first document in history establishing relations between a great power and a smaller country on the basis of equality and non-interference in each other's internal affairs, friendship and mutual respect.

The significance and effectiveness of this treaty have been borne out by the decades that have passed since it was signed. Those were troubled decades for the Afghan people, when often only the frontier with the Soviet Union remained tranquil.

## USSR Aid

All this came to my mind when my neighbour, an Afghan returning home from the GDR, had mentioned the name by which the northern border of his country was known among his fellow-countrymen. We spoke about Berlin, Moscow and Kabul and discussed political problems, including the West's hysterical reaction to Soviet military aid for the Afghan revolution.

---

*"In 1921 a Soviet-Afghan treaty was signed. . .establishing relations between a great power and a smaller country on the basis of equality and non-interference in each other's internal affairs."*

---

"Oh yes," said my neighbour with a smile, "there are many people in the West now, ever so 'solicitous' about our independence and anxious about the future of Islam in Afghanistan. True enough, many of them had no idea until recently where Afghanistan was or never saw a praying Moslem in their lives. One can't help asking why they have become so enamoured with the Afghans, when before it did not worry them one bit that millions of Afghans lived in abject poverty and medieval stagnation. We Afghans know what this concern is worth. After all, the whole world knows whose support helped to keep the Shah of Iran in power for so long, that slaughterer of hundreds of thousands of Moslems. And who but the United States is threatening not only Afghanistan, but many other Moslem countries as well today.

He let a cigarette and went on:

"Soviet assistance, the response to our request, is a matter between Afghanistan and the Soviet Union. Such mutual assistance is stipulated by the Treaty of Friendship between our two countries and by the UN Charter, which records the right to individual and collective self-defence from aggression. The armed bands sent into Afghanistan from abroad, the demolished power lines, ruined roads, the dead bodies of school teachers and peasants buried alive—what is this if not a full-scale aggression?" . . .

## The Soviet Army

Two of my fellow-travellers on the flight from Moscow to Kabul were Soviet army officers, a colonel and a major, returning to Afghanistan after a week at home. There were few passengers on the plane and it was not long before we started talking. Towards the end of flight we felt as if we had known one another for a long time. During the several hours that the flight took we were able to discuss many topics. Naturally, we spoke about the Soviet military contingent in Afghanistan and the Afghans' attitude to the Soviet men and officers.

"The enemies spread all sorts of preposterous tales about us Soviet soldiers," the Colonel said, his outward composure hardly concealing his seething indignation. "And I must say that under that influence of this systematic indoctrination by the imperialist propaganda machine and the Chinese hegemonists, some people did give in at first to suggestion and threats. But not many people and not for long. Today the doubters are leaving their doubts behind. As for the truth about us and our presence, people know all about that today. The masses learn the truth not only from the statements made by leading party and government figures, but also by observing us. They make comparisons, you know."

---

*"The history of Afghan-Soviet relations is daily enriched with fresh manifestations of brotherhood and friendship."*

---

"Dushmans [Afghan guerrillas] burn down schools, kill civilians, teachers and school children, they rob peasants and steal their cattle," the Major, who only a minute before had been telling me enthusiastically about the classical records he had managed to buy, broke in fervently. "We, on the other hand, take

nothing from them. We don't interfere with their affairs. We protect them from the dushmans. We help them every way we can. This gets through even to the most suspicious."

"I'll tell you just one thing," the Colonel added. "It may look like a trifling matter, but I think it speaks volumes. In January 1980 the peasants, with whom we were in constant contact, were friendly with us from the start, but the shepherds kept clear of us. Now, however, they often hang around and are friendly too. They say they are sick of dushmans. They see us as their protectors and friends and think that we are generally good fellows. You would do well to go to a meeting of Soviet armymen and local people. These meetings are unforgettable."

## Brotherhood and Friendship

The history of Afghan-Soviet relations is daily enriched with fresh manifestations of brotherhood and friendship. It is not just good-neighbourliness now, but an intimate, sincere and steadfast friendship, imbued with the spirit of comradeship, revolutionary solidarity and all-round co-operation.

Soviet-Afghan co-operation is a daily reality of Afghanistan today, expressing itself in the most diverse forms. I attended a joint exhibition of Soviet and Afghan artists, the opening of a new section of a highway, and the ceremonial commissioning of the new installations of the Kabul house-building plant, and I have seen for myself that Soviet people in Afghanistan, just as everywhere else, do a lot of good not only as skilled experts, but as exponents of new ethical values. By their example, they contribute to positive changes in the minds of the Afghan people and in their everyday life. This positive example set by Soviet people in Afghanistan bears out once again the profound appraisal of the work done by Soviet people abroad, given from the rostrum of the 25th CPSU Congress by Leonid Brezhnev.

"The international activity of the CPSU involves the whole people," he stressed. ". . . Thousands of Soviet people are doing work abroad—as staff members of embassies and other missions, geologists and builders, doctors, and teachers, metallurgists and chemists, transport workers and other specialists.

"To all these comrades the Central Committee expresses its sincere appreciation for their profound understanding and conscientious performance of their internationalist duty."

I remember hundreds of Soviet people of different trades and professions: oilmen discovering riches in the Afghan subsoil, builders of industrial enterprises in Kabul, Kandhar and Mazari-Sharif; hardworking builders of roads across the mountains and valleys, engineers and designers, teachers and agronomists. These ordinary people have come here from afar, leaving their homes to fulfil their internationalist duty, their profoundly humanitarian mission which deserves to be admired. . . .

Ronald Reagan's statement on the intention to give military aid to the Afghan counter-revolutionaries has had a sinister outcome. It can be seen in such concrete steps as the allocation in 1981 of almost a hundred million dollars for equipping and training bandits in special camps on Pakistan's territory, the attempts of Secretary of State Alexander Haig, during his recent visit to Peking, to make China a trans-shipment base for supplying American weapons to Afghan counter-revolutionary organisations and the active involvement of Britain in financing and delivering weapons, which has already contributed more than two million pounds sterling to the "kitty." Also taking part in anti-Afghan operations are Egypt, Saudi Arabia and certain other countries. Not long ago the France Press reported that the US Central Intelligence Agency was coordinating between all partners in the anti-Afghan alliance, in particular to provide weapons for the counter revolutionaries. . . .

*"I believe in the just cause of the Afghan revolution because it is supported by the Soviet Union, other socialist countries and the progressive forces of the whole world."*

The revolution in Afghanistan is going full steam ahead. The most gallant sons of the nation have now all rallied around its banners. . . .

I cannot but believe in the radiant future of the people, who are led by such men—unselfish, brave and persistent. I believe all this because I myself saw how people changed and embraced the revolution, those very people, who had been in dread of the dushman and the landlord but a month before. I believe in the just cause of the Afghan revolution because it is supported by the Soviet Union, other socialist countries and the progressive forces of the whole world.

*Boris Petrov is a Bulgarian journalist who writes on international affairs.*

*"And now . . . a Poland of tanks and underground leaflets, where the structures of control are in place, but just barely—a crumbling facade with a scaffold around it."*

# Overview: Martial Law in Poland

John Darnton

Dusk, with a steady, bone-chilling drizzle. An abandoned concrete watchtower sits at one end of the bridge. The car slowly dodges the potholes.

The span over the Oder is ugly and dilapidated. Neither the East Germans on one side nor the Poles on the other would dream of repairing it, a sign of their mutual disdain. The river below is a thin brown stream, disappointing, considering the bloody course it has wended through history.

The East German guardhouse squats on the other side, technically on Polish ground. Eric Ambler would love it here. The reek of black tobacco, the hard stares at the passport held under the gooseneck lamp, the inquisitions, the rubber stamp pounded down with an executioner's swing.

But the waiting is nerve-racking, hours and hours behind the drone of windshield wipers. The East Germans are being relentless. Car panels torn out; body searches. The guards hold up each piece of paper and read it, sometimes upside down. This is strange, for it is February 1982 and Poland, plunged into martial law, is supposedly once again a reliable "fraternal" nation. The Poles returning from visits abroad look nervous. They are bringing in coffee, soap, meat wrapped in plastic bags that bleed on the wet pavement. Many, you are sure, are smuggling in gold, clothes to sell, zlotys purchased in West Berlin at one-tenth the official rate. There are guns everywhere; officials moving with abrupt darting motions; a pervasive sense of fear.

And then, incredibly, it is over. The road beyond is deserted and dips around a bend into a forest. It is dark.

Half a mile ahead, five men in Polish Army uniforms step out of the bushes. Their bayonets gleam in the headlights. The commander flags you down ferociously. He leans against the roof, demands to know your nationality, where you are coming from.

Then he reaches into his pocket. He thrusts something through the window. It is an old, crumpled French note, 100 francs. "I was wondering," he says, "if you would be good enough to exchange this for dollars. I'll give you a good rate."

## Inscrutable Country

You have left behind the Oder, the efficiency, the stares, and you are back in Poland, the same old inscrutable, confused, troublemaking, muddling-through Poland, martial law or no martial law.

It is also the third Poland I have seen in my nearly three years here. First, there was the Poland of Edward Gierek, the former party chairman, with his ambitious development schemes, who is now in disgrace. That was a time of cynicism, apathy and pretense—and of prosperity disappearing before everyone's eyes like milk down a drain. Then there was the Poland of Solidarity and Lech Walesa. It was a time when horizons suddenly opened up, the blinkers came off, and there was hope of creating a livable, productive, nonschizophrenic society within the Soviet bloc. And now the Poland of Gen. Wojciech Jaruzelski, a Poland of tanks and underground leaflets, where the structures of control are in place, but just barely—a crumbling facade with a scaffold around it. In this new Poland, the fear and the dream commingle and everyone waits for something to happen—*something. . . .*

## August 1979

Confusing—this moonscape. On our first day in Poland, my wife, Nina, and I dine at Bazyliszek, the one luxury restaurant in the Old Town section of Warsaw. An atmosphere of faded Viennese elegance, with crystal chandeliers, brass samovars, wild boar on the menu and a string quartet in the corner playing Mozart. Outside, on the cobblestones of Market Square, sits a young woman with straight blond hair, a gold star pasted under one eye and a guitar. She sings an old Dave Van Ronk song in strangely accented English. The words rise up, distinct between the spaces in the Mozart: "Baby, you been away *too-o-o* long."

The Old Town is, for my money, the most magnificent nub of any city in the world. In Nuremberg, Cracow and Prague, the medieval buildings totter and list with authentic age. Here they are as neat as picket-fence slats, instant Gothic, dating from the 1950's, when the Government decided to rebuild the heaping ruins of the Nazi-occupation era brick by brick. Crafts that had died out a century ago were revived; old Canaletto paintings were copied to re-create the archways, gutters and gargoyles.

---

*"Party membership has become a scarlet letter."*

---

Later, I drive by the sprawling housing developments on the outskirts of Warsaw. Huge concrete slabs are scattered about like giant cinder blocks, monotonous in design and appalling in their cheap regard for living space. The priorities sink in: the sense of a golden, royal past, a desperate attempt to climb backward in time, and a gray future that crawls ahead without a vision of what shall be or should be. I have been here three weeks and I have yet to meet a self-professed Communist.

But, house-hunting, I discover the moneyed operators. In the exclusive Mokotow section, I come up against the same landlord four times. It is illegal in Poland to own more than one house. He feels compelled to explain. One house belongs to his wife; another, to his sister; a third, to his son. His son, I learn later, is in primary school.

The landlord shows me an upstairs bedroom. Its window has been bricked down to the size of an envelope. Regulations, he explains: This way, it's only a storage room. In the living room, metal rods hang down from the ceiling, so low that we have to stoop. Technically, he has reduced the room's dimensions so that it's not a room at all. Don't worry, he assures me; the rods will come down as soon as the inspectors come and go.

The rent for the house, officially set at 9,000 zlotys ($300) a month, will be paid to the state, but he wants five times that sum for himself, in dollars, under the table. Also, to reduce the Government's take, he proposes that we say we are sharing the house. He begins to pace off "his" half of the kitchen. I protest. The deal falls through. I hear him mutter, "Idiot. Doesn't know what country he's in."

An official guide is showing me around. He seems a bit defensive about my interest in the 500,000 Jews who lived in Warsaw before the Holocaust. He shows me where the tracks were of the trains that took them off to Treblinka. The raised foundations of earth under the high-rise apartments of the former ghetto still contain human bones. The monument to the heroes of the ghetto uprising is built with the very same granite that Hitler had planned to use to commemorate the liquidation of Poland's Jews. The monument is impressive. But it is the only one in Warsaw without flowers.

## The Agony of Eastern Europe

The guide then takes me to a church. He guides me stealthily down an aisle to plaques on the wall in memory of the war dead. Lists and lists of names, towns, dates. Finally one name leaps out: "Katyn."

"The date, the date, look at the date," whispers the guide.

I see the year 1940. I realize he is telling me the church believes that the Katyn Forest massacres of an estimated 15,000 Polish prisoners of war took place at a time when the area was in Soviet hands—that it was Stalin's work, not Hitler's, as Moscow claims. And the deeper meaning that this is the agony of Eastern Europe, where Germans kill Jews and Russians kill Poles, where the flagstones are steeped in blood, and where thousands can slip into graves unnoticed by history.

The next day, I go into a furniture store to buy a chair.

*"Nie ma"* ("There are none"), says the saleswoman, barely looking up from her newspaper.

But how about all those chairs in the window?

*"Dekoracja"* ("Decoration"), she says, mumbling something to herself. I think I hear that word again: "Idiot."

## Angry Miners

The town of Czechowice-Dziedzice, in the mining region of Silesia. A flat landscape of blackened smokestacks, dirty red-brick buildings and concrete high-rises, with an occasional clump of sad, scraggly pines. There has been an explosion at a mine. Two men are dead and 20 are trapped in a tunnel 600 feet underground, where a methane-gas fire is still raging.

It is the third mine disaster in the past month; in all, some 43 lives have been lost. The accidents coincide with a new brigade system that keeps the mines going 24 hours a day, seven days a week. The Government is desperate for foreign exchange; it is squeezing the miners for more and more of its "black gold."

Appointments with officials at the mine are made for me at the Mining Ministry office in Katowice, 32 miles away; they send me off with handshakes. I arrive at Czechowice-Dziedzice and something has gone wrong. The official has been called away, the gate is locked. I bounce back and forth for two days. A local party secretary finally loses patience and tells me to get the hell out of town. My car is followed by a Polonez, the favored model of the U.B., the secret police.

My translator and I find a small bar named Barborka, after St. Barbara, the patron saint of miners. We enter a smoky cavern smelling of beer and sweat, and the bawl of conversation stops. Hostile eyes rimmed with coal dust turn to the stranger in a necktie. No one moves to ease our path to the bar.

## A Mass of Lies

Two beers later, my translator explains to the nearest table that I am an American journalist who has read about the mine disaster and has come to see what happened. A miner lurches up; his face is three inches from my own.

"First thing," he says, "you've got to realize that all the papers in this country are crap—crap and lies."

"They're scared of the truth and they're scared of us," says his companion. "And, by Christ, the Government better do something and do it fast, or we'll do something ourselves."

There follows, over the next hour, an unremitting stream of complaints, threats and curses, despite the presence of a shadow who creeps in and sits down nearby. Rarely have I encountered such burning anger, a pure, white-hot, we're-going-to-get-the-bastards anger. And these are the miners, the elite of the Polish work force, coddled with special meat shops and goods unavailable to others. These are the men who refused to join in the anti-Government upheavals of 1956, 1970 and 1976.

We toast cousins in Chicago. Leaving, I see the Polonez sitting empty down the street.

The next morning, I return to the mine. The party secretary tells me I got his workers drunk to elicit the kind of information spies are interested in.

And the fire in the mine? "None of your business," he says. "And don't you worry. Everything here is under control."

Three days later, they bring up the dead bodies.

## August 1980

When the revolt comes, it is deeper and more disciplined than anyone expected. At the Lenin shipyard in Gdansk, the strikers' faces are dirt-streaked but radiant, solemn and lighthearted at the same time. The workers lounge about on the grass, listening to their leaders on loudspeakers, and, on transistor radios, to the BBC, Voice of America and Radio Free Europe. They marvel at the speed of news when it flows freely; they can take a vote and hear it come back over the little box within the hour.

The hall swarms with delegates from other factories joining the strike. A life-size plaster statue of Lenin gazes reflectively into the distance. To my surprise, I am given a seat on the raised stage of the strike committee. The delegates sit at long tables, as at a banquet—dockworkers, shipbuilders, tool-die machinists, assembly-line workers, bus drivers. Some write the names of their factories on placards as if they were attending a Rotarian convention.

More strikes are announced. Somewhere in the list, after an electrical factory in Elblag, I hear: *"The New York Times."* A cheer goes up. With everyone expecting an attack by armed troops, the foreign press seems to offer a glimmer of protection. At least, the world will know.

Food is brought to the locked gate by well-wishers. Overhead, a plane drops leaflets proclaiming the strike over.

Lech Walesa is rushing around, bobbing his head in hurried conferences, giving orders, grabbing the microphone to calm the workers with joking patter. Only a month ago, he was an unknown, unemployed activist for the minuscule Baltic Coast Free Trade Union. I talk to Anna Walentynowicz, the 50-year-old crane operator whose dismissal sparked the strike. She describes the agony of 1970, when workers were shot down. She got into trouble later for passing a hat to buy flowers to their memory. This time, it will be different, she says. No more marching through the streets; stay close to the machines and wait. I ask her for her political views. "I'm a democrat," she says. "But mostly, I believe in God."

## Church Support

The strikes are still on. Stefan Cardinal Wyszynski, the Primate of Poland, delivers a sermon that is actually broadcast over state television. A group of workers in the Gdynia shipyard are huddled in a room, hanging on his every word. He is their spiritual monarch, for 30 years the only authority they have respected.

---

*"One reason the military takeover came as such a surprise sounds a bit ludicrous in retrospect. There was no provision in the Polish constitution for a state of emergency."*

---

Cardinal Wyszynski calls for peace, calm, reason, respect. True, he criticizes the Government, but he warns that strikes could pose a threat to the nation; he pleads for workers to be patient and postpone some of their demands. He refers to the partitions of Poland: "Let us remember with what difficulty we regained our freedom after 125 years." All this mixed in with religious metaphors honed to perfection from his decades of slipping elliptical meanings past the

Communist authorities.

The speech is of critical importance. The church, in so many words, has told the workers to stop. What effect will it have?

The room is silent. A strike leader strides to the front and flips off the television. "Friends," he says, "as we have just heard, the Primate supports us right down the line."

---

*"The police spread the word that anyone passing petitions or information to Western journalists is liable to be charged with treason."*

---

A roar of applause and cheers. I learn, at that moment, a fundamental truth about the Roman Catholic Church in Poland. It resides so deeply in the people's hearts, in those recesses of nationalism and legend, that it can never be uprooted. When its words come into conflict with its own image, they are not ignored, they are magically transposed. The image is stronger; it is, in a sense, the real church.

Five days later, Solidarity is born.

## October 1980

The country is opening up—a headlong tide. New groups are forming. Liberals, reformers, even radicals, are taking over institutions, such as the journalists' union, that have been instruments of party control. Yet all this is unfolding peacefully, methodically, even democratically. It all seems part of what Jacek Kuron, the brilliant, barrel-chested long-time dissident, calls a "self-limiting revolution." The idea is to turn the authorities upside down without overthrowing them; to transform Poland without disturbing the geopolitical balance and bringing in the Russians. It is a tricky business.

Newspapers, incredibly, are printing news. I am having tea in the house of a friend, a former Polish ambassador, when a political activist arrives. Breathlessly, he pulls a typewritten document from his coat lining and says conspiratorially, "Have you seen the latest demands?"

My host answers graciously, "Thank you, I have. They're in today's newspapers."

Even the security apparatus seems a bit more human. Janusz Onyszkiewicz, Solidarity's national spokesman, is on the telephone talking to a friend in London about whether a Polish exile should return. "Tell him it's safe," Onyszkiewicz says.

"I don't know," says the friend.

"Tell him everything's changed now," says Onyszkiewicz.

"I'm not sure."

A third voice cuts into the line. "For God's sake, tell him *we* say it's O.K."

I go to a political cabaret. There is a curious mix in the audience, dissident intellectuals seated across the room from party and Government officials. But one central table up front is empty until the final moment. When it fills, there is a stir; eyes turn, waiters rush to push in chairs; people drift by, hoping for a nod of recognition. The latecomers are steel-mill workers and Solidarity activists. They are the new celebrities.

Something of a social revolution is underway. It is consummate paradox to feel the winds of class warfare in a Communist state. It is as if all those statues of "worker heroes" had suddenly come alive.

The party is widely seen as the agent of exploitation. People are leaving it in droves. Across the country, workers strike to back up demands that hospitals, clinics, rest homes and vacation spas reserved for the police and party elite be given to "the people." Fancy cars left on the streets overnight are likely to have their windshields smashed.

At the Ursus tractor factory outside Warsaw, thousands gather in the movie hall to prepare for a strike. The issue is the "Narozniak affair," the arrest of a Solidarity volunteer for disseminating a classified state document. Tempers are rising. A lanky political dissident gives advice on how to stand up under police interrogation. Another reads a poem about the glory of dying for Poland; it sends shudders of excitement through the hall. One young man grips the mike earnestly and begins with a gaffe—"Comrades," he calls out. Twitters and chuckles. He blushes deeply and recovers, but two minutes later he slips again—"Another thing we should remember, comrades...." This time there are howls of laughter. Flustered and red-faced, he can only sit down. Party membership has become a scarlet letter.

## December 1980

Things are moving fast. Films previously banned by the censor are playing on television. Universities are preparing to choose their own rectors by democratic elections. Parliament is becoming fractious. There is a kind of national euphoria; the whole country resembles a university coffeehouse plunged into frenetic discussions about unions, socialism, society. It seem that no meeting can adjourn before 3 in the morning.

Passports for travel abroad are available almost for the asking. It's as if the world has suddenly opened up. No matter that the neighboring "fraternal" countries have sealed their borders: Who wants to go *there?* Poles are coming back from the West to sniff the breezes—writers and scholars who left in official disgrace in 1968, émigrés who had vowed never to set foot in the country again.

New Year's Eve is a frenzied round of parties. The toasts become more and more outrageous, the champagne spills onto the floor. Men kiss each other on the cheek, women hug each other and exchange wishes in intimate tones. Jan, my sardonic friend, raises his glass and says: "And to you, as a journalist, I wish a Soviet invasion." Our friends laugh. It is too unthinkable.

Walking home in the middle of the street, we meet other groups of revelers. Beautiful Ania, who had looked so drawn and sad in the picture taken years before for a passport that never came, sighs and breathes deeply of the dank air. She opens her arms, as though to the night, and says: "All my life I've wanted to live in a free country. And now, just to think, my own country is becoming free."

## January 1981

Breakfast with Lech Walesa at the Solec Hotel, a sort of rundown Polish version of a Holiday Inn. Two busloads of Soviet tourists pull up. They enter— bulky, chattering, the big-bosomed women, the men in their crinkly suits. How will they react when they see Walesa, the devil incarnate, the man threatening to bring down their empire?

They sit down. They order breakfast as if they own the place. They eat. Nothing happens. Of course they know the name, but not the face: He is so dangerous that they've never been shown a picture of him.

## Walesa: An Enigma

I look at Walesa and I realize that I know the fact but not the man. How many times have I interviewed him? Maybe 10 or 15. How many times have I seen him sitting in his office, presiding at meetings, speaking to crowds? Maybe 30 or 40. And yet he remains elusive.

He has become such an international superstar there seems to be little left over. The legend of Walesa as dyed-in-the-wool worker, churchgoer, folk hero is beginning to overshadow the man. He is, without doubt, a gifted leader—courageous, instinctive, articulate. But there is a darker side to his nature—his dictatorial tendencies, his pettiness, his intolerance. These traits have been coming to the fore, affecting his leadership. Some of his top lieutenants are becoming disenchanted; the movement is in danger of splitting.

Walesa repeatedly says that it is unity—millions of unarmed workers standing shoulder to shoulder against the state—that has made Solidarity into what it is. If that goes, the union is lost.

## Tomb of the Unknown Soldier

The Tomb of the Unknown Soldier is in Warsaw's Victory Square. The tomb, containing the ashes of a Polish soldier who died in the fighting that repelled a Soviet invasion in 1920, has become a rallying point for all kinds of demonstrations. It is guarded at all times by four Polish soldiers standing erect and immobile. Every few hours, they are replaced by four others, who goose-step from a garrison across the square. On this day, Rural Solidarity, the new independent farmers' union, has been refused legal status by the courts. The farmers, large men with calloused hands, whose Sunday suits are rumpled from all-night bus trips, are confused and angry. They march to the tomb.

The crowd grows; there are thousands. Speeches start up. Tough, defiant words are shouted. Suddenly, from across the square come the guards. They march straight for the tomb, right toward the crowd—they have no choice. They get closer, 10 feet away, five feet.

Suddenly, the crowd parts, an aisle opens up, and, as the soldiers march through, a chant rises: "Long live the army!"

The soldiers take their places. I look at one of them. He is ramrod stiff and expressionless. But tears flow down his cheeks.

## Visions of Revolution

The lines in front of the stores seem endless. They practically merge into each other. The huddled, shivering figures conjure up visions of revolution and turmoil. In reality, the country is remarkably quiet, even subdued. The shortages are so bad that conspiracy theories develop. The Government, it is rumored, is intentionally holding goods off the market to blacken Solidarity. One writer tells his tablemates he has it on good authority that the goods are being stored in a secret tunnel constructed by the Nazis during the occupation. It's hard to tell if he's joking.

*"There is a laxity and inconsistency to the crackdown that seems in keeping with the Polish character."*

The strikes continue sporadically. They sound worse when they are read about outside the country, making it seem that the whole place is swirling in a vortex. But many of the strikes are local affairs, undertaken to oust a local administrator, or to get a police building converted to a clinic, or just to test muscle. I suspect they're not as detrimental to the economy as the Government makes out. I'm at one factory when a one-hour strike ends. The workers move dutifully over to the assembly line, but the conveyor belt doesn't move. "We don't have any parts, anyway," one worker explains.

But the economy, strapped for foreign exchange because of Gierek's live-now, pay-later borrowing policy, is in a state of collapse. A group of farmers from the south persuade the Solidarity chapter at the Ursus factory to build tractors for them on weekends. They go to another chapter and borrow the money, which is to be repaid with potatoes and cabbage. It's the only way to get anything done: Bypass the state altogether.

Mismanagement and inefficiency are rife. Goods are shipped to the wrong places, essential parts are missing, things are ordered and don't arrive. Cigarettes almost run out because there is no glue. Writers, who are guaranteed an allotment of paper, are composing novels on the backs of rejected manuscripts. I hear of a chocolate factory where no chocolates are being produced because there is no paper to wrap them in. But everyone goes to work, punching the time clock in and out.

## December 1981

Back in August 1980, our maid, Kasia Trzcinska, suggested matter-of-factly that I should meet her son, Jurek. I put her off. A few weeks later, she raised the subject again. I explained that I would love to meet her son and her whole family, but that I was up to my neck trying to write about Solidarity and all the changes shaking Poland.

*"[This] is the image of Poland I carry away with me—oppressor and oppressed standing side by side, watching the theater of their country's disintegration."*

Not long after that, her son telephoned. "I'm coming to Warsaw tomorrow," he announced.

"Good," I said, not very enthusiastically.

"I'll be driving down with some other people," he said. "Lech Walesa, Bogdan Lis, a few others. You see, we have this new union we're trying to get registered."

## Solidarity's Goals

Jurek Trzcinski, it turned out, was a top Solidarity leader. A large man with a rakish mustache, he had a bemused expression that he put on to parry my queries about Soviet intervention. From Jurek I derived my respect for the integrity, courage and basic level-headedness of the Polish working class. Night after night, he explained the goals—not to drag Poland out of the Warsaw Pact, not to overthrow the state, but to set things right. "We just want a decent country," he would say.

Jurek often visited us with Bogdan Lis, Walesa's right-hand man. One day, they came from a meeting with striking farmers. Lis pinned a new button, a green Solidarity badge, on the lapel of my youngest daughter, 7-year-old Liza. She stood straight, eyes wide and solemn.

"Do you know about Solidarity?" Lis asked her.

"Yes," she replied.

"And what it it?" he prodded.

"Solidarity wants to make the Polish people free."

With a whoop of pleasure, he hugged her and spun her into the air.

For some reason, that scene flashed through my mind when my phone and telex went dead at 11:10 on the night of Dec. 12, 1981, and I drove through the streets to file a story and encountered police vans closing off both ends of the block where Solidarity's Warsaw headquarters is located.

## December 13, 1981

Martial law came down like a sledgehammer. It caught everyone off guard. Solidarity's leaders, who had arrived at Gdansk for a general meeting, were brought meekly down the stairwells of the hotels, their hands behind their backs. Many of our friends were dragged out of bed, some not even given time to put on their shoes. When Walesa was seized at his Gdansk apartment in the early hours of Dec. 13 and flown to Warsaw, he was convinced, reliable sources told me later, that he was going to be thrown out of the plane.

Jurek evaded arrest and went into hiding. But shortly afterward, four policemen with a dog came to his apartment for his wife. She shouted at them: "Criminals, bandits! I will not go with you—you'll have to shoot me right here." Her 8-year-old daughter screamed, "Mama!" and her 87-year-old mother threw herself at a policeman's feet, begging them to leave her daughter alone. But they arrested Jurek's wife and dragged her away.

## The Illusion of Democracy

One reason the military takeover came as such a surprise sounds a bit ludicrous in retrospect. There was no provision in the Polish Constitution for a state of emergency; a bill that would allow for one was being prepared for Parliament. Until the bill passed, the thinking ran, a military crackdown couldn't happen. So great was the illusion that democracy had already taken root that it was difficult to imagine the authorities acting illegally.

The key to the operation was isolation. The whole nation was cut off from the rest of the world and plunged into a blackout. All communications were severed, all travel banned, all meetings prohibited. Every household was isolated from every other, every factory, every division within a factory. The power of the union lay in numbers and concerted action, which depended on communication, openness and visibility. Once these were blotted out with curfews, roadblocks, dead telephones and jammed radio broadcasts, the power dissipated.

The generals did more than arrest 6,000 Solidarity leaders and supporters. Figuratively, they placed the entire population under arrest.

Everyone is slumped in a moral depression. Journalists are being fired left and right. Universities are being purged. People direct their energies toward schemes to get out of the country. No one seems to be doing any work.

A campaign is under way to boycott the regime. Intellectuals and professionals withhold their services. One actor I know works as a waiter in a coffeehouse. A well-known singer is pumping gas. A woman television broadcaster in Wroclaw is selling ice cream at a small stand in the market square.

## Pervasive ZOMO

There is an occupation-regime atmosphere about everyday events. A soccer game between a Soviet team and a Polish one is held under tight security; ZOMO troops with automatic weapons ring the stadium; the stands are divided into quadrants by uniformed police. On flights of the Polish airline, a ZOMO with his hand on his AK-47 stands at the back of the cabin, on the lookout for hijackers.

On the other hand, there is a laxity and inconsistency to the crackdown that seems in keeping with the Polish character. One man I know who is in hiding comes up from time to time for a meal at his favorite restaurant. Another public figure in hiding, the former head of the journalists' association, is said to have received heart medication, through an intermediary, from an official in the Ministry of the Interior.

In Victory Square there is a huge cross, made entirely of flowers, lying on the flagstones. Twice the police have removed it, and each time it has been reconstituted, bigger than before. Near the cross is a small shrine to nine miners shot by the police at Wujek in December. One day, someone brought a marble plaque with the nine names engraved on it. The police removed it. The next day, there were nine lumps of coal. They, too, were removed. The next day, there were nine crucifixes. And so it goes.

Last month, a British diplomat was walking across the square when he chanced to see a young man picked up by two ZOMO while kneeling beside the cross. The man did not resist as he was led away into a police van. Once inside, he was beaten savagely with nightsticks. The diplomat, peering through a window, counted 26 blows to the head and stomach before he was spotted and ordered to move on. He felt certain that the young man must have died. . . .

## The Turning Point

In retrospect, the critical turning point came in March 1981, when the union voted a nationwide general strike to protest police beatings in Bydgoszcz. That was a do-or-die moment, when the union's strength was at peak, the resolve of the authorities shaky and Moscow's intentions unclear. A general strike, if won, might have forced the authorities into honest cooperation.

Instead, Walesa and a few other negotiators bypassed the union's democratic decision-making procedures to negotiate a last-minute settlement. This opened up fissures in the movement and strengthened hard-liners in the party. Union

negotiators said afterward that the authorities had informed them that the Russians would invade if they did not give way. History may never know if that was true or not. . . .

---

*"A general strike, if won, might have forced the authorities into honest cooperation."*

---

Official thuggery is on the rise. On May 3, during pro-Solidarity demonstrations, policemen bashed heads all over the place. Clouds of tear gas billowed from one end of town to the other. Late in the evening, I went to meet someone at the train station. At an underground track, where there is a television set fixed to the wall, a crowd had gathered for the evening news. Four ZOMO were standing in the center, their nightsticks still bent and scuffed. Around them were young men, obviously demonstrators. Everyone was watching the clashes on the news—in effect, watching themselves.

That is the image of Poland I carry away with me—oppressor and oppressed standing side by side, watching the theater of their country's disintegration. I do not know what will happen here; no one does. What everyone knows is that the conflict and the anguish are far from over.

*John Darnton is a Pulitzer Prize-winning journalist and bureau chief in Warsaw for* The New York Times.

*"Solidarity. . . insisted on a completely free market in which the government would under no circumstances intervene."*

viewpoint 56

# Martial Law Suspended Poland's Trend Toward Capitalism

Sidney Lens

When General Wojciech Jaruzelski placed Poland under martial law in December, he committed a crime and created a tragedy. It was a crime because his martial law regime reversed a process of democratization that had been under way for a year and a half. It was a tragedy because it halted, at least for the present, a hopeful trend toward decentralized communism that had attracted attention around the globe.

The blame for this serious setback belongs, first of all, to the Polish Communist leadership, which clung stubbornly to an economic program that many Polish economists had long warned could lead only to bankruptcy. The Party's glacial pace in instituting even the most obviously needed reforms played no small part in bringing the Polish crisis to a head. But some of the blame must be allotted, too, to Poland's insurgent trade union movement, Solidarity.

Certainly Solidarity had good reason to demand shorter hours and higher wages for Polish workers. But without a restructuring of the economy to achieve higher productivity, any gains in wages or reductions in hours were bound to be pyrrhic victories, swiftly wiped out by uncontrollable inflation and the black-marketing of goods in short supply. (The nationwide total of monthly wages, I was told in Warsaw last year, was 145 million zloty higher than the nationwide value of monthly production.)

Furthermore, Solidarity put forth two demands to which the Polish government could not possibly agree: In its negotiations for a system of worker self-management, the union insisted on a completely free market in which the government would under no circumstances intervene. Not even Adam Smith—or the most zealous American libertarian—could have

gone along with such a scheme: There are moments of crisis—natural disasters, economic dislocations, emergencies of many sorts—when state intervention is unavoidable.

## Call for a Referendum

A second, even less acceptable proposal, reflecting the strains of a prolonged stalemate, was Solidarity's call for a national referendum on the nature of the Polish form of government. No regime, and especially not one caught up in the kind of crisis confronting Poland in 1981, could be expected to consent to such a plan.

It's too bad Lech Walesa and his comrades in Solidarity failed to come to grips with these realities. Poland presented an extraordinary opportunity to bring about a form of what the Czechs in 1968 called "socialism with a human face." A Polish version of the sort of system that has evolved in Hungary or Yugoslavia would not only have amounted to a great step forward for the Poles; it would have had incalculable consequences for the Soviet Union itself, and for all the rest of the Communist world. And it could not have failed to strengthen the prospects of international peace.

The Poles will probably have another chance—as the Hungarians did after the Soviet invasion of 1956. The regime of Janos Kadar, imposed after Soviet tanks struck down thousands of Hungarians who demanded a decentralized, humane socialism, pursued a harsh line for a couple of years. But then it began to release political prisoners, and it introduced a democratic agrarian system and an economic program that have given Hungary a considerably higher standard of living and made the nation a showcase of the Eastern bloc.

General Jaruzelski is likely to set out on a similar course, but the Polish reforms of 1980 are sure to be held in limbo for at least a year or two, and when they are officially revived they will take a less radical

Sidney Lens, "Second Act in the Second World," *The Progressive*, March 1982. Reprinted by permission from *The Progressive*, 409 East Main Street, Madison, Wisconsin 53703. Copyright © 1982, The Progressive, Inc.

form than seemed attainable before the crackdown.

Regardless of the crisis in Poland, however, a strong and irreversible tide is running within the socialist world—including the People's Republic of China—toward an anti-Stalinist, decentralized kind of communism. Even the Soviets have been caught up in that tide. Immediately after Stalin's death in 1953, hundreds of thousands were released from the forced-labor camps, and Premier Georgi Malenkov introduced the "New Course," which encompassed the conversion of some heavy industry to light industry, a sharp increase in the production of consumer goods, an easing of rules governing sales by collective farmers, and a substantial boost in farm income. Workers, too, were promised higher wages and lower prices.

---

*"Regardless of the crisis in Poland, . . . a strong and irreversible tide is running within the socialist world."*

---

Some other Communist states rushed to follow the Soviets' New Course in the 1950s, but it was abandoned after a short time when Nikita Khrushchev forced Malenkov from power. Nonetheless, efforts to introduce "socialism with a human face" continued in East Germany, Poland, Hungary, and Czechoslavakia.

So long as the Eastern bloc economies could draw on a pool of unemployed or underemployed labor in the rural areas, they were able steadily to increase production despite inefficiency and poor worker morale. But now that surplus labor pool has been drained, and Communist planners must improve both efficiency and morale if they are to achieve levels of production commensurate with those prevailing in the West. That will require the regimes to grant both democratic rights and material incentives to workers and managers.

Communist leaders are aware of these considerations. When I was in Poland during last year's Communist Party convention, a magazine editor told me about a luncheon he had just attended with two members of the Soviet central committee. Referring to the workers' struggle in Poland, one of the Russian officials had said, "Our system at home also needs grass-roots pressure to shake it up."

## Decentralized Communism

The conflict between centralized (Stalinist) communism and decentralized (worker self-managed) communism is certain to grow more acute. It will continue in Poland, it is under way in China, and it will surely arise sooner or later in every Communist nation. It has, in fact, been a crucial issue for half a century and more.

Toward the end of the 1920s, the Soviet Union under Stalin adopted an economic model that was, in effect, geared to an imminent expectation of war. Stalin, convinced that the capitalist West was about to mount an attack against the Soviet Union like the invasion of 1918-20, restructured the Soviet economy to give top priority to production of weapons and munitions. He stressed heavy industry and neglected consumer goods. He forced peasants from their farms into collectives, so that their crops could readily be gathered up and exported to raise the hard currency needed to pay for foreign machinery. He sent living standards into a sharp decline.

Whether there was real justification for such draconian measures is still a matter of conjecture and debate. But the fact is that Stalinist economic planning was the *worst* kind of planning, subordinating considerations of quality, efficiency, and cost to the quantitative goals of "the plan." All decisions about prices, wages, and production goals were left in the hands of the government bureaucracy. There was no such thing as consumer choice, and no incentive for managers or workers to improve efficiency or quality.

One consequence was that the Soviet Union—and the Communist nations which came into being with a Russian shove after World War II—lagged behind the capitalist world in providing consumer goods. Theirs were economies of perpetual shortage, and the evidence has been on display to every visitor—empty shelves in the stores, or long lines for such items as meat, cigarettes, and sugar. At Warsaw's best hotel, the Victoria, where the daily rate is $100 (in hard currency), there was no orange juice, fresh or canned, when I was there, and half the items on the menus of the best restaurants were unavailable. Because the system is not obliged to worry about competition or profitability, it can let such things slide.

## Beneficial Competition

In 1948, when Yugoslavia was expelled from the Soviet bloc and cut off from trade with its members, Marshal Tito's government was forced to turn to the West. That meant suddenly competing with far more efficient economies. If Yugoslavia hoped to sell its wares in London or Vienna, it had to produce better goods at lower cost. This was the challenge that impelled Tito, over the next few years, to develop the system of worker self-management that provided material incentives at the factory level. In a sense, Tito was replicating the socialist workshop plans devised a century earlier by Louis Blanc.

Compared to the Stalinist standard, Yugoslav self-management was remarkably decentralized. Prices and production goals were set by workers' councils and management committees in each enterprise, rather than by the State. The central government got out of the business of detailed planning; instead, it laid down targets—for example, "increase shoe production by 8 per cent"—and attempted to guide the economy toward achievement of its goals by offering such inducements as credit or foreign exchange.

Most important, Belgrade gave workers and managers a greater degree of autonomy than could be found in any Stalinist state—the right to travel, to quit one job and take another, to seek work abroad, and to exercise at least a measure of free speech.

Hungary adopted much of this format in the mid-1960s, about a decade after Soviet tanks had rolled into Budapest to crush a revolution. And Poland, until the imposition of martial law, was clearly in the early stages of a similar (perhaps even more sweeping) transformation. In Poland, a popular movement obviously provided the catalyst for change: Five times in the last thirty-six years—in 1956, 1968, 1970, 1976, and 1980—the Poles have rebelled against their shortage economy. On each occasion the government promised reform, but each time it merely tinkered with the Stalinist system, leaving its essential components in place.

## Modernizing Heavy Industry

In 1970, for example, when Eduard Gierek replaced Wladislaw Gomulka as head of the Polish party and government, he introduced a grandiose development plan designed primarily to modernize and expand heavy industry. To finance the scheme, Poland was able to borrow $26 billion from Western governments and Western banks. By 1976, almost one-third of Poland's yearly national income was devoted to economic development. Respected Polish economists cautioned Gierek that trouble was coming: The industrialization program couldn't work because Poland still lacked both the raw materials and the productive efficiency required to compete with the West.

For several years, Polish living standards rose at an annual rate of about 6 per cent, but the increase was illusory, fueled by the heavy influx of foreign funds. The bubble burst in 1975, and by 1978 Poland was buying four times as much grain from the West—on credit—as it had in 1971. Polish exports did not begin to pay for such imports, or even to service Polish debts. Fifty major projects and hundreds of small ones were abandoned in mid-course for a lack of capital or raw materials or foreign exchange.

In 1980, when the government tried to raise prices without public notice or discussion, a full-scale revolt erupted. The regime had no choice but to make concessions to the militant new union, Solidarity, and it had to find a way to pay for those concessions and for the debts that had been incurred by Gierek. The government and Solidarity agreed that a program of self-management would be an essential element of any system devised for Poland but they differed significantly on the details. Solidarity wanted workers to run the factories; the Communists insisted that ownership had to be vested in the State. Solidarity called for a totally free market; the Communists insisted on the State's right to intervene at times of crisis. When negotiations collapsed and the regime's fate seemed to be in jeopardy, martial law was imposed. How and when the process of reform is to be resumed remains to be seen.

Around the world in China, changes now taking place may ultimately have a more profound effect on the Communist world—and on the entire world—than anything that has been happening in Poland. China's transformation is a gradual one, but there, too, the trend is toward a new form of communism, distinct from but akin to the self-management models that have been established in Yugoslavia and Hungary.

## Easing Pressures

There are hopeful signs in the "readjustment and reform" program China's new leaders have mounted in the last few years. China is still a rigidly regimented society, but pressures on the people are easing, living standards are going up, material incentives have been offered to spur production, farmers are being permitted for the first time to sell on the open market the grain and animals they raise on their tiny private plots, some individual initiative is being allowed and even encouraged in enterprises ill-suited to state management, and wide-spread cultural changes are readily apparent in such visible areas as fashion and the arts....

---

*"Poland presented an extraordinary opportunity to bring about a form of what the Czechs in 1968 called 'socialism with a human face.'"*

---

What had been denounced as "capitalistic" during the Cultural Revolution is now officially encouraged. In handicrafts, commerce, and service industries, small private businesses have been chartered, provided they employ five or fewer persons; in 1979, there were 300,000 such enterprises, and by the end of 1980 the number had grown to 810,000. In the Maoist catechism, these are transgressions against socialism, but their impact has been to make more goods and services available and to raise living standards after years of stagnation.

But the most significant changes in China are system-wide and structural. Directors of some 6,000 large plants (which account for 60 percent of the nation's manufacturing output) have been given latitude in buying raw materials, setting production goals, and selling the goods they produce. When the cutbacks in heavy industry went into effect a few years ago, for example, the director of an aircraft plant set aside part of his production line for the manufacture of electric fans; such decisions had previously been made only by higher-ups in the appropriate ministries in Beijing. Furthermore, local directors are now allowed to retain and reallocate some of the profits earned by their enterprises.

In most of the factories that now enjoy this measure of autonomy, workers' congresses have been elected. Some of these organizations exist only on paper, and others confine themselves to receiving reports and offering suggestions. But the trend is toward giving workers an important and perhaps even controlling voice in economic decision-making.

## On a Steady Course

At the same time, the principles of decentralization have spread to provinces and cities, which now hold on to some of their funds to pay for construction projects they design and manage on their own. There have been problems: Last year, while the central government was attempting to cut down on capital investment, the cities and provinces were increasing it. Nonetheless, China's new course seems steady and bound for still wider application.

The Chinese leaders have made no secret of the fact that they are favorably disposed toward self-management and want to move in the direction that has been chosen by Yugoslavia and Hungary. In vast and diverse China, the transformation is likely to be a gradual process—especially since it is already encountering serious resistance. High military leaders are said to oppose the rapid dismantling of Maoism, and millions of Communists are also reluctant to change direction. Some would lose power under decentralization, and others might lose their jobs in a system that placed a greater premium on performance and efficiency.

However, the shift toward a different kind of communism has begun in China, too, and long before that shift has run its course the impact will be immense—for China, for Eastern Europe, and probably for all of us.

*Sidney Lens is senior editor for* The Progressive.

*"Since the Soviets seem quite prepared to apply regularly the required dose of force, they are likely to prevail indefinitely."*

viewpoint 57

# Martial Law Destroyed Poland's Trend Toward Capitalism

### Charles Krauthammer

Shortly after the Soviet invasion of Afghanistan President Carter said he had learned more about the Soviets in a week than he had in his previous three years in office. Carter's remark was ridiculed and attributed to his naiveté and general "softness." Ronald Reagan, on the other hand, made a career of toughness and called upon Americans to face the facts about the "enemy." And the facts, as he sees them, are that an unholy alliance of Communists and terrorists has an exclusive franchise on the devil's work on earth. Yet when Reagan was asked in an unguarded moment about the Red Brigade's kidnapping of General James Dozier, he answered with visible anger that those "cowardly bums" don't even have the guts to stand up one on one in a fair fight. It is curious for a man with such a hardheaded, conspiratorial view of the world to become indignant upon learning that terrorists disregard Marquis of Queensberry Rules in pursuit of their political objectives. Reagan appeared genuinely shocked that the punk revolutionaries of this world do not live by a High Noon code of honor, just as Carter was shocked that the Russians violated the cardinal postwar rule that superpowers are not to annex neutral neighbors. Reagan and Carter may have disagreed on whether an international code of conduct derives from frontier justice or Sunday school morality. But both found it hard to believe that for many in this world such a code counts for little or nothing.

At least since Wilson's Presidency, the American penchant for mixing morality with realpolitik has been an enduring source of wonder—and dismay—to the world, particularly to the Europeans. But this surfeit of morality also produces a certain moral blindness, an inability to grasp, even imagine, the nature of radical evil. How prone we are to view evil through liberal democratic eyes is apparent in the casual way we use the language of enormity. "Genocide" was a word used to describe the Atlanta murders. "Fascist" was the word Norman Mailer used to characterize a society unwilling to take chances on literary murderers. Senator Larry Pressler was detained by the Polish police for half an hour during his visit to Warsaw a couple of weeks ago, and came back saying that now he understands how repressive martial law can be. The air traffic controllers claimed for months that they were being treated the way unions are treated in Poland, a claim not heard very much lately.

Having trivialized our vocabulary, it is not surprising that we are unprepared when real enormities like the Polish repression occur. Early Western reports first characterized martial law as an attempt to purge extremists from both the Communist Party and Solidarity. Even as thousands of Solidarity members were being jailed, General Jaruzelski was viewed as a patriot trying to save "socialist renewal" from Soviet tanks. Some editorialists spoke sympathetically of Jaruzelski's "burden." There was a general unwillingness to believe that the Polish authorities fully intended to destroy Solidarity and the social movement it represented.

## The Force of Arms

We reacted with disbelief not only because such repression violated our ideas of what is right but also because it violated our ideas of what is possible. Ever since Vietnam, we have come to believe that popular national movements cannot be suppressed by force of arms. They have a certain inevitability to them; even if they are temporarily contained, they ultimately prevail. A widely held corollary is that force itself is somehow obsolete: the day of the superpowers is gone, and with it gunboat and jackboot diplomacy. In

Charles Krauthammer, "A Panglossian Warsaw," *The New Republic*, February 10, 1982. Reprinted by permission of THE NEW REPUBLIC, © 1982, The New Republic Inc.

a modern age, battles are won and lost in other arenas—economic, ideological, spiritual.

To believe that is to think it impossible that Jaruzelski would ever attempt, let alone succeed at, a brutal counterrevolutionary putsch. Even as the first news of the success of martial law began to filter into Western news reports, it was hard to believe that a mass workers' movement, ten million strong, could be suppressed by force. How could a mere army turn back the clock on a national revolution so deep and wide as Poland's?

---

*"The Polish authorities appear to be operating quite successfully under the archaic notion that force can prevail."*

---

This belief in the triumph of the will is derived from recent American national experience: the success of the civil rights and antiwar movements on the one hand, and of Vietnamese nationalism on the other. But to universalize that experience is to misread history. Nonviolent mass movements like Martin Luther King's succeed, indeed exist, almost exclusively in tolerant liberal societies. In other societies the "spirit" had best be armed, disciplined, and backed by a superpower (precautions that Hanoi wisely took). But the struggle of an unarmed people against a militarized totalitarian regime is an unequal contest. There is nothing inevitable about the triumph of the spirit in those conditions, as Hungary and Czechoslovakia showed.

Yet so ingrained are our neo-Hegelian habits of thought that some Western intellectuals were loath to abandon them even after Jaruzelski's coup and the evidence that Solidarity had indeed been crushed. A week after the imposition of martial law in Poland, Lewis Lapham wrote that the events in Poland (and the Israeli annexation of the Golan) demonstrated that the time for superpower control of the world is over: "(I)t is the smaller states that make the rules of what used to be called, in a more spacious and optimistic age, 'the game of nations.'". .

## Military Censorship

That news has yet to reach Warsaw, perhaps because of military censorship. The Polish authorities appear to be operating units quite successfully under the archaic notion that force can prevail. Now, it is true that force may prevail only in the short run. But if the short run means a generation or two, after which, as Keynes noted, we are all dead anyway, then that kind of short run victory seems substantial indeed. And if the short run means, say twelve years (the biorhythmic cycle of East European explosions) then, since the Soviets seem quite prepared to apply regularly the required dose of force, they are likely to prevail indefinitely.

Another corollary of the Western view that force is obsolete is that if force does become absolutely necessary, then the proper response is to use it with restraint. Hence the theory of escalation, the use of force commensurate with the enemies'. . . .

The Soviet bloc has a different doctrine: overwhelming force. The Jaruzelski coup, one of the first cases of total takeover of an advanced industrial society, is a classic example. It involved all the elements of the strategy of overwhelming force. First, a massive show of military might to demoralize the population and make resistance unthinkable. Second, absolute control of all information and interruption of all independent communication to atomize the opposition, whose strength lay, literally, in its solidarity. Third, the immediate seizure of all opposition leaders, to decapitate the movement and render it directionless. Fourth, and possibly the most important, the use of force to induce betrayal. The *New York Times* reported that at one factory the police offered striking workers safe passage out if they allowed them to arrest their leaders. The workers complied out of fear. Like Orwell (in *Nineteen Eighty-Four* Winston Smith is broken when tortured into betraying his lover), the Polish authorities know that betrayal, even more than brute force, has the exquisite capacity to demoralize.

In the United States we were slow in responding to the Polish coup primarily because we couldn't believe it. We have a habit of failing to imagine the world as it is. At the end of World War II, the U.S. Ambassador to China, Patrick Hurley, reported to the State Department that both the Chinese Communists and the Kuomintang "are striving for democratic principles." Jefferson would have recognized neither as his spiritual descendants, but Hurley, like many Americans since, suffered from the tendency to see everyone as just like us. Barbara Tuchman notes that the Hurley cable "reflects the characteristic American refusal to recognize the existence of fundamental divergence." And the principal divergence we refuse to recognize is between those who share our view of what force can and ought to be used for, and those who don't. Tuchman adds that Hurley's cable is one of the least sophisticated judgments in American diplomatic history. Her words were written in 1972, long before the Polish coup and before any American had gotten around to writing about Jaruzelski, the Polish patriot who had to destroy his country in order to save it.

*Charles Krauthammer is a senior editor for* The New Republic.

*"In spite of constant government propaganda against the American position, [the Polish people] understand why it is being done."*

# US Support for Poland Is Sincere

*Christianity Today*

Poland is by far the largest and most populous of Russia's European satellites. Among the latter it is also the least pliable and the most religious, with more than 90 percent of its population Roman Catholic and about 1 percent Protestant. It is said that Poland has a higher percentage of people in church on any given Sunday than any other country in the world.

Poland's Communist overlords, pragmatic about the existence of more religion than they cared to see, had been uneasily aware since the summer of 1980 of a new independent spirit in the country's legislature. Not unconnected with the strides made toward a free trade union, this was also boosted psychologically by an expatriate Pope in Rome who could never quite forget his Polish origins.

## A Jewish Scapegoat

The other Warsaw Pact countries, three of which form Poland's land frontiers, were aghast at the danger signals. They reduced essential supplies to their wayward ally, already the victim of economic mismanagement, in the hope of starving it into submission. To explain this dismal state of affairs, Radio Warsaw dredged up for a new generation an old crudity: the Jews were to blame. They were wrecking the economy by hoarding goods, stirring up unrest in universities, and "collaborating with international Zionism." Never mind that supporting evidence was totally lacking; it had the makings of a useful diversion, designed to rekindle ancient antipathies between Roman Catholics and Jews. *Divide et impera* has been a useful weapon through the centuries in the tryannical armory.

Moscow chipped in with a complementary version, attributing Polish problems to American support of dissident groups and Solidarity extremists. It was

unthinkable, of course, that the workers should seek salvation through any source other than the Communist party. Was not the good of the working classes the party's overriding concern, and its very *raison d'etre?* Writing history books for the Communist young would become a nightmare! How could you explain the revolt of ten million workers against a government of the workers, by the workers, and for the workers?

Happily for the establishment, Solidarity became the victim of its own momentum. Instead of strategically pacing itself, it presented a head-on challenge to the Communist machine. On December 13, then, the tanks rolled—as they did on that other day of infamy 25 years earlier in Hungary, when they crushed another people's inalienable right. Solidarity should perhaps have realized, as President Reagan put it two Sundays later, "that they were asking one thing that a Communist government cannot allow." Marshal Viktor Kulikov, commander of the Warsaw Pact forces, had been on hand in Warsaw. Reports are that he gave General Jaruzelski the ultimatum, "Either you go in, or we do." Jaruzelski did, and the oncoming winter exacerbated the suffering, misery, and depression that ensued.

## Western Reaction

Ten weeks passed. It is not the first time Western Europe has been frustrated and divided in its reaction to brute force and intimidation. As always, there is no lack of excellent reasons for doing nothing; ironically, the most dramatic response came from Polish ambassadors in two major world capitals, who sought political asylum.

President Reagan's imposition of sanctions has received wholehearted support nowhere among his European allies. Many Americans became exasperated at what they regarded as Europe's pussyfooting. This, they held, was no time for self-interest. Was not the plight of the Poles more

*Christianity Today*, "The Plight of Poland: News Behind the News," March 5, 1982. Copyright © 1982 by CHRISTIANITY TODAY. Reprinted by permission.

important than the financing of a pipeline from Siberia? For their part, Europeans pointed out that if we Americans were a few thousand miles farther east our outlook would be different. In any case, in his refusal to reimpose an embargo on grain exports to the Soviet Union, Mr. Reagan's motives were domestic politics rather than international justice.

Moreover, on prominent display in the Free University of Amsterdam during last November's World Council of Churches meeting was a quotation attributed to an American admiral and taken seriously by Dutch peace lovers: "We fought World War I in Europe. We fought World War II in Europe. And if you dummies will let us, we will fight World War III in Europe." We agree with the incensed Hollanders. Any American admiral who said that should be court-martialed.

## A Detour Around Calamity

Many of the details of the present Polish situation are still not known: the plight and prospects of the many thousands who are detained; the extent of the ongoing Soviet involvement; the future of Solidarity; the nature and duration of military rule. And what of the indomitable Lech Walesa? We recall his rousing words at an outdoor rally in the fall of 1980: "We cannot surrender, for those who will follow us will say, 'They were so close, and they failed.' History would not absolve us then." Thank God for Walesa. When the story of the decline and fall of the Russian empire comes to be written, Solidarity's valiant part will not be forgotten.

There are two major factors on the Polish scene. One of these is the enigmatic Wojciech Jaruzelski. Has the general who in 1970 was arrested for refusing to order his troops to fire on striking workers, and who was again in trouble in 1976 for similar reasons, had a radical change of mind? Is he merely the dupe of Soviet tyranny, as many Russians believe? Or are the Europeans and large sections of the Polish citizenry right? Could he not rather have aimed to draw the teeth of the Russians and deprive them of a pretense for invasions because of the very effectiveness of his December 13 action? As one commentator put it, "A successful military autocracy might prove a far more deadly thorn in Russia's side than a free trade union. Its dangers are much less obvious, but in the end, they are more devastating to Communist expansion. Military rule stemming from the Communist party's inability to cope is itself a standing rebuke of the Kremlin."

## The Pope Is Right

The other prime factor in this situation is the position of the church. Both the dominant Roman Catholic body and the Protestant and evangelical churches of Poland are requesting help. They are, after all, without food and suffering from hunger. Moreover, they desperately fear any move that would bring a Russian military invasion closer. Minor relaxations of the Polish army's harsh grip were widely advertised within a month, but a price was being paid—as Pope John Paul II was quick to point out. In order to deep their jobs, Poles were being forced to sign loyalty statements that conflicted with their consciences. "Violation of conscience," the pontiff told a crowd of 30,000 in Saint Peter's Square, "is a grave act against man. It is the most painful blow inflicted on human dignity, and in a certain sense it is worse than inflicting physical death."

It would be heartening to find this ringing appeal for liberty and human rights endorsed unequivocally by that sizable segment of Protestantism represented by the World Council of Churches. In the words of one leading British Socialist: "Those so justly vociferous about the denial of freedom in Africa, Asia, and Latin America have over the years been uncharacteristically reticent about repression in Eastern Europe. Now they must speak out or be condemned as hypocrites. Silence for them in this situation is a form of complicity."

But they won't speak; they do not really prize human liberty. The goal of the World Council is not primarily freedom and justice, but change in the social, and especially the economic, structure of society.

## Imposing Sanctions

Political decisions are not within our competence. Is Walesa simply moving too fast? Is General Jaruzelski a Soviet minion, or is he a patriot driving a hard bargain while choosing the lesser of two evils?

If the U.S. and Western European nations were to impose sanctions, would this drive the Russians to an immediate invasion of Poland? Or would they back away from their hard line to permit more freedom?

---

*"Only Western food can keep from hunger a land that has long been one of the breadbaskets of Central Europe."*

---

In the long run, is it better to push Russia so that it shows to all the world how utterly destructive to freedom communism really is? Or would it be better not to force that nation's hand?

If we work to create a more secure world for the Russians, would this encourage them to remove the barriers to freedom throughout Poland and even the entire Communist empire? Or would such action merely unleash capability for further spread of Soviet repression to new quarters?

We must leave these decisions to the President and his advisers. We trust that God, in his good providence, will overrule their mistakes and guide them to work for the good of the Polish people and of all the peoples of the world.

But there are some things we can do.

We can begin by taking seriously our own obligation as American citizens. We live in a free democracy—imperfect, to be sure—yet still a democracy, and relatively free. For that reason we must assume some responsibility for the decisions of our own rulers. When things go wrong, we cannot simply blame Carter, or Reagan, or anonymous "politicians." We are responsible for the politicians we elect. It is our duty to vote for good leaders—leaders of intelligence and vision and moral convictions and courage. But voting is not enough. Some of us must heed God's call into politics, and all of us must participate actively in the politcal process to the degree that we can as private citizens. . . .

## To Those Who Thirst

The Polish situation has brought Western Christians face to face with a very practical dilemma: Shall we withhold food and supplies from hungry, suffering people in order to punish a repressive government? The position of the American government is equivocal. There will be no official support or provision of supplies, but the government will not forbid private groups from meeting these human needs.

*"By sending food and supplies, America simply shows all too clearly that communism simply is not worth it."*

We believe this is wrong. We do not argue over the political nuances of whether or not this will in some indirect way aid the Communist regime. As a matter of fact, we believe a good case can be made that it will not. A committed Polish evangelical, who is also a devout supporter of Solidarity, explains the viewpoint of his people. In spite of constant government propaganda against the American position, they understand why it is being done; but they are hungry, and their children are hungry. They think it is a mistake. They and the whole world have witnessed a breakdown in the Communist government because of a revolt of the workers. Now only Western food can keep from hunger a land that has long been one of the breadbaskets of Central Europe.

And the evidence seems to support the view that Jaruzelski is at heart a Pole who bends as little as he can, but as much as he must, in order to prevent a bloodbath of Poles at the hands of ruthless foreign troops. By sending food and supplies, America simply shows all too clearly that communism simply is not worth it.

Christianity Today *is a monthly magazine concerned with national and international issues.*

# US Support for Poland Is Patronizing

Leopold Tyrmand

This was a roundtable conference. The subject was Poland—a country that has recently contributed more to the conference industry than any other on earth. It was held a mere eighty miles from the Polish border, in West Berlin. While we may assume that the distance was of little significance either actually or symbolically, it meant a lot to me. . . .

Having spent most of my life under Hitler and Stalin, I see Nazism and Communism not as abstractions but as personal enemies. I tend to anthropomorphize them in a way that appears unintelligible to those who have not shared the experience.

Although there is, I agree, a bit of phoniness in the posture of a better-informed victim, I firmly believe that the understanding of a totalitarian reality is inseparable from an organic and empirical relationship with it. My fellow Americans in particular (since I am now one of them) seem uncomprehending when I try to describe my former condition. For them freedom is like breathing, and they no more notice its presence than they notice the presence of oxygen in their air supply. Americans are not the only ones who find it hard to understand the nature of totalitarian reality. Soon after I defected, I talked in Paris to a prominent Polish editor in exile who had spent his life in the West doing battle (and quite successfully) against Communism. Our conversation took place at the time of a state visit to France by a top Polish Communist who had been directly instrumental in my Warsaw miseries and humiliations. "You understand nothing," I told my interlocutor, "you weren't *there.*" "Would that guy who's talking in the Elysée Palace with the French President understand you any better?" sneered the editor. "Of course," I said, with no hesitation. "The

hunger and his prey are linked by an identical sense of reality; they both know something others don't." . . .

## The Communists and the Poles

The majority of my fellow conferees, even the most insightful among them, used the plural "Poles" when speaking of Polish Communist officialdom, apparently not cognizant of the fact that in Poland, since 1945, the Communists have been considered a category apart from the rest of the nation, a subgroup without clear-cut national definition. They may call themselves Poles, but in those deep layers of collective consciousness where the sense of a commonly accepted propriety resides, a distinction is made between *them* and *us,* and they are referred to almost universally in the third person.

This distinction, sealed into the very fabric of the Polish reality, somehow escapes the recognition of Westerners. Thus, no American is able to comprehend the bitter frustration of a Pole on reading daily headlines like "Poland Takes Action Against Striking Miners." What Poland? Why should those who slaughter miners be designated *Poland* just because they hold brutal sway over the nation's territory and have stolen and falsified Polish national emblems and signs?

Like the citizens of my mutilated former homeland, I still retain a nonpolitical approach to politics. That is why I felt so apart from the other conferees, as they painstakingly scrutinized every detail of the interplay among the Communist party, the Church, and Solidarity, and drew minute distinctions among the various factions and individuals within these bodies. My table partners were perfectly ready to agree that the basic struggle in Poland is between the society as a whole and Communism. They seemed to have understood that the intangibles of personal yearning, suffering, and alienation form the very core of this fight; but somehow the crux of the matter was

Leopold Tyrmand, "What Do the Poles Want?" Reprinted from *Commentary,* June 1983, by permission; all rights reserved.

lost as they noted all the other aspects to be pondered, negotiated, and perhaps even resolved by the combined impact of Western economic help, political maneuvering behind the scenes, and tough but "pragmatic" dialogue with the supreme supervisor in Moscow. *"No,"* I constantly wanted to shout, "there is *one* issue only, that of Communist power, whose legitimacy the Poles have refused to accept ever since Yalta, and will never accept. The West must do something about *that* essential factor, and if it doesn't, it's the West that will be the loser."

---

*"I suddenly felt myself in the same company as all the well-heeled Western sympathizers with the 'oppressed,' babbling about the new order from the safety of America's shores."*

---

There was more too that I wanted to add: that the West must honestly and thoroughly reevaluate its notion of Communist power, something it has never really done, and that only then will it finally understand—for the good of the so-called "captive nations" but for its own good as well—that the main principle of Communist strategy is never *really* to negotiate anything with anybody, even while pretending to do so. The Hungarians and the Czechs tried unsuccessfully to tell the world about the fraudulence of Communist negotiations, but only the Poles have succeeded, though only to a limited extent, in making the issue more visible. The Poles have lost the latest round, but they will never stop knocking at the walls of the dungeon, which is, actually, not the Pole's but the West's problem. Yet none of this did I succeed in making clear, since my views were emotional rather than analyses of changing political realities.

## Dangerously Naive Proposition

Instead, I listened as a West German representative of one of the major parties involved in the formulation of *Ostpolitik* got up and delivered a sensible, kindhearted plea for priority aid to the Poles at any cost and through every possible channel of assistance. Here was a gentleman overwhelmed by the spirit of sharing who was perverting the idea of giving. What he said sounded both humanitarian and honorable, but for all his solicitude, it was actually an appeal for unconditional maintenance of the political status quo, whereas the whole point of the Polish effort was the positive rejection of the status quo. Following the German, there arose an Englishman of methodical cast of mind who asked the speaker whether he actually knew what the Poles really wanted, or was offering his compassion and generosity without consulting their wishes. The German theoretician ducked the question: he insisted good-naturedly on finding a solution whereby all parties would be reconciled and happy. I tried to say something myself on this sunny but dangerously naive proposition, but the sheer effort of describing the chasm between East and West made me sound in my own ears a trifle incoherent.

It is true that, *en masse,* the Poles, like everybody else, want peace, security, a decent living. But above all what they want is a modicum of purposeful and effective control over their own lives. For the individual, the central question of human existence in Communism is the all-pervading sense of the futility of *any* endeavor. It is not even political freedom that is at stake, but simply the freedom to exist on one's own terms, that rudimentary natural right established in 18th-century Europe and America as an immutable human privilege and accepted in all democratic society as a given. This freedom to pursue individual happiness within the framework of agreed-upon laws is what Communism abolishes the instant it is installed in power. Yet the organic human claim to it will not be obliterated. Marxism-Leninism may have relegated this claim to the dustbin of history, but the Poles have dug it out again, whisked off the dust and filth, and polished it into a shining crucifix behind which they have already marched three times and will march again—regardless of settlements made among the reigning powers.

Along with the German *Ostpolitik* ideologist, I heard some engaging remarks at the conference from a high-powered West German banker, deeply enmeshed in the $30-billion Polish debt to the West. He gave an honest and detailed account of past mistakes and miscalculations, as well as present options, and closed his statement with the astonishing assertion that the one thing the German bankers had not anticipated was the personal like they had come to feel for the Polish banking officials in charge of doing business with the West. This was a moving confession, sentiment being so rarely invoked as a factor in financial catastrophes. Still, I remarked that *Stimmungspolitik* (mood politics) may be as unreliable as *Realpolitik,* and that the German bankers had found themselves in the same situation as Napoleon, who based his attitude toward the Poles on the lovableness of one Polish lady. . . .

## The Voice of America

Yet it seems that in 1982, during an interview with the Voice of America, commenting on Solidarity's apparent defeat, I outdid myself with enthusiasm for its indestructible achievement. I lauded the glory of those who had shown the world the real face of socialism, even if they had now suffered a temporary setback and were too sunk in gloom to acknowledge their historic accomplishments. Many months later, I received a letter from a bright young journalist, a fierce and dedicated Solidarity man who had been badly scarred as a prisoner in the detention camps set up by Jaruzelski after the crackdown. He wrote: "I listened to you. My memory of your words still hurts me. You made some clever phrases about what a weird people we Poles are for grieving at this moment instead of rejoicing at the historic victory we had won. It was strange listening to your voice on that December night, from far-away, unreal America. Where did you ever find reasons for such euphoria, and what was all that talk about history? In the Poland of those days history was like outer space to us.... How could you of all people have addressed yourself to the inevitable logic of history—you, who were also trampled with dirty boots in the name of those same immutable historical laws?"

He was right. Reading his words, I suddenly felt myself in the same company as all the well-heeled Western sympathizers with the "oppressed," babbling about the new order from the safety of America's shores. There is such a thing as taste in the exercise of political conscience, and I had violated it, showing myself guilty of that moral tactlessness which is the besetting sin of the liberal mentality. But how could I possibly convey any of this to the conference without blatant exhibitionism?

## Purging Anti-Marxism

All over the West, an effort has already gotten under way to purge the Polish experiment of its anti-Marxian and anti-socialist substance. The energies of one important sector of the non-Communist Left have been harnessed to demonstrate through periodicals, books, and other channels that what Solidarity represented was a heroic attempt to salvage the Holy Grail of Marxian socialism from the paws of Communism but still retains the socialist creed and hopes for a better life under the sun of a collectivized, bureaucratic system of governance and values. Many of the cliches of leftist melodrama have been taken out of storage for this purpose, turning the Polish shipyard worker into a proletarian hero out of Bertolt Brecht or Pete Seeger—all this on the shaky theory that Polish Catholicism is politically radical and Polish trade unionism is organically anti-capitalist.

When I keep proposing that what the Polish worker wants is capitalism, pure and simple, I routinely confront the most acrimonious disbelief. Small wonder, for to say such things is to spoil the reveries of the many nice people who spent some time in Solidarity's Poland and came back full of certainties about the new socialist dawn. Which Poles did they talk to, I wonder? Not the seamstresses who conduct semilegal business on the economic fringes of big cities, or the workers in small factories that produce marmalade or plumbing accessories, or the laundry operators, vegetable sellers, and street vendors of belt buckles and umbrellas. Nor, I imagine, did they ever

go to the dingy bars where the Poles who try to work at three jobs during twenty-four hours drink their vodka, or sit with them on Sundays at their soccer matches in provincial towns. Had they done so, they would know what those people want is the freedom to make a living, exactly as in America or West Germany; that capitalism is associated in their minds with a purposeful and effective life, while the very word "socialism," over recent decades, has acquired a connotation of utter hostility toward the most commonplace human needs and unlimited power to destroy lives.

## The Ordinary People of Poland

The ordinary people of Poland have experienced the injustices and indignities that for forty years have been coterminous with the word socialism, and they know that these plagues are infinitely worse than anything capitalism could ever inflict upon them. Just give them a truly free election, and see what happens.

During the entire Solidarity saga, the Polish Church was treated with veneration by the Western Left, a puzzling attitude when one considers that some crassly reactionary elements are still alive and well within the Church and are still propounding their view that the Freemasons are conspiring with the Communists to erect a kingdom of godlessness on this planet. Indeed, until not so long ago it was this portion of the clergy which determined the Polish Church's direction. It fell to one man, Cardinal Adam Sapieha, Archbishop of Cracow before and during World War II, to achieve a qualitative change in the chemistry of Polish Catholicism and a redirection of its spiritual assets and energies.

*"When I keep proposing that what the Polish worker wants is capitalism, pure and simple, I routinely confront the most acrimonious disbelief."*

This does not mean that notions of the rebirth of Catholic doctrines of social commitment had not already been floating around in the Polish Church: yet those ideas were usually parochial and reductive, tinged with the modish anti-Semitism of the 1930 s, and confined to quasi-totalitarian visions of the homogenous, autocratic, corporate society. Western observers of today's Poland are thus mistaken to think that the church has always been the central repository of Polish national identity and ethos. During the war years the Church would not have been visible at all as a moral force had it not been for Cardinal Sapieha, who defied the Nazis by saving Jewish children, and Father Maximilian Kolbe, a prewar semi-fascist whose heroic behavior at

Auschwitz was a desperately needed gesture of moral grandeur. In the postwar period, too, the influence of the Church on Polish life would probably have been modest had it not been, ironically enough, for Communism which, after 1945, forced it into the spiritual mobilization whose effect we see today....

---

*"The West has never really understood the make-up of the Polish intelligentsia as a coherent class."*

---

The West has never really understood the make-up of the Polish intelligentsia as a coherent class or pursued any real attempt to win it over as an ally, despite the fact that this group, obsessed with independence and dignity, is anti-Communist to its core. To be sure, every Western journalist has done his share of marveling over how, in Poland, novelists, poets, and critics enjoy so much respect and social influence. But the underpinnings of this phenomenon have never been investigated.

## Discrepancy in Stereotypes

During the 50s, some perceptive American diplomats detected the discrepancy between the stereotype of the Polish intelligentsia (romantic-religious-nationalist) and its nonconformist tendency to subvert Communism through offbeat behavior and manners (as by adopting Western clothes and music). This should have served notice of a serious demand for social and political influence, yet the opportunity was squandered when the United States turned its attention instead to a group of "revisionist" Communist functionaries who had embarked upon a mission impossible to reform Communism and give it a human face. Grants and fellowships were showered on these people, trips abroad were facilitated by the American embassy, to expose them to civilized democratic existence and, in turn, make them amenable to political compromise. In fact, some of them actually defected to America. Most, however, returned to the party fold in brand new Brooks Brothers blazers and with Zenith stereos, smilingly assuring the Americans (who were footing the bills) of their good intentions, and then going on to expedite any vile assignment handed down by Gomulka or his successor, Gierek, Two decades later, most of Poland's eccentric intellectuals ended up among Solidarity's strategists and theoreticians, while the prime representative of the revisionists, Vice Premier Rakowski—whom the State Department had wined and dined and brought together with President Kennedy for a friendly chat—became Solidarity's hangman....

The crux of Communism's superiority over us is that it has both a scenario for how to do us in *and* the faith that it can be done. Why bother to wage war if we can be brought to our knees by a combination of hard-core strategic harassment and subtle self-doubt implanted into the very fabric of our civilization and culture? No one in the West has given serious thought to destroying Communism since 1918, while the Communists, ever since the October Revolution, have been thinking both methodically and strenuously about how to liquidate democratic capitalism. After World War II, when the Communist expansion hit like the outbreak of a dangerous disease, the West had no choice but to resist Communism by force; yet even this decision was soon negated in Cuba, Vietnam, and Angola, and we are now witnessing its negation in Central America as well. Here again Gramsci offers a clue to the way our own liberal sentiments have induced in us a kind of ideological daze, so that the mere *wish* to destroy Communism is decried as a horrendous one, not just perhaps feasible, but abjectly improper, something no decent man ought even to think. Communism after all is an idea, a dream, a promise; it may be flawed, it may indeed have killed 60 million people, but is it not contemptible to think of killing an idea, of murdering a dream?

The Communists are free from this sort of philosophical agonizing. They picture capitalism quite straightforwardly as an obscene, fat slob with a repulsive cigar, which makes it quite easy to visualize killing him. Our own cartoonists, by contrast, have been forcibly restrained—by some invisible hand—from conceiving a graphic metaphor for Communism as evil. The best they can do is caricature its leaders and spies—rather benignly for the most part.

## An Elusive Policy Toward Poland

This is why we have never had a relevant policy toward Communism, Soviet Russia, or the satellite arrangement, and why all efforts toward such a policy seem, at least for the moment, futile. Many maintain that there is no need to worry since the Soviet Union needs our existence more than it needs our destruction. Perhaps they are right. In any case, nothing our enemies may do to us could equal what we have done to ourselves.

*Leopold Tyrmand, vice president of the Rockford Institute and editor of the journal* Chronicles of Culture, *came to the United States from Poland in the mid-1960s.*

# The US Media Does Portray Soviet Life Accurately

David K. Shipler

Autumn is the saddest season in Moscow. It comes too soon, furtively, dissolving the fleeting summer warmth in a haze of gray and rain. In the collective farmers' markets the crude wooden counters begin to lose their splashes of bright greens and reds, shifting into somber shades as squashes and nuts and potatoes appear, heaped in front of peasant men and women who have come on crowded trains and buses in the aching hours before dawn. In coarse padded jackets they stoop over their wares, their faces the color of burlap. Occasionally a gold tooth flashes in a clucking, coaxing smile of salesmanship, like the glint of gilt on a church's onion dome against the sunless city. The smells of the aging summer turn musty.

On such a day in September 1975, less than a week after I had arrived in Moscow, the sky seemed as if it would be forever sheathed in lead, and the city was cast in a chill gloom that confirmed the worst stereotypes I had brought with me, images of overpowering drabness and cheerlessness. From my second-story office window I looked across a narrow street to a wall of bleak dun buildings, a view of what I imagined to be the monotony of Russian life.

Suddenly down the small street poured a stream of little schoolgirls, running, laughing, tripping, pulling at each other's long braids, all in matching brown dresses with pinafores starched and gleaming white in honor of the first day of school, all with pristine, elegantly tied ribbons in their hair. They were like fresh blossoms bursting out of a field of slate, their neat prettiness testimony to the devotion of a dozen mothers somewhere behind the austere walls.

## Forms of Rebellion

It was a surprise, a quick glimpse of a richer, warmer vein of Russia. And just as quickly the girls were gone, the street gray again and quiet. Of course,

they were an illusion, too, a mirage of uniformity and orderliness and gaiety, a neat veil prettily masking the diversity and hardships of Soviet life. Even the meticulously dressed schoolgirls, as I learned much later, wear subtly patterned stockings with their uniforms—a technical violation of the rules, overlooked by teachers—as a faint form of rebellion into individual expression. At an early age they acquire the technique of dodging and weaving in and around authority without confrontation, a skill vital in their adult lives.

As the illusions and images are peeled away one by one, Soviet society reveals itself as having grown more complex than it appears from outside. The variety of political thought is more extensive, the literature and theater and film more creative and truthful, the press more critical than many Americans imagine. It took me a full four years of living and traveling in the Soviet Union to arrive at some understanding of how minds are shaped, of how political values and social attitudes are absorbed by the young, of how it is to grow up in Russia long after the zeal of revolution has died.

Remarkably, beneath the state hierarchy's tough rules, many Russians have lost their heroes and their faith, their faith in their ideology and in their future. Some respond by retreating into their personal lives, neglecting the collectivism that is supposed to govern the country's social structure. Others idealize an irretrievable past rooted in rural simplicity and moral purity, a search for Russianness, as it can be called. These are more than drawing-room philosophies nourished by small handfuls of Moscow intellectuals; they catch a groundswell of tension and yearning that runs across the full sweep of Soviet society. They are played out through Russia's three great forces of Communism, Christianity and Patriotism, and through a rising Russianist movement that mobilizes the frustrations and dreams that those forces contain. What they signify—the conflicts, the ambiguities, the overlapping of one ideology with its opposite—is a profound crisis of belief.

## Communism

Twice a year, on November 7 and May 1, Red Square is cordoned off. The parades on the anniversaries of the Bolshevik Revolution and on May Day are pageants of military might and worker solidarity, done in the name of the common man, but not open to him. Admission is by ticket only, a ticket carefully provided to those deemed worthy.

---

*"Beneath the state hierarchy's tough rules, many Russians have lost their heroes and their faith, their faith in their ideology and in their future."*

---

In the vast square before the rust brick of the Kremlin walls, the Politburo climbs the steps of the red-granite Lenin mausoleum, faltering with age, waving stiffly to the diplomatic corps, the crowd, ascending to the balcony to survey royally the spectacle below. The troops in greatcoats march in perfect ranks. The tanks and missiles sweep into view, filling the square with clatter and blue exhaust, followed by card shows and precision drills like football halftimes. Then the workers come, carrying banners, pushing floats adorned with slogans: "We Put the Decision of the 25th Party Congress Into Reality"; "All Power to the Soviets"; "We Are the First on Earth to Create Developed Socialist Society. We Are the First to Build Communism."

Does anybody read these slogans? Do they speak to the people? Do they have meaning? This is a special sort of Soviet fantasy, a synthetic world created by the sentences that flow endlessly from newspaper columns and radios, from toasts and speeches, from the banners and signs that deface streets and factories like some state-subsidized graffiti. All carry a unanimous, heroic, self-congratulatory message that all is well and getting better. The product is Communist surrealism. In this milieu, the mark of a mature citizen is his ability to know the real truth from the synthetic truth, to slice himself neatly in half and to keep his divided personality properly split.

## Private Thoughts

A Soviet journalist can tell his private joke—"Communism is just over the horizon but the horizon is an imaginary line and as you approach it, it recedes"—so long as he writes openly about the inexorable advance toward Utopia. A violinist attends political lectures every other week, knitting and reading while the lecturers drone on, to get the required check mark by her name so she can go on

the orchestra's scheduled tour of Western Europe. A linguist wrinkles his nose as he describes the zeal of the party committee in his Moscow district, which organizes two weeks of daily indoctrination lectures every year or so for residents of the neighborhood; he says he sits through the exercise reading science fiction.

One evening in a drab apartment not far from mine, among a few young people discussing life, there were two young women: Suzanna, 19, pudgy, Jewish, a second-year student in an engineering institute specializing in the control of air pollution, and Maria, the slender, sinewy daughter of an exiled Spanish Communist. Both were born in Moscow, Maria because her father had taken refuge there in 1949. She had been brought up a Soviet girl, and now, in her late 20's, her eyes flashed with rebelliousness behind her tinted glasses.

She worked for 100 rubles a month (about $150 at the official exchange rate) at the Institute of the Working Class, as part of a seven-member team studying Trotskyism. But never had she been allowed to read a word of Leon Trotsky's writings, except for some of his letters. The Trotsky collection in the institute's library was off limits to her and her colleagues; they were restricted to the proclamations and newspapers of Trotskyist parties in the West, and their task was to analyze this material appropriately, always delineating the incorrectness of the parties' position.

## A Hundred Rubles

Maria found herself agreeing with some of what the parties said, but she wrote what her boss wanted. "I sell my soul for a hundred rubles," she said.

By contrast, Suzanna seemed to require delicate handling. She took the issues rather seriously. When she tried to remember the questions intrinsic to studying Marxist ideology—"First, the distance between quantity and quality, or, when does quantity become quality?"—the others in the room, including her cousin Yuri, cut her off with laughter. When I asked Maria if she considered herself a Communist, like her father, she cast a glance at Suzanna. "If I had lived in Spain," Maria said slowly, "maybe I would have been a Communist. But not here. Excuse me." She smiled wryly, bowing in sarcastic apology toward Suzanna.

I had the feeling that Suzanna's crystal world was close to shattering. She reminded me of a wellbred churchgoer, flushed with a naive fervor that couldn't stand the simple question "How do you know there is a God?" It was the shallowness of her convictions that was striking, and yet how desperately she clung to them. When pressed, she could not say honestly whether or not she was a Marxist; perhaps she was, though she could not be sure, because, she confessed, she had no clear grasp of what Marxism was. She could recite definitions, but had decided that she would have to be older to understand them thoroughly.

While this may have had a ring of humility and tolerance, her views were quite otherwise. She would not entertain the notion of competing structures of ideology, and she fell into a sharp disagreement with her more liberal cousin Yuri, who studied at a teachers' college. To his complaints about the absence of open discussion in classes, she replied in a scolding tone, saying that it was as it should be. Teachers must know clearly what to teach, she explained pedantically, because students are too young to think for themselves. If you don't have a firm system of ideas to teach, then young people might end up having a variety of ideas, which would be terrible. She grew quite agitated at the thought of competing ideas flying wildly around the classrooms.

As she explained herself further, I began to see that it was not the nature of the idea that appealed to her but its singularity. Her allegiance was to conformity; she valued the common direction of her peers and figures of authority, and her displeasure with Yuri was not at all ideological, it was social. She seemed to believe in nothing but good behavior.

Here was a pressure point of the new society; the pulse could be felt beneath the surface like a fluttering, elusive truth. Here was what it had all added up to, all the blood and suffering, all the fierce hope and the angry dreams of the distant Revolution, now blurred in a misty past. Drained of passion, empty of desire, the Revolution now stood motionless.

## The Siberian Wasteland

We had been traveling for days in the subarctic wasteland of western Siberia, a group of American journalists, pressing government officials in charge of oil production with our relentless questions on the capacity and future yield of the country's most plentiful oil region. The questions had become crucial to knowing where the Soviet Union was headed, for the United States Central Intelligence Agency had just issued a report predicting a decline in production that would ultimately throw the Russians into the world market as buyers, no longer exporters, with all the political and military ramifications of that dramatic shift in roles. Officials in Moscow had arranged our trip to counteract the C.I.A.'s projection, yet all the local administrators we interviewed were too jittery to speak candidly. Nervously, evasively, they parried our questions, like men in the dock.

These were all government officials, not party officials. Virtually all of them were in the party, to be sure, but their salaried jobs were as executives in various branches of governmental operation, including oil production. Despite their rank, they displayed a striking anxiety, an opaque style of practiced blandness.

We were on our way home to Moscow, frustrated, between planes at the Tyumen airport, when a neat man in a dark suit, white shirt and conservative tie emerged from a black Volga sedan and entered the V.I.P. lounge. One of our local guides, a Soviet newsman, recognized him as Sergei D. Velikopolsky, first secretary of the party committee of the city of Nizhnevartovsk, the administrative capital of the Samotlor oil region, one of the most important in the country. He was catching a plane for some distant point in the region, and we doubted that he would grant our request for a few minutes of his time.

## A Crown Prince

But we tried him, and, to our surprise, he seemed rather pleased to find a herd of American reporters in this unlikely spot. He stood in our midst for a long time while we peppered him with questions, and he responded with calm candor, revealing the statistics that had been so elusive, discussing future production curves and shortcomings with the open confidence of a man clearly in charge. He was only 41, yet he wore authority with impressive ease, the crown prince of a remote and vital place.

*"Drained of passion, empty of desire, the Revolution now stood motionless."*

This was the characteristic of party officials—those paid to conduct party affairs, as opposed to those workers, teachers, scientists and farmers who were also members of the party, as in the West they might also have been members of a church. The party professionals were very different from the rank and file: well-groomed and well-spoken, urbane and expert, comfortable with power. They were more difficult to meet than government officials, and more rewarding, for in my experience they were generally men with whom one could have an intelligent conversation and a genuine exchange of views, an impression I found shared by diplomats and other journalists. Their counterparts in Western societies occupy the board rooms of corporations: They are the conservative elite dedicated to the smooth functioning of the existing system, and to their own careers.

The party, the supposed "agent of history," has evolved into an unrevolutionary political watchdog and, perhaps more important, into a management and efficiency board. Its local committees—at every factory and hotel, on every farm and faculty—are charged with making things run properly, a job so consuming (and futile, evidently) that it overwhelms most ideological activity. "Our first task is to see that things work better," said a young woman party member and Intourist guide in Tallin, Estonia. You could almost hear the bones rattle as Marx and Engels spun in their graves.

## Focus on Work Performance

This focus on work performance lends a strangely apolitical cast to party affairs, especially at lower echelons, where soporific lectures and empty slogans make political activity into a stylized ritual. As politics permeates all spheres of life, it grows mundane and unimportant, like background music in a restaurant. One party member in Tbilisi, a factory engineer, blushed with embarassment when asked to name the 13 members of the Politburo at the time; he couldn't get beyond six. I once asked a musician with the Bolshoi to what extent his party membership involved him in things political. "Political?" he laughed. "Ha. There's no politics at all. What do I do as a party member? Be a good example at work. And at party meetings discuss work discipline, especially of members."

At the same time, party members, and especially the professional *apparatchiki,* are subjected to close and continuing scrutiny, and not only on the job. A party member is not thought of highly, I was told, if he goes out often to a restaurant or dancing. Even in this divorce-ridden society, a divorce can wreck a high party official's career, a Soviet journalist observed. Central Committee members are pressed by their colleagues to weather marital crises, lest they risk their positions in the hierarchy, he said; the exemplary Communist is one whose marriage is in order, or at least appears to be. "We are the Puritans," said a party member, trying to explain to an American.

---

*"As politics permeates all spheres of life, it grows mundane and unimportant, like background music in a restaurant."*

---

"The party is just a police force," sneered a young woman studying to be a teacher. Her brother belonged, but not out of any conviction. He had been enticed into joining by superiors in the courthouse where he worked, who told him that if he did so, he could go with a group of tourists to Western Europe for a few weeks. A woman scholar was advised to join the party if she wanted to become a full professor.

It rarely has to be put so bluntly that the good jobs, the state prizes, the trips abroad, the key promotions—and with them the access to better housing and the special shops that are closed to the public—tend to flow to those who are supposed to be the best and the brightest, the Communists. A young Muscovite looked at me quizzically when I asked why he wanted to join, as if I had asked why the sun comes up each morning. "For my career," he said simply.

## Sensation of Momentum Crushed

It is an article of conviction among Soviet intellectuals that the Bolsheviks who made the Revolution were men of ideas, creative thinkers whose vision possessed their fellow Russians and inspired the country with a sense of forward movement. Lenin, Trotsky, Plekhanov, Bukharin were more than skillful activists; they were theoreticians for whom ideology lived, grew, developed, matured and ripened within an evolving reality. Their mission, as they saw it, was pure, holding a promised future guaranteed by inevitable history: feudalism to capitalism to socialism to communism, the inexorable progress of mankind. The exciting sensation of momentum lasted for Russians long after the ideal was crushed for most adherents in the West, dashed by the oppressive example of the Russians themselves.

Today, in those engaging discussions and debates around Moscow kitchen tables, the bloom of faith is still recalled with a painful pleasure. Socialism, with its state control of the economy, was to be but an intermediate stage between the downfall of capitalism—the abolition of "bourgeois property"—and the advent of communism. As the proletariat took the reins of productive power in Marx's utopia, the class antagonisms that had determined the course of history would disappear, the state would wither away and the abundance of material goods would allow for a proper relationship between a man's work and his wage. The socialist dictum, "From each according to his abilities, to each according to his work," would be replaced by the Communist principle, "From each according to his abilities, to each according to his needs."

Many Russians can remember when they believed in this, when they genuinely foresaw the advance of their society toward the flowering of communism. The recollection of the hope puts a bitter edge on today's despair. Something has died. The ideology still shapes perceptions of events—particularly in the outside world—but the vital sense of forward motion is gone. The country feels aground, stuck in the phase of gigantic socialism, "state capitalism," as it is termed disdainfully. Soviet Communists have become conservatives as their party has evolved from an agent of historical change into a guardian of the status quo.

*David K. Shipler,* The New York Times *correspondent in Jerusalem, reported from Moscow from 1975 to 1979.*

*"What we experienced in the Soviet Union was so far from what we read in the US media,...one is tempted to doubt one's own observations and findings."*

viewpoint 61

# The US Media Does Not Portray Soviet Life Accurately

Farley W. Wheelwright

Rule No. 1: Anyone who goes to the Soviet Union for whatever reason, under whatever auspices, comes home an expert in all matters socialist. I am no exception. Therefore, it is important to be careful what one says and how one says it. Expertise does not imply credibility back at the ranch!

Rule No. 2: Anyone who goes to the Soviet Union for whatever reason, under whatever auspices, takes his/her prejudices with them and inevitably comes home convinced by what they have seen. One generally sees only those things which confirm previously-held convictions. I have tried not to be victimized by this rule.

## Rejection of Propaganda

I was never one of those persons who thought that everything the Soviets tell you is propaganda fed by some gigantic thought-machine which originates in a computer buried next to Lenin in the Kremlin. I can smell propaganda, whether it emanates from a chamber of commerce, the State Department or the Soviet Union. I am fairly expert at rejecting it.

At some point we must develop our own critical faculties. This is one of the blessings of being a Unitarian-Universalist—to listen, to observe, to think for one's self, to make one's own decisions. These are the hallmarks of our faith. These are the rules I tried to apply to the trip Virginia and I took this summer to the Soviet Union, in the company of about 150 people with as varied a political and theological complexion as you would meet in a Unitarian-Universalist society. I was glad to have most of them as traveling companions.

I had an advantage over most of the group. In 1954 I had taken one of the first tours to the Soviet Union after the second world war, busing from Brest-  .

Litovsk through Minsk and Smolensk to Moscow and thence to Novgorod, Leningrad, Helsinki, and home. This was the same route across the Pripet Marshes to Moscow that both the Napoleonic and Hitler's armies journeyed. The countryside had not markedly changed in the past 150 years as far as I could tell.

## A 29-Year Miracle

The return to the USSR last summer was like visiting another country. In 1954, the Soviet Union was starting its recovery after surviving a war that took 20-million lives. Then, none of the country villages had electricity or running water, or any other of the amenities you and I call necessities. None of the cities had luxuries we consider necessities: cars, telephones, private bathrooms or personal privacy.

Twenty-nine years had worked miracles. Now, every country village we passed as we cruised down the Don and Volga rivers had electricity; most had television antennae on the roofs of prosperous-looking farm cottages. Mine was a journey of constant surprise.

I was not prepared to see so many smiling faces; so many healthy babies; so many smartly dressed women with painted toenails and high-heeled shoes; so much prosperity; so little poverty; so much new housing; so many indications of a deeply religious people. These sights were doubly confusing when I considered the skid-rows, the crime in the streets, gang wars back home, or the inability of my own government or private capital to rebuild our burned-out urban housing in Watts, Hough, South Bronx, and elsewhere, while finding ample funds with which to build glass skyscrapers for luxury hotels, executive offices for multi-national corporations and banks. The one bank I had occasion to visit in Moscow looked more like a Los Angeles welfare office than a bank. I was treated there with as much courtesy as a welfare client is treated in Los Angeles.

Farley W. Wheelwright, "I Was Taken In," *The Churchman*, January 1984. Reprinted by permission of *The Churchman*, 1074 23rd Ave. N., St. Petersburg, FL 33704.

Early on the tour I stopped playing the game of comparing "them" to "us." That is a no-win game. There is no question of being "better than." It is rather, "different from." We were warned by our Soviet hosts that they live under a different system of government, which affects everything we see and makes comparisons irrelevant. Although lifestyles may differ, human natures do not.

## US-Soviet Myths

In our country we live under a system whose great myth is that everyone has the opportunity to become President, or at least a millionaire if he or she is honest and works hard. The Soviets live under a system whose great myth is that they live in a classless society, one into which all persons are created equal. Way back when we had our revolution, we once had the same dream. Whatever the system of government, human hungers and material fantasies remain essentially the same.

> *"The major differences between the Soviet government and ours are philosophical rather than actual."*

We live in a society in which almost everyone wants an automobile, a computer, a color television and a stereo, a telephone, and two bathrooms in every home. The Soviets live in hopes of acquiring a piano, a color television and a stereo, and one private bathroom in every apartment. All of these wants make Uncle Ivan as much of a materialist as Uncle Sam. There are good reasons why the Soviets are not as car-crazy as we. Cars there are very expensive, and the high cost is a way of controlling both consumption and emission pollution. Public transportation everywhere we visited was fast, easily available, cheap, and clean. Few people make a case for the necessity of owning an automobile, as is the case with us, because our public transport is slow, generally unavailable, expensive, and dirty.

The pervading impression of the Soviet Union which I brought home with me was of a nation longing for peace. Perhaps this was because we were guests of the Soviet Peace Committee, but I do not think so. Everywhere we went there were signs and posters proclaiming *Mir Mira Mir*—Peace in the World, Peace. Except for the daily English press, we did not experience any anti-Americanism. Even the press was more anti-Reagan administration than it was anti-American.

## Philosophical Differences

The major differences between the Soviet government and ours are philosophical rather than actual. Theirs is a controlled economy, ours is *laissez-*

*faire*. Theirs is a so-called closed society, ours so-called open. However, these generalizations do not stand up to close scrutiny. All the labels to which we attach the Soviet lifestyles—repression, indifference to the needs of the people, communist lies, thought control, etc., etc.—simply do not fit in with the observations we were free to make on the scene. To be sure, the Soviet system is not perfect; it came as a surprise to hear the Russian resource people assigned to us freely admit as much. Here are a few things we learned about the Soviet Union which commend it to me, which really took me in:

Full employment. Everybody works, even though many people are under-employed and many people dislike the jobs they are doing. I thought of our 10-million unemployed, of our 20% black Americans, 56% black teenagers who are unemployable, and envied the Soviet record.

Economic control means that although few people are rich, everybody gets by. And the few people who do amass fortunes may be farmers, not the nabobs of industry. The average salary in the Soviet Union is 180 roubles a month (about $250.00). Since most women work and there is equal pay for equal work, the average family lives on $500.00 a month, which seems enough.

## A Controlled Economy

The dollar figure tells you nothing. One must count other benefits of a controlled economy. Rent is held to about $20.00 a month, utilities (including telephone) to about $5.00 more. Transportation costs are negligible (from three to five kopeks a ride—five to seven cents depending on whether you ride the trolleys or the Metro), and fares are collected on the honor system. The only cheats we saw were Virginia and myself when we boarded a bus with no change and didn't know how to ask for it!

Another major prerequisite to life in the Soviet Union is freedom from worry about health care or education. It comes with residency there. From cradle to grave, all medical care is free. From daycare centers to post-graduate education in the universities, all education is free.

Children are a precious commodity which is apparent in myriad ways, both statistically and to the casual observer of kids on the streets and in the parks. In heavily populated republics, the average family is two children; in sparsely populated republics, more (the Soviet Republic of Tajikistan has the highest birthrate in the USSR with an average family of five children).

Parenthood is the responsibility of the parents, of course, but parents receive special legal, moral, material support from the state. The size of the apartment depends upon the size of the family. Over half the Soviet workforce is women, and they are given four months' fully-paid maternity leave, as well as part-paid leave to nursing mothers until the child is a year old. Working mothers are entitled to shorter hours, a shorter work-week and, when it can be arranged, work at home.,

## Healthy Children

Pre-school centers are vital to the well-being of children, as are the marvelous playgrounds which were integrated into every housing project we visited. Children were uniformly healthy and well-fed, well-dressed, and happy looking. These observations are in sharp contrast to the 1954 children I saw who lived in circumstances of inadequate food, clothing, and shelter. As a matter of fact, everybody in the Soviet Union is manifestly better fed, clothed, and sheltered than they were in 1954. I wonder if we can say the same thing about our country?

An outstanding impression to every visitor to the Soviet Union has to be its housing. Still in short supply, still looking jerry-built, the massive public housing in this country is just a wonder of the world. The Great Patriotic War, which is what the Soviets call World War II, left the Soviet Union devastated, with millions of people homeless. Housing was a No. 1 priority, and one more talisman of a government responding to the needs of the people.

The city of Kiev lost 60% of its housing in the German bombardment; Volgograd (then Stalingrad) was totally levelled. Leningrad fared better with a 30% building loss, but worse with 800,000 dead in a city of one and a half million people. The Soviet government, in the last forty years, has done a gargantuan job building houses. In Leningrad alone there are 50,000 new apartments being built each month, and still there is a housing shortage and still the people grumble it is not being completed fast enough.

## Lack of Consumer Goods

Department stores were crowded with people with money to spend but very few consumer goods to purchase. One result of the arms race and the apartment-building boom is a sad lack of consumer goods.

The people are hungry for consumer goods, for the U.S. lifestyles they see on their television and in cinemas. That the government is trying to respond to the wants of the people is evident. In some shops, cheap souvenir-type products are beginning to appear, imported from India. Even in the dollar shop (Beryoshka) I bought a couple of Russian babushkas, and when I got home I was disappointed to read on the label, "Made in Japan." Young Soviet boys will almost sell their souls for T-shirts and blue jeans, young girls their virtue for hair dye and facial makeup. "We adore everything American," a young man told me, "except for your nuclear bombs."

The Soviet press and TV covered us and we became known from coast to coast. Everywhere we went, people recognized our conspicuous Peace buttons, and loved us for our mission to their country. The United States press was invited to attend but failed to show up. The U.S. Embassy in Moscow acknowledged the happening by branding it with two words: "A fake." Of the big peace rally in Moscow there was not a word in our mass media. Thousands of Soviet citizens marched with us.

## "Proud" Atheism

All of the Soviet resource people who led our workshops as we sailed down the Don and Volga rivers were unrepentant atheists. They wore their atheism unobtrusively but proudly. Religion was not much discussed, yet I found the ambience throughout our trip profoundly religious (etymologically, a binding together, which is what this word was intended to mean in its root or radical form).

People looking for normative Judaism or Christianity found it. While practice of the Russian Orthodox religion is discouraged, it is far from forbidden. The Soviet government has gone to great lengths to preserve and renew the historic grandeur and gold leaf of the great cathedrals. I shall speak at another time specifically to the Jewish situation, about which more heat than light is shed by anti-Soviet U.S. propaganda. Suffice it to say here that Jewish members of our tour attended synagogue services there.

---

*"Everybody in the Soviet Union is manifestly better fed, clothed, and sheltered than they were in 1954."*

---

In Moscow, a city of over eight million people, there are only 17 Russian Orthodox churches open to the public. The great Kazan Cathedral in Leningrad is now the Museum of Religion and Atheism and in *Fodor's Guide Book* is not recommended for sensitive Christians who would be offended to see displayed atrocities committed in the name of Jesus Christ. Virginia and I attended matins in Moscow. The music, provided by a pick-up choir, was magnificent. The church was sparsely attended by men and women of all ages. The grounds were not well kept and the cemetery was a disgrace, in marked contrast to the secular graves of Soviet heroes killed in the war.

## Deeply Religious

Protestants in our group attended the Baptist Church in Moscow, the same church at which Billy Graham a year ago extolled religious freedom in the Soviet Union. There are about five thousand Baptist churches spread throughout the country and about five thousand members in the Moscow church. There are three services each Sunday which, I was told, are full at every service. Many young people are in attendance. In the Soviet Union people are as free as they are here not to attend church at all. You can't take the religious pulse of a country by counting the number of people who go to church or temple. How do I know these are a deeply religious people? Let me count the ways:

---

*"An outstanding impression to every visitor to the Soviet Union has to be its housing."*

---

Their love and respect for nature and protecting the environment; over 60% of the city of Kiev is in parks and gardens for the people. In every apartment complex there is breathing space as well as play space for children, chess tables set out for oldsters. One looks in vain for broken beer bottles, trashing, graffiti.

Their respect for each other; public places, public transportation are spotlessly clean. In queues people patiently wait their turn. No one seems to jostle another for position in line, even for goods in short supply.

## Concern for Children

Their care and concern for children as previously noted.

Their care and concern for their dead; cemeteries are holy places, especially cemeteries for war heroes. Here brides and grooms come after their marriage ceremony and picture-taking. They come in remembrance of the dead and they lay their wedding flowers on graves before taking off for their wedding reception in some rented hall (their wedding rites looked every bit as romantic and middle-class as those over which I preside here at home).

Their intellectual curiosity; people read as they ride the subways. Everywhere there are kiosks and libraries (3,000 in Kiev alone). The books they buy and/or read are classics, art books, good novels. Many of them are by American authors. Favorites include Jack London, Mark Twain, F. Scott Fitzgerald. Adult bookstores in the Soviet Union are just what they claim to be!

The absence of violence in the cities; we felt perfectly safe to walk everywhere alone at night, on streets, in the parks. Pornography and violence to women are outlawed.

## Longing for Peace

The people seem to make a religion of peace. As I said, the signs are everywhere—*Mir Mira Mir.* There is nothing phoney about this religious longing for peace. Although no Sovietsky would use these words, they come tumbling down the ages and reflect what I

felt to be the mood of the people in the streets of the Soviet Republic of Russia: "Blessed are the peacemakers, for they shall be called children of God."

What we saw, what we experienced in the Soviet Union was so far from what we read in the U.S. media or what our President has to say about the Soviet Union, one is tempted to doubt one's own observations and findings. The questions then are raised: Who benefits from telling lies about the Soviet Union? If our system of government and our way of life are so superior to theirs, why must we jeopardize them by spending 44% of our national budgeted income on a military complex to protect them? Why in these United States do we not have sufficient resources to look after our own people?

Working hand in hand rather than hand on bombs, the USA and the USSR could build such a beautiful world. We need each other for friends, not for enemies. As friends we can learn so much from each other, help each other. That one day we may become friends is my prayer and hope for the future. May it come to pass. *Mir Mira Mir*—Peace in the world, Peace!

*Farley W. Wheelwright is a minister in the Unitarian-Universalist Society in Sepulveda, California.*

# The Soviets Manipulate US Media

Roy Godson

Although we sometimes take for granted our vigorous and free press, we tend to react strongly against attempts to manipulate free expression, either by legal means, or by overt or covert pressure from governments or groups which espouse particular ideas. We generally assume that left to its own devices, and given freedom and time, the press will deliver to us truthful, objective information and analysis that contributes to rational policymaking. Recently, however, we have begun to learn about a relatively new threat to objective media reporting: that we may be reading, seeing and hearing a version of events which not only is inaccurate and downright false, but one which has been manufactured to distort our perception of reality and to influence us. This afternoon I would like to discuss this issue.

## Creative Propaganda

Let me begin with a major and telling example. In the Spring of 1982, the world press and particularly the American press was flooded with stories about the former Soviet KGB Chairman, Yuri Andropov, who some months later succeeded Leonid Brezhnev as the major Soviet leader. When Andropov headed the KGB from 1967 until the early 1980's, his image in the Western press was that of a hardline secret police boss, who used the largest and perhaps the most effective secret police and intelligence service in the history of the world to ensure the Communist Party's continued control of the Soviet people. Indeed, under his regime, the KGB, in a fit of creativity that surely rivals that of Heinrich Himmler and Joseph Mengele, developed the use of psychiatric hospitals to control Soviet dissidents.

But in the Spring of 1983, Andropov's public image in the West began to suddenly and radically change.

Roy Godson, "Soviet Manipulations of the Media" from a speech delivered to the Commonwealth Club of California in San Francisco on March 15, 1985.

Let me recall for you just a few of the stories and descriptions of Andropov that appeared in many newspapers.

## Andropov Makeover

One major East Coast daily headlined a story from Moscow with: "ANDROPOV SEEN AS CLOSET LIBERAL." That paper had previously reported Andropov to be an unimpressive "five feet eight inches," but now elevated him to "tall," and added urbane, well-educated, and enlightened. Another major East Coast paper noted that Andropov "stood conspicuously taller than most" Soviet leaders, and that "his spectacles, intense gaze and donnish demeanor gave him the air of a scholar." He was credited with knowledge of foreign languages— English, German and even Hungarian. He was described as a "witty conversationalist," a "bibliophile," a lover of jazz, romantic novels and connoisseur of modern art. There were even hints that he might be partly Jewish. In short, as the liberal magazine, *The New Republic* put it, "a short, burly thug almost overnight became a tall, dapper Chubby Checker fan."

Let me cite a few more examples of stories which I believe have a less obvious but nonetheless common thread:

—CIA SEEN INVOLVED IN GANDHI ASSASSINATION
—REAGAN PRESIDENCY LEADS TO STRAINED RELATIONS WITH MOSCOW
—U.S. IMPLICATED IN PLOT TO TIE SOVIETS TO POPE ASSASSINATION
—KOREAN AIRLINER ALLEGED TO BE U.S. SPYPLANE

How and why did these and other similar stories— of very dubious authenticity—appear on almost every continent? Why did the electronic and print media from Washington to Wellington give international currency to them? All are sensational and have damaging implications far beyond their apparent subject matter.

Of course, it is entirely possible that the media, on its own, in various parts of the world and at about the same time, came to similar conclusions on the basis of highly contentious "evidence." It is also true that many journalists are not sympathetic to the United States or to its current Administration, and that it is by no means unusual for stories about the U.S. to be negative in tone and content.

---

*"There is a massive and ongoing effort to affect political behavior in the West through the world media—and the Soviet Union and its allies are largely responsible."*

---

There is however, another possible explanation—namely that the headlines and the stories just cited—and many like them—are the result of a conscious effort to manipulate the media. Proponents of this view differ on how extensive this manipulation is and how successful it has been, but they believe there is a massive and ongoing effort to affect political behavior in the West through the world media—and that the Soviet Union and its allies are largely responsible.

I have been studying this subject together with a colleague on the faculty at the Fletcher School for several years, and we recently published a book—*Dezinformatsia*—about it, convinced that the weight of evidence supports the view that manipulation can and does take place.

*I want to be very clear about what I am saying, however. I do not believe, as some do, that most of the world's media are controlled or manipulated systematically and that every or almost every negative story about the United States is the result of Soviet manipulation. Nor do I mean to imply that ALL attempts to make use of the media succeed.* What I would like to propose and submit evidence to support is the proposition that there is a massive attempt by the Soviet Union to influence and use the media as well as other important Western governmental and private sector opinion leaders; that sometimes these attempts are successful; that the campaign is ongoing; and that by being aware of it, by speaking the truth about it, a free society can in large part neutralize its effects.

How can such conclusions be substantiated?

## Manipulation of the Media

First, we have learned a great deal from information provided by Soviet bloc officials who now live in the West. This information has been cross-checked by scholars and Western government officials. These defectors tell us that the manipulation of the media is part of what in Moscow is referred to as "active measures" (aktivnyye meropriatia). These are attempts to actively influence Westerners to act in ways designed to further Soviet interests.

A variety of tactics are subsumed under the term "active measures." Among the most important are the use of the media to influence, mislead, or deceive the target so that he acts in a way favorable to Moscow. This is done through overt propaganda and manipulation, as well on covert means including the use of secret agents of influence and forgeries—or a combination of the two—KOMBINATSIA—as the Russians sometimes call it. This also involves the use of information which is basically true, as well as intentionally false information, or disinformation.

Based on the eyewitness accounts of those who received their orders to engage in these activities from top Soviet leaders, we can be fairly sure that Moscow believes that the use of "active measures" and particularly media manipulation and disinformation is an important means of shifting what they call the "correlation of forces" further in their direction.

The institutions or organizations in Moscow and throughout the world that engage in these activities are directed from the very top echelons of Soviet government. They involve a vast array of techniques, fuelled by an unprecedented level of financial and human resources.

## The US Peace Council

The most important Soviet institutions that control and carry out these activities are the International Department of the Central Committee of Communist Party of the Soviet Union—the CPSU. The International Department is perhaps one of the most important and least studied parts of the Soviet government. It controls, to a significant degree, more than ninety Communist parties around the world and 13 major international fronts, the most important of which—the World Peace Council—has affiliates in every major western country including the U.S. Peace Council. The International Department also works to influence Western scholars, young political leaders, trade unions, women's groups, and lawyers around the world.

The second organ of the CPSU is the International Information Department. Created in the late 1960's this institution coordinates the Soviet media in Moscow and the Soviet media and press throughout the world. It passes on the information in the 3,000 plus hours of Soviet radio broadcasts to the world in eighty languages each week. It coordinates the themes of the hundreds of Soviet "journalists" stationed throughout the world. It would be as if the Republican Party controlled and coordinated the entire media in the U.S., and every U.S. journalist overseas.

A third institution in the Soviet active measures

apparatus is the press section of the Ministry of Foreign Affairs. It accredits Western correspondents in Moscow, and has a great deal of day-to-day control over their access to and contacts with Soviet officials and citizens. Through Soviet embassies and consolates abroad, it also seeks to influence journalists in non-communist countries.

## KGB Directorates

Two other institutions that play an important role in Soviet manipulation are the KGB's First Directorate and a section of the KGB's Second Chief Directorate. The First Chief Directorate works almost exclusively to spy on and to influence the non-communist world. It has a special staff in Moscow, now known as Service A, whose function is to assist in secretly influencing the media and other important sectors of our society.

Abroad, the First Chief Directorate of the KGB and other Soviet bloc intelligences have headquarters in every country, usually based in embassies, missions, and consulates. In addition to engaging in espionage and buying—or stealing—technology, they also carry out "active measures." In Western Europe, for example, at any one time there are approximately 14,000 legal Soviet bloc officials, 30-40 percent of whom work for the KGB and its sister services. Of these ½ or approximately 3,000 work in what Moscow calls Line PR—that is political espionage and influence operations. In the United States there are about 2,200 legal Soviet bloc officials, so using the 30-40 percent figure, this means about 700 are intelligence officers, and 300 of them in Line PR, engaged in political spying and influence operations.

In addition to thousands of "legal" spies and active measures specialists, Moscow also has an unknown number of illegal or deep cover agents embedded in Western society. In recent years for example I was startled to learn that a student at my own university was a second generation illegal. That is, his parents had been sent by the KGB to be illegal agents first in West Germany and Canada. Then his parents went to live and work as photographers in the suburbs of New York in the 1970's and they sent their son to Georgetown University. In addition to his regular studies, the son was being trained in the summers to be a deep cover illegal and it was expected that after graduation he would seek a position in the U.S. government. While he was at Georgetown, Moscow also asked him to identify fellow students who were planning to join the CIA, as well as keep an eye on Chinese students studying on the campus.

## Counterintelligence

Another section of the KGB in Moscow, the Second Chief Directorate, is concerned with counter-intelligence, but has a special section to study, assess, and manipulate the Western press stationed in Moscow. I have talked with a former Soviet official who worked in this section and he has described in detail how he went about his work.

In terms of manpower, it is estimated that these institutions employ somewhere between ten and fifteen thousand people in Moscow and another ten to fifteen thousand throughout the world. Their annual budget the U.S. government now believes is in the range of 3-4 billion dollars.

## Controlling the Media

To influence and manipulate the western media, the Soviet apparatus uses a combination of overt and covert instrumentalities, and old tried and true methods together with new public relations techniques. For example, in Moscow, because they completely control access to all important government officials and all Soviet media, they are in a position to assist a journalist to become a star reporter—first with the news. Take the case of the liberalization of Yuri Andropov. How did this come about? Let me cite the seminal story in the East Coast newspaper in 1983. "While largely unknown in the West, East Europeans who have met with Andropov"—because the Western journalist could not—"have described him as an affable and efficient man who has managed to place considerable restraints on the KGB." Note that this report about Andropov is the story about the same man who crushed the Hungarian Revolution in 1956, who innovated the use of psychiatric hospitals and drugs, and who was responsible for the KGB at the time there were attempts on the life of the Pope and probably Lech Walesa. Clearly, someone in Moscow was planting rumors.

*"Moscow believes that the use of 'active measures' and particularly media manipulation and disinformation is an important means of shifting. . .forces further in their direction."*

Some columnists and reporters are conscious of this Soviet technique. For example, Joseph Kraft recently pointed to various published stories about current Soviet leaders as emanating from a journalist "long in Moscow, who is thought to have KGB ties. A second was a planted rumor which blazed through the diplomatic community and was then traced back to a KGB source." Other journalists, particularly those under pressure from their editors for dramatic news from Moscow, may be less careful and more susceptible to influence and rumors. This is a tried and true Soviet gambit, and I have discussed the technique involved with specialists who used it.

Other documented methods of Soviet influence

include actually recruiting and controlling a journalist, a government press spokesman, a news service, or even a newspaper as well as circulating and recycling forgeries. One example which shocked France in recent years was the conviction of journalist Charles Pathe in the late 1970's, who had been working for the KGB for nearly twenty years. Pathe was a well-connected journalist who wrote under his own and other names. He also published a newsletter, which the Soviets helped finance, received by a small but influential readership. The newsletter consistently attacked the U.S. and sought to detach France from the NATO Alliance. Now in other European countries, the public is learning that a recent press spokesman at the Norwegian Ministry of Foreign Affairs has been working for the KGB for many years, and that a major Greek daily newspaper was influenced by, if not completely financed by the KGB, and is consistently anti-U.S.

---

*"Another favorite covert Soviet bloc tactic is the production and dissemination of forgeries."*

---

Another favorite covert Soviet bloc tactic is the production and dissemination of forgeries. This long time favorite apparently was halted in the 1970's during the Watergate investigations, but in the late 1970's the pace of Soviet bloc forgeries picked up and now hardly a month goes by without the U.S. government finding forgeries designed to influence the media. Sometimes these forgeries are crude, quickly spotted and do little damage, such as the fake Ku Klux Klan letters last summer designed to intimidate African and Asian athletes. Sometimes however they damage the reputation of the U.S. and are recycled in the press year after year in spite of being identified as forgeries.

## Western-style Press Conferences

In addition to these covert and traditional methods of media manipulation, Moscow also sometimes is more open and innovative. One new technique is the Western-style press conference. One of the more sensational examples was the appearance of the then head of the Soviet General Staff before the world press after the Soviets again shot down an unarmed civilian airliner, this time in September, 1983. The news conference was unprecedented. The General's speech and charts received extensive coverage and confused many as the Soviets sought to exculpate themselves from intentionally shooting down the Korean civilian airliner, whose many passengers included a U.S. Congressman. During the course of the press conference and in the ensuing propaganda barrage, the Soviets sought to sow doubt about the

benign nature of the flight, and tried to suggest that the United States was somehow implicated in the massacre of innocent travelers.

Another recent technique is the veritable parade of Soviet "journalists" and "scholars" who now appear as invited guests regularly on Sunday morning and late night TV talk shows, live coast-to-coast radio programs—as well as instant commentators on special occasions such as the inauguration of President Reagan. All of them speak very good English, appear very much at home on the U.S. media, and are excellent propagandists. All of these gentlemen, however, are part of the Soviet active measures apparatus. Their appearances and the themes they espouse are coordinated by the International Department and IID of the Central Committee. They are completely paid Soviet government propagandists, even though their U.S. radio and TV talk show hosts usually describe them to the U.S. audience as "journalists" and "scholars." I am not suggesting here that they should be denied free time on the U.S. media. What I am saying, however, is that we should recognize them for what they are—part of a massive and increasingly sophisticated effort to use the media to influence us.

Now what does Moscow hope to achieve with all this effort and money? It is not always easy to understand Soviet motivation, but based on careful reading and analysis of Soviet overt and covert propaganda and disinformation, as well as numerous interviews with former Soviet specialists who sought to manipulate the Western press, Moscow appears to have both long-term objectives which they pursue year in and year out, as well as short-term objectives geared to specific events and opportunities.

## Discrediting the US

Over the past several decades, and there is no indication that this is about to change, whether we are in a period of detente or a period of more strained relations, Moscow seeks first and foremost to weaken and discredit the U.S. We are, they teach their KGB and other active measures personnel, the "main enemy," (glavnyy vrag) and one of their main tasks is to diminish U.S. military, economic, and political power throughout the world. Second, they seek to split the various strategic alliances we have built up, particularly the NATO Alliance. They want to separate—to decouple—the U.S. from Britain, France and Germany, and to separate the major European allies from each other, as well as to weaken our alliance with Japan, Australia and New Zealand. Should they succeed, they would be in a position to dominate each continent.

Third, Soviet leaders seek to enhance the reputation of politicians and parties that help achieve these objectives, and denigrate if not destroy those politicians, parties, and movements that don't. Their attempt to enhance Andropov's reputation and denigrate Reagan's in recent years, was preceded in the 1960's and 1970's with active measures campaigns against politicians such as the conservative Franz Joseph Strauss in Germany, and supportive of center right candidate Giscard d'Estaing against Socialist Mitterand in France. In other words, they don't only support left-of-center politicians. They support those whom they believe are useful. In their view, Giscard was more useful and Strauss and Mitterand less valuable in splitting and weakening the NATO Alliance.

Finally, they seek to affect Western attitudes and behavior on important issues, particularly military preparedness. They engaged in a massive, and they believed, successful campaign to stop NATO deployment of the so-called neutron bomb in the late 1970's. They are still in the midst of seeking to influence the peace movement to prevent the modernization of U.S. and NATO forces.

## Short-Term Objectives

In addition to pursuing these long-term objectives, Moscow also pursues short-term gains. In the coming months, for example, they will seek to influence the media so that (1) the new Indian Prime Minister, scheduled to visit the U.S. in June, 1985, does not develop closer relations with the U.S., (2) ensure attention is drawn away from the evidence that more and more links Moscow and the Bulgarians' intelligence service to the shooting of the Pope; and (3) ensure that the 40th Anniversary of the ending of World War II is perceived as a result of Soviet efforts and that the cause of the war and the use of the atomic bomb can be laid at the feet of Western politicians.

Not all these campaigns—and others they will mount—will be successful by any means. Moscow doesn't expect them to be. They are, however, an important means, in addition to diplomacy and military power, that the Politburo uses to exert its influence.

*"Let us simply make ourselves as aware as possible of how and through what means Moscow is seeking to manipulate the media and to disinform us."*

What can and should be done about this attempt to manipulate the press and distort our understanding of reality? There are no simple solutions. We are and wish to remain a free, pluralistic society which allows freedom of expression. Hence, we will remain vulnerable to manipulation, in ways which closed totalitarian systems—where the media is totally controlled—are not.

At the same time there are a number of measures, each with advantages and disadvantages, that can be taken to limit the deleterious effects of Soviet manipulation.

The most appealing option we have is truth. Let us simply make ourselves as aware as possible of how and through what means Moscow is seeking to manipulate the media and to disinform us. To a large extent this already is happening. Seven or eight years ago those in government, the press and the academic community who stated that there was cause to study Soviet active measures techniques and disseminate information about them were ridiculed or called McCarthyites and right-wing fanatics.

But beginning in the last year of the Carter Administration and now continuing in the Reagan Administration, the U.S. government is making available information on Soviet attempts at manipulation. This should be continued and expanded. I am glad to see that other Western governments such as the West Germans are beginning to do the same.

On the non-governmental side, academics, novelists and journalists, more and more are taking the subject seriously and alerting the public and their colleagues. Much more needs to be done.

*Roy Godson is professor of government at Georgetown University.*

# The Soviets Do Not Manipulate US Media

Chip Berlet

For years a furtive group of leftovers from the McCarthy period have been publishing newsletters and newspapers, holding meetings, sponsoring debates on whether or not Teddy Kennedy is a Soviet agent, and generally networking a disgruntled audience of cold warriors who long for the day when Negroes still knew how to serve a drink with the appropriate deference—that is, before the Communists coaxed Dr. Martin Luther King into stirring up trouble.

I once infiltrated a John Birch Society meeting in 1971 where we all sat around with tea and cookies watching a slide show on how the Council on Foreign Relations was a gigantic communist conspiracy to facilitate Soviet control of America. It was held at a modest home in southwestern Colorado with about one dozen friendly geriatrics whose watery eyes lit up when the talk turned to plots and conspiracies.

The basic line of reasoning was simple: if the major media were not a part of the worldwide communist conspiracy to destroy the American Way of Life, then the real truth about the commies and their troublemaking at home and overseas would be revealed to all God-Fearing citizens. If these citizens could then be motivated to take action, it would be possible to restore America to its greatness. In the dark corners of the room a few would politely probe you for your views on how much could be blamed on militant Blacks and Jews.

## Paranoid Vision

They seemed harmless enough at the time, especially since the natural order of things would eventually carry their paranoid vision of reality into the relative safety of the grave.

Somewhere, somehow, something went wrong. Terribly wrong.

Charges that the media is part of the Soviet plan for world conquest have escaped the confines of conservative living rooms and are now ringing in the halls of Congress. Adherents of this point of view are members of Congress now, and some of them control a Senate Committee which is holding hearings into Soviet manipulation of the corporate media, progressive media and social change groups. Even the President and his advisors are echoing the charges in muted form.

A plethora of publications on the Right are calling for investigations into how alternative media groups are part of KGB disinformation campaign. Among the media and publishing groups named so far as logical targets are: The Institute for Policy Studies, *Mother Jones* magazine, the North American Congress on Latin America (NACLA), Pacific News Service, Pacifica Radio, *Covert Action Information Bulletin, Counterspy* magazine, and journalists who "may engage in subversive activities without being fully aware of the extent, purposes or control of their activities," according to a report by the right-wing Heritage Foundation.

## Smear Campaign

The corporate media have already capitulated to the new political reality and are reporting these ravings as if they held even a scintilla of sanity. *The New York Times* Magazine printed an attack on the Institute for Policy Studies that was full of innaccuracies, misquotes and historical revisionism. Lengthy interviews with several key figures in the campaign to smear progressives have appeared in numerous publications. The novel by Arnaud de Borchgrave and Robert Moss, *The Spike,* which supposedly elaborates how the Soviet KGB disinformation network is controlled and functions in the U.S., has hit the bestseller charts and is now in paperback. It is as if we have collectively been transported by Time Lord Dr. Who to the 1950s

Chip Berlet, "The Big Liars Are Back in Town," *Alternative Media,* Fall 1981. Reprinted by permission of the author.

when McCarthyism and its witch hunts swept America. The alternative media could be in big trouble quite soon if this trend continues.

There is another way to tell this story. It involves a careful analysis of changing political and economic conditions, and shows how in periods of economic crisis and political uncertainty there is a tendency toward simplistic solutions. These solutions appeal to a nervous citizenry who prefer the solidity of a clear crisp answer—even if it is the wrong answer—rather than facing the complex and troubling questions which have no easy answers. Such is the approach of the academics. It leads to a certain detachment; a use of the passive voice. The American Civil Liberties Union took this approach at first, warning that an overreaction to the Senate Subcommittee on Security and Terrorism and other gears in the Reagan repression machine would be inappropriate, even counterproductive.

That was before one of Reagan's top advisors called the ACLU a criminals' lobby. Suddenly the ACLU felt it was necessary to call attention to the authoritarian and repressive trend that is threatening our civil liberties. Well, tardy awareness is better than no awareness at all. So this article is a warning not couched in the genteel tones of the careful academic nor the objective journalist, this is a warning trumpeted in no uncertain terms.

## Anesthetized to Threats

The jackals are at the door.

Actually, the jackals are behind several doors:

The newly-established Senate Subcommittee on Security and Terrorism has already held several sets of hearings including one where author de Borchgrave announced that many reporters have been "anesthetized" to Soviet threats by Soviet "disinformation specialists."

---

*"Charges that the media is part of the Soviet plan for world conquest have escaped the confines of conservative living rooms and are now ringing in the halls of Congress."*

---

There is a major drive to re-establish the House Un-American Activities Committee by several right-wing groups, including the network of individuals around John Birch Society stalwart Congressman Larry McDonald. McDonald's crowd has repeatedly identified various alternative publications as subversive and part of the communist conspiracy.

The Justice Department has already moved to restrict information released by the FBI under the Freedom of Information Act, and legislation has been introduced that would severely curtail the ability of journalists to use the FOIA to obtain information from federal agencies. The CIA has requested a complete exemption from disclosure requirements under the FOIA, and the FBI is expected to put forward a similar request. . . .

## CIA Searches

CIA Director Colby has asked Congress to authorize his agents to launch surprise searches of newspaper offices to seize the notes and papers of reporters being investigated for unauthorized disclosure of information identifying covert agents. This in anticipation of the passage of some form of the Agents Identities legislation.

Exciting and challenging times are ahead. The rallying cry is National Security. The wagons are being circled. The alternative press is outside the circle, folks. Just how far outside the circle is made clear by reading what right-wing publications have to say about "disinformation" especially as outlined in *The Spike.* The ultra-right American Security Council newsletter headlined an interview with *Spike* co-author de Borchgrave "Soviet Disinformation Program," and a note informs the reader:

> The best-selling novel *The Spike* describes how the Soviet intelligence agency, KGB, conducts the disinformation program and how it places distortions and lies in the American press and the federal government in such a way as to mislead the American people and influence U.S. foreign, military, and economic policy in a way favorable to the communist cause. *The Spike* also explains the links between the disinformation program and other forms of communist subversion and terrorism worldwide.

## Alleged KGB Tactics

According to de Borchgrave, the Soviet KGB, "encouraged by the general attack on authority in Western countries" developed a plan to accomplish the "strategic defeat" of the U.S. using seven tactics:
– "Increased recruitment of agents of influence in Western countries;
– character assassination campaigns to discredit Western leaders;
– sponsored strikes and demonstrations;
– the spreading of false information to drive a wedge between the U.S. and Europe and between the industrial West and the Third World;
– the infiltration and manipulation of new left groups;
– covert support for terrorism;
– the manipulation of the Western media."

It is this conspiratorial theory that is being given credence by the Senate Subcommittee on Security and Terrorism which wants to investigate journalists who allegedly may not even be aware of their manipulation by the KGB. It's for our own good, mind you. After all, wouldn't we want to know that the KGB secretly supplied us with information for our articles on Reagan's economic policies, or the arms race?

Let's focus on the arms race; the Senate Committee already has. When de Borchgrave was asked to name one component of the KBG apparatus in America he singled out the Mobilization for Survival, a group dedicated to ending the nuclear arms race. According to de Borchgrave (and follow this logic carefully), the Mobilization for Survival is a coalition of many groups including the Communist Party USA, and the U.S. Peace Council which has members who are known communists and are thus doing the bidding of the Soviet Union. Therefore the entire Mobilization for Survival is a component of the KGB disinformation apparatus. Follow that? Wait, it gets better. According to some of the adherents of the Soviet disinformation theory, since the Soviets support terrorism worldwide, then components of the KGB disinformation apparatus are part of the terrorist infrastructure. Now, if an alternative newspaper publishes an interview with a member of the Mobilization for Survival it becomes an unwitting dupe of the KGB disinformation campaign and an accomplice to worldwide terrorism. Pretty neat, huh?

## Far-Fetched Ideas

Find all this far-fetched? Try this one: according to *Spike* co-Author Robert Moss, America lost the Vietnam war because of a KGB disinformation campaign that succeeded in eroding public support for the war through the press. Moss warns archly, "If the news media can be manipulated to bring about America's defeat in a war to which it had dedicated over 50,000 lives and billions of dollars to win, then they can surely be manipulated in other important areas too."

These peculiar statements came in a letter urging membership in the right-wing media criticism group Accuracy in Media. Potential members were being offered a free copy of *The Spike* for joining AIM. This promotion was sent to the 13,000 members of the Christian Anti-Communism Crusade, the leader of which has identified abortion, busing for racial integration, sex education, and homosexual rights as part of the communist agenda to weaken the moral fiber of America. The cover letter from the Christian Anti-Communism Campaign tells us that "The communists regard information as an important weapon" and that Accuracy in Media "often shows how Soviet disinformation is accepted and published by major news outlets within the U.S.A."

OK, now we have alternative newspapers that carry articles on reproductive rights, sex education, busing, and homosexuals as part of the Soviet KGB disinformation terror network. Maybe the Senate Committee will give us the benefit of the doubt when they haul us before the panel and allow us to beg forgiveness because until we read the *Spike* we didn't know any better.

The glue that binds together the disparate elements

of the right-wing network promoting the "disinformation" theory is the steadfast belief that anyone working for progressive social change in America is a communist, a willing accomplice of communists, or an unwitting dupe of communists. Since that level of hysterical anti-communism became somewhat unacceptable following the wretched excesses of the McCarthy period, the ultra-rightists developed a protective response—secrecy and a new vocabulary.

*"The glue that binds together the disparate elements of the right-wing network promoting the 'disinformation' theory is the steadfast belief that anyone working for progressive social change in America is a communist."*

Secrecy in the sense that their honest assessments regarding the KGB disinformation terror network are not aired in public hearings or newspaper interviews, but are reserved for circulation in their newsletters and promotional mailings. The new vocabulary consists primarily of substituting the word terrorist for communist whenever possible; and note that it is the Senate Subcommittee of Security and *Terrorism*, despite the FBI reports on the decline of terrorism in the U.S.

In the '50s headlines such as "Communist Network Menaces Atomic Energy Facilities" were popular. Now it's "Terrorist Network Menaces Atomic Energy Facilities." Of course, real terrorist violence is despicable, and no sane person wants a real terrorist to have The Bomb, so the ultra-right is preying on the fear of terrorism to convince Americans that investigations into Soviet-backed terrorist infiltration of U.S. social change organizations are valid. Who knows what terrorist lurks behind the cover of a group protesting U.S. nuclear policies or Reagan's actions in El Salvador?

## Terrorist Hype

The implication, however, is that anti-nuclear organizing or protesting U.S. intervention in El Salvador is a cover for terrorism—just as in the '50s and '60s Ban the Bomb and civil rights organizing were victimized by charges that marching orders came from Moscow.

The bottom line here is that no matter what the stated goals of Congressional investigative committees such as HUAC or the new SST, the actual goal is to preserve and protect the status quo. The hearings are used to smear social change organizers with outlandish charges designed to neutralize their organizational effectiveness.

Part of the program is designed to intimidate journalists away from providing coverage of social change activities. Since this is a major component of alternative publications, this is a threat we cannot ignore. Alternative publications must not allow the ravings about the Soviet/KGB/Terrorist disinformation network and the threat of being called before a Congressional Committee to have an effect on coverage of social change issues.

More important is the need to educate readers about the threats to civil liberties posed by the Congressional committees, attempts to use National Security scare tactics to unleash the FBI and CIA, and the general repressive agenda of the right-wing network. Right now these forces, though vocal, are a relative minority in Congress and across the nation. Authoritarian movements grow like weeds in the fertile soil of economic crisis, however, and actions must be undertaken now to prevent these maniacs from implementing their paranoid agenda.

We must not allow another era of witch hunting. If we do not act now, the alternative press is likely to be among the early victims.

*This viewpoint originally appeared in* Alternative Media.

*"The principal result [of trade with the Soviet Union] has been that the Soviet Union is now a mortal threat to the security of the United States and to freedom everywhere."*

# US/USSR Trade Endangers the US

Roger Donway

One wintry day a Woodman was tramping back home from his work when he saw something black lying on the snow. When he came closer he saw it was a serpent, to all appearances dead. But he took it up and put it in his bosom to warm while he hurried home. As soon as he got indoors he put the serpent down on the hearth before the fire. The children watched it and saw it slowly come to life again. Then one of them stooped down to stroke it, but the serpent raised its head and put out its fangs and was about to sting the child to death. So the woodman seized his axe, and with one stroke cut the serpent in two. "Ah," said he, "no gratitude from the wicked."

—Aesop's Fables

Each of Aesop's fables ends with the appropriate moral learned, by one character or another. But in real life, it seems, we are not such apt pupils. Again and again the West has nurtured the Soviet serpent with trade, only to be stung in return, again and again. What is it that keeps us from learning the simple lesson: do not aid your enemies?

Principally, I think, we are blinded by three illusions about the Soviet Union. The first illusion is simply that the Soviets do not critically need our trade. For obvious reasons, this is the illusion preferred by the Soviets themselves, and they have developed a number of techniques to foster it. One of the more effective techniques works likes this:

## The CoCom Charade

America and its allies try to agree on which high-tech goods to keep from the Soviets, and they do this through an informal organization known as the Coordinating Committee for Multilateral Export Controls—CoCom, for short. In past years, the Soviets typically responded to a CoCom embargo by producing a catalogue from an upcoming trade show. In the catalogue would be a picture of a Soviet-made

"Soviet Trade: The Bosom Serpent," by Roger Donway, *On Principle*, February 18, 1985. Reprinted from ON PRINCIPLE, a pro-capitalist newsletter published bi-weekly by Amwell Publishing, Inc., Princeton Professional Park, 601 Ewing Street, Suite B-7, Princeton, NJ 08542. Subscriptions are $45.

version of the good that CoCom had just restricted. "Why won't you sell this to us," the Soviets would then ask plaintively. "You see that we can make it for ourselves."

This worked fairly well until August, 1983, when police arrested Eugene Michiels for selling information to the Soviet Union. Since 1971, Michiels had been head of the European Coordinating Service of the Belgian Foreign Ministry, and had complete access to CoCom discussions. From Michiel's information, the Soviet Union was hastily printing up catalogues that featured non-existent goods—Soviet goods indeed, in a deeper sense than the Soviets intended.

## No Such Thing as Soviet Technology

Our knowledge of Soviet dependence on Western trade now goes beyond the anecdotal. The subject has become a scholarly field unto itself, and the leading scholar is writer Anthony Sutton, formerly a research fellow at the Hoover Institution of Stanford University. Sutton has written a three-volume work called *Western Technology and Soviet Economic Development*, and also a more popular one-volume summary, aptly titled *National Suicide*. His conclusion in these works is nothing less than astounding: "There is no such thing as Soviet technology. Almost all—perhaps 90-95 percent—came directly or indirectly from the United States and its allies. In effect, the United States and the NATO countries have built the Soviet Union." Or as an earlier work on the same subject put it: *East Minus West Equals Zero*.

What has become of Sutton's information? Richard Pipes, Baird Professor of History at Harvard University, writing in *Commentary* magazine (August, 1984), summarized the fate of Sutton's books in this way: "Sutton comes to conclusions that are uncomfortable for many businessmen and economists. For this reason his work tends to be either dismissed out of hand as 'extreme' or, more often, simply ignored." And so the illusion endures that East-West trade is not critical for the Soviets.

## Trade Will Not Foster Peace

The second illusion that keeps us nurturing the Soviet Union is that trade will somehow mellow their system. Philosophically, this illusion embodies the error of trying to reverse cause and effect: peaceful nations trade; so if we trade with the Soviet Union, it will become peaceful. Historically, this illusion is the oldest one in the book.

In 1918, shortly after Russia's revolution, but before the Bolsheviks had consolidated their hold on the country, a message was sent to the U.S. State Department by Edwin Gay, then a member of the U.S. War Trade Board, later Dean of the Harvard Business School. According to State Department files for 1918: "Mr. Gay stated the opinion that it was doubtful whether the policy of blockade and economic isolation of these portions of Russia which were under Bolshevik control was the best policy for bringing about the establishment of a stable and proper government in Russia. Mr. Gay suggested to the Board that if the people in the Bolshevik sections of Russia were given the opportunity to enjoy improved economic conditions, they would themselves bring about the establishment of a moderate and stable social order."

Since 1918, Edwin Gay's policy of mellowing the Soviets with trade has been carried out with few interruptions and no successes. The principal result has been that the Soviet Union is now a mortal threat to the security of the United States and to freedom everywhere.

## Surviving Obvious Failures

How has this policy survived its obvious failures, such as Afghanistan and Poland? By a neat trick. When faced with failure, the policy's advocates say: True, trade did not mellow the Soviets, but suspending trade will only make them worse. In his latest book, *How Democracies Perish,* Jean-Francois Revel gives a striking example of this switch.

In June, 1982, six months after the crushing of Solidarity, a Western economic summit was held at Versailles. At that summit, America asked its allies— not to suspend their loans to the Soviet Union—but to suspend the preferential rate on those loans. As Revel says: "There would have been nothing wild and dangerous in such a stance; in dealing with a Communist world tormented by its inner contradictions, it might have been reasonably effective."

But the Europeans refused, and Revel concludes, "So, after a dozen years of pleading that economic aid to the East bloc would pacify the Soviet Union, the Europeans in 1982 declined to reduce that aid because it would not make the Russians less belligerent. . . . That's a fine blind maze we've shut ourselves into; appeasement and reprisal, we find, are equally incapable of making the Communists behave themselves and of slowing their aggressive drive. By this reasoning, our only choice is whether we're going to pay to be rolled, and we are opting to die paying."

## No Regard for Individual Rights

Finally, there is a third illusion that permits us to go on nurturing the Soviets, and that is the illusion that the Soviet Union is "just another social system." It's hard to know how to respond to this. The Soviet Union is responsible for murdering many tens of millions of its own citizens. It holds at least a dozen other nations in chains by direct military force. Its animating philosophy preaches the complete denial of the individual. Its practice seeks to dictate the whole being of Soviet citizens, from their inner-most beliefs to their simplest needs. In all these respects, the Soviet Union is more evil, by many orders of magnitude, than the common ruck of brutal dictatorships now defacing the globe. All these facts about the Soviet Union are easily learned. Yet, here is what was said of the Soviet empire and of dealing with the Soviet empire by Thomas Theobald, head of Citibank's international division: "Who knows which political system works? The only test we care about is: can they pay their bills?"

*"Businessmen and others need a policy that leaves no doubt about their moral and patriotic obligations."*

There is no adequate way to respond to such a remark, except perhaps with the words of the 19th century writer Lysander Spooner: "The men who loan money to governments, so called, for the purpose of enabling the latter to rob, enslave and murder their people, are among the greatest villains that the world has ever seen." Perhaps by some such moral condemnation, bankers and businessmen may be impelled to think through the illusion that their Russian customers represent "just another political system."

## Export Administration Act Expires

At any rate, these three illusions will be much heard during 1985, as the question of Soviet trade becomes a hot political issue. The Export Administration Act of 1979 expired last March, and President Reagan had to invoke his emergency powers to continue the Commerce Department's export-control authority. Such a stop-gap remedy cannot last. According to the *New York Times* (1/1/85): "Without an act in force, a senior Congressional aide said, there is so much uncertainty over the program's legality that 'I would be very surprised if there is not a frontal attack from an exporter during the period.'"

---

*"The long-term policy of private American citizens should be to express their abhorrence of the Soviet system through a complete boycott of the Soviet empire."*

---

In short, the new Congress must start work on a new export-control act. And when Congress begins to hold hearings on such a bill, it is going to be strongly lobbied, by high-tech companies, to make the controls as lax as possible. Last April, the state Secretary of Economic Affairs for Massachusetts, Evelyn Murphy, said: "We don't see any other issue hurting the high technology industry as much as this one." Under these conditions, it is predictable that the illusions about the Soviet Union will flourish.

## Legitimate Reasons for Fewer Export Controls?

Nevertheless, there may be legitimate reasons for restricting the scope of export control. At present, there are about 300,000 items on the Commerce Department's restricted list, and some people argue that a shorter list would be more effective, for two reasons. First, they say, it would be possible to watch fewer items more carefully. (A Customs Service crackdown, begun in October, 1981, and known as Operation Exodus, has had the effect of putting a sieve in what was before a more or less clear channel.) Second, it would be possible to get more complete allied agreement on a shorter list, which is indispensable to an effective embargo.

There is also a third argument for restricting export controls, namely, that America is a free society, not at war with the Soviet Union. Certainly, America can prohibit its citizens from selling Russia items of direct military use, on the same principle that it can prohibit the sale of guns to convicted criminals. But it is not clear how far a free society can go in banning the sale of non-military goods.

## Two Moral Trade Policies

Even more important than a new law is America's need for a new national policy on Soviet trade. Businessmen and others need a policy that leaves no doubt about their moral and patriotic obligations, however ambiguous their legal obligations may be.

Such a policy should rest on four basic facts. First, the Soviet Union is a totalitarian society, the moral equal or inferior of Hitler's Germany. Second, totalitarian societies stifle creativity and are therefore essentially stagnant societies. Third, because of their stagnation and because of their anti-human philosophies, totalitarian societies are perpetually driven toward war, and so constitute a standing threat to the peace. Fourth, the U.S.S.R., alone among totalitarian societies, is in the same military league as the United States, and so is a unique threat to American security.

These four facts should, in turn, give rise to two simple policies. The long-term policy of private American citizens should be to express their abhorrence of the Soviet system through a complete boycott of the Soviet empire: no trade, no cultural exchanges, no scientific meetings, no athletic competitions, *no cooperation at all.* The long-term policy of the American government should be the extirpation of Soviet totalitarianism, the break-up of the Soviet empire and indeed of the Soviet Union itself. Or as Barry Goldwater asked more than twenty years ago: Why not victory?

Fortunately, a policy of victory is not so rare as it was twenty years ago. Gregory Fossedal, an editorial page writer for the *Wall Street Journal,* recently reviewed four books that seek to define the positions of the Right, and he noted that all four seek the defeat, rather than merely the containment, of the Soviet Union. This policy, of course, is just the counterpart of Russia's; as Lenin noted long ago, the only question is: "kto kogo?" "Who [will defeat] whom?"

## Best Weapon Is Soviet Stagnation

In seeking victory over the Soviet Union, our best weapon will always be the intrinsic stagnation of the Soviet system. For that system, if left to itself, is a disaster waiting to happen. To the extent we can, therefore, we should deny to the Soviets all the fruits of our free society—not only by a legal ban on military goods, but by a *voluntary* ban on all trade. A private boycott of East-West cooperation, desirable for moral reasons, should also be the central feature of our government's Soviet policy.

To promote such a boycott, the President could do many things, starting with the following: first, he could publish a dishonor roll of companies and groups who continue to deal with the Soviet Union. Second, he could make clear to such organizations exactly why it is in their interests to stop such dealings. And for this last task, the President might well draw on the words of Shakespeare: "I fear me you but warm the starved snake, who, cherished in your breasts, will sting your hearts."

*Roger Donway wrote this viewpoint for* On Principle, *a bi-weekly newsletter devoted to economic and related issues.*

*"If we get sufficiently interlaced economically, we will probably not bomb each other off the face of the planet."*

# US/USSR Trade Is Mutually Beneficial

## Thomas H. Naylor, William D. Marbach

*Editor's note: Part I of the following viewpoint was written by Thomas H. Naylor. Part II is taken from an article in* Newsweek *written by William D. Marbach and other* Newsweek *staffers.*

### I

At a time when United States-Soviet relations are improving, increased trade could draw the two superpowers even closer together.

Secretary of Commerce Malcolm Baldridge has indicated that our trade deficit for 1984 may nearly double last year's record of $69.4 billion. Increased foreign competition, the strong dollar and severe import restrictions imposed by third world nations have aggravated the problem. Although the economy has recovered substantially, many of our smoke-stack industries have not. And the record number of bank failures and the enormous third world debts carried by American banks have put great stress on the nation's financial institutions.

It is not surprising that some American companies are looking for new markets in such places as the Soviet Union and Eastern Europe. A trade delegation of 250 American business leaders visited Moscow in November 1982. This meeting was considered so important by the Soviet Union that it took place during the period of mourning for Leonid I. Brezhnev. In a reciprocal visit in May 1984, 40 Soviet trade officials met with these same American executives in New York.

Trade between the United States and the Soviet Union fell from $4.5 billion in 1979 to $2.3 billion last year. According to one estimate, American companies are losing at least $10 billion a year in

Thomas H. Naylor, "For More Trade with the Russians," *The New York Times*, December 17, 1984. Copyright © 1984 by The New York Times Company. Reprinted by permission.

William Marbach, "A Closed Door Policy," *Newsweek*, November 12, 1984. Condensed from *Newsweek*. Copyright © 1984 by Newsweek, Inc. All Rights Reserved. Reprinted by permission.

sales to the Soviet Union because of Government restrictions, causing the Russians to buy in greater quantities from Western Europe than ever before. The large French agribusiness firm Interagra sold the Soviet bloc nearly $750 million worth of food and agricultural products last year and recently completed a deal involving the sale of 1,800 tons of inexpensive table wine. And to raise hard currency to finance imports, the Soviet Union's Moscow Narodny Bank, in London, recently offered a $50 million bond issue in what is believed to be the first Soviet foray into the Eurobond market.

Meanwhile, there is evidence that the economies of the Soviet bloc are becoming more market-oriented. I visited 10 economic research institutes in Moscow in 1982 in which Soviet scientists were evaluating the effects of market-oriented planning in the Soviet Union. Cynics have said this was nothing new and had little to do with the way Soviet enterprises actually conduct business. But recent discussions with more than 30 Soviet-bloc executives suggests that what I observed in Moscow was only the tip of the iceberg.

### Soviets Turning to Marketplace

In varying degrees, Bulgarian, Czechoslovak, Hungarian, Polish, and Soviet executives are all singing the same tune. The old ways don't work, and they are turning to the marketplace to raise the level of innovation and productivity. Each of Budapest's three first-rate international hotels is owned by the Hungarian Government, financed by private Austrian capital and managed by a United States hotel chain. Hungary has taken the largest steps toward the West, the Soviet Union the smallest. But the direction is the same.

Critics contend that the Russians want increased trade with the West to obtain our technology for military gains. This overlooks the virtual impossibility of preventing American technology from finding its way into the Soviet bloc. It is hard to prevent neutral nations like Austria and Finland from selling technology to whomever they please. Blocking third world countries from selling technology to the Russians is equally impossible. William C. Norris, founder of Control Data, has noted that they have some very good technology of their own: "It's not in commercialized form—it's research results. And that's really the most important thing of all." And with its recent Soviet grain deals, the Administration has shown little sympathy for the view that rejects all trade with the Russians on strategic grounds.

## Economic Interlacing for Peace

There may be some unique opportunities for American business leaders to contribute to global peace by assuming a stronger leadership role in East-West trade and joint ventures. Rather than resisting global interdependence, we should embrace it. As John Naisbitt, author of *Megatrends,* says: "If we get sufficiently interlaced economically, we will probably not bomb each other off the face of the planet."

## II

Last January, Teltone, Inc., of Kirkland, Wash., won a $250,000 order to supply telephone-switching gear to the government-run phone system in a NATO country in northern Europe. As required by law, it applied to the U.S. Commerce Department for an export license, in the past a routine matter. Teltone officials were stunned when Commerce held up the application because the system's tone-to-pulse converter was on a list of technologies considered vital to U.S. security. "I can't for the life of me understand how they can classify a 20-year-old technology as 'high technology' " says Arne Midtskog, Teltone's international sales director. "I *would* understand if these things had a shadow of military or strategic use." Six months later, Teltone finally got its license—only to fight another long battle for the right to ship a $750 order to the Far East. "We are losing business because of this nonsense," says Midtskog.

## Good Fences Make Bad Neighbors

Teltone officials are not alone in their exasperation. In an effort that began under Jimmy Carter and intensified in the Reagan administration, the United States is trying to stop exports of American technology that could contribute to the military potential of the Warsaw Pact. Administration hardliners, led by Richard Perle, the assistant secretary of defense for international-security policy, sought to go even further, not only restricting exports of such familiar equipment as the Apple II computer, but also banning foreign nationals from U.S. research labs and limiting discussion of even unclassified research at technical conferences. And good fences make bad neighbors: last summer the United States enraged its allies by seeking tighter regulation of computer exports from Europe and Japan as well.

There is little doubt that the Soviet Union has benefited from Western technologies. According to Stephen Bryen, Perle's deputy at the Pentagon, the Soviets during the detente period built a dozen semiconductor factories with Western equipment. And experts say that many components of Soviet weapons systems are of Western origin or design. But with the crackdown since the Export Administration Act of 1979, the East bloc has turned more to smuggling: in a highly publicized case last year, authorities intercepted a shipment of VAX minicomputers bound for the Soviet Union that had been smuggled through dummy corporations in South Africa. Customs officials now routinely search outgoing shipments for proscribed equipment.

## Restrictions More Damaging to US

But critics believe that restrictions will ultimately do far more damage to the United States than to the Warsaw Pact. For one thing, there is no U.S. commercial monopoly on technology. "In fact, about 75 percent of the high-tech goods sold in Free World markets in 1982 were made outside the United States," says General Electric's Boyd McKelvain, vice chairman of the Industry Coalition on Technology Transfer. Heavy restrictions reward foreign competitors, with losses to American firms perhaps running into billions of dollars.

*"If we lock up our basic research we will do far greater damage than if we allowed the leakage."*

Even more important in the long run, technological progress is threatened. In mid-1982, the Pentagon forced researchers to withdraw more than 100 technical papers from a symposium of the Society of Photo-optical Instrumentation Engineers, on the ground that East bloc scientists were scheduled to attend. In July 1983, the Pentagon forced withdrawal from an Alaska conference on permafrost of six unclassified papers on pipeline construction, the performance of off-road vehicles and the maintenance of roads and airfields in permafrost conditions. Bryen justified the action by pointing to disrepair in the Soviet military infrastructure; he did not think the Pentagon should "brief the Russians on how to maintain their airfields in Siberia."

The scientific community finds such single-mindedness alarming. "If we lock up our basic research we will do far greater damage than if we allowed the leakage," says Michael Dertouzos, director of MIT. "Free communication between science, technology and the high-tech companies is what gives us our strength." Adds Wolfgang Panofsky, director of the Stanford Linear Accelerator Center and a member of a commission studying technology transfer: "We found no discernible impact on Soviet [capabilities] from the acquisition of know-how through scientific channels."

The attempts to exclude non-U.S. citizens from scientific meetings or to consider discussions with them "exports" that are subject to license also ignore fundamental realities. Today nearly half the students receiving Ph.D.s in engineering in U.S. universities are foreigners, and many of the strongest U.S. technology firms have research labs and operations all over the globe.

## Indiscriminate Critical Technologies List

One of the biggest problems is the Pentagon's 700-page Militarily Critical Technologies List, the MCTL. The Pentagon drew up the classified list under the Export Administration Act (since expired), but in a case of bureaucratic overkill, the document became a laundry list—not a careful catalog of truly critical technologies. Moreover, the list reportedly ignored the fact that many of the so-called critical technologies are available in commercial markets all over the world.

Thus, the administration tried to block exports of some kinds of "embedded microprocessors"—the computer chips now used in thousands of commercial products—because the Soviets could convert them to other uses. The Pentagon blocked sales of digital-telephone-switching systems to the Soviet bloc, on the grounds that they would allow the Soviet defense ministry to pre-empt civilian users and convert the telephone network over to a military command and control system. And Pentagon officials sought to tighten restrictions on aircraft and jet-engine sales, inertial navigation gear—and drydocks. . . .

Some suspect the hard-liners of believing that the Soviet regime will collapse if denied Western technology. That may be a vain hope. In 1565, King Sigismund of Poland wrote a letter to Elizabeth I imploring her to prevent British merchants from trading with Russia: "We repeat once more to your Majesty that the Tsar of Moscow, enemy of all liberty, increases his forces day by day through the advantages of trade and by his relations with the civilized nations of Europe. . . . Our only hope rests in our superiority in the arts and sciences, but soon he will know as much." Four centuries later, only the names have changed.

*Thomas H. Naylor is professor of economics and business administration at Duke University's Fuqua School of Business. William Marbach, a writer for* Newsweek, *wrote the second part of this viewpoint with the assistance of several other* Newsweek *staffers.*

*"Western technology [is] the target of a massive, well-coordinated Soviet acquisition effort. . . aimed at those technologies which promised the highest military payoff."*

# Technology Transfer Threatens the US

William Schneider Jr.

Many of you will recall, as I do, the euphoric days of the early 1970s—the heyday of detente in East-West relations. The Soviet Union and the United States had just signed a strategic arms limitation agreement, perceived at the time as an important milestone in limiting arms expenditures and as the prime indicator of relaxation of Soviet-American tensions. President Nixon and Premier Brezhnev exchanged visits and signed numerous agreements. Our allies joined in to create a widespread spirit of East-West detente.

Economic relations, naturally, played a major part in the new atmosphere. The West liberalized its credit terms, and the Soviets took advantage of this liberalization to increase their purchases of strategic technology and equipment that they either could not make or could make only with radical shifts in existing patterns of resource allocation, such as truck assembly lines, entire chemical plants, and innumerable pieces of capital equipment.

The theory underlying detente was that a web of economic, scientific, cultural, and political relationships would so interlink Soviet and Western societies that their views on security and other core issues would tend to converge. It was believed that the tangible benefits flowing from economic and other interchanges would encourage Soviet restraint in foreign policy. In a word, it was believed that our two societies would become "interdependent," thereby diminishing the possibility of any serious conflict.

## Unfulfilled Hopes of Detente

These hopeful views of East-West relations regrettably were not fulfilled. The Soviets, in the late 1970s and after, failed to live up to the hopes of a decade earlier. Their sponsorship of Cuban adventures in Africa, their continuing activities in Indochina, their invasion of Afghanistan, their crackdown in Poland, and their involvement in Central America were visible indications that their fundamental values and policies had not been changed by a more lenient, friendly, and cooperative attitude on the part of the West. Most recently, we have seen another brutal reaffirmation of Soviet values—the Korean Air Lines tragedy—which has cost 269 innocent lives.

Underlying these aggressive acts, of course, is the massive and unrelenting Soviet military buildup that went far beyond any reasonable notion of what would be needed to defend the U.S.S.R. In retrospect, it is clear the Soviet Union used detente as a tactical device to slow the modernization of U.S. forces and lull the West into a false sense of security while they carried on the largest, costliest, and most threatening military buildup in history.

As we slowly disabused ourselves of the belief that we and the Soviets shared a common objective, we became increasingly critical of the ease with which the Soviets could obtain advanced Western technology. We increased and focused our information gathering and analysis to try to determine what technology the Soviets were getting and what the military impact might be. The results were dismaying. Evidence grew that Western technology was the target of a massive, well-coordinated Soviet acquisition effort, orchestrated through legal and illegal methods and aimed at those technologies which promised the highest military payoff.

## Technology Targets

Make no mistake—U.S. companies and equipment are a prime target of the largest intelligence organization on earth. They are determined, well financed, and increasing their efforts. There is no end

William Schneider Jr., "East-West Relations and Technology Transfer," speech delivered before the Federal Bar Association of Newton, Massachusetts on March 29, 1984.

in sight for the struggle which this forces upon us. This struggle is complicated by the fact that industry is overwhelmingly in the civil, rather than the military, domain. As a consequence, the ability of the Federal Government to directly control the dissemination of this technology to the Soviet Union is a vastly more difficult task than controlling the critical technology of a generation ago—nuclear weapons—which was entirely in the military domain.

---

*"Soviet acquisition efforts have become more systematic and effective over the past 15 years."*

---

The Soviet acquisition effort is planned and approved at the highest governmental and party levels. Much of the Soviet acquisition of Western equipment, know-how, and training applicable to the military has been through entirely legal and open means, such as commercial sales, business and research seminars and symposiums, commercial visits, and academic exchange programs. This effort is complemented by the extensive and growing use of Soviet and East European intelligence services through a variety of clandestine and illegal means.

Continued problems in Soviet domestic technological capabilities—due in part to the Soviet system itself, which tends to discourage innovation—strongly suggest they are not likely to decrease their dependency on Western equipment, technology, and know-how.

## Soviet Acquisition Efforts

Soviet acquisition efforts have become more systematic and effective over the past 15 years and a number of trends have become clear.

• Weapon-related acquisitions increasingly are more selective, focusing on critical components and materials necessary to achieve greater performance.

• Greater emphasis is being placed on acquiring Western production technology and equipment, as opposed to end products. This reflects the Soviet need to become self-sufficient and to increase the efficiency of large-volume production. Much of this technology and equipment is subject to export controls, and its acquisition often is accomplished through intelligence-directed trade diversions.

• Increasing priority is being given to dual-use commercial technologies and emerging high technologies, perhaps indicating the military value placed on them by the Soviet Union, as well as their greater vulnerability to intelligence acquisition methods.

• Acquisitions of U.S. technology are being stepped up beyond U.S. borders.

• The role of East European intelligence services

has increased steadily since Western sanctions against the Soviet Union were initiated following Afghanistan and Poland.

## Soviets Benefit

We believe these acquisitions have benefited the Soviet Union by increasing the pace of Soviet weapons systems development; reducing military research-and-development costs and risks; expediting the development of effective countermeasures against Western military systems; and modernizing and expanding critical sectors of the Warsaw Pact defense industry and support base. These payoffs are very critical to the Soviets, who continue to forge ahead with their military buildup, despite a deteriorating economic growth rate.

The qualitative advances made by the Soviet military by means of acquiring Western technology increase the burden that we and our NATO allies must share in maintaining qualitative superiority over the Warsaw Pact.

The Reagan Administration has given top priority to fighting this massive Soviet effort at increasing its military power with the fruits of Western technology. However, a great deal of damage has already been done that has saved the Soviet Union millions of dollars in research-and-development costs and has cost the West billions of dollars in forcing an accelerated pace of arms modernization.

## The U.S. Response

The U.S. Government has had to ask itself a number of important questions in facing this problem. How shall we meet this challenge? What priority should it receive, among the many threats to our interests? What should we expect of our allies, who are increasingly capable of producing the technologies of concern? What should our private sector do?

This administration has sharply increased the priority and the resources assigned to this problem. We intend to sustain and increase our efforts to minimize the acquisition of militarily useful technology by our potential adversaries. As the problem is a long-term one, rooted in Soviet ambition and weakness, it is essential that our response be sustained.

One way, I believe, has been through the creation of an interagency organization that has assumed great importance in the Administration's efforts to stem the flow of strategic technology to our adversaries—the Senior Interagency Group on the Transfer of Strategic Technology. Since its advent in the summer of 1982, several exciting developments have taken place. It was created to bring all U.S. Government agencies with strategic technology programs or interests together at a policymaking level for the purpose of coordinating the many facets of the government's technology transfer activities. Eighteen agencies or offices are members. . . .

The Senior Intelligence Group has. . .opened major bilateral dialogues with our key high-technology allies, seeking enhanced government awareness of the technology transfer issue and a strengthening of their national control systems. . . .

Yet another project of the group has been the raising of intelligence priorities within allied intelligence agencies. We have had consultations with at least 12 countries so far. They began looking at what they had largely ignored before and did not like what they saw. Of the approximately 80 expulsions or arrests of Soviet intelligence officers in 1983 in the industrial democracies, we believe more than half were involved in strategic technology collection.

In taking the overview of the strategic transfer issue, we discovered early on that there were some problems in our own system of protection and control. One response was to strengthen the visa mechanism. It was clear that there is a group of people entering the United States every year with the intent of acquiring controlled U.S. technology illegally, and yet it was unclear what the government could do. We put the issue under intensive study in 1982-83. In April we reached the conclusion of this process, adopting a new policy of denying and restricting visas when we have evidence that this is justified.

Another of our efforts has been to enhance U.S. public awareness of the transfer problem. This is what today's appearance by myself and my colleagues is all about. We have been actively pursuing this goal through opportunities presented by public speaking invitations, media appearances, and dissemination of unclassified government reports. A more specific aspect of this program is to brief industrial, commercial, and research-and-development institutions that we believe may be high on the Soviet priority list. I am happy to report we have had a generally positive response to our presentation of the problem to defense contractors, civilian firms, trade associations, and even the universities. A great deal has been accomplished in this area and efforts are even now being intensified. One of our next steps will be to press friendly governments to follow our example with awareness programs of their own.

## Coordination of Export Controls

As you know, the role of our allies is also vital to our success. The organization through which we work to coordinate U.S. and allied export controls is COCOM. COCOM has been in existence since the late 1940s when the United States realized is was essential to achieve a fundamental agreement among the major Western industrial powers concerning their trade in militarily relevant technology to the Soviet bloc. . . .

COCOM's present membership comprises all of the NATO members except Iceland and Spain, plus Japan. It was created by informal agreement of its members and has no formal treaty or executive agreement basis. The members, therefore, have no legal obligation to participate in COCOM or to abide by the commitments made there. However, there have been relatively few instances when a member nation has exercised its sovereign right to deviate from decisions reached in COCOM. This may be in part because all important COCOM decisions are made on the basis of unanimity.

Traditionally, COCOM has had three major functions:

*The first* is the establishment and updating of the three lists of embargoed products and technologies—the munitions list, the atomic energy list, and the international list which covers dual-use items with both civil and military applications. Although the COCOM lists are not published, they become the basis for the national control lists administered by member governments. . . .

*Second,* COCOM acts as the clearinghouse for requests submitted by member governments to ship specific embargoed items to specified end users in the proscribed countries. (The COCOM-proscribed countries are the Soviet Union, the other Warsaw Pact countries, Albania, and the communist countries in south Asia.)

*"The qualitative advances made by the Soviet military by means of acquiring Western technology increase the burden that we and our NATO allies must share in maintaining qualitative superiority over the Warsaw Pact."*

*Third,* COCOM serves as a means of coordinating the administration and enforcement activities of the member governments, largely through its Export Control Subcommittee. . . .

In brief, COCOM has been reasonably effective over the years in coordinating national export control policies and restrictions. Without COCOM, competition among Western exporters would have escalated so that even more high-technology sales to the Soviet Union and other communist countries would have taken place. . . .

## Cooperation with the Private Sector

A final way to sustain our response to the Soviet threat is through our continuing cooperation with our own technical and business communities, for the private sector is at once the source of creativity and the engine of our society. With your good will and support, we will be able to manage our own technology losses and bring increasing pressure on our allies to conform their export policies to ours. Without your participation, we will enter a world where all compete to increase their own insecurity. We will, to paraphrase Lenin's chilling prophecy, sell the rope to hang ourselves.

*"We will, to paraphrase Lenin's chilling prophecy, sell the rope to hang ourselves."*

In closing, a society such as ours, which values individual freedom and private initiative, is bound to suffer some disadvantage when confronted with an attempt to utilize our openness, our lack of secrecy, and the military utility of our commercial technologies against us. But we also have certain strengths, which, in my view, more than outweigh these disadvantages—our technical creativity, the speed and breadth of our technical advances, and, most of all, the spirit of responsibility with which our private citizens have always responded to challenges. I have no doubt that we shall meet this challenge as we have met all others, for the future belongs to the free.

*William Schneider Jr. is Under Secretary for Security Assistance, Science and Technology. This viewpoint was delivered as an address by Michael B. Marks, in Mr. Schneider's absence, before the Federal Bar Association.*

*"The Reagan administration's technology policy toward the Soviet Union has been almost entirely defensive, and has ignored the potential for American gain from Soviet brains."*

# Technology Transfer Can Benefit the US

John W. Kiser III

Russia, British historian Thomas Carlyle wrote more than a century ago, is a "big, dumb monster." The Reagan administration obviously agrees with Carlyle. Acting on the assumption that the Soviets are desperate for American technology and know-how, this administration has sought to build new barriers to block Soviet access to Western ideas and machinery that they think the Russians cannot live without. The Soviet Union needs us, the Reagan administration contends, but we don't need the Soviet Union.

But if the U.S.S.R. is so backward, how has it managed to build titanium submarines capable of going 40 miles an hour underwater—faster than any of ours? Why are companies such as Bristol Myers, Dupont and 3M buying new patented drugs and surgical devices from the U.S.S.R.? Why are Kaiser Aluminum and Olin Corp. acquiring sophisticated manufacturing know-how from the Soviets?

I am in the business of trying to acquire Soviet and East European inventions and know-how that have commercial potential for American companies. I got into this field after doing a number of studies for the federal government and others on Soviet and East European technology. My experience has left me modestly impressed with Soviet technological strengths—but powerfully impressed by American ignorance of them. When I tell new acquaintances what I do, they often are astonished that U.S. companies could find anything of technological value in the communist bloc.

This perception of the Soviet Union is perhaps understandable. Americans have been exposed to a stream of publicity about the Soviet theft of U.S. industrial and military secrets, and there is ample evidence that the KGB and other Soviet intelligence

agencies have an active illegal technological acquisition program throughout the West. Like other countries, the Soviets also openly buy specialized Western technology, from cigarette-making machines to chemical processing technology and truck factories.

## Soviet Union Not Backward

But we should not infer from this that the Soviet Union is hopelessly backward, or that we have little to learn from its scientists, engineers and inventors. The Soviet Union, to be sure, is a nation plagued with economic problems. Its consumer goods and its industrial products often don't measure up to Western standards. But we should not be misled by this.

A great deal of the country's innovative laboratory research, creative product design and excellent applied science never show up in final products because of bureaucratic inertia and bottlenecks. Good product designs get degraded in production by inadequate manufacturing methods and poor quality control. These problems are not self-correcting in a system where a factory call sell virtually anything it produces due to chronic shortages and lack of competition.

In other words, there is a Soviet technology gap—but it is mostly within the Soviet Union itself. It is a technically highly advanced society, but one that is constantly frustrated by problems rooted in its system of economic incentives and industrial organization.

It is true that shopkeepers in Moscow and Kiev still use the ancient abacus to tote up the bills of customers. But Soviet hydroelectric power stations operate with sophisticated Soviet-made computers. If Americans had an opportunity to see Soviet shipyards, visit a continuous steel casting plant in Novo Lipetsk, or inspect an electroslag melting line in Dneprospetstal, they would get a view of sophisticated industrial technology at work.

John W. Kiser III, "Technology: We Can Learn a Lot from the Soviets," *The Washington Post*, August 14, 1983. Reprinted by permission of the author.

If we fail to grasp the true nature of the Soviet economy and Soviet technological capabilities, we will fall into facile miscalculations—like the belief that the West could bring Russia to its knees through all-out economic warfare. In almost every case in which the West has denied specific technologies to the Soviets, they eventually have developed capabilities of their own. Examples range from synthetic industrial diamonds, (now a major Soviet export item) to vacuum remelting furnaces that make the high alloy steels for aerospace.

We tend to judge Soviet accomplishments by our standards rather than theirs. We stress appearance, while they frequently stress simplicity and functionalism. As a result Soviet equipment often looks crude and unfinished to American eyes. And that distracts Westerners from a more fundamental question: does it do the job?

## Soviet Achievements

Soviets understandably resent the fact that Westerners don't give them credit for their very real achievements. For example, Russians have drilled the world's deepest bore hole—a geological experiment in the Komi Peninsula that goes nine miles into the earth. The Soviets have pioneered development of lasers, laid much of the groundwork for current high energy physics and accumulated more experience manufacturing industrial materials in space than the United States.

Yet the Reagan administration's technology policy toward the Soviet Union has been almost entirely defensive, and has ignored the potential for American gain from Soviet brains. It has focused public attention on the threat to national security posed by Soviet acquisition of American science and technology. It has tended to lump together the illegal espionage activities of the KGB and the ordinary activities of scientific communication and legitimate industrial information gathering of the kind that all countries engage in.

---

*"The Reagan administration has been excessively concerned about the 'threat' posed by visiting Soviet scientists."*

---

The Reagan administration has been excessively concerned about the "threat" posed by visiting Soviet scientists. Yet for American businessmen and scientists these visits can be opportunities to learn. For example, in 1981, engineers at the Varian Corp. in Palo Alto got the idea of using infrared light beams to anneal (remove stress from) computer chips from papers presented at Albany, N.Y., by Soviet scientists describing their work using lasers for this purpose. These papers motivated the U.S. engineers to do the

same thing, though using a somewhat different technique.

Dr. Walter Gilbert, who won a Nobel Prize for his work on DNA research while at Harvard, has acknowledged that the research that led to his award benefited from ideas stimulated by the visit of Andrei Mirzabekov, a Soviet biophysicist.

## Scientists Share Knowledge

People who think the Soviet-American scientific exchange are always a one-way street are ignorant about what motivates scientists. Scientists are inherently interested in sharing their research results and getting comments and reactions from peers, regardless of nationality. Respect from peers is one of the main "incomes" that scientists have. It cannot be obtained without contributing to the pool of knowledge. I am not aware that real Soviet and East European scientists are any different from others in this respect.

When American or Japanese specialists go to the Soviet Union, it is not only their brains that are picked. The idea of putting infant pigs in wire cages that can be stacked on top of each other for more efficient use of space came from observing the practice in the Soviet Union, according to Roger Gerrits, a swine specialist at the U.S. Department of Agriculture. U.S. producers are now using this technique, and U.S. equipment manufacturers are providing the special cages.

The Japanese firm, Mitsui Mining, began using hydraulic techniques for mining coal after visiting mines in the Soviet Union where highly pressurized jets of water were used to cut coal from the seam and to transport it from the mine. Mitsui has since transferred some of this technology to Kaiser Resources Ltd. of Canada.

Julian Sturdevant, a biochemist at Yale, uses a differential scanning microcalorimeter based on a design developed by a scientist at the Institute for Biophysics in Puschino. This instrument measures heat transfer inside of cells. Sturdevant learned of the new design, which permits more sensitive measurements than before, while visiting colleagues in the Soviet Union.

## Quality Soviet Technical Information

Soviet scientific literature is not the desert some think. While articles are often sketchy and their ideas not reproducible, some Soviet open technical literature is of high quality. Roderick Scott, the former chief scientist at Perkin Elmer, a U.S. high-technology firm, has reported that the Soviet Journal of Spectroscopy is a valuable source of ideas and was regularly read at his company.

According to an engineer at Kaiser Aluminum, roughly half of all articles on nonferrous metallurgy that the company abstracts come from Soviet literature.

In its 1981 annual report, Varian Corp. acknowledged the value of Soviet articles describing work on gyrotrons. Nuclear fusion research in Japan and the United States, based on the so-called Tokomak or "donut" magnetic containment design, originated directly from Soviet work and publications on the subject.

Yet, according to Eugene Rivin, a Soviet emigre engineer who is now a professor at Wayne State University, very little of the Soviet technical literature is being tapped. In an April, 1983, article in Mechanical Engineering, Rivin cites numerous examples of high-quality Soviet publications in fields such as super plastic forming, squeeze casting and titanium alloys. Rivin echoes an opinion of many knowledgeable U.S. scientists that the level of much Soviet research is very high—considerably higher than is reflected in the level of their consumer products and commercial machinery.

In Rivin's specialty, manufacturing engineering, Russian books on the subject are of excellent quality and often are more detailed than American ones. Yet much of this valuable Soviet information is missed by American companies that tend at best to subscribe only to foreign technical journals, not books.

## Soviet Liberality

Part of the U.S. problem in exploiting foreign technology is, of course, self-imposed. Our ignorance of foreign languages amounts to unilateral linguistic disarmament. Few American scientists can read Russian, let alone Japanese. Translations of foreign technical journals typically are poorly done and expensive. Underpaid, technically unqualified translators don't, as a rule, produce good translations of material that they would barely understand if it were in their native language.

U.S. business is learning. But only relatively recently have politicians and journalists begun to realize what industry has long known: We aren't the best in a lot of things, and we can and must learn from others.

Ironically, the Soviet bloc is surprisingly liberal about the technologies it is willing to sell to the West. In some cases the technology that has been made available has obvious military and strategic applications. There are technologies which, if the shoe were on the other foot, the U.S. government would be unlikely to approve for export to the Soviet Union.

Universal Oil Products, for example, imported a Soviet cold rolling mill in the 1970s to expand capacity for making hydraulic tubing for the Air Force; East German photogrammetric cameras used for making extremely precise measurements are being used to attach wing sections to the F16 fighter at General Dynamics' Fort Worth plant; Soviet electroslag hollow ingot technology sold to Cabot Corp. can be used for making rocket engine casings

and gun barrel tubes as well as for more benign products such as rings and couplings. The highly efficient Soviet flash butt welding technology sold to J.R. McDermott of New Orleans for welding large diameter pipe will greatly improve the efficiency of pipeline construction by reducing the time and manpower required to weld 56-inch pipe.

For the most part, American companies buy the Soviets' technology for the same reason they buy ours. If someone else has already solved the problem, why reinvent the wheel—if the price is right?

## Question of Priorities

The issue isn't brains, but economics and priorities. Advanced technology can only be assimilated by countries that are themselves technologically advanced. One of the reasons the Soviet Union is capable of benefiting from our technology is that it *is* advanced.

---

*"We aren't the best in a lot of things, and we can learn from others."*

---

As long as we can run faster than our competitors, we shouldn't worry too much about what others are learning from us, and that includes the Soviet Union. Unless we can focus our attention on the real problems facing U.S. industry, our concerns about the leakage of U.S. technology will amount to an idle diversion. The real problem is the lack of competitiveness of some U.S. industry.

Unfortunately the attitude of the government (and parts of industry) toward Soviet technology is symptomatic of a more wide-spread U.S. arrogance and parochialism born largely from competing in a postwar world when our natural competitors were devastated and Europe's best brainpower flowed to the United States. America became psychologically accustomed to being number one in everything that counted. And that led us to overlook the opportunities provided by foreign countries—including our leading adversary.

If we view the Soviet Union as technologically backward, struggling to catch up with the West by buying—or stealing the West's know-how, that will lead to different policies than if we perceive a more accurate picture: a Soviet Union that possesses tremendous scientific capabilities, even if they are translated unevenly or inefficiently into everyday practice inside the U.S.S.R.

*John W. Kiser III is a Washington consultant who specializes in technology and government research.*

*"The Soviets have acquired militarily significant technologies and critically important industrial Western technologies."*

viewpoint **68**

# Western Technology Has Significantly Advanced the USSR

### Central Intelligence Agency

The United States and its Allies traditionally have relied on the technological superiority of their weapons to preserve a credible counterforce to the quantitative superiority of the Warsaw Pact. But that technical superiority is eroding as the Soviet Union and its Allies introduce more and more sophisticated weaponry—weapons that all too often are manufactured with the direct help of Western technology. Stopping the Soviets extensive acquisition of military-related Western technology—in ways that are both effective and appropriate in our open society—is one of the most complex and urgent issues facing the Free World today....

Since at least the 1930s, the Soviet Union has devoted vast amounts of its financial and manpower resources to the acquisition of Western technology that would enhance its military power and improve the efficiency of its military manufacturing technology. Today this Soviet effort is massive, well planned, and well managed—a national-level program approved at the highest party and governmental levels.

This program accords top priority to the military and military-related industry, and major attention is also given to the civilian sectors of Soviet industry that support military production.

The Soviets and their Warsaw Pact allies have obtained vast amounts of militarily significant Western technology and equipment through legal and illegal means. They have succeeded in acquiring the most advanced Western technology by using, in part, their scientific and technological agreements with the West to facilitate access to the new technologies that are emerging from the Free World's applied scientific research efforts; by spending their scarce hard currency to illegally purchase controlled equipment,

as well as to legally purchase uncontrolled advanced Western technologies having military-industrial applications; and by tasking their intelligence services to acquire illegally those US and Western technologies that are classified and export controlled.

## Blend of Legal and Illegal

The Soviets have been very successful in acquiring Western technology by blending acquisitions legally and illegally acquired by different government organizations. The Soviet intelligence services—the Soviet Committee for State Security (KGB) and the Chief Intelligence Directorate of the Soviet General Staff (GRU)—have the primary responsibility for collecting Western classified, export-controlled, and proprietary technology, using both clandestine and overt collection methods. They in turn make extensive use of many of the East European Intelligence Services; for their efforts in acquiring Western technology, these countries are paid in part with Soviet military equipment and weapons.

Clandestine acquisition of the West's most advanced military-related equipment and know-how by the KGB and GRU is a major and growing problem....

As a result, the Soviets have acquired militarily significant technologies and critically important industrial Western technologies that have benefited every major Soviet industry engaged in the research, development, and production of weapon systems.

Soviet acquisition mechanisms include: *legal means* through open literature, through legal trade channels, and through student scientific and technological exchanges and conferences; *illegal means* through trade channels that evade US and Western (i.e. CoCom) export controls, including acquisitions by their intelligence services through recruited agents and industrial espionage. While a large volume of technology is acquired by nonintelligence personnel, the overwhelming majority of what the United States

Central Intelligence Agency, from "Soviet Acquisition of Western Technology," unclassified report, April 1982.

considers to be militarily significant technology acquired by and for the Soviets was obtained by the Soviet intelligence services and their surrogates among the East European intelligence services. However, legal acquisitions by other Soviet organizations are important since it is often the combination of legally and illegally acquired technologies that gives the Soviets the complete military or industrial capability they need.

---

*"Soviet assurances that legally purchased dual-use technology will be used solely for civilian applications can seldom be accepted at face value."*

---

Because of the priority accorded to the military over the civilian sectors of the Soviet economy, Western dual-use technology—i.e., technology with both military and civilian applications—almost always finds its way first into military industries, and subsequently into the civilian sectors of industries that support military production. Thus, Soviet assurances that legally purchased dual-use technology will be used solely for civilian applications can seldom be accepted at face value....

## Acquisitions and Exchanges

Both legal and illegal acquisitions of US and Western technology and equipment are coordinated with information obtained through the complex network of international governmental scientific and technical agreements and exchanges that the USSR maintains with the advanced industrial nations. These include know-how, equipment, and computer data base collection activities of Soviet scientists and engineers who participate in academic, commercial, and official S&T exchanges. Visiting Soviet and East European technical and student delegations to the United States generally consist of expert scientists, many of whom are connected with classified work in their home countries. Such was the case with the Soviet scientist who managed to get assigned to fuel-air explosives work. When he finished his US study programs, he almost certainly returned to the USSR to work on related weapons. Other Soviet and East European scientists have come to the United States to work in the aerohydrodynamic, cryogenic, optic, laser, computer, magnetic bubble computer memory, nuclear, microelectronic, and structural and electronic material areas. Given the military importance of these fields to the Soviet Union, it appears likely that a high percentage of these scientists will work on military-related programs in these areas after they return home....

The Soviets correctly view the United States and several other Western countries as a continuing source of important and openly available scientific and technical information, which they take every opportunity to obtain access to. Some of the unclassified documents so acquired are previously classified materials which had been downgraded to unclassified through US procedures providing for automatic declassification after a stipulated period. When collected on a massive scale and centrally processed by the Soviets, this information becomes significant because it is collectively used by Soviet weapons designers and weapons countermeasure experts.

The Soviets also regularly attend high-technology trade shows, and attempt to visit commercial firms in the West, particularly small and medium-sized firms that are active in developing new technologies. These apparent trade promotion efforts often mask Soviet attempts to acquire emerging Western technological know-how before its military uses have been identified and government security controls have been applied. Emerging technologies are particularly vulnerable to foreign collection efforts of this type....

## Soviet Dependence on Western Technology

Today's recognition of the crucial role of Western technology in the development and production of Soviet weapon systems and related military equipment is not unique. Soviet dependence on Western technology was visible and clear-cut in the years immediately after World War II, when the Soviets stole Western nuclear secrets leading to their development of a nuclear weapon capability, and copied a US bomber in its entirety leading to production of their TU-4. To achieve major improvements in their military capability quickly, they exploited captured scientists and industrial plants and resorted to a combination of espionage, stealing, and copying Western systems.

Since that early period of near-complete reliance in the 1950s, the Soviets' dependence on Western technology to develop their weapons has decreased. Nevertheless, despite several decades of Soviet priorities focused on science, technology, and weapon systems, the Soviets, because of their inability to be innovative and effectively apply new technology to weapons developments, still depend on Western technology and equipment to develop and manufacture some of their advanced weapon systems more quickly.

Today, Soviet military designers carefully choose the Western designs, engineering approaches, and equipment most appropriate to their deficiencies and needs. These needs are still substantial and pervade almost every area of weapons technology and related manufacturing equipment.... In certain areas, notably the development of microelectronics, the

Soviets would have been incapable of achieving their present technical level without the acquisition of Western technology. In other areas, acquisitions have allowed the Soviets to reduce the indigenous effort they would otherwise have had to expend. . . .

## Soviet Gains

Thus, the Soviets and their Warsaw Pact allies have derived significant military gains from their acquisitions of Western technology, particularly in the strategic, aircraft, naval, tactical, microelectronics, and computer areas. This multifaceted Soviet acquisitions program has allowed the Soviets to:

• Save hundreds of millions of dollars in R&D costs, and years in R&D development lead time (see inset).

• Modernize critical sectors of their military industry and reduce engineering risks by following or copying proven Western designs, thereby limiting the rise in their military production costs.

• Achieve greater weapons performance than if they had to rely solely on their own technology.

• Incorporate countermeasures to Western weapons early in the development of their own weapon programs.

*"Today's recognition of the crucial role of Western technology in the development and production of Soviet weapon systems and related military equipment is not unique."*

These gains are evident in all areas of military weapons systems. While difficult to quantify, it is clear that the Western military expenditures needed to overcome or defend against the military capabilities derived by the acquisition of Western technology far outweigh the West's earnings from the legal sales to the Soviets of its equipment and technology. . . .

## Future Efforts

Future Soviet and Warsaw Pact acquisition efforts—including acquisitions by their intelligence services—are likely to concentrate on the sources of such component and manufacturing technologies, including:

• Defense contractors in the United States, Western Europe, and Japan who are the repositories of military development and manufacturing technologies.

• General producers of military-related auxiliary manufacturing equipment in the United States, Western Europe, and Japan.

• Small and medium-size firms and research centers that develop advanced component technology and designs, including advanced civil technologies with future military applications. . . .

The task of stopping Soviet Bloc intelligence operations aimed at Western military and industrial technologies already poses a formidable counterintelligence problem, both in the United States and abroad. . . . In response, the West will need to organize more effectively than it has in the past to protect its military, industrial, commercial, and scientific communities.

*The Central Intelligence Agency (CIA) is part of the Executive branch of the US Government. Its activities include collection and evaluation of intelligence information, coordination of intelligence activities with other government departments, and various covert and overt intelligence operations throughout the world.*

*"Soviet chances of surpassing the West now seem far more remote than they did at the time of Stalin's death."*

# Western Technology Has Not Significantly Advanced the USSR

Bruce Parrott

Almost exactly 26 years ago the Soviet Union launched Sputnik, the first man-made earth satellite, and sent the American public into a paroxysm of despair. Sputnik ignited American fears that the Soviet Union would soon surpass the United States technologically—if indeed it had not already done so—and pose an unprecedented economic and military challenge to American security. Today, however, American views of Soviet technological capacities have swung almost to the opposite extreme. Although many Americans are apprehensive about the expanding Soviet military capabilities, many also believe that the Soviet system is technologically stagnant and that without infusions of American know-how it might collapse....

## Stalin's Policy

The strengths and weaknesses of contemporary Soviet technology are primarily the result of institutions and policies that crystallized during the Stalin era. When Stalin and his supporters took control of the Soviet government in the late 1920's, an enormous gap separated the Soviet Union from the technological level of the capitalist powers. Determined to eliminate this gap, the Stalinists embarked on a program of forced development that caused vast human suffering but produced very rapid economic growth. Virtually all the growth was in industry, especially heavy industry, because the party leaders were striving desperately to construct a military shield against the outside world.

The Stalinists were convinced that for strategic as well as internal political reasons they must make the Soviet Union independent of the world economy. This conviction led to lavish Soviet spending on domestic research and development (R&D) during the

1930's—spending that far exceeded the proportion of gross national product (GNP) that most semideveloped countries today devote to R&D. The Stalinists, however, were also convinced that the risk of a major war within the decade was so great that they could not wait for domestic R&D to become an independent source of technological advance.

Therefore, during the early 1930's, they drew very heavily on imported capital equipment, external assistance in designing new factories, and other forms of technology transfers from abroad. Their aim was to make a quick transition from Western technology to native research and production, and as the decade progressed they turned decisively toward economic autarky.

## Successful Military Technology

The realm in which the Stalinists achieved their greatest technological successes was military weaponry. In the military sphere, they effectively combined early access to foreign technology with a dynamic R&D program. During the early 1930's, the regime was able to purchase models of Western weapons together with necessary manufacturing technology, and it used this know-how as a basis for further indigenous innovation. A fast pace of domestic weapons development was possible because military R&D enjoyed an overriding political priority that enabled innovators to surmount widespread shortages of supplies, skilled manpower and other administrative bottlenecks. In weapons production, unlike other industrial sectors, the "consumer," i.e., the military establishment, had the necessary clout to reject unsatisfactory output. Moreover, centrally organized competition among the designers of prospective weapons systems spurred an unusually high rate of indigenous innovation.

Lacking these special benefits, other industrial branches did not fare so well....

Despite these problems, Soviet industry grew at a

Bruce Parrott, "Technology and the Soviet System," *Current History,* October 1983. Copyright 1983 Current History, Inc. Reprinted with permission.

very rapid rate under Stalin. The principal reason for this was the regime's exceptional ability to mobilize and channel investments and manpower into more productive economic sectors. This mobilization capacity, which depended on rigorous central planning and a ruthless willingness to sacrifice popular consumption for the sake of industrial expansion, had special utility at a stage of economic development when many resources like agricultural labor and mineral deposits were still underutilized. In addition, the heavy commercial infusion of Western technology during the early 1930's (and to a lesser extent, American Lend-Lease assistance during World War II and the confiscation of German and Japanese technology at the end of the war) helped compensate for the barriers to native research and innovation. . . .

## Soviet Innovation Needed

In the post-Stalin period, however, innovation at operating enterprises has become more urgent. The aging of the factories built during an earlier era has heightened the need to modernize old technology. In addition, Stalin's successors, seeking to reduce internal pressures and to improve popular welfare, have fundamentally modified Stalin's draconian concentration on heavy industrial investment. President Leonid Brezhnev, especially, slowed the growth of capital investment and channeled more available investment resources into consumer-oriented sectors like agriculture. Since investment is now expanding more slowly and a smaller proportion of it is going into new industrial enterprises, the need for energetic innovation at established plants has become correspondingly greater. The recent slackening of growth in the labor force adds another complication. When less growth can be obtained by mobilizing new investment and labor for preferred industries, more widespread technological change is necessary to sustain an adequate rate of economic growth.

> "Many of the problems that bedevil domestic innovation also make it difficult to obtain maximum results from foreign equipment and know-how."

These circumstances should not cause us to ignore genuine Soviet technological accomplishments. Under Stalin, the country substantially reduced the gap separating it from the developed West. It made impressive advances in several basic industries, like iron and steel and electric power transmission, where progress does not depend heavily on scientific research; and in some segments of those industries it is now close to being on a par with Western technical achievements. The Soviet system also managed to

make very large advances in military weaponry, the research-intensive sector that enjoyed supreme political priority.

However, in other research-intensive industries, like chemical production and electronics, it has performed much more poorly and remains far behind Western standards. Thus, on balance, the country has made little if any progress since the late 1950's in catching up to the West. Although Soviet technology has continued to advance, Western technology has moved at least as fast, and Soviet chances of surpassing the West now seem far more remote than they did at the time of Stalin's death.

## Western Technology

The gradual recognition of this fact provoked considerable dismay among Stalin's successors, and they responded in two ways. One response, advocated by many economists and specialists, was to seek large new transfers of Western technology to bolster Soviet progress. The rapid postwar growth of intra-Western trade and technology transfers was providing important new economic gains to the Soviet Union's main Western rivals, thereby increasing the competitive burden of Soviet technological isolation. The regime's second form of response to its persisting technological lag was to restructure domestic research and industry in order to accelerate indigenous innovation. Adumbrated in the Khrushchev years, both impulses became more pronounced under Brezhnev.

To date, neither response has had a major impact on Soviet economic performance. For one thing, the infusion of Western technology has not been so large as is popularly believed. Soviet imports of Western capital equipment have climbed sharply over the last 15 years, but they began from a very low level and still constitute a modest share of Soviet domestic investment in equipment—roughly five to seven percent of the total in the late 1970's. This share is far smaller than it was in the first years of Stalin's industrialization drive. Transfers of unembodied technology—know-how in the form of licenses, technical literature, and exchanges of experts—are also limited. For political reasons the regime remains wary of economic dependence on the West and is especially hesitant to participate in the extensive international exchanges of people and information that facilitate the diffusion of advanced technology. More than most Western critics of technology transfers to the Soviet Union realize, the regime's attempts to avoid ideological contamination from the West have hampered its efforts to absorb Western technical knowledge.

Another reason that the infusion of Western technology has not yielded more is that many of the problems that bedevil domestic innovation also make it difficult to obtain maximum results from foreign equipment and know-how. In the 1970's, Western and Soviet observers both arrived, with different emotions, at the conclusion that Western technology could serve as an effective substitute for domestic reform in the Soviet Union. This conclusion, however, exaggerates the possibility of overcoming the system's defects simply by obtaining more Western inputs. Soviet economists, for instance, have traditionally complained that many domestically engineered factories are inefficient because construction takes so long that basic designs become outdated before the plants start operating.

## Assimilation Problem

The same problem has affected the assimilation of recent capital imports. A study of large industrial installations imported from Great Britain shows that the elapsed time between the signing of an import agreement and the commissioning of the installation was two or three times the interval required for comparable British exports to other Western countries. Labor productivity at these installations also tended to be lower than at similar facilities in the West—no doubt partly because Soviet plant managers still felt compelled to hoard surplus labor as protection against unexpected demands from the central planners.

It remains true that capital imports from the West have been installed faster than Soviet-made equipment, and they have undoubtedly conferred real gains in productivity in comparison with indigenous Soviet technology. But these gains are limited by the internal inefficiencies of the economic system. Although the recent influx of Western technology has probably added something in the vicinity of half a percentage point to Soviet industrial growth each year, this has been far from sufficient to stem the country's steady loss of economic momentum.

Only by improving domestic research and innovation will the Soviet Union significantly upgrade its ability to benefit from Western technology and—above all—its ability to move beyond the levels of that technology....

## Technological "Carrots" and "Sticks"

The past American efforts to use technological "carrots" and "sticks" to shape Soviet political behavior have not been entirely without effect. In the early 1970's, for example, the Brezhnev administration allowed many Soviet Jews to emigrate, and it seems evident that one motive for this unusual step was to obtain greater access to United States technology by placating an aroused American public. On the whole, however, the political results of American economic blandishments and punishments have been extremely limited.

To begin with, Soviet leaders have vigorously resisted accepting any overt linkage between trade and their own conduct. In addition, United States

policy has been inconsistent; its focus has oscillated between the Soviet regime's domestic and foreign behavior, and it has tried to elicit major Soviet concessions in exchange for relatively small amounts of technology. Finally, most of the Western technology exported to the Soviet Union has not come from the United States (in contrast to Western exports of agricultural goods). The American share of Western high technology exports to the Soviet Union was only 13.3 percent in 1974 and by 1979 had declined to a mere 6.5 percent. Many other Western nations supplying such technology are reluctant to attach political conditions to East-West trade, and this has worked to the Soviet Union's advantage. President Ronald Reagan's unsuccessful effort to block European technical assistance for construction of the Soviet gas pipeline to West Europe is a vivid example.

---

*"Only by improving domestic research and innovation will the Soviet Union significantly upgrade its ability to benefit from Western technology."*

---

In the future, Western technology might conceivably become a more useful instrument for influencing Soviet conduct if the members of the Western alliance were able to move toward agreement on more stable and consistent criteria governing the provision of technical assistance to the Soviet Union. To approach this goal, however, will require more give-and-take among NATO (North Atlantic Treaty Organization) members and a much greater American willingness to sacrifice lucrative grain deals with the Soviet Union when asking the Europeans and Japanese to cut back their trade with the U.S.S.R. in high technology.

## Military Technology

The role of technical assistance in East-West diplomacy also raises the issue of military technology. In the last decade, some Western officials have become convinced that growing transfers of Western know-how are contributing to the steady advancement of Soviet military weaponry. In this view, the current export controls administered under the 1950 CoCom agreement (in which NATO members and Japan agreed on a nonbinding basis to restrict strategic exports to the Communist world) have failed to block this development. Some officials have urged a large expansion of the list of exports prohibited under the CoCom agreement.

With congressional authorization, the United States Defense Department also attempted to devise new ways to restrict the Soviet acquisition of military-related "critical technologies" through active forms of transfer such as Western training of Soviet bloc personnel, extensive contracts among technical specialists, and the like. There can be no doubt that important lapses in the control of weapons-related technologies have occurred. Probably the most serious was the export to the Soviet Union of micro ball bearing grinders that could be used to enhance the accuracy of Soviet missile guidance systems.

*"The political results of American economic blandishments and punishments have been extremely limited."*

The problem is to decide how to obstruct direct Soviet military applications of Western technology, which all the Western allies oppose in principle, without inflicting unacceptable costs on the Western countries themselves. Widening the list of prohibited exports is not the answer. This step could divert attention from control of the most vital military-related technologies and would undermine Western cooperation by exacerbating West European suspicions that the United States is pursuing economic warfare against the Soviet Union rather than trying to control the technology directly applicable to weapons production.

## Creating Undesirable Obstacles

The critical technologies approach also has major drawbacks. In practice, it has proved difficult to apply, and there is a serious danger that it will gradually be expanded to encompass not only Western commercial knowledge but also the findings of unclassified non-commercial research. The effect would be to create obstacles to scientific discussion and communication within the West that could easily harm the pace of technological development in the United States more than it inhibited the progress of Soviet weaponry.

Rather than move in this direction, the United States government would be wiser to put the emphasis on other measures: increasing the number and expertise of Western officials monitoring commercial flows of technology to the East; urging the Western allies that do not include their defense ministries in decisions on such transfers to do so; and improving Western governments' understanding of the potential military impact of specific transfers by underwriting ongoing, across-the-board studies of Soviet manufacturing technologies.

These are only partial solutions. But in dealing with the problem the United States should not weaken its own capacities for technological innovation, which constitute one of the principal American strengths in the long-term competition with the Soviet Union.

*Bruce Parrott is Associate Professor of Soviet Studies at the School of Advanced International Studies, Johns Hopkins University.*

*"We in the Soviet Union are for safeguarding and broadening human rights."*

# The Soviets Have Basic Human Rights

## Georgi A. Arbatov interviewed by Willem Oltmans

*Editor's note: The following viewpoint is an excerpt from* The Soviet Viewpoint, *in which Dutch author Willem Oltmans interviews Georgi A. Arbatov, the Russian director of the Institute of USA and Canada.*

**Arbatov:** How can one be against human rights nowadays? It's the same as to be against motherhood. So to do more than repeat political platitudes you have to be concrete and specific. Speaking about the USSR, I would like to stress our deep and long-standing commitment to human rights. It's for human rights that we made our Revolution and then defended it against foreign intervention and a Nazi invasion. More than that—it fell to the Soviet Union to develop a new, broader approach to human rights by including social rights largely neglected before that time, but vitally important for the overwhelming majority of our people and other peoples as well. It took the world community half a century to recognize the significance of those rights in the form of the U.N. covenants.

**Oltmans:** Would you say that in the field of social rights the Soviet Union is more advanced than the West?

**Arbatov:** Yes, and this is only natural. At the time of the Revolution in Russia, social rights and freedoms were of prime importance for people who were hungry and lived in conditions of abject poverty, and for the illiterate peasants constituting the majority of the population. These were the right to work, the freedom from hunger and starvation, the right to have a shelter, the right to have land to till, the right to be educated, the right to receive medical care, and so on. And for a country devastated first by World War I, then by a civil war and the intervention of Western powers, the right to live in peace was of the greatest importance. These and many other social

rights still occupy the highest places in the set of values of our society. Of course, our constitution guarantees the usual political rights just as well, including freedom of speech, freedom of conscience and religion, freedom of the press, and freedom of assembly, although the understanding of these rights and freedoms here differs from, say, the standard American approach. In general, I am sure that, given a serious balanced approach, there could be a thorough and useful dialogue about human rights. Unfortunately, in the United States and in the West as a whole, this very important and complex question was turned into a symbol of a fierce propaganda campaign against the USSR.

## Petty Priorities

**Oltmans:** But it is inexplicable to Westerners that a large and powerful nation like the Soviet Union should be so petty in not allowing citizens who prefer to leave to obtain a passport and go.

**Arbatov:** Well, Mr. Oltmans, every state and government acts in accordance with its own understanding of its interests, priorities, and attitudes toward problems. And you cannot escape here from the influence of historic traditions and historic experiences. There is a great difference in this respect between the United States and the Soviet Union. With the exception of the American Indians, who were forced from their land and almost completely annihilated, Americans are a nation of immigrants or descendants of immigrants, and it is quite logical that other peoples' freedom to emigrate has become sort of a natural right in their minds. But in this country, attitudes and sentiments are different. During its history the Soviet Union witnessed two waves of large-scale emigration. The first wave occurred right after the Revolution and the civil war. These emigrés were, for the most part, bitter enemies of our new society. They had participated in an armed struggle against the new Soviet power, hand in hand with foreign invading forces. Among those who emigrated in the second wave—during and after World War II—were a lot of collaborators with the Nazis and war criminals. As a result, a very definite attitude was formed against those who wanted to leave the country. And the word *emigrant* became almost synonymous to the word *traitor*.

**Oltmans:** Is this still a widespread attitude?

**Arbatov:** The situation began to change gradually, first as a result of migration across the borders shared with socialist countries, then through mixed marriages and family reunions and changes in the political atmosphere due to detente. Later, as you know, there was increased emigration to Israel, or, under that pretext, to the West. But this doesn't mean that the traditional attitude has disappeared completely. Speaking frankly, those who emigrate are still far from being regarded as exemplary citizens and patriots. And I think you wouldn't dispute that there are good reasons for such an attitude.

**Oltmans:** What do you mean?

## Emigration Is Rejection

**Arbatov:** Emigrating from here to the United States is not like leaving, say, Holland for the United States or the United Kingdom. When somebody leaves this country for the West, it means that he or she rejects the whole set of social values and ideals of the Soviet nation, which were born, developed, and defended through many hardships and ordeals. This also creates certain emotions at the grass roots. The same could be true, to a certain extent, of America. I am sure that a decision to emigrate to a Western European country or Canada would be treated with tolerance. But imagine the reaction of a sheriff from Texas or even an ordinary law-abiding and church-going citizen in a small midwestern town to the news of a neighbor planning to leave for the Soviet Union, Bulgaria, or the German Democratic Republic.

---

*"It's for human rights that we made our Revolution and then defended it against foreign intervention and a Nazi invasion."*

---

On the whole, whether we like it or not, certain restrictions on emigration and immigration exist in practically every country. The United States, for instance, has severe restrictions on immigration, which is no less a humanitarian problem than emigration.

**Oltmans:** Only in Utopia will all restrictions cease to exist someday.

**Arbatov:** Of course, everything is on the move, things change. I firmly believe that the time will

come when all restrictions on international migration of people will be lifted. But until then we obviously should treat this matter with a lot of understanding, realizing that it involves some serious problems, which should be reckoned with and not turned into a propaganda trump card. At the same time, I'm sure that our relations and rules concerning emigration are really not the heart of the matter in the campaign for human rights launched a few years ago by the United States.

## Human Rights Pressure

**Oltmans:** What do you mean?

**Arbatov:** I mean that this human-rights campaign has different purposes: to put pressure on the USSR, to arouse anti-Sovietism, to improve the American image around the world, and to restore the foreign policy consensus inside the United States. Human rights themselves were not what the Carter administration cared about very much. The United States often turns out to be the staunchest supporter of authoritarian regimes. And whenever such a regime is toppled—in Kampuchea, Iran, Nicaragua, or Afghanistan—why is Washington so enraged and vengeful?

**Oltmans:** But no matter how Washington interprets human rights, the problem itself remains vital.

**Arbatov:** Of course it's important. We in the Soviet Union are for safeguarding and broadening human rights. It's part of our ideology, our laws, our entire outlook. But when the human rights rhetoric is deliberately used to foment distrust and hostility in Soviet-American relations, to undermine detente, it has nothing to do with human rights as such. The noble idea is perverted and abused.

I think Americans should try to understand that if they are so strongly for human rights, this implies they must also be for detente. War and preparation for war, international tensions and crises—these are the factors most detrimental to democracy and social progress. The McCarthyist witch-hunts of the late forties and early fifties would not have been possible without the cold-war atmosphere.

I think it was Harvard University sociologist Daniel Bell who once said that, during the heyday of the Cold War, America was a "mobilized society." By the same token, the CIA and the FBI were set up in periods of tensions to fight an "external enemy." All their methods of operation, subversive activities, and psychological warfare, developed for cold-war purposes, were then turned against Americans themselves, including, as Watergate revealed, even political opponents within the elite. It may be remembered, by the way, that the Watergate "plumbers," when asked in the court about their profession, replied after some hesitation that they were "anticommunists." The same logic is unfurling now that the second edition of the Cold War is being issued from the White House. In a cold war-type situation, governments like those of Chile, South Korea, Pakistan, or El Salvador can afford to do whatever they please with civil liberties and still get American aid and support.

## Discredit the USSR

**Oltmans:** Even if American concern about human rights should be thoroughly political and self-serving, why wouldn't the Soviet Union try to outmaneuver Washington, "disarm" it, if you will, by changing its mind on some of the sore points that Americans keep pointing to?

**Arbatov:** To change our minds on some of the sore points would change nothing. One has to realize that in this human rights campaign we deal with an attempt to modify through constant, ever-increasing pressure our domestic order according to Western liking, and at the same time to discredit the USSR before the world public. Specific demands might sometimes look rather modest—to let N or M out of jail (though they were convicted strictly according to the Soviet law), to permit X or Y to emigrate (the reason of refusal being, as a rule, that their former jobs involved access to classified information), to change a procedure of importation and sales of some Western periodicals, and so on. But we have learned through hard experience that with every concession grows an appetite for further demands and pressures. This is quite understandable, because for many organizers of this campaign these demands do not reflect a sincere concern over human rights, but serve as a pretext for stepping up an attack against our institutions and values. There were times when a real war was waged to crush this system. Then came the Cold War, and now other devices, including the human rights campaign, are being utilized.

**Oltmans:** Are you not exaggerating? Could it be a manifestation of the Soviet paranoid attitude to the West?

## Basic Internal Changes

**Arbatov:** Not at all, I assure you, Mr. Oltmans, and, please, don't think that I attach a great importance to this campaign as such; but the point is it can't be viewed in isolation. It should be seen against the background of certain military efforts, foreign policy maneuvers, and other propaganda campaigns. It would be proper to recall, for instance, that in some key American foreign policy documents, like NSC-68, basic changes in our internal structure were put forward as a *sine qua non* for peaceful coexistence. Many actions in U.S. foreign policy in recent years reflect those guidelines. More than that—somewhere deep in the American political conscience there still lives the thought that we are something illegitimate, created not by God but by the Devil, and that our existence in its present form should be ended somehow.

**Oltmans:** This is too intangible.

**Arbatov:** Well, take a specific example—"Captive Nations' Week," celebrated every July by the U.S. Congress. As if this were not enough, the president personally signs a solemn declaration, which has been a routine practice for many years now. But what is its real message? It means, as explained in many U.S. commentaries, that, in the opinion of the United States, the Soviet Union lawlessly holds in its grip fourteen republics, which, therefore, should be "liberated." These include vast territories in Siberia—called DVR—the "Cherkessia," "Idel-Urals,"

---

*"For a country devastated first by World War I, then by a civil war and the intervention of Western powers, the right to live in peace was of the greatest importance."*

---

and "Kazakia." I really don't know what all these crazy names mean, but my feeling is that they include the Urals, the Lower Volga basin, the Kuban River region, Don, Northern Caucasus, and some other regions. In other words, we are left with an area extending approximately from Moscow to Leningrad, north to south, and from Smolensk to Vladimir, west to east. I wonder how Americans would react if our Supreme Soviet and President Brezhnev issued solemn proclamations supporting a campaign questioning U.S. sovereignty beyond, say, an area from Boston to Washington and from Baltimore to Detroit, declaring that all the rest should be "liberated"? One could argue that the southern states were kept in the union only by means of war, that others were taken by force from France and Mexico, and that the whole territory originally had been stolen from the most captive nation of all—the American Indians.

## Goal of Continued Progress

**Oltmans:** But most Americans ignore "Captive Nations' Week." Why do you take it so seriously?

**Arbatov:** We far from exaggerate its importance. But neither can we completely ignore such things. To finish this theme I'd like to summarize.

We consider the matter of human rights very important. A lot has been and will be done in this area in our country. We know that we haven't reached an ideal situation yet. Who has? The continued progress of democracy remains our basic goal.

Another point: the propaganda campaign launched in connection with human rights by the United States has in fact nothing to do with those rights. We see it as one of the instruments of anti-Soviet policy, and let there be no illusions about our yielding to it. What the West really wants from us in this field is that we help with our own hands to organize anticommunist, anti-Soviet activities aimed at undermining our own social and political system. We aren't going to cooperate in destabilizing our social institutions, just as we would not expect the American government to do so if we were to make such demands on them.

A third point: what makes this campaign look particularly dubious to us is that the United States, in our view, has no right whatsoever to teach others the basics of human rights, because, as is true with many other problems, this one begins at home. It is very difficult for us, for instance, to believe in the value of the American system of free speech when the American news media have become such huge private enterprises, strongly motivated by profit, and catering to the tastes of their owners and the interests of corporate advertisers rather than to the interests of the public.

## Harassment in America

Denied access to the mass media, you can scream almost anything you want in America without being heard, though sometimes at the risk of being spied upon by the FBI or the CIA, like those young people who were persecuted for their opposition to the war in Southeast Asia. We in the Soviet Union have read about congressional inquiries into the illegal activities of the CIA regarding the Watergate scandal. We know that President Lyndon Johnson used J. Edgar Hoover to spy not only on communists and other radicals, but on respected congressman as well. Richard Nixon even had a list of enemies drawn up. We know that if the authorities in the United States deem it necessary, they not only harass people, but even kill them. This happened, for example, to leaders of the Black Panthers, a number of whom were murdered in cold blood by the police. Not to speak of assassins who killed or wounded dozens of civil rights leaders from Martin Luther King to Vernon Jordan. And those responsible seldom get punished. Remember Kent State University? And what happened to the American Indian movement? What about numerous black activists sentenced and kept in prison for years on trumped-up charges? You would agree that this can only make us more skeptical toward the United States as a mentor on the subject of human rights.

**Oltmans:** Yes, but in spite of these alarming examples it is still possible for a dissident CIA agent like Frank Snepp to publish a book on the crimes perpetrated by Americans in Vietnam and elsewhere. Such a publication in the Soviet Union would be unthinkable.

**Arbatov:** Publication of Frank Snepp's book was possible a couple of years ago. Whether it would be possible now is doubtful. By the way, while Frank Snepp did get his book published, the CIA retaliated through the courts, and he's been severely punished financially. As a result of the legislation passed by Congress in 1980, I'm afraid that he and others like him may suffer much greater hardships. There are numerous indications that the wave of revelations has come to an end. The recent changes in the status of the intelligence bodies and secret police are a throwback to the status quo ante. On the other hand, when you talk about the Soviet Union, you forget that the practices of our security organs underwent very critical scrutiny and revision at a time when the CIA and FBI were still considered sacred cows. In the fifties, the Soviet Communist Party openly stated that the security organs had violated laws and abused power. There were court proceedings against high officials of those bodies, and those found guilty were severely punished, in some cases with the death penalty. The organs were restructured and put under effective party control. Whenever these matters are discussed by the big Western media, there is a clear double standard applied. No matter what changes occur in our country, no matter what we do, we are accused of being undemocratic. At the same time, violations of human rights in the West are always minimized and regarded as exceptions to the rule.

**Oltmans:** Without defending the violence in American society, Americans have never experienced anything close to the Gulag Archipelago.

---

*"Speaking about the USSR, I would like to stress our deep and long-standing commitment to human rights."*

---

**Arbatov:** I do not consider it proper, Mr. Oltmans, or in good taste, to refer to the tragic events of our past, so painfully remembered by the Soviet people, using a term that has become a cliché of anti-Soviet propaganda. As I've mentioned earlier, the party took strong measures to correct the situation and to punish those who were guilty. But since you've touched upon this problem, I would like to emphasize that one of the main conditions that made possible the repressions in Stalin's time was the very hostile environment that our country then had to deal with.

**Oltmans:** The threat from Nazi Germany?

## Intense Internal Struggles

**Arbatov:** The Nazi threat was perhaps the high point. But the situation was pretty rough even before that. You see, our country lived through a period of intense political struggles after the 1917 Revolution. The counterrevolution would not give up. It was fighting dirty, and it was assisted from the outside on a large scale. Some of our leaders and ambassadors were assassinated. There were repeated military incursions into our territory. Foreign intelligence services were actively operating within the country. We were expecting a big war to erupt sooner or later, and, of course, after Hitler came to power on an anticommunist and anti-Soviet platform, the external situation deteriorated dramatically. Those were the special historical external conditions that made mass repression and crimes against our constitution and ideals possible.

---

## "We know that we haven't reached an ideal situation yet. Who has?"

---

We have not forgotten those tragic events and do not expect others to do so. What we are against are the attempts to interpret our whole history in the light of those events. For us, their meaning even back in those hard times was quite different. We have a lot of truly historic achievements on our record, achievements of worldwide significance. We have made economic, social, and cultural progress at a speed unknown to man before. There has been a rebirth of a people who used to be among the most oppressed and exploited of all the civilized nations. There was the victory over Nazi Germany and the removal of that threat to humanity. There have been a number of tremendously important firsts— economic planning, social developments such as equality of nationalities, equal rights of women, making medical care and education available to the whole population, and many, many other things. There is a lot in our history we can be proud of.

### Costs of Progress

**Oltmans:** Have you ever tried to compare the costs of progress in different societies?

**Arbatov:** Well, this is an extremely difficult task. Human history is too complex and multidimensional to quantify. There is hardly any developed methodology for such comparisons. But I have no doubt that the costs of progress in a capitalist society were higher. First, you have to take into account the wars under capitalism. It was only capitalism, with its inherent drive for technology, first of all military technology, coupled with insatiable lust for markets and sources of raw materials, that made wars both worldwide and unprecedentedly devastating. This alone accounts for the loss of millions of human lives. Second, there was colonialism, which preceded capitalism, but which became a worldwide phenomenon and a precondition for rapid development and accumulation of the wealth of most capitalist countries. The cost again was many millions of human lives, as well as brutal exploitation, colonial wars, and political oppression, keeping a majority of mankind in a condition of backwardness. Third, capitalism has not always been associated with liberal democracy. In many countries this social system has taken the most oppressive political form—fascism with its bloody terror, military dictatorships, and other features of ruthless totalitarianism.

*Georgi A. Arbatov is director of the Institute of USA and Canadian Studies in Moscow. Willem Oltmans is a Dutch author and lecturer.*

# The Soviets Do Not Have Basic Human Rights

Yuri Tuvim interviewed by Robert James Bidinotto

*Dr. Yuri Tuvim emigrated to America from the Soviet Union in 1976. A research scientist who now lives and works in the Boston suburbs, Tuvim is passionately concerned about what he sees as deadly misconceptions Americans hold about the nature of the Soviet system....*

*Tuvim was interviewed recently by Robert James Bidinotto [contributing editor to* On Principle, *a publication dedicated to "reason, human rights, and capitalism"].*

**Bidinotto:** You have often said that the entire Soviet system is based on a lie, and that their biggest fear is that their nature will be uncovered. What do you mean?

**Tuvim:** The Soviet authorities pretend that whatever they do is for the well-being of their people. The reality is that they have no concern other than the well-being of the officials.

Soviet people can have a comparatively tolerable life—if they don't make waves, if they have the connections to get decent clothing, a better apartment, better food. But if you raise your voice to fight injustice, you immediately find yourself in trouble.

All the Soviet newspapers are full of unpleasant facts about Soviet life. But there is an unwritten law: You cannot generalize. Yes, they say, there are some unpleasant facts, bad deeds, injustices—but only in single cases. They are not the product of the system. They are the product of bad management, or some isolated bad authority. But the system as a whole is absolutely perfect; it only needs to be improved in these isolated cases. And they pretend it is the most democratic system in the world.

But look at the facts. They can't feed their own people. They have shortages of everything. Labor morale is terrible. Medical care is "free"—but of dismal quality. Education is "free"—but to get into a university, you have to have connections, or be absolutely outstanding and non-Jewish. And they have never had a free election. There is only one candidate on the ballot for each office. The Party authorities "advise" the local officials to select these particular persons. You actually don't "run" for office: if they select you, it means you are already elected.

They use all the democratic appearances—it's like a staged play. The democratic terminology is retained just as a matter of historic tradition, and as a camouflage.

## Inhuman Acts

**Bidinotto:** Soviet actions are often so inhuman as to be inexplicable by our own interpretation of self-interest. How do they perceive their interests? What basically motivates the men in the Kremlin?

**Tuvim:** Compare how the two systems work. There is no way for our President to remain in office after January 20th of his final term. And the outgoing President is still respected; he retains his dignity and possessions; he is a person.

But once the Soviet leaders are out of office—they are nothing. So the well-being of the so-called Soviet leadership is completely interwoven with the well-being of their *system*. They have a primary interest in remaining in power, because this power gives them *everything*—and without it, they lose everything.

Power itself is very attractive. Also, to be in charge means to have a very good life, unlike most people in the Soviet Union. They travel abroad, their offspring can enter the universities, very warm places are secured for them in the state apparatus, they have very good apartments. It's like a caste society—a caste of rulers. And the only way for them to survive is to continue the existence of the system, which gives them everything. It's like riding a tiger: try to get off.

"Meeting the Soviet Threat—An Interview with Yuri Tuvim," by Robert James Bidinotto, *On Principle*, August 20, 1984. Reprinted from ON PRINCIPLE, a pro-capitalist newsletter published bi-weekly by Amwell Publishing, Inc., Princeton Professional Park, 601 Ewing Street, Suite B-7, Princeton NJ 08542. Subscriptions are $45.

**Bidinotto:** In other words, they're slaves to their own system.

**Tuvim:** Yes. And also, they cannot introduce any democratic changes to their own system. Because if they start to introduce some little bit of liberalization, this process, once started, cannot stop; and as a result of this process, they will be out. They could be eventually tried for crimes against humanity or whatever. So they are slaves of the system.

How can we force them to make their system even a little more human? We should apply tremendous pressure on them. They should feel the public opinion of the world, through all the pores of their skin, that they are not legitimate members of the world community. They are criminals.

**Bidinotto:** Then what function does communist propaganda and ideology serve? Does anybody there still believe any of it—or is it just an abstract way to legitimize an essentially criminal system?

## Cynical Obedience

**Tuvim:** You answered your own question. Nobody believes in communist ideology; it is dead. But they use it, because they are very sophisticated. We in the West condemn our own faults so outrageously, that they use our own accounts in our press to support their ideological points: the capitalist society is unfair; it's brutal; it's for the rich and against people. They use our press to brainwash their own people.

The Soviet people are cynical; but the rulers aren't afraid of cynical people. Cynical people do not threaten the well-being of the system: they obey. And all the rallies, meetings, condemnations of Sakharov or the United States have only one internal purpose: the authorities are holding their hands on the pulse of the people. If you participate in the rallies and are obedient, the authorities have no reason to be afraid of you. They want you to ruin your self-esteem. Because nobody wants to be at the rallies, and 99% do not believe what they say and hear. But if you go to the meetings and participate, and condemn imperialism and Solzynitsyn and dissidents—now you are "reliable." Just read Orwell: the "minute of hatred"—that's what they're doing.

**Bidinotto:** You've said that "we are dangerous for them simply because we exist." What kind of threat does our mere existence pose for the Soviet Union?

**Tuvim:** All human beings are looking for justice and dignity. The existence of the free world, and the capitalist system of free enterprise—the example of a society where human rights are preserved—is very seductive. Also, the Soviet people know that the material level of life in the West is very much higher than that in the Soviet Union. They know that democracy and capitalism are successful in making life here better every day.

Because our democratic system is turned inward and looking for ways to make life here better, we have no external call. But a totalitarian system— which cannot produce enough for the people, and cannot produce a decent society internally—can only survive if its major thrust is turned outward.

So the Soviet Union simply cannot afford peaceful co-existence. Their instinct for self-preservation tells them that if peaceful co-existence is permitted—if countries start to exchange ideas, if people travel— then that will be the first day of the end of the Soviet system, or of any totalitarian empire.

*"They have never had a free election. There is only one candidate on the ballot for each office."*

Their goal is to continue their existence. But they can achieve their goal only through the destruction of democracy.

## World Domination

**Bidinotto:** Are they primarily interested in world conquest, in the accumulation of people and territory—or are they just trying to stamp out any system whose existence exposes the lie that underlies their own system?

**Tuvim:** I don't think that they are interested in world conquest. They are interested in world domination. I think that there is a difference. Conquest means that Soviet troops will be in the United States and Europe. And they are realists, they are professionals, they understand that 260 million people cannot conquer the whole world.

But they *can* ruin democracy. They can dominate the world. They can make a big production source out of the United States. And people will live here and work, and will obey orders from the Kremlin, and will not challenge the Kremlin's rulers. There are a lot of misguided people here who will work for the Soviets, just like the pacifists of Europe. There are a lot of dissatisfied people here who don't like the capitalist system, who say more socialism would be better—and who don't realize that they would be the first ones eliminated.

**Bidinotto:** So you see their aim as world domination...

**Tuvim:** Yes—commanding obedience, and doing anything to undermine democracy. Look, they claim to be the world's greatest democracy. But what did they do in the Falkland War between Great Britain and Argentina? It was absolutely obvious that Argentina was an aggressor, and one of the most brutal juntas in recent history. But the Soviet Union supported Argentina. Why? Argentina was not threatening the Soviet system—because Argentina was not a democracy. Great Britain was the democratic party. So—with whom to side? Side with the brutal junta against democracy.

**Bidinotto:** Same thing with the Hitler-Stalin Pact.

**Tuvim:** Same thing with the Hitler-Stalin Pact.

## Brother Dictatorships

**Bidinotto:** Those things really shock those who take communist ideology seriously. But you're saying that such dictatorships are essentially brothers under the skin, and don't pose the threat to each other that freedom does.

**Tuvim:** Look at Rumania. Rumania, in foreign policy, behaves much more independently than, say, Czechoslovakia. But the Soviets have no intention of invading Rumania, because internally, Rumania is a very harsh totalitarian country. But the first sign of liberalization in any of the countries of Eastern Europe immediately arouses Soviet vigilance, and sooner or later they do something about it.

**Bidinotto:** On the one hand, you say they are out to destroy democracy. But on the other, they seem to *need* the spectre of an external enemy or threat. How do you explain this irony?

**Tuvim:** That's very simple. Even if they had no external enemy, their system would still be a failure. But how would they justify the shortages of everything? They need the external enemy to keep people under control and to justify hardship. They say, We cannot produce enough butter because we have to produce missiles; and we have to produce missiles because the United States is going to attack us tomorrow.

---

*"It's like a caste society — a caste of rulers."*

---

**Bidinotto:** I sense from your comments that you don't think the Soviet rulers believe a nuclear war is winnable.

## Threat, Not War, Needed

**Tuvim:** No, I don't think the Kremlin is going to start a war. They are not suicidal; they are not idiots; they are reasonable—in *that* sense. And they don't *need* war. Why would they need a war—look at the world map. The Soviet empire is growing. They are now in Aden, Mozambique, Ethiopia, Angola, Cuba, Syria, and so on. They are enslaving more and more territories and peoples, by themselves or through proxies. So why do they need war? They need the *threat* of war—to intimidate people here to obey their commands, and not insist on human rights.

American so-called "liberals" say: The problem of war and peace is the primary concern of ours; so let's talk about war and peace. Human rights? Yeah, it would be better if the Soviet Union preserved human rights; but look what *we* are doing with the world. We are also not very good about human rights.

They distract public attention from the main problem—human rights—to this secondary issue of the fear of war. So people are talking about war, and the nuclear freeze, and we're spending all our time and resources discussing all these secondary issues. But the primary issue is human rights. Because if the people of the Soviet Union had the chance to express their opinion openly, the Soviet Union would no longer be a threat to the world, and the threat of war would be immediately eliminated.

**Bidinotto:** Why do they spend billions on propaganda, and then do things which are an affront to world public opinion?

## Unscrupulous Monsters

**Tuvim:** They are slave drivers—unscrupulous monsters. In any choice between bad publicity or saving the system, they choose the system. They know that we are not persistent, that we are polarized, that we have a lot of fellow travelers here who will whitewash their actions. Two years after the invasion of Czechoslovakia, we started "detente" and were ready to forgive and forget. Afghanistan? How long did it take for us to lift our grain embargo—two years? So they know it takes only about two years for Western public opinion to forget and forgive.

**Bidinotto:** The Korean airliner—already we've forgotten about that.

**Tuvim:** They know that Western public opinion has no endurance. Sakharov—we don't know if he's alive or dead in Gorky, yet the French president still decided to go to Moscow because he was concerned about war and peace. So why should Moscow care about its public image?

The policies of detente and peaceful co-existence have an inherent flaw. They do not address the root of the problem: the situation *inside* of the Soviet Union, the nature of the Soviet system, human rights. What did we reach after all the years of detente? Now we are facing their enormous military build-up. And our inconsistency has made the Kremlin absolutely aware that whatever they do, they will come through unpunished. Our appeasing and conciliatory concessions simply provoke their aggressive, blatantly belligerent behavior.

Is the well of our patience unlimited? How long can we allow them to challenge us? I think there is a big danger of miscalculation. We are sending them very confusing signals; and they might interpret this as weakness and do something really serious. And we will be forced to respond, as a result, and have a war. So appeasement actually brings war closer.

**Bidinotto:** Would you address the issue of the so-called peace movement?

**Tuvim:** I can only repeat what (Soviet dissident) Vladimir Bukovsky said in his essay, "The Peace Movement and the Soviet Union." The peace movement is very convenient for the Soviet Union because it distracts public attention from the primary problem. The key to war and peace is in Soviet hands—and the peace movement is marching in New York. Maybe they feel that they are doing something. Actually, they've done nothing but send the Soviet Union another very bad signal. And the Soviets use the peace movement in their internal propaganda. Worse, the movement treats the United States and the Soviet Union as on the same moral level. But the nature of the two countries is totally different. It is a big disservice to compare them.

> *"They need the threat of war to intimidate people here to obey their commands, and not insist on human rights."*

Everything starts with terminology. If you use the wrong word, the chain of logic will bring you to the wrong conclusion. Look at our terminology. We say "President of the Union of Soviet Socialist Republics" when none of those words are true. I think it was Stalin who said, when he was asked why they had chosen such a long name for the country: "Every time the people repeat it, it will serve our propaganda." Because there is no union; the Soviet— or council of deputies—is just window dressing; there is no socialism; there is no republic. It is a dictatorship. There is no President—he was never elected. The terminology we use only legitimizes and white-washes their system.

## Source of Evil

We must call things by their right names. I think President Reagan was absolutely right when he said the Soviet Union was the source of evil, and he should have elaborated more. The biggest task of American officials is to preserve this country. To do that, they need to explain the nature of the Soviet Union to the American people.

Our military buildup is a necessary but not sufficient answer to the Soviet threat. What is necessary is a consensus of public opinion about the danger. The best formula for survival is not appeasement, concessions, detente, or even "peace through strength" (which is much better)—but knowledge, will, and strength. We have to know our enemy; we have to develop a national will to resist— and learn when and how to resist; and we need military strength. As the old proverb put it, if you want to have peace, be ready to fight.

*Yuri Tuvim emigrated to the US from the Soviet Union in 1976.*

*"The State Planning Committee, the Communist Party and the managerial elite are hardly likely to give up their control over the labor force."*

viewpoint 72

# The Soviet Government Is to Blame for the Oppression of Its People

David E. Powell

A number of Soviet sociologists and industrial psychologists have pointed out that the lack of industrial democracy—Soviet workers have virtually no influence over their wages, hours or working conditions—has given rise to feelings of powerlessness. Such feelings in turn present a major barrier to job satisfaction and to raising productivity. These specialists argue that industrial morale will improve only if a more democratic "microclimate" is established at individual enterprises—if, that is, "everybody, regardless of his position, feels that he is significant and necessary." Some have urged that workers be permitted, even encouraged, to acquire a sense of ownership, and have called for their participation in industrial planning and management. Such an approach would involve bringing ordinary workers into the decision-making process in individual shops and factories, thus encouraging personnel at all levels to help eliminate production bottlenecks and to participate in the setting of work norms and wage rates.

However laudable these proposals are, and whether or not they could help raise the level of labor satisfaction and thus increase labor productivity, it is highly unlikely that there will be anything more than cosmetic change in this sphere. Just as Marx observed a century ago that "no ruling class ever voluntarily gives up state power," the State Planning Committee, the Communist Party and the managerial elite are hardly likely to give up their control over the labor force. Furthermore, the Yugoslav experience with workers' councils, as well as the more recent Polish experience with the independent trade union, Solidarity, cannot help but reinforce the determination of Soviet officials to cling tenaciously to their power.

David E. Powell, "Social Trends and Social Problems," *Bulletin of the Atomic Scientists,* November 1982. Reprinted by permission of THE BULLETIN OF THE ATOMIC SCIENTISTS, a magazine of science and world affairs. Copyright © 1982 by the Educational Foundation for Nuclear Science, Chicago, IL 60637.

The post-Stalin relaxation of controls on population movement has resulted in large-scale voluntary shifts of people from the countryside to the cities and from one area of the country to another that seems more desirable. According to official data, 62 percent of the population live in urban areas; but the Soviet conception of "urban areas" and "urban-type settlements" suggests a much less concentrated pattern of residence than is normal elsewhere. Still, a massive exodus from the villages has undeniably occurred—an exodus that until very recently showed no signs of slowing.

## Urban Migration

Annually for the past 20 years some 1.5 to 2.0 million rural dwellers have migrated to the cities. The movement was not spontaneous or unexpected; indeed, it resulted primarily from official policy. Committed to a program of industrial development that required the skills of a large, urban labor force, and perhaps sharing the contempt of Marx and Engels for "the idiocy of rural life," the government had actively encouraged peasants and their children to leave the countryside. Until a decade or so ago, the authorities welcomed urbanization, viewing it as a prerequisite for industrialization and economic development as well as a means of increasing social mobility and bringing "backward" citizens into the socioeconomic mainstream. Now, however, they are reassessing their unqualified endorsement of the process and eventually may place rigid restrictions on this movement.

## The Best and Brightest

Rural-urban migration is primarily a movement of teenagers and those in their twenties and early thirties. In the main, it is "the best and the brightest," the young people with energy, ambition and skills, who abandon the farm and make their way to the city. Machine operators (tractor drivers, truck drivers, combine operators, for example), as well as members of the rural intelligentsia (such as schoolteachers, librarians, agronomists and economists), are especially anxious to leave. Those who go to the countryside on obligatory assignments after finishing their education in the city generally leave as soon as their period of required service is up.

In a classic study of Soviet migrants and potential migrants, T.I. Zaslavskaia found that most respondents pointed to the quality of life in the city as the primary inducement to leave home. In particular, they cited the diversity of the urban environment, better working conditions, more interesting and remunerative jobs, more and better services and better opportunities to continue their own education or that of their children. Zaslavskaia was bold enough to add that younger men and women not only found farm work uninteresting but also were frustrated because they were not "masters of the land."

## Socialized Agriculture

While her point is well taken, it is difficult to believe that the sytem of socialized agriculture will soon be abandoned. The last vestiges of private agriculture—the minuscule plots of land that remain in the hands of peasant families—are highly productive, yielding approximately one-fourth of total agricultural output on only 3 percent of the land. But collectivization was introduced for *political* rather than economic reasons, and the same factors that mandate Party control over industry ensure that socialized agriculture will persist for the foreseeable future.

---

*"Solidarity cannot help but reinforce the determination of Soviet officials to cling tenaciously to their power."*

---

Although authorities still view the rural exodus as "a historically legitimate, progressive process," one required by "the objective laws of social development," Soviet officials and scholars alike are becoming increasingly uneasy with some of its consequences. There are four major areas of concern.

First, there is the apparent irrationality of migration patterns. Rural dwellers tend to move to the city from precisely those areas (Siberia and the Urals) which already suffer from manpower shortages, while villagers in areas of surplus manpower (Central Asia, Moldavia and the Caucasus) have been the most reluctant to leave for the cities. Few individuals, whether peasants or urban residents, are anxious to move to the energy-producing areas of Siberia or to the Sino-Soviet border.

Second, rural out-migration has led to certain

demographic changes that the regime finds troublesome. People who reach the city tend to marry later and to have smaller families than those who remain in the village. There has also been a sharp decline in rural birth rates, largely because of the departure of men and women in their twenties and early thirties. In view of the labor shortage, official concern is clearly warranted.

## Urban Problems

Third, the dramatic influx of citizens into Soviet cities has led to or exacerbated a wide array of urban problems, ranging from crowded housing, crime and delinquency to emotional disorders and marital instability. To be sure, urbanization everywhere seems to engender certain distinctive forms of social pathology. Cut off from traditional sources of family and social support, large and heterogeneous groups come together in strange surroundings and are subjected to new and threatening stimuli. Although the overwhelming majority of migrants increase their earnings substantially after arriving in the city, many are unable to cope with their new responsibilities and opportunities. Statistics on crime and delinquency continue to be a state secret (as they have been since 1927), but increasingly frequent and pointed press coverage of such matters strongly suggests that anti-social behavior among the young is getting out of hand.

Finally, uncontrolled rural out-migration has been found to be "in conflict with the needs of agricultural production." The most competent and promising youngsters abandon the land, leaving the farms to older, less skilled and less productive workers. Soviet studies showing a decrease in the rural population generally have revealed an even sharper drop among those of working age. In fact, most research actually *underestimates* the disparity between young and old, since persons listed as "able-bodied workers" on some collective farms include women whose husbands work at nearby enterprises. These women remain on the farms to cultivate their private plots for family needs, contributing little to the collective's effort.

## Shortage of Food

While we are here looking primarily at the social aspects of rural-urban migration, the phenomenon is of even greater importance economically. The shortage of animal feed and food for the population has required the expenditure of some $8 billion in each of the past three years to make up the lack.

Over the past several decades, there has been a dramatic increase in alcohol consumption almost everywhere in the Soviet Union and among almost all population groups. Soviet sources acknowledge that between 1940 and 1980, when the country's population increased by some 36 percent, sales of alcoholic beverages (corrected for price changes) increased almost eightfold. From 1970 to 1980, when the population grew by 9 percent, alcohol sales rose by 77 percent. These figures indicate that current levels of alcohol consumption are more than just a modern version of the traditional "drink problem." Indeed, according to U.S. economist Vladimir Treml, the Soviet Union now ranks first in the world in consumption of distilled spirits. Treml has found that total *per capita* consumption of all alcoholic beverages has been increasing by 5.6 percent annually over the past 20 years.

An increase in consumption levels, even of this magnitude, does not necessarily imply a commensurate increase in alcohol abuse or alcoholism. Yet there has, in fact, been an enormous increase in problem drinking. A professor at the Academy of the Ministry of Internal Affairs reported in 1980 that 37 percent of the country's male workers "abuse" alcoholic beverages, and other Soviet analysts have expressed dismay at the rapid growth of alcohol-related crime, motor vehicle accidents, on-the-job injuries, birth defects and similar misfortunes.

## Russian Alcoholics

According to Boris M. Segal, a physician who carried out a large-scale study of the drinking habits of the Soviet population in the 1960s, the highest incidence of drinking and alcoholism occurred in the Russian Republic. There, 91 percent of the adult population were "drinkers" (that is, not abstainers), and 11 percent of the population over the age of 15 and 13 percent of those over 21 could be classified as alcoholics. The other two Slavic republics, Belorussia and the Ukraine, showed rates of alcoholism almost as high, while the three Baltic republics (Estonia, Latvia and Lithuania) ranked fourth, fifth and sixth. Throughout the country as a whole, Segal's data indicated, 44 percent of citizens 15 years of age or older drank, in contrast to 95 percent of those of Russian nationality. In regions of high wine consumption, primarily the Caucasus and Moldavia, there was a striking discrepancy between "the relatively high incidence of drinking and the relatively low incidence of alcoholism." The lowest figures for drinking and alcoholism were found among Jews and among Moslems residing in the Central Asian republics.

Alcohol abuse is particularly widespread among poorly educated and relatively unskilled urban blue-collar workers, although other groups are by no means immune. In recent years, in fact, the incidence of both drinking and problem drinking has risen in all social strata. But what seems to be especially troublesome to the authorities is the growing problem of alcohol abuse among women and teenagers. Scientists, scholars, journalists and public health and law enforcement officials have expressed genuine alarm at this phenomenon, arguing that problem drinking poses a grave threat to society and to the economy.

In the Soviet Union today, alcoholism and associated diseases are the third leading cause of death; only cardiovascular diseases and cancer rank higher. In fact, given the close correlation between heavy drinking on the one hand and cardiovascular problems and cancer on the other, many specialists are inclined to place alcoholism first.

## Alcoholics and Birth Defects

There is perhaps even more concern about the link between alcoholism and birth defects. The dramatic rise in alcoholism among women—far more rapid than among men—has been accompanied by increasing numbers of miscarriages, premature births, small babies and brain-damaged children. Medical journals and the popular press note that among the offspring of female alcoholics there is a higher incidence of infant mortality, mental retardation and a variety of serious physical defects.

*"Most people in the Soviet Union live out their lives either in a state of 'quiet desperation' or in pursuit of their personal ambitions."*

Many other ills are associated with alcohol. For example, approximately half of all divorces are attributed to drinking problems: in study after study, drunkenness is cited more than any other factor as a reason for the wife initiating divorce proceedings. Suicide, too, is often linked with alcohol. Soviet researchers have determined that more than half of all men and women who take their own lives are not sober when they do so, and one investigation found that almost half of those who committed or attempted suicide were alcoholics.

Lastly, the consumption of alcoholic beverages is closely associated with crime and delinquency. Data from the 1920s indicate that 23 to 25 percent of persons convicted of crimes were drunk when they committed the act; today, approximately half—estimates range from 45 to 63 percent—of all crimes are committed by people who are intoxicated. Certain categories of criminal behavior are especially strongly correlated with drunkenness. Some 60 percent of all thefts and more than 80 percent of all robberies are attributable to intoxicated individuals. Figures for crimes against the person conform to this pattern: 74 percent of all premeditated murders, 76 percent of all rapes and more than 90 percent of all acts of "hooliganism" (a highly elastic term which covers behavior ranging from "disturbing the peace" to "assault" and "assault and battery") are the acts of people who were drunk at the time.

It is unclear whether the authorities can prevent the situation from getting worse. They have raised the price of alcoholic beverages repeatedly; reduced the number of retail liquor outlets; introduced a wide array of criminal and civil penalties; disseminated anti-alcohol propaganda in the mass media, at schools and at workplaces; and have tried in many other ways to curb the people's desire to drink. But none of these measures has been successful, and even some sort of "dry law" would be unlikely to do the job. The existing problem of illicitly manufactured liquor would only grow worse, and in turn lead to public health and law enforcement difficulties that the regime prefers not to face. Besides, the sale of alcoholic beverages is highly remunerative, providing the single largest source of budgetary revenue for the state.

## Engineering Change

Turmoil has marked Russian and Soviet society since the beginning of the century. Before the Bolshevik coup, most of this turmoil consisted of anomalies—disruptive incidents and episodes that appeared against a backdrop of conservative institutions and processes. By contrast, the Communist Party has deliberately sought since 1917 to engineer a social and economic transformation, and to this end has consciously revolutionized the country.

---

*"The shortage of consumer goods has led to widespread corruption and a flourishing black market."*

---

As the years have gone by, however, and as the regime has consolidated itself, it has been increasingly inclined to pursue conservative rather than radical policies. The authorities reward hard work and obedience, while punishing those who deviate from prescribed norms. Personal values and behaviors are also, in the main, highly conventional. Children go to school, are taught to be respectful toward their elders, and to seek good grades, admission to an institution of higher learning and a comfortable white-collar job. Adults tend to be highly family-oriented, anxious to obtain a better apartment, a new car or various other consumer goods that are in short supply.

Although the shortage of consumer goods has led to widespread corruption and a flourishing black market, it would seem that most people in the Soviet Union live out their lives either in a state of "quiet desperation" or in pursuit of their personal ambitions. In this they behave much as their counterparts in other countries do.

*David E. Powell is a lecturer in the department of government at Harvard University, Cambridge, MA. He is the author of* Antireligious Propaganda in the Soviet Union *and a book on the subject of alcohol abuse in the Soviet Union.*

*"Why does the Russian regime feel the need to impose authoritarian restraints on its citizens?...First, an overriding fear of war."*

# The US Is to Blame for Soviet Oppression

Sidney Lens

The young man we met outside the Intourist Hotel one evening last summer was a specialist in Third World languages who also spoke English and French. He had come to Moscow from Kiev to spend a few days with the young woman at his side, a computer programmer. They were members of the Soviet Union's urban postwar generation—educated, sophisticated, stylish, and possessed of aspirations quite different from those of their parents and grandparents.

The two were standing on the sidewalk, trying to gain admission to the hotel so they could dance and have a few drinks, but a guard barred the door to anyone who could not produce a hotel card listing a room number. My wife and I asked the couple to join us, and our magic card swept all four of us past the guard.

At the downstairs bar (which requires payment in dollars, not rubles), I complimented the computer programmer on her striking dress and observed that women's apparel seemed much more attractive than on my last visit to Moscow several years ago.

"Maybe," she said, "but this dress is Italian. I bought it from a tourist. The nicest dresses you will see here are bought from foreigners."

## Talk of Travel

That remark led to talk of travel. She had been to many places in the Soviet Union but never out of the country, "not even to Bulgaria," she said. Would she like to travel abroad? "Of course," she replied, making it clear that cost was not a problem; her income, she assured us, was quite high by Soviet standards. The young man said he, too, had never been out of the country.

Many Soviet citizens have been abroad, within the East Bloc or outside it, but many more would like to travel if they could obtain permission. Other socialist countries have a more liberal attitude. Hungarians, for instance, are allowed to spend $300 a year for travel in Western Europe or the United States. But the Russians still impose rigid curbs on the right to travel.

It seems to make no sense: In this age of instantaneous worldwide communications, why should the Soviet government fear what its citizens might learn on a visit to London, Paris, or Milan?

The morning after our encounter with the computer programmer and her linguist friend, we had a long talk with a *refusenik*—a dissident who had been denied permission to emigrate. Born and raised in Chicago, he had come to the Soviet Union in 1932 with his parents and sister—all dedicated communists—to "help build socialism."

During the Stalinist purges of the late 1930s, his father had disappeared "and we never heard from him again." Though members of his family were afraid to inquire about the father's whereabouts or even to discuss his disappearance with friends, they didn't lose their faith in communism; they thought a ghastly mistake had been made, and their father would ultimately be returned to them. Eventually, the mother, too, was arrested; she died of cancer while in prison.

## Potential Émigrés

Some years ago, the *refusenik's* sister was allowed to leave the country, and he himself had received official permission to emigrate to Israel with his Russian-born wife and son in 1975. They quit their jobs and shipped out all of their belongings. At the airport, however, they were prevented from boarding the plane. Government officials claimed that the wife, a chemist, could not leave because she had been working on "secret" research, though her

Sidney Lens, "Fear But Not Loathing," *The Progressive,* December 1984. Reprinted by permission from *The Progressive,* 409 East Main Street, Madison, Wisconsin 53703. Copyright © 1984, The Progressive, Inc.

supervisor later acknowledged this was not the case.

Again, it seems to make no sense: Why keep this man and his family in the Soviet Union? He no longer calls himself a communist—"I became disillusioned slowly in the course of years, hardly realizing I was losing faith"—but he has long since paid his dues to the regime. His parents died as a result of official actions that the present government admits were illegal. He himself was wounded fighting for the Soviet Union in World War II. He is seventy-two years old, unlikely to pose any threat to the regime from abroad. Why hold him? His own explanation is that he is being used as "a deliberate warning to others who might want to emigrate."

---

*"[The Soviets] believe that they are under siege, and must therefore preserve 'national unity' at any cost."*

---

What makes the Soviet government so nervous, not only about its own citizens but also about visiting foreigners? My wife Shirley has been to the Soviet Union twice, and on each occasion she was detained by the police for half an hour or so—once because she was carrying, though not using, a camera in an old section of town, and a second time, this year, because she was walking with another American who snapped a photo of a poster.

## Soviet Restrictions

Why does the Soviet government still impose such severe restrictions on speech, on the press, on the arts, on travel? The simplistic answer we hear so often, especially from the right-wing media and politicians in the United States, is that the Soviet Union is "a slave society," "an evil empire," "a totalitarian dictatorship." But that sort of rhetoric merely begs the question of persistent Soviet insecurity and defensiveness.

My observation, shared by most foreigners residing in the Soviet Union, is that the government has overwhelming popular support. People gripe about the long lines for food and other necessities, about shortages, about shoddy goods, about many annoying and burdensome aspects of everyday life. The standard of living is low, even in comparison to conditions in East Germany, Czechoslovakia, or Hungary. But life is steadily improving, and there is obvious expectation that it will continue to do so. The vast majority of the people boast of their society's achievements and bask in their country's "greatness." "We won the war," they say. "Without us, Hitler would have conquered the world, including the United States."

"There were practically no private cars in Moscow before the war," Yuri Zhukov, columnist for *Pravda*

and head of the Soviet Peace Committee, told me. "Now there are two million." Before 1941, he added, "90 per cent of our city people lived in communal apartments [where five or six families shared one flat]. Now 80 per cent have their own apartments." That may not strike Americans as a great achievement, but for the Russians it is a long step forward.

## Economic Development

The Soviet Union is no underdeveloped wasteland. It produces about a million automobiles a year, and Moscow's wide boulevards are often jammed with traffic. The capital's subway system is cleaner and more efficient than those of Paris, New York, or Chicago. Shopping on Gorky Street is not like shopping on Fifth Avenue in New York or on Bahnhofstrasse in Zurich, but it isn't like shopping on Hester Street or Maxwell Street, either. The display of fashions in a department store window 100 yards from the Intourist Hotel was far more attractive than anything I had seen in previous visits.

There is no unemployment—the government guarantees everyone a job. To fulfill this fundamental commitment, the system inevitably permits and even encourages some make-work, but Russians regard this as a small price to pay for avoiding the kind of economic insecurity experienced by workers in our Pennsylvania steel towns.

## No Rat Race

"We don't have a rat race like you do," says a senior researcher at the Institute of U.S. and Canadian Studies—and in some respects he is right. Medical care in the Soviet Union may be poor, as resident Americans attest, but it is absolutely cost-free. Pensions, available to workers at age sixty or thereabouts, amount to more than half their pre-retirement pay. Vacation resorts, parks, and cultural events are abundant at little or no cost.

The school system is superior to ours and children are better educated, particularly in the sciences and mathematics. Nowhere in the United States can one see so many people reading books as on the Moscow subway. Education, including higher education, is free; a student admitted to college need not beg or borrow tuition or housing costs as in the United States.

The average Soviet citizen is not waiting eagerly for a change of government—as people wait, for example, in South Africa, Chile, Pakistan, or Uruguay. Whatever opposition exists is confined to small, clandestine groups committed to single issues, such as the independent peace movement that opposes Soviet as well as American militarism or the *refuseniks* who demand the right to emigrate. Undoubtedly, these efforts have many covert sympathizers, but they have not coalesced into a significant opposition and they are not likely to do so soon.

## Authoritarian Restraint

In such circumstances, Ronald Reagan's image of a Soviet state collapsing under the weight of public opposition is a fantasy. But the question remains: Why does the Russian regime feel the need to impose authoritarian restraints on its citizens?

There are, it seems to me, two reasons:

*First, an overriding fear of war.* For almost seventy years, with only two brief periods of detente in the 1930s and the 1970s, the Soviet state has been at war or under the threat of war. In our century, no other nation has been subjected to such pressure.

*Second, deepening apprehension about a stagnating Soviet economy.* An antiquated system of planning and an entrenched bureaucracy increasingly frustrate the rising expectations of the citizenry. Though the economy is still improving, it is growing at an ever-slower pace. Sooner or later, something will have to be done.

Since the civil war of 1918-1920, when the new Bolshevik government was compelled to deal with internal insurrection and a seventeen-nation Western invasion, the Soviet Union has relied on severe measures to preserve a measure of social cohesiveness. During the civil war, Lenin imposed "war communism"—rigidly centralized control—to save the state from disintegration.

His successor, Stalin, was determined to repel any "second intervention," and imposed such draconian measures as collectivization of farms, expansion of the secret police, liquidation of opponents within the Communist Party, purge trials, and forced labor camps—all of the repressive paraphernalia associated with Soviet communism.

## Preventive War

These totalitarian impulses were reinforced by the devastation wrought in World War II and by the new tensions introduced as the Cold War took hold between the Soviet Union and the United States. Such highly placed U.S. officials as General Orville Anderson and Secretary of the Navy Francis Matthews spoke openly of waging "preventive war" and mounting a nuclear attack on the Soviet Union.

We tend to dismiss such reckless talk as empty jingoist rhetoric, but it is taken seriously in Moscow. The Soviets have spent huge sums attempting to counter-balance US. military might. They believe they are under siege, and must therefore preserve "national unity" at any cost.

In the United States, antiwar demonstrations are organized by groups and individuals who see themselves as hostile to the Government and its policies. In the Soviet Union, the government encourages and sponsors antiwar demonstrations—though these are directed, of course, at the U.S. role in the arms race, not at the Soviet role.

In October 1983, for instance, Zhukov's peace committee called on people in thirty-five regions to rally for disarmament and detente; some 800,000 Soviet citizens participated. Each year, hundreds of thousands visit great war memorials like the one at Khatin in Byelorussia to recall the horrors of war and pledge themselves anew to the pursuit of peace.

The Soviet leadership, obsessed with the fear that an American President might press the button that brings on nuclear annihilation, believes that in this perpetual state of siege, dissent is a luxury a responsible government simply cannot tolerate. Most governments take that stance toward dissent in time of war; they impose a requirement of conformity so they will have an unchallenged mandate for military preparedness. War demands sacrifice, and public disagreement with official doctrine comes to be viewed as an intolerable indulgence.

## "National Security" Rationale

Our Government's attitude differs only in degree. In the United States as in the Soviet Union, "national security" becomes the rationale for internal surveillance, for secrecy, for censorship, and for official deception. In our country, too, dissidents have been denied the right to travel abroad and have faced prosecution for their political views.

The authoritarian impulse is certainly more restrained here than in the Soviet Union, but I suspect that is the case primarily because our fears are less acute. We have, after all, been at war or under threat of war for only sixteen years of the last seventy, and have suffered far fewer casualties than the Soviet Union's twenty million. Despite the shrill rhetoric employed by our Government and parroted by the mass media, most of us do not feel nearly as threatened as the Soviets do.

*"In this perpetual state of siege, dissent is a luxury a responsible government simply cannot tolerate."*

Furthermore, the Soviet regime finds it necessary to shield its citizens, to whatever extent possible, from knowledge of the "better life" available in the capitalist world, so that they will not raise demands that cannot be met without compromising "national security."

During my stay in Moscow, I repeatedly found myself wondering what the Soviet Union would be like if the threat of war were not constantly poised over it. I doubt that it would have had the same leaders or gone through the same evolution.

No less than the political system, the economy is profoundly affected by the persistent foreign threat.

A huge share of the nation's resources—a much greater share, proportionally, than in our case because the Soviet gross national product remains smaller—is allocated to military production, making it necessary to postpone, time and again, the fulfillment of domestic needs.

The effect of the military threat on economic planning is even more pernicious. "National security" serves as an excuse for stifling innovation and creativity.

---

*"Most of us do not feel nearly as threatened as the Soviets do."*

---

The Russians know their economy is stultified and antiquated. A top economist who has the ear of high-ranking Soviet officials told me frankly that the economy is on the wrong track: "We have been depending on an extensive form of economic development; we should have gone over to an intensive form years ago."

What he meant is that the Soviet economy has based its growth on added manpower rather than on improved technology. That system worked so long as a surplus of labor existed in the villages—millions of marginal peasants who could easily be lured to the cities by the promise of a steady income. European factory workers might be twice as productive as their Russian counterparts, but that made no difference so long as the Soviet Union could assign two laborers to the task performed by one in Paris or Turin.

## Shortage of Workers

Though the Soviets received neither loans nor massive aid from the West (except during World War II), their gross national product has increased at a phenomenal rate during most of the period since the Revolution. But now the surplus of labor is gone, and the nation suffers from a shortage of workers. Future increases in the GNP will depend on technological innovation—computers, robots, better equipment, all of the components of *intensive* economic development.

In 1961, when Premier Nikita Khrushchev predicted that the Soviet Union would overtake the United States in economic development by 1980, his country's annual rate of growth was still remarkably high—8 or 9 per cent. The U.S. rate, according to the Institute of World Economics, was 2.3 to 2.7 per cent. It seemed obvious to Khrushchev's economic theorists that the Soviet Union would forge ahead of its superpower rival within a single generation.

But the American economy, relying on intensive technological advances, performed at a much higher level than the Soviet economists had anticipated, and the Soviet economy, unwilling or unable to change,

saw its rate of growth fall steadily—to less than half of what it had been in 1961.

## Government Economist

The Soviet economist who explained all this to me was critical of his government's planning process: "Our mechanism for planning was made for the 1930s, not the 1980s. We refuse to depreciate equipment rapidly enough to put in new and better equipment. We also need to decentralize decision-making, as in Hungary."

He harbored no illusion that such change would come easily. Managers and workers would have to be given a greater role in the planning process, he understood, and once people are given a real voice in decision-making, they must be able to speak and move about more freely, so that they can exchange ideas and learn from other cultures.

The economist spoke approvingly of Yugoslavia's system of self-management (which the Poles have tried, unsuccessfully so far, to emulate), but he was more impressed with the Hungarian model of decentralization. Given the opportunity, he would bring back some of the private enterprise that existed under Lenin's New Economic Policy in the early 1920s. This, he said, was the direction in which the entire communist world should be heading.

"Does anyone listen to you?" I asked him.

"Everyone," he said, "and they practically all agree."

"Why, then, is the pace of change so slow?"

"We have a massive apparatus of party officials, trade union leaders, and an entrenched management that is hard to change," he said, choosing his words carefully. "Everyone agrees with the principle of decentralization, but no one implements it. One of our major problems is psychological. The leader of a collective farm, for instance, has become accustomed to giving orders; he doesn't want to give up that power. It is easier to change equipment than people."

## The External Factor

And then, he added, there was the "external factor." American foreign policy "has forced the Soviet Union to increase military expenditures. The emphasis is on this sort of production, so that we tend to be careless about the quality and quantity of consumer goods. No one is punished for doing a bad job." The bureaucracy, presumably, hangs together, and can always invoke "national security" as a rationale for retaining the status quo.

Sooner or later, my economist friend insisted, a wave of change would break down the dam of resistance. "My generation of intellectuals," he said, "is now in its fifties. It has a university education and has traveled abroad. It is aware of the problems."

Small reforms have already been instituted. A team system being introduced in some factories, for instance, permits groups of workers to "contract" with management to produce specified quantities of goods at an agreed-upon price. The workers supervise themselves, impose their own discipline, and maintain their own program of quality control.

## Trend Toward Decentralization

In agriculture, the trend toward decentralization is reflected in a system called RAPO—a regional agro-industrial complex encompassing collective farms, factories, and local government units. Party leaders claim this structure gives the grass roots greater autonomy in production, storage, transport, and processing. Each RAPO complex is responsible for deciding what to produce and has the right to retain a share of the profits.

Such measures are the first small, inadequate attempts to address the Soviet Union's domestic impasse—the ultimately irreconcilable conflict between people's rising expectations and an inflexible, centralized system that cannot supply their needs.

As in Czechoslovakia's brief 1968 experiment with "socialism with a human face," two separate currents are beginning to flow together: on the one hand, the demands of dissidents for greater freedom and a better life, and on the other, the growing need to wring greater productivity from an economy stalled on dead center.

*"American foreign policy 'has forced the Soviet Union to increase military expenditures.'"*

Like the Yugoslavs, Hungarians, Chinese, and others who are experimenting with forms of self-management and decentralization, the Soviets will eventually come under heavy pressure to relax their stringent controls on speech—even dissident speech—and travel. I believe that those aspects of Soviet life that strike us—and the Russians—as most objectionable today are likely to improve within the next few years.

If the United States has any real interest in such change for the better, it can accelerate the process dramatically by calling a halt to the arms race.

*Sidney Lens is the senior editor of* The Progressive.

*"I feel God's presence nowhere so strongly as I do in Russia."*

# The Soviets Have Religious Freedom

Anthony Ugolnik

Despite sporadic media attention to the problems of Christianity in Russia, I am troubled that Americans know so little of Russian Christians. It is not right that our brothers and sisters in the Soviet Union should be faceless. They deserve to have us see, briefly, a small slice of their spirit.

The church is everywhere in the Soviet Union. Let me assure you that Christianity, especially in its Orthodox form, is pervasive in Russia. Many Russians identify themselves quite frankly as "believers," a term much more frequent than "Christian." They pray. If a working church is within commuting distance, they worship openly. If there is no church close by, they go to great trouble to find one.

## Pervasive Religion

Westerners can be blind to the Spirit in Russia because they do not recognize his Orthodox form. Believers and nonbelievers are not quite so incessantly polarized as we might suspect. The Russian grandmother babysitting in the park is likely to be a Christian and to teach her granchildren the sign of the cross and basic prayers before they ever learn the official atheist line. Families often split along theological lines—a brother is a believer, an aunt belongs to the Party, a grandmother is piously observant (all too many of the grandfathers died in the war), yet a daughter is ignorant of religious matters but believes, somehow, in a God.

Lenin is as omnipresent an image in Russia as are the well-fed, dazzle-smiled models who symbolize the good life in U.S. advertising. Any of these images can stand in the way of the gospel, but none of them can kill it. Our Christian social movement in the United States has been shaped in reaction to the consumer

culture. Under socialism, surrounded by idealized images of the worker, burdened by antireligious legislation, the Spirit in Russia has taken on his own subtle shades that can instruct us as we discern them.

Clearly, the ministry of the church in Russia is very different from our own, at least in its emphasis. Christians take contradiction totally for granted. Pecherskaya Lavra, the Monastery of the Caves in Kiev famous among Orthodox as the cradle of Russian Christendom, is now a museum complex. At the entrance to the caverns where the hallowed monks are buried, guides assemble the groups they will lead through the caves.

I watched a Russian group from Leningrad. They nodded agreeably as the guide recited, in a bored monotone, the "superstitions" of the monks and the supposed miracle that preserved the bodies in the dry, natural embalming that the caves provided. Some even took notes.

## Religious Resistance

Out of curiosity, and with some Orthodox outrage at the tone of the guide and the simplistic antireligious slogans on the walls, I tagged onto the end of the single-file procession through the narrow, twisting caves. I was not prepared for what I saw. The guide, far ahead, was well out of sight. The Russians at the end of the line crossed themselves. Many bowed, as is our custom, before the relics. Some left petitions for prayer scratched on shreds of paper, stuffing them into the icon-studded niches in the walls. And these were the same people who nodded so agreeably to the guide. Their resistance takes a different form, you see, from our own.

Christians in Russia begin by taking the last place at the banquet. Western visitors to Russia often conclude that the churches are filled with the old and uneducated. Seldom do they discover, unless they worship and converse with believers, that Christians dress like and have the demeanor of the old and the rejected. Believers in Russia "dress down" for church, in direct contradiction of our own custom.

Christianity in Russia is incompatible with success. Those who desire the Soviet equivalent of rising the corporate ladder can hardly speed that rise with membership at the right parish. To become a regular worshiper is to choose the way of Christ over the way of the world. As the psalm goes, chanted at the beginning of every Orthodox liturgy in Russia, "Put not your trust in princes, in sons of men, in whom there is no salvation" (Psalm 146:3).

## The Beatitudes

Following that psalm, the Russian choir intones the beatitudes, which draw the congregation into their spell. They are the laws of the kingdom proclaimed in the liturgy, and they embody the spirituality of the Russian church. It is hard to convey the joyous spirit, the almost palpable faith at the monastery in Zagorsk as the masses of pilgrims join the choir in singing "Blessed are you when men shall revile you, and persecute you, and say all manner of evil against you falsely, for my sake, for great is your reward in heaven."

---

*"Christianity, especially in its Orthodox form, is pervasive in Russia."*

---

I feel God's presence nowhere so strongly as I do in Russia. The Soviet posters proclaim the worker triumphant over the material conditions of his being. The Soviet church has incorporated some of the same consciousness and, in the grand ideological transformation (or subversion) typical of our faith, the church has transfigured it. Christ the worker, Christ the peasant, Christ the fool triumphs over the powerful, the rich, and the wise.

Christians in Russia focus upon the self-emptying of God, the divine condescension of Christ in becoming human, as their spiritual model. Mary, the *Bogoroditsa*, "Birth-giver of God," is a manifestation of God imminent in the humble.

## Daily Prayer

Yuri is a solemn young engineering student in Leningrad. He scowls when he walks, as do many Russians—you've met these faces in our media portraits of Soviets. Daily, you will find him with that same round, Slavic face rapt in prayer before an icon of the Mother of God in one of Leningrad's churches.

Yuri had only a copy of the Gospels, not in modern Russian but in the liturgical language of Old Church Slavonic, which he studied to better understand the Word. Given a Bible as a gift, he scanned the modern Russian text through tears of gratitude. (Those scowling Russians can be intensely emotional.)

In serious conversation he professes to prefer his own dilemma to ours. "It is difficult for us, especially in the outreaches like Siberia and Central Asia. No Bibles, no churches—but we survive. With us, the choices are plain. But from what I know of you, the choices seem insidious. Materialism among us is an ideology. We can combat it. But with you, it seems to me, materialism is a hidden presumption. Your battle is the harder to fight." If you pray for Yuri in his struggle, remember also that he prays for you.

## A Russian Nun

Yuri's choices, however difficult, have not involved him in radically open declarations of faith. I first saw Olga at vespers services in a central Russian city. Her dress drew my attention. Though it is common for young believers to dress simply—babushkas or shawls for the women and nondescript, coarse dark coats for the men—Olga was dressed in a modified nun's habit with a long dark dress and a veil pinned beneath her chin. She clutched in her hand a long black staff. Crossing herself, bowing deeply through the long litanies of the evening service, she was known to the other worshipers and frequently interrupted her devotions with a smile to one, or a few kisses, Russian style, to another.

Olga is a "nun in the world." With opportunities to enter the monastic life severely limited, this becomes an option in Soviet Russia. Although she was educated for a clerical profession, her radical choice to be so open a believer has committed her to another way of life. She is content in a menial job, that of a street sweeper, which occupies her early morning hours. She is able, then, to attend the daily liturgies that take place in most Orthodox churches in the Soviet Union. Though she punctuates her conversation with signs of the cross and expressions of faith, she is a product of modern Soviet education. She has willingly taken upon herself the contemporary equivalent of an ancient Russian choice: to become a "fool for Christ," a poor person, a pilgrim who gives to others her testimony to the fullness of the Spirit.

These younger believers exist in increasing numbers. Many of them are, in a sense, converts to the faith of their forebears. Most of them were once "good Soviet kids" who, like many of us, found emptiness in the world.

*Anthony Ugolnik is an associate professor of English at Franklin and Marshall College and a member of the board of directors of the American Academy of Ecumenists.*

# The Soviets Do Not Have Religious Freedom

David K. Shipler

The dark-haired girl of 16 was a Komsomol activist and the daughter of two Communist Party members. In the middle of an afternoon, at the end of the school day, she walked gracefully from the hard, gray streets of Baku into the gold and candlelight of a church. Dusky icons hung framed in gilt, dim images suggesting mystery beyond the dancing gold reflections of the tiny flames. A trace of incense hung in the placid air. She crossed herself, lit a candle and bowed her head in prayer.

It was a frequent after-school routine, kept secret from her mother and father. The church calmed her, gave her delicate sensations of faith, warmed her as nothing had outside. But these important feelings were held closely, the magic of her double life. I asked how she could reconcile her Communist affiliation with her religious faith. "It's easy," she said brightly. "At the Komsomol committee, when they ask if I believe in God, I say no."

Thus do Communism and Christianity coexist, intertwining through the layers of belief and disbelief, binding conviction with hypocrisy. Party members sometimes even have their children baptized, clandestinely; the K.G.B. puts agents in the clergy. Nothing is ever as it seems. There are priests who do not believe in God, and Communists who do.

## A Drifting Vacuum

The longer I lived in the Soviet Union the less surprised I was by the drawing power of the Russian Orthodox Church. Christianity can exert a special hold on Russians yearning for an enveloping truth, on those once inclined, in earlier, fervent years, to give themselves to Communism as a full system of explanation and belief. And so in the drifting vacuum left by failing Communism, the church holds

*Russia: Broken Idols, Solemn Dreams,* by David K. Shipler. Copyright © 1983 by David K. Shipler. Reprinted by permission of Times Books, a division of Random House, Inc.

potential power—not institutionally, but spiritually—that Soviet authority watches warily and seeks to contain.

Not all attraction to the church is profound or complete. Some, merely esthetic, turns on a taste for richer ceremony than that provided in the state's austere wedding halls and crematoria. Communist authorities have worked hard to create "new socialist ritualism," as Pravda called it. In the Krasnodar region on the Black Sea, a ceremonial registration of newborn babies was introduced in an effort to supplant baptism. The Ukraine formed a committee to manufacture new rituals, with appropriate costumes and pageantry to "help put bright and colorful finishing touches on ceremonies connected with various events in people's lives," Pravda said. But the effort does not quite work, at least not for everyone.

## Shame at a Wedding

A young friend of ours was so ashamed of her state wedding ceremony that she didn't invite my wife, Debby, and me, fearing that, as Americans used to church weddings, we would find hers plain and boring, worthy only of mockery. It was precisely the same as many other weddings she had attended, and that we had also seen. Presiding was a woman civil servant seated before the hammer-and-sickle emblem, reading a dry text in the unfeeling tones of having done it many times. Once the rings were exchanged, attendants hurried the party out to make room for the next couple on the assembly line. "'It was awful," said our friend. "I hated it."

Church weddings have become quite a fashion as an alternative of candlelight and vestments and gold, chanting and incense and organ music. The state does not recognize the religious ceremonies, on the ground that the Soviet Constitution provides for strict separation of church and state, so the couple must still have a state ceremony or at least register the marriage with state authorities. Most try to keep their church weddings secret to avoid damage to career. The phenomenon thus becomes unmeasurable, taking on the appearance of a vast, partly hidden celebration, contributing to an impression of religious renaissance.

Sometimes the church attracts the way a fad does, in a thin, fleeting whim of pleasure and naughtiness. Icons and compositions of liturgical music are admired as art, and are also collected or played and heard for their overtones of mystical defiance. The infatuation is a teasing dance with authority, for officialdom also values icons, even to the point of enforcing strict prohibitions against their export. The treasures of the Russian heritage are precious, needing preservation; the churches of the Kremlin, although museums now, are fussed over, scrubbed and painted and gilded again with gold leaf so that they shine among the taller towers bearing the ruby-red stars and the red flags fluttering. The icon and the golden dome are symbols with multiple meanings, connecting the intricate lines of what is Russian and what is Soviet, bringing the great Russian past into some strange harmony with the powerful Soviet present.

## A "Withering Away" of the Church

Basic Soviet theory envisions the natural withering away of the church, as the aged men and women raised in its traditions die off and the younger breed of "Soviet man" rises into adulthood. This may be why the elderly are usually left to worship openly, mostly old women hunched and bundled in heavy coats, muttering prayers, kneeling on stone floors, carrying candles in trembling hands—images of a supposedly dying rite. The young and middle-aged, however, are the focus of official concern. To lure the young away from midnight Easter services, state movie houses usually run American and West European films that can never be seen any other time; the only showings are at midnight. And for good measure, Komsomol activists and plainclothesmen ring the churches, letting through the old and screening out the young. Names are taken, and there are repercussions at schools and places of employment for those younger people caught trying to enter.

The original Soviet Constitution of 1918 permitted "freedom of religious and antireligious propaganda." If this reflected a certainty that the antireligious would prevail, the confidence soon ebbed, and the passage was amended in 1936 to "freedom of religious worship and antireligious propaganda." The church was thus deprived of its right to propagandize—to transmit its creed and values formally. No group study, no Sunday schools, no evangelism. The party, on the other hand, was free, even obligated, to preach atheism.

The Stalin Constitution of 1936 also contained an article that was retained in the revised Constitution of 1978, Article 52, which declares that "the church in the U.S.S.R. is separated from the state." This separation principle is observed only at the convenience of the authorities; organized religion is utterly dependent on the state. The church has no property and receives its candle wax, vestments, buildings and land from the state. Whether Christian, Jewish, Moslem or Buddhist, no congregation may be organized, no worship service held, no religious publication issued, no charity undertaken without permission of the state. The Council on Religious Affairs, whose chairman and four deputy chairmen are all party members, acts on behalf of the state to register congregations, issue Bibles in severely limited and overpriced editions and otherwise regulate and restrict religious activity.

## Atheism Is Everywhere

The message of atheism is everywhere, from biology textbooks to nightclub acts. The basic biology text for 9th and 10th grades is laced with antireligious references describing belief in God as antiquated, unscientific and incompatible with the theory of evolution and other modern thought. A newspaper in Soviet Georgia printed a satirical poem portraying priests as drunken and dishonest. In a nightclub in Tallin's Viru Hotel, Debby and I watched as a group of chorus girls, dressed as nuns, suddenly tore off their habits to reveal multicolored tights, in which they ground and writhed as a singer did a rock version of a hymn full of "glory, glory hallelujahs."

*"Repeated, heavy fines are levied against those who hold unregistered worship services in their apartments."*

Russia's Christians include some fundamentalist Protestant sects, such as Baptists, Pentecostals and Seventh-day Adventists; they are relatively small in number and their members are usually treated more roughly than Russian Orthodox observers. Repeated, heavy fines are levied against those who hold unregistered worship services in their apartments. Religious leaders are sentenced to long terms in prison and Siberian exile. In rural areas, particularly, the authorities have removed children from their parents' custody—this under the guise of protecting the health and welfare of minors forbidden by their families to engage in dancing, look at television or belong to the Pioneers or the Komsomol.

But Russian Orthodox activists have sporadic trouble, too. Two prominent priests were arrested in the fall and winter of 1979-80: Gleb Yakunin, who had organized a small committee to press for religious rights and to publicize harassment and imprisonment, and Dmitri Dudko, whose popular, outspoken sermons had packed his Moscow church in the early 1970's. The authorities forced the Moscow Patriarchate to deprive Father Dmitri of his church and to reassign him to a rural parish just outside the city. He gave his sermons there, too, boldly.

*"The message of atheism is everywhere, from biology textbooks to nightclub acts."*

"The church in our country," he said, as I sat with him in his apartment in Moscow's northern suburbs, "will always exist because our country, by its Christian nature, has the richest soil now for Christianity. Here are suffering and persecution. It is not those wallowing in luxury who clutch at a straw. I look upon this optimistically: We and the Communists must find a common language, and this common language is not the language of nonbelief but of belief."

## An Outspoken Priest

A short, balding, stocky elf of a man with a gray beard and penetrating eyes, Father Dmitri was of the view that the Russian Orthodox Church in our time has been too timid, too anxious, too compliant. "Believers avoid priests," he said. "Priests run from believers, or betray the interests of believers. This is our misfortune. They are afraid of each other." Sermons are not supposed to deal with the real world, and so they and the rites become spiritually empty. "Outwardly, splendor. Inwardly, emasculation."

When Father Dmitri was arrested two years after our talk, it was apparently because his sermons continued to excite interest among young Russians. An even sadder event occurred five months later: The priest appeared on Soviet television to read a statement of confession and apology. "I have seen that I yielded to those propaganda voices that are directed at undermining our system," he read. "I repudiate what I have done and assess my so-called struggle against godlessness as a struggle against the Soviet power." I was already in Jerusalem at the time, but when I saw the news reports of his confession, I felt how deeply his parishioners must have been grieving for him.

*David K. Shipler,* The New York Times *correspondent in Jerusalem, reported from Moscow from 1975 to 1979.*

# Soviet Soldiers Are Treated Fairly

### B. Viktorov

Even during the war, in severe frontline circumstances the Soviet Command paid serious attention to the conditions of the officers and men. Reminiscences of the Soviet military leaders, front-line soldiers, documents of the war years prove this. Thus, a directive of a political department issued late in 1943 and addressed to the political workers read in part:

"It is necessary to display constant concern for the preservation of the soldiers' strength and health. Regular, uninterrupted provision for the men of hot meals and boiled water should be an inviolable rule. It is vital to exercise the strictest control to see that everything the state issues to the officers and men should invariably reach them. People who are careless and slack in this respect will be held strictly responsible for their actions."

Concern for the welfare of the servicemen is a manifestation of the policy pursued by the Communist Party and the Soviet Government. The cardinal aim of this policy is maximum satisfaction of the people's material and cultural needs.

## Good Living Conditions

The living conditions of the officers and men are an important factor contributing to the combat readiness of the land and sea forces. For instance, ships of the Soviet Navy make extended ocean cruises. Therefore, it is important to maintain the morale and keep up the physical strength of the crews so that they would be able, at all times, not only to stand up to tremendous physical and psychological stresses, but also to accomplish the most difficult missions.

Living conditions on a ship is a broad term. It covers provision of meals, clothing and medical services, and creation of the best possible conditions for the performance of service duties.

B. Viktorov, "Living Conditions in the Navy," *Soviet Military Review,*
September 1983.

The material and living conditions of Soviet servicemen, including naval personnel, are being constantly improved. The Soviet state adequately meets their needs. The commanders and political workers see to it that all supplies and other means made available to the officers and men are used effectively to improve the conditions of the servicemen.

In 1977 a special All-Army Conference was held on the improvement of the welfare and living conditions of the forces. Its recommendations were of considerable practical assistance to the commanders, political workers and personnel of the fleet logistical services.

## A Floating Home

Based on the results of scientific research, the pertinent authority drafted sanitary health standards which naval architects and designers take into account in designing new ships. Thanks to the creative cooperation of scientists, engineers, designers and medical personnel the habitability standards aboard ships are being steadily improved. The modern Soviet warship—whether it is a cruiser, submarine, landing or antisubmarine ship—is rightly regarded as a floating home.

The cabins and crew's accommodations are cozy and clean. The ventilation and heating systems are effective. The wardrooms are attractively decorated. The officers assemble here for meals and also relax, when off duty. At sea the wardroom is also used as a working room by officers. They can gather in it for official functions and for leisure. They exchange views and chat here. The commanders, political workers and Party activists try to keep it clean, to maintain within it an atmosphere of goodwill and comradely concern.

Much is being done to improve the diet of the personnel aboard ships. Here too the pertinent authority took into account scientific recommendations. Naval rations are characterised by adequate calorific value.

Submarine crews are subject not only to physical strain. They have to spend many days running in the close quarters of their ships. These factors tend to exercise a negative effect on the men's appetite. That is why the submarine rations are extremely varied. They include (taking into account possible substitutes) over 70 items.

*"There has never been a complaint or even expressions of displeasure about the quality of the food."*

However, in the provision of meals aboard a ship, more than in any other department of the supply service, a lot depends on the personal initiative of the officers and men concerned. Here is a case in point. While the patrol ship *Bezukoriznenny* was visiting a foreign port, a customary reception ceremony was held on board. After the function one of the guests approached Captain 3rd Rank Yu. Rykov, commanding officer, and introduced himself as the owner of a local hotel. He said:

"I own a hotel and know a good meal when I see one. Admit that the meal you served us was prepared in a restaurant."

The commanding officer was compelled to introduce Mitchman I. Mishchenko, the ship's chief cook, to the guest. He was a master of his trade, of course, author of many recipes. The dishes he makes give pleasure to the entire crew. There has never been a complaint or even expressions of displeasure about the quality of the food regardless of the conditions of the cruises.

## Training the Cooks

The navy pays serious attention to the training of ship's cooks. The nominees are trained at special classes. Once in a while at more or less regular intervals ship's cooks' conferences are held at which they share their "secrets" with one another.

Auxiliary farms make a major conbribution to improvement of rations. As a rule, an officer of the supply service heads the farm which grows vegetables and fattens porkers. Such farms play a particularly large role in improving diets in the Far North and the Far East.

The garment making industry has considerably improved the quality of naval uniforms and special work clothes. Each officer and man has several uniforms, namely full-dress, semi-dress, service and fatigue dress. There are also many various types of special and protective clothing which is being constantly improved, for the weaponry, combat equipment and service conditions are changing, too.

Servicemen, just like all Soviet citizens, enjoy free medical service. Medical checkups for seamen and petty officers are conducted regularly twice a year, before the winter and summer training periods. The purpose is to establish the physical condition and development of the crews and to identify those who need treatment or simply recreation before a ship is sent on an extended ocean cruise. Officers, mitchmans (commissioned warrant officers) and extended service petty officers are required to undergo a medical checkup at least twice a year. The medical officer reports to the commanding officer the results of the checkup and his proposals for the execution of necessary measures for improving the health of the crew.

It is also the duty of the medical officer to monitor the conditions in the crew's accommodations, and in the working rooms, to check the quality of the food, change of underclothes, attendance of the bath and the ship's water supply.

Other officers of the ship contribute to the crew's welfare and good living conditions. However, the main role here is played by the commanding officer. He is the master of the ship, so to say, and all matters aboard, including those bearing on the welfare and living conditions are his concern.

Marshal of the Soviet Union Dmitry F. Ustinov, Minister of Defence of the USSR, said:

"In dealing with matters of material and everyday support of the forces it is vital always to see the purpose of all this effort. Our purpose is to ensure a high level of combat readiness..."

This is the approach displayed in the Soviet Navy towards these questions.

*B. Viktorov writes for* Soviet Military Review.

*"If combat action began, one half of the
company might shoot the other."*

# Soviet Soldiers
# Are Not Treated Fairly

Andrew Cockburn

Soviet youths are liable for service once they turn
eighteen, but to simplify matters the authorities
simply draft all men whose birthdays fall before July
1 in May and June, and those born after that date in
November. Once he has put on his uniform,
according to virtually all the émigré accounts, a
draftee is shut off in an incomparably harsher world
than he has known at home.

Soviet soldiers have little or no opportunity to see
their families, read newspapers, or even leave their
bases. Food is bad and undernourishing. One
survivor reported having been served dried fish for
supper every night for two years. Vitamin-related
diseases like night blindness and running sores are
common. "The whole year they are fed on rotten
potatoes," remembers Alex Rantinor, a lieutenant
drafted in August 1973. "Even in the summer they
are not given fresh vegetables. Much of the food is
canned, but the men don't even get the full amount
because the soldiers who work in the kitchen steal it
and pass it on to their friends."

## Rampant Stealing

Stealing, in fact, seems to have been one of the
main occupations of these soldiers. A Soviet conscript
is paid next to nothing—3.5 rubles a month, which is
the rough equivalent of about $6.50. A first-term
volunteer in the U.S. Army, by contrast, gets paid
$573 a month plus housing and other allowances.
Since a packet of cheap cigarettes can cost half a
ruble, and the soldiers have to buy their own
cleaning equipment, there is little or nothing to spare
out of their stipends. This does not mean that Russian
soldiers do not have extra cash—simply that whatever
they have comes either in the mail from home or
from stealing and selling state property.

It is hard to find a former draftee prepared to
reminisce about his own thefts of military equipment,
but every veteran remembers someone else in his
unit who stole. "Fur-lined winter helmets for tank
crews are in great demand among civilian
motorcylists, or anyone who has to work in the
open," a former tank officer remembers, "so that the
moment they were issued, any platoon commander
who knew his business would take them and hide
them under his mattress or in some such safe place.
Otherwise they would quite certainly be stolen and
sold by the men."

The consensus among former soldiers is that guns
and ammunition are off-limits for the most part,
because they are closely guarded and stealing them is
a capital offense. Otherwise, anything goes. The
standard protective suits for use in case of attack by
chemical weapons are made of rubber, and command
a high price from Soviet fishermen. Gasoline is ready
to hand and always assured of a market.

Westerners, accustomed to thinking of the Soviet
Union as a law-and-order state, may find it hard to
accept that crime could be such a serious problem,
especially where the country's defenses are
concerned. Yet stories like this one from a former
anti-aircraft radar specialist are common:

If a soldier is supposed to guard the store and, since
he's only human, he wants to sleep, he will go into his
booth. At this someone who needs spare parts, tires,
for example, will go into the store and steal what he
needs. The crew of the vehicle will discover that they
have no wheels. If war were to start now, such
deficiencies would become apparent in the Soviet
Army. In the unit where I served, for example, I had
a radar. According to regulations I should have had
two of them. But only one of them actually worked,
and then only half the time. Why? Because the officers
in my unit liked to drink, and to get extra money, and
how are they going to get it? They would immediately
think of selling spare parts. What kind of parts? Cables,
various generators for the radar, various kinds of radio
equipment that is in short supply in civilian stores, but

Andrew Cockburn, "Ivan the Terrible Soldier," *Harper's*, March 1983.
Reprinted by permission of the author.

that is available in the army. As a result the station would work only for a short time and then die out...my equipment was on its last legs. The second radar would not work because there was no generator—the officers sold it, and drank away the money.

## Illegal Drinking

Drink is illegal for the conscript rank and file, although officers are allowed to buy it. This attempt to keep the men sober does not meet with much success, judging by all personal accounts.

Barred by law from possessing drink, the troops exhibit tremendous ingenuity in getting hold of it. There are three basic solutions to the problem: having it sent from home through the mail, buying it off base with funds generated through the sale or barter of military equipment, or falling back on indigenous means of intoxication. Viktor Belenko, a Russian pilot who defected in his Mig-25 fighter to Japan, has given a vivid account of what went on at his Siberian air base:

> Except for a television set, no recreational facilities of any kind were available to the men (or the officers, for that matter), and there was little they could do. They were forbidden to listen to a transistor radio, to draw pictures of women, to listen to records, to read fiction, to write letters about life in the service, to lie or sit on their bunks during their free time (there was no place else to sit), to watch television except when political or patriotic programs were shown, and to drink. But drink they did, in staggering quantities, for alcohol was the only commodity available in limitless quantities.
>
> To fly seventy minutes, the maximum time it can stay aloft without refueling, a Mig-25 needs fourteen tons of jet fuel and one-half ton of alcohol for braking and electronic systems. So wherever Mig-25s were based, huge quantities of alcohol were stored, and in the Soviet Air Force the plane was popularly known as "The Flying Restaurant."

Other planes may not carry as much alcohol as the Mig-25, but they all carry tanks of alcohol de-icing fluid for the cockpit canopy. A favored stratagem for pilots is to take off on a training mission and falsely report that they are encountering icing conditions and therefore activating their de-icers. Then they land with a full tank of this alcohol, which has officially already been used, and take it home for a party.

Ordinary soldiers are sometimes reduced to spreading shoe polish on bread, leaving the bread out in the sun so that the alcohol content in the polish soaks into the bread, and then consuming it. Eau de cologne, on the rare occasions that it goes on sale in some camp commissaries, is sold out within fifteen minutes. Antifreeze for trucks, brake fluid from all kinds of vehicles—it seems there is nothing the Soviet soldier will disdain in his quest for oblivion.

## A Relentless Search

The soldiers' relentless search for intoxicants may have serious effects on their equipment. A modern military organization has an enormous number of machines that need constant cleaning. In the Soviet Union such cleaning is done with an alcohol-based fluid. Viktor Sokolov, an émigré Soviet journalist, spent his military service as a member of a specialist construction crew working on the ring of air defense radars around Moscow. He remembers how the fluid issued for cleaning the moving parts in the big radars was regarded as being far too valuable for such purposes, so the men would substitute gasoline instead. When gasoline is wiped on metal it makes a nice shiny gleam, but it also causes it to corrode.

---

*"One survivor reported having been served dried fish for supper every night for two years."*

---

We can only guess at the precise effect of the epidemic of alcoholism on the Soviets' ability to fight. The men who fought their way across Europe, from the Volga to Berlin, were accompanied not by field kitchens (they were expected to look after their own cooking), but by field stills, and yet they won the war. On the other hand, German officers who fought against them have described occasions on which a Soviet unit was easily overcome because every man in it was drunk. A former lieutenant in the Strategic Rocket Forces told Enders Wimbush, a Rand Corporation researcher: "The time for the Americans to attack would be New Year's Eve, because everybody was drunk and there was no one on duty." But then he paused and added, "New Year's Eve wasn't that much different from any other time."

## Lack of Food

Drink and lack of food can weaken Soviet combat strength, but the miseries inflicted on conscripts also have more subtle and far-reaching consequences for the defense of the U.S.S.R. Western armies with or without the draft rely on a core of experienced "lifers," men who are not officers but who have chosen the service as a career. They become the sergeants and master sergeants, regarded as the backbones of our military. When only one third of these men were reenlisting in the U.S. forces after completing their contracted tour of duty, it was considered a cause for alarm. Such problems seem pale in comparison with the problems facing the Soviets. So unpopular is life in the ranks that only about one percent of the draftees reenlist at the end of their two years, despite considerable blandishments for them to do so in the form of pay and benefits.

The lack of professional NCOs means that the command structure of Soviet forces works differently from that of Western armies. The Russian system of officer ranks looks like the Western model; there are colonels, majors, lieutenants, and so on, in a line of authority descending through senior and junior sergeants, corporals, and first- and second-class private soldiers. The reality, however, is different. Authority in the lower ranks emanates not from a sergeant's stripes but from the oldest and strongest soldiers—regardless of their actual rank.

The social customs of this unofficial chain of command have been vividly described by a former draftee, Kyril Podrabinek, who served in a regiment stationed in the Central Asian republic of Turkmenistan between 1974 and 1976. Between leaving the army and his arrest as a dissident, Podrabinek composed a memoir of his service life called *The Unfortunates,* which was smuggled to West Germany:

## The Unfortunates

You and I, reader, are in Turkmenistan, in a Soviet Army barracks. Let's go straight to the heart of the matter. In the barracks there is a strict hierarchy by years of service and date of conscription. . . .

The Soviet draft takes place every six months. The soldiers in their first six months of service are called the "youngsters." This is the lowest caste. Having served six months the youngsters become "fishes," although, from the point of view of rights, the fishes have no advantage over the youngsters. The "regulations" for a fish are exactly the same as for a youngster. But he has served longer and gets a lesser share of washing the bosses' leggings and of scrubbing the barracks at night and so on. . . . A year goes by, and a fish has turned into a candidate. He is not a candidate for some office, but a candidate to become a boss. The functions of a candidate are basically repressive— police work. They persecute the youngsters and the fishes so the first-year soldiers don't get out of hand. Bluntly, they are responsible for "order." Having served another six months, the candidates become bosses. . . .

For bosses the custom is to relax. They do persecute the youngsters, but it's by way of private initiative or personal interest, and not for the sake of order, like the candidates. Then there's the highest rank of power, to be a "grandfather." Grandfathers are soldiers who have received their discharges but who have not yet left for home.

---

*"So unpopular is life in the ranks that only about one percent of the draftees reenlist at the end of their two years."*

---

Rations, austere as they are, are shared unequally between the "old men," as they are sometimes called, and the "weaklings." Podrabinek describes the scene at the dining table:

Not one weakling dares take bread, butter, sugar, the evening piece of fish, or anything until the older soldiers have served themselves. After that the youths pounce on the leavings. Those sitting near the bosses are in a more advantageous position for this than those sitting further away. Every seat around the table is strictly regulated; it corresponds to social standing, determined by strength, resourcefulness, submissiveness to the second-year soldiers, chutzpah, and orneriness. And so, all the food is allocated.

## Ruthless Beatings

All accounts of these customs agree that they are backed up by physical force—ruthless beatings administered in the barracks after lights out. Civilians to whom I have retailed these accounts of vicious hazing sometimes flippantly suggest that it is of little significance, since it occurs in all armies. It is true the custom is not unique to the Soviet system. It is untrue to suggest it is irrelevant to the combat capability of an army.

Virtually every military authority agrees with the proposition that cohesion is the most important factor in creating a successful fighting force. This truth is usually summed up in the aphorism "You don't take a hill for your country but for your buddies." The unofficial organization of Soviet units, in which at any time half the strength is being brutalized and exploited by the other half, is hardly likely to foster the trust and mutual confidence that makes for cohesion. Podrabinek goes so far as to suggest that "if combat action began, one half of the company might shoot the other."

*Andrew Cockburn is a contributing editor of* Defense Week.

# Russian Emigrés Consider US Freedom Challenging

Jane Anderson

Outside, one of Harvard University's grassy quadrangles is nearly deserted. Inside a brick dormitory building on the quadrangle, resident tutor Misha Tsypkin and his wife, Elena, enjoy the quiet afternoon in their apartment while their 16-month-old son, Lyosha, takes a nap.

For the Tsypkins, who emigrated to the United States from the Soviet Union seven years ago, life in this tranquil environment is a release from anti-Semitism and political constraints. But the bitter memory of life in Russia has not faded.

"I couldn't stand living there anymore. I couldn't go into the street—I almost suffocated from rage," Mr. Tsypkin says. "I still haven't forgotten. I wake up every morning and bless God I'm not there. Life there is life without dignity, without purpose.

"Most of the time, I was unemployed or underemployed. Before we applied to leave, we had to quit our jobs. My employer was taking a risk by hiring a Jew in the first place, and I didn't want to make his life more miserable. Half of our friends stopped saying 'hello' and would cross to the other side of the street," he recalls.

## Now Tutors at Harvard

When the couple first arrived in Boston, Misha Tsypkin worked in a bookstore for the first four months. Soon afterward he began taking political science courses. Now he tutors at Harvard and is earning his doctorate in government. Elena Tsypkin is a free-lance writer, but, at present, devotes most of her time to caring for their son.

"We would never have had children if we stayed there," says Misha Tsypkin. "We wouldn't breed into captivity."

On a softer note he observes, "People are kind here—they aren't afraid of each other. People in Russia can be kind, but only to a select few close friends and relatives."

"In this country you have every chance," Elena Tsypkin adds. "If you don't use it, it's your fault."

The Tsypkins are among some 250,000 Soviet citizens who were allowed to emigrate from Russia during the decade ending in 1981. About 100,000 of those emigrés, most of whom are Jewish, settled in the United States.

## Stranded in Soviet Union

Since 1979 the number of Soviet emigrés to this country has fallen dramatically with the disintegration of detente. In some instances, spouses or other close relatives hoping to join family members in the United States are stranded in the Soviet Union indefinitely.

Twenty-eight-year-old Alla Golbert, who emigrated last year, waited four years to join her mother in New York City. She sympathizes with friends who are waiting to emigrate.

"They are in the same position I was in," she says. "I led a very difficult life for four years. I understand their lives perfectly well.

"To be Jewish in Russia is not good for you. I left because I didn't feel like a normal human being there. They say everyone is equal, but that is not true. You always feel you are not secure. You always feel that something terrible may happen to you because you are Jewish."

Still, she retains a warm feeling for her homeland.

"Russia is a good country. It might be very different under other conditions. Many people love Russia, but they cannot live there."

When she first arrived in the United States, "I was prepared for the worst," she says with a laugh. Initially, she was aided by the New York Agency for New Americans (NYANA), one of the largest national resettlement agencies assisting Jewish and non-Jewish

Jane Anderson, "Russian Emigres," *Christian Science Monitor*, August 30, 1984. Reprinted by permission from *The Christian Science Monitor.* © 1984 The Christian Science Publishing Society. All rights reserved.

Soviet emigrés in their adjustment to New York and the United States. She also received a great deal of support from the Jewish community.

## "I Like Life Here"

"Coming to America, I feel like I've come home," says Golbert, who has just completed a course in computer programming and is applying for jobs. "I like life here; I like the people here. I will try to do my best to work for this country. I want to give."

Professionally, some Soviet emigrés find greater opportunities for advancement than were possible in the Soviet Union.

Mark Kuchment, a noted science historian, emigrated to this country in 1975 with his wife and four-year-old daughter to escape anti-Semitism and growing frustration with the Soviet regime. The move has proved to be a fruitful one for both Kuchment and his wife.

With his buoyant manner, Kuchment fits easily into his job teaching classes on modern Soviet society at Boston University. He also give seminars around the country and is a fellow at the Russian Research Center at Harvard. A few years ago, he received national press coverage when he pieced together clues revealing that an American engineer who had achieved remarkable success in Soviet military research was actually a high official in the Soviet military.

---

*"People are kind here—they aren't afraid of each other. People in Russia can be kind, but only to a select few close friends."*

---

Kuchment's wife, a violinist, plays with the Harvard chamber orchestra and takes part in international competitions. She also teaches violin at the New England Conservatory of Music in Boston.

Looking out over the Charles River from the Boston University campus, Kuchment compares the professional lives of Soviets and Americans.

"Russians may be more idealistic but more unreasonable than Americans, because they cannot achieve certain things you can in this country," he says. "Things that were an impossible dream in Russia I could achieve here because my American friends show me how to do it. Here, you can do certain things that would be impossible or illegal in Russia.". . .

According to Evelyn Cohen, director of family services at NYANA, "Most Russian emigrés find jobs, but at a lower level than they had in the Soviet Union. Writers, poets, painters, and musicians—if they are good—can carve out quite interesting careers for themselves. . . ."

At NYANA, incoming emigrés are given furniture and living allowances according to need. English classes and vocational services are also available.

## Emigrés Stay in New York

Generally, Cohen notes, Russian newcomers tend to stay in New York City and to congregate in areas such as Brighton Beach, Brooklyn, Queens, and the Bronx.

Coming from a society where information about the United States is altered or unavailable, many emigrés arrive in this country with unrealistic expectations. Further, says Cohen, "Since there is no immigration to Russia, Russians don't have a notion of what it means to be a newcomer to a society."

Despite any disillusionment, most Russian emigrés work hard to build new careers and lives in this country, according to Cohen. "We're not trying to say all these people are heroes," she says, "but very few sit around dreaming of the old country."

For some Soviet Jews, emigration can mean a turning point in their religious lives.

Tamara and Abraham Ainbinder of New York City emigrated in 1976 seeking educational opportunities for their three children. In the Soviet Union, there are severe restrictions on Soviet Jews entering universities.

## Future for Children

"Our goal was a future for our children," says Tamara Ainbinder, who works for American Express. "We achieved that goal, but we also got more than we expected."

Welcomed into the Jewish community, the Ainbinders learned how to practice their religion more fully.

"In Russia we didn't know who we were—we were deprived of our identity. It's very important to know your roots. If you don't have that you don't have strength, you are nobody," she says.

Educationally, their children have achieved remarkable success. Boris graduated with a Ph.D. from Harvard and is a professor at Tufts University. His twin brother, Joseph, is earning a doctorate at Columbia University. Galina, 19, is working for a degree in computer science at Columbia.

To the Ainbinders, their children's achievements are secondary to their spiritual rebirth.

"The children have also become deeply religious," Tamara Ainbinder says. "When I see my son at morning prayers, it is so delightful.

"I think it's wonderful we can live here," she says.

*Jane Anderson writes for the* Christian Science Monitor.

*"The best that can be said for Dr. Wolpe [a Russian emigré] is that she died trying to return to her homeland."*

# Russian Emigrés Consider US Freedom Terrifying

Tim Wheeler

Every Thanksgiving, I spread out on our dining room table the pink and gold linen tablecloth given to us seven years ago by Dr. Anna Wolpe, a Jewish emigré from Leningrad. The cloth has the distinctive sheen of the highest quality linen and is embroidered with two stylized roosters, a traditional Russian motif.

This year, I will remember Dr. Wolpe with more than the usual poignance because of Svetlana Alliluyeva's (Stalin's daughter) successful repatriation to the Soviet Union. The best that can be said for Dr. Wolpe is that she died trying to return to her homeland.

I first met Dr. Wolpe when she visited my office in the National Press Building in the spring of 1977. She was a half-starved graying wraith of a woman with large, haunted blue eyes. Her bony fingers trembled as she sat telling me how she had made the fateful decision to leave Leningrad where she had been director of a neighborhood polyclinic. Her eldest son, she said, a restless, malcontented person, was an inveterate listener to the Voice of America and a year or so earlier had emigrated to the U.S. where he settled in the Washington suburbs. He bombarded her with letters, telegrams and phone calls urging her to renounce Soviet citizenship and join him in the U.S.

## Visa Approved

Finally, longing to see her son, she decided to accept his proposal. She applied for an exit visa and soon it was approved. She flew to the U.S., leaving her younger son behind.

"I found my son was a changed person," Dr. Wolpe said. "All he and his American wife talked about was money. All they were interested in was buying more and more things. In his letters, he promised I could resume my medical practice. But when I got here, I was told my credentials were worthless. They gave me a job emptying bed-pans at a home for the aged."

Her son pressured her to attend meetings of Soviet emigrés sponsored by an anti-Soviet Zionist relief agency in Washington. The officials of the agency urged her to agree to appear at Congressional hearings and news conferences to testify on "Soviet anti-Semitism."

"I could not agree," Dr. Wolpe said, speaking in fluent though Yiddish-accented English. How, she asked, could she denounce as "anti-Semites" neighbors who had shared their starvation rations with her during her teenage years under Nazi siege? How could she accuse of "anti-Semitism" a nation and government that enabled her to become a medical doctor?

## She Lost Her Job

When she refused to appear at the Congressional hearings, all offers of assistance ended. She lost her job. Her son was so hostile, she moved out of his home into a seedy, downtown hotel. Her meals, when she took them, were at a gospel mission for the homeless.

"Have you ever been to Leningrad?" she suddenly asked me. "I believe it is the most beautiful city in the world. In summer, the sun never sinks below the horizon. We call it 'white nights.' The light is like gold." She was overcome by emotion. Tears welled in her eyes. "I don't believe I will ever see my beautiful city again. I cannot live as you live here, where money is everything. I only want to be useful. All my life I have been useful. I just want to go back home to my city."

She suggested that she write an article for the *Daily World* about her ordeal and I agreed that she should. I promised to read it and send it to the editors.

Tim Wheeler, "A Cold War Casualty," *Daily World,* November 21, 1984.

Dr. Wolpe had granted an interview to Yuri Barsukov, the Soviet correspondent for *Izvestia* newspaper. After she left my office, I telephoned him and he confirmed that, yes *Izvestia* had published his interview with her. I telephoned an official in the Soviet Embassy who told me Dr. Wolpe had indeed filed for permission to return to the Soviet Union. Her appeal, he said, is under "active review." It is just a matter of time, he said. "But she must be patient. Her case is complicated because she is no longer a citizen. It will take time to process her application for a reversal."

## Last Ray of Hope

I saw Dr. Wolpe perhaps once a week after that for two months or more. Sometimes we had lunch together in a nearby cafeteria. Then, one Friday afternoon in November, she came by briefly to deliver her article for the *Daily World*. I read it carefully over the weekend. It was so incoherent, her English so broken, I knew it could not be salvaged even by a complete rewrite. When she returned to my office that Monday morning, I broke the news to her. She seemed crushed, as if a last ray of hope was blotted out by darkness. To ease her disappointment, I urged her to join us for Thanksgiving dinner that Thursday.

*"When I got [to the US], I was told my credentials were worthless."*

She joined us that chill, bright day in Baltimore. She was so grateful that we had lifted, even for one day, the crushing burden of loneliness that she had brought a gift. It was the tablecloth. After my wife, Joyce, had opened the package, Dr. Wolpe took it into the dining room and spread it out on the table, smoothing away every crease.

We joined our neighbors for a turkey feast and Dr. Wolpe's spirits seemed to rise, especially when I recounted a trip Joyce and I had taken to Leningrad four years earlier. Her eyes sparkled like the Neva itself as I rhapsodized over the glory of the "Venice of the North." As she left to return to Washington that afternoon, I suggested that I interview her as a substitute for the article. She embraced me. "We should do this," she said. "Perhaps others will learn to avoid my mistake."

## No Valid Passport

I never saw her again. She did not keep the appointment we had made for our interview. Several months later, Yuri Barsukov visited my office. Usually a sunny, sociable person, he was weighed-down and withdrawn as he sat down. "Have you heard the news about Anna Wolpe?" he asked me. "She bought a ticket on a cruise ship that stopped in Leningrad. But when she attempted to board the ship in New York, the ship's officer discovered she had no visa or even a valid passport. She was not permitted to board the ship. The vessel sailed. A few hours later, Dr. Wolpe leaped into the harbor and was drowned. "I just learned at the embassy that her application to return home was to be approved," Yuri said, shaking his head sadly.

This Thanksgiving I will, as usual, unfold the linen tablecloth from Leningrad and remember gentle Anna Wolpe, a casualty of cold war anti-Sovietism.

*Tim Wheeler is the Washington, DC, correspondent for the* Daily World, *the daily newspaper for the United States Communist Party.*

*"There should be no question where the blame lies for the lack of an agreement. It is not in Washington."*

# The Failure to Negotiate Lies with the Soviets

*National Security Record*

President Carter's National Security Adviser, Zbigniew Brzezinski, has warned of "naive escapism" in dealing with the Soviet threat. Unfortunately, Mr. Brzezinski and other Democrats who show a clear understanding of the nature and extent of that threat have had little impact on those who continue to call for a nuclear freeze, and moratoriums on the testing and deployment of new U.S. weapons. Such steps, if combined with the proposed cancellation of the MX and B-1 programs, would mark the end of the long-term effort to modernize the U.S. strategic deterrent.

Meanwhile, the President is being criticized for having signed no arms accord with Moscow. But look at the record—a massive and inexorable Soviet buildup of nuclear striking power over the past dozen years, since the signing of SALT I, which was supposed to limit increases in just such weapons. New Soviet weapons have consistently been developed and deployed, regardless of unilateral U.S. restraint. The only variation on the Soviet side has been in rhetoric, which is friendly when the West imposes moratoriums on its weapons, and bellicose when it does not.

## The Defense of NATO

Consider what a freeze would mean for the defense of NATO. The Soviets began deploying their powerful and accurate new ballistic missile, the SS-20, in 1977. As SS-20 deployments increased, NATO decided in 1979 to deploy a new U.S. intermediate-range ballistic missile, the Pershing II, and ground-launched cruise missiles (GLCMs) to counter the growing number of SS-20s. At the same time, the West sought the total elimination of these weapons, or at least genuine reduction in their levels, through the Intermediate Nuclear Force (INF) negotiations.

As early as 1979, the Soviets claimed that a balance of theater nuclear forces existed in Europe, even while proceeding to deploy more SS-20s. At the beginning of the INF talks in November 1981, the U.S. proposed a zero-zero option—no long range INF missiles on either side. The Soviets were not interested. In March 1983, the U.S. modified its position, proposing an interim agreement limiting U.S. and Soviet warheads on such missiles on a global basis. In September 1983, the U.S. suggested limits on aircraft as well as missiles, to meet Soviet concerns. Two months later, as the first nine Pershing II missiles were being deployed (and the 360th SS-20), the Soviets walked out of the negotiations, proclaiming them dead.

The "walk in the woods" formula favored by some critics of the Administration, was rejected two years ago by the Soviet Union. That idea would have cut Soviet SS-20 deployment against Europe to 75 3-warhead missile launchers, while the West would have been limited to 75 GLCM launchers with four cruise missiles each. Despite the numbers, that would be an uneven agreement for the West, since the slower GLCM cannot be compared to the SS-20, which strikes with ballistic missile speed. Even so, the Soviets rejected the idea first, apparently determined not to cut any of the SS-20s they had already fielded, and showed no willingness to discuss the concept further.

## Clear Soviet Goals

The Soviet goals throughout the talks were clear and constant—the prevention of *any* Western deployments and the rupture of the Western Alliance. When NATO remained united and went ahead with the deployments—despite four years of Soviet propaganda and two years of fruitless negotiations— the Soviets picked up their chips and left the table. For them, the game was over. But if a unilateral U.S. freeze now is applied to deployment of the Pershing

*National Security Record.* "Arms Control Negotiations—Soviet Style," October 1984. Reprinted by permission.

IIs and GLCMs, the Soviets would gain through the U.S. election a victory they could not win during the past four years through either negotiations or intimidation of the Western allies.

Criticism has been leveled at the Administration for not reaching an agreement in the Strategic Arms Reduction Talks (START). In fact, the Administration has made a major effort to reach an accommodation with Moscow in a way that would both assure U.S. security and reduce the risk of war. It was the Soviets who suspended the talks and, suffering through a long-term leadership crisis, have been unable or unwilling to return. President Reagan, by meeting with Foreign Minister Gromyko and personally repeating the U.S. offer of new ideas and flexibility, has tried to ease Moscow's return to the talks.

The START Talks began in May 1982 with a U.S. offer to negotiate genuine reductions of the most threatening weapons, intercontinental ballistic missiles (ICBMs). The U.S. proposed substantial reductions in ballistic missile warheads, to a ceiling of 5,000 for each side, with a sub-ceiling of 2,500 land-based ICBM warheads. Deployed ballistic missiles would be limited to 850, with a sub-limit of 210 medium and heavy missiles. Heavy bombers would be limited to 400, including the Soviet Backfire, which was not included in SALT II, and there would be reductions in missile throw-weight.

## Soviet Violation of SALT

The Soviets were not interested in major reductions in either warheads or throw-weight. Instead, they proposed reducing the SALT II limit on strategic nuclear delivery vehicles (SNDVs—a catch-all category including ballistic missiles and bombers) from 2,250 to 1,800. This was a strange proposal, considering that the Soviets have not honored the present SALT II ceiling of 2,250 SNDVs (which the U.S. has scrupulously respected) and as of last January had 2,524 SNDVs deployed, exceeding the SALT II limit by 274, despite Brezhnev's commitment not to jeopardize SALT II.

The Soviet negotiators agreed that ceilings on nuclear warheads should be considered in the talks, but would not discuss specific limits. The data they provided indicated they had in mind a warhead ceiling of 11,400 compared to the U.S. proposal of 5,000. With about 7,900 Soviet ballistic missile warheads now deployed, the U.S. proposal would result in a 37 percent reduction, while the Soviet ceiling would permit a 45 percent *increase* in these weapons.

During the five rounds of START talks that ran from June 1982 to December 1983, chief U.S. negotiator Ambassador Edward L. Rowny persistently tried to find solutions to Soviet concerns. In response to Soviet complaints that the proposed reduction in throw-weight would require a restructuring of Soviet forces, the U.S. offered to explore alternative ways of

reducing throw-weight. ...

With over 2,500 strategic nuclear delivery vehicles deployed in the USSR versus 1,900 in the U.S., a build-down would give the Soviets greater flexibility in retaining their most modern weapons. Even so, the Soviets were not interested. Apparently seeing no reason to agree to *any* reductions in their strategic forces, they publicly rejected the build-down concept. In December 1983, shortly after the Soviets walked out of the INF talks, Moscow announced that the NATO deployment of new intermediate range missiles would also require a reexamination of its START position, and refused to set a date for round six of the talks.

---

*"New Soviet weapons have consistently been developed and deployed, regardless of unilateral US restraint."*

---

Last year, President Reagan offered to explore possible trade-offs with the Soviets in an effort to make progress toward an agreement, an offer he repeated in his recent meeting with Foreign Minister Gromyko. Since last December, Ambassador Rowny has been ready to discuss possible trade-offs, including a limitation on the deployment of U.S. air-launched cruise missiles (a matter of Soviet concern) in return for a reduction in the 3 to 1 Soviet advantage in ballistic missile capacity. But Moscow, in the midst of a continuing leadership crisis, has been trying to change the agenda.

With a clear superiority in ICBMs and throw-weight, Moscow is not eager to negotiate reductions in offensive missiles. Instead, the Soviets have been concentrating on what they see as America's greatest strength—the application of modern technology to develop strategic defenses against their offensive forces. Thus, the Soviets want to talk about stopping the deployment of U.S. space and anti-satellite weapons, but not about reducing their own large and destabilizing ICBMs. And the Soviet pre-condition for these talks is a U.S. moratorium on the testing of an anti-satellite weapon, a weapon the Soviets already possess.

The issue now is whether and when Moscow will accept the President's offer to return to the negotiations. But whether they do or not, there should be no question where the blame lies for the lack of an agreement. It is not in Washington.

*The* National Security Record *is a monthly newsletter from the Heritage Foundation.*

*"The Government of the USA has not responded to any of these (arms reduction) proposals with any gesture of goodwill."*

# The Failure to Negotiate Lies with the Americans

## Mikhail Gorbachev

The exchange of opinions we had with the leaders of the parties and states who are members of the Warsaw Treaty Organization gives us grounds to assert with confidence: We are unanimous in the belief that the Warsaw Treaty Organization is to continue to play, as long as the NATO block exists, an important part in upholding the positions of socialism in Europe and the world and is to serve as a dependable instrument for preventing nuclear war and strengthening international security.

The Soviet Union will, persistently and with a sense of purpose, continue to strengthen mutual ties and develop cooperation with other socialist countries, including the People's Republic of China. Our position on this matter is well-known and it remains in force.

We favor the further expansion of all-round cooperation with the countries of Asia, Africa and Latin America. The CPSU and the Soviet state invariably support the right of all peoples to shape their social and economic present in accordance with their own choice and to build their future without any interference from outside. Any attempts to deny the peoples this sovereign right are hopeless and doomed.

### Political Settlements

We invariably come out for the development of normal, equal relations with capitalistic countries. Disputed problems and conflict situations should be settled by political means. This is our firm conviction.

The Politburo proceeds from the belief that inter-state documents from the period of detente, including the Helsinki Final Act, have lost nothing of their significance. They offer an example of how international relations can be built if the states are guided by the principles of equality and equal security and existing realities in the world, and if they do not seek any advantages but look for mutually acceptable solutions and accords. In connection with the tenth anniversary of the Conference on Security and Cooperation in Europe, it appears advisable that the will to overcome the dangerous tension and to develop peaceful cooperation and constructive principles in international affairs should be expressed in Helsinki again on behalf of the states that signed the Final Act.

The Soviet Union comes out for fruitful and all-round economic, scientific and technical cooperation based on the principles of mutual benefit and excluding any discrimination; it is ready to continue to broaden and extend trade relations, to develop new forms of economic ties based on the mutual interest of the sides concerned in jointly using scientific, technical and technological novelties, designing and building plants and developing new material resources.

In posing the question this way, it is necessary to carefully analyze the state of our foreign economic relations, to take a closer look at them with an eye to the future. Despite international tensions there are favorable opportunities in this field. Our approach to mutually beneficial economic ties in foreign trade should be broad, large-scale and oriented to the future.

### Mutually Beneficial Cooperation

We stand for extensive and diversified mutually beneficial cooperation with Western European states, Japan and other capitalist countries:

Everybody knows our readiness to improve our relations also with the United States of America, for mutual benefit and without any attempts to infringe on each other's legitimate rights and interests. There is no fatal inevitability of confrontation between the

Mikhail Gorbachev, from an address at the Plenary meeting of the Central Committee of the Communist Party of the Soviet Union on April 23, 1985.

two countries. An analysis of both positive and negative experience in the history of Soviet-American relations, in both remote and recent history, shows that the most reasonable thing is to look for ways to straighten out relations, to build a bridge of cooperation but build it from the two sides.

But the completed first stage of the Geneva talks already indicates that Washington does not seek agreement with the Soviet Union. This is to be seen if only from the fact that it refuses, in general, to discuss the question of preventing the arms race from spreading to space simultaneously with the discussion of the question of nuclear arms limitation and reduction. It thus violates the agreement reached in January on the interconnection of the three subjects—prevention of an arms race in space, nuclear strategic arms reduction and reduction of medium-range nuclear armaments in Europe.

## US Ambitions

The questions arises: How do you explain such a position? It is to be explained by the fact that certain circles in the USA still want to attain a dominant position in the world, especially militarily. We have told the American side more than once that such ambitious plans are hopeless. The Soviet Union, its friends and allies and, properly speaking, all other states favoring peace and peaceful cooperation do not recognize the right of any state or group of states to supremacy and to imposing their will on the other countries and peoples.

*"The completed first stage of the Geneva talks already indicates that Washington does not seek agreement with the Soviet Union."*

The Soviet Union, for its part, has never set itself, and does not set now, such an aim.

We should like to express the hope that the present position of the USA will be corrected, which would create an opportunity for achieving mutually acceptable accords. We, for our part, are prepared for this.

This is evidenced by the Soviet Union's proposal for the two sides to impose, for the entire duration of the talks, a moratorium on the development of space arms and for freezing strategic nuclear arsenals. In pursuance of this line, the Soviet Union unilaterally announced a moratorium on the deployment of medium-range missiles and on implementation of other response measures in Europe. This decision was received throughout the world as important and constructive, one contributing to the success of the talks.

It should be recalled that this is not the only step of its kind. The Soviet Union's unilateral pledge not to use nuclear weapons first has been in force since 1982. In 1983, it announced a unilateral moratorium on first deployment of antisatellite weapons in space. The Government of the USA has not responded to any of these initiatives with any gesture of goodwill. On the contrary, it is trying in every way possible to give a distorted view of the Soviet Union's actions aimed at reducing the war danger and at reaching agreements, and tries to arouse distrust of them. In short, everything is being done to avoid taking positive steps in response.

One cannot help but find surprising the haste with which the American Administration responds with its standard and customary 'No' to our proposals, a fact clearly showing the United States' reluctance to lead matters to reasonable results. I would say only one thing: it is impossible to reconcile an arms race and disarmament talks. This is clear if one does not indulge in hypocrisy and does not try to mislead public opinion. The Soviet Union will not encourage such a course, and let this be known to all those who are now engaged in a political game and not serious politics. We would not like to have a recurrence of the sad experience of the previous talks.

The Soviet Union, for its part, will consistently seek concrete, mutually acceptable agreements in Geneva that would help not only put an end to the arms race but also push forward the matter of disarmament. What is needed today, more than ever before, is political will in the name of peace on Earth, in the name of a better future.

*Mikhail Gorbachev is General Secretary of the Central Committee of the Communist Party of the Soviet Union.*

*"Soviet-American relations are in the worst state of repair in over 30 years. . . . The responsibility for this state of affairs lies with both sides."*

# The Failure to Negotiate Lies with Both Sides

### Robert J. Bresler

Soviet-American relations are in the worst state of repair in over 30 years. No serious negotiations are presently under way. Ronald Reagan has assumed villainous proportions in the mind of the Soviet leadership. The Soviets seem determined to take whatever steps they can to diminish his chances for reelection and to embarrass him—hence their boycott of the Olympics.

The responsibility for this state of affairs lies with both sides. It predates the election of Reagan, and begins with the Soviet decision to modernize their European missile force by adding the more accurate MIRVed SS-20's. The West had taken no steps to warrant such a Soviet move. Yet, the NATO response announced in December, 1979, to station American Pershing II's and ground-launched cruise missiles (GLCM's) in Western Europe was an overreaction. The reassignment of more Poseidon submarines to NATO would have been a sufficient, less threatening reaction.

Once the December, 1979, decision was made, the Soviets saw less promise in the SALT II Treaty, which they hoped would lead to a permanent ban on all cruise missiles. Thus, when the Soviets moved into Afghanistan on Christmas, 1979, they must have anticipated it would kill any chances of SALT II ratification by the U.S. Senate. This was the price, in light of the NATO decision, they were apparently willing to pay. One wonders if they also realized that their Afghanistan adventure would help to pave the way for the election of Ronald Reagan.

### The "Evil Empire" Speech

Indeed, Reagan did not immediately help matters. He denounced the SALT II Treaty as "fatally flawed"

and engaged in a series of sustained political attacks on the Soviet leadership, including his famous "evil empire" speech. Against this climate, it was no surprise that the arms control negotiations in 1981-83 failed to achieve any results.

Reagan's initial proposals, renamed START (Strategic Arms Reduction Talks), would have required the Soviets to reduce their cherished land-based missile force by 60%. Strobe Talbott, the *Time* magazine diplomatic correspondent, described the offer as something "the Soviet Union could do nothing other than refuse." The Soviet proposals, which involved only a slight reduction of the SALT II ceilings, were dependent upon the U.S. not stationing any intermediate range missiles in Western Europe. Both proposals were non-starters.

By early 1982, the European missile negotiations, known as the Intermediate Nuclear Force Talks (INF) were also going nowhere. In the summer of 1982, a chance to break the deadlock appeared and was tragically flubbed by the Reagan Administration. In a series of informal talks in Geneva, the chief American negotiator, Paul Nitze, and his Soviet counterpart, Yuli Kvitsinsky, constructed a compromise. The Americans would be permitted partial deployment of some cruise missiles in Europe, but no Pershing II's. In exchange, the Soviets would agree to reduce their SS-20 missile force aimed at Western Europe and freeze those SS-20's stationed in Asia.

### Influential Sub-Cabinet Members

The President was persuaded by two young, but influential, sub-Cabinet officials—Richard Burt, the Assistant Secretary of State for European Affairs, and Richard Perle, the Assistant Secretary of Defense for International Security Policy—to reject the Nitze-Kvitsinky deal. Burt and Perle apparently persuaded Reagan that the sacrifice of the Pershings II's was too high a price to pay for an agreement.

Robert J. Bresler, "Can We Bridge the Arms Control Impasse?" Reprinted from *USA Today*, September 1984. Copyright © 1984 by The Society for the Advancement of Education, Inc.

This decision may turn out to be one of the most serious misjudgments of the Reagan Administration, for now that some Pershings and the GLCM's have been deployed, any future agreement will be much more difficult to negotiate. In fact, the Soviets, in response to this deployment, suspended both the INF and START negotiations.

Presently, not only are the START and INF talks going nowhere, but the entire fabric of arms control, built up through agreements negotiated over a 21-year-period, may be torn apart. The Soviets, petulant over the American failure to ratify SALT II, are pushing their compliance to the SALT Treaties to the outer limits. For example, it is not clear whether the Soviets are developing two new types of ICBM's (only one new type is permitted by SALT II); whether the large new radar tracking station in Siberia is in violation of SALT I; or whether their encoding of ICBM and SLBM tests is in violation of SALT II. Since we have yet to ratify SALT II, the Soviets assert we have no right to quibble over the finer points of the treaty. However, if the Soviets are straining the SALT agreements, the Reagan Administration is proposing programs involving the militarization of outer space that could utterly destroy both the SALT I ABM Treaty and the 1967 Outer Space Treaty. Such is the sorry state of Soviet-American affairs.

## Looming Arms Control Threats

Other threats to the arms control process loom in the immediate future. By the end of 1985, the SALT II Treaty will expire. If neither side agrees to continue to abide by its terms and should no other agreement be negotiated in its place, the arms race could take a dangerous and irretrievable step forward. The Soviets could increase significantly the number of warheads on their powerful SS-18 and SS-19 ICBM's. The U.S. could begin a massive addition of cruise missiles to its nuclear force, complicating verification and opening up a new area of arms competition. The Pentagon is presently contemplating the deployment of almost 4,000 sea-launched cruise missiles (SLCM's).

---

*"The entire fabric of arms control, built up through agreements negotiated over a 21-year-period, may be torn apart."*

---

Can this situation be brought back under control? What possible initiatives could the U.S. take? An attempt by a bipartisan group of moderates in Congress, working with the Reagan Administration to develop a new approach to the START talks, only elicited a contemptuous response from the Soviets. This proposal, known as the "build-down," involves a somewhat complex method for reducing nuclear

warheads. In more precise terms, the build-down works this way: for every new MIRVed ICBM warhead each side adds to its arsenal, it would have to retire two older ICBM warheads; for every two new SLBM warheads added, three older warheads of that category would have to be retired. The proposal aims for an eventual reduction to 5,000 warheads on each side—down from the current 8,000-9,000 presently in each superpower's arsenal.

## Merits of a Build-down

The build-down has some merits. If adopted, it would encourage both sides to reduce its vulnerable, yet increasingly accurate, MIRVed ICBM's. Any attempt by either side, under the rules of the build-down, to add heavy missiles with larger numbers would result in the concentration of more ICBM warheads on fewer missiles. For example, by adding just one MX missile with its 10 warheads, the U.S. would be required to dismantle seven Minuteman III's. This makes no strategic sense. The logic of the build-down is to push each side toward the replacement of its MIRVed ICBM's with less vulnerable single-warhead ICBM's.

Even in the best of times, the Soviets react cautiously and suspiciously to any new arms control proposal. In the present climate, it is highly unlikely that any new idea will receive even a respectful hearing from the Soviets. In fact, their first reaction to the build-down was to brand it as unacceptable.

What, then, should be done? Rather than begin with a whole new order of complex negotiations, we should propose to the Soviets a series of relatively simple steps. First, we should offer to reconstruct the Nitze-Kvitsinky formula for breaking the INF deadlock. Second, we should offer to ratify SALT II as a gesture of good will. Third, we should propose a new treaty that involves a continuation of the formula embodied in SALT II. This treaty would set an over-all limit on missile warheads of 5,000 and reduce the SALT II ceilings on missile launchers. There would be an additional ceiling on long-range bombers and on air-launched cruise missiles. Both sides would have to forego future deployment of SLCM's and GLCM's (beyond those allowed to remain in Europe). The problem is complex enough, and thus we should try to make our solution as simple and comprehensible as possible.

*Robert J. Bresler, national affairs editor of* USA Today, *is chairman of the Public Policy Program, Pennsylvania State University, Capitol Campus.*

# Poor Agreements Are Worse than No Agreements

### Eugene V. Rostow

Francois Mitterand has characterized the nuclear impasse at Geneva as the most serious East-West crisis since the Berlin airlift and the Cuban missile crisis. He understates the case. This time, the Soviet Union is not trying to take over an outpost along the boundary of the two systems—a pawn in what the Soviet Union still treats as the Great Game of old-fashioned European imperialism. On the contrary, the Soviet leaders are playing for checkmate, and without cost or risk to themselves.

It has long been conventional wisdom that the key to the difference between the Soviet and the American styles in foreign relations is that chess is the Russian national game and poker the American. There is some truth in that old wheeze, but not much. Despite decades of costly international experience, the American mind still dreams about the golden century of isolationism between 1815 and 1917, and doesn't accept the implacable fact that we have no choice but to play the Great Game of world politics ourselves every day, and not in fits and starts. We have not yet learned to think like a great power. Meanwhile, the Soviet Union plays hard and well, on the basis of meticulous preparation, in the ancient tradition of chess.

It is clear what the Soviet leaders are up to. While the Russians distract us by secondary though important moves in the Caribbean and the Middle East, they are lunging to neutralize Western Europe by detaching it from the United States. Arms agreements at Geneva are the weapons on which the Soviet leaders are relying to bring about this mutation in world affairs.

The Soviet gambit recalls a classical form of Chinese warfare in which each army is deployed in battle array while the two generals watch and drink

tea. After each studies the deployments and maneuvers, one says to the other, "You have won," and surrenders.

## Wise Warning

The Western publics expect too much of arms control agreements. They have forgotten the wise warning of Salvador de Madariaga, who lived through the futile efforts of the League of Nations to achieve disarmament before World War II. Disarmament can be achieved, de Madariaga said, only in a generally peaceful world. "Otherwise, disarmament conferences invariably result in agreements to have more armaments." Good arms control agreements can be useful adjuncts to an effective Western foreign policy for achieving stability, but poor agreements can do a great deal of harm in preventing the United States from doing what is necessary to assure the peaceful protection of its national security interests.

The goal of the Soviet negotiators at Geneva is to obtain agreements that acknowledge the Soviet Union's "right" to nuclear superiority and thus make it impossible for the United States to prevent or offset such superiority. The Soviet Union is hoping that political pressure in Europe, Japan, and the U.S. will force President Reagan or his successor to swallow nuclear arms agreements on Soviet terms. If the Soviet leaders should succeed in achieving this goal, they rightly believe, American security treaties and other guarantees would lose all deterrent credibility. Bowing to the inevitable, Western Europe, Japan, China and many other countries under the American nuclear umbrella would make appropriate accommodations to Soviet nuclear hegemony. The United States would of necessity pull back from military positions in Europe, the Mediterranean, the Persian Gulf, the Far East, a good deal of the Atlantic, and even parts of the Caribbean. The world balance of power would be irrevocably changed, and the U.S.—besieged, impotent, and furious—would

Eugene V. Rostow, "The Russians' Nuclear Gambit," *The New Republic,* February 20, 1984. Reprinted by permission of THE NEW REPUBLIC, © 1984, The New Republic, Inc.

lose its capacity to have a foreign policy at all. By default, world politics would be organized on the principle of *pax Sovietica.* The Soviet Union would have achieved victory without war.

---

*"Because of major errors made by the US in negotiating both the Interim Offensive Arms Agreement of SALT I and SALT II, the Soviet Union now has a 3-to-1 lead over the US in the number of ICBM warheads."*

---

If, on the other hand, the Western countries behave with even a moderate degree of rationality, the Soviet bid will surely fail. In that event the Soviet Union would be no worse off than it is now, and probably somewhat better off.

The Soviet strategy is an exercise in muscular diplomacy based on a new and potentially decisive factor in world politics: the exploitation of nuclear fear as a political, as distinct from a military, weapon. People have an altogether reasonable horror of nuclear war; and in the democratic world that horror has the potential of becoming an overwhelming political force. To help make that potential real, the Soviet Union is conducting a campaign based on two programs: the creation of a nuclear arsenal that would make a devastating nuclear threat plausible; and propaganda designed to transform nuclear concern into panic, and thus keep the West from taking the peaceful, effective countermeasures that are within its power.

## No Guarantees

Although no one can guarantee that a nuclear war is impossible, the risks of such a catastrophe are lessened to the degree that two critical conditions are satisfied: first, that the United States retain an adequate nuclear deterrent and the solidarity of its alliance systems; and second, that the world prevent widespread nuclear proliferation, especially to irrational political leaders like Qaddafi and Khomeini. General nuclear proliferation would make world politics unpredictably volatile.

It does not follow, however, that nuclear weapons can be ignored as if they were flying pyramids, badges of prestige of no relevance to the ongoing political life of the state system. Nuclear weapons can intimidate even when they are not exploded. That is the point of Mitterrand's sardonic comment that the present world crisis is particularly hard to manage because the Soviet Union produces weapons while the West produces pacifists.

Why is the Soviet Union building so many nuclear weapons? The answer to that question is widely

resisted in the West: the two superpowers have different doctrines about the political and military utility of nuclear weapons.

The American nuclear arsenal has been planned and built as a deterrent against aggression. All that American deterrence requires is a convincing second-strike nuclear capacity—that is, a capacity to inflict unacceptable damage if our vital interests are attacked. The criteria for deterrence cannot be static, given the inevitability of endless change in technology, and in the size and composition of the Soviet forces. Deterrence is thus difficult to define with precision, except as a defensive capacity to retaliate against aggression, distinguishable from an offensive capability principally in size.

## Nuclear Blackmail

For the Soviet Union, however, the function of nuclear weapons is altogether different, and therefore Soviet nuclear building programs and negotiating positions are altogether different from those of the U.S. Soviet nuclear doctrine is not defensive but offensive. The Soviet government has long understood that it does not face the risk of armed attack. It views its nuclear forces as an engine of nuclear blackmail—the ultimate sanction behind a foreign policy whose aim is the indefinite expansion of Soviet influence. To achieve such a position, the Soviet Union is trying to attain a credible first-strike nuclear capacity—that is, a capacity for an unanswerable preemptive attack on the military power of the U.S. and especially on its nuclear power. Only one hypothesis is consistent with such a policy—that the Soviet goal is not to deter aggression against the Soviet Union, but to facilitate Soviet aggression against others, and to weaken and finally destroy any conceivable Western resistance to its program of expansion based on the aggressive use of conventional forces, proxies, and terrorists.

The centerpiece of the Soviet Union's drive for such a first-strike capacity is its quest for permanent superiority in ground-based ballistic missiles. It has been evident for several years that the growing Soviet lead in this area is the source of the waves of nuclear anxiety now transforming the politics and public opinion of the Western nations.

The American nuclear arsenal is divided into three nearly equal parts—ground based, sea based, and airborne. That division—the nuclear triad—protects our force against the unknowable risk of scientific change, and corresponds to the bureaucratic structure of our defense establishment. The Soviet Union, on the other hand, decided after a long and careful study during the 1950s to put at least 75 percent of its nuclear forces into ground-based missiles. Such nuclear weapons are extremely accurate, swift, and destructive. They can be used without warning; and, so far, they admit no possible defense except the repulsive idea of preemptive attack or the equally repulsive notion of launch-on-warning.

In 1972, when the SALT I agreements were signed, the United States and the Soviet Union were approximately equal in the number of warheads on ground-based ballistic missiles of intercontinental range (ICBMs). The Soviet force of intermediate-range weapons of this type was still small. Because of major errors made by the U.S. in negotiating both the Interim Offensive Arms Agreement of SALT I and SALT II, the Soviet Union now has a 3-to-1 lead over the U.S. in the number of ICBM warheads and a 4-to-1 lead in ICBM throw-weight. The Soviet Union's intermediate-range force of this type, spearheaded by the mobile SS-20s, has reached the level of 378 deployed missiles and 1,134 deployed warheads, and is growing at roughly the rate of 1 new missile with 3 warheads per week. The Russians have a monopoly of this class of weapons, and have been trying desperately to keep that monopoly by preventing the deployment of the new American cruise missiles and Pershing IIs in Europe.

The Soviet lead in ground-based ballistic missiles implies, or will soon imply, the theoretical possibility of a first-strike—a bolt out of the blue. It is now mathematically possible for the Soviet Union to destroy all of our ICBMs, our submarines in port, and our planes on the ground with something like a quarter of its ICBM force, holding the rest in a paralyzing reserve that would make it nearly inconceivable for us to use our submarine-based or airborne nuclear weapons at all.

## Soviet Advantage

The Soviet advantage in ground-based ballistic missiles does not necessarily increase the possibility of nuclear war. There is no need for the Soviet Union to consider the risky and unpredictable course of actually firing nuclear weapons. They are doing well by using them politically, because a Soviet first-strike capacity casts doubt on the credibility of our guarantees to use either conventional or nuclear forces in defense of our interests, and therefore increases the nervousness of Europeans, Japanese, Chinese, and others who face the growing menace of the Soviet intermediate-range SS-20s.

This whipsaw effect of Soviet superiority in both classes of ground-based ballistic missiles is eroding the foundations of the political system we have built since 1947. Every chancellery and foreign office of the world is haunted by the comments of Richard Nixon and Henry Kissinger that "no great power commits suicide for the sake of allies," and that the change in the Soviet-American nuclear balance since 1973 has made it impossible for any President to do now what Kennedy did during the Cuban missile crisis of 1962 or what Nixon himself did during the Mideast crisis of 1973. These comments, which both men have repeated a number of times, reflect the conclusion that the American nuclear deterrent is worthless, except as an ultimate protection for American soil.

This defeatist view is entirely unjustified, but it is becoming more and more popular. To embrace it leads straight to policies of retreat, appeasement, and withdrawal in the United States, and to corresponding politics both of resignation and of ultra-nationalism and militarism elsewhere in the West. Senator Howard Baker says that a new Mansfield Resolution calling for the withdrawal of American forces from Europe and other forward bases would go through the Senate like wildfire. There are many serious indications of comparable import both at home and abroad. Isolationism has not been stronger in American politics since the 1930s, when Franklin Roosevelt failed to overcome it in time to prevent war. In every part of the political spectrum, Americans, like Europeans, are looking for a rabbit hole through which to escape from a particularly unpleasant moment in history.

*"The only way the United States can hope to protect this most vital of its vital interests is through the methods of concerted alliance diplomacy based on deterrent military power."*

Those who advocate policies of American isolation and neutrality speak and write as if our security guarantees to Europe, Japan, China, South Korea, Israel, and other key nations and areas of the world are acts of philanthropy for the benefit of friendly democratic countries, matters of choice we can elect to continue or abandon at will. No illusion could be more dangerous. Since the final collapse of the Concert of Europe in 1945, we have made treaties and other security arrangements with countries around the world not only because we are linked to them by ties of blood and culture but also because it would endanger the primitive security of the United States to allow those areas, people, and resources to come under Soviet control.

## Geopolitical Reality

We did not support Stalin against Hitler because we thought Stalin was a closet democrat. And we are not supporting China against the Soviet Union because we are under any illusions about the nature of the Chinese government. Strongly as America should always encourage and support the progress of democracy, the foreign policy of the U.S. must be based on geopolitical reality. Its first goal is to protect the security of the U.S. by achieving a balance of power and respect for the rules of world public order needed to maintain the stability of a balance of power.

The only way the United States can hope to protect this most vital of its vital interests is through the methods of concerted alliance diplomacy based on deterrent military power. These were the essential ideas first applied by President Truman and Secretary of State Dean Acheson a generation ago. They have been carried forward and developed with varying degrees of success by all their successors. For the U.S., a foreign policy based on these principles is not an option to accept or reject. It is a necessity.

*"Soviet negotiators. . .always say that there is equilibrium now, which would be altered by the introduction of modern American weapons."*

In this perspective, it is not difficult to understand the tenacity of the Soviet Union in seeking to preserve its lead in ground-based ballistic missiles through the Geneva negotiations on intermediate-range and intercontinental nuclear weapons. Throughout the West, many well-intentioned people persist in believing that the impasse in the Geneva nuclear arms negotiations is based on mutual misunderstanding, which could be cleared up by a high-level super-negotiator, a summit meeting, or a few clever changes in language. These naive views are contradicted by the history of Soviet-American relations since 1945. Moreover, they patronize the able and serious men who direct the Soviet Union. The Soviet leaders are not crude peasants who need a little reassurance about how well-intentioned the U.S. really is. They understand the difference between Soviet and American foreign policy very well indeed. And they have no intention of giving up the policy of expansion the Soviet Union has pursued since 1917 unless the West makes that policy unacceptably risky.

There is one issue in the I.N.F. and START negotiations, and it is extremely simple: whether Soviet-American nuclear arms agreements should be based, as the United States contends, on Soviet-American equality, or on what the Russians call the principle of "equal security."

## Equal Security

Like many Orwellian phrases in the Soviet vocabulary, "equal security" means just the opposite of what it seems to say. The Soviet Union wants the United States formally to acknowledge that the Soviet Union has the right to a nuclear arsenal equal to the sum of all other nuclear arsenals and potential arsenals in the world—American, British, French, Chinese, Israeli, Indian, Argentine, etc. This is not a recipe for "equal security" between the Soviet Union and the United States, but for Soviet hegemony: total security for the Soviet Union and total insecurity for everybody else. An agreement based on Soviet ideas would concede to the Soviet Union a nuclear advantage comparable to the one we had at the time of the Berlin airlift or the Cuban missile crisis: the capacity to control the escalation of crises and therefore to use conventional force at will. Truman and Kennedy used this kind of power for defensive purposes; the Soviet Union is trying to achieve it as the foundation for its foreign policy of aggressive expansion.

## Realistic Position

In both the I.N.F. and START talks, the United States' position is based on a new and more realistic unit of account than the one used in SALT I and SALT II. Instead of agreements about the number of missile launchers on each side, the United States now proposes that agreements should deal primarily with the number of actual weapons—that is warheads—and take fully into account the differences in their destructive capacity.

In the I.N.F. talks, which began in November 1981, the United States has put forward a series of offers based on the principle of Soviet-American equality in this sense. The first was the "zero option," involving the complete abolition of intermediate-range ballistic missiles—zero for each side. When the Soviet Union said for the fiftieth time that it would never accept a zero-zero outcome, the United States suggested equal limits on each side at any level the Soviet Union elected, both in and near Europe and in the Far East. That was the essential idea of the trial balloon floated by Ambassador Paul Nitze and his Soviet colleague, Ambassador Yuli Kvitsinsky, after their famous walk in the woods during the summer of 1982. The Nitze-Kvitsinsky approach, which I strongly supported, was vehemently rejected in toto by the Soviet Union. The United States had a number of amendments to suggest, but took the position that it wished to keep the channel open and to discuss the ambassadors' formula. Since 1982, the United States has put forward a number of proposals based on the principle of the 1982 balloon. They have all been turned down by the Soviet Union. The Soviet position has been and remains that the Soviet Union should keep all or nearly all of its weapons in the European area; that an I.N.F. agreement should not deal with the security of the Far East at all, despite the fact that the Soviet SS-20 is mobile; and that the United States should not deploy any of its modern ground-based weapons in Europe. I don't know any Western expert in the field who regards the Soviet position in the I.N.F. talks as serious.

The chief nominal justification for the astonishing posture of the Soviet Union is the existence of the British and French nuclear forces, among which may be found only eighteen ground-based ballistic missiles in any event. But the Soviet position is openly cynical. Soviet spokesmen freely concede that the British, French, and Chinese nuclear forces do not constitute a significant military threat to the Soviet Union; no nation holding thousands of nuclear warheads can possibly be afraid of an attack by countries that possess at most a couple of hundred weapons of this kind. The British, French, and Chinese systems exist for quite different purposes—as ultimate protectors of national sovereignty in the event the United States elects a weak President and world politics degenerates into general war.

## The Missile Gap

Sometimes the Soviet Union proposes agreements based on equal Soviet and American reductions in each category of nuclear weapons. It doesn't take a mathematical genius to realize that such an approach would increase the gap between the Soviet Union and the United States in the critical area of ground-based ballistic missiles. If the ratio in a given class of weapons is 8 to 4, and 3 is subtracted from each side, the ratio becomes 5 to 1.

The other arguments advanced to justify the Soviet bargaining approach are those of arithmetical acrobatics. By counting some American weapons and omitting similar Soviet weapons, the Soviet negotiators always reach the same conclusion, and have been doing so for six or seven years, despite the steady increase in the number of Soviet weapons: they always say that there is equilibrium now, which would be altered by the introduction of modern American weapons.

One of the many fallacies commonly used in the debate over intermediate-range weapons is the notion that equilibrium in that category of weapons is attainable at all, since there is no law of physics that would prevent Soviet intercontinental-range weapons from being targeted on London, Tokyo, or Hamburg. The significance of the SS-20s is primarily political; from the strictly military point of view they are part of the much larger problem of credible nuclear deterrence to protect the entire range of American security interests.

Soviet-American differences in the START talks are equally simple. The heart of the American START proposal is in itself a major concession to the Soviet Union because it would count ground-based and sea-based ballistic missiles of intercontinental range together, although submarine-based weapons are still less accurate than ground-based missiles, and less vulnerable to a first strike. Each side has about seventy-five hundred warheads of these types, the Soviet Union having more ground-based weapons, and the United States more submarine-based weapons. The American proposal is that the total number of warheads in the combined category be reduced to five thousand, of which no more than half could be in ground-based ballistic missiles. This

proposal would require the United States to dismantle more sea-based weapons, and the Soviet Union to dismantle more ground-based weapons. It would be a long step toward political stability.

The Soviet Union has rejected this proposal with the same tenacity it has shown in the I.N.F. talks, and for the same reason: it would reduce the destabilizing Soviet advantage in ground-based weapons, an advantage which exists to defeat deterrence.

## The Impasse in Geneva

Having failed thus far to stampede European opinion, the Soviet Union is now relying on the dynamics of the American election process to compel President Reagan to accept nuclear arms agreements based on Soviet notions of "equal security." Since the Soviet walkout at Geneva, those pressures have been building rapidly. Senator Glenn has suggested that it would be only fair to take British and French nuclear arms into account. Mr. Mondale advocates a freeze which would accept and legitimize the Soviet advantage in ground-based missiles and thus make our security problems nearly insoluble. Every Op-Ed page and radio and TV talk show produce another formula which its sponsors believe would persuade the Soviet Union to come back to the bargaining table—a summit meeting; a special envoy; the combination of the I.N.F. and START negotiations; negotiating on the basis of the Soviet proposals; and many others. In short, we assume that the impasse in Geneva is our fault, and are busily negotiating with ourselves rather than with the Russians.

---

*"The United States is being widely accused of taking a 'hard line' in the nuclear arms talks. The charge is without merit."*

---

The assumption behind these frantic activities is that nuclear arms agreements with the Soviet Union are almost magically important as guarantees of peace, and that it would be better to have bad I.N.F. and START agreements than none at all. In view of the accelerating Soviet drive for expansion since SALT I and SALT II were negotiated, such claims are either acts of political deception or manifestations of hysteria.

We have been negotiating and signing nuclear arms agreements with the Soviet Union for more than ten years while most of our politicians and experts assured us that such agreements would induce "restraint" in Soviet behavior, and help move world politics toward "detente" and even "peace." In 1972, when the SALT I agreements were signed, Nixon even proclaimed that "detente" had been achieved, and "cooperation" with the Soviet Union substituted for "confrontation." The history of the last decade makes those claims embarrassing. The Soviet Union treated its formal guarantee of the Indochinese peace agreement, dated March 2, 1973, as a scrap of paper. In the Middle East, Soviet behavior was equally a betrayal; in May 1972, the Soviet Union promised Nixon full support for cooperative efforts to achieve peace between Israel and its neighbors in accordance with Security Council Resolution 242. One month before, the Soviet Union had promised to help Egypt launch the aggression of October 1973—a promise it

---

*"The heart of the American START proposal is in itself a major concession to the Soviet Union."*

---

carried out faithfully. The record has been the same, with minor variations, in Africa, Afghanistan, and Kampuchea. Thus the 1970s and early 1980s turned out to be the worst period of the cold war, marked by Soviet and Soviet-sponsored aggression throughout the Third World on a larger and more serious scale than the probes and feints of the late '40s, and by the emergence of the Soviet attempt to separate the U.S. from Western Europe, Japan, and China through the achievement and acknowledgement of the Soviet nuclear hegemony.

## An Issue of Principle

The United States is being widely accused of taking a "hard line" in the nuclear arms talks. The charge is without merit. Thus far in Geneva the United States has been firm as to its goal in the talks, but conciliatory and flexible in its bargaining tactics. Obviously we cannot and must not repeat the mistakes we made in SALT I and SALT II by departing from the principle of equality between the Soviet Union and the United States as the basis for agreements which would be compatible with true detente. But the Soviet Union has not budged from its insistence on agreements that would preserve and even increase its capacity to execute a first strike. The issue at Geneva is thus a simple issue of principle, and it cannot be solved by verbal ingenuity, summit meetings, or other gimmicks.

Is there any chance the gap can be bridged? That is, that the Soviet Union can be brought ultimately to accept genuinely peaceful co-existence as the basic rule of international society—peaceful co-existence based on reciprocal respect for the rules of world public order embodied in the United Nations Charter? I should answer this question affirmatively—more affirmatively now than when I became Director of the Arms Control and Disarmament Agency in 1981. Of course we should

not expect the leaders of the Soviet Union to abandon their imperial ambitions if they are not required to do so by the restoration of effective Western policies of deterrence, containment, and collective security. That goes without saying. But on that assumption, I think the chances for a change in the direction of Soviet policy are not hopeless.

## Soviet Leaders

The leaders of the Soviet Union are intelligent and expert. Their main preoccupation is the maintenance of their own power. They are not romantics about war, like Napoleon and Hitler. And they must know what is obvious in the recent experience of Germany and Japan—that powerful nations accomplish far more for their people by encouraging them to make economic and social progress than by ordering them to make war. The Soviet leaders realize better than anyone else that the social and political problems of Poland and Eastern Europe—and of Russia itself, for that matter—can no longer be solved by the methods of Stalin, and that there is no real hope for them to rule their own peoples indefinitely unless they move away from perpetual mobilization toward policies of pluralism and relaxation of tensions. Above all, they know that Khrushchev was right when he said that the nuclear weapon does not respect the differences between socialism and capitalism. Despite their addiction to military doctrines of "surprise attack with all weapons" and other ideas designed to make our flesh crawl, the leaders of the Soviet Union must know as well as we do that nuclear war is unthinkably and unpredictably dangerous, and that the development of nuclear weapons has resulted in an insanity from which mankind can be delivered only by Soviet-American agreement.

## A Marriage of Necessity

There are marriages of love and marriages of convenience. There are also marriages of necessity. The Soviet Union and the U.S. are inextricably bound together in the coils of the nuclear weapon. There can be no assured firebreak between conventional and nuclear war. There can therefore be no real assurance against the risk of nuclear war until the Soviet Union gives up its policies of expansion, and decides to live according to the rules against aggression of the U.N. Charter. Until it reaches that decision, the West will have to muddle along with policies of nuclear deterrence, containment, and collective security, as it has for nearly forty years. But the Western governments should stress, both to their own people and to the Soviet Union, that the alternative of East-West cooperation for peace is always available, and would always be welcome.

*Eugene V. Rostow is Sterling Professor of Law at Yale University. He was director of the Arms Control and Disarmament Agency from 1981 to 1983.*

*"U.S. officials squandered solid opportunities to stabilize the arms buildup at lower levels of armament. In so doing, they have badly damaged U.S. security."*

viewpoint 84

# Any Agreement Would Be Better than No Agreement

Robert C. Johansen

Despite new rhetoric about arms control and a more constructive relationship with Moscow, the Reagan administration's past actions may be the best indication of future policy. Throughout most of its first term, the administration indulged in acrimonious attacks on the Soviet leadership and criticized arms control agreements that had been favored by previous Republican and Democratic administrations. For many officials, detente and the arms control efforts of the 1970s were naive policies that had lulled the electorate into a false sense of security. Arms negotiations on many subjects were avoided or, if belatedly entered into, viewed as opportunities to scale down Soviet forces disproportionately. To highlight their interest in "real" arms control, U.S. officials dispensed with the arms limitation of SALT (the Strategic Arms Limitation Talks) and began the arms reduction of START (the Strategic Arms Reduction Talks). This new approach brought neither limitation nor reduction. Instead, it shattered efforts both inside and outside negotiations to restrain the arms buildup.

When the Reagan administration took office, three treaties, already signed by the United States and the Soviet Union, awaited Senate approval. The administration opposed ratification of all three: the Threshold Test Ban treaty prohibiting the testing of nuclear devices with yields exceeding 150 kilotons; the Peaceful Nuclear Explosions treaty governing underground testing for peaceful purposes; and the SALT II treaty limiting strategic missile launchers, intercontinental bombers, and MIRVs (multiple independently-targetable re-entry vehicles.) In addition, the administration chose not to conclude the final negotiations to establish a comprehensive test ban, even though such a ban had been supported by

every other U.S. president, regardless of party, over the past 30 years. The Reagan administration simply did not want to halt nuclear tests. As Eugene Rostow, then director of the Arms Control and Disarmament Agency, told the Senate Foreign Relations Committee, "We are going to need testing . . . for weapon modernization."

## Lost Opportunities

While letting those past arms control efforts languish, the administration put forward no new proposals of its own during its first 16 months in office. And those that it did finally advance were so one-sided as to be non-negotiable, according to independent experts and seasoned arms control negotiators from earlier Republican and Democratic administrations. At the START talks, the United States tried unsuccessfully to press the Soviet Union to restructure its arsenal while the United States would have retained its current configuration of strategic forces. The number of warheads permitted for each country—five thousand—would have been equal. But in fact the U.S. proposals were profoundly unequal. The United States asked the Soviet Union, a land power, to dismantle more than half of its new, relatively invulnerable land-based missiles and to shift a major portion of its arsenal to submarines, where U.S. technology, including anti-submarine capability, has exceeded the Soviet Union's by substantial margins.

At the Intermediate-range Nuclear Force (INF) negotiations, the United States asked for a reduction of Soviet intermediate-range nuclear missiles to zero in return for a U.S. pledge not to deploy its Pershing II and land-based cruise missiles. After leaving office, former Secretary of State Alexander Haig commented that "the fatal flaw in the zero option . . . was that it was not negotiable. It was absurd to expect the Soviets to dismantle an existing force of 1,100 warheads, which they had already put into the field

Robert C. Johansen, "The Future of Arms Control," *World Policy Journal,* Spring 1985. Reprinted by permission.

at a cost of billions of rubles, in exchange for a promise from the United States not to deploy a missile force we had not yet begun to build." Even so, the Soviet Union did move partway toward zero, offering to reduce its SS-20s and other intermediate-range missiles to the level of British and French deployments, an offer the Reagan administration declined.

---

*"When the Reagan administration took office, three treaties, already signed by the United States and the Soviet Union, awaited Senate approval. The administration opposed ratification of all three."*

---

The Reagan administration's START and INF proposals were primarily a public relations exercise—a tool to sway public opinion and to mask the deleterious effect of U.S. military policies on future arms control. Drawing firm, hard lines to stop future weapons was anathema to President Reagan and his advisers. The administration's first-term arms control record shows approximately 2,000 new nuclear weapons added to U.S. arsenals, sizeable increases in Moscow's forces as well, and a surging stream of technologically new, even exotic, weapons.

## Easy Concessions

In contrast, consider what the Reagan administration could have achieved merely by responding positively to publicly-known Soviet positions. To begin with, it is likely that the entire intermediate-range nuclear arms buildup in Europe could have been halted. In 1983, if the United States and NATO had agreed to forgo the deployment of 108 Pershing II missiles in West Germany and 464 ground-launched cruise missiles in several NATO countries, the Soviet Union would have cut its arsenal of new, European-based, triple-headed SS-20 missiles in half, to 120. The United States could have maintained its Pershing I nuclear missiles and its nuclear bombs on aircraft in Western Europe, as well as Poseidon and Trident submarines off the coast. European security would not have been jeopardized in any way. Instead, the West now faces approximately 250 SS-20s, the first deployments of SS-22s and SS-23s in East Germany and Czechoslovakia, and new, long-range cruise missiles off the coast of the United States, with more to come on both sides of the Atlantic.

The United States could also have achieved at least a 10 percent reduction in Soviet strategic missile launchers, and reductions in the U.S. arsenal to an equivalent level, simply by ratifying the SALT II

treaty—which the Reagan administration pledged to honor even while refusing to ratify it—and by accepting Moscow's offer for a 10 percent cut now and further cuts after the first had been implemented. But Washington chose to leave the door completely open to new deployments. The rationale: by building the MX and the Trident II missiles and using them to "bargain from strength," Washington would be softening up Soviet officials for bigger cuts later on. The result: no reductions have been achieved, the United States now plans three new long-range missiles—the MX, the Trident II, and Midgetman—that if deployed will violate the SALT II ceilings, and the Soviet Union is developing several new competing systems. By not working to extend the SALT II treaty, the administration has virtually ensured that when the Soviet Union deploys its equivalent of the Trident II, a submarine with precisely guided multiple-warhead missiles, Washington will resurrect the "window of vulnerability" as a pretext for further U.S. armament. In addition, if the SALT II restraints are not maintained, Moscow will no longer be required to halt the deployment of even its heaviest intercontinental ballistic missiles (ICBMs)—which have been the main concern of U.S. officials.

## Possible Ban on Cruise Missiles

The United States could probably also have achieved a complete ban on land- and sea-launched cruise missiles by extending the SALT II protocol that had suspended their testing. Because Washington has led Moscow by several years in the development of cruise missiles and because the Soviet Union has for many years expressed interest in prohibiting such systems, one can reasonably assume that the extremely destabilizing missiles could have been totally banned. Washington's refusal to pursue this course will cause an unending series of nightmares for anyone attempting to devise overall controls on nuclear weapons: because cruise missiles are quite small and mobile, they will create new verification problems that will make arms control agreements much more difficult to conclude. Moreover, since they will number in the thousands, their manufacture and deployment will reduce the significance of existing ceilings on ICBMs. Any time Moscow wishes, it can deploy new Soviet cruise missiles in great numbers off U.S. shores, just two or three minutes from all U.S. coastal cities. Thus by rejecting an across-the-board halt to these systems, the Reagan administration not only chose a military route with no end in sight, but also brought the nuclear threat closer to the U.S. homeland than ever before.

The United States could also have achieved a mutual moratorium on the testing of antisatellite (ASAT) missiles. Soviet leaders, eager to prevent a quantum leap in U.S. space warfare technology, initiated a unilateral moratorium on the testing of

Soviet ASATs in August 1983. At that time, the United States claimed that verification was impossible and refused to enter negotiations on these systems rather than begin talks to work out ways to improve verification. Yet if the administration conducts tests planned for later this year, Washington will irretrievably pass the point where verification of a ban on such weapons is most feasible. Had Washington been willing to reciprocate the Soviet moratorium—which still awaits a U.S. response—it is likely that by now the United States could have secured a treaty banning field tests of the guidance technology essential for ASATs, a treaty that independent scientists say would be verifiable. Negotiations for banning all weapons in space could also have been far advanced, if not completed.

## Badly Needed Credibility

The United States could also most likely have halted the testing of *all* nuclear explosives for weapons purposes if the Reagan administration had not pulled out of negotiations for a comprehensive test ban when they were nearly completed. The Soviet Union had provisionally accepted some on-site inspection to assure compliance. Thus if the real reason for the administration's refusal to negotiate had been inadequate verification provisions, it would have made more sense to focus further negotiations on how to strengthen verification, instead of simply abandoning negotiations. Had the United States agreed to halt tests, the possibility of either country building new war-fighting systems would have been substantially reduced. The superpowers' policies of limiting the worldwide proliferation of weapons would also have gained some badly needed credibility.

Finally, the Reagan administration ignored an important opportunity to reduce the risk of war in Europe by refusing to reciprocate the Soviet Union's unilateral declaration that it would not be the first party to use nuclear weapons in combat. U.S. officials have correctly pointed out that no promise is ironclad. Yet if the United States had reciprocated Moscow's no-first-use pledge, it could have pursued steps to turn both sides' declared intentions into concrete actions. For example, Washington could have offered a withdrawal of NATO tactical nuclear weapons to positions at least 300 kilometers from the East-West border in return for a similar withdrawal by the Soviet Union. Such an initiative would have greatly reduced the likelihood of miscalculation or preemption in a European conflict.

The meaning of this profoundly negative record can hardly be exaggerated. Although the Soviet Union is still interested in arms control, suspicions run deeper and hopes for major progress appear thinner than during the 1960s and 1970s. Major new weapons systems such as the president's Star Wars plan have gathered a bureaucratic momentum that will be difficult to stop; other destabilizing systems such as cruise missiles are already being deployed. In sum, U.S. officials squandered solid opportunities to stabilize the arms buildup at lower levels of armament. In so doing, they have badly damaged U.S. security.

## Erosion of Existing Arms Constraints

But the Reagan administration has not simply wasted good chances to implement new arms restraints; it has also begun to jeopardize the most important restraints that are now in place. Current plans for the deployment of the MX, Pershing II, long-range cruise missiles, the Trident submarine and D-5 missile, the Stealth bomber, and space weapons will, if enacted, undermine or violate present arms control agreements, encourage new Soviet armament, and increase the likelihood of instability in U.S.-Soviet relations during times of crisis.

Particularly in danger are four existing boundaries of arms restraint that presently regulate international conduct: the SALT II ceilings on strategic launchers; the SALT I restrictions on antiballistic missile (ABM) systems; the traditional norm against deploying weapons for warfare in space; and the time-honored firebreak between conventional and nuclear arms.

*"START and INF proposals were primarily a public relations exercise—a tool to sway public opinion and to mask the deleterious effect of US military policies on future arms control."*

The main bulwark against a totally unregulated offensive arms competition—the SALT II limits on offensive strategic weapons—now threatens to collapse under the onslaught of current U.S. armament. Although the SALT II treaty has not been ratified by the United States, President Reagan has promised to abide by the treaty's provisions as long as the Soviet Union does also. Yet in March 1984, the Reagan administration announced that it was considering launching a seventh Trident with submarine-launched ballistic missiles (SLBMs) during 1985 without retiring any existing submarines—an action that would violate the limits established in the Interim Agreement (SALT I) and SALT II treaty for strategic submarines, submarine missiles, and multiple warhead missiles. In his news conference on January 9, President Reagan implied that the United States would keep within established limits, but he and the State Department subsequently denied that the issue of retiring Polaris submarines had been resolved. In the absence of a firm U.S. commitment to honor the treaty, the threat to violate it remains, needlessly stimulating the arms race.

The SALT II treaty also stipulates that each superpower is allowed to test and deploy only one new ICBM. Yet the Reagan administration intends to develop and deploy both a completely new, multiple-warhead ICBM, the MX, and a new single-warhead ICBM, the Midgetman. Although the Midgetman will not be tested before the treaty's scheduled expiration in 1985, plans to develop it have crushed hopes that the treaty's restrictions would be extended beyond 1985 and maintained indefinitely until a gradual reduction from the SALT II baseline could begin.

## Lack of Respect

The administration shows no greater respect for SALT I than for SALT II. The ABM treaty, signed by President Richard Nixon in 1972 and duly ratified by the Senate, severely restricts the development of defensive weapons that can attack offensive missiles. By committing both the United States and the Soviet Union not to "develop, test or deploy ABM systems or components which are sea-based, air-based, space-based or mobile land-based," it flatly bans any nationwide defense against missile attack. It also prohibits the testing of such systems, a measure that Moscow and Washington agreed on to improve the treaty's verifiability. Both nations undertook the ABM treaty because they recognized that defensive missiles would stimulate the expansion of new offensive arsenals, making any future reversal of the arms race much more difficult. For more than a decade the treaty has successfully averted a dangerous competition in defensive missiles.

Four U.S. programs now threaten to violate this agreement. First, the $26-billion Strategic Defense Initiative (SDI), announced by President Reagan in his Star Wars speech in 1983, calls for accelerated research on space-based lasers and particle beam weapons that could be used to destroy Soviet missiles in flight. The administration is apparently unwilling to halt this program even if offered the chance to negotiate a ban on such weapons with the Soviet Union. For example, there is a passage in the secret 1984-88 Defense Guidance statement, leaked to the press, that specifies that the United States will initiate "the prototype development of space-based weapons systems...so that we will be prepared to deploy fully developed and operationally ready systems." Furthermore, in January 1984, President Reagan signed a National Security Decision Directive that requires those working on the space warfare program to conduct four major tests of critical missile technologies before 1990. The tracking and pointing component of the space-based laser, called Talon Gold, is scheduled for testing aboard the space shuttle in 1987 and 1988. These steps would clearly violate the ABM treaty.

A second threat to the ABM treaty is posed by an earlier U.S. program for ballistic missile defense. In his 1983 testimony before Congress, Major General

Grayson D. Tate reported that the planned High Altitude Defense System includes homing experiments with the "primary objective" being "flight test demonstrations of high altitude optical homing and nonnuclear kill." Independent experts have concluded that these activities "appear inconsistent with the treaty limits on air- or space-based ABM component development and testing."

*"The United States could probably also have achieved a complete ban on land- and sea-launched cruise missiles by extending the SALT II protocol that had suspended their testing."*

The development of ASAT weapons to be launched from F-15 fighters puts the United States on a third collision course with the ABM treaty. Although the treaty does not ban weapons for use against satellites, the targeting technology for such weapons can be adapted to ABM systems, which *are* regulated by the treaty. President Reagan opposed even the brief delay that Congress requested on U.S. ASAT tests scheduled for late 1984 and early 1985. As noted earlier, he has also refused to reciprocate the Soviet Union's unilateral moratorium on testing ASAT weapons. Several days after the presidential election, while officials talked about new prospects for arms control, the United States carried out another test of the ASAT missile. Continued U.S. testing may force Moscow to resume tests of its own ASAT weapon or even to withdraw from the ABM treaty. By increasing the likelihood of such actions, the Reagan administration is beginning to turn the ABM treaty into a dead letter—and in the process it will nullify much of the domestic opposition to the Strategic Defense Initiative.

## Assault on the ABM Treaty

The Reagan administration is waging yet a fourth assault on the ABM treaty, by developing antiballistic missiles designed for use against aircraft and *tactical* ballistic missiles. Although such short-range weapons are not regulated by the ABM treaty, the targeting technology they utilize is applicable to the longer range sytems that *are* proscribed. Programs to determine whether the Patriot and Hawk missiles can serve as antitactical missiles violate the understanding, insisted upon by the United States in the 1972 treaty, that nonstrategic missiles must not be tested in an ABM mode.

If the United States does not immediately halt field tests of all these antimissile and antisatellite weapons, it is difficult to take seriously the promise Secretary Shultz reportedly made at Geneva that the United

States would not violate the ABM treaty for the next three years. Apparently he meant that field tests of Star Wars weapons were three years away, for tests of these other weapons will, if they proceed as scheduled, bring the United States into violation of the ABM treaty during 1985. And in any case, to talk openly about violating a treaty in three years' time will hardly encourage the Soviet Union to avoid violations of its own.

As Ambassador Gerard C. Smith, former director of the Arms Control and Disarmament Agency and chief U.S. arms negotiator at the time the treaty was signed, has concluded: "We are already in an anticipatory breach of contract." The weapons programs described above cannot be reconciled with the provisions of the ABM treaty. Nor can the treaty be amended, as U.S. officials have proposed, to permit the very weapons that it was written to prohibit, since this would in practice be little different from abrogation of the treaty.

In addition to breaking positive treaty law, current U.S. military policy undermines the customary international norm of keeping space free of weapons. The Strategic Defense Initiative and military facets of the space shuttle program represent the greatest threat in this area. They are matched by the Reagan administration's pronounced reluctance to negotiate a ban on weapons for use in space—a sign of its intention to militarize the only remaining sphere of the human environment that has never known war.

---

*"Washington has moved the purpose of arms control away from comprehensive arms restraint toward the development of an extensive war-fighting capability."*

---

Finally, the United States has also severely eroded the time-honored boundary that separates nuclear from conventional arms. Tactical nuclear and "dual-capable" weapons, the implications of which will be discussed below, are being introduced in large numbers throughout all the armed forces. By deploying more numerous tactical nuclear weapons, more destructive conventional arms, and weapons that can carry either conventional or nuclear explosives, the United States is both lowering the threshold at which nuclear weapons are considered legitimate to use in war and eroding the firebreak that divides conventional from nuclear combat. U.S. security and the international code of conduct are suffering as a result.

## The Demise of Arms Control

Like a bull in the arms control china shop, the Reagan administration is shattering treaty restrictions and arms control practices that have been painstakingly established over many years. By pursuing deployment of the very weapons that these norms were designed to prohibit, the administration is actively undermining almost all constraints on nuclear arms and is making it more difficult to reach future agreements. These actions have already begun to erode Soviet confidence in U.S. pledges, making Soviet leaders less inclined to restrict their own arms programs. Soviet officials cannot be confident that the United States wants a treaty genuinely limiting U.S. technological advances; that a treaty, if signed, would be ratified; or that a treaty, if ratified, would be maintained beyond the time that it takes the United States to prepare for its next technological leap forward. If Washington violates old rules, the Soviets may ask, why should Moscow sacrifice to establish new ones?

## Confirming Fears

As if to confirm Soviet fears, none of the areas in which the United States holds a technological edge—such as new cruise missiles, stealth bombers, submarines, or space weapons—is being offered for reduction. These, after all, are the weapons needed to fulfill the Defense Guidance's goal of prevailing in a protracted nuclear war. In recent weeks the administration has redoubled its lobbying efforts for all these programs, including the president's Star Wars plan, arguing that they are needed to strengthen the U.S. bargaining position.

Apparently, the Reagan administration has convinced itself that the Soviet Union will not negotiate an arms agreement if the United States suspends plans to deploy its next generation of weapons. Conversely, the administration has argued that Moscow *will* negotiate an agreement if U.S. testing and deployment continue. But this approach has failed in the past and is likely to fail again. Given Moscow's determination to maintain parity with the United States, the best time to strike a deal with the Kremlin is before U.S. weapons have actually been tested and deployed. New U.S. weapons are far more likely to fuel a Soviet counter-buildup than they are to force Soviet concessions at the negotiating table. Consequently, if an arms control agreement is somehow reached despite existing procurement policies, it will no doubt permit much higher and more dangerous levels of armament than the administration could have obtained in an agreement several years ago.

To varying degrees over several decades, officials have tried to increase U.S. security by following this now familiar formula of preparing for war through an arms buildup and negotiating toward strength under the banner of arms control. Subordinated to the pursuit of a military edge, arms control policies have at best sought to limit a few specific weapons systems without reducing reliance on weapons in general. This emphasis has severely restricted the security benefits of arms negotiations. Even arms control's greatest successes—the 1963 Test Ban treaty, the 1972 ABM treaty and Interim Agreement, and the 1979 SALT II treaty—did not halt the development or deployment of a single new weapon system that was on the Pentagon's drawing boards at the time. In this sense, the Reagan approach to arms control has merely perpetuated a 30-year trend: even if Moscow had accepted the entire set of U.S. START proposals, the resulting treaty would not have banned any of the major new weapon systems planned by the United States or their Soviet counterparts.

## The Breaking Point

The Reagan approach has brought arms control to the breaking point. As doctrine has shifted, Washington has moved the purpose of arms control away from comprehensive arms restraint toward the development of an extensive war-fighting capability. Officials use arms control to legitimate a more offensively armed and less secure East-West relationship. Compared with existing weapons systems, the weapons being sanctioned by Reagan's arms control policies will be more numerous, more difficult to verify and to detect in flight, more likely to be placed on hair trigger, and more prone to drive escalation out of control. Policy-making proceeds backwards. Officials adjust arms control proposals to accommodate war-fighting doctrine and military procurement, rather than adjust an offensive doctrine and procurement program to conform to a security-enhancing arms control policy.

The adverse effects of doctrinal constraints on arms control have been magnified by a rapidly changing technology that entices military strategists with ever more exotic weapons and that makes the verification of arms control agreements ever more difficult. Official strategists like Zbigniew Brzezinski and Max Kampelman, for example, claim that the United States needs a new generation of space-based defensive weapons because verification problems will make arms control unable to limit the newest offensive weapons. But the same officials who now favor Star Wars weapons previously opposed mutual constraints that would have prevented the deployment of MIRVs, or that would have averted the problems posed by dual-capable cruise missiles. Without weapons such as these, the Strategic Defense Initiative would have no rationale at all. Policymakers thus use the consequences of their own past obstruction of arms restraint to justify the acquisition of new weapons that, in turn, will derail future verification efforts. Rather than actively pursuing bilateral restraints on destabilizing technological innovation, Washington has narrowed the scope of negotiating proposals by deciding to develop new weapons to protect old ones.

In part, officials support antimissile weapons in space because of arms control's limited success in stopping deployment of offensive forces. Yet by forcing open the gates of new military technology with plans for Star Wars, these individuals will only hasten the demise of arms control. If the administration would instead ackowledge that testing such weapons is inconsistent with the broader purposes of arms control, the conclusion of far-reaching agreements permanently banning space weapons would undoubtedly be possible. Policymakers who ignore this point assume that arms control must weakly submit to a technological imperative, when, in fact, technological innovation is a result of unwise policy decisions for which they are partly responsible.

## An Instrument of Deception

In view of these obstacles to effective arms control, many strategists agree with Brzezinski that the prospects for achieving "a comprehensive and complex U.S.-Soviet arms control agreement...are increasingly slim." Indeed, "it is quite possible that arms control as we have known it has come to the end of the road." But it may be premature to sound the death knell for arms control. If nothing else, arms control serves as an insrument of deception and self-deception in the political process: negotiations help soothe the leadership and the public into believing that Washington is doing all it can to end the arms race, even as it proceeds with new weapons. This purpose is reflected in the administration's appointment of two vocal advocates of space-based weapons—Kampelman, an influential Democrat, and John Tower, a prominent Republican and former Chairman of the Senate Armed Services Committee—to head the new U.S. arms control delegation. As negotiators, these men will be in a strong position to urge Congress to vote for new U.S. weapons, in part to enable the United States to "bargain from strength." With negotiations in progress, officials appear justified in advocating new weapons, which are rationalized as bargaining chips or as promising technological advances in "defensive" ability.

*"The administration is actively undermining almost all constraints on nuclear arms and is making it more difficult to reach future agreements."*

Thus as long as U.S. negotiating options remain constrained by current strategic doctrine and plans for weapons procurement, the "umbrella" talks and other future arms control initiatives have little hope of reversing the arms buildup. If the administration insists on "bargaining from strength," it will continue to rule out balanced, broadly restrictive proposals designed to end the arms buildup through mutual concessions. By attempting to threaten the Soviet Union into agreement, Washington will stimulate the development of new weapons systems. By reaffirming all of its concrete military programs, the administration has nullified its newly expressed interest in arms control.

Even if the next round of talks does yield a U.S.-Soviet agreement, a new treaty can hardly come close to sewing up as much arms control fabric as Reagan unravelled during his first four years. Development programs will proceed while negotiations linger, producing at best an arms agreement that may regulate older weapons or temporarily delay one or two new ones, while channeling further energy and resources into more advanced long-range cruise missiles, stealth bombers, a mobile land-based ICBM, ASATs, and laser and particle beam weapons for space warfare. These weapons will prepare the way for yet another wave of offensive weapons.

In this way, U.S. arms control policies provide the wrapping for a package of U.S. doctrine and procurement policies—which will destablilize East-West security and further escalate the arms race. Unless officials change the direction of U.S. policy in a far more imaginative manner than any yet suggested by the administration, arms control has no worthwhile future.

*Robert C. Johansen is a senior fellow of the World Policy Institute and editor-in-chief of* World Policy.

*"[Americans] offer assurances that they favor a reduction in world tensions but only. . .by intensifying military preparations."*

viewpoint 85

# The US Arms Buildup Hinders Negotiations

### Andrei A. Gromyko

United efforts were and are still needed today in order to build the postwar world. For it is the major lesson of World War II that states must stand together in the fight against war. It is common knowledge however that while the war-ravaged earth was still smoldering and thousands of towns and villages lay in ruins, the international atmosphere once again began to deteriorate and ultimately to become critical.

The blame for this lies with those who, in their quest for world hegemony, began to behave in a way that contravened obligations as allies in the anti-Hitlerite coalition, oblivious to the lessons of the past.

In disregard of the lofty purposes and principles of the United Nations Charter, to which they too had just affixed their signatures, a group of states set out to escalate their military preparations by piecing together a system of aggressive military blocs with the North Atlantic alliance as its pivot. These states pledged themselves to a policy based on a position of strength, a policy of brinkmanship. It is they who are responsible for the beginning of the cold war, which for so long stemmed the normal flow of international life for which the peoples of the world yearned.

## The Postwar Years

As a result, in the postwar years the world has been in a state of fever. And whenever international relations have been marked, as was the case in the period of detente, by the rise of cooperation between states with different social systems, no effort was spared to undermine these positive processes. And, thanks to the NATO military bloc, this is exactly what happened.

It is precisely this approach in world politics that has led to the situation that marks the international climate today: the threat of war has grown, and the foundations of world peace have become more shaky. This course, which is more than ever such a marked feature of the current policies of the United States and of those who have chosen the role of its accomplices, is opposed by a broad front of peace-loving states, peace-loving forces.

## The Talks in Geneva

Our country strove for a ban on nuclear weapons, both before it possessed them and after it had developed these weapons. The U.S.S.R. continues to favor immediate measures to reduce and ultimately to eliminate nuclear weapons totally. This is the goal of a comprehensive set of initiatives put forward by the Soviet Union.

It took Washington a long time to send its representatives to the negotiating table in Geneva. However, at these talks the U.S. side followed a scenario not designed to lead to agreement. How else can one describe the fact that while negotiating the limitation of nuclear arms in Europe, our partners did exactly the opposite. Beforehand, they set the date—I repeat, beforehand!—they set the date for deploying new U.S. missiles of medium range on the territories of several West European states. We were told to either accept the U.S. position or there will be no agreement. So there is no agreement.

It was Washington's deliberate intention to wreck the negotiations on nuclear arms, both medium-range and strategic. And it did succeed in this.

Now they are rejoicing that they were able to embark on the deployment of their missiles in Europe as planned. Even here, in the course of the General Assembly, you can meet representatives of Western European states who are rubbing their hands with pleasure at the fact that the plan for the deployment is being implemented.

The United States must remove the obstacles it has erected to the holding of talks. Unless these obstacles

Andrei A. Gromyko, from an address to the United Nations General Assembly on September 27, 1984.

are removed, of course, these talks will not take place—and this is what the U.S. has in mind.

Quite often it is asked: since it is difficult for the time being to arrive at a radical solution of the problem of nuclear arms, would it not be possible to take steps which would create a favorable atmosphere for this by raising the level of trust among states and reducing international tensions. We are convinced that this is both possible and necessary.

## For a Freeze on Arsenals

An effective measure of this kind would be the implementation of our proposal, endorsed by the United Nations, for a quantitative and qualitative freeze on nuclear weapon arsenals by all states which possess them. This could be done first by the U.S.S.R. and the U.S.A. on a bilateral basis. I repeat: the U.S.S.R. and the U.S.A. on a bilateral basis by way of an example for other nuclear powers. Why shouldn't we do this?

We are proposing to Washington: let us set this example.

## On Weapons in Outer Space

In view of its particular urgency, it is necessary to single out the question of preventing the race in nuclear and other weapons in outer space, which some people want to turn into a springboard for waging war. And we know who this is, who these people are.

The extension of the arms race to outer space, unless checked in time, could become an irreversible process.

It is our belief that the U.S.S.R. and the U.S.A., as the leading powers in the field of outer space exploration, should do everything in their power to keep outer space peaceful and, in particular, with the view to accomplishing this task, to lay the foundations for multilateral agreement. And we believe this idea is alive in many states.

But responsibility for the failure to hold the talks lies wholly with the U.S. side. Washington is unwilling to engage in the talks.

---

*"While negotiating the limitation of nuclear arms in Europe, [the US] did exactly the opposite."*

---

We urge the U.S. Government to recognize that the militarization of outer space threatens the whole of mankind, including the American people themselves. We express the hope that the United States of America will refrain from actions which would render irreversible the process of turning outer space into the arena of military rivalry and that it would be willing to engage in talks with a view to reaching agreement. For its part, the U.S.S.R. continues to favor the idea of starting such talks as soon as possible.

In seeking to do everything possible to promote this goal, the Soviet Union proposes the inclusion on the agenda of the current session of the General Assembly as an important and urgent item, an item entitled, ''The Use of Outer Space Exclusively for Peaceful Purposes, for the Benefit of Mankind.''

## Non-Use of Force

The idea first and foremost is to ban immediately and for all time the use of force in and from outer space against the earth, as well as from the earth against targets in outer space. In other words, agreement must be reached on the prohibition and elimination of space-attack weapons of all systems and kinds, whatever their mode of basing, designed to destroy targets in case. Above all, this applies to states with a major space capacity.

Surely the implementation of a proposal by the socialist countries to conclude a treaty on the mutual non-use of military force in relations between the states of the Warsaw Treaty and the North Atlantic Alliance would help to dissipate mutual apprehension. And it would be welcomed if an obligation not to be the first to use either nuclear or conventional weapons against the other—in other words, not to use force—if such an undertaking were entered into by states whether they belong to military alliances or are of a neutral or nonaligned status.

We have tabled these and some other major proposals at the Stockholm conference as well. They have been submitted in combination with certain confidence-building measures in the military field.

However, the representatives of NATO countries, in actual fact, have taken up what amounts to an obstructionist position with regard to these proposals. What is proposed under the guise of military and technical measures is a program drawn up by them of barely disguised espionage.

The NATO countries are avoiding businesslike discussion of cardinal questions, above all those dealing with arms reductions. But without such discussions there can be no genuine strengthening of security and stability on the European Continent.

At the Vienna talks, too, there should be no room for any kind of political maneuvering, of which our negotiating partners are so fond.

## A Readiness to Negotiate

Our country expresses its readiness to take part in multilateral negotiations on the limitation of naval activities and naval armaments, and on the extending of confidence-building measures in seas and oceans, particularly for those regions with the busiest sea lanes, the regions with the highest likelihood of conflict situations.

We have originated a proposal—and it's worth recording this—for an agreement on appropriate measures, including measures applicable to particular regions such as, for example, the Indian, Atlantic or Pacific Oceans; the Mediterranean or the Persian Gulf.

The U.S.S.R., together with other Warsaw Treaty states, has put forward a proposal to the North Atlantic bloc to begin talks on the question of the increase in military expenditures and the consequent reduction of them.

However, so far there has been no response from NATO, and this is no accident.

If by using the most sophisticated technology available today a photograph were to be taken showing the magnitude of worldwide military preparations by the United States and its allies on a planetary scale, it would reveal a panorama which would be mindboggling to any thinking person: a palisade of missiles, strategic bombers, naval armadas flying the seas and oceans, hundreds of military bases scattered all over the globe—hundreds of military bases—and colossal stockpiles of weapons of every description.

## An Involuntary Buildup

Some may say that we in the Soviet Union also have weapons—on land, in the air, on and under water. Our answer is yes, we do. But this is not our choice. The objective facts of postwar history make it undeniably clear that it was not the Soviet Union, not socialism, but the other side that started the arms race, and each new spiral in this arms race. This is where the truth lies.

Forced to take countermeasures, our country only did so in response to, and to the extent commensurate with, the protection of its own security and the security of its friends and allies. We have never sought, nor do we seek, superiority. What we want is to maintain the equilibrium, and at the lowest possible level.

## Soviet Proposals

Of our own free will and unilaterally, we have assumed a number of obligations ranging from the non-first use of nuclear weapons through practical steps limiting our armed forces and armaments in Central Europe.

Yet no matter what proposal or argument we put forward, our opposite numbers would say, no, not acceptable. They would swear that they favor a halt in the arms race, but only through the modernization of them, of these weapons, and through the improvement and stockpiling of these weapons.

It's absurd, yes it's absurd. But it's what underlies their policy. They offer assurances that they favor a reduction in world tensions but only by establishing ever more military bases, by intensifying military preparations, by militarizing outer space, by deploying new types of U.S. nuclear weapons in Europe.

What is necessary to prevent hunger and disease from claiming the lives of countless millions of people? According to the logic of NATO countries, it would appear that this can be achieved by throwing as much money and as many resources as possible into the insatiable maw of the war industry.

It would appear that there's no other path towards insuring peace than war preparation. This is perverted logic, the logic of out and out militarism. All states must clearly realize why none of the important and urgent international problems has found a solution so far. And this applies above all to nuclear weapons and to the arms race.

*"The extension of the arms race to outer space, unless checked in time, could become an irreversible process."*

Even elementary decency is lacking in cases where representatives of the two powers—the U.S.S.R. and the U.S.A.—have met to discuss something or other. Everything the U.S. side says is designed to secure unilateral advantages for the United States. Therefore, from the very outset, everything is doomed to failure.

## Moscow's Future Policy

The Soviet delegation is authorized to state in this high forum that the U.S.S.R. will follow precisely the same policy it has been pursuing up to now, namely, a policy of peace, disarmament, the limitation and subsequent elimination of nuclear armaments and the solution of other urgent problems of the day.

*Andrei A. Gromyko is the Foreign Minister of the USSR.*

*"The Soviet Union respects military strength. Its incentive for negotiating an agreement is greater when the positions taken by its negotiating partner [are] supported by that strength."*

viewpoint 86

# The US Arms Buildup Aids Negotiations

### Max M. Kampelman

When the Helsinki Final Act was signed in 1975, the 33 European signatory countries plus the United States and Canada acted on the assumption that the agreement reflected a condition of *"detente,"* a process toward peace and cooperation. The military, economic, cultural, scientific, and humanitarian provisions of that agreement were designed to cover the totality of East-West relations. The Madrid meeting was a follow-up meeting whose original purpose was to carry forward that process of *detente.*

But by the time Madrid began, there was no *detente.* The invasion of Afghanistan exacerbated tensions as it became clear that the Soviets behaved as if they had never signed the Helsinki accords. . . .

The question has been raised by some experts as to whether confrontation is consistent with serious negotiation. Negotiation without confrontation, where the objective facts require blunt talk, is not a serious negotiation at all; it is a charade. A purpose of negotiation is obviously to reach agreement. The negotiating process must also be used to communicate concerns where they exist; so as to lessen the likelihood of ambiguity. Absent this clarity, there is no reason for the other side to take seriously the depth of our commitments and perceptions. . . .

### Strength in Unity

What is necessary is constantly to keep in mind that it is our values that tie us together and that it is those values that are under attack. In a real sense our task is to raise the vision of the West above the minutiae of our relations, important as they may appear to be at any moment. It is vital we prevail in that effort in the face of a massive Soviet onslaught to divide and weaken the alliance.

Let me make an assertion about dealing with the Soviet Union that is based on conviction and on my

experience. The Soviet Union respects military strength. Its incentive for negotiating an agreement is greater when the positions taken by its negotiating partner have the added dignity of being supported by that strength.

The Soviet Union is an aggressive society seeking, with its massive military and police power, to expand its influence, and a repressive society determined to defend its totalitarian power, whatever the human cost. We know it is a major challenge to our security and values. How do we constructively face this reality? I suspect that we and our friends who value freedom will pay a heavy price and suffer great anguish as we come to grips with this challenge. The integrity and character and strength of our society and of our people will undergo the greatest challenge of our history as we learn how to live with Soviet military power, meet it, challenge it, and simultaneously strive to maintain the peace as we remain constant in our ideals.

### World Leadership Role

We still look upon ourselves as a young and developing society, even though we are now one of the oldest, stable systems in the world. We did not seek the role of world leadership, and our people today still tend to shy away from it. By the end of the war, we were somewhat like a young giant among nations. And being a giant is not easy. It is not easy living with a giant, and our friends are learning that. It is hard to find shoes to fit if you are a giant; and the bed is always too short. Being strong, the giant can afford to be gentle, but he is also, at times, awkward. His good intentions are not always so interpreted by others.

We make mistakes because we are unaccustomed to and hesitant about the responsibilities of leadership. As a result, our behavior is at times one of fits and starts and it frequently tends to confuse. We talk a great deal about values and about liberty.

Max M. Kampelman, from an address to the Aerospace Industries Association of America in Williamsburg, Virginia on May 24, 1984.

Some of our more sophisticated friends see this linkage of values with world *realpolitik* as a form of naivete. We, of course, talk about the values of liberty because to us, they are not abstract. We also know they are not abstract to those unable to enjoy them.

Our founding fathers, by cool calculation, informed by history and inspired by a passion for liberty, knew that idealism and realism were a tightly woven warp and woof. They made a sturdy constitutional fabric. We just again treat them as mutually reinforcing. Our values distinguish us from the totalitarians and authoritarians of the world. They are our strength.

## Democracies Subvert Soviets

As we reaffirm our faith, however, we must understand that we thereby implicitly threaten the Soviet Union. Like any dictatorship, the Soviet ruling class is deeply concerned about the subversion of its power—power accumulated not by consent but by military and police force alone. Where there is no legitimacy; where there is repression coupled with traditional national and cultural differences; where there is an obvious failure of the system to meet the needs of its peoples—these obviously contribute to Soviet insecurity. The very fact that there are neighboring free societies creates a powerful draw and attraction for those who live under totalitarian rule. By example, democracies inevitably tend to subvert Soviet authority.

---

*"The Soviet leadership appears frightened and somewhat disorganized."*

---

Thus, the challenge. There are some who respond to the danger to us represented by Soviet military power and theology by ignoring or denying its existence. That would be fatal for us. There are others who are so overwhelmed by the difficulties as to place all of their trust in military power and its use alone. That view can be fatal to us as well.

We dare not and cannot blow the Soviet Union away. We cannot wish it away. It is here and it is militarily powerful. We share the same globe. We must try to find a formula under which we can live together in dignity.

## Soviets Must Change

We must engage in the pursuit of peace without illusion, but with persistence, regardless of provocation. Thus, in Madrid, we attended, talked, debated, negotiated, argued, dined, condemned, talked some more. We achieved some results in words. We have not yet achieved a change in patterns of behavior. That will only come, if it ever does come, when the Soviet Union concludes that it is in its interest to change, and when its leadership

decides that the change is necessary to keep itself in power.

The Soviet Union is not likely to undergo what Jonathan Edwards called "a great awakening," or see a blinding light on the road to Damascus. Yet the imperatives for survival in the nuclear age require us—through the deterrence that comes from military strength, through dialogue, through criticism, through negotiation—to persist in the search for understanding, agreement, peace.

Today, the prospects for understanding seem remote. The Soviet leadership appears frightened and somewhat disorganized—threats, coupled with infrequent smiles, and techniques of traditional Soviet political offensives. This time, however, the threats seem more desperate and despairing.

## Soviet Credibility Collapses

The "correlation of forces" has moved against the Soviet Union. The credibility of its system as a viable alternative has collapsed for sensible people.

The growing military strength of the United States is of further concern to an aging and unstable Soviet elite. It is now engaged in a massive and frantic program to intimidate the world half to death.

The totalitarian cause would be a lost one, considering the added burden of its economic and social failures, were it not for its belief that the West is divided, lazy, comfortable and increasingly pacifist. They doubt the will of the West to resist the intimidating power of its military bluster. Soviet submarines enter Swedish waters to warn and scare as well as gain intelligence. They train and finance terrorists all over the world to destabilize the rest of us. The deep involvement of the Bulgarian secret police in the attempted assassination of the Pope, which would not have been possible without KGB complicity, is an illustration of that criminal irresponsibility. . . .

In a letter smuggled to the West from his exile in Gorky, where his own life and that of his wife Ilene Bonner are now in jeopardy, Andrei Sakharov warned that "the world is facing very difficult times and cruel cataclysms if the West and the developing countries trying to find their place in the world do not now show the required firmness, unity and consistency in resisting the totalitarian challenge. . . ." I believe that with this kind of understanding, free societies will be able to survive the multiple assaults of totalitarianism and establish the conditions for genuine peace.

*Max M. Kampelman is ambassador and chairman of the US Delegation to the Madrid Conference on Security and Cooperation in Europe.*

*"Our fundamental goal is to defend our freedom and that of our allies and to reduce the risk of war, especially nuclear war."*

viewpoint 87

# Arms Negotiations: US Goals

George Shultz

Our fundamental goal is to defend our freedom and that of our allies and to reduce the risk of war, especially nuclear war.

The prerequisite of successful arms control—and world peace—is the deterrent strength of the United States. This strength has been the basis of international stability and security for the past 40 years. The defense policy of the United States and the North Atlantic alliance has been to have that strength necessary to convince any potential adversary that aggression will not pay. The democracies cherish peace; we would prefer to go about our lives without devoting huge effort and treasure to arming ourselves. But as long as there are others in this world hostile to freedom and willing to use force to impose their own system, we must be willing to defend what we hold dear. As President Truman expressed it in 1946: "Peace has to be built on power for good. Justice and good will and good deeds are not enough."

For a time in the 1970s, in the wake of Vietnam, we tended to turn away from this reality, and we neglected our defenses. But the Soviet buildup continued without breaking stride. The Soviets passed the United States in the number, size, and destructive power of offensive missiles; they proceeded to develop more and more modern systems. We essentially froze the number of our missiles; our modernization programs slowed down. As this process continued, the improvements in the Soviet ballistic missile force—including the prompt hard-target-kill capability of its giant ICBMs (intercontinental ballistic missiles)—increasingly threatened the survivability of our own land-based retaliatory forces and our national command structure. The Soviets spent significant resources on passive defensive measures to improve the survivability of their own forces, and they continued to develop active defenses that might eventually be able to counter the surviving U.S. retaliatory forces. These Soviet moves were slowly, but very surely, eroding our capability for swift and effective retaliation—on which depends our ability to deter any attack. Our concern was heightened by mounting evidence of Soviet violations of previous arms control agreements.

## Ensuring Deterrence

The arms control process has always had as a main goal to ensure deterrence by enhancing stability and balance in the strategic relationship. These Soviet actions were undermining that very goal. The United States had an inescapable responsibility to work to maintain the basic conditions for stability and balance.

To strengthen our deterrent and restore the military balance, President Reagan has moved to modernize our strategic and conventional forces across the board. The MX Peacekeeper missile is a vital element of this policy. I cannot stress too much the importance of continuing on course with this program.

But the American eagle holds arrows in one hand and the olive branch in the other—and his eyes look toward the olive branch. Our goal is peace, and, therefore, we are always ready for serious dialogue with our adversaries on ways to control and reduce weapons. The Soviets have now returned to the bargaining table for new negotiations, after their failed attempts to divide us at home and from our allies. Earlier this month, the President dispatched three distinguished Americans—Max Kampelman, Mike Glitman, and Texas' own John Tower—to lead our side on these crucial negotiations. With a strengthened deterrent, an alliance that has withstood Soviet pressures, and the impressive vote of

George Shultz, from an address before the Austin Council on Foreign Relations in Austin, Texas on March 28, 1985.

confidence given by the American people last November, we are now in a good position for successful arms control. Our steadfastness and our continuing commitment to serious negotiations have brought us to this promising moment. This is a lesson we must not forget in the arduous months and years ahead.

## Objectives at Geneva

What are our objectives in these new negotiations? Our four basic aims are stability, reductions, equality, and verifiability.

• First, we seek arms control measures that enhance strategic stability. An agreement, if it is truly to promote security, must decrease and minimize the incentives one side might have to preempt or strike first in a crisis. By this means, arms control can help reduce the danger of war.

---

*"Our goal is peace, and, therefore, we are always ready for serious dialogue with our adversaries on ways to control and reduce weapons."*

---

• Our second objective is reductions. Our arms control proposals represent a historic and systematic effort to reduce the levels of nuclear weapons substantially—rather than, as in the past, only legitimize their increase. When the SALT I (strategic arms limitation talks) negotiations began in 1969, the Soviet Union had about 1,500 strategic nuclear weapons. Today, the Soviet arsenal has grown to more than 8,000 strategic nuclear weapons, yet it still remains within most of the limits of the SALT I and SALT II treaties. The radical reductions that we seek today would reverse the arms buildup and result in a more stable balance at lower levels of forces on both sides.

• Our third objective is equality. Reductions must leave both sides with equal or equivalent levels of forces. An agreement that leaves one side with a unilateral advantage could only create instability. Soviet strategic power is centered in its land-based missile force; American strategic power is spread more evenly over each element of our triad of land-based missiles, submarines, and bombers. We recognize these differences and are prepared to be flexible and reasonable in taking them into account.

• Our fourth objective is verifiability. No American would favor an accord which lacked provision for effective verification of compliance by the parties. Questions about our ability to verify the SALT II Treaty were one reason it encountered such opposition. All our efforts to resolve the many complicated issues of stability, reductions, and equality will come to naught in the absence of effective terms of verification. The evidence of Soviet violations or probable violations of existing arms control obligations—including verification provisions of SALT II—makes this an inescapable necessity.

In the new Geneva talks, our negotiators will discuss offensive and defensive weaponry with the Soviets in three broad areas: strategic offensive nuclear systems, intermediate-range offensive nuclear forces, and defense and space arms. The President has instructed our negotiators to bargain seriously and vigorously. We will judge the results by the strictest of standards—whether they would maintain the security of the United States and our allies, ensure deterrence, enhance strategic stability, and reduce the risk of war. We are prepared to be flexible, however, about ways to achieve our objectives. We will meet the Soviet Union halfway in finding a mutually acceptable approach.

## Strategic Arms

In the field of strategic arms, our negotiators are authorized to explore ways of bridging differences that separated the two sides' positions in the earlier strategic arms reduction talks (START). In those talks, we offered to explore alternate ways to reduce ballistic missile throw-weight, in response to Soviet criticism that our proposals would require restructuring of Soviet forces. We were willing to consider indirect limits such as those we originally proposed, direct limits if the Soviets preferred, or any other serious Soviet proposals. In response to the Soviet criticism that the original U.S. proposal was not comprehensive, we dropped our two-phased approach and proposed a draft treaty. This treaty included equal limits on heavy bombers and held the number of air-launched cruise missiles allowed on each bomber to a level below that of SALT II.

We remain ready to explore trade-offs between areas of U.S. and Soviet advantage in order to begin the process of reducing overall numbers, particularly the numbers of the most destabilizing systems—highly MIRVed (multiple independently-targetable reentry vehicles) ICBMs. For our part, we are ready to limit the potential capabilities of our heavy bombers.

With regard to intermediate-range nuclear forces (INF), we believe the position that we outlined in the fall of 1983 in the earlier INF talks provides a framework for a fair agreement. Our ultimate objective has been and remains a zero-zero outcome—the complete, global elimination of this entire class of longer range INF missiles. The continuing Soviet deployment of SS-20 missiles, now with over 1,200 warheads, makes this goal all the more important. We are also ready to consider interim steps, such as a balance at equal levels of warheads in a global context. The United States is prepared to consider foregoing deployment of its full global allowance in Europe. We are ready to talk about possible aircraft limitations and to be flexible on other points as well. We look to the Soviets to be equally flexible.

There remains a third area under discussion at the new Geneva talks, namely defense and space arms. Here we seek a dialogue on how both sides together may begin to move from the current strategic situation toward a more stable framework for deterrence, one relying more and more on non-nuclear defense systems. In these discussions, we will present our concerns about the erosion of the Anti-Ballistic Missile (ABM) Treaty regime, including Soviet actions that have called that agreement's premises into question. In turn, we will provide the Soviets with a comprehensive rationale for our Strategic Defense Initiative—or SDI—and be prepared to address the entire question of defense and space weapons.

## The Strategic Defense Initiative

For at least the past 30 years, deterrence has rested on the ultimate threat of offensive nuclear retaliation; the United States and the Soviet Union have each been hostage to the nuclear forces of the other. Our retaliatory deterrent has enabled us to live in peace with freedom. We strive to deter war with the minimum level of military power consistent with that purpose. If there is no alternative to the threat of offensive nuclear retaliation, then this is the necessary and moral course. But if, with adequate defenses, we could deny the potential aggressor any hope of achieving his objectives through military power, so that neither side's population was at risk to the other, then that would become the preferable and moral course.

Effective defenses against ballistic missiles would enhance deterrence by reducing or eliminating the efficacy of the attacking weapons. Such defenses, with the ability to intercept first-strike missiles, would take away incentives for an aggressor to attack first in a crisis. They would also provide an insurance policy, in the remote possibility that deterrence failed, by shielding us and our allies against attack.

In his seminal speech of March 23, 1983, President Reagan proposed that we explore the possibility of countering the awesome Soviet missile threat with defensive measures. He offered a vision of a world in which the mutual hostage relationship might eventually be replaced by something more secure—by systems that could intercept and destroy missiles before they strike their targets. Such a strategic world would be not to any single nation's advantage, but to the benefit of all. As the President asked, "Wouldn't it be better to save lives than to avenge them?"

## Nuclear Retaliation Threat

We recognize that deterrence will have to rely on the threat of offensive nuclear retaliation for many years to come—though at sharply reduced levels, if the Geneva talks succeed. With this understanding, we now begin a major research effort: the SDI. We believe that it will provide the basis for a considered judgment, sometime in the next decade, on the feasibility and practicality of providing a shield for the United States and our allies against ballistic missiles.

Defenses, if feasible, will also aid our objective of deep reductions in offensive missiles. A strategic balance at sharply lower levels is more vulnerable to the risk of cheating. The lower the agreed level of arms, the greater the danger that concealed deployments could be of a magnitude to threaten the other side's forces. But with feasible defenses in place, so many illegal missiles would be required to upset the balance that significant cheating could not be concealed.

Indeed, this very point was made by Foreign Minister Gromyko, who told the UN General Assembly in 1962 that anti-missile defenses could be the key to a successful agreement reducing offensive missiles. They would, he said, "guard against the eventuality. . .of someone deciding to violate the treaty and conceal missiles or combat aircraft." Mr. Gromyko and other Soviet leaders in the past have often discussed the value of defenses. I would hope that he and his colleagues would review those statements and come to acknowledge again the merit of our position today on the potential value of strategic defense.

*"Our arms control proposals represent a historic and systematic effort to reduce the levels of nuclear weapons substantially—rather than, as in the past, only legitimize their increase."*

I have emphasized that the defenses would have to be feasible. Feasibility means, first, that any new defensive systems must be reasonably survivable; if not, they might themselves be tempting targets for a first strike. Second, it means not just that the systems must work but that they must be cheaper to produce than would the new offensive systems needed to overcome them. In short, they must be cost effective; otherwise, it would make sense to produce offensive weapons in numbers sufficient to overwhelm the defenses.

A change in the cost relationship of offensive to defensive forces would have revolutionary and potentially quite beneficial effects. Cost-effective defenses would change the marginal incentive for investment away from offensive to defensive systems. In turn, even an imperfect but cost-effective defense system would vastly complicate any aggressor's first-strike planning and further reduce his temptation to consider a preemptive nuclear attack.

## A New Strategic Environment

The road to this safer world would have to be traveled with care. In making the transition from today's near total reliance on offense, our objective would be to deploy defensive systems which, at each step of the process, make a first strike even more difficult. By doing so, we would not only enhance stability but also provide further incentives for reducing offensive forces.

---

*"The road to this safer world would have to be traveled with care."*

---

The feasibility criteria we have adopted—survivability and cost effectiveness—are designed precisely to ensure that any transition period is a stable one. Thus, survivability means less temptation and incentive for either side to attack these new defensive systems at a moment of political crisis during the transition period. Phasing in of truly cost-effective defensive systems will mean that offensive countermeasures—such as piling up more missiles to swamp the defenses—are a losing game.

SDI is not a bid for strategic superiority; on the contrary, it would maintain the balance, in light of the rapid Soviet progress in both offensive and defensive systems. Nor is SDI an abrogation of the ABM Treaty. President Reagan has directed that the research program be carried out in full compliance with the treaty. He has also made clear that any future decision to deploy defenses that were not permitted by treaty would have to be a matter of negotiations.

This does not mean giving the Soviets a veto over our defensive programs, any more than the Soviets have a veto over our current strategic and intermediate-range programs. But our commitment to negotiations does reflect a recognition that we should seek to move forward in a cooperative manner with the Soviets. Given the early stage of our research, many of the details of such a transition are, by necessity, still unclear. Nonetheless, we look forward to discussions in Geneva with the Soviets on the implications of new defensive technologies for arms control and strategic stability and on how best we can both manage any transition to such defenses.

Thus far, the Soviets have not accepted the idea of such a cooperative transition. This should neither surprise nor particularly dismay us. At this point, the Soviets still are seeking to undermine our domestic and allied support to SDI research while they proceed with their own efforts. They are tough-minded

realists, however. As our research proceeds and both nations thus gain a better sense of the future prospects, the Soviets should see the advantages of agreed ground rules to ensure that any phasing in of defensive systems will be orderly, predictable, and stabilizing. The alternative—an unconstrained environment—would be neither in their interest nor in ours.

## Enhancing US Security

Our SDI program is designed to enhance allied as well as U.S. security. A decision to move from research to development and deployment would, of course, be taken in close consultation with our allies. As the U.S. and Soviet strategic and intermediate-range nuclear arsenals declined significantly, we would seek to negotiate reductions in other types of nuclear weapons. If we could develop the technologies to defend against ballistic missiles, we could then turn our energies to the perfection of defensive measures against these other nuclear weapons. Our ultimate objective would be the elimination of them all.

By necessity, this is a very long-term goal. For years to come, we will have to continue to base deterrence on the ultimate threat of nuclear retaliation. And that means we will continue our modernization programs to keep the peace.

This long-term goal also poses special challenges. Were we to move toward the sharp reduction or elimination of nuclear weapons, the need for a stable conventional balance would come once again to the fore. To maintain NATO's security, continued modernization of conventional forces will be essential—just as it is in the present conditions of the strategic balance. At the same time, we must continue to press for reductions in conventional forces—in particular, for mutual and balanced reductions in troop levels in Europe. The world community should also devote urgent attention to the need to limit and, indeed, eliminate the menace of chemical weapons. We have made such a proposal with a draft treaty presented by Vice President Bush last spring in Geneva to the Committee on Disarmament.

We must remember as well that deterrence would continue to be the basis of our security, even were we to make this transition to a defense-dominated world. The difference would be that, rather than resting on the threat of mutual assured destruction, deterrence would be based on the ability of the defense to deny success to a potential aggressor's attack—whether nuclear or conventional. The President has called this strategic relationship mutual assured security.

## The Debate Over SDI

Some urge against SDI. They say the balance of terror has worked, so why tamper with it? They also say SDI will lead to an offensive arms race as the Soviets move to counter our defense—as if the Soviets have not been engaged for the past 20 years in the greatest offensive buildup in history, one far beyond legitimate security needs.

These critics overlook two other central points.

• The first is that the pace of technological advance in offensive weapons—such as increasing missile accuracy and mobility—could, over time, undermine the principles on which the mutual hostage relationship has rested. SDI is a prudent and wise investment in our future safety. It would enhance, not undercut, deterrence.

• The second point the critics overlook is that the Soviets have their own version of an SDI program and have had it for years, long before ours. Behind the propaganda about the alleged "militarization of space," you will find the expenditures, the military and research personnel, the laboratories, testing grounds, and weapons of an ambitious Soviet strategic defense program.

The Soviet Union has always placed great reliance on strategic defense. Over the past 20 years, the Soviets have spent approximately as much on defense as on their massive offensive program. They have long made major investments in civil and air defense; they have the world's only operational antisatellite weapon system and the only operational ABM system around Moscow. The 1972 ABM Treaty permits one such system; we abandoned ours, but they have maintained and modernized theirs. The Soviet Defense Forces—one of their five military services—number 500,000 strong, more than the Soviet Navy or Strategic Rocket Forces.

## Laser Program

We have persuasive evidence that the Soviets have long been investigating the defensive technologies in which our SDI research will focus. Their high-energy laser program is considerably bigger than ours and continues to grow. There is also much evidence of a major Soviet research effort in the development of particle-beam weapons.

The ABM Treaty limits the deployment of ballistic-missile early-warning radars to locations along the periphery of the national territory of each party and requires that they be oriented outward. At Krasnoyarsk, almost 400 miles inside the frontiers of the Soviet Union, a new radar, oriented across Soviet territory, is under construction in violation of the treaty. Other Soviet activities suggest that the Soviet Union may be preparing a nationwide ABM defense—an action which, of course, would entirely negate the ABM Treaty. Twenty-three Democratic members of the House of Representatives just sent a letter to General Secretary Gorbachev, pointing out that if the Krasnoyarsk matter "is not resolved in a satisfactory manner, it will have serious consequences for the future of the arms control process." Halting and reversing this erosion of the ABM Treaty is another objective we have set for the Geneva talks.

My point here is clear: the United States is not alone. We are not starting another arms race. We are starting a research program that complies with the ABM Treaty. Rather than asking what will be the Soviet response to SDI, critics ought to be asking: given the Soviet Union's major strategic defense effort and its huge offensive forces, what are the consequences for deterrence, stability, and Western security if we do not pursue an adequate research effort?

## Prerequisites for Successful Arms Control

These are the issues we intend to pursue in Geneva. They represent a full agenda. The United States is committed to seek progress; we hope the Soviets have the same commitment. We in the West can facilitate progress if we bear in mind what progress depends upon. History suggests there are three prerequisites.

The first, which I explained earlier, is the need to keep up our guard and our strength. In the past, we have had a tendency to focus either on our military strength or on negotiations. To succeed, we must treat them both in tandem as two essential components of a sensible national security strategy. That is the plain reality of international politics. Talk without strength to back it up is just that: talk. The Soviets must understand that in the absence of an equitable, verifiable agreement, we will be as strong as necessary to maintain our freedom and deter war.

The other two prerequisites are patience in seeking the agreement we desire and unity both at home and with our allies.

---

*"We are not starting another arms race. We are starting a research program that complies with the ABM treaty."*

---

We are embarked on the most complex and comprehensive negotiations to limit arms in the history of man. In these talks, we face Soviet diplomats who are practiced, patient, and determined. They will try to wear us down. They will also try to undermine our positions by deceptive propaganda, by specious appeals to public opinion here and in Europe, by subtle and not so subtle threats, just as they did for 2 years during the START and INF talks.

## Need for Patience

The opening of the Geneva talks a few weeks ago, like my meeting with Foreign Minister Gromyko in

January, received much publicity and attention. This is understandable. It reflects the hopes of all people, hopes we share. But if we are ever to attain those hopes, we must be patient. We must recognize from experience that the talks may be long and arduous. Every negotiation has been protracted. The talks that led to the 1963 Limited Nuclear Test Ban Treaty took 8 years; the 1968 Non-Proliferation Treaty took 4 years; SALT I, almost 3 years; SALT II, nearly 7 years. Ever since bilateral nuclear arms control negotiations with the Soviet Union began some 30 years ago, the Soviets' rigid perception of their military requirements and their hostility to proper measures of verification have been significant obstacles. But we, for our part, are ready to move ahead as fast as possible. We will not be the obstacle.

*"We must be careful not to permit our revulsion against war to lower our guard."*

The third and, perhaps, most important prerequisite is unity, both at home and with our allies.

Many of our problems in the past 15 years have resulted from divisions here at home. Probably the greatest cost of the Vietnam war, after its terrible toll in lives, was the shattering of the national consensus on defense that was forged in World War II and that carried us through the most difficult days of the cold war. Today, I believe a new consensus is emerging—a growing majority behind the need for a strong defense coupled with serious and realistic efforts for reliable arms control agreements with the Soviets. And we see a new patriotism, a new pride in America.

## Responsibility to Cooperate

Last November, the American people overwhelmingly expressed their confidence in President Reagan and his policies. The Administration has the responsibility to consult with the Congress, and we are doing all we can, in a spirit of cooperation. Congress has the duty to debate and criticize, to approve expenditures, and to consult in the formulation of general policy. We in the executive branch have the constitutional responsibility to conduct the negotiations. To aid Congress in its role, we had with our delegation at the opening of the Geneva talks a distinguished bipartisan group from both Houses. Should a treaty be negotiated, it will require the Senate's advice and consent to ratification. But if the Congress does not back us in many other ways, we may not have a good treaty to bring home for advice and consent.

The same principle applies to our relations with our allies. The Soviet attempt to prevent the deployment of Pershing and cruise missiles in Europe failed utterly because we allies stood together, as we have for decades. The Soviets may make this attempt again, in the context of the new talks. We must continue to stand together if we want these talks to succeed. The Soviets will be watching closely for signs of differences and disarray in the West. If they see such signs, they will only be encouraged to step up their political warfare while prolonging negotiations and waiting for unilateral concessions. But if they see us united, we will have hastened the day of serious negotiation and furthered the prospects of success.

The Geneva talks will be of unprecedented complexity. We must be careful not to permit our revulsion against war to lower our guard. We must not let our hopes, noble as they are, blind us to the daunting realities of the arms control process. But there are favorable factors at work. America is recovering its economic vitality, it military strength, and its self-confidence. We stand firm with our staunch allies. If we in the West are patient and united, combining resolution with flexibility, then we have good prospects of success. We can attain the goal we all share: reducing the danger of war and building a constructive and secure relationship with the Soviet Union in the nuclear age.

*George Shultz is secretary of State for the United States.*

*"In the opinion of the USSR, it is above all essential to attend to security. To check the arms race to begin with, and prevent its spread to outer space."*

# Arms Negotiations: USSR Goals

Vladlen Kuznetsov

In the opinion of the U.S.S.R., it is above all essential to attend to security. To check the arms race to begin with, and prevent its spread to outer space. To ensure that the Geneva talks result in mutually acceptable agreement, the U.S.S.R. proposes to the U.S. the introduction, for the entire duration of the talks, of

—a moratorium on the development (including research), testing, and deployment of space strike weapons;

—a freeze on the strategic offensive arms of both sides;

—a halt in the deployment of the U.S. medium-range missiles in Europe and in the buildup of countermeasures on the part of the U.S.S.R. and its allies.

As has been the case so many times before, the Soviet Union is displaying good will in this crucial period in the development of international relations. It has declared a moratorium on the deployment of its medium-range missiles and suspended other countermeasures in Europe. The moratorium will be effective until November this year. Whether it will be prolonged or lifted depends on the United States, on whether Washington will follow the Soviet example and display restraint, stop the further deployment of its medium-range missiles in Europe.

## New Soviet Initiatives

The Soviet Union's new initiatives are an invitation to carry forward the Geneva talks with all speed to the productive stage, the achievement of a mutually acceptable agreement. The U.S.S.R. seeks at these talks not one-sided advantage, but an honest outcome that would satisfy both itself and its socialist allies and the United States and its NATO partners, an outcome satisfactory to all who want to see the war danger reduced. Moscow is not out to outmanoeuvre the negotiating partner. It wants the common cause of peace to be the gainer.

The U.S.S.R. went to Geneva not to engage in some futile philosophical debate on abstract disarmament themes divorced from the realities. And still less does it regard the talks as a course of lectures on the supposed merits of dubious strategic "initiatives." The Soviet delegation has been instructed to work for the achievement, within reasonable, acceptable time limits, of agreements in the spirit of the understanding in principle that the problems of nuclear and space weapons would be examined in their interrelations on the basis of equality and equal security.

The Soviet initiatives have been met the world over with deep satisfaction and hope that a glimmer of light will appear on the international political horizon. Only in official Washington are these concrete manifestations of good will described as "propaganda." If the U.S. and in general Western official quarters really wish to help strengthen world peace they should make a radical reappraisal of their negative attitude to the proposals of the U.S.S.R. and the other socialist countries. As it is, everything that comes from the U.S.S.R. is said to be prompted by ulterior motives. As can be seen from press comment, world opinion demands that the governments of the NATO countries, and primarily the U.S. Administration, stop brushing aside Soviet proposals and reciprocate.

## Peaceful Development

Aware of the significance of the state of its relations with the U.S. for world peace and international security, the Soviet Union has urged concentrating on a search for mutual understanding, on peaceful development excluding hostility and confrontation. In view of this, Moscow regards as useful also a summit

Vladen Kuznetsov, "In Which Direction?" *New Times*, April 1985.

meeting that could give a serious impulse to Soviet-American relations.

Between the U.S.S.R. and the U.S. there is no gulf that cannot be spanned by a bridge leading to lasting peace. But that bridge has to be built in both countries. Thus everything depends on political good will, on whether that will exists or not. "That will exists on the Soviet side," Mikhail Gorbachev stressed in his talk with the Speaker of the U.S. House of Representatives Thomas O'Neill. "If the American side displays that will, many concrete issues that now divide our countries will gradually find their solution."

The Soviet Union is often accused of pursuing an "over-ideologized" foreign policy determined by nothing short of a striving towards "world revolution." But what is the real state of affairs?

## Peace vs. Ideology

The U.S.S.R. has made it plain that it is against carrying ideological differences over to the inter-state sphere. Its socialist ideology in no way prevents it from building its relations with the U.S. on the basis of common interest in preserving and safeguarding peace. Neither differences between social systems nor the contrariety of ideologies are an impediment to this.

The foreign policy of a number of Western states, and primarily of the U.S., is increasingly determined not by the interests of world peace but by ideological differences with socialism. Some government leaders are so obsessed with the "crusade" against socialism that it sometimes looks as if even their instinct of self-preservation is ceasing to work. It is precisely in these quarters that the watchword is "better dead than Red."

---

*"The Soviet Union is ready for genuine political reconciliation with the US and other NATO countries on the basis of renunciation of confrontation."*

---

The Soviet Union, on the contrary, is ready for genuine political reconciliation with the U.S. and other NATO countries on the basis of renunciation of confrontation and of the use of force, on the basis of equality and equal security and joint effort to put an end to the arms race.

The question of whether outer space is to remain peaceful or is to be turned into a military springboard has latterly acquired particular urgency. In Mikhail Gorbachev's interview to Pravda and his talk with the Speaker of the U.S. House of Representatives the emphasis was laid on the necessity of Washington abandoning its provocative schemes for carrying the arms race into outer space.

However, Washington has taken the bit between its teeth. It has officially proposed to 17 of the United States' NATO and other military blocs allies that they take part in research within the framework of the "strategic defence initiative" programme. Moreover, the proposal was couched in a form nothing short of an ultimatum.

Perhaps Washington recognizes the right of free choice on this very serious issue requiring independent and responsible consideration? Nothing of the kind. The White House, State Department and the Pentagon undertake to do the thinking for their allies, out of which both up-to-date technology and financial resources would be squeezed. The allies are under an incessant and heavy propaganda barrage, with the big guns like Weinberger, Burt, Perle, Rogers, Abrahamson, Scowcroft, Nitze and others brought into play. They are trying to force upon the West as its common platform Reagan's "strategic defence initiative" the object of which is to create a hermetically sealed, "total defence" in order to be able to deliver the nuclear first strike with impunity, as it is hoped.

At the Geneva talks the U.S. delegation is reluctant to discuss the space issue, which was brought to the fore two years ago by Washington itself. It is legitimate to ask: is not the U.S. insisting on the militarization of outer space because it has no intention of trying to reach mutually acceptable agreements?

It is to the credit of a considerable segment of world public opinion that it has seen through Washington's design. This, of course, is not to the liking of the architects of these schemes. Not a day passes without official Washington spokesmen eulogizing them, serving them up as a boon for all humanity.

## A Hawk Dressed as a Pigeon

The casuistry resorted to knows no bounds. They claim that the idea is to create a purely defensive system, and at the same time they build up the U.S. first-strike potential. They argue that they are out to "destroy the missiles" and "protect millions of people"—and at the same time they press on Congress for appropriations for the production of that mass destruction weapon, the MX missile. They contend that the "strategic defence initiative" is "arms control" and at the same time escalate the deadly arms buildup subject to no limitation and fraught with unpredictable consequences. They give assurances of their peaceful intentions and appeal for trust, but refuse to follow the example of the U.S.S.R. and undertake the commitment not to be the first to use nuclear weapons. They seek to persuade some, to dissuade others, to refute still others, and to fool them all. The fact is glossed over that from this dubious "defence" it is only one step to aggression. In a word, the hawk is being dressed up as a pigeon.

But the most insidious propaganda is powerless to cover up nefarious designs.

It is plain to see that participation in U.S. "technological programmes," which is being pressed upon its NATO partners, is participation in a dubious, risky undertaking. Those who are tempted by the prospect of finding "protection" against Soviet nuclear weapons, including the SS-20 missiles, under the "space umbrella" are risking finding themselves under a sword suspended on a very slender thread.

One of Washington's arguments is that the Soviet Union is doing the same things as the United States. The allegation is too crude to warrant refutation; suffice it to say that the U.S.S.R. has the wherewithal to counter these dangerous plans. But it would not want to extend military rivalry to outer space. The Soviet Union has proposed to the United States that agreement be reached already now on a reciprocal basis on the prohibition of all types of space weapons. The U.S. is expected to undertake no more than the commitments the U.S.S.R. is ready to undertake. Would this not be the best solution? After all, those out to gain technological and military superiority will gain neither the one nor the other. The Soviet Union will see to that.

## Scientific Projects

There is still another aspect of the matter. Washington indulges in exhortations not to discontinue scientific research, not to impede progress in inventive thought. True enough, progress must not be halted. But those who use it against peace and humanity can and must be stopped. And no amount of rhetoric can induce normal people to applaud "star wars" technology. The Hiroshima and Nagasaki victims will not allow it to be forgotten that the Manhattan project which produced the atom bomb also was only a scientific project at first. How, then, can political and government leaders who are aware of their responsibility for the fate of peace allow themselves not to give thought to the consequences of technical projects? It would be a crime to abandon the fate of peace and the security of the peoples to the mercy of militarism. It is not military technology but reason that should prevail in human society. Ask any sober-minded person and he will tell you which is preferable—military space research fraught with terrestrial and star wars, or peaceful space research which opens truly boundless prospects of progress and well-being.

The United States' allies too will have to decide which is better—to participate in peaceful space research or to be a party to the militarization of space, which would blast all hopes for success at the Geneva talks, all hope of limiting and reducing nuclear armaments.

The Soviet Union is convinced that security lies at the heart of East-West relations. And for much-suffering Europe it is the issue of issues. Given reliable security it will be easier to build interstate relations, to cooperate, to trade, to maintain contacts of all kinds. The greater the security, the more confidence, the lack of which makes itself so keenly felt today in international relations.

## Nuclear-Free Europe

Security must be created and ensured by the joint efforts of East and West. As regards the Warsaw Treaty countries, they have a concrete programme of military detente in Europe. It envisages ridding Europe completely of nuclear weapons, both medium-range and tactical, and of chemical weapons as well. It provides for a whole complex of other large-scale political and military measures, including the reduction of military spending by both the Warsaw Treaty and NATO countries, and the creation of nuclear-free zones in various parts of Europe.

*"The Soviet Union has proposed to the United States that agreement be reached already now on a reciprocal basis on the prohibition of all types of space weapons."*

The Warsaw Treaty countries are strengthening their own security without impairing anyone else's. In general it must be said that this nuclear missile and space age erases, as it were, the distinction between one's own security and that of others. Peace is indivisible, and so is security. He who seeks to undermine the security of others is jeopardizing his own.

Which direction, then, are things to take? The Soviet Union has no doubts on this score. It is necessary to seek agreement on the decisive questions of war and peace, to end the arms buildup, to work for mutual understanding and trust, for detente and all that word stands for. People who have lived through and remember the two world wars merit a better fate than to live between war and peace. They deserve the right to live in conditions of secure peace guaranteed against the danger of war.

*Vladlen Kuznetsov is a writer for* New Times, *a weekly magazine published in the Soviet Union.*

*"Treaties, pacts and conventions mean
no more to them than they did to Hitler
and his Nazis."*

# The Soviet Threat Impedes Peace

## William Rusher & Patrick Dillon

*Editor's note: Part I of the following viewpoint is by
William Rusher and Part II is by Patrick Dillon.*

### I

Just what sort of conduct do you suppose it would
take on the part of the Soviet Union to outrage liberal
opinion in the Western world?

Granted, bringing this outlaw nation to book for its
crimes is something else again, for it is extremely
powerful and therefore dangerous. But there is no
risk, from the standpoint of liberals living in perfect
freedom on this side of the Iron Curtain, in at least
expressing an appropriate moral fury at the conduct
of the despots who rule Russia. Yet such liberals
apparently will overlook any outrage, and keep on
calling for a deeper ''understanding'' of these
villains—as if we did not understand them very
well already.

What kind of Soviet behavior, I repeat, would
really get to such people? The Kremlin's total
suppression of internal dissent is clearly not
enough—that has been going on for 65 years, and
everybody takes it for granted. The Soviet Union's
systematic destabilization and subversion of other
sovereign nations, from Cambodia and Mozambique
to Nicaragua, is positively applauded—at any rate
until the local liberals in such places, who typically
helped the communists seize power in the first place,
come bounding out and report breathlessly that
things are actually worse than before.

Not even the outright Soviet invasion of another
country, as in the case of Afghanistan, can rouse the
world's liberals to more than a purely pro forma
protest. To this very day the U.N. General Assembly
has never been able to bring itself to identify by

nationality the ''foreign forces'' for whose withdrawal
from Afghanistan it has meekly called. Yet this sort
of pusillanimity is scarcely so much as criticized in
the West.

Very well, then, would Western opinion be deeply
roused by a Soviet-inspired attempt to assassinate the
pope? Such an attempt was actually made, and nearly
succeeded, and the would-be killer now has
implicated a whole raft of Bulgarian intelligence
agents, not one of whom would dream of tying his
own shoelaces without the prior knowledge and
permission of the KGB. What's more, the head of the
KGB at the time has just taken over the chairmanship
of the self-elected little committee that runs Russia—
and we are invited to butter him up on the theory
that he is a ''closet liberal.''

What's left? How about waging highly sophisticated
chemical warfare against the native populations of
backward but refractory nations like Afghanistan and
Cambodia? Would that at least, if proved against the
Russians, rouse the sluggish conscience of Western
liberal opinion?

Apparently not; the first American charges about
Soviet use of ''yellow rain'' were attacked and
dismissed by our liberal media as too insubstantial to
credit. The most recent official State Department
report on the subject, being far too detailed and well-
documented to dismiss that way, has been given the
absolute minimum of media attention.

And by the way, don't fall for the liberal excuse
that they see no point in making heavy weather over
misdeeds of foreign countries that ''the United States
can't do anything about.'' We couldn't ''do anything
about'' Hitler in the 1930s, either, but that didn't
prevent the world's liberals from yelling bloody
murder—and rightly—about his domestic persecution
of Jews and his foreign aggressions. One can imagine
just how lively their reaction would have been if
there had been comparable evidence that Hitler had
tried to assassinate the pope or had resorted in

William Rusher, ''Does Nothing the Soviets Do Bother Western Liberals?''
*The Washington Times,* January 3, 1983. Reprinted by permission of
Newspaper Enterprise Association, Inc.

Patrick Dillon, ''Soviet Mercenaries Must Be Stopped,'' *The Union Leader,*
March 26, 1981. Reprinted with permission.

combat to "yellow rain."

I conclude that there is absolutely nothing the Soviet Union can do—no outrage against the moral order that it can commit—that would tease from Western liberal opinion one-tenth of the anger that any decent person would normally feel. The reason, though obscure, is not altogether incomprehensible; what we call "liberal" opinion in the Western world is in fact essentially democratic socialist opinion. As such, it has many of the same philosophical and rhetorical enemies as communism: capitalists, multinational corporations, the "upper classes," Big Business, exploitative colonial powers, etc. This common demonology prevents it from evaluating the Soviet Union altogether objectively. Whatever its "excesses," communism isn't—in pure theory liberals would stress (if they dared to be candid)—entirely wrong.

Fortunately, liberals are becoming steadily less able to speak for the West. And that is why the Soviet Union may yet receive what it so richly deserves: the wholehearted moral condemnation of mankind.

## II

The time of pandering to the "peace at any price" one-worlders, our current crop of domestic marxists and other ill-assorted brotherly love intellectuals is past. What some may consider to have started out after World War II as a game of ideological chess has now clearly resolved itself into an exercise in survival and there can now no longer be any question whatsoever that we are rapidly approaching the point of no return in the balance of our contest with the growing menace of Communist imperialism....

Let me leave no doubt in your mind that the king-sized problem with the Russian dictators—and please do not confuse this elite group with either the population of the Soviet Union or its captive nationals—we have been trying to talk ourselves out of over the past 35 years will not go away. In fact, it will get worse if we don't start thinking straight and doing something about it now. What we have to cope with will take more than band-aids and brinkmanship; more than dollops of aid and advice and a good deal more than half a dozen helicopters and a carload of carbines. Of course, we've been this route before in Southeast Asia and it cost us 50,000 dead and left us $20 billion in the hole. That was the best war the U.S.S.R. ever arranged for us to lose and we fell right into their trap, hook, line and sinker. This time we have no alternative but to take the initiative and strike at the source of the disease before it assumes the proportions of a hemispheric epidemic.

## Communist Malignancy

For starters, the malignancy of Castro's Cuba must be excised if we want to purge the festering sores of communism by proxy in the Caribbean area. And we had better make up our minds to win this time regardless of the squeals of the causists and the howls of the paid Marxist moles in our midst. Make no mistake about it, we are going to hurt but the privation and suffering amongst the millions already caught up in the Communist net both on our doorstep and in the rest of the Soviet Empire will be even worse. The cleansing of their homelands from the venom and pestilence of a vicious self-perpetuating dynasty of unprincipled fuhrers will call for massive endurance and much physical suffering but there is no alternative if we want to survive in a free world. As a keen observer of the West's roller coaster ride towards the political and economic oblivion of a Marxist Police State, I realized many years ago that the avenues of containment through statesmanship and diplomacy were about as impressive to the Communist rulers as watering the Sahara Desert with a garden hose.

*"The Soviet Union may yet receive what it so richly deserves: the whole-hearted moral condemnation of mankind."*

Treaties, pacts and conventions mean no more to them than they did to Hitler and his Nazis. They are used only as instruments to wither and destroy our democratic institutions and ultimately, all the freedoms that this great country has fought for so long to preserve. They are totally irreconcilable in their determination to impose their cruel Godless cult over every living soul on the face of this earth regardless of how long it takes and they will lie, cheat and use every dirty trick known to achieve this end. Ever since the Big Three conference at Yalta in February of 1945, the Soviet leadership has been laughing up its sleeves at our naive attempts to compromise, rationalize and cooperate in the makings of a new world free of the terrors of war. Its agents, planted amongst us, sponsored and promoted the false images of benign tolerance towards Marxist egalitarianism while their masters busied themselves sowing the seeds of political dissent and economic ruin in every country that could become a ready target for destabilization.

## Subversive Infection

How deeply we have become infected by subversive propaganda is exemplified by the following piece of witless pedestrianism by none other than Walter Mondale, our ex Vice-President. "I'm very worried about U.S.-Soviet relations. I cannot understand—it just baffles me—why the Soviets these last few years have behaved as they have. Maybe we have made some mistakes with them. Why did they have to build up all those arms?

Why did they have to go into Afghanistan? Why can't they relax just a little bit about Eastern Europe? Why do they sprinke their influence around Ethiopia? Why do they try every door to see if it is locked?" No wonder Brezhnev and his henchmen were rooting for another four years of Carter!

## Courting Political Insanity

With the proliferation of international gang warfare fostered and supported by the U.S.S.R. and its pack of underdogs we had better clear our heads and get into where this crowd is coming from before we are isolated and brought to our knees. It makes no sense at all for us to dribble a few dollars' worth of aid to countries already targeted by the Communists for subjugation while, at the same time, courting financial ruin by lending billions to other countries that have been locked into the Soviet orbit for several decades. So deeply is the West committed to some of these satellite dictatorships that we are now obliged to lend them rent money to pay the interest on their loans. The sheer brilliance of the international banking set behind this fiscal insanity should make us all sick with envy!

Nor does it make any sense for us to trade brains and industrial expertise with the Communist Empire or any country that will act as a pipeline to it. Does anyone really believe for one minute that this might lead to a mutually profitable interchange of talent and scientific skills for the general benefit of all mankind?

*"It makes no sense at all for us to dribble a few dollars' worth of aid to countries already targeted by the Communists for subjugation."*

Only by the Grace of God is their system of government so oppressively inefficient that despite some of the richest agricultural soil in the world, they can neither feed themselves nor their slave empire. And what do we dumb fools in the West do? We send them wheat and grains at bargain basement prices while, at the same time, paying our own farmers millions not to make use of their land to grow crops that might alleviate either our dependency on imported oil or the misery of famine amongst our allies in Asia and Africa—what's left of them. In all truth, there seems to be no end to our stupidity—or is it faithless treachery from within our own walls by those who would aspire to the delusions of temporal power in a society bereft of spiritual greatness?

*William Rusher is a syndicated political columnist who appears regularly in* The Washington Times. *Patrick Dillon's columns appear in* The Union Leader *of Manchester, New Hampshire.*

*"We make a caricature of foreign policy when we let our 'habitual hatred' of the Soviet Union becloud our sense of the complexity of the world predicament."*

viewpoint 90

# The Myth of the Soviet Threat Impedes Cooperation

George W. Ball

One of the sagest admonitions in George Washington's Farewell Address was that we Americans should beware of "inveterate antipathies against particular nations."

"The nation," he said, "that indulges toward another an habitual hatred...is in some degrees a slave. It is a slave to its animosity...which is sufficient to lead it astray from its duty and its interests." And he added: "Antipathy in one nation against another disposes each more readily to offer insult and injury, to lay hold of slight causes of umbrage, and to be haughty and intractable when accidental or trifling occasions or disputes occur."

That advice has particular relevance today, for our government is exhibiting toward the Soviet Union such an "habitual hatred" as to make it, in Washington's phrase, "to some degrees...a slave to its animosity."

No sensible American would, of course, contend that the rivalry that exists between the West and those nations and peoples dominated by Moscow is without substance or that it should be taken lightly. The competition between two great power centers, each armed to the teeth with nuclear weapons, is indubitably a central element of international relations. But it should not become such an all-consuming element as to obscure the other diverse problems that now face us.

The world of the late twentieth century is enormously complex and intricate, and nothing can more seriously throw us off course in conducting international relations than to ignore that fact. Yet our foreign policy today is dominated by a passion for oversimplification, largely because living with complexity is forbiddingly difficult. It requires skill, patience, thought and a spacious view that can be

achieved only with a comprehension of history and the application of sustained effort.

## Movie Plot Politics

The easy, escapist resort is to let our "habitual hatred" of Moscow dictate our policy and to adopt a Manichean view that sees our foreign policy as an eternal struggle between America as the embodiment of righteousness and the Soviet Union as the "focus of evil." That view is heavily influenced by the movies, which base many story lines on an inevitable shoot-out between the good guys and the bad guys, the black hats and the white hats. But that is the fantasy of scriptwriters, who can always assure that right prevails and that the ending is happy. In real life there are an appalling number of subplots, while motivations and emotions are so much conditioned by history and geography—by political and economic disparities; ethnic, religious, tribal and family disputes and differences—as not to permit substituting a comforting dichotomy for complex analysis and hard decisions.

Thus we are stultifying ourselves when we base our policy on President Reagan's expressed assumption that, if the Soviet Union did not exist, the world could live in relative tranquility without "hot spots." The facts emphatically deny this. During the whole of the past decade, the developments that have most critically jeopardized and harmed Western interests have resulted from movements, actions and policies with which Moscow has had nothing to do.

OPEC's precipitate price increases dislocated the world's economy and helped bring about a global recession. That was an initiative not of the Politburo but of a group of Third World nations exploiting their monopoly of a key source of the world's energy. Nor did the Soviets overthrow the Shah of Iran. He was pushed off his throne not by external forces, but because he had, from good motives and bad, managed to alienate almost every sector of Iranian society. Even the most paranoid ideologues cannot blame Moscow for the Iran-Iraq war. Nor is Moscow in any way the cause of the festering Arab-Israeli struggle, or the agonies of Lebanon, the communal bloodshed in India, the menacing racial tensions in South Africa,the religious feuding in Northern Ireland, the quarrel between the Moroccans and the Polisario in North Africa, Libya's threat to the Sudan, the comic opera conflict in the Falklands—or any of numerous other "hot spots," as the President calls them.

## Simplistic Interpretations

So we make a caricature of foreign policy when we let our "habitual hatred" of the Soviet Union becloud our sense of the complexity of the world predicament. Most troubles between nations are local or regional in nature. More than 40 shooting wars are now in progress around the globe, and all but a tiny number result from ethnic or religious conflicts, racial animosities, intolerance and repression in all its forms, inequities and inequalities, ancient boundary disputes, and historic arguments that are not less bitter for having lost all discernible relevance to today's realities. The reaction of our government, almost by conditioned reflex, to force everything into the oversimplified mold of the East-West struggle—to bend and push and pull and distort parochial disputes to fit the doctrinaire concept of the polarized conflict known as the Cold War—is not only factually dishonest but a fatuous delusion.

---

*"Let us avoid being led by our habitual hatred for the Soviet Union to imitate its practices."*

---

Not the least of the dangers in such a foolish exercise is that it could prove self-fulfilling. If we insist that long-running, complex, factional feuds are intricately related to the quarrel between the United States and the Soviet Union as the "source of all evil," we shall go on repeating the error of Vietnam, where we confused a combination of Tonkinese imperialism and civil war having anti-colonialist overtones with a deliberate aggression by the major Communist powers. And we shall go on producing humiliating fiascos such as that we suffered in Lebanon, where we sought to justify our own careless involvement in an environment of long-standing factional conflict by portraying Syria as a mere Soviet puppet. We shall pay heavily for the damage and dislocations we mindlessly encourage.

Washington presciently anticipated current developments when he told us that an habitual hatred can lead to slavery. Not only are we exhibiting an aspect of slave mentality by imitating the Soviets;

we are also validating an old French adage that we acquire the visage of our adversary. In our obsession with the Soviet Union, we are adopting its principles and aping its practices—and diminishing our country in the process.

## US "Brezhnev Doctrine"

Consider, for example, our conduct in Central America and the Caribbean. In 1968, when the Kremlin moved its army into Prague, the Soviets sought to justify that action by the so-called Brezhnev Doctrine, which holds that Moscow is entitled to interfere in the affairs of any socialist state within its sphere of influence if that state shows signs of succumbing to Western ideas. Today our government, without admitting it, is pursuing its own particular form of the Brezhnev Doctrine.

How do we justify trying to overthrow the government of Nicaragua? The people of that country, so our leaders say, have been captured by a political and economic system that is anathema to us. Moreover—and this is quite unforgiveable—the Nicaraguan government draws support from Cuba and the Soviet Union. Since we have historically, if never explicitly, regarded Nicaragua as within our sphere of influence, we claim the right to overthrow its government and install one more to our liking. Of course that is not the public rationale. Our government is visibly working with and supplying arms, money, training and ammunition to the "contras"—Nicaraguan emigres, including ex-Somoza followers—whose sole objective is to overthrow the Nicaraguan government and take over themselves. Yet the Administration insists that it might abandon the contras—"betray"is the harsher term—if the Sandinista government would only stop shipping arms to the Salvadoran rebels. But even if that is really our position, does it justify our intervention? Are we entitled to claim the right to export our revolution to Nicaragua and overthrow its government solely to prevent Nicaragua from exporting its revolution to El Salvador and trying to overthrow its government?

## Gunboat Diplomacy

If we are honest with ourselves, we will recognize that our assumed right to depose (or, to use the euphemism, "destabilize") distasteful Latin American governments is merely an atavistic manifestation of gunboat diplomacy. Although we now claim to have outgrown that practice, we still pursue it and, in the process, leave the people of target countries in worse condition than before:

• As far back as the 1920s, when we sent our Marines for the second time to Nicaragua because its government was, we claimed, falling under Bolshevik influence from Mexico, we saddled that country with the Somoza regime which repressed the people and bled them white for the next four decades.

• When, under the Eisenhower Administration, we overthrew the duly-elected Arbenz government in Guatemala, we bequeathed that country a succession of military juntas punctuated by assassination.

• When we sought in the early 1970s to overthrow the Allende government in Chile before it overthrew itself by its own incompetence, that nation fell under the Pinochet regime, which has set an odious mark for brutality.

• Finally, when we launched the Bay of Pigs operation to try to depose Castro, we succeeded only in establishing his control of Cuba more firmly than ever.

Today we are not only pursuing a Brezhnev Doctrine of our own, but, driven by our habitual hatred of the Soviet Union and all its works, we are even imitating Soviet methods. There is no way we can reconcile our avowed national principles with such outrageous conduct as mining harbors and interrupting international traffic into Nicaragua—a clear act of war against a government with which we maintain formal diplomatic relations. We are behaving even more odiously when we reject the arbitrament of the World Court—again an action slavishly imitating the nation we habitually hate.

## Rationalizing Odious Behavior

Of course, our government defends such unworthy activities by the banal casuistry with which evil has been justified since time immemorial. It is the argument of last resort by every schoolboy caught with a slingshot in his pocket: We have to use such tactics because other kids use them.

Such a rationale for aping Soviet methods is not only contemptible but stupid. The Soviets can use covert tactics far better than we can because their system is cursed with the very qualities we most scorn, including a Byzantine addiction to secrecy. America's commitment to an open society, on the other hand, disqualifies us from competing in that league. The conclusion that emerges from all this is that no nation can act effectively when it is violating its own principles and traditions.

That, however, is only one of the reasons why we should avoid such squalid tactics. By resorting to them we squander our most valuable advantage as a democratic state—our reputation for freedom, honesty and decency—which clearly sets us apart from the Soviet Union. That nation faces a dreary future. Its system simply is not working. The Soviet standard of living is miserable and scarcely improving. Soviet leaders face a serious struggle even to keep their vast country together, for the Russian element in the population is about to become a minority, and ethnic unrest poses critical problems. Meanwhile, the Eastern European nations that form the balance of COMECON (Council for Mutual Economic Assistance) grow progressively more discontented, as is underlined by the current agonies of Poland.

Not only do the Soviets face deep troubles within their empire but their system also has largely lost its appeal in the Third World. Initially, many leaders of the nations that emerged from the ruins of the great colonial empires were attracted by the Soviet model—influenced in part by their desire to show their independence of the Western powers that had kept them in colonial status. But the Soviet model has now lost its glamour.

*"Not only are we exhibiting an aspect of slave mentality by imitating the Soviets; we are also validating an old French adage that we acquire the visage of our adversary."*

Wiser American policy would fully exploit our inherent advantages. We have a system that works and has given us unparalleled economic power. In addition, we possess a great potential asset in the appeal of our nation to the new generations of Third World leaders just now moving into positions of power and authority. But to benefit from that asset we must validate it in practice, and that means acting in accord with our principles and not behaving like an international thug. We must be true to our own avowed principles, respecting the sovereignty of countries no matter how small, supporting and trying to advance human rights and showing by our actions as well as our words that we are firm in our commitment to freedom and diversity. We must make clear that we are not ideologues doctrinally committed to fixed patterns of life and structure, but respect the right of any nation to adopt whatever system it may prefer even though we think it is making a mistake.

We must, in other words, act in character, displaying the qualities of tolerance and understanding which have inspired other nations from our earliest days as a republic. America still has a large residue of respect and confidence remaining all over the world, even though in the last 20 years we have recklessly depleted it.

Throughout the Third World many young men and women are still singing our songs rather than the Internationale and are still quoting Thomas Jefferson more than Felix Dzerzhinsky. The shot heard round the world is still loudly and effectively ricocheting. So let us by all means reconsider what I fear we are now doing—trying to combat the communist powers on their own level and with their own instruments.

Let us avoid being led by our habitual hatred for the Soviet Union to imitate its practices. And finally,

let us avoid the seductive glibness of oversimplification. We live in a complex world and we shall
succeed only if we acknowledge that fact and shape
our plans and meet our obligations in those terms.

*George W. Ball was a United States ambassador to the
United Nations.*

# The USSR Is Paranoid

## Robert G. Kaiser

Well, what about the Russians? Do they share what we consider basic human values or not? Are they part of our world or not? Are they just international gangsters?

The fate of Flight 007 raises all the old questions with brutal abruptness. What sort of society will cavalierly dispose of 269 human lives to preserve its sense of national pride? How could they do something so *stupid?*

Aha—there's the key to it. For this particular "they"—the men who run the Soviet Union—shooting down Flight 007 does not seem stupid. It was characteristic and predictable behavior that reflects a value system and a society that are profoundly different from our own, despite our stubborn efforts to will it otherwise.

In all likelihood, the decision to shoot down Flight 007 was made out of fear of the consequences if it were *not* made. Orders are to shoot down intruders; there are no asterisks for benign intruders, because Russians are disinclined to believe that any intruder could be benign. As in any army or police department, a Soviet line commander's best defense is always, "I was just following orders." To take responsibility for making an exception to the standing orders would be irresponsible.

But why not at least say you're sorry after the fact? Why not offer to pay compensation to the victims' families? Surely it would now be smart to do that?

### Preserve the System

No, not from a Soviet point of view. It is crucial to understand that in Soviet society, one value is paramount: to preserve the system as it exists, and the autocratic power of those who rule it. The system is built on myths, and one of the most important of them is the myth of the infallible Communist Party.

The Soviet response to the death of those 269 people is fully consistent with the demands of loyalty to party and system. These Soviet leaders see nothing to apologize for.

Foreigners may make mistakes, but the Soviet Union does not.

Of course this is ridiculous. Soviet history is riddled with examples of appalling official behavior—Joseph Stalin's great terror, for example.

But there is no acknowledgement of this in the official version of Soviet history, the one taught in school. Stalin's enormous crimes against his own people are dismissed as a "cult of personality," a term that makes no sense until you realize that it was invented to absolve the Communist Party of responsibility for Stalin. His acts were the personal aberrations of one man, not the responsibility of the party—that's the party line. How could the party leave him in power for more than 20 years? The schoolbooks don't answer that question.

### Soviets Can't Acknowledge Wrongs

If we begin acknowledging errors or regrets, where do we stop? That is the question that would trouble a Soviet leader. The best answer to it is not to acknowledge anything that might put the system in a bad light.

The mentality of Soviet officials in somewhat like the mentality in big-city American police departments in the 1960s, when police chiefs stood steadfastly if blindly by policemen who were too quick to use force in tense black ghettos. Sure, maybe the men sometimes went too far, but no good chief would admit that—he had to be loyal to the beleaguered troops, to keep up morale. When citizens demanded civilian review boards to evaluate police behavior, the chiefs staunchly refused to consider the idea. Then the cities exploded in riots, and most big-city police departments changed their ways.

Confronting past errors and attempting to correct

Robert G. Kaiser, "To Deal with Soviet Paranoia Americans Must Understand It," *The Minneapolis Tribune,* September 19, 1983. Originally published in and reprinted by permission of *The Washington Post.*

them is the pragmatic American way. But for Russians this is an abnormal notion, particularly when the authorities are involved. Ask an American you know who has traveled to the Soviet Union if he ever met a Soviet guide or official who volunteered that his government ever made a significant mistake. Generations of foreign travelers to Russia have been frustrated by the fact that such admissions are virtually never heard.

## Russian Terror

Yes, these Russians are part of our world, no matter how uncomfortable that makes them. But they are also terrified of us and our world, and react to us as only the fearfully insecure can react. They would like us to admire and respect them, but are confident that we will not; so as a second-best alternative, they want us to be afraid of them.

*"The credulity of the Soviet populace is one of the most baffling aspects of that baffling culture."*

The Soviet relationship with the rest of the world is like that '60s American police department's relationship with the ghetto—nervous, defensive, self-protective. Our world is alien and hostile territory to the Soviet leaders. That is one reason why they won't let their people—with few exceptions—visit our world, and why they jam the radio broadcasts we beam at the U.S.S.R. They are afraid of us, a fact that we have to understand to deal effectively with them.

To ask the Soviets to apologize for shooting down a foreign civilian airliner is to ask them not only to admit a mistake, but also to cower before foreign pressure—or so it would seem to them. It requires a sense of security to admit fallibility or to accept criticism from abroad, but the Russians do not have a sense of security. On the contrary, they are riddled with the most profound insecurity in their dealings with us.

Russians feel they have unassailable historical reasons for hypersensitivity about their homeland. Centuries of invasions and abuse by foreigners have persuaded them that protecting "the Motherland" is rightly a paramount consideration. Anyone who has suffered the indignity of a Soviet border guard's search of baggage and person will be familiar with the mentality at work here.

## Full-Blown Paranoia

But there is more than pragmatic anxiety about the intentions of hostile outsiders. The Russians have allowed security-consciousness to evolve into full-blown paranoia. The Soviet Union publishes no accurate map of its own territory—every town,

railroad line and river has been moved ever so slightly on the published maps, to throw off foreigners who might try to use them to plan a military attack. Apparently because the security police could not monitor all the calls, the Soviets dismantled an advanced direct-dialing system for international telephone communications that they installed for the 1980 Olympic Games (to show how up to date they were).

This strikes us as paranoid behavior; after generations of acculturation, it strikes most Russians as normal and proper. The distinction explains why Soviet citizens interviewed on the streets of Moscow in recent days all seem to support their government's actions in shooting down Flight 007.

Those same Soviet citizens also tend to believe their government's explanations for what happened in the airplane incident. They probably tend to believe the official contention that the nasty Americans were behind the whole thing. The credulity of the Soviet populace is one of the most baffling aspects of that baffling culture, but again, we have to understand it to deal with it effectively.

It is not a totally unquestioning credulity. Ordinary Russians do know from personal experience that the government says things that are not true. Moscow is always buzzing with rumors of events great and small that are not reported in the news media, some true and some fanciful. This incessant rumor-mongering is evidence that human skepticism survives in the Soviet Union. So is the popularity of Western radio broadcasts in Russian. But most people have been so immersed in the official Soviet view of the world that they find it impossible to escape its grasp.

Moreover, the government may not be universally popular, but it is accepted as the legitimate guardian of the nation's security. A government assertion that security was in jeopardy is widely accepted.

## The Lie as a Pillar of the State

Soviet leaders have a lot of confidence in their own ability to sell a concocted story. They have been doing it for many, many years. Alexander Solzhenitsyn once wrote that in the Soviet Union, "the lie has become not simply a moral category, but a pillar of the state." He is absolutely correct.

The legitimacy of the Soviet regime is built on mythology, particularly the great myths about Vladimir Ilyich Lenin, the Bolshevik Revolution and World War II ("the Great Patriotic War"). The party line on the history of the Soviet Union has been rewritten time and again to suit the needs of those in power. Today, a serious Soviet citizen literally could not find a true account of the history of his own country in officially-published historical materials.

By now the distinction between true and false has been blurred beyond recognition. Joseph Brodsky, the greatest Russian poet of this generation (and now an American who writes his Russian verse on a stipend from the MacArthur Foundation) once observed that the Soviet Union is now characterized by a kind of doublethink:

"By doublethink I do not mean simply, 'I-say-one-thing-I-do-another,'" Brodsky wrote. "I mean the rejection of a moral hierarchy, not for the sake of another hierarchy but for the sake of nothing.... I mean not the mutual destruction of the two basic human categories—good and evil—as a result of the struggle between them, but their mutual decomposition as a result of coexistence...."

In this case the senior officials—probably the members of the Politburo—who decided (after the incident occurred) how the Soviet Union would handle the crisis of the Korean plane, passed on their decision to the propagandists whose job it is to produce the official explanations. Some of these men are extremely talented, but in the Soviet Union system even they would not have full access to the facts. They are propagandists, after all—they have no need to know all the facts. Their job is to take the leaders' decision and make it sound plausible.

This probably explains why the propagandists have stuck to the assertion that Flight 007 had its lights off, even while the recording of the Soviet pilots' voices confirmed that the lights were on. Nobody told that to the propagandists in the beginning, so they got stuck with a bad story.

The Soviets will pay a price—conceivably a high price—in the diplomatic arena for shooting down Flight 007. Anti-Soviet forces all over the world have been strengthened by this episode; negotiations with Moscow will be more difficult and less likely to succeed. The Soviets are trying to minimize this damage with their current propaganda counter-offensive, but it is not likely to be a big success.

## Artificial Sense of Siege

At the same time we should realize that there is a kind of domestic fringe benefit for the Soviet leaders in this episode. For many years, an artificially exaggerated sense of siege has been a key tool for Soviet leaders seeking to maintain firm control over their huge and diverse country and empire. The presence, real or imagined, of hostile foreign dangers has been used to justify rigid internal controls.

For some time the Soviets have worried that the Reagan administration would force them into a painfully expensive new round of the arms race. Many of them now consider this inevitable. An incident like the intrusion of Flight 007 will contribute to the atmosphere the Soviet leaders will want to encourage to justify further sacrifices to a Soviet public whose standard of living has already stopped improving as predictably as it did in the '60s and '70s.

Our own misreading of the Russians has fostered the theory in Washington that the old men in Moscow should be grateful to Ronald Reagan for reacting to this crisis so benignly. According to this naive American theory, the Russians should be able to see past the harsh American rhetoric to perceive what they like to call "objective realities"—that Reagan imposed no tangible sanctions on them; therefore he was signaling his willingness to carry on with other important business.

Here is a case where Americans can imagine how Russians might react. What would we do in a comparable situation? The rival superpower is conducting—with great success—an international campaign to isolate us as inhuman renegades guilty of crimes against civilization. Would we turn the other cheek? No, and neither will the Russians. They won't accept our verbal spankings as gentle treatment, even if they do happen to be fully justified. Because the Soviet leaders are insecure men, especially in their relations with foreigners, the campaign to vilify and isolate them on this issue will aggravate their deepest anxieties about Reagan, which were deep indeed already.

In fact, the successful humiliation of the Russians will have more significant consequences in Moscow than would a new grain embargo or the cancellation of other commercial contracts. The Russians know they can cope with sanctions, because they have survived them already. But in this phase of Soviet history, when the Russians are striving to establish themselves throughout the world as the legitimate second superpower, humiliation and isolation will be painful. They will look for ways to strike back. And they are now most unlikely to invite Ronald Reagan to Moscow for a summit meeting in 1984.

---

*"Because the Soviet leaders are insecure men, especially in their relations with foreigners, the campaign to vilify and isolate them... will aggravate their deepest anxieties."*

---

What does this episode portend? Should we now expect the Russians to act like gangsters all over the globe? Have we learned something about them we didn't know before?

## Predictable Behavior

The answer to that last question ought to be no. The crucial fact about the decision to shoot down Flight 007 is that it was predictable. If you had outlined the circumstances in advance—overlapping flights by a Korean jetliner and an American spy plane, then an invasion of Soviet air space by the jetliner that took it over two highly sensitive military areas in the course of a two-hour flight—virtually any student of Soviet behavior would have predicted this outcome.

Of course this kind of behavior is abhorrent. By our standards the Soviet system is abhorrent. And the range of predictable Soviet actions in the next few years includes events that would further appall us. If the situation in Poland falls apart, the Russians will invade Poland. If offered an "honorable" way out of Afghanistan, the Soviet Union will probably decide to stay there anyway. There's no use kidding ourselves about these possibilities.

## "There will be times when their interests and ours will coincide."

But suicidal Soviet behavior is not likely. The Russians will continue to avoid high-risk adventures outside their empire. They will not try to take over the Western world by threat of nuclear war, and they will remain interested in negotiated agreements on nuclear arms and other issues where they feel they can advance their interests. And there will be times when their interests and ours will coincide.

The Soviet Union will remain part of our world, and we will have to deal with that fact, just as they will.

*Robert G. Kaiser is an associate editor of* The Washington Post *and a former Moscow correspondent.*

# The US Is Paranoid

### Philip Zwerling

Once upon a time, Paul Revere rode his horse from Cambridge to Concord, crying, "The British are coming, the British are coming." And John Hancock and Sam Adams and other of the revolutionary leaders had to go into hiding. Militia men reached for their weapons, and assembled at Lexington Green and Concord Bridge. The alarm was real, the British were coming. The battles that followed led directly to war. Today, we have another rider on horseback, galloping from his ranch in Santa Barbara to Washington, DC, telling us, "The Russians are coming, the Russians are coming." The alarm is raised, but instead of muskets, the new arms that we reach for are thousands of nuclear-tipped missiles poised in underground silos, missiles which are aptly named, "Minute Men." The alarm is raised that we face traitors within, new Benedict Arnolds, whom today the CIA and FBI must be allowed to investigate, whose phones must be tapped, whose mail must be opened, whose meetings must be monitored—even as this church was under surveillance in years past.

### Unite Against Threat

For, if the Russians are coming, not only must we be armed with all of these missiles, but we must also be united before such a threat, and any of those who question government policy, or any aspect of the status quo, give aid and comfort to the enemy. This time, the cry is raised, the alarm is given, and nothing happens. No foreign troops invade our land. No shots are fired. And people ask, "Where is the enemy?"

And then we must ask, "Who has turned in this false alarm?" Who has frightened us into surrendering our freedom? Who has endangered our

lives with ever bigger stockpiles of nuclear weapons?

"The Russians are coming, the Russians are coming!" we were told, and so we invaded Russia in 1919, to fulfill Winston Churchill's words that, "The baby Bolshevism must be strangled in its crib," and 7,000 U.S. troops joined troops from Japan, Britain, France and ten other countries in landings in the Baltic and in Siberia in an effort to tip the balance against the Communists in the Russian Civil War. I think it is interesting in retrospect, to see that the countries that are identified today as our enemies— Russia, China and Cuba—are countries that have never invaded the United States, but have in fact, each in their time, been invaded and occupied by the United States: Russia in 1919, China in 1900, Cuba in 1898 and again in 1961.

With the victory of the Red Army in Russia and the failure of the American Expeditionary Force there in 1920, U.S. foreign policy became one of containment of Communism. In foreign policy that meant the Cold War, U.S. intervention in Korea in 1950, in Vietnam in 1961, in Cuba in 1961, Santo Domingo in 1965, and CIA coups in Iran in 1963, in Guatemala in 1954, in Chile in 1973. And at home, it meant the repression of dissent: The Palmer Raids in 1921 and the destruction of the Industrial Workers of the World by the jailing of its leadership and 2,000 of its members; the mass deportations of foreign born, Socialists and Anarchists, like Emma Goldman; the 1927 executions of Anarchists Sacco and Vanzetti; the hysteria of McCarthyism of the 1950's and the House Un-American Activities Committee inquisitions; the government loyalty oaths, more deportations; and the executions of Julius and Ethel Rosenberg.

"The Russians are coming, the Russians are coming," said Attorney General A. Mitchell Palmer in 1921, as he rounded up the Anarchists. "The Russians are coming," said Secretary of State Sumner Wells as he helped Anastasio Somoza and Fulgencio Batista to power in Nicaragua and Cuba, respectively,

Philip Zwerling, "The Russians Are Coming! The Russians Are Coming!" *UU-World,* September 15, 1982. Reprinted by permission of the Unitarian Universalist Association.

in 1933. "The Russians are coming," said Senator Joe McCarthy as he held up a list, supposedly containing the names of fifty Communists in the U.S. State Department, in a speech at Wheeling, West Virginia, in 1950. "The Russians are coming," said Lyndon Johnson as he surveyed 55,000 American dead in Vietnam. "The Russians are coming," says Secretary of State Al Haig as he tells us that Soviet-Cuban-Nicaraguan forces threaten our Salvadoran military junta, even as that government "improves" its human rights record every day!

## Fears Manipulated by Scoundrels

For sixty years we have been told that the Russians were coming. For sixty years Americans have died in places like Korea and Vietnam, and for sixty years we have been told to be quiet and to sacrifice. For sixty years the alarm has been spread, and now it is finally time to say, "Enough!" to say that we see no Russian troops on Wilshire Boulevard; to say that we are more afraid of the nuclear madness of those who say they are defending us than we fear peace; to say that it is finally time to talk about changes from Wall Street in New York to the Skid Rows that exist in every city in this country. It's time, finally, to see how our fears and our patriotism have been manipulated by scoundrels. It's time to see how absurd and desperate these machinations have become; to see how every ill in our society is blamed on our supposed Soviet enemy.

---

*"Fear of communism has more often than not poisoned us to our roots."*

---

Do we have a drug problem in this country? Well, we can't blame our friend, the country of Colombia, because they are allied with us. So the *Los Angeles Times,* two weeks ago, had a story about how the Cubans are responsible for our drug problems. Smugglers from Colombia take the cocaine to Cuban waters, where it is transferred to Cuban ships and brought into Florida. Our imagination is so limited, that our government believes that because we turned Batista's Cuba into the whore and drug capitol of the Caribbean, that the Cubans would do the same to us.

And what plays on a national scale to a national audience is bound to have its local imitators. This is a clipping from the *Los Angeles Times* of last January, an official report of the Los Angeles Police Department, and I quote:

> Due to the advanced state of forensic psychology and psychiatry in the Soviet Union, many knowledgeable people are of the opinion that the Soviets are collecting dangerous criminals and sending them to the United States as refugees via the Jewish immigration quota. The Soviets realize that they can aggravate our crime problem in this manner.

So now, even the crime problem is a Communist trick.

Is the economy bad? Are inflation and unemployment rising? Are people's savings being wiped out? Then we can take solace in this full page ad in the *Los Angeles Times,* paid for by the Glendale Federal Bank, (an ad showing the Russian flag) telling us that no matter how bad things may be, we are still lucky not to live under the 'Hammer and Sickle.' A notion that I am sure will warm the hearts of those on Skid Row!

## Excuse for Expenditures

"The Russians are coming!" The worst part of this alarm is, of course, that it is an excuse for incredible expenditures for so-called defense, and an excuse for the very real possibility of global war. Today we are seeing the resurrection of civil defense systems, air raid shelters, evacuation plans, and talk of a limited nuclear war, because peace is unpatriotic when "the Russians are coming."

In the words of the author William Styron, whose books include *Nat Turner's Rebellion,* and *Sophie's Choice,* speaking to a graduating class, within the last year, at Duke University:

> Fear of Communism has more often than not poisoned us to our roots. Fear of Communism degraded us by murdering Sacco and Vanzetti. Fear of Communism caused countless deaths and mutilations in the Labor Movement in the years before World War II. This terrible fear, inflamed by Senator Joe McCarthy, turned friend against friend, wife against husband, brother against brother and ruined the lives and reputations of hundreds of innocent men and women, thirty years ago. Most catastrophic of all, encouraged by industrial profiteers, our fear has led us into wars in places we never belonged; wars whose dismal outcome can show little or no gain, moral or physical, for the fact of our participation. Hideous and bloody stalemates like Korea, or far worse, Vietnam, where thousands and thousands died utterly futile deaths, or returned home maimed and brutalized in body and spirit. A nation becomes the more vulnerable to fear, and falls prey to the terror of witches and demons.

Who are the demons who fill us with fear? The 270 million people of the Union of Soviet Socialist Republics are not the warlike barbarian hordes pictured in media caricatures. They are people and people who, quite unlike people in the United States, have seen first hand, in their own country, the horrors of war, with the Nazi invasion of World War II. Just think of these figures which come from a book by Sydney Lens, entitled *The Forging of American Empire.* Consider these statistics, and what happened to the Soviet Union during the Nazi invasion: 20 million people dead, fifteen major cities destroyed, 1,700 towns destroyed, 70,000 villages destroyed, 6 million buildings demolished, 10,000 power plants destroyed. It was the devastation of a people and of a country that we cannot even imagine occurring in the United States.

Who are the demons? Let us ask questions. Who

built and used the first atomic weapon? Who built the first hydrogen bomb? The answer, we did. Ask who, today, feels surrounded by 365 hostile military bases along its borders? The answer must be the Soviet Union. Ask which country deploys most of its armed forces along its own borders, and the answer is the Soviet Union. Then ask which country deploys its arms and its soldiers in 2,000 bases around the world. The answer is *we* do.

## Naming the Demons

The first part of any ceremony of exorcism is to name the demons. And today we must name them. They are Imperialism, and they are Capitalism. And *their day is done.* Let us not be distracted any more by theories of foreign devils. Let us say, "Let the Russians come, let the Mexicans come, let the Salvadorans come, and let us live in peace together." Let us look, not at the Soviet Union, but at Skid Row; not at El Salvador, but at County Hospital. Let us look at what we must do; let us raise a new cry. Let us say that *we* are coming, that change is coming.

Let us say, quoting that subversive Rabbi from Nazareth, "The first shall be last, and the last shall be first."

*"The first part of any ceremony of exorcism is to name the demons."*

Let us say that our enemies are poverty and hunger and unemployment, and let us say, as did the Disciples Peter and John, that we wish to live in a society where:

> There was not a needy person among them, and distribution was made to each as any had need.

One of the most moving letters in the New Testament was the Apostle Paul's letter to the churches at Galatia, in which he wrote:

> There is neither Jew nor Greek. There is neither slave nor free. There is neither male nor female. You are all one.

And we add that there is neither Russian nor American, for all are one. "All are Abraham's offspring. All are heirs, according to the promise."

*Philip Zwerling is a minister at the First Unitarian Church of Los Angeles.*

*"It is the United States that has always been the initiator of the arms race."*

# US Military Strength Threatens Peace

### Sergei Sokolov

*Editor's note: The following viewpoint is taken from a Soviet press release in which Defense Minister Sokolov answers questions from a Tass correspondent.*

**Q:** *Comrade Defense Minister, how do you assess statements by U.S. leaders to the effect that they allegedly come out in favor of ensuring security on the basis of strategic defensive systems while the Soviet Union, they say, conducts a race in strategic offensive arms?*

**A:** It is the United States that has always been the initiator of the arms race. For forty years after the Second World War it has been trying to achieve military superiority. However, the Soviet Union has thwarted these attempts in time by effective reply measures.

The existing military-strategic balance between the USSR and the USA, between the Warsaw Treaty Organization and NATO, is a historic achievement of the socialist community, an indispensable prerequisite of its security. It objectively exists today, and no one will be able to disprove this fact if one does not engage in deception. The existence of the balance deters the imperial ambitions of the USA, and prevents it from achieving world dominance. This is precisely why Washington leaders are trying to upset the parity, to acquire a military edge over the USSR and its allies.

In these conditions their statements concerning some kind of transition in military construction matters to orientation toward defensive systems sound strange, to put it mildly. Facts prove that the present Administration thinks of anything but "defense." On the contrary, it banks on acquiring the capability of the first disarming nuclear strike.

For that purpose efforts are under way to improve the accuracy of U.S. nuclear systems capable of hitting our retaliatory strike forces, primarily intercontinental ballistic missile (ICBM) silo launchers. Conditions are being created for a sudden nuclear attack with the help of Pershing II missiles being sited in Western European countries and long-range cruise missiles of different basing modes being deployed near the territory of the USSR. Different means are being used to camouflage U.S. missiles and bombers in flight to limit the possibility of their detection to the maximum.

The Pentagon is developing at an accelerated pace new strategic offensive systems—two types of ICBMs, submarine-launched ballistic missiles (SLBM), and two types of heavy bombers. Secretary of Defense Caspar Weinberger does not bother to conceal that, while developing a space antiballistic missile system, the United States will also have a powerful strategic triad for dealing a devastative nuclear strike that threatens the existence of the Soviet Union. Evidently, the case in point is not orientation toward defense systems but a relentless buildup of U.S. strategic offensive potential.

## "Strategic Defense Initiative"

Now the Pentagon is longing to get into space. What for? Again it is to try and achieve military superiority over the USSR this time through space. The so-called "Strategic Defense Initiative" of President Ronald Reagan is called "defensive" only for coverup purposes, but actually it is aimed at the development of a new class of weapons—strike space systems.

Trying to place strike weapons in space, some U.S. public figures, in contradiction to facts, maintain that militarization of outer space allegedly has begun with the appearance of satellites for different military uses and that the USSR has allegedly been engaged in an arms race in space since that time. This is not true. Communication, navigation, missile attack warning

Sergei Sokolov, "Answers given by the Minister of Defense...to Questions from a Tass Correspondent," press release on May 6, 1985.

and other satellites which both sides have are not strike space weapons. Neither the USSR nor the United States has weapons in space at the present time.

Space militarization, which is a danger to humankind, will begin when strike systems designed to hit objects in space or from space are placed there. It is then that a race in space arms will unfold. And the USA is working toward exactly that.

---

*"The Soviet Union is resolutely opposed to the arms race on Earth and to its spreading to outer space."*

---

The Soviet Union is resolutely opposed to the arms race on Earth and to its spreading to outer space. That is why it proposes the only natural and sensible thing: to freeze nuclear arsenals of the sides, to terminate preparations for the production of weapons for deployment in space and, on that basis, to pass right away to the reduction of the existing arms stockpiles. To prove its sincerity and goodwill, more convincingly, the USSR has announced that it has discontinued unilaterally, from April 7 until November 1985, further deployment of its intermediate-range missiles and suspends implementation of other countermeasures in Europe.

This decision reaffirms the striding of our country to do everything necessary to curb the arms race. The road from moratorium toward reduction is open. But the United States, as is known, rejected the Soviet initiative out of hand, thus calling into question the sincerity of its statements concerning readiness to reach agreement concerning nuclear arms reduction.

## Irresponsible US Pronouncements

Now Washington officials are making irresponsible pronouncements to the effect that the moratorium announced by the USSR is allegedly not being observed. Let me put it straight: This is deliberate and malicious disinformation. The USSR sticks by its words. It is not and will not be adding a single missile or a single plane to its intermediate-range forces in the European part of the country for the duration of the moratorium.

**Q:** *The U.S. Administration maintains that the acceptance of the Soviet proposal for a moratorium would allegedly "solidify superiority of the USSR" in the field of strategic offensive weapons and intermediate-range nuclear systems. Does such superiority really exist today?*

## USSR "Nuclear Superiority" Is Myth

**A:** There is no "nuclear superiority of the USSR" in either strategic offensive weapons or intermediate-range nuclear systems. There is an approximate

balance in such systems. Washington resorts to the distortion of facts in order to justify its unprecedented military programs and arms buildup and to conceal its reluctance to reach agreement in Geneva on nonmilitarization of space and a radical reduction of nuclear weapons.

The balance between the USSR and the USA in the field of strategic arms has been thoroughly verified and recognized by the sides when SALT I and SALT II agreements were being negotiated. At the present time the USSR has a bit more delivery vehicles, while the USA has an edge in the number of warheads. But, in general, approximate equality exists.

The approximate parity is confirmed by the Joint Chiefs of Staff of the U.S. Armed Forces. Their 1985 report to Congress says that at this time approximate nuclear parity exists between the United States and the Soviet Union. According to official data from the Washington Administration itself, the USSR and the USA have approximately equal number of warheads on ground- and sea-launched ballistic missiles. But the USA has many more heavy bombers than the USSR and, correspondingly, more nuclear weapons on them. So, if there exists an imbalance in the field of nuclear warheads on strategic delivery vehicles, it is in favor of the USA.

In intermediate-range nuclear forces NATO countries now have an edge both in delivery vehicles (missiles and planes) and in the number of warheads lifted by these vehicles in one launching (the USSR has 850 delivery vehicles and about 2,000 warheads, and NATO—990 delivery vehicles and more than 3,000 warheads).

## Distorted Facts

How is the real state of affairs being distorted in Washington? No account is made of British and French missiles and medium-range planes and the aircraft carrier-based aviation of the USA (in total about 550 delivery vehicles and almost 1,500 nuclear warheads). All of the Soviet Union's systems are taken into account, even those that are deployed in the eastern part of the country and have no relation to the balance of forces in Europe.

Such are the facts concerning nuclear parity. Under such conditions the introduction of a moratorium on the nuclear arsenals of the sides and on the development, including research, or strike space weapons is a timely, effective and right measure from the point of view of curbing the arms race. It agrees with the spirit of the accord reached in January. Such a step would make it possible to prevent the situation from deteriorating and to embark on the resolution of questions of reducing nuclear arms.

**Q:** *Washington leaders describe plans for the development of a space antiballistic missile system as "humane" and allege that it will make ballistic missiles "unnecessary" and deliver humankind from nuclear weapons. What is the true substance of the U.S. "Star*

*Wars" plan?*

**A:** The USA has put into circulation assertions concerning the "humaneness" of space plans to mislead the public and distract its attention from the danger which these plans pose to humankind.

What are they in Washington really up to? They seek to create an antimissile shield over the United States, and to simultaneously deploy strategic first-strike offensive armaments, new strategic space-based forces intended to hit targets on Earth, in the sea, in the atmosphere and in outer space. It is not difficult to see that if such plans of the United States materialize, then Washington's strategists may be tempted, under the cover of the space antimissile shield, to risk using nuclear and space weapons for dealing a strike at the Soviet Union and its allies, counting on it to go off with impunity. According to the Pentagon's designs, the antimissile shield is called upon to frustrate the retaliatory strike from the USSR, to, so to say, "finish it off" by taking out the Soviet missiles which survived the American first nuclear strike.

Pronouncements of the U.S. Administration as to the "deliverance of humankind from nuclear weapons" are, in this connection, outright demagogy. If, as the U.S. Administration assures, "Star Wars" is the way to the destruction of nuclear weapons, why then is the United States building up strategic offensive armaments in huge proportions, creating other newer nuclear systems, deploying Pershing and cruise missiles in Europe, and leading the production of 37,000 new types of nuclear ammunition? Common sense prompts the need to freeze nuclear arsenals of the sides and to switch to reductions. This is exactly what the Soviet Union proposes.

In Washington they act differently. There they say: It is now necessary to continue deploying strategic nuclear armaments. Besides, it is necessary to militarize outer space, to create a space antimissile system, that is, strike offensive space armaments. And only then, when all that has been done, "possibly in many decades" it might become possible, as they say, to reduce or even eliminate nuclear armaments.

## Reduce Arms by Multiplying Them?

It turns out that in order to liquidate nuclear weapons, it is first necessary to multiply their stockpiles many times. The way to nuclear disarmament, if one follows this logic, comes only through the buildup of strategic offensive armaments and militarization of outer space, and it will take scores of years besides. There appears to be no other way out.

Why is this being done? To deceive people, to divert their attention from the need of undelayed and efficient steps to reduce nuclear arsenals. The

dangerous consequences of such a course are thoroughly hidden from the public. They conceal the objectively existing mutual link between the offensive and defensive armaments which underlies the 1972 Soviet-American treaty of unlimited duration on limitation of ABM systems.

Nothing is said about the fact that creation of one of the aspects of the large-scale antimissile system breaks this mutual link, destabilizes the strategic situation and impels the other side to restore the situation either by the buildup of its strategic offensive armaments, or by supplementing them with antimissile systems or, most likely, both.

## Undermining International Security

In other words, the truth is that the outer space antimissile system being created by the United States programs the arms race in all its directions, leads to undermining the international security. That conclusion was clearly formulated by General Secretary of the Central Committee of the Communist Party of the Soviet Union Mikhail Gorbachev in his conversation with the *Pravda* editor: "Just as the appearance of nuclear arms did not eliminate conventional types of weapons and only generated an accelerated race in the manufacture of both nuclear and conventional arms, the creation of space arms will have only one result—the arms race will become even more intensive and encompass new spheres."

---

*"There is no 'nuclear superiority of the USSR' in either strategic offensive weapons or intermediate-range systems."*

---

From the military viewpoint, the American "Star Wars" plan is the inseparable component part of the U.S. nuclear strategy, the first-strike strategy. The real meaning of that plan is to obtain the capability of making a nuclear attack with impunity and to ensure conditions for the constant nuclear blackmail of the Soviet Union and other countries. Since the United States categorically refuses to undertake the obligation not to be the first to use nuclear weapons, such intentions of the United States are a real threat to peace. . . .

The U.S. course of militarizing outer space will extremely negatively influence the military-political situation in the world, and will complicate, if not make impossible, the solution of the problem of reduction of nuclear armaments. Creation of strike space weapons will bring about, and is sure to bring about, the lessening of the security of the United States itself and its allies. Such an outcome should not be forgotten by the initiators of "Star Wars" and those who are being urged to comply with that provocative program.

## USSR Wants to Live in Peace

The Soviet Union—and this was repeatedly stated in our country at the highest level—does not seek to attain any unilateral advantages over the United States and NATO countries. We do not need that since we do not intend to threaten them or to impose our will. But we want to live with them in peace, to maintain normal, good relations. Our aim is an end to the arms race and the full destruction of nuclear weapons everywhere....

---

*"It turns out that in order to liquidate nuclear weapons, it is first necessary to multiply [US] stockpiles many times."*

---

"We offer the Government of the United States," said General Secretary of the CPSU Central Committee Mikhail Gorbachev, "the opportunity to conduct the matter in such a way that it would be obvious to all, to our peoples, to other countries, that the political courses of the USSR and the United States are oriented not at hostility and confrontation but at the search for mutual understanding and peaceful development."

*Sergei Sokolov is the Soviet Minister of Defense.*

> "If the United States government would withdraw its threat of nuclear attack... the Soviet threat against the cities of the allies...[would] make the world safe for the Soviet army."

# USSR Military Strength Threatens Peace

### Edward N. Luttwak

In recent years, entire books have appeared which argue that the Soviet armed forces are much weaker than they seem. Citing refugee accounts or personal experience, they depict the pervasive technical incompetence, drunkenness, corruption, and bleak apathy of officers and men. Drunken officers and faked inspections, Turkic conscripts who cannot understand orders in Russian drowning in botched river-crossing tests, the harsh lives of ill-fed, ill-housed, and virtually unpaid Soviet conscripts, and a pervasive lack of adequate training fill these accounts.

It is odd how all these stories (each true, no doubt) contrast with the daily evidence of the routine operations of the Soviet armed forces. Merely keeping its warships seaworthy and supplied in distant and often stormy waters demands a great deal of discipline and expertise from the officers and men of the Soviet navy. Even more skill is needed to carry out successfully the missile launches and gunnery trials that are also part of the Soviet naval routine. Likewise, we have the evidence of Soviet air operations; they too require a great deal of competence, both in the daily training sorties of the fighters and in the long-range flights of the bombers and transports.

Nor can the Soviet army fake all the disciplined maintenance, tight planning, and skills needed to assemble, move, and operate the many thousands of complicated armored vehicles, hundreds of helicopters, and countless smaller weapons in its exercises. It only takes a little drunken inattention or technical incompetence, or mere apathy by maintenance crews, to cause an aircraft to crash; a little more can sink a ship; and the delicate gear box of a battle tank is easily wrecked.

It is true that at fairly regular intervals we learn of spectacular failures in the upkeep of the Soviet armed forces. Breakdowns at sea lead to much photography of submarines adrift in the ocean and to much speculation over possible radiation leaks. Word of plane crashes reaches us now and then, and most recently there was solid evidence of huge explosions in the weapon stores of the Northern Fleet in the Kola peninsula. It is perfectly probable that Soviet standards of maintenance are lower than those of the United States, but the difference is scarcely of dramatic consequence. All armed forces, including those of the United States, have their collisions, their air crashes, their catastrophic breakdowns. The Soviet armed forces may well have more than their share. Yet it was never by superior efficiency that first Russia and then the Soviet Union became so very powerful, but rather by a combination of numbers, persistent strategies, and a modest technical adequacy.

### Battles Won by Supremacy of Forces

When the actual record of war is assessed, not from official accounts but from the testimony of those who were there, it becomes quite clear that battles are not won by perfection but rather by the supremacy of forces that are 5-percent effective over forces that are 2-percent effective. In peacetime, when all the frictions of war are absent, when there is no enemy ready to thwart every enterprise, effectiveness may rise to dizzy levels of 50 or 60 percent—which means, of course, that filling in the wrong form, posting to the wrong place, supplying the wrong training times, selecting the wrong officers, and other kinds of errors are merely normal. Matters cannot be otherwise, because military organizations are much larger than the manageable groupings of civilian life that set our standards of competence; and because their many intricate tasks must be performed not by life-career specialists like those who run factories, hospitals,

Edward N. Luttwak, *The Pentagon and the Art of War.* New York: Simon & Schuster, 1984. Copyright © 1984 by Edward N. Luttwak. Reprinted by permission of SIMON & SCHUSTER, Inc.

symphony orchestras, and even government offices, but by transients who are briefly trained—short-service conscripts in the case of the Soviet armed forces.

*"In the five possible war theaters of the North Atlantic alliance . . . it is clear that the ground forces of both the United States and its allies . . . would be outnumbered, outgunned, or both."*

Actual alcoholism, in the severe, clinical sense, is now epidemic in the Soviet Union, where so many lead bleak lives, no longer alleviated by the once vibrant hope of a fast-approaching better future. So drunkenness is no doubt pervasive in the Soviet armed forces. But Russians have always been great drinkers. Drunk they defeated Napoleon, and drunk again they defeated Hitler's armies and advanced all the way to Berlin. All these stories of corruption are also undoubtedly authentic. But no great military empire is likely to be undone by generals who procure villas through corrupt dealings, nor by sergeants who take the odd ruble off a conscript; Anglo-Saxon morality makes much of these things, history much less. Corruption in the higher ranks can demoralize the troops—but not if it is accepted as a normal part of life. . . .

## Sheer Numerical Strength

So far nothing precise has been said about the most obvious attribute of the Soviet armed forces: their sheer numerical strength. The gross totals are well known, and mean little. As against the 30 large divisions of the U.S. army and marine corps, active and reserve, the Soviet army has 194 divisions, smaller by a third on average but just as heavily armed. One-third are fully manned, one-third are half and half, and the rest are mostly manned by reservists—but all Soviet divisions are fully equipped, even if not with the latest and best, and all have a full-time professional cadre, even when their line units are manned by reservists. The Soviet tactical air force has some 6,000 strike aircraft, fighters, and fighter-bombers, less advanced on average but also of more recent vintage than the 5,600 or so equivalent aircraft of the U.S. air force, navy, and marines. Another 1,250 interceptor-fighters serve in the territorial air defenses (along with more than 9,600 anti-aircraft missiles), and the Soviet navy's land-based aviation also includes some fighter-class aircraft.

For the Soviet navy, one ship list prepared by the U.S. navy shows 1,324 "surface combatants," as against its own 285 surface warships; 367

submarines, as against 99; and 770 auxiliaries, as against its own 105 logistic and support ships. The figures are of course grossly inflated, but even the most sober count that excludes the old, the inactive, and the small would sitll list 290 major Soviet surface warships, 119 nuclear and 157 diesel-attack submarines, and 360 land-based naval bombers, of which 100 are modern machines of transoceanic range. . . .

## USSR Superiority in Critical War Theaters

In the five possible war theaters of the North Atlantic alliance—northern Norway, the "central" front in Germany, northeast Italy, the Thrace frontier of Greece and Turkey with Bulgaria, and the Turkish border with the Soviet Union in remote eastern Anatolia—it is clear that the ground forces of both the United States and its allies, those already deployed in peacetime and those to be mobilized, would be outnumbered, outgunned, or both. By adding absolutely everything on the books—including Turkish infantry and the American National Guard, in addition to the manned forces actually in place—the total number of alliance divisions for the five theaters rises to 144, as against a combined Warsaw Pact total of 170. That is scarcely a catastrophic imbalance, and the situation looks even easier for the alliance when we recall that the Warsaw Pact total includes the divisions of rebellious Poland, unwilling Hungary, restive Czechoslovakia, doubtful East Germany, and uncooperative Rumania.

If we make a somewhat finer comparison however, including only tank and mechanized divisions on the alliance side, thus removing a mass of ill-armed and immobile infantry forces of low military value, while at the same time eliminating *all* the non-Soviet forces of the Warsaw Pact, 80 divisions of the alliance remain, while the Soviet army alone has 109—*after* leaving 78 Soviet divisions to face the Chinese border, occupy Afghanistan, and control Iran's long border. These 109 Soviet divisions are smaller than the Western divisions, but no longer by much, and they do belong to one army under one central authority, whereas the Western total is split among the armies of the United States, Canada, Britain, Norway, Denmark, West Germany, Holland, France, Portugal, Italy, Greece, and Turkey—and the French divisions are not under alliance command and not necessarily available, the Greek divisions are of uncertain allegiance, and the American reserve forces must first be mobilized, then filled out and updated in training, then transported across the ocean.

If we include the non-mechanized forces of high military value (such as the American and Soviet airborne divisions), and exclude alliance forces not rapidly available for reinforcement, the realistic alliance count is on the order of 56 divisions, the Soviet, 114.

The situation in the air over the European fronts is similar: by the fullest count, the Soviet Union alone could muster 4,700 fighters, fighter-bombers, and interceptors, without reinforcement from other theaters; the Western air forces in Europe hold a total of 3,045, of which not more than two-thirds can be considered modern, including all the 594 American fighters and fighter-bombers.

To consider the military balance in the Persian Gulf, with Iran as the possible theater of war, no computation is even needed: against a maximum of four or five American divisions that could eventually be deployed with great difficulties and greater risk, the Soviet Union could send 20 with great ease.

On the last of the "continental" fronts, which cuts across the peninsula of Korea—where sudden war is all too possible, but where a large Soviet intervention now seems most unlikely—it is the Korean forces on both sides that now make the balance. But should Moscow choose to do so, it could add much more to the North Korean strength than the United States could add to that of South Korea.

Thus on every possible major front we encounter the powerful arithmetic of the Soviet army. . . .

## Soviet Nuclear Tactics

So far, not a word has been said about the entire subject of Soviet nuclear weapons. This separation and implied downgrading of the matter corresponds to the strategic logic of the Soviet position against the West. Moscow's protestations of reluctance to use nuclear weapons against the West (China is another mattter) may be perfectly sincere. Just as the invader is always peaceful—for he seeks only to advance and not to fight, while it is his victim who causes war by resisting—so the Soviet Union has every reason to avoid nuclear war, because it is now stronger than the West in non-nuclear military forces. Fully able to invade Europe, Iran, or Korea without having to use nuclear weapons, the Soviet Union now needs its nuclear weapons mainly to neutralize the nuclear deterrence of the United States, Britain, and France. Just as it is always the victim who must make war to resist aggression, so the West must rely on the fear of nuclear war to obtain security, by threatening nuclear attacks against invading Soviet forces if they cannot be stopped by non-nuclear arms.

To deter such "tactical" attacks—that is, to inhibit the first level of the Western nuclear deterrent in order to restore the full value of its armies for intimidation or actual invasion—the Soviet Union has built up its own "tactical" nuclear forces, in the form of artillery shells, rockets, short-range missiles, and bombs for fighter-class aircraft and strike bombers. The Soviet Union can therefore reply in kind should its invading armies have their victories spoiled by nuclear attacks.

If the West begins to strike at invading Soviet columns with tactical nuclear weapons, the Soviet Union can, in a simple military calculation, use its own tactical nuclear weapons to blast open paths through the alliance front, so that even badly reduced and shocked invasion columns can continue to advance, eventually to reach and "hug" the cities—thereby forcing the alliance to stop its nuclear attacks. In the far more meaningful political calculation, the mere existence of large and very powerful Soviet tactical nuclear forces should inhibit to some extent any Western use of the same weapons.

## Western Defensive Character

But the alliance has a most significant advantage that arises from its purely defensive character: at this first level, the entire onus of beginning a war rests on the Soviet Union; it is by *its* decision that the movement of the armies would begin; it is by *its* decision that the invasion of Western territory would continue so that tactical nuclear weapons would be used against its forces, raising the conflict to the second level. Hence the Soviet tactical nuclear forces are not sufficient to dissuade Western use of the same weapons. The Soviets could only use them to achieve physical results (blasting gaps through the front) that would not begin to remedy the catastrophic deterioration of their position from a successful non-nuclear invasion to a nuclear conflict in which no good result could be achieved.

*"Just as it is always the victim who must make war to resist aggression, so the West must rely on the fear of nuclear war to obtain security."*

Therefore, to inhibit Western tactical nuclear forces much more powerfully, the Soviet Union maintains another category of nuclear weapons of longer ("intermediate") range, which threaten the cities of Europe, as well as large military targets in the deep rear, such as air bases. At present, the celebrated SS-20 ballistic missile is the main weapon in this category, which also includes Soviet strike aircraft such as the Su-24 ("Fencer"). With these weapons the interaction between Soviet and Western military power reaches its third level.

Of late, the alliance has begun to deploy intermediate-range cruise and Pershing-2 missiles in Britain, West Germany, and Italy (more are to be deployed in Belgium and Holland). Because they are widely regarded as an entirely different category of weapons, they *are* different politically: the huge controversy surrounding their deployment may enable the cruise and Pershing-2 missiles to have a counter-intimidation impact since public opinion views them as an answer to the SS-20s. To that extent, they are *politically* distinct from the far more abundant aircraft bombs and all the other nuclear weapons officially described as tactical. In addition, the new missiles may be more reliable in reaching their targets than strike aircraft with nuclear bombs.

---

*"The United States must rely on believeable threats. . . to offset the Soviet Union's non-nuclear superiority and 'tactical' nuclear parity."*

---

But *strategically* the cruise and Pershing-2 missiles are *not* different from the tactical nuclear weapons of the alliance: they too serve to neutralize the non-nuclear strength of the Soviet army, and they too are neutralized in turn by the Soviet nuclear counterthreat against the cities of the alliance. As a matter of physical fact, the cruise and Pershing-2 missiles do not threaten anything not already threatened by alliance weapons classified as tactical; specifically, they do not threaten Soviet cities any more than the tactical nuclear bombs of longer-ranged alliance strike aircraft. Both those aircraft and the new missiles could reach cities in the western part of the Soviet Union; neither is meant to be used against those cities; for both, the relevant targets are Soviet military forces and their bases and command centers.

## Third Strategic Level

To neutralize the Soviet third-level threat against the alliance cities in Europe, the new missiles would have to counterthreaten Soviet cities with an equal certainty of complete destruction; because of their vulnerability and range limits, the new missiles cannot do that. Hence the new missiles cannot take the strategic interaction to a fourth level, where the Soviet invasion potential is once again neutralized. The third level thus leaves the Soviet Union in control of the situation, because with or without the cruise and Pershing-2 missiles, the alliance can protect its frontal defenses only at the risk of provoking Soviet nuclear attacks against the cities that those same frontal forces are supposed to protect.

It takes a fourth level to restore a war-avoiding balance, in which this Soviet third-level nuclear threat is itself deterred by American intercontinental nuclear forces capable of inflicting catastrophic destruction on the Soviet Union. Then the Western "tactical" nuclear forces can once again deter a Soviet (non-nuclear) invasion, and the Soviet Union's invasion potential yields neither war options nor the power to intimidate the European allies of the United States.

The Soviet response would be to seek a fifth level of strategic interaction, where the American deterrent would be neutralized by the threat of destroying the intercontinental nuclear force if any were used against Soviet military forces, and American cities if any Soviet cities were destroyed. If the United States government would withdraw its threat of a nuclear attack on the Soviet Union in response to a Soviet attack on European cities, or if American intercontinental nuclear forces could not plausibly threaten the Soviet Union, the strategic interaction would revert to the third level, in which the Soviet threat against the cities of the allies inhibits the West from using its tactical nuclear forces, thus making the world safe for the Soviet army. . . .

## "Parity" Would Harm US

One could add details and nuances to the estimate of the Soviet Union's intercontinental nuclear strength and homeland defenses, but the result would not change, for the two forces do not have the same task. The United States must rely on believable threats to use its intercontinental nuclear forces to offset the Soviet Union's non-nuclear superiority and "tactical" nuclear parity. Otherwise matters would stand at the third level, where there is nothing to stop Soviet military intimidation of America's allies—who then could scarcely remain allies. The Soviet Union by contrast need only make the American intercontinental nuclear threat unbelievable in order to recover the invasion potential of its armies, thus restoring their power to intimidate or actually invade. To do that the Soviet Union does not even need intercontinental nuclear superiority, which it is striving so hard to achieve. But the United States does need a margin of intercontinental nuclear strength merely to keep the overall military balance duly balanced.

Hence "parity" (shorthand for strategic-nuclear parity) is or should be fundamentally unacceptable to the United States. Any true parity between the intercontinental nuclear forces of each side must leave the United States militarily inferior in all the continental theaters where the Soviet army can muster its power—namely Europe, Iran (and thus the Persian Gulf), and Korea. And that is the situation that now prevails, the true cause of today's anxieties for world peace.

*Edward N. Luttwak is a senior fellow at the Center for Strategic and International Studies, Georgetown University. He is also a professional defense consultant and author of many articles and books about foreign policy.*

*"For our part, we do not seek... a trial of strength. The very thought of it is alien to us."*

# The USSR Desires Peace

### Yuri Andropov

The Soviet leadership deems it necessary to make known to Soviet people, other peoples and all those who are responsible for shaping the policy of states its assessment of the course pursued in international affairs by the present U.S. Administration.

Briefly speaking, it is a militarist course which poses a grave threat to peace. Its essence is to try and assure for the United States dominant positions in the world without reckoning with the interests of other states and peoples.

Precisely these aims are served by the unprecedented build-up of the U.S. military potential, the large-scale programmes of manufacturing weapons of all types—nuclear, chemical and conventional. Now it is planned to project the unrestricted arms race into outer space as well.

American military presence thousands of kilometers from U.S. territory is expanded under spurious pretexts of all kinds. Bridgeheads are set up for direct armed interference in the affairs of other states, and for the use of American weapons against any country which rejects Washington's diktat. As a result, tensions have grown the world over—in Europe, Asia, Africa, the Middle East and Central America.

Other NATO countries are increasingly being involved in the implementation of these dangerous plans of Washington. More, efforts are being made to revive Japanese militarism and hitch it to the bloc's military-political machine. In doing so, people are being induced to forget the lessons of the past.

## Policy Judged by Actions

The peoples judge the policy of a government primarily by its actions. That is why when the U.S. President grandiloquently holds forth from the United Nations rostrum about commitment to the cause of peace, self-determination and sovereignty of peoples, these are mere declamatory statements that can convince no one.

If anyone had any illusions about a possible evolution for the better in the policy of the present American Administration, such illusions have been completely dispelled by the latest developments. For the sake of its imperial ambitions, that Administration goes to such lengths that one begins to doubt whether Washington has any brakes at all to prevent it from crossing the line before which any sober-minded person must stop.

The insidious provocation involving a South Korean plane engineered by U.S. special services is also an example of extreme adventurism in politics. We have elucidated thoroughly and authentically the factual aspect of this act. The guilt of its organizers, however they might prevaricate and whatever false versions they might put forward, has been proved.

The Soviet leadership has expressed regret over the loss of human lives due to that unprecedented, criminal subversion. Those lives are on the conscience of those who would like to arrogate to themselves the right not to reckon with the sovereignty of states and the inviolability of their borders, who masterminded and carried out the provocation, who literally on the following day hastily pushed through Congress colossal military appropriations and are now rubbing their hands in glee.

## Phony "Humanism"

Thus, the "humanism" of the statesmen who are seeking to blame others for the death of the people aboard the plane is materialized in new mountains of weapons of mass destruction—from MX missiles to containers with nerve gas.

In their striving somehow to justify their dangerous, inhuman policies, these same people heap

Yuri Andropov, "Statement," *New Times*, October 1983.

slander on the Soviet Union and on socialism as a social system, with the tone being set by the U.S. President himself. One must say bluntly—the spectacle of the leaders of a country like the United States resorting, with the aim of smearing the Soviet people, to what amounts well-nigh to obscenities alternating with pharisaical preachments about morality and humanism is an unattractive sight.

> "Can the [United Nations]. . . remain in a country where an outrageous militarist psychosis is being implanted?"

The world knows well the worth of such moralizing. In Vietnam morality, as understood by Washington leaders, was introduced with napalm and toxic agents, in Lebanon it is being hammered in by the salvoes of naval guns, in El Salvador this morality is being imposed by genocide. And the list of crimes could be continued. So, we have something to say about the moral aspect of the U.S. policy as well: both by recalling history and speaking about the present time.

Today in Washington, together with morality, elementary norms of decency are being trampled and disrespect shown not only for statesmen and states, but also for the United Nations Organization. The question arises: can the international organization, called upon to maintain peace and security, remain in a country where an outrageous militarist psychosis is being implanted and the good name of the organization besmirched?

## Anti-Communism Ploys

Under the cover of anti-communism, the claimants to the role of arbiters of the destinies of the world are seeking to impose their order wherever they do not encounter a rebuff.

The concepts used to justify such a manner of action would not in themselves merit attention if not for the fact that they are preached by leaders of a major power, and not merely preached, but are carried out in practice.

The transfer of ideological contradictions to the sphere of interstate relations has never benefited those who resorted to it in external affairs. To do so today, in the nuclear age, is simply absurd and inadmissible. To turn the battle of ideas into military confrontation would be too costly for the whole of mankind.

But those who are blinded by anti-communism are evidently incapable of grasping this. Starting with the bogey of a "Soviet military threat," they have now proclaimed a "crusade" against socialism as a social system. Attempts are made to persuade people that in general there is no room for socialism in the world.

True, they do not specify that what they mean is the kind of world Washington would wish to see.

But wishes and possibilities are far from being the same thing. It is given to no one to reverse the course of history. The U.S.S.R. and other socialist countries will live and develop according to their own laws— the laws of the most advanced social system.

## Stoic Soviet State

In the six and a half decades of its existence the Soviet state has successfully withstood many trials, including severe ones. Those who attempted to encroach on the integrity of our state, its independence and our system found themselves on the garbage heap of history. It is high time that everybody to whom this applies understood that we shall be able to ensure the security of our country, the security of our friends and allies under any circumstances.

Soviet people can rest assured that our country's defence capability is maintained at such a level that it would not be advisable for anyone to stage a trial of strength.

For our part, we do not seek such a trial of strength. The very thought of it is alien to us. We do not set the well-being of our people, the security of the Soviet state apart from, let alone counterpose them to the well-being and security of other peoples, other countries. In the nuclear age one should not look at the world through the narrow prism of one's selfish interests. Responsible statesmen have only one choice—to do everything possible to prevent a nuclear catastrophe. Any other position is shortsighted, more, it is suicidal.

The Soviet leadership does not hesitate in deciding what line to follow in international affairs in the present acute situation too. Our course continues to be projected at preserving and strengthening peace, lessening tension, curbing the arms race and expanding and deepening co-operation between states. This is the immutable will of the Communist Party of the Soviet Union, of all Soviet people. These are, we are convinced, also the aspirations of all peoples.

Of course, the malicious attacks on the Soviet Union produce here a natural feeling of indignation, but we have strong nerves, and we do not base our policy on emotions. Our policy rests on common sense, realism, a sense of profound responsibility for the destinies of the world.

We proceed from the premise that mankind is not doomed to destruction. The arms race can and must be terminated. Mankind deserves a better fate than living in a conflict-rent world, suffocating under the burden of deadly weapons.

## Concern for World Security

In advancing far-reaching proposals on limitation and reduction of nuclear armaments, both strategic and medium-range, in Europe, we show our concern not only for the security of the U.S.S.R., the states of the socialist community, but also for the security of all other countries.

As regards U.S. policy, its growing militarization is manifested also in the unwillingness to conduct serious talks of any kind, to reach agreement on questions of curbing the arms race.

The Soviet-American talks on the burning problem—reduction of nuclear armaments in Europe—have been going on for two years now. The position of the Soviet side is directed at finding mutually acceptable solutions on a fair, just basis, solutions which do not infringe on anyone's legitimate interests. At the same time, these two years have made it clear that our partners in the talks at Geneva are by no means there to reach an accord. Their task is different—to play for time and then start the deployment in Western Europe of ballistic Pershing 2 and long-range cruise missiles. And they do not particularly try to conceal this.

All they do is prattle about some flexibility of the United States at the Geneva talks. Another portion of such "flexibility" has just materialized. And this time too the inbuilt deception is clear. Leaving details aside, the essence of the so-called new move in the U.S. position, vaunted as "superb," boils down to the proposal to agree, as before, on how many Soviet medium-range missiles should be reduced and how many new American missiles should be deployed in Europe, in addition to the nuclear potential already possessed by NATO.

In short, we are asked to talk about how to help the NATO block to upset to its advantage the balance of medium-range nuclear systems in the European zone. And this move is blandly presented as something new.

## American Advantage, European Expense

The operation of stationing these American nuclear missiles in Europe is seen from the Washington control tower as perfectly simple and maximally advantageous for the United States—advantageous at the expense of Europe. The European allies of the U.S. are regarded as hostages. This is a frank, but cynical policy. But what is really unclear is this: do those European political leaders who—disregarding the interests of their peoples, the interests of peace—are helping to implement the ambitious militaristic plans of the U.S. Administration give thought to this?

Here nothing should be left unsaid. If, contrary to the will of the majority of people in West European countries, American nuclear missiles appear in the European continent, this will be a major move fundamentally inimical to peace on the part of the U.S. leaders and the leaders of other NATO countries who act at one with them.

Neither do we see any willingness on the American side to tackle in earnest the problem of limiting and reducing strategic armaments. In the American capital they are busy launching the production of ever new systems of these armaments as well. And on the approaches are types of these weapons that may radically upset the concept of strategic stability and the very possibility of effective limitation and reduction of nuclear arms.

No one should mistake for a sign of weakness the Soviet Union's good will and desire to reach agreement. The Soviet Union will be able to make a proper response to any attempt to disrupt the existing military-strategic balance, and its words and deeds will not be at variance.

However, we are in principle opposed to competition in the production and stockpiling of weapons of mass annihilation. This is not our path. It cannot lead to the solution of any of the problems facing mankind, i.e. economic development of states, preservation of the environment, creation of at least elementary conditions for people's life, nourishment, health and education.

## Struggle Against Militarism

Release of the material resources recklessly squandered on the arms race, and the unfolding of man's boundless creative potentialities—this is what can unite people, what should determine the policy of states at the turn of the 20th and 21st centuries. For all this to be realized, the forces of militarism must be checked, and the world be kept through concerted effort from sliding into an abyss.

All peoples, every inhabitant of our planet, should realize the danger that threatens. Realize, in order to join efforts in the struggle for their own survival.

Mankind has not lost, nor can it lose, its reason. This is clearly manifested by the great scope of the anti-missile, anti-war movement which has developed in the European and other continents, a movement in which people of different social, political, and religious affiliation participate.

All who raise today their voice against the senseless arms race and in defence of peace can be sure that the policy of the Soviet Union, of other socialist countries, is directed at attaining precisely these aims. The U.S.S.R. wants to live in peace with all countries, including the United States. It does not nurture aggressive plans, does not impose the arms race on anyone, does not impose its social order on anyone.

Our aspirations and strivings are implemented in concrete proposals directed at effecting a decisive turn for the better in the world situation. The Soviet Union will continue to do everything possible to uphold peace on earth.

*Yuri Andropov was the General Secretary of the Central Committee of the Communist Party of the Soviet Union.*

# The US Desires Peace

### John W. Vessey Jr.

The principal reason that the United States needs military health is the threat posed by the Soviet Union and its military forces. The most significant and certainly the most dangerous trend over the last 25 years has been the unrelenting growth of Soviet military power. The Soviets have armed themselves to the teeth. They continue to do so at a rate far in excess of legitimate defense needs. We need not theorize regarding their motives.

In his acceptance speech on assuming the duties of Secretary-General of the Communist Party in November, Yuri Andropov said, "We well know that peace cannot be achieved by begging from the imperialists. It can be defended only by relying on the invincible might of the Soviet armed forces." Mr. Andropov failed to mention that the battlegrounds of their "defense of peace" have included Hungary, Czechoslovakia, Cuba, Nicaragua, Afghanistan, and Poland, to say nothing of those "imperialist" nations of Estonia, Latvia, and Lithuania.

## Soviet Quest for Military Superiority

I find it difficult to believe that anyone could want war. Yet we know that the Soviets are building the forces they believe are needed to achieve their war objectives. This relentless Soviet quest for military superiority achieved new levels during the past year across all areas of strategic and conventional forces. They:

• Began test flights of a new land-based, solid-propellent intercontinental ballistic missile, while continuing to modernize their SS-17, SS-18, and SS-19 missiles. In 1982, they fielded more MX-quality warheads in their forces than we are asking to deploy in our entire ICBM modernization program. Their preparations to begin testing of other new ICBMs

continue—we'll probably see them next year. Yet, we face the sad dilemma of trying to surmount opposition to the MX program.

• Test flew their new strategic, manned bomber, the Blackjack—larger than our own B-1. But, our B-1B will not deploy until 1985, after years of research and development, false starts, and acrimonious controversy.

• Added more than 80 mobile SS-20 intermediate-range ballistic missile launchers, each with three nuclear warheads, so that more than 330 launchers and reloads are now arrayed against Western Europe, Japan, and China. We have no comparable systems.

• Now conduct Atlantic, Pacific, and Indian Ocean operations with three Kiev-class aircraft carriers, and a fourth ship has been launched. Development continues on a newer, larger class of aircraft carriers. Their navy took delivery of several new classes of submarines. While we maintain an edge of superiority in these areas, it is decreasing from year to year at an alarming pace.

• Continued development of a new long-range heavy-lift transport aircraft. The prototype, just completed, is comparable to our own C-5.

• Ran their high-energy laser program at three-to-five times the United States level and geared it to the development of specific laser weapon systems, including land-based and sea-based air defense.

• Showed a new approach to combined arms combat with the introduction of special high-speed, tank-heavy raiding forces. The Soviets continue to increase the number of modern T-64/72/80 tanks facing NATO.

• Have begun deployment of a MiG variant, the Foxhound, their first interceptor with a true look-down/shoot-down capability. Two more fighters with this capability are in development and will probably enter service soon.

The trends are clear. The Soviets view military modernization and advances in science and

John W. Vessey Jr., "The World, the Threat, and the JCS," *Defense/83,* May 1983.

technology as interrelated to the point of being one and the same.

The Soviets pursue the acquisition of our technology through legal and illegal sales, third-world transfers, and a highly organized espionage system. Customs Commissioner William von Raab explained that the Soviets "...have come to depend on the US electronics industry as a major source of both components for their own military systems and for manufacturing equipment with which to develop new systems." Let there be no doubt about the quality of our own systems. But, never expecting to outnumber our potential enemies, we now find the qualitative edge we once enjoyed dissipating at an alarming rate.

---

*"The most significant and certainly the most dangerous trend over the last 25 years has been the unrelenting growth of Soviet military power."*

---

We must deal with the reality of Soviet military power. Their forces are large—about five million active in contrast to our two million. Their forces are also well organized, well trained, and well equipped for a full range of military operations. Soviet leaders continually say that they don't want war, yet when we look at the forces they've built, the threat of war seems very real.

As we in the United States go about our business in this world of nation states, we don't want to be coerced by Soviet power or to have our friends coerced. We don't want war, but as we pursue the political, economic, social, and cultural objectives that "We the People" choose to pursue, we don't want to be paralyzed by the fear of war.

## US Strategy Is Prevention

The strategy of the United States is the prevention of war. Let me state unequivocally that neither I nor any member of the Joint Chiefs of Staff want war, not a conventional war and certainly not a nuclear war.

On the contrary, we are in the business of "waging the peace." The modern jargon word is "deterrence," dissuading one's potential enemies from starting a war by making it self-evident that war aims cannot be attained—that the cost will be too great. Many people have suggested that we announce a "no first use" policy for nuclear weapons. President Reagan restated our policy in 1981, and it was reaffirmed last year by the NATO ministerial council: "No NATO weapons, conventional or nuclear, will ever be used in Europe except in response to an attack." Our fundamental strategy is defensive.

Our strategy reflects a global perspective, centering on alliances and forward deployed forces in East Asia and Europe; strong naval forces to control sea lanes from our island nation; a central reserve of flexible land, sea, and air forces comprised of active forces and reserve units; the necessary strategic mobility capability; the command and intelligence systems; and on the North American continent and in the oceans of the world the most important ingredient in our ability to prevent nuclear war—our strategic nuclear forces.

We want to make it clear that we can and will retaliate to a Soviet nuclear attack by destroying Soviet forces in such a way that guarantees their war aims will not be achieved. To do so, the United States must and will maintain a modern strategic Triad—intercontinental ballistic missiles, submarine-launched missiles, and strategic bombers—with the required readiness, accuracy, warhead effectiveness, warning systems, and command arrangements. Modernization of our strategic nuclear forces to counter the dangerous and growing nuclear warfighting potential of the USSR is essential for deterrence and peace now, for the hope of strategic arms reductions talks, and for a more stable peace in the years ahead.

*John W. Vessey Jr. is the Chairman of the Joint Chiefs of Staff, the ruling committee of the armed forces of the United States.*

*"We have to convince [the Soviet Union] that they cannot win a war and that the rewards of peace are infinitely greater than anything they could gain from war."*

# Only US Strength Can Contain the US/USSR Conflict

## Anthony Harrigan

Ladies and gentlemen: In line with the theme of this meeting, I want to explain why, in my view, confrontations with the Soviet Union are inevitable so long as the U.S. government is committed to the security and freedom of our people.

Undoubtedly, there are many Americans who would be shocked at the statement that confrontations are inevitable. [They believe] that confrontations are *not* inevitable, that if the United States were, as they see it, to display greater reasonableness and a spirit of accommodation, negotiations on nuclear armaments would be resumed and overall relations with the Soviet Union would improve.

### Dangerously Naive Views

I regard those views as dangerously naive as they fail to take account of the history of Soviet behavior for almost 70 years. No American administration can avoid confrontations with the Soviets unless it is prepared to accept the Soviet agenda and act on it as the Soviets want us to act. In our dealings with the Soviet Union, we always must bear in mind that we are not dealing with a nation state that shares our values. A nation that uses chemical weapons in Afghanistan, that sponsors terrorist acts around the world, that organizes its governmental system for subversive warfare abroad, that wages war against its own people to prevent the emergence of any trace of freedom, is not a nation that can be expected to engage in civilized diplomacy.

President Reagan has been criticized at home and abroad for referring to the Soviet Union as an "evil empire." The characterization is deserved. How else would one characterize a country that has slaughtered and imprisoned millions of its own

people, not to speak of the captive nations who suffer under Moscow's thralldom? It is interesting, by the way, that the Marquis de Custine, after visiting Russia in the 1830s, referred to Russia as "the Empire of Fear." Also consider that Americans don't hesitate to speak of Hitler's Third Reich as an evil empire; it was precisely that. The Nazi concentration camps have been closed down for 39 years; the Soviet Union's Gulag Archipelago continues to operate across the vastness of Siberia. So let's not shy away from realistic rhetoric and the characterization of the Soviet Union as an evil empire. If we don't recognize the moral reality of the Soviet Empire, we are psychologically disarmed to a dangerous degree.

There's no question in my mind but that *many* Americans *are* psychologically and morally disarmed so that they don't support a strong deterrent aimed at the Soviet Union. There has been a decades-long-struggle to enlighten the American people as to the Soviet reality. During this same period, however, apologists for the Soviet Union have been at work in our country, in the Old Left and the New Left, to sanitize the Soviet image and prevent the American people, especially young college-educated people from understanding the Soviet reality.

### History's Lessons

For a few minutes, let me go back in time some 40 years. It always is well to do that, especially in a university, to examine history and to search out the misjudgments that were made by people in high places. What happened in the past has relevance for our decisions today and tomorrow.

This thought occurred to me the other day while I was doing some research on U.S.-Soviet relations. I came across a copy of *Soviet Asia Mission,* former Vice President Henry A. Wallace's account of four weeks he spent touring Soviet Asia in 1944. This book is a reminder of how fortunate the American people were that Franklin D. Roosevelt replaced

Anthony Harrigan, "Confrontations with the USSR," from a speech before the Institute for Soviet and East European Affairs, John Carroll University in Cleveland, Ohio on July 10, 1984.

Henry Wallace with Harry Truman when he chose a running mate for a fourth term. If Mr. Wallace had been vice president when Mr. Roosevelt died, the United States would have been in the hands of Stalin's most important dupe.

Mr. Wallace managed to spend a month in the Soviet regions that were a giant prison camp—the Gulag Archipelago in Solzhenitsyn's phrase—and thought everything was as nice and happy as an Iowa agricultural fair. He completed his Siberian tour with unqualified praise for the Soviet Union, saying: ''I must say that my personal impressions surpass all my expectations. I am enraptured by the scope of building and the great achievement.'' He telegraphed Stalin, stating that '''The governmental' policy of the Soviet Socialist Republic which has made this progress possible is a glowing tribute to a distinguished and talented statesmanship.'' This tribute to Stalin was rendered six years after Stalin had conducted his purge trials which finally awakened thousands of believers in the Soviet experiment to the communist tyranny.

The hopelessly naive vice president of the United States, who would later run for president with communist support, said in his account of the journey: ''The people of Siberia today are a hardy vigorous race, but not because they are whipped into submission. The only whip driving them is the necessity to master a vast new land.'' When he wrote these words, millions of captive Soviet peoples were being starved, tortured and otherwise brutalized in the slave labor camps of Siberia. Women and children were being tossed from railroad freight cars into deep banks of snow.

Vice President Wallace's inability or unwillingness to recognize Soviet reality is much more than an historical footnote. It is a reminder that the dupe or the apologist for totalitarian tyranny is a real type. Thank heavens we don't have them in high places in the U.S. government today, but they are numerous elsewhere. For example, a thousand professors signed an advertisement protesting the U.S. removal of the Marxist thugs in Grenada.

## Soviet Dupes

Two months ago, I heard a professor at a leading Southern liberal arts college praise Cuba and Nicaragua and hail the former for ''eliminating hunger.'' He didn't have a word to say about forced labor in Cuba, Castro's imprisonment and torture of opponents, or the Soviet use of Cuba as a military base. His remarks were a chilling reminder that the Soviet dupe still exists in the United States, and the rest of the Western world. He represents a continuing threat to democratic interests.

A little more history, if you please. When Mr. Wallace failed to receive the vice presidential nomination for President Roosevelt's fourth term, he was appointed Secretary of Commerce and held that position until September 1946, when he was forced to resign because of his open opposition to President Truman's foreign policy—the policy of firm resistance to Soviet expansionism. After a brief term as editor of *The New Republic*, Mr. Wallace launched a new Progressive Party, which charged the Truman administration with responsibility for the cold war.

*''In our dealings with the Soviet Union, we must always bear in mind that we are not dealing with a nation state that shares our values.''*

What has this to do with current confrontations involving the Soviet Union and the United States? Well, Mr. Wallace is long gone from the scene. But his naivete lives on in a new generation of political aspirants and writers.

They are unyielding in their belief that confrontation *isn't* inevitable, that a most sincere commitment to peace and good will produce a cooperative response from the Soviet Union. And they are prepared to make substantial concessions in terms of U.S. national security in the hope of gaining that response.

Organizations such as the Institute for Policy Studies, which the *Washington Post* refers to as a leftist think tank, work very hard to encourage the naivete and the belief in strategic and political concessions which stems from such an attitude. Rael Jean Isaac and Erich Issac, in their new book, *The Coercive Utopians*, point out that the IPS has assumed a major role in the disarmament movement. Let me quote the following passage from that book:

> One of the IPS' most innovative projects was a joint disarmament program with the Soviet Union's Institute for the U.S.A. and Canada and the USSR-USA Friendship Society, with the first session in Minneapolis in May 1983. Soviet defectors have estimated that 40% of the staff of the Institute for the U.S.A. and Canada consists of intelligence officers or individuals working under the direct supervision of the KGB and the FBI has reported that the USSR-USA Friendship Society is used by the Soviet Union for 'active measures' directed against the U.S.
>
> While IPS announced that the purpose of the conference was to come up with 'new ideas' on disarmament, the most apparent purpose was *to convey to the American public an idea shared by all three organizations sponsoring the program, namely that the United States is primarily responsible for the arms race.*

## US Threat to World Peace?

Let me spell out here what are some of the concessions proposed by those who regard the U.S., not the USSR, as the chief threat to peace. The July issue of *Harper's* features an article by Rep. Ron Dellums of California's 8th congressional district, which includes Berkeley. He says that ''the Era of

Pax Americana is over" and urges elimination of the MX missile, the Pershing II missile, the Trident II missile, and ground and sea-launched cruise missiles. He would eliminate the Rapid Deployment Force in the Middle East and cut the Marine Corps. He would reduct the U.S. Army to 8 divisions (the Soviets have 194) and cut the U.S. Navy to less than half the ships it had 5 years before Pearl Harbor. He also would get rid of the B-1 bomber and the M-tank. He would eliminate all economic and military aid to El Salvador and Honduras. All this means that the U.S. would have to withdraw from the NATO alliance and other efforts to preserve the free world. The Dellums hit list could not be more to the liking of the Soviets if drawn up in the Kremlin.

The Soviets have enjoyed considerable success in their disinformation campaign to put across the idea that the United States *is* primarily responsible for the arms race and that it also *is* responsible for the breakdown in negotiations on strategic weapons. It's only a short step from there to persuading Americans that they must make amends for what the Left refers to as strident rhetoric and "cowboy diplomacy."

---

*"Apologists for the Soviet Union have been at work in our country. . . to sanitize the Soviet image and prevent the American people. . . from understanding the Soviet reality."*

---

It's very difficult to get across to the American people that there hasn't been any arms race in the past decade, that the Soviets had a crash program of developing and deploying new weapons systems while America's defenses deteriorated and only recently began to be rebuilt to some degree. Instead of gaining a new measure of realism regarding the Soviet Union, many of our most influential people have become gripped by an ideology of fear. The subliminal suggestion of those who present themselves as workers for peace is that we must not make any statement or action that could provoke a reaction by the Soviet Union—even if it means abandonment of the cause of freedom within or without the Western world.

Obviously, Western resistance to the Soviet Union cannot continue without some risk-taking. The self-styled peace advocates want the U.S. and its allies to adopt a no-risk policy. What they fail to realize is that even total surrender to the Soviet Union—acceptance of all its demands—would not end the risk of human life. On the contrary, surrender most certainly would mean a blood bath for all Westerners who defend the cause of freedom.

It is very important that more attention be devoted to the consequences of a policy of concessions rather than confrontations. I suspect that many of those who urge concessions—who urge acceptance of a posture of military inferiority on the part of the United States (in order not to be provocative)—imagine that the West can continue to enjoy, with this policy, the same degree of freedom and independence that it had during a generation of deterrence and resistance. It's hard to understand how they rationalize this belief, given the unwillingness of the Soviet authorities to permit any measure of freedom within those countries of Eastern Europe where they have a commanding influence. Would the Western advocates of a policy of nonprovocation be willing to settle for that measure of freedom and independence enjoyed by Hungary and Rumania, for example, with a token measure of independence, let us say?

## Ideology of Fear

Of course, we should recognize that there are those advocates of concessions who, while they don't admit it to the world, apparently *are* prepared to surrender freedom and independence for the level of those qualities one finds in the less oppressed of the Soviet satellite countries. I am not referring here to those who have a sympathy for the Soviet world order or revolutionary movements in general, but who, simply, are so concerned about nuclear war that they would make any sacrifice.

This outlook is not new. In the 1930s, when the weapons of war were much less destructive, there were many influential people who were willing to accept Nazi dominance in order to avoid another world war. The ideology of fear was very strong in the 1930s. Fortunately for the survival of Western civilization, this fear did not cripple the Western will to resist Nazi totalitarianism.

Now, to be sure, the threat of destruction in war is vastly greater, and the fear of a nuclear holocaust is correspondingly great. Is the United States prepared to abandon resistance to Soviet totalitarianism because of the more awesome character of weapons? Is it the will of the people to reach whatever accommodation is required to eliminate the nuclear war threat from Moscow and to settle for some sort of passive resistance in a Soviet-controlled world?

## American Commitment to Freedom

I don't believe that the American people, or the people of Western Europe, for that matter, are prepared to take any such steps or adopt the outlook that lies behind them. They have lived with the spectre of a Soviet nuclear threat for a generation and have not been shaken by it. The commitment of our people to freedom is profound. I am convinced that Americans cannot conceive of life without freedom. Americans would not be slaves, no matter what the danger to free men. Moreover, death is not a collective experience; it happens to each man and woman. The East German man, woman or child who attempts to cross the Berlin Wall or similar deadly barriers makes the choice for freedom over the threat of death and possible extinction of a family. These individuals reject the ideology of fear.

We would not be much of a people if our actions were ruled by an ideology of fear. Indeed what would our future be if fear ruled us and shaped our choices and destiny? Since the dawn of time, man has lived with risks. Thousands of years ago, tiny bands lived on the edge of the European glacier. Their existence could not have been more precarious, their chances of survival more slim. They endured; they survived; they accepted the risk of their era and place; and we must do the same.

We cannot be less than our adversaries in the world. In May of this year, former President Nixon told the assembled newspaper editors of the country that "the Russians are a great people. They are strong; they are courageous." I don't doubt that. And he added: "We have to convince them that they cannot win a war and that the rewards of peace are infinitely greater than anything they could gain from war." That, in brief, is what we hope to gain in a confrontation with the Soviets, in standing up to them, that is. If the Soviets thought that the ideology of fear characterized the American people as a whole, and not merely one ideological segment, they would have cause for believing that they could win a war against us. The incentive for the Soviets to go to war would be considerable. They undoubtedly would judge that they had more to gain from war than from peace.

## Soviet Inner Life

The American people need to understand the inner life of the Soviet Union, for it is part of the equation. Nora Beloff, in an essay entitled "Calling the Soviet Bluff" (London, 1982) warned that the Soviet people "are kept in a permanent state of psychological mobilization. Banners stretched across the roads and buildings are couched in military language: 'Smash barriers'; 'Build bulwarks'; 'Defeat obstacles.'"

One of the hopes of those Americans who favor a strictly non-provocative policy towards the Soviet Union is that a soft approach will have a favorable effect on the Soviet people. Time and again, we hear the statement from those returning travelers from the USSR, who urge concessions, that the Soviet people don't want war. Certainly, but they don't know what is going on at home or abroad and they don't have any input into Soviet decision-making.

To quote Miss Beloff again: "Secrecy in the USSR is enforced not only towards foreigners but also between the Soviet people themselves. The prohibition against conveying information unless specifically permitted, is an invaluable prop for the authorities. This keeps the population on the defensive, makes them easier to manipulate, and facilitates propaganda campaigns. And that is why no one knows the Soviet system can take seriously the unilateralist contention that the Soviet public could force their leaders to change course."

## Structure of Soviet System

One of the gaps in understanding of the Soviet Union, among those who urge concessions for peace, is a failure to take note of the structural organization of the Soviet regime, which is set up to wage political and ideological war against the Western world. The warfare system is at the apex of Soviet organizational arrangements. Active Measures, by which one means overt and covert techniques for influencing the behavior of foreign countries, are institutionalized in the USSR. At the top is the CPSU Politburo. Under that is the CPSU Secretariat, served by three major organs. Briefly, the International Information Dept. handles Tass and other orthodox channels. Service A, 1st Chief Directorate, KGB, deals with espionage, terrorism, insurgency, etc. The International Dept., however, is in many ways the most interesting and significant organ, for it directs international front organizations, national front organizations (US Peace Council, for example), and the Academy of Sciences. The organizations it directs include the World Peace Council, Afro-Asian People's Solidarity Organization, International Union of Students, International Institute For Peace, International Organization of Journalists, Christian Peace Conference, International Assn. of Democratic Lawyers. Most of these groups were first established in the 1940s. So long as these organizations and this organizational structure is part of the Soviet system, it is foolish to imagine that any real progress towards peace can be achieved. These, after all, are combat organizations that are aimed at the morale of the West.

*"We cannot be less than our adversaries in the world."*

The self-proclaimed peace organizations in the West take no note of this structure. Of course, they also fail to acknowledge, as Dr. Roger Scruton and Baroness Caroline Cox said in a recent article on peace studies, that the Soviet system is "a system without legal opposition, without limited or constitutional government, without representations, without any corrective device other than those applied to it from outside." This is a design for tyranny. And given these facts and this structure, how can the self-styled peace groups expect the Soviet Union to respond to a diplomatic policy in which the free world walks the extra mile for peace? A regime without internal restraints isn't likely to practice restraint in its external relations. The language of power and firmness undoubtedly is the only language such a regime understands.

## Fear Is the Only Restraint

All this has a bearing, I believe, on the way blame is apportioned to the United States and the Soviet Union for the breakdown of negotiations on nuclear weapons. A significant element in the major media tends to say that the United States is most to blame, or at least, equally to blame. This element fails to address the question as to which is the greater threat to peace—a society based on free association and representative government, or a society based on totalitarian control? The United States government is under tremendous internal and international pressure to modify and weaken its negotiating stance in order to arrive at a position acceptable to the Soviets. For their part, the Soviet leaders face no comparable internal or external pressure, as the Soviet peoples have no voice in the shaping of Soviet policy; and Soviet bloc countries certainly are not in a position to oppose or even question the decisions of the Soviet leadership. Fear, then, is the only restraint on Soviet policy or action.

*"One of our first and foremost tasks is to reject the notion that there is a political and moral equivalence between our open democracy and the closed oligarchical system in the Soviet Union."*

As we consider our posture with respect to the USSR, we certainly need to avoid the error of judging the roadblock to agreements and to a wider peace to be a faction in the Kremlin. This is what columnist Joseph Kraft did when he said that our difficulties lie with "the inner gang of hard-liners grouped around Foreign Minister Andrei Gromyko and Defense Minister Dimmitri Ustinov and the military brass." This is a mistaken approach: there is no dove versus hawk dispute in Moscow. Differences may exist as to timing and tactical methods, but no one reaches the Politburo without sharing the same outlook and commitment to the structure and strategy of the Soviet regime. However, we can reasonably expect the members of the Politburo to adjust their position to the external power realities, to respond to resistance, in other words, in terms of altering the *pace* of Soviet action. And it is to that end that our policy should be directed.

That's a limited goal, but an attainable one. We should not expect any dramatic breakthrough on any front, as the status quo is solidly established.

This reality is a world away from the hopes and dreams of those in the United States who think a new measure or reasonableness will produce a dramatic breakthrough for the cause of peace. Those who have such extravagant hopes should review the history of the Soviet Union and of Russia itself. Whenever I am puzzled by the enigma of the Soviet Union, I turn to the Marquis de Custine's account of his visit to imperial Russia in the early 19th century. His description and analysis of Czarist Russia also bears on the successor Soviet regime. Russia, the Marquis said, is "a country which differs from all others." And he went on to say that "Russia sees in Europe a prey which our dissension will sooner or later yield to her."

Let's hope our country will grow in awareness of the Soviet reality, namely that we shall continue to be confronted by intrinsically hostile Soviet leaders who will resort to any method to divide and weaken us. We are in a very long-term struggle, and one of our first and most important tasks is to reject the notion that there is a political and moral equivalence between our open democracy and the closed oligarchical system in the Soviet Union. If we understand these matters correctly, we should be able to maintain a sound negotiating posture that doesn't yield our freedoms and vital interests.

*Anthony Harrigan is president of the US Business and Industrial Council.*

*"Indirect means of containing or balancing Soviet power are as important as our direct dealings with the Soviets."*

# A Flexible, Moderate Strategy Can Manage the US/USSR Conflict

Joseph S. Nye Jr.

Looking ahead, there are grounds to hope for improvement in our management of relations with the Soviet Union. Public opinion at the mass level is still centrist in its demands for a policy that balances "peace and strength," though mass public opinion does not weigh international issues very intensely and events can pull the non-internationalist opinion (of those little concerned on a daily basis) back and forth between its dual concerns. . . .

The first requirement for successful long-term management is a flexible strategy that combines a sensible vision of the future and definition of our interests with appropriate means in a manner that can sustain domestic support. Since 1947, there have been variants of one basic strategy—containment. The broadest choice in strategy is between containment and totally new approaches. If one assumes that options such as isolation or a U.S.-Soviet condominium are not feasible in domestic or international politics, then there are two basic alternatives to containment; one in the direction of a more active confrontation with the Soviet Union and the other in a direction of a less active American role.

## A Less Active Role?

Those who are deeply pessimistic about our ability ever successfully to manage Soviet relations might be tempted to urge a less active American role. From this point of view, the only sensible strategy is to encourage the development of a multipolar world in which Soviet power will be balanced and contained by others as much as by the United States. So long as nuclear bipolarity is combined with ideological rivalry, the American public will remain obsessed with the Soviet Union, and election campaigns will press politicans toward exaggerations in the

formulation of policy. In a truly multipolar world, one would logically have to consider the Soviet Union as a potential partner in shifting coalitions balancing Chinese, Japanese and European power. In such circumstances, our domestic politics could show less of a fixation on the Soviet Union, and policy might be easier to manage.

There are a number of problems with such a strategic vision. Our experience of multipolar balances comes from the pre-nuclear age. There may be greater dangers of miscalculation in the management of deterrence if coalitions shift quickly in the nuclear age. Moreover, even if the end result were desirable, it might be destabilizing to try to get from here to there, since the process could well involve the massive nuclear arming of Germany and Japan with uncertain effects on Soviet perceptions. In fostering such proliferation, we might be throwing wide open the lid on Pandora's nuclear box as others rush to emulation. Moreover, the benefits in terms of American politics and policies toward the Soviet Union may prove to be ephemeral. After all, there were ideological hostility and wide oscillations in our policies toward the Soviet Union in the period of multipolar balance before World War II. . . .

## Confrontation Strategy?

The other major alternative to containment is an active policy of confrontation designed to force change in the Soviet Union. . . . Those who urge a confrontation strategy offer a long-run vision of a Soviet empire in decline. Economic growth has slumped from six percent to roughly two percent a year. Corruption and inefficiency are rampant. Demographic trends could exacerbate the nationalities problem inside the Soviet Union, and there is restiveness in the empire in Eastern Europe. In these circumstances, it is argued, curtailment of trade and scientific exchanges and the threat of a new arms race could force the Soviets to change, or at

Joseph S. Nye Jr., "Can America Manage Its Soviet Policy?" Excerpted by permission of *Foreign Affairs*, Spring 1984. Copyright 1984 by the Council on Foreign Relations, Inc.

least force the Soviets to turn from expensive external adventures to domestic economic reforms.

This strategy also raises fundamental questions. Is it prudent in a world of nuclear-armed powers to try to press an opponent to the wall? The reckless performance of Austria-Hungary on the eve of World War I would indicate that declining empires can be very dangerous actors in a balance of power. Moreover, do we really know how to bring about reform in the Soviet Union? Is there good reason to believe that faced with a choice, the Soviets will choose butter rather than guns? Or that they can be prevented from producing adequate guns? A recent CIA report indicates that "the ability of the Soviet economy to remain viable in the absence of imports is much greater than that of most, possibly all, other industrialized countries....Consequently the susceptibility of the Soviet Union to economic leverage tends to be limited....

Thus the difficulties of the alternatives, both in terms of the uncertainty of their goals and the feasibility of their means, drive us back to the historically proven center ground of containment. But there are many paths among which to choose in the center, and the slogan of containment can be misleading. If containment is thought of as balancing Soviet power by a variety of political and diplomatic means, then it is merely the traditional common sense of international politics. But if containment implies a broad definition of American interest that leads to efforts to counter every Soviet or Soviet-allied action in the Third World, it would soon surpass our means, including the critical resource of domestic political support. The lesson of Vietnam is that an overly ambitious definition of interest which creates a gap between ends and means can lead to severe oscillations in foreign policy attitudes. One might label a centrist strategy as "containment with communication" or a "managed balance-of-power" approach.

## Conflict Is Inevitable

The important point is that conflict with the Soviet Union is endemic in the structure of the bipolar relationship. Hopes to terminate the conflict quickly by accommodation or victory are unlikely to be realized. The problem is one of long-term management. At the same time, successful management of a balance of power requires communication and negotiation among the opponents. And a successful foreign policy for managing such a balance requires reliance upon multiple sources of strength—economic, political, military—and a selectivity in goals which relates ends and means. There are three principles to guide such a strategy.

*First is the importance of a moderate design to insure that policy can be durable and robust.* Some aspects of our policy process can be improved, but others are deeply rooted in our political culture and institutions. Our problems are more constitutional than organizational. There are no quick fixes. A basic principle for a durable strategy is to cut the coat of foreign policy to fit the rather rare eighteenth-century domestic cloth that we have inherited. The importance of this principle cannot be overstated: fine-tuning is impossible, secrecy difficult, oversimplification likely, and pluralism of views of the Soviet Union unavoidable. Thus a successful strategy must be moderate in three ways: in its definition of American interests; in its cautious rather than optimistic expectations of Soviet behavior; and in its assessment of American politics—meaning a hardheaded appraisal of what resources the electorate will devote to what interest and for how long. This does not mean a low profile in countering Soviet power. On the contrary, it means recognizing that only a moderate strategy will be robust enough to survive our domestic climate and durable in the face of any tendency toward pendular swings in attitudes. Only a moderate strategy will allow leaders to close the gap between ends and means. The point seems obvious until one reflects on how often we have failed to achieve it.

## Evolving USSR

*A second principle is that the Soviet Union is also unlikely to change quickly, but it does evolve slowly and unevenly.* We will continue to be faced with a closed and secretive society which is difficult to understand. On the other hand, the Soviet Union has opened up somewhat over the past 30 years. There are more contacts. There are more pinholes letting light into the black box. Moreover, recognition of this second principle helps with our domestic politics. Specifying a broadly shared long-range goal is an important precondition for giving legitimacy to the policy choices needed to undergird a durable strategy.

---

*"The important point is conflict with the Soviet Union is endemic in the structure of the bipolar relationship."*

---

Avoiding nuclear war by balancing Soviet power and gradually reducing the risks associated with nuclear deterrence is such a goal. If misperception and miscalculation are the conditions most likely to foster a breakdown of nuclear deterrence, then one of the long-term security objectives in our strategy should be to encourage that process of evolving transparency and communication.

The Soviet Union remains opaque to us, as a number of legislators noted when trying to decide on how to vote on the MX missile. "When you play cards against someone," noted Congressman Dan

Glickman of Kansas, "you ought to know something about them. Unfortunately, our judgments turn out to be highly subjective for the most part." Or in the words of Senator Richard Lugar of Indiana, "We try to figure out where they're coming from, but it could well be the blind leading the blind." Increased contact and communication can help to poke holes in the "black box" of Soviet society and gradually increase its transparency.

*"The difficulties of the alternatives. . . drive us back to the historically proven center ground of containment."*

Change inside the Soviet Union will be gradual and hard to gauge, and we can at best encourage, rather than hope to guide it. Nonetheless, this possibility suggests that a managed balance-of-power strategy should involve routine and regular communication. From this point of view, our tactics should include engaging the Soviets in prolonged strategic discussions; holding talks at high level on force structure and stabilization measures; and efforts to consider crisis prevention techniques, not necessarily in the expectation of signing formal agreements, but as a means of enhancing transparency. It also follows that trade, scientific and cultural exchanges, and tourism should be evaluated by the same standard and not solely by the current criteria of economic benefits and short-term security interests. A managed balance-of-power strategy does not rest on expectations that increasing engagement will win Soviet trust or greatly constrain Soviet actions. Nor does it rest on any immediate liberalizing effects of "goulash communism." In the first instance, it rests on the importance of enhancing transparency and communication.

## Indirect Containment Through Economics

*The third principle to guide a more consistent strategy is that indirect means of containing or balancing Soviet power are as important as our direct dealings with the Soviets.* Both because the Soviets will resist efforts to change them quickly, and because our politics tend to undermine our own persistence in pursuing such efforts, our direct efforts will often face frustration. An indirect approach is more likely to succeed both at home and abroad. We may be most successful in containing Soviet power by constraining their opportunities in the rest of the world. Maintaining the Western Alliance has been the key to the success of containment thus far, and this is an area where the pluralism of American institutions can be a help

rather than a hindrance by providing multiple points of access and reassurance.

The growing complexity of world politics, with more actors and issues, and the inevitability of turmoil in the Third World mean that we can never hope to completely control the milieu of world politics as an element in a strategy of containment. But a recognition of these problems and of the diffusion of economic power to our allies should reinforce our attention to the indirect dimensions of our policy in managing relations with the Soviet Union. A strong world economy with effective linking among the non-communist market economies may be a more robust economic strategy than one which tries to fine-tune East-West trade. An effective strategy rests on the comparative advantage of America's economic power and presence in the world economy as well as on the traditional political and military aspects of balancing Soviet power.

In addition to these basic principles, a managed balance-of-power strategy has important implications for dealing with the main issues in the relationship: defense, crisis management, trade and human rights. Managing the defense and nuclear issues is basic. A strong defense and clear signals are essential for an effective policy of deterrence toward the Soviet Union, and domestic and allied confidence in the strength of our deterrent is a necessary condition for all the rest of policy toward the Soviets. Uncertainty about security exacerbates the domestic debate and hinders effective steps toward arms control. The practice of exaggerating the Soviet threat as a means of generating support for the defense budget encourages inconsistency when the public eventually reacts to the exaggeration. To counter this tendency requires improving estimates, integrating arms control with defense planning, negotiating in smaller (but related) packages, and avoiding the rhetorical excesses that prove disruptive to retaining allied and domestic support for a consistent defense program over the long term.

## Avoid Dramatics

In the area of crisis prevention and crisis management we should eschew large dramatic gestures and formal agreements such as those of 1972 and 1973, but engage the Soviets in quiet discussions of classic technics (neutralization, buffer states, spheres of concern) for avoiding crisis escalation. Such talks could extend or be related to discussions of nonproliferation of nuclear weapons or of particularly dangerous conventional weaponry. Equally important will be efforts at home to redefine our interests in the less expansive terms of selective containment. As originally outlined by George Kennan, the most cost-effective way of containing Soviet power was through reliance on the nationalistic currents of other states. This entails learning to live with disagreeable regimes, and distinguishing those Third World situations where our interest would be deeply involved (e.g., Saudi Arabia) from those where they are less centrally involved (e.g., Southeast Asia)....

As for the economic component of a managed balance-of-power strategy, we must avoid too ambitious an approach. While it is important to control a narrow set of technologies where we are sure of the direct military relevance, we know too little about the net effect on the Soviet economy and have too poor a grasp of our own or of allied political processes to engage in a policy of detailed linkage or fine-tuned leverage. The signals we would try to send would inevitably come across as too confusing to justify the costs that we would incur in trying to send them. Because interest groups will always be hard to control and the effects of restrictions on the Soviet Union are debatable, it is better to focus controls on those situations (such as trade in technology that shortens military lead times) where a clear and present danger is demonstrable....It is critical that disputes over East-West economic ties not be allowed to disrupt an effective intra-Western trading system. In short, the American comparative advantage lies in strengthening the open international economy in which we loom large and the Soviets small, rather than squandering Western unity over futile efforts to prevent the Soviets from gaining any benefits from that economy.

## Caution and Realism

Finally, we need caution and realism in our expectations of bringing about social and political change in the Soviet Union. An idealistic concern for human rights is a domestic American reality which a managed balance-of-power strategy must accept. Americans cannot live by balance of power alone. Nonetheless, a confrontation human rights policy is likely to be counterproductive in terms of the interests of Soviet citizens. Sometimes, however, minor improvements can be made through quiet diplomacy. In general, the fate of human rights in the Soviet Union is adversely affected by the worsening of the overall climate of U.S.-Soviet relations. Government actions that promote social contact and quiet diplomacy rather than public government efforts targeted at individuals or Soviet policies are more likely to serve both human rights and our long-term objective of enhancing the degree of transparency and communication in the relationship....

The implications of this simple-sounding proposition are very significant. It means that there will always be limits to the types of strategies that we can successfully follow. As stated earlier, our ability to manage the Soviet relationship is less a matter of organization than of choosing an appropriate strategy. The basic principle for a durable strategy is to cut the foreign policy coat to fit our domestic political cloth.

This does not mean appeasing the Soviet Union or failing to balance Soviet power. Quite the contrary. What it means is that if we pick an inappropriately ambitious strategy, we will fail in the long run, because the American domestic political process will produce oscillations and inconsistency. In a nuclear age, we ignore such reality at our peril.

## Appropriate Strategy

An appropriate strategy must be modest enough to fit our domestic capabilities; it must focus on indirect effects through maintaining our alliances as much as on the direct bilateral relationship with the Soviet Union; and it should combine balancing Soviet power with economic engagement and continual communication. Over time, such a strategy may

*"In the area of crisis prevention and crisis management we should eschew large dramatic gestures."*

gradually increase the transparency in the relationship, reducing the dangers of miscalculation and increasing somewhat our understanding of what goes on within the opaque Soviet society. Our strategy should not only manage the current threat of Soviet power, but should gradually seek to improve the conditions that make it so difficult for a society organized such as ours is to manage the relationship with the Soviet Union.

*Joseph S. Nye Jr. is a professor of government at Harvard University and was formerly Deputy to the Under Secretary of State for Security Assistance, Science and Technology. He has written numerous books and articles on US foreign policy.*

*"We cannot ignore the fact that in most cases these problems [between the US and the USSR] are the result of Soviet misconduct."*

# To Build Trust, the USSR Must Change

### Lawrence S. Eagleburger

Leonid Brezhnev is dead, and Yuri Andropov governs in his place. And for many Western pundits the way is now open, if we Americans, they say, but have the wit and will, to bring about a fundamental change in the relationship between the United States and the Soviet Union. I am here tonight to tell you that, though I might wish it were so, I do not believe it to be so.

The reality is that while, of course, personalities are influential in setting the course the two superpowers will follow, the divergence of views, history, and interests is so basic that no one man, indeed, no group of men, can affect, except at the margins, the fundamentally competitive nature of our relationship....

Our policy toward the U.S.S.R. starts from the fact that both of us have weapons of almost unimaginable destructive force. Each of us can do mortal damage to the other in an afternoon. Our weapons are not the result of failed judgment or of a military-industrial complex spinning out of control. We arm because the Soviet Union is armed and aggressive.

## Deeply Rooted Differences

The differences between the Soviet Union and the Western world are deeply rooted. We have radically different political values, visions of the proper social order, and aspirations for the future of the international system. While we in the West are fundamentally committed to individual liberty, to free elections, the accountability of those who govern to the governed, to economic freedom, and to a world order that fosters those values, the Communist Party of the Soviet Union is just as fundamentally opposed to all of those principles.

But even more ominous than these differences is the Soviet decision to translate our philosophical rift

Lawrence S. Eagleburger, remarks before the World Jewish Congress in Washington, DC on February 1, 1983.

into a global, military competition. They have made us rivals.

We are rivals not because the Soviets do not respect our interests but because they respect only their own. Our moral commitment to the rule of law, to peaceful change, and to the safety of the weak from domination by the strong compels us to view the Soviets not only as our rival but as the rival of a humane world order.

We cannot wish these differences away. And we will not abandon our values. In fact, we are determined to advance them. This administration welcomes an open and peaceful competition between our visions of man's future. President Reagan has recently launched a program to promote democratic values and institutions abroad; it is a program that has already drawn substantial Soviet fire, so its potential effectiveness must worry them.

Our rivalry, then, must continue so long as our two nations remain true to the principles upon which they were founded. But because our arms make the rivalry so dangerous, we must keep it within bounds. We and the Soviets have few common interests. But, so long as the West remains strong, we do share one fundamental interest—that of avoiding war. American policy toward the Soviet Union must fall between the impossible and the unacceptable; we must steer a middle course between the friendship we cannot have and the war we must not have.

## Requirements for Cooperation

The aim of this administration is plain. We want relations with the Soviets that are as cordial and cooperative as our deep differences permit. But such a relationship has two fundamental requirements.

*First, there must be a military balance.* History offers few clear lessons for those who manage our nation's affairs, but one of them surely is that an imbalance of military power between two rivals leads to trouble. Where such an imbalance exists for long, the stronger party talks while the weaker listens. Soon the stronger makes demands and the weaker submits.

Over the past decade, America's investment in defense lagged behind that of the Soviet Union. During the 1970s, we spent between 4% and 5% of our gross national product on defense; the Soviets spent 12-14% of theirs. In that decade, our defense spending declined in real terms. Theirs increased by 4-5% per year. These facts have clearly affected the course of Soviet conduct for much of the past ten years. We have, then, little choice but to increase our defense effort to make up for the ground we have lost.

*"To the extent that the Soviets continue to act as international outlaws, we will meet the challenges they present."*

Our efforts are designed to assure equality in the military relationship. We do not seek an arms race, but we will not, we cannot, accept second best. We are not trying to spend the Soviet economy into the ground. Indeed, we would not mind at all if the Soviets improved their economic condition by spending less on their military. We arm for a single purpose: to deter the use of Soviet arms against us or our allies.

Our effort to maintain a stable military balance is entirely consistent with our goal of improved relations with the Soviet Union. In fact, the one is clearly necessary for the other, a reality that some, of late, seem to have forgotten. There is great wisdom in the story of the first-time visitor to Jerusalem who tells an Israeli he meets that he is surprised to see so many weapons in the land of the Bible. "It is true," the Israeli tells him, "that the Bible says that on the day of days the lion shall lie down with the lamb. But," he continues, "the day of days hasn't come yet. And even then," he adds, "I'd rather be the lion than the lamb."

## Soviets Must Change

*The second fundamental requirement for an improved relationship with the Soviet Union is simply stated: the Soviet Union must observe certain basic standards of national conduct.* We do not insist that the Soviet Union abandon legitimate national interests or its standing as a superpower. But what possible legitimate Soviet interest would be threatened were they to live up to standards that are plainly written into documents they themselves have signed—the Helsinki accords, the U.N. Charter, even their own constitution? Yet these standards have been violated time and time again. The Soviet occupation of Afghanistan, the suppression of the popular desire for reform in Poland, the Vietnamese imperial control of

Kampuchea at the behest of the Soviet Union, their Cuban proxy's promotion of instability in southern Africa and Central America, the denial of basic human rights to their own citizens—all these acts demonstrate that the Soviets have not only failed to abide by the rules of civilized societies; they have failed to keep their word.

When the Soviet buildup far exceeds any legitimate defense requirement; when they deploy forces in Eastern Europe, the Far East, and the Indian Ocean that have no conceivable defensive mission; when they intimidate our European and Asian allies to try to prevent them from taking measures that their own unwarranted military initiatives have made necessary, it is difficult to credit the Soviet Government with peaceful intentions. When the Soviets threaten Japan with nuclear devastation on the heels of Prime Minister Nakasone's visit here, are they not to be taken seriously? When elementary human rights are denied where Communist governments hold power; when Anatoli Shcharansky is cruelly imprisoned instead of being allowed to emigrate and Andrei Sakharov is held under house arrest far from his home under no formal charge; and when one of the first acts of the new Soviet leadership is to threaten the distinguished historian Roy Medvedev, we in the West, for whom human rights are of paramount importance, must not pretend that more cordial East-West relations will be easy to achieve.

## Soviet Provocation Harms Relations

It is these policies, undertaken by the Soviet Union and its allies, that have poisoned East-West relations. This is the crucial point that some in the West are too ready to forget. Our relations have been bad because Soviet aggression and provocation have made them bad. When aggression and provocation cease, relations will improve. . . .

We stand ready to cooperate in arrangements that would reduce the differences between us and bring the Soviets into the family of responsible nations. Ours is not an agenda for humiliating the Soviet Union. It is a formula for more cordial, constructive Soviet-American relations. Soviet leaders constantly complain that we do not give them the respect they deserve as a superpower; but the possession of great power carries with it special responsibilities, including the obligation to respect the rights of others, to show restraint, and to live up to universally recognized standards of conduct. The Soviets cannot earn our respect by amassing and misusing power; they can earn it by responsible behavior.

What conclusions can be drawn from this analysis? You may well find reason for pessimism in my remarks. After all, my main themes would have been pertinent at almost any moment during the past thirty-five years. We find ourselves in the position of the man in the small Jewish community in eastern

Europe in the last century whose job it was to sit at the village gate all day waiting for the approach of the Messiah. "Isn't your job boring?" someone asked. "Sure it's boring," he replied, "but at least the work is steady."

The work of trying to moderate Soviet conduct over the last three decades has been anything but boring. I wish it might have been otherwise; international affairs could use a little more tedium. But bored or excited, we are determined to take the steps necessary to protect our friends and ourselves from aggressive Soviet conduct. We will maintain our alliances, despite the difficulties that such international partnerships always involve. We will sustain the balance of military power, despite the sacrifices that this imposes on our citizens, and despite Soviet attempts to undermine popular support for this policy. And we will stand firm on our principles and steady in our position in disputes with the Soviets, although this taxes our patience and our national impulse for problem solving.

## Soviets Must Remove Obstacles

We are prepared to work with the Soviets in search of solutions to the problems between us, though we cannot ignore the fact that in most cases these problems are the result of Soviet misconduct. If the Soviets try in earnest to remove the obstacles to a better relationship, they will find us ready for relations of mutual respect, for cooperation in areas of mutual interest, and for insuring that competition remains peaceful where our interests conflict.

To the extent that the Soviets continue to act as international outlaws, we will meet the challenges they present. The American people are committed to this course over the long term; not just for the life of this administration but for as long as necessary. Like the job of standing at the village gate, we will bring steadiness and perseverance to the task of leading the West.

---

*"It is these policies, undertaken by the Soviet Union and its allies, that have poisoned East-West relations."*

---

Whatever course the Soviet Union chooses to follow, we will work on our own and with our friends to build a world order compatible with our values and our interests. The U.S.S.R., is, admittedly, a major player on the world scene. But we must not be mesmerized by that fact. There are other issues, other weighty problems that we can and will deal with no matter what the Soviets do.

We will continue our efforts to revitalize the institutions of international economic cooperation, to spur recovery and promote domestic and

international economic growth. We will continue our efforts to resolve dangerous conflicts. I need not remind this audience of our deep concern for peace in the Middle East. That concern is the basis for the president's September initiative. We are committed to the security of Israel within defensible borders; we will work for a peaceful, united Lebanon and a just resolution of the Arab-Israeli conflict. We will continue our global efforts to make the peaceful settlement of disputes the normal international practice. We will, as well, remain dedicated to the protection of human rights throughout the international community, a goal which is threaded throughout our entire foreign policy.

## Toward Humane International Relations

These endeavors will proceed with or without Soviet cooperation. These efforts must be made whatever the state of U.S-Soviet relations. And the more peaceful, prosperous, and humane the international community becomes, the fewer opportunities there will be for Soviet mischief and the stronger the pressure of Soviet leaders to moderate their conduct and eventually accept a role as a great and responsible nation.

My message tonight is not a dramatic one. I cannot promise sweeping changes in U.S.-Soviet relations. There is no basis for such a promise. I cannot tell you when modest improvements will take place. That is up to the Soviets. And I must caution you that improvements, if they do come, are bound to be modest. We will not see the day of days with the Soviet Union. Our rivalry will, I fear, outlive all of us in this room. But we can hope, and work, to see days more tranquil, less heavy with menace, than those of the recent past.

*Lawrence S. Eagleburger is Under Secretary of Political Affairs.*

*"U.S.-Soviet relations have deteriorated so seriously that little can be done... until the political leadership of both superpowers makes the repair of the relationship its top priority."*

# To Build Trust, Both the US and the USSR Must Change

Richard J. Barnet

U.S.-Soviet relations have deteriorated so seriously that little can be done to improve them until the political leadership of both superpowers makes the repair of the relationship its top priority. An essential step in that direction is to change the foreign policy and military doctrine of both nations to reflect the two fundamental realities of the nuclear age: that nuclear weapons are militarily and politically useless except to threaten retaliation against a nuclear attack; and that the security of the United States cannot be improved by inducing greater insecurity in the Soviet Union, and vice versa.

U.S. strategy, however, has depended greatly on communicating just the opposite message: that in a crisis the United States would be more prepared to begin a nuclear war than the Soviet Union would. Nuclear weapons have been viewed as critical to what is called the most effective instrument for "managing" relations with the Soviet Union: threat manipulation. The U.S. military buildup and the increasing integration of nuclear and conventional forces in the U.S. arsenal have been designed for "escalation dominance," to use the chilling jargon of the war planners. Moreover, the idea that nuclear weapons could be used effectively in the Third World has by no means been abandoned.

To encourage greater trust in U.S.-Soviet relations, the United States should renounce the illusions about nuclear weapons that have guided its national strategic planning. Nuclear weapons cannot be used to "manage" crises or to compensate for local military or political weaknesses, and nuclear threats, whether conveyed by word or by deed, produce not a properly cowed Soviet leadership but a vengeful, nervous, and error-prone Politburo. The United States should renounce these dangerous policies, and the

Richard J. Barnet, "Why Trust the Soviets?" *World Policy Journal,* Spring 1984. Reprinted by permission.

Soviet Union, in turn, should bring its military doctrine and deployments unequivocally into line with the "no-first-use" pledge adopted by the Soviet government in 1982.

## Avoiding War as Principal Goal

In addition, each superpower must convince the other that the avoidance of nuclear war is its principal goal and that its strategy for accomplishing this is to reduce, not to increase, its military threat to the other. The superpowers can build mutual trust only by convincing one another of their strong self-interest in moving in this direction. This requires demonstrated changes in their current foreign policy practices, a clear shift in domestic priorities, and a marked change in rhetoric. Although U.S. experts may disagree on the extent to which Soviet behavior can be explained by feelings of insecurity, the theory that "keeping the Soviets off balance" makes the United States more secure is not supported by historical evidence. The more paranoid the political atmosphere becomes, the more easily aggression can be justified as "defense." (It is instructive to recall how the tiny island of Grenada suddenly became a "national security threat" to the United States.) By the same token, the security of the Soviet Union depends on its being able to reassure the United States that it plans no military aggression. Public declarations of intention are useful, but they are clearly inadequate unless backed up by specific, visible changes in military doctrine, training, and deployment that confirm that a historic shift in strategic thinking is indeed taking place.

Another key to moderating the images of hostility on both sides—images that keep the arms race going and that create areas of confrontation between the superpowers around the world—is for the United States to make it unmistakably clear that the Soviet Union is and will be treated as a legitimate superpower with rights and responsibilities commensurate with those of the United States. We cannot expect the Soviet Union to accept responsibilities for stabilizing political settlements in critical conflict areas, such as the Middle East, until it has been granted a legitimate role as a guarantor of the peace. It is a short-sighted triumph to exclude from negotiations a power that retains the incentive and the capability to upset, or at least to harass, any political settlement that is achieved without it.

*"The superpowers can build mutual trust only by convincing one another of their strong self-interest in moving in this direction."*

U.S. concern that the Soviets have fished and will fish again in the troubled waters of the Middle East is legitimate. But the Austrian State Treaty and the Quadripartite Agreements on Berlin and Germany suggest that where mutual interest exists the Soviets can be trusted to act as reliable stabilizers of the peace. In any event, the proposition that Soviet incentives and behavior can be positively influenced by U.S. attitudes and policies should at least be tested. The Soviets have often imitated U.S. behavior in the past. There may be room now for the United States to influence Soviet behavior both by explicit agreement and by example.

## Recognition of USSR Status

U.S. recognition of the Soviet Union's legitimate status and responsibility as a superpower could well proceed in stages. The United States should tone down its poisonous rhetoric, change its nuclear doctrine, and end its self-defeating efforts to restrict economic relations between Western multinationals and Soviet government. If the Soviets were foolish enough to regard these steps as a "green light" for expansionism, as anti-Soviet hawks relentlessly argue, then the process of moderating tensions would end right there. This, presumably, the Soviets know. Any effort to establish greater trust between the superpowers unavoidably must rest on the assumption that the Soviets have an interest in doing so. They have, as already noted, recently made major decisions on the assumption that relations with the West will not deteriorate. The objective risks of war, the staggering cost of the arms race, and the deteriorating quality of life inside the Soviet Union due to the pressures of military spending lend credibility to the protestations of Soviet leaders that they genuinely do seek a more cooperative relationship with the United States. . . .

The most likely arena of superpower conflict is the Third World, and the most likely scenario for a

nuclear war by miscalculation is the escalation of a conventional conflict in some designated strategic area of the world when one side fails to back down when its bluff is called. For this reason, the superpowers' common interest in avoiding war requires a clarification of intentions and policies with respect to the Third World. . . .

## Possible Areas of Agreement

To ask the superpowers to give up their rhetorical commitments to "democracy," "free enterprise," and "socialism" in the Third World, however, would be utopian—and unnecessary—despite how grotesquely divergent from these ideals some favorite protectorates and aid recipients around the world may be. But both could agree to give up specific activities, such as military intervention, which now block the development of a more secure relationship. It is a quintessential requirement for building trust in the U.S.-Soviet relations that the two superpowers avoid sending their own forces into other countries. Given the price both powers have paid in Vietnam, El Salvador, Afghanistan, and Czechoslovakia, such an understanding, tacit or explicit, may not be as utopian as it appeared in the era of Pax Americana and Khrushchevian optimism, both now long gone.

Moreover, the superpowers should agree to acquire no new foreign military bases and to initiate a process of withdrawal from those bases that they presently occupy. These bases are a source of instability. They engage the prestige of the superpowers in volatile areas. In a crisis, they would pose them with the unenviable choice between military escalation to defend them and the humiliation of abandonment. The United States has by far the greater spread of bases around the world. Many of them, those in the Philippines, for example, are potential political hostages more than military assets. Most of the U.S. "forward bases" around the Soviet Union were acquired before the era of the transcontinental bomber and the intercontinental ballistic missile. They are far more objectionable to the Soviet Union than they are militarily useful to the United States. They could therefore be used to negotiate away some aspect of Soviet deployments that is most objectionable to the United States, such as the high state of readiness of Soviet forces in Europe.

## Ending Arms Shipments

Arms shipments to governments fighting nationalist insurgencies and arms shipments to insurgents, as in Central America, should also be halted unilaterally by both superpowers as a step toward building trust. Until each reassesses the risks involved in tying its prestige to the outcome of Third World struggles for national independence, it will not be able to make credible its desire for a new relationship between the superpowers. That relationship cannot be, as some critics charged at the time of detente, a condominium to control the world. It must be a mutual recognition that most of the world cannot and need not be controlled by the superpowers. Until the superpowers are secure enough to live with considerable diversity and political chaos in the world, both of which are inevitable, they will not be secure enough to live with one another.... 

A relationship of trust between the superpowers cannot be stabilized if either attempts to play the role of armed "peacekeeper" unilaterally in any area of the world, even in regions traditionally treated as "backyards," such as Central America or Eastern Europe. The superpowers already maintain a heavy military presence in these regions: U.S. naval forces in the Caribbean and Soviet divisions in Poland, Czechoslovakia, and Hungary. Both should make immediate unilateral declarations to stop harassing maneuvers and to freeze further deployments in Central America, Eastern Europe, and elsewhere. This would specifically preclude either superpower from conducting maneuvers on the borders of Nicaragua and Poland for purposes of political intimidation. These declarations should then be ratified by the Congress, by the Supreme Soviet, by all political parties in the United States that qualify for federal matching funds, and by the Soviet Communist Party.

The role of negotiations in U.S.-Soviet relations also needs to be rethought. A precondition for successful negotiations is a set of agreed goals. The two superpowers will not achieve agreement unless they share common expectations that are politically realistic. The SALT process was based on a shared objective that was not realistic. The negotiations sought to manage the arms race so that each side would be free to build the weapons it wanted while remaining protected against some unpleasant surprises and pressures to build anything more. Because the continuation of the arms race requires the expenditure of scarce resources, domestic political concerns in both countries make such an ambivalent relationship unstable. To obtain military appropriations and to keep the forces in fighting trim, the potential adversary must continually be presented as a threat. This tends to undermine political support for even the most minimal of agreements.

## Negotiations Record

The record of U.S.-Soviet relations suggests that successful negotiations are either a ratification of independent initiatives taken by the two sides because it is in their common interest to do so—the Partial Test Ban Treaty, for example, was a ratification of a mutual moratorium on atmospheric testing—or a reflection of a newly discovered common interest after more ambitious goals have been abandoned—the Austrian State Treaty, for example. In recent years, however, the negotiating process has become a prime instrument of Cold War politics which each superpower has used not only as a weapon against the other, but as an instrument for maintaining political hegemony over its respective sphere. Negotiations have thus become a means of monopolizing East-West relations and of discouraging independent initiatives across the blocs.

## Deteriorating Relations

As in the Stalin era, the negotiating process over the last few years has itself led to a worsening of relations, negotiations are seen as instruments of competition rather than as instruments for resolving mutual security problems. It is hard to see how any future U.S.-Soviet arms negotiations can succeed outside of a larger political settlement. Their success seems to require that they be preceded by unilateral steps on both sides, such as redeployments, the cancellation of threatening weapons programs, evidence of a shift in national priorities away from an increased reliance on the military, and certainly a cooling of rhetoric.

To build trust in the negotiating process, each superpower should undertake to reassure the other that it is a reliable long-term partner. One way to do this is to spell out both a set of shared objectives and a framework within which individual agreements can be reached....

*"A relationship of trust between the superpowers cannot be stabilized if either attempts to play the role of armed 'peacekeeper' unilaterally in any area of the world."*

Arms negotiations will not succeed unless their significance is seen as primarily political rather than technical. Tinkering with numbers of weapons cannot accomplish much in itself as long as our arsenals remain far above the crucial threshold of removing the threat to the inhabitability of our planet. Negotiations will improve U.S.-Soviet relations only if they are used to communicate nonthreatening intentions on both sides. The "bargaining chip" theory of negotiations does just the opposite. We need to ask ourselves why a U.S. military buildup should be expected to make the Soviets readier to compromise on security questions, as the president maintains, when the United States responded to the Soviet military buildup in exactly the opposite way. The perception of the Soviet buildup of the 1970s played a critical role in destroying the U.S. political consensus behind detente.

Within the United States, the issue of whether the

Soviets can be trusted has been influenced by concerns over Soviet performance under past agreements. The Reagan administration has charged the Soviets with violating the SALT agreements, but it has neither disclosed its evidence to the public nor resorted to the procedures specified by the treaties for raising such charges. The Soviets have been accused of supplying chemical weapons for use in Kampuchea and Afghanistan—the so-called yellow rain—and of producing biological weapons in violation of agreements or unilateral pledges. There is a large literature in which these charges have been defended and disputed. Yet neither guilt nor innocence has been established. All that is clear at this point is that both superpowers, in dealing with these issues, have demonstrated a greater interest in the political utility of propaganda than in building a basis for trust.

> "In the end, the building of a minimal trust between the superpowers will depend on how much each is willing to make the betterment of relations its top priority."

The United States has concluded more than 100 treaties with the Soviet Union. In general, the record of Soviet performance has raised no doubts about Soviet trustworthiness. In commercial dealings, U.S. businessmen report that the Soviets have been reliable partners—tough bargainers who keep the bargains they make. The agreements that have raised such doubts are of two kinds. The first are declarations of high principle couched in language that is easily susceptible to differing interpretations. Part of the Helsinki Declarations on Human Rights falls into this category; it should have been evident that the Soviets never intended to change their internal practices to the extent that the United States says the wording implies. The second are narrow arms agreements with built-in ambiguities. Under SALT II, for example, it is now disputed whether a certain weapon is a "new" missile and hence proscribed by the treaty, or a modification of an "old" missile and hence permitted.

## Pushing to the Limits

Both sides have been reckless in pushing the wording of existing arms agreements to the outermost limits. Whether or not the Soviet Union has actually violated weapon agreements, as the Reagan administration has charged, it certainly has stretched them. But in announcing plans to develop space warfare capabilities and an anti-ballistic missile system, the United States has demonstrated a cavalier

attitude toward existing arms control agreements that does nothing to build faith in American dependability. The more comprehensive the agreements and the less peppered they are with exceptions and modifications, the less frequently exploitable ambiguities and gray-area violations will arise. . . .

In the end, the building of a minimal trust between the superpowers will depend on how much each is willing to make the betterment of relations its top priority. In recent years, other priorities have taken precedence: ideological warfare, the pursuit of an ephemeral influence in the Third World, and the perverse pleasures of humiliating, outwitting, or frightening the adversary. There is, unfortunately, no historical precedent for what is now required: the subordination of rankling historical memories, power fantasies, and missionary zeal to the requirements of survival. But never before has this necessity been so obvious.

*Richard J. Barnet is a Senior Fellow at the Institute for Policy Studies in Washington, DC. He has written numerous books and articles on international relations.*

# chronology

1945 The Yalta conference establishes basis for occupation of Germany and returns to the Soviets land taken by Germany and Japan. US President Franklin Roosevelt, British Prime Minister Winston Churchill, and Soviet ruler Joseph Stalin participate.

Roosevelt dies and is succeeded by Vice-President Harry S. Truman.

The Potsdam conference makes plans for reconstructing post-war Germany. Truman, Churchill, and Stalin participate.

1946 In a speech at Fulton, Missouri, Churchill warns that an Iron Curtain of communist aggression has descended across Eastern Europe.

Soviet Foreign Minister Andrei Gromyko refuses US proposals for controlling atomic energy development.

1947 Truman announces the containment doctrine, aimed at preventing communist expansion, and requests aid for Greece and Turkey.

US Secretary of State George C. Marshall announces the Marshall plan for European economic recovery; the Soviets refuse to participate.

The US State Department discloses the full terms of the 1945 Yalta and Potsdam agreements, including giving the Kurile islands and Sakhalin peninsula to the Soviets in exchange for their participation in the war against Japan. At Potsdam, Truman and Churchill agreed to the admission of the Ukraine and White Russia as separate voting members of the United Nations.

The Soviets announce they have formed the Cominform, an alliance of communist countries which will coordinate communist activities and information in Bulgaria, Czechoslovakia, France, Hungary, Italy, Poland, Rumania, USSR, and Yugoslavia.

1948 The USSR invades Czechoslovakia as communists seize control of the government.

Marshall Tito ends Yugoslavia's alliance with the Soviet Union, and Yugoslavia is expelled from the Cominform.

The Soviets set up a land blockade of West Berlin, which is lifted six months later after Western allies have airlifted food and supplies to West Berlin.

1949 The Soviets set off their first atomic bomb.

The US, Canada, and ten West European nations establish the North Atlantic Treaty Organization (NATO).

1950 China's new communist government and the USSR sign a 30-year friendship treaty.

The Korean War breaks out when the North Korean army crosses the 38th parallel, which was set up as the partition between North and South Korea.

1952 The Soviets declare US Ambassador George Kennan *persona non grata* after Kennan's comments that conditions in the USSR reminded him of being interned in Nazi Germany.

Dwight D. Eisenhower is elected US President; Richard M. Nixon, Vice-President.

The US explodes its first hydrogen bomb.

1953 Workers in East Berlin demonstrate and the Soviets intervene with tanks.

The armistice ending the Korean War is signed; some US troops remain in South Korea.

Stalin dies. Georgi Malenkov takes over as Premier and first secretary of the Communist Party. He soon resigns his first secretary position and Nikita Krushchev becomes secretary.

The USSR explodes its first hydrogen bomb.

Stalin's ally and former chief of secret police Lavrenti Beria is dismissed from the government and the Communist party and later executed with six colleagues for high treason.

1955 Malenkov loses premiership; Nikolai Bulganin takes over as Premier.

The Soviet Union and Eastern bloc nations establish the Warsaw Pact as a counterpart to NATO.

Ten years after occupying Austria during World War II, Soviet, American, French, and British troops leave the country after agreeing Austria's foreign policy will be nonaligned.

Treaty between East Germany and USSR gives East Germany sovereignty.

1956 Uprising in Poznan, Poland is crushed and Soviet attempt to prevent Gomulka's victory in the Polish Communist Party fails.

Hungarians revolt, announce neutrality, and appeal to the United Nations for help. Soviet troops soon suppress Hungarian uprising; at least 7,000 are killed.

Krushchev advocates "peaceful coexistence" with US.

At the 20th Party Congress meeting, Krushchev denounces Stalin's "personality cult" and dictatorial excesses.

The Cominform is dissolved as a gesture of good will towards Tito.

Egypt's leader Gamal Abdal Nasser expels British oil and embassy officials, and nationalizes the Suez Canal zone. After Egypt refuses to let Israel use the canal, war breaks out. The US and Britain withdraw their financial support for building the Aswan High Dam; the Soviets respond by providing technical help and money for the project.

The Eisenhower Doctrine advocates aid to Mideast countries which resist Communist aggression.

The Soviets develop their first intercontinental ballistic missile.

The Soviets put first satellite in space (Sputnik I), beginning the space race between the US and the USSR.

Malenkov and V.M. Molotov are kicked out of government posts and the Presidium of the Communist Party.

1958    Bulganin resigns as premier; Krushchev replaces him.

Krushchev announces a seven-year economic plan, aimed at making the Soviet economy surpass the US economy.

1959    Krushchev becomes the first Soviet communist leader to visit the US.

Fidel Castro overthrows Cuban dictator Batista and takes over the Cuban government.

1960    The American U-2 spy plane is shot down over Russia. Krushchev responds by cancelling Paris summit meeting. The plane's pilot, Francis Gary Powers, is imprisoned for two years in the USSR until he is exchanged for a Soviet spy held in the US.

The Soviets send up first manned space flight.

The Soviets and Communist China break their alliance and cut off diplomatic relations.

John F. Kennedy defeats Nixon and becomes US President.

1961    US President John F. Kennedy orders an invasion of Cuba in an attempt to overthrow Castro. This Bay of Pigs attempt fails disastrously.

To stop the exodus of its citizens, East Germany builds a fortified wall between East and West Berlin.

Soviet cosmonaut Yuri Gagarin makes the first orbital flight around the world.

The USSR and Albania break relations and Albania aligns itself with China.

1962    Kennedy reveals the Soviets have built an offensive supply of missiles in Cuba; in response he orders a naval blockade of Cuba. Krushchev backs down and the crisis is defused.

1963    A telephone hotline is established between Washington and Moscow.

The US, USSR and Britain agree to a treaty banning nuclear weapons tests.

Vice-President Lyndon B. Johnson becomes President after Kennedy is assassinated in Dallas.

1964    Krushchev is forced into retirement as Leonid Brezhnev becomes First Secretary of the Party and Aleksei Kosygin becomes Premier.

The US Congress passes the Tonkin Gulf Resolution, which extends the President's power to send troops to intervene in conflicts. Johnson sends more US soliders to Vietnam to help South Vietnam fight against communist North Vietnam.

1965    The US begins bombing raids on North Vietnam in an effort to stop the flow of weapons and soldiers to Vietcong guerrillas fighting the South Vietnamese government.

The US Embassy in Moscow is attacked twice by demonstrators protesting US bombing raids on North Vietnam.

1967    The Six-Day War breaks out in the Middle East between Israel and Egypt, Syria, and Jordan. The US supports Israel while the Soviets support the Arab nations.

Stalin's daughter, Svetlana Alliluyeva, defects from the USSR and comes to New York.

1968    After the Czechoslovak government adopts reforms aimed at instituting "humane socialism," the Soviets invade Czechoslovakia. They justify the invasion by issuing the Brezhnev Doctrine, stating allied countries may intervene to defend communism.

Nixon defeats Hubert Humphrey and becomes US President.

1970    Alexander Solzhenitsyn wins the Nobel Prize for Literature. His works are banned in the USSR.

1972    The US and the Soviets sign the largest trade deal to date between the two nations; the US will export $750 million of grain to the Soviets.

US President Nixon visits the USSR for summit talks, which conclude agreements on strategic arms limitation. Called SALT I, the talks set a ceiling of 200 anti-ballistic missiles for both sides and freeze Soviet ICBMs at 1,618 and US ICBMs at 1,054. The USSR's numerical advantage in submarine missiles is balanced by allowing the US more warheads on its more accurate missiles.

After breaking with the Soviets, Egyptian President Anwar Sadat orders Soviet military advisers out of Egypt.

1973    The US calls a world-wide nuclear alert after the Soviets threaten to intervene to help Egyptian forces in the 1975 Arab-Israeli war.

1974    The Soviets condemn Solzhenitsyn's *Gulag Archipelago*, which reveals Soviet crimes. After its publication in the West, Solzhenitsyn is arrested and expelled from the Soviet Union.

After two years of Congressional investigations into the Watergate scandal in the Nixon administration, Nixon resigns and Gerald R. Ford becomes President.

Congress passes the Jackson-Vanik amendment which bars trade privileges and credits to communist countries that do not permit free emigration.

1975    The Final Act of the Helsinki Accords is signed. Among its provisions are articles calling for nations to respect human rights and not intervene in each other's internal affairs.

The level of Soviet space capability is openly demonstrated for the first time by a 44-hour linkup of Soviet Soyuz space vehicle and US Apollo spacecraft.

The US protests Soviet and Cuban involvement in the Angolan civil war.

1976    James E. Carter becomes US President and Walter F. Mondale Vice-President after defeating incumbent President Ford.

1977    A nuclear non-proliferation pact is signed by 15 countries, including US and USSR.

US President Carter announces human rights policy and protests Soviet arrests of dissidents.

The Soviets charge Anatoly Scharansky, Jewish human rights activist, with treason.

1979    A temporary ban is set on export of high technology goods to USSR as part of President Carter's protest against jailing of Soviet dissident Aleksandr Ginzburg. Ginzburg and four other Soviet dissidents are exchanged for two Soviet spies held in the US. The highest number of Jews (51,320) ever allowed in a year emigrates from the USSR.

The SALT II agreement is signed by Carter and Brezhnev in June.

The US refuses final ratification of SALT II agreement after the Soviets invade Afghanistan in December.

1980    In response to Soviet invasion of Afghanistan, Carter orders an embargo on grain shipments and high-technology equipment to the USSR. He also announces the US will boycott the Summer Olympics, hosted by Moscow for the first time. US, Canada, Japan, and all western allies, except France and Italy, boycott the Olympics.

The Soviets send dissident nuclear physicist Andrei Sakharov and his wife Dr. Yelena Bonner into exile in Gorki.

After a national strike is settled, Polish workers form the labor union Solidarity.

Ronald Reagan defeats incumbent Carter and becomes US President.

Soviet Prime Minister Aleksei Kosygin resigns.

1981    Reagan announces plans to develop and stockpile neutron bombs: weapons which leave buildings intact while killing humans. Within a week the Soviets announce plans to develop neutron bombs.

Negotiations on reducing medium-range nuclear missiles begin. Reagan offers a "zero-option": the US will cancel its planned missile deployments in Europe if the Soviets dismantle their existing medium-range missiles. The Soviets reject the offer.

The Reagan administration releases a "White Paper," which claims the Soviets and Cubans have been using Nicaragua to ship arms to rebels fighting to overthrow the Salvadoran government.

A military government takes over in Poland, imposes martial law, and represses the labor union Solidarity. In response, Reagan orders economic sanctions against Poland and the Soviet Union including an at-

tempt to block an agreement between the Soviets, Western Europe, and Japan to construct a gas pipeline.

1982    Strategic Arms Reduction Talks (START) begin in Geneva.

Resolutions calling for a freeze on nuclear weapons development are introduced in Congress.

Reagan proposes cutting the number of warheads on US and Soviet land-based missiles by one-third. Brezhnev argues the proposal would cut Soviet forces more than American forces and offers a proposal to freeze weapons during arms negotiations.

The US charges the Soviets are using chemical warfare in Afghanistan.

Brezhnev dies in November and is succeeded by Yuri Andropov.

In response to US plans to deploy the MX missile, the Soviets announce in December a plan to deploy new ICBMs in the same class as the MX.

1983    Reagan calls the Soviet Union "the focus of evil in the modern world."

Reagan proposes developing an anti-ballistic missile defense system, saying that the system he wants would not violate the ABM treaty with the Soviets.

Soviet military planes attack a South Korean commercial airliner which had strayed over Soviet air space, killing all 269 passengers aboard.

The US advocates a "build-down" program for arms reductions. Each deployment of new missiles would have to be accompanied by destroying a greater number of old missiles.

The Soviet Defense Ministry announces it will deploy tactical nuclear weapons in East Germany and Czechoslovakia if the US carries out its plan to deploy cruise missiles in Western Europe.

The US starts delivering cruise missiles to be deployed in Europe, provoking large anti-nuclear demonstrations in Europe. The Soviets break off all arms negotiations with the US.

1984    Soviet Foreign Minister Gromyko calls the US the main threat to peace in the world.

Andropov dies in February and is succeeded by Konstantin Chernenko.

Reagan announces his intention to pursue the development of antisatellite weapons and says a ban on such weapons with the Soviets would be impossible to verify. The Senate votes to halt full testing of the weapons until Reagan certifies he is seeking negotiated limits on them.

The US Defense Department releases figures that the Soviets have 8,000 more warheads than the US has.

Soviet dissident Sakharov begins a hunger strike to publicize his demand for medical attention for his wife.

The Soviets and all Eastern bloc nations except Rumania boycott the Los Angeles Summer Olympics.

The US State department announces that advanced Soviet fighter aircraft may be on board a Soviet freighter docked in Nicaragua. The USSR and Nicaragua deny the claim.

Reagan meets with Foreign Minister Andrei Gromyko, marking the first time in his administration Reagan has met with a top Soviet leader.

1985    Secretary of State George Shultz and Gromyko meet in Geneva to negotiate an agenda for arms control talks. The Soviets demand space weapons be included in future negotiations.

The Soviets suggest a no-first use policy be put in a treaty at a Stockholm disarmament conference. The US refuses to negotiate the treaty.

Chernenko dies in March and is succeeded by Mikhail Gorbachev, who is named General Secretary of the Communist Party.

A Soviet guard shoots US Army Major Arthur Nicholson Jr. near a military site at Ludwigslust, East Germany.

John Walker, a retired US Navy officer, and other members of his family are arrested in May on charges of selling classified documents to the Soviets.

After Nicaraguan leader Daniel Ortega visits the Soviet Union in May, Congress reverses an earlier vote and decides to send money to the *contra* rebel forces fighting to overthrow Nicaragua's government.

# organizations

### Afghanistan Relief Committee
345 Park Ave., Suite 4100
New York, NY 10154
(212) 355-2931

The Committee, a private group, was established to help the Afghan victims of Russian aggression. Through the media and in meetings with concerned groups in the US and abroad, the Committee seeks to keep the Afghan refugee cause active. Their private assistance, sent to war victims within Afghanistan, is the only humanitarian aid entering that country.

### American Committee on East-West Accord (ACEWA)
227 Massachusetts Ave. NE, Suite 300
Washington, DC 20002
(202) 546-1700

The Committee is composed of a group of prominent individuals from the academic and business communities, former ambassadors, labor leaders, and public interest spokesmen. Their purpose is to reduce tensions (and thereby the possibility of nuclear confrontation) between East and West by furthering public understanding of strategic arms agreements and mutually beneficial programs in science, trade, and culture, with special emphasis on US-USSR relations. ACEWA publishes the *East/West Outlook,* as well as books and occasional papers.

### American Friends Service Committee
1501 Cherry St.
Philadelphia, PA 19102
(215) 241-7000

The Committee supports arms control and opposes the Star Wars program. AFSC's purpose is to relieve human suffering and to find new approaches to world peace and nonviolent social change. Their resource catalog includes the books *Nuclear Illusion and Reality, The Freeze Economy,* and *The Arms Race and Arms Control,* and also includes films such as *Survival . . . Or Suicide* and *In The Nuclear Shadow: What Can the Children Tell Us?*

### Americanism Educational League (AEL)
P.O. Box 5986
Buena Park, CA 90622
(714) 828-5040

The League, founded in 1927, conducts public education to promote the private enterprise system and protect citizens' freedom from internal and external threats. AEL periodically publishes position papers and pamphlets on national defense issues.

### American Security Council (ASC)
Washington Communications Center
Boston, VA 22713
(703) 825-8336

The Council was founded in 1955 to support national research and information on national security. The ASC maintains a Washington bureau and broadcasts Radio Free Americas, a daily Spanish language program on over 38 stations throughout the Americas. It organizes and serves as program secretariat for Coalition for Peace Through Strength. The Council publishes two monthly publications, the *Coalition Insider,* and *Washington Report.*

### Amnesty International (AI)
304 W 58th St.
New York, N.Y. 10019
(212) 582-4400

Amnesty International monitors human rights in the USSR as it does everywhere. AI is a worldwide movement which is independent of any government, political faction, ideology, economic interest, or religious creed.

### Arms Control and Foreign Policy Caucus (ACFPC)
US Congress
501 House Annex 2
Washington, DC 20515
(202) 226-3440

The ACFPC is a bipartisan caucus made up of members of the United States Senate and House of Representatives who are concerned with foreign and military policy. The Caucus publishes background papers, fact sheets, and memos.

### Arms Control Association (ACA)
11 Dupont Circle NW
Washington, DC 20036
(202) 797-6450

The ACA does not have a formal program in US-USSR relations but rather a strong and continuing interest in facilitating and strengthening relations between arms control and security specialists of the two countries through participation in other programs and by taking advantage of opportunities as they arise. The Association publishes books, pamphlets such as "What about the Russians?" and Films/Slide Presentations like *Security, Strategy, and New Technology.*

**Cardinal Mindszenty Foundation**
P.O. Box 11321
St. Louis, MO 63105
(314) 991-9490

This anti-communist organization was founded in 1958 to conduct educational and research activities concerning communist objectives, tactics, and propaganda through study groups, speakers, conferences, and films. The Foundation publishes the monthly *Mindszenty Report.*

**Carnegie Endowment for International Peace (CEIP)**
11 Dupont Circle NW, Suite 900
Washington, DC 20036
(202) 797-6400

The Endowment seeks to educate the American decision-makers and the public about the complexities of Soviet foreign policy. The issues covered include foreign policy, arms control, military balance, and Soviet policy towards Western Europe and the Middle East. The CEIP publishes the 4 volume book, *Future of Arms Control.*

**Central Intelligence Agency (CIA)**
Office of Public Affairs
Washington, DC 20505
(703) 351-7676 Office

The CIA collects, produces, and disseminates foreign intelligence and counterintelligence, advises government bodies and makes recommendations about national security matters, and conducts special activities approved by the President. Write for a list of publications.

**Christian Anti-Communist Crusade (CACC)**
PO Box 890
227 E. Sixth St.
Long Beach, CA 90801
(213) 437-0941

The Crusade, founded in 1953, sponsors anti-subversive seminars "to inform Americans of the philosophy, morality, organization, techniques, and strategy of communism and associated forces." The CACC publishes a free, semi-monthly newsletter.

**Citizen Exchange Council (CEC)**
13 E. 41st St. #1900
New York, NY 10017
(212) 889-7960

The CEC seeks to promote mutual understanding between American and Soviet citizens. The Council emerges in cultural, educational, and professional travel programs for Americans in the USSR and by providing programs and hospitality for Soviet visitors in the US in an attempt to address all issues pertinent to their goal. The Council publishes the biannual *Communique* and pamphlets.

**Committee for National Security (CNS)**
2000 P St. NW
Washington, DC 20036
(202) 833-3140

In the area of US-USSR relations, the goal of the Committee is to provide general educational information, analyses, and negotiation proposals for public and private sector use. The Committee publishes books and periodicals.

**Committee on the Present Danger (COPD)**
1800 Massachusetts Ave. NE
Washington, DC 20036
(202) 466-7444

The Committee directs attention to the unfavorable military balance between the United States and the Soviet Union. The COPD publishes occasional papers dealing with this issue.

**Continuing the Peace Dialogue USA/USSR**
Valle Vista
Carmel Valley, CA 93924
(408) 429-6584

The goal of Peace Dialogue is to add momentum to friendship and understanding between people of the United States and the Soviet Union. It publishes a quarterly newsletter and a pamphlet on travels in the USSR.

**Council for the Defense of Freedom (CDF)**
1275 K St. NW, Suite 1160
Washington, DC 20005
(202) 789-4294

The Council is an educational organization which disseminates information on communism in order to combat it and protect national security. It supports the Star Wars and civil defense programs. The Council's weekly paper, *The Washington Inquirer,* repeatedly deals with the arms race and US failure to take measures to overcome a lack of preparedness. The CDF also publishes the monthly *Bulletin.*

**Department of Defense (DOD)**
Office of Public Affairs, Public Correspondence Division
Room 2E 777
Washington, DC 20037
(202) 545-6700

The DOD is responsible for defending the country and maintaining the armed forces and military arsenal. The Department plans for the development of conventional and nuclear weapons.

**Educators for Social Responsibility (ESR)**
639 Massachusetts Ave.
Cambridge, MA 02139
(617) 429-1764

The goal of ESR is to de-demonize the Soviets in order to educate the next generation of students so that it will understand the Soviet people, negotiate with them, and survive together. The ESR publishes a newsletter, the *Forum,* and books on the issues they are concerned with.

**Federation of American Scientists**
307 Massachusetts Ave. NE
Washington, DC 20002

The Federation campaigns to urge members of Congress to travel to the USSR and invites reciprocal visits by Soviet political leaders. It publishes a bi-monthly journal at the cost of $25 per year.

**Fellowship of Reconciliation (FOR)**
Box 271
Nyack, NY 10960

The FOR, founded in 1915, is a pacifist organization, made up of religious pacifists drawn from all faiths. The Fellowship "attempts, through education and action, to substitute nonviolence and reconciliation for violence in international relations." It publishes pamphlets, books, and the monthly magazine *Fellowship* dealing with disarmament and nonviolence.

**Forum for a US-Soviet Dialogue**
22 Hemlock Hill
Amherst, NH 03031
(603) 673-8639

The Forum coordinates annual exchanges of young people, independent of special interest groups, to discuss US-Soviet relations in education, science, economics, and disarmament. It publishes, bimonthly, *The Forum* and an annual report.

**Foundation For Economic Education, Inc. (FEE)**
Irvington-On-Hudson, NY 10533
(914) 591-7230

The Foundation supports freedom through an understanding of the free market, private property, and limited government. ''To this end, FEE has remained a consistent proponent of the ideal concept of human liberty and a critic of collectivism in any of its forms.'' FEE publishes the monthly journal, *The Freeman*.

**Fund For Peace**
345 E. 46th St.
New York, NY 10017
(212) 661-5900

The Fund, in the area of US-USSR relations, seeks ways to improve understanding and to reach an accord between the two superpowers. The Fund plans to develop a program of direct communication and exchanges between individuals in both countries. Its publications are the three monthlies, *The Defense Monitor, First Principles,* and *In the Public Interest.*

**Global Education Associates**
552 Park Avenue
East Orange, NY 07079
(201) 675-1409

GEA ''seeks ways to enable US leaders and people and Soviet leaders and people to transcend simplistic ideological perceptions of each other and to recognize their common self-interest in developing effective international institutions as a necessary framework for achieving true security in today's interdependent world.'' The GEA focuses on the military and economic insecurity of both superpowers. It publishes books and pamphlets.

**Ground Zero Pairing Project, Inc.**
P.O. Box 19049
Portland, OR 07219
(503) 245-3403

The objective of the Ground Zero Pairing Project is to pair American and Soviet cities as a basis for establishing bridge-building programs so that citizens in both countries may learn more about each other. They publish books and pamphlets and the bi-monthly newsletter *Linkages.*

**W. Averell Harriman Institute for Advanced Study of the Soviet Union**
420 West 118th St.
New York, NY 10027
(212) 280-4623

The overall goals of the Harriman Institute's US-USSR programs are the training of graduate students for scholarly and professional careers in Soviet Studies and the promotion of research in the Social Sciences and Humanities related to Russia and the Soviet Union. The Institute touches on virtually every aspect of USA/USSR relations. It publishes the monthly, *Newsnotes.*

**The Heritage Foundation**
214 Massachusetts Ave.
Washington, DC 20002
(202) 546-4400

The Heritage Foundation seeks to examine the nature and extent of the Soviet challenge to Western nations and institutions. The Foundation looks at military, political, economic, and cultural dimensions of the East-West relationship. The Foundation publishes books and the monthly *Policy Review.*

**Institute for Policy Studies (IPS)**
1901 Q St. NW
Washington, DC 20009
(202) 234-9382

The Institute's program on national security provides both factual analysis and critical alternatives of foreign and military policy. From its earliest years, analysis of US-USSR relations has been a part of this. Their goal has been to unravel the myths of the Cold War and provide a more balanced view of relations. The IPS has a joint exchange with the Institute for the Study of the USA of the USSR Academy of Sciences. The Institute publishes several books on these subjects.

**Liberty Lobby**
300 Independence Ave. SE
Washington, DC 20003
(202) 546-5611

The Lobby, founded in 1955, is a group of ''nationalists and populists interested in political action on behalf of 98 issues which are pro-individual liberty and pro-patriotic.'' They support less government spending, protective immigration laws, and withdrawal from the United Nations. They oppose federal aid to education, foreign aid, and ''unfair'' foreign competition, recognition of Red China, and world government. The Lobby publishes the weekly *Spotlight,* the *Congressional Handbook,* and *Liberty Ledger.*

**National Council of American-Soviet Friendship**
162 Madison Ave.
New York, NY 10016
(212) 679-4577

The Council was founded in 1943 to encourage better relations between the US and the Soviet Union to help bring about world peace and guard against nuclear destruction. The Council publishes the quarterly *Friendship News.*

**National Education Association (NEA)**
201 16th St. NW
Washington, DC 20036
(202) 833-4400

The Executive Office of the National Education Association maintains contact with the Soviet Embassy in Washington and with the Educational and Scientific Workers Union of the USSR. The general purpose of its relationship with the Soviet teacher unions is the promotion of international cooperation and understanding, the exchange of information on education trends, concepts, and experiences, and the establishment of personal relationships between the leaders of the two teacher organizations. The NEA publishes the *NEA Today,* the annual *Handbook,* and the annual *Today's Education.*

**Physicians for Social Responsibility**
639 Massachusetts Ave.
Cambridge, MA 02139
(617) 491-2754

This organization of medical doctors has more than 100 chapters in cities throughout the country. The group holds periodic symposia to alert people to the medical consequences of nuclear war.

**SANE: Committee for a Sane Nuclear Policy**
711 G St. SE
Washington, DC 20003
(202) 546-7100

SANE works ''to reverse the international arms race through negotiated arms reduction agreement, to shift funds from the military to domestic needs, to convert defense facilities and industries to civilian production, and to organize citizen political action toward these ends.'' They publish *SANE Action* and *Sane World,* monthly, as well as pamphlets and articles.

**Socialist Workers Party**
14 Charles Ln.
New York, NY 10014
(212) 242-5530

The Party's views include a call for an end to imperialist
intervention abroad. They publish the weekly newspaper *The
Militant.*

**Soviet Embassy**
Information Department
1706 18th St. NW
Washington, DC 20009

Speeches and statements on disarmament and Soviet foreign policy
are available. It is best to ask for a specific speech or publication.

**Young Americans for Freedom**
P.O. Box 1002, Woodland RD.
Sterling, VA 22170
(703) 450-5162

Young Americans for Freedom is a youth organization (up to age
39) that promotes the conservative philosophy of free enterprise
and a strong national defense. YAF publishes the quarterly
magazines *New Guard* and *Dialogue on Liberty.*

# bibliography

The following bibliography of books, periodicals, and pamphlets is divided into chapter topics for the reader's convenience. The topics are in the same order as in the body of this Opposing Viewpoint *SOURCES*.

*Many periodicals which focus on the Soviet-American debate are not widely found. Below is a list of some of the most useful, less available publications with information about where to obtain them.*

**Daily World**
Official newspaper of the American Communist Party.

Longview Publishing Co.
239 West 23rd Street
New York, NY 10011

**The Guardian**
An independent radical newsweekly.

33 West 17th Street
New York, NY 10011

**In These Times**
An independent Socialist newspaper.

1300 West Belmont Avenue
Chicago, IL 60657

**New Times** and **Soviet Military Review**
News magazines published by the USSR.

Imported Publications
320 West Ohio Street
Chicago, IL 60610

**The People**
A weekly newspaper published by the Socialist Labor Party.

914 Industrial Avenue
Palo Alto, CA 94303

**Problems of Communism**
A monthly magazine produced by the US Information Agency.

Superintendent of Documents
US Government Printing Office
Washington, DC 20402

**Revolutionary Worker**
A weekly radical newspaper.

Box 3486 Merchandise Mart
Chicago, IL 60654

**Soviet Life**
A monthly photo and feature-news magazine published by the USSR Embassy.

1706 18th Street NW
Washington, DC 20009

## Historical Chapters

R. Aron — *The Imperial Republic: The United States and the World, 1945-1973.* Washington, DC: University Press of America, 1982.

Winston S. Churchill — *The Second World War.* (6 volumes) Boston: Houghton Mifflin, 1948-1953.

Stephen F. Cohen, Alexander Rabinowitch and Robert Sharlet, eds. — *The Soviet Union Since Stalin.* Bloomington: Indiana University Press, 1980.

W. Phillips Davison — *The Berlin Blockade: A Study in Cold War Politics.* Salem, NH: Ayer Co., 1980.

Department of State — *American Foreign Policy: Current Documents.* US Government Printing Office, annual.

*Documents on American Foreign Relations* — New York: Council on Foreign Relations and Harper & Brothers, annual.

Herbert Feis — *Between War and Peace: The Potsdam Conference.* Westport, CT: Greenwood Press, 1983.

Herbert Feis — *Churchill, Roosevelt, Stalin.* Princeton, NJ: Princeton University Press, 1967.

D.F. Fleming — *The Cold War and Its Origins, 1917-1960.* (2 volumes) New York: Doubleday, 1961.

John L. Gaddis — *The United States and the Origins of the Cold War, 1941-1947.* New York: Columbia University Press, 1972.

John L. Gaddis — "The Rise, Fall and Future of Detente," *Foreign Affairs,* Winter 1984.

Robert A. Goldwin — *Readings in American Foreign Policy.* New York: Oxford University Press, 2nd Edition revised by Harry M. Clos, 1971.

Norman A. Graebner — *The Cold War.* Lexington, MA: Heath, 1976.

Louis J. Halle — *The Cold War as History.* New York: Harper & Row, 1971.

A. Hanak — *Soviet Foreign Policy Since the Age of Stalin.* Boston: Routledge & Paul Kegan, 1972.

| Jerry F. Hough | *Soviet Leadership in Transition.* Washington, DC: Brookings Institute, 1980. |
| Marty Jezer | *The Dark Ages: Life in the US, 1945-1960.* Boston: South End Press, 1982. |
| George F. Kennan | *The Nuclear Delusion.* New York: Pantheon Books, 1982. |
| Robert F. Kennedy | *Thirteen Days.* New York: W.W. Norton, 1967. |
| Basile Kerblay, trans. by Rupert Swyer | *Modern Soviet Society.* New York: Pantheon Books, 1983. |
| Jonathan Kwitny | *Endless Enemies: The Making of an Unfriendly World.* New York: Congdon and Weed, Inc., 1984. |
| Walter Lafeber | *America, Russia and the Cold War, 1945-1960.* New York: Random House, 1980. |
| Martin McCauley, ed. | *The Soviet Union After Brezhnev.* New York: Holmes and Meier Publishers, 1983. |
| Jay Martin | *Winter Dreams.* Boston: Houghton Mifflin, 1979. |
| J.P. Nettl | *The Eastern Zone and Soviet Policy on Germany.* New York: Octagon, 1977. |
| Joseph S. Nye Jr., ed. | *The Making of America's Soviet Policy.* New Haven: Yale University Press, 1984. |
| Martin Sherwin | *A World Destroyed: The Atomic Bomb and the Grand Alliance.* New York: Alfred A. Knopf, 1975. |
| Arkady Shevchenko | *Breaking with Moscow.* New York: Alfred A. Knopf, 1985. |
| Robert W. Tucker | *The Radical Left and American Foreign Policy.* Baltimore, MD: Johns Hopkins, 1971. |
| Adam Ulam | *Expansion and Coexistence: The History of Soviet Foreign Policy 1971-1967.* New York: Praeger and Co., 1974. |
| Bernard A. Weisberger | *Cold War, Cold Peace: The United States and Russia Since 1945.* New York: American Heritage/Houghton Mifflin, 1984. |
| Thomas P. Whitney, ed. | *Krushchev Speaks: Selected Speeches, Articles, and Press Conferences.* Ann Arbor: University of Michigan Press, 1963. |

## Communism & Capitalism

| Hannes Adomeit | "Capitalist Contradictions and Soviet Policy," *Problems of Communism,* May—June 1984. |
| Doug Bandow | "The Decline and Fall of Communism," *Conservative Digest,* April 1985. |
| David L. Barnett | "Communism: The Great Economic Failure," *US News & World Report,* March 1, 1982. |
| Peter L. Berger | "Democracy for Everyone?" *Commentary,* September 1983. |
| John B. Dunlop | *The Faces of Contemporary Russian Nationalism.* Princeton, NJ: Princeton University Press, 1983. |
| Yuri Gudkov | "Ready to Go All the Way," *New Times,* August 1984. |
| Sidney Hook | *Marxism and Beyond,* Totowa, NJ: Rowman and Littlefield, 1983. |
| Irving Howe | "Intellectuals, Dissent & Bureaucrats," *Dissent,* Summer 1984. |
| Nikolai Ovcharenko | "The Party of Revolutionary Renewal," *New Times,* May 1984. |

| The People | "The Death Throes of US Imperialism," December 10, 1984. |
| Boris N. Ponomarev | *Communism in a Changing World,* New York: Sphinx Press, Inc., 1983. |
| Jerry W. Sanders | "Breaking Out of the Containment Syndrome," *World Policy Journal,* Fall 1983. |
| Fred Schwartz | *Why I Am Against Communism.* Pamphlet available from the Christian Anti-Communist Crusade, P.O. Box 890, Long Beach, CA 90801. |
| Fred Schwartz | *Why Communism Kills: The Legacy of Karl Marx.* Pamphlet available from the Christian Anti-Communist Crusade, P.O. Box 890, Long Beach, CA 90801, February 15, 1985. |
| Aleksandr Solzhenitsyn | "Communism at the End of the Brezhnev Era," *National Review,* January 21, 1983. |
| *Soviet Military Review* | "Complying with the Laws of Friendship," November 12, 1984. |
| *US News & World Report* | "Communism Doesn't Fit a Modern Industrial Society," Interview with Ernst Kux, February 4, 1985. |
| Caspar Weinberger | "The Imperatives of the Soviet System," *Defense,* February 1985. |
| C.H. Mike Yarrow | "Toward Understanding the Soviet Union," *Friends Journal,* June 1/15, 1984. |

## Afghanistan

| Richard Bernstein | "Remaking Afghanistan in the Soviet Image," *New York Times Magazine,* March 24, 1985. |
| Robert James Bidinotto | "Afghanistan and the Soviet Mind," *On Principle,* December 20, 1984. Available from *On Principle,* Princeton Professional Park, 601 Ewing St., Suite B-7, Princeton, NJ 08542. |
| Chris Blatchley | "Dispatch From Afghanistan," *Intervention,* Winter 1985. |
| Henry S. Bradsher | *Afghanistan and the Soviet Union.* Durham, NC: Duke Press Policy Studies, 1983. |
| *Bulletin of the Atomic Scientists* | "Afghanistan," June/July 1983. |
| Jimmy Carter | "Soviet Military Intervention in Afghanistan," *Vital Speeches of the Day,* January 15, 1980. |
| Gerard Chaliand | *Report From Afghanistan.* Translated by Tamar Jacoby, New York: The Viking Press, 1982. |
| Mike Davidow | *Afghan Diary.* Moscow: Novosti Press Agency Publishing House, 1984. |
| Jere Van Dyk | "Journey Through Afghanistan," *New York Times Magazine,* October 17, 1982. |
| Felix Ermacore | *Report on the Situation of Human Rights in Afghanistan.* Available from the United Nations Office at Geneva, Palais des Nations, Geneva, Switzerland, February 1985. |
| Roger Fenton and Maggie Gallagher | "Inside Afghanistan," *The New Republic,* August 29, 1983. |
| Robert Herr | "A Stillborn Olympics," *The New Republic,* February 16, 1980. |
| Jerry F. Hough | "Why the Russians Invaded," *The Nation,* March 1, 1980. |
| Robert E. Hunter | "Afghanistan's Agony Calls for Less Caution by America," *Los Angeles Times,* January 4, 1985. |

Syed Jhabbir Hussain and others — *Afghanistan Under Soviet Occupation.* Islamabad: World Affairs Publications, 1980.

Anthony Hyman — *Afghanistan Under Soviet Domination, 1964-1981.* New York: St. Martin's Press, 1982.

Jeane J. Kirkpatrick — "Afghan Situation and Implications for Peace," *Department of State Bulletin*, January 1982.

Edward N. Luttwak — "After Afghanistan, What?" *Commentary*, April 1980.

Claude Malhuret — "Report from Afghanistan," *Foreign Affairs*, Winter 1983-84.

Girish Mathur — *New Afghanistan.* New Delhi: Sterling Publishers Private Limited, 1983.

Boris Petkov — *Afghanistan Today: Impressions of a Journalist.* New Delhi: Sterling Publishers Private Limited, 1983.

Earl C. Revenal — "After Afghanistan: Sitting on Our Hands," *The Libertarian Review*, September 1980.

Alvin Z. Rubinstein — "The Soviet Union and Afghanistan," *Current History*, October 1983.

Harrison E. Salisbury — "A Boon for the K.G.B.," *The New York Times*, January 31, 1980.

Viktor Suvorov — *The Liberators: My Life in the Soviet Army.* New York: W.W. Norton & Co., 1981.

Ludmilla Thorne and David Friend — "Prisoners of the Afghans," *Life*, February 1984.

Gherman Ustinov — "Who is Fanning the Flames?" *New Times*, May 1985.

*The World Today* — "The Afghanistan Stalemate," April 1985.

## Poland

Timothy Garten Ash — "Poland: The Uses of Adversity," *New York Review*, June 27, 1985.

Abraham Brumberg — "We Can Only Sit," *The New Republic*, March 24, 1982.

Cassandra — "The Soviets Annex Poland," *Washington Inquirer*, May 10, 1985.

Alexander Furenko — "Code-Named Argonaut," *Soviet Life*, March 1985.

Jacek Kalabinski — "For the Poles, Solidarity Lives On," *New York Times*, May 7, 1985.

Michael T. Kaufman — "The Importance of General Jaruzelski," *New York Times Magazine*, December 9, 1984.

Vladlen Kuznetsov — "In Which Direction?" *New Times*, April 1985.

Walter Laqueur — "What Poland Means," *Commentary*, March 1982.

Jan Jozef Lipski and Witold Jedlicki — "Trials of a Polish Resister," *The Nation*, May 26, 1984.

George D. Moffett III — "US-Polish Ties Are Strained, but Not Broken," *The Christian Science Monitor*, May 8, 1985.

Lucia Mouat — "Is US Too Tough on Poles Seeking Asylum?" *The Christian Science Monitor*, February 6, 1985.

Adam Przeworski — "Marshall Plan for Poland," *Bulletin of the Atomic Scientists*, March 1982.

Zdzislaw M. Rurarz — "The Sovietization of Poland, *Washington Times*, April 9, 1985.

*Time* — "Curtain Up," December 10, 1984.

Lawrence Ueschler — "Poland: Three Years After," *Harper's*, December 1984.

Zdzislawa A. Walaszek — "The Polish Crisis and the Communist Malaise, *Society*, March/April 1982.

James H. Wolfe — "Winter in Poland," *USA Today*, March 1982.

## Media

Stephen F. Cohen — "Sovieticus," *The Nation*, May 12, 1984.

Lloyd N. Cutler — "Foreign Policy on Deadline," *Foreign Policy*, Fall 1984.

G.L. Dexter — "The U.S.: Target of Communist Propaganda," *Conservative Digest*, March 1985.

William A. Dorman — "Soviets Seen Through Red-tinted Glasses," *Bulletin of the Atomic Scientists*, February 1985.

Anatoliy Golitsyn — *New Lies for Old*, New York: Dodd, Mead & Co., 1984.

Ellen Goodman — "Sadly Distorted Images in Unofficial Eyes," *St. Paul Pioneer Press*, May 10, 1985.

Sally G. Greenway — "America's Constricted 'Voice,'" *New York Times*, March 19, 1984.

David Maraniss — "New Fronts in the Old War Against Leaks and Disclosure," *Washington Post National Weekly Edition*, November 28, 1983.

Elizabeth Pond — "The West Wakes Up to the Dangers of Disinformation," *The Christian Science Monitor*, February 28, 1985.

John Rees — "Moscow's Friends at the Institute for Policy Studies," *American Opinion*, November 1983.

Richard H. Shultz Jr. and Roy Godson — *Dezinformatsia: Active Measures in Soviet Strategy.* Arlington, VA: Permagon-Brassey's, 1984.

G. Solovyov — "Behind the Web of Anti-Sovietism," *Soviet Military Review*, April 1984.

Gene Tagle — "How Media Manipulate Workers' Minds," *The People*, December 8, 1984.

Mikhail Taratuta — "The U.S. Media's Role in Anti-Sovietism," *Daily World*, March 9, 1984.

James L. Tyson — *Target America.* Chicago: Regnery Gateway, Inc., 1981.

James D. Van De Graaff — "Soviet Disinformation: The Threat to an Open Society," *Conservative Digest*, October 1984.

Vladimir Voinovich — "The Trouble with Truth," *The New Republic*, November 28, 1983.

## Trade

Ralph Kinney Bennett — "The Great Russian Raid on US Technology," *Reader's Digest*, March 1984.

Lester R. Brown — "US and Soviet Agriculture," *WorldView*, December 1982.

Lester R. Brown — "US & Soviet Agriculture: The Shifting Balance of Power," *The New Republic*, August 16 & 23, 1982.

*Businessweek* — "A Paradoxical Push to Build Trade With the Soviets," June 4, 1985.

Nick Butler — "The US Grain Weapon: Could It Boomerang?" *The World Today*, February 1983.

*Conservative Digest* — "Soviet Spies Desperate to Get Our Technology," Interview with Author John Barron by Barbara Reynolds, March 1984.

| | |
|---|---|
| *Conservative Digest* | "Corporate America is Fueling the Soviet War Machine," October 1983. |
| Roger Donway | "Selling Out," *On Principle.* Monthly newsletter available from Princeton Professional Park, 601 Ewing Street, Suite B-7, Princeton, NJ 08542. |
| Henry Eason | "Soviet Spies: Your Firm Could Be Their Next Target," *Nation's Business,* June 1983. |
| Philip Hanson | "Foreign Trade Policy: The USSR, The West and Eastern Europe as an Eternal Triangle," *The Soviet Union After Brezhnev.* New York: Holmes and Meier Publishers, Inc., 1983. |
| Dale R. Herspring | "Technology and the Soviet System," *Problems of Communism,* January/February 1985. |
| Orr Kelly | "High-Tech Hemorrhage: From US to Soviet Union," *US News & World Report,* May 7, 1984. |
| Roy Kaufman | "Life Trade Embargoes, Avoid Further Economic Disaster, *US-USSR Friendship News,* Summer 1983. |
| Linda Melvein, David Hebditch, and Nick Anning | *Techno-Bandits: How the Soviets Are Stealing America's High Tech Future.* Boston: Houghton Mifflin Company, 1984. |
| Sasha Rakoczy | "Nuclear Bandits Face Aid Cutoff," *The Spotlight,* June 3, 1985. |
| Warren Richey | "High-tech Firms May Soon Self-Police Exports of Sensitive Goods," *The Christian Science Monitor,* September 19, 1984. |
| William A. Root | "Trade Policy: The US Needs to Listen to Its Allies . . ." *Businessweek,* November 21, 1983. |
| Erwin A. Salk | "Hostages of Mythology: Facts on US-USSR Trade and Economic Relations," *Minnesota Council of American-Soviet Friendship Newsletter,* July/August 1982. |
| Tad Szulc | "US Wheat May Leaven Soviet American Relations," *The Los Angeles Times,* September 23, 1984. |
| Karl-Eugen Wadekin | "Soviet Agriculture's Dependence on the West," *Foreign Affairs,* Spring 1972. |
| James D. Watkins | "Technology Transfer," *Vital Speeches of the Day,* March 15, 1983. |
| Gennadi Zhuravlyov | "World Says Yes to Soviet Trade," *Soviet Life,* July 1985. |

## Human Rights

| | |
|---|---|
| Igor Bestuzhev-Lada | "The Family: Past, Present and Future," *Daily World,* December 13, 1984. |
| Alva Buxembaum | "A Marxist View of Women's Oppression," *Daily World,* March 7, 1985. |
| Lawrence Elliott | "The Persecution of Andrei Sakharov," *Reader's Digest,* November 1984. |
| George Feifer | "Russian Disorders," *Harper's,* February 1981. |
| Si Frumkin | "We *Can* Make the Soviets Comply on Human Rights," *Los Angeles Times,* March 27, 1985. |
| Bill Gertz | "Pentagon Report Details Unrest in Soviet Union," *Washington Times,* June 6, 1985. |
| Marshall I. Goldman | *USSR in Crisis.* New York: W.W. Norton & Company, 1983. |

| | |
|---|---|
| Robert L. Heilbroner | *Marxism: For and Against.* New York: W.W. Norton & Company, 1980. |
| Louis Menashe | "The New Wave from Russia," *New York Times Magazine,* May 5, 1985. |
| Stephen Miller | "God and Man in the Soviet Union," *Catholicism in Crisis,* January 1985. |
| L. Mikhailenko | "Children, the Privileged 'Class,'" *Soviet Military Review,* June 1984. |
| Seth Mydans | "Corruption Campaign in Soviet Union Takes Its Toll," *New York Times,* February 8, 1985. |
| Darya Nikolayeva | "The Way We Live: Who Is Head of the Family?" *Soviet Life,* March 1985. |
| Norman Podhoretz | "The Terrible Question of Aleksandr Solzhenitsyn," *Commentary,* February 1985. |
| Elizabeth Pond | *From the Yaraslavsky Station.* New York: Universe Books, 1981. |
| James P. Scanlan | "Doublethink in the USSR," *Problems of Communism,* January/February 1985. |
| Serge Schmemann | "Standing in Line Persists as Scourge of Soviet Life," *New York Times,* February 6, 1985. |
| David K. Shipler | *Russia: Broken Idols, Solemn Dreams.* New York: Times Books, 1983. |
| Jaryl Strong | "Soviet Union Continues Its Campaign Against Believers," *Christianity Today,* February 15, 1985. |
| Georgi Vins and Lydia Vins | "The KGB Lurks Behind Many Soviet Altars," *Washington Times,* February 13, 1985. |

## The Issue of Freedom

| | |
|---|---|
| Doug Bandow | "Sinking the Hopes of Political Refugees," *The Wall Street Journal,* August 28, 1984. |
| David A. Bell | "The Jews Left Behind," *The New Republic,* February 18, 1985. |
| Janice A. Broun | "Mosque & Kremlin," *Commonweal,* March 22, 1985. |
| Janice A. Broun | "Soviet Monasticism," *America,* March 9, 1985. |
| Helen Carriere, trans. by George Holoch | *Confiscated Power: How Soviet Russia Really Works.* New York: Harper & Row, 1980. |
| Anita Deyneke and Peter Deyneke Jr. | "Life on the Soviet Precipice," *Christianity Today,* March 1, 1985. |
| Jim Forest | "Icons and Miracles: An Intensity of Faith," *Christianity and Crisis,* May 27, 1985. |
| Robert O. Freedman, editor | *Soviet Jewry in the Decisive Decade, 1971-80.* Durham, NC: Duke University Press, 1984. |
| Billy Graham | "100 Million in the Soviet Union Profess Belief in God," *US News & World Report,* October 8, 1984. |
| Billy Graham | *Special Report of the Soviet Union Trip,* October 1984. Pamphlet available from Promoting Enduring Peace, P.O. Box 5103, Woodmont, CT 06460. |
| Charles E. Grassley | "A Visit with Soviet Jews," *The Saturday Evening Post,* September 1983. |
| Kevin Klose | *Russia and the Russians: Inside a Closed Society.* New York: W.W. Norton & Company, 1984. |
| *The New Republic* | "Not Only Jews," April 8, 1985. |

| | |
|---|---|
| Maureen Perrie and Andrew Sutton | *Home, School, and Leisure in the Soviet Union*. Winchester, MA: Allen and Unwin, 1980. |
| Benjamin Pinkus | *The Soviet Government and the Jews, 1948—1967*. New York: Cambridge University Press, 1984. |
| *Policy Review* | "The Atlas of Freedom: The Right to Emigrate." Winter 1985. |
| Vladimir Rubtsov | "'Freedom of Information' Paradoxes," *New Times*, December 1983. |
| George Shultz | "Soviet Jewry and U.S.-Soviet Relations," *Department of State Bulletin*, December 1984. |
| Thomas B. Smith | *The Other Establishment*. Chicago: Regnery Gateway, Inc., 1984. |
| Gary Thatcher | "Despite Official Scorn, Interest in Religion Rises in Soviet Union," *The Christian Science Monitor*, December 10, 1984. |
| Anthony Ugolnik | "The Godlessness Within: Stereotyping the Russians," *The Christian Century*, November 9, 1983. |
| Pat Zaharopoulos | "Adversarial Facet Absent from Soviet Justice," *San Diego Union*, February 5, 1984. |

## Negotiations

| | |
|---|---|
| Kenneth L. Adelman | "Toward a Defense Strategy, *New York Times*, March 10, 1985. |
| Tom Bethell | "The Mugger's Deal in Geneva," *National Review*, March 8, 1985. |
| Harold Brown | "Reagan's Risky Approach," *New York Times*, March 10, 1985. |
| Danny Collum | "Bluff and Bluster in Geneva," *Sojourners*, March 1985. |
| George J. Church | "Only a Step, but an Encouraging One," *Time*, January 21, 1985. |
| Earl W. Foell | "At a Teflon Summit, can Reagan and Gorbachev Make any Bargain Stick?" *The Christian Science Monitor*, March 19, 1985. |
| Alton Frye | "Strategic Synthesis," *Foreign Policy*, Spring 1985. |
| Colin S. Gray | "Moscow Is Cheating," *Foreign Policy*, Fall 1984. |
| Max M. Kampelman and George Urban | "Can We Negotiate with the Russians?" *Encounter*, February 1985. |
| Michael T. Klare | "Securing the Firebreak," *World Policy Journal*, Spring 1985. |
| Steven Kull | "Nuclear Nonsense," *Foreign Policy*, Spring 1985. |
| Marx Lewis | "The Hazards of Negotiating with Communists," *Washington Inquirer*, February 1, 1985. |
| Richard Lugar | "U.S. Must Show 'Credible Will' in Arms Talks," *US News & World Report*, February 4, 1985. |
| Paul N. Nitze | *The Objectives of Arms Control*, Current Policy No. 677, March 28, 1985. Available from Bureau of Public Affairs, United States Department of State, Washington, DC 20520. |
| Ronald Reagan | "Address to the United Nations: U.S. and U.S.S.R. Negotiations," *Vital Speeches of the Day*, October 15, 1984. |
| David B. Rivkin Jr. | "What Does Moscow Think?" *Foreign Policy*, Summer 1985. |
| Dimitri Simes | "Nothing Is Going to Change Radically," *US News & World Report*, March 25, 1985. |

| | |
|---|---|
| Marvin Stone | "When Soviets Run Scared," *US News & World Report*, March 18, 1985. |

## The Future of US-Soviet Relations

| | |
|---|---|
| Georgi A. Arbatov and Willem Oltmans | *The Soviet Viewpoint*. New York: Dodd, Mead and Company, 1983. |
| Michael H. Armacost | "Reflections on US-Soviet Relations," Available from the Bureau of Public Affairs, Department of State, Washington, DC 20520, May 1985. |
| Charles T. Baroch | "The Mirror-Image Fallacy: Understanding the Soviet Union," *The Backgrounder*, June 29, 1982. |
| Thompson R. Buchanan | "The Real Russia," *Foreign Policy*, Summer 1982. |
| James L. Buckley | "Freezing Chances for Peace," *Department of State Bulletin*, December 1982. |
| Arthur Burns | "Reflections on East-West Relations," *Department of State Bulletin*, January 1985. |
| Andrew Cockburn | *The Threat: Inside the Soviet Military Machine*. New York: Random House, 1984. |
| John Alexis Crane | "Does War Make Sense?" *The Churchman*, November 1981. |
| Edward Crankshaw | *Putting Up With the Russians*. New York: Viking Press, 1984. |
| Richard D. DeLauer | "Countering the Soviet Threat," *Defense*, June 1983. |
| I.M. Destler, Leslie H. Gelb, and Anthony Lake | *Our Own Worst Enemy: The Unmasking of American Foreign Policy*. New York: Simon and Schuster, 1984. |
| Richard Gillett | "Demystifying the Russian Threat," *The Witness*, March 1984. |
| Sanford Gottlieb | *What About the Russians?* Published by the Student/Teacher Organization to Prevent Nuclear War, Box 232, Northfield, MA 01360, 1982. |
| William G. Hyland | "Clash with the Soviet Union," *Foreign Policy*, Winter 1982—83. |
| Max Kampelman | "Can the US and Soviet Union Coexist?" *USA Today*, March 1985. |
| Max Kampelman and George Urban | "Can We Negotiate with the Russians?" *Encounter*, February 1985. |
| George Kennan | *Soviet American Relations: Breaking The Spell*. Published by the Council for a Livable World, 11 Beacon St. Boston, MA 02108, reprinted from the *New Yorker*, October 3, 1983. |
| Edward N. Luttwak | *The Grand Strategy of the Soviet Union*. New York: St. Martin's Press, 1983. |
| Robert Moyer | "The Enemy Within," *Psychology Today*, January 1985. |
| Paul H. Nitze | "Living with the Soviets," *Foreign Policy*, Winter 1984-85. |
| Joseph S. Nye | *The Making of America's Soviet Policy*. New Haven: Yale University Press, 1984. |
| Richard Pipes | "How to Cope with the Soviet Threat," *Commentary*, August 1984. |
| Richard Pipes | "Can the Soviet Union Reform?" *Foreign Affairs*, Fall 1984. |
| *Policy Review* | "Beyond Containment? The Future of US-Soviet Relations," Winter 1985. |
| Harry Rositzke | *Managing Moscow: Guns or Goods*, 1985 |
| Ronald Reagan | "United States—Soviet Relations," *Vital Speeches of the Day*, February 1, 1984. |

| Jonathan P. Sanders | "Why Russians Fear, Yet Admire Americans," *Scholastic Update,* April 15, 1983. |
| George P. Shultz | "Managing the US-Soviet Relationship Over the Long Term," *Department of State Bulletin,* December 1984. |
| Dimitri Simes | "America's New Edge," *Foreign Policy,* Fall 1984. |
| Viktor Suvorov | *Inside the Soviet Army.* New York: Macmillan, 1982. |
| Michael Voslensky | *Nomenklatura: The Soviet Ruling Class.* Garden City, NY: Doubleday & Company, Inc, 1984. |
| Thomas J. Watson Jr. | "Dealing With Moscow," *The New York Times,* January 19, 1981. |
| W. Bruce Weinrod and Manfred R. Hamm | "Assessing US-Soviet Relations," *Mandate for Leadership II.* Published by the Heritage Foundation, 1984. |
| Tom Wicker | "Beware of 'Gaposis,'" *The New York Times,* January 9, 1981. |
| Aaron Wildavsky | *Beyond Containment: Alternative American Policies Toward the Soviet Union.* San Francisco: Institute for Contemporary Studies, 1984. |
| Alan Wolfe | *The Rise and Fall of the Soviet Threat.* Published by the Institute for Policy Studies, 1901 Q St. NW, Washington, DC 20009, 1979. |
| Donald S. Zagoria | "US-Soviet Relations: The Arms Race and Coexistence," *Worldview,* January 1983. |

# index